NORMAL FAMILY PROCESSES

NORMAL FAMILY PROCESSES

GROWING DIVERSITY AND COMPLEXITY

FOURTH EDITION

Edited by

FROMA WALSH

THE GUILFORD PRESS
New York   London

© 2012 The Guilford Press.   Preface to the Paperback Edition © 2016.
A Division of Guilford Publications, Inc.
370 Seventh Avenue, Suite 1200, New York, NY 10001
www.guilford.com

Paperback edition 2016

Printed in the United States of America

This book is printed on acid-free paper.

Last digit is print number: 9   8   7   6   5   4

Library of Congress Cataloging-in-Publication Data

Normal family processes : growing diversity and complexity / edited by
Froma Walsh. — 4th ed.
    p. cm.
    Includes bibliographical references and index.
    ISBN 978-1-4625-0255-4 (hardcover: alk. paper)
    ISBN 978-1-4625-2548-5 (paperback: alk. paper)
    1. Families—Research.   2. Family assessment.   3. Families.   I. Walsh, Froma.
HQ728.N83 2012
306.85—dc23

                                                          2011041949

ABOUT THE EDITOR

Froma Walsh, MSW, PhD, is the Mose and Sylvia Firestone Professor Emerita in the School of Social Service Administration and the Department of Psychiatry at the Pritzker School of Medicine, University of Chicago. She is also Co-Founder and Co-Director of the University-affiliated Chicago Center for Family Health. Dr. Walsh is a past president of the American Family Therapy Academy and past editor of the *Journal of Marital and Family Therapy.* She has received many honors for her distinguished contributions and leadership in the field of family therapy, including awards from the Division of Family Psychology of the American Psychological Association, the American Family Therapy Academy, the American Association for Marriage and Family Therapy, the American Orthopsychiatric Association, and the Society for Pastoral Care Research. Her books include *Strengthening Family Resilience, Second Edition*; *Spiritual Resources in Family Therapy, Second Edition*; *Living Beyond Loss: Death in the Family, Second Edition*; and *Women in Families: Framework for Family Therapy.* She is a frequent speaker and international consultant on resilience-oriented professional training, practice, and research.

CONTRIBUTORS

Carol M. Anderson, PhD, Department of Psychiatry, University of Pittsburgh Medical Center, Pittsburgh, Pennsylvania

Edward R. Anderson, PhD, Department of Human Development and Family Sciences, University of Texas at Austin, Austin, Texas

Deidre Ashton, LCSW, Princeton Family Institute, Princeton, New Jersey

Leah Bloom, MSMFT, The Family Institute, Northwestern University, Evanston, Illinois

Nancy Boyd-Franklin, PhD, Graduate School of Applied and Professional Psychology, Rutgers, The State University of New Jersey, Piscataway, New Jersey

Carrie Capstick, PhD, private practice, New York, New York

Carolyn Pape Cowan, PhD, Department of Psychology and Institute of Human Development, University of California, Berkeley, Berkeley, California

Philip A. Cowan, PhD, Department of Psychology and Institute of Human Development, University of California, Berkeley, Berkeley, California

David S. DeGarmo, PhD, Oregon Social Learning Center, Eugene, Oregon

Janice Driver, PhD, Eastside Parenting Clinic, Inc., Bellevue, Washington

Malitta Engstrom, PhD, LCSW, School of Social Service Administration, University of Chicago, Chicago, Illinois

Marina Eovaldi, PhD, The Family Institute, Northwestern University, Evanston, Illinois

Celia Jaes Falicov, PhD, Department of Family and Preventive Medicine and Department of Psychiatry, University of California, San Diego, La Jolla, California

Mona DeKoven Fishbane, PhD, Chicago Center for Family Health, Chicago, Illinois

Marion S. Forgatch, PhD, Oregon Social Learning Center, Eugene, Oregon

Peter Fraenkel, PhD, Department of Psychology, City College, City University of New York, New York, New York

Chelsea Garneau, PhD, Family and Child Sciences, School of Human Sciences, the Florida State University, Tallahassee, Florida

John M. Gottman, PhD, The Gottman Institute, Inc., Seattle, Washington

Robert-Jay Green, PhD, Rockway Institute for LGBT Psychology, California School of Professional Psychology, Alliant International University, San Francisco, California

Shannon M. Greene, PhD, Department of Human Development and Family Sciences, University of Texas at Austin, Austin, Texas

E. Mavis Hetherington, PhD, Department of Psychology, University of Virginia, Charlottesville, Virginia

Evan Imber-Black, PhD, Ackerman Institute for the Family, New York, New York, and Marriage and Family Therapy Master's Program, Mercy College, Dobbs Ferry, New York

Melanie Karger, MA, Graduate School of Applied and Professional Psychology, Rutgers, The State University of New Jersey, Piscataway, New Jersey

Carmen Knudson-Martin, PhD, Counseling and Family Sciences, Loma Linda University, Loma Linda, California

Jay Lebow, PhD, The Family Institute, Northwestern University, Evanston, Illinois

Cassandra Ma, PsyD, The Family Institute, Northwestern University, Evanston, Illinois

Monica McGoldrick, MSW, PhD(Hon.), The Multicultural Family Institute, Highland Park, New Jersey

Kay Pasley, EdD, Family and Child Sciences, School of Human Sciences, Florida State University, Tallahassee, Florida

Cheryl Rampage, PhD, The Family Institute, Northwestern University, Evanston, Illinois

John S. Rolland, MD, Department of Psychiatry and Center for Family Health, University of Chicago, Chicago, Illinois

Gina Miranda Samuels, PhD, School of Social Service Administration, University of Chicago, Chicago, Illinois

Alyson F. Shapiro, PhD, School of Social and Family Dynamics, Arizona State University, Tempe, Arizona

Tazuko Shibusawa, PhD, Silver School of Social Work, New York University, New York, New York

Erica L. Spotts, PhD, Division of Behavioral and Social Research, National Institute on Aging, National Institutes of Health, Bethesda, Maryland

Catherine B. Stroud, PhD, The Family Institute, Northwestern University, Evanston, Illinois

Amber Tabares, PhD, private practice, Bellevue, Washington

Froma Walsh, PhD, School of Social Service Administration, Department of Psychiatry, and Center for Family Health, University of Chicago, Chicago, Illinois

Catherine Weigel Foy, MSW, The Family Institute, Northwestern University, Evanston, Illinois

PREFACE TO THE PAPERBACK EDITION

Since the publication of the fourth edition of *Normal Family Processes* in 2012, families worldwide are continuing to become increasingly diverse, complex, and fluid in composition and living arrangements. "New normal" families vary in structure, gender arrangements, multicultural makeup, socioeconomic conditions, and life-cycle patterns. Many strains in family life are generated by larger societal forces and by disruptive transformations in the global economy. Vast social and economic disparities affect marriage prospects, family stability, and wellbeing, especially for racial and ethnic minorities and others facing marginalization and discrimination. Yet, as research in this volume documents, most families raise their children well and show remarkable resilience in surmounting their challenges and forging creative new pathways forward.

There is increasing recognition and normalization of the wide spectrum in human sexuality, including gender identity, sexual orientation, and relational bonds for gay, lesbian, bisexual, and transgender persons. A growing body of research finds that children of lesbian and gay parents function as well as—and often better than—those of heterosexual parents in terms of mental health and parent–child relationships (Fedewa, Black, & Ahn, 2015; Green, Chapter 8, this volume). Most noteworthy, in June, 2015, the United States Supreme Court ruled in favor of nationwide marriage equality for same-sex couples in *Obergefell* v. *Hodges*. This landmark decision will help same-sex partners clarify their mutual commitments and obligations, and improve their ability to take care of and provide for one another and their children in times of illness or death. And yet, serious barriers persist. For instance, many states lack legal protections against discrimination in employment and housing. Many same-sex couples (especially those in conservative religious groups) face rejection, discrimination, or violence from their families and communities. Thus, challenges remain ahead.

The state-of-the-art research and clinical perspectives in this volume are attuned to our times and varied social contexts. By illuminating the varied challenges today's couples and families face and the relational processes that enable them to adapt and thrive, they enrich our understanding of effective family functioning and can inform our best approaches to strengthening families in distress.

REFERENCE

Fedewa, A. L., Black, W. W., & Ahn, S. (2015). Children and adolescents with same-gender parents: A meta-analytic approach in assessing outcomes. *Journal of GLBT Family Studies, 11*, 1–34.

PREFACE (2012)

The changing landscape of family life in a turbulent world has become "the new normal." As families face unprecedented challenges and stitch together a growing diversity and complexity of relational patterns, we need to understand their struggles and their strivings. Drawing on the most current research and practice perspectives, this volume illuminates the strengths and challenges in the broad spectrum of contemporary families, identifying the family processes that foster well-being, adaptation, and resilience.

The first edition of *Normal Family Processes*, published in 1982, was hailed as a landmark volume in the clinical literature. It was the first text to examine normality from a family systems orientation, presenting pioneering research and conceptualization of well-functioning families. With traditional clinical training and practice focused on family dysfunction and blind to family strengths, I remarked that a "normal family" might be defined as one that had not yet been clinically assessed! In drawing attention to transactional processes in "nonclinical" average families and high-functioning families, the book was influential in rebalancing the skewed clinical perspective from family deficits to family strengths and resources.

The second and third editions (1993, 2003) advanced our understanding of family functioning as families and society were becoming increasingly diverse. In the mental health field and the larger society, those who did not conform to the reified standard of "the normal family" tended to be pathologized and stigmatized, reinforcing their sense of failure and deficiency. Interventions often aimed inappropriately to mold all families into a "one-size-fits-all" model that didn't fit their lives. Postmodern theory heightened our awareness of the profound influence of socially constructed views of normality, filtered by cultural and professional values and biases.

This fourth edition updates and expands our knowledge and perspectives on couples and families in the second decade of the 21st century. As clinicians, researchers, and social policy formulators move beyond assumptions of a single model for healthy families, it is essential for efforts to be informed by the most current research and conceptual advances. This volume examines family life in sociocultural and developmental contexts and identifies key processes in healthy functioning and resilience under stressful conditions. Chapters in this volume address the challenges and strengths in the broad spectrum of families today, considering their diverse cultural orientation and socioeconomic circumstances; and their varied and fluid structural arrangements, gender roles, sexual orientation, and passage over the life course and across the generations. Whereas sociological surveys of family demographics can track population trends such as marriage and divorce, this volume is unique in its focus on the interior of family life, examining shared belief systems, organizational patterns, and communication/problem-solving processes. Chapters describe how families navigate their life challenges and the transactional processes that can enable them to thrive. Implications for clinical and community practice are woven throughout.

The authors in this new edition are at the forefront of research, theory building, and clinical training. They present the latest data, identify trends, and offer useful frameworks to guide intervention and prevention efforts to strengthen families. Part I critically examines assumptions about normal families. Chapter 1 grounds the volume in a systemic framework, with ecological and developmental perspectives on family processes, adaptation, and resilience. A broad conceptualization of the family is inclusive of diverse values and structures, varied household composition, and extended kinship networks. Through a sociohistorical lens, emerging trends in couple and family life are highlighted, revealing the challenges and vitality of today's families in adapting to their changing social, economic, and global environment. Chapter 2 examines clinical perspectives on "normal" (i.e., average) and "healthy" (i.e., optimal) family functioning as they influence assessment of family dysfunction and therapeutic goals. The shift in focus from family deficits to family strengths and resilience in family therapy theory and practice is described, with recommendations for clinical training, practice, and research.

Parts II, III, and IV address the diversity and complexity of patterns in family functioning relative to varied structural forms, life challenges, and sociocultural and developmental contexts. Family risk, coping, adaptation, and resilience are considered in relation to the interplay of intrafamilial and environmental stressors. As the chapters demonstrate, some family patterns and adaptive strategies may be more functional than others in mastering a particular set of challenges—be it dual-earner families, stepfamily integration, transnational migration, or conditions of poverty, racism, or other forms of discrimination. Drawing on research and clinical experience, three questions frame the discussion:

1. What are the "normal" (i.e., common, expectable) family challenges and adaptive strategies under various conditions or stressors?

2. Can we identify key family processes that enable coping and mastery of challenges (e.g., in successful single-parent families; in resilient postdivorce families; among people with serious illness or disability)?
3. How can scholarly findings and insights inform clinical practice?

Part II, "Varying Family Forms and Challenges," includes topics such as interactional patterns in successful couple relationships, by Janice Driver and Gottman research colleagues; navigating work and family challenges in dual-earner families, by Peter Fraenkel and Carrie Capstick; risk and resilience after divorce, by Shannon M. Greene and research colleagues; single-parent households, by Carol M. Anderson; remarriage and stepfamily life, by Kay Pasley and Chelsea Garneau; gay and lesbian family life, by Robert-Jay Green; kinship care, by Malitta Engstrom; and adoptive families, by Cheryl Rampage and colleagues. In Part III, "Cultural Dimensions in Family Functioning," the topics include culture and concepts of normality, by Monica McGoldrick and Deidre Ashton; race, class, and poverty, by Nancy Boyd-Franklin and Melanie Karger; immigrant family processes, by Celia Jaes Falicov; changing gender norms, by Carmen Knudson-Martin; and the spiritual dimension of family life, by Froma Walsh. Part IV, "Developmental Perspectives on Family Functioning," includes topics such as the family life cycle, by Monica McGoldrick and Tazuko Shibusawa; family resilience, by Froma Walsh; normative family transitions, couple relationship quality, and healthy child development, by Philip A. Cowan and Carolyn Pape Cowan; family challenges with illness, disability, and genetic conditions, by John S. Rolland; and the value of rituals in family and community life, by Evan Imber-Black.

In Part V, "Advancing Family Systems Research and Practice," Jay Lebow and Catherine B. Stroud survey the state-of-the-science in assessment of couple and family functioning. The concluding two chapters affirm the importance of a biopsychosocial systems orientation in family research, theory, and practice. Erica L. Spotts examines gene–environment interplay and family processes and Mona DeKoven Fishbane addresses neurobiology and family processes.

This volume is designed to serve as a core textbook for clinical training and practice in psychology, social work, marriage and family therapy, counseling, psychiatry, and nursing; as a sourcebook for practitioners in a wide range of mental health, healthcare, and human service professions; for scholars and students in the social sciences; and for those formulating family policy in public and private arenas. It is intended as a resource for all who strive to improve the quality of family life and the well-being of all family members from the newborn to the eldest. The cutting-edge knowledge and perspectives presented here, all by distinguished authors at the forefront of the field, can inform and enrich intervention and prevention efforts, family research, social policy, and community-based programs, shifting focus from how families fail to how they can succeed.

ACKNOWLEDGMENTS

On behalf of all the authors, I would like to express our deep appreciation to the families who have let us into their lives, informed our research, and enriched our teaching and practice. We are also grateful to our loved ones and close friends who support and encourage our endeavors and nourish our spirits. I want to thank the staff of The Guilford Press, particularly Senior Editor Jim Nageotte and his assistant, Jane Keislar, for their valuable contributions to this new edition. I also wish to thank Claire Whitney for her keen eye and insightful feedback on chapters in this volume.

This new edition is dedicated to the everyday families who strive to do their best and to care lovingly for one another, as they navigate the stressful challenges of family life and weather the economic turmoil of our times.

CONTENTS

PART III. CULTURAL DIMENSIONS
IN FAMILY FUNCTIONING

PART IV. DEVELOPMENTAL PERSPECTIVES
ON FAMILY FUNCTIONING

PART V. ADVANCING FAMILY SYSTEMS RESEARCH
AND PRACTICE

PART I
OVERVIEW

CHAPTER 1

THE NEW NORMAL

Diversity and Complexity
in 21st-Century Families

FROMA WALSH

All happy families are alike; every unhappy family
is unhappy in its own way.
—TOLSTOY

All happy families are more or less dissimilar;
all unhappy ones are more or less alike.
—NABOKOV

Families and the world around them have changed dramatically over recent decades. Many traditionalists, sharing Tolstoy's view, have contended that families must conform to one model—fitting a cultural standard of "the normal family"—to be happy and raise children well. As families have become increasingly varied over a lengthening life course, our conceptions of normality must be examined and our very definition of "family" must be expanded to encompass a broad spectrum and fluid reshaping of relational and household patterns. This is the "new normal." Supporting Nabokov's view of happy families, a substantial body of research attests to the potential for healthy functioning and well-being in a variety of family arrangements. In our turbulent times, family bonds are more vital than ever. It is important to understand the challenges families face and the family processes that can enable them to thrive.

This overview chapter seeks to advance our knowledge of the diversity and complexity of contemporary families. First, we consider the social construction of family normality and clarify four major perspectives from the clinical field and the social sciences. The value of a systems orientation is highlighted, to understand "normal" family processes in terms of average and optimal family functioning. Next, a sociohistorical lens is used to survey the emerging trends and challenges for today's families. Chapter 2 then examines the influence of assumptions about family normality and dysfunction in clinical training and practice.

WHAT IS A NORMAL FAMILY?

The Social Construction of Normality

Clinicians and family scholars have become increasingly aware that definitions of normality are socially constructed, influenced by subjective worldviews and by the larger culture (Hoffman, 1990). Most influential theory and research on the family were developed by white, middle-class scholars and professionals, predominantly male, and from a Euro-American cultural perspective. Family therapists have become wary of the term "normal," taking to heart Foucault's (1980) criticism that too often in history, theories of normality have been constructed by dominant groups, reified by religion or science, and used to pathologize those who do not fit prescribed standards. Notions of normality sanction and privilege certain family arrangements while stigmatizing and marginalizing others.

The very concept of the family has been undergoing redefinition as profound social, economic, and political changes of recent decades have altered the landscape of family life (Coontz, 1997). Amid the turmoil, individuals and their loved ones have been forging new and varied relationship patterns within and across households as they strive to build caring and committed bonds. These efforts are made more difficult by questions about their normality. Our understanding of family functioning—from healthy to average to dysfunctional—must take into account these challenges and changes in family life in our changing world.

Although some might argue that the growing diversity and complexity of families make it impossible or unwise even to address the topic of normality, the very subjectivity of constructions of "the normal family" makes it all the more imperative. They powerfully influence all clinical theory, practice, research, and policy. It is crucial to be aware of the explicit and implicit assumptions and biases about normal families that are embedded in our cultural, professional, and personal belief systems.

Varied Conceptions of Family Normality

Defining family normality is problematic in that the term "normal" is used to refer to quite different concepts and is influenced by the subjective position of the observer and the surrounding culture. The label may hold quite different meanings to a clinician, a researcher, or a family concerned about its own normality. Our language confounds understanding when such terms as "healthy," "typical," and "functional" are used interchangeably with the label "normal." In an overview of concepts of mental health in the clinical and social science literature, Offer and Sabshin (1974) were struck by the varied definitions of a "normal" person. Building on their synthesis of views of individual normality, four perspectives can be usefully distinguished to clarify conceptions of a normal family: (1) normal as problem-free (asymptomatic); (2) normal as average; (3) normal as healthy; and (4) normal in relation to basic transactional processes in family systems.

Normal Families as Problem-Free

From this clinical perspective grounded in the medical/psychiatric model, the judgment of normality is based on a negative criterion: the absence of pathology. A family would be regarded as normal—and healthy—if members and their relationships are asymptomatic. This perspective is limited by its deficit-based skew, focused on symptoms of distress and severity of problems, and inattention to positive attributes of family well-being. Healthy family functioning involves more than the absence of problems and can be found in the midst of problems, as in family resilience (Walsh, 2003; see also Walsh, Chapter 17, this volume). As Minuchin (1974) has emphasized, no families are problem-free; all families face ordinary problems in living. Thus, the presence of distress is not necessarily an indication of family pathology. Similarly, freedom from symptoms is rare: As Kleinman (1988) reported, at any given time, three out of four persons are "symptomatic," experiencing some physical or psychological distress. Most define it as part of normal life and do not seek treatment.

Further problems arise when therapy is used as the marker for family dysfunction, as in research comparing clinical and nonclinical families as disturbed and normal samples. "Nonclinical" families are a heterogeneous group spanning the entire range of functioning. What is defined as a problem, and whether help is sought, varies with different family and cultural norms. Worrisome conflict in one family might be considered a healthy airing of differences in another. Distressed families most often attempt to handle problems on their own, more frequently turning to their kin or spiritual resources than to mental health services (Walsh, 2009d). Moreover, as mental health professionals would avow, seeking help can be a sign of health.

Normal Families as Average

From this perspective, a family is viewed as normal if it fits patterns that are common or expectable in ordinary families. This approach disengages the concept of normality from health and absence of symptoms. Since stressful challenges are part of everyday life, family problems or distress would not necessarily signal family abnormality or pathology. Yet family patterns that are common are not necessarily healthy; some, such as violence, are destructive.

Social scientists have traditionally used statistical measures of frequency or central tendency in the "normal distribution," or bell-shaped curve, with the middle range on a continuum taken as normal and both extremes as deviant. Thus, by definition, families that are atypical are "abnormal," with negative connotations of deviance too often pathologizing difference. By this standard, an optimally functioning family at the high end of a continuum would be abnormal. Given the multiplicity of family arrangements in contemporary society, the normal distribution is no longer a bell-shaped curve, and no single predominant model is typical. Rather the curve has flattened, with many peaks along the broad spectrum, reflecting the many, varied ways that ordinary, average families organize and experience family life.

Normal Families as Healthy, Ideal

This perspective on normality defines a *healthy* family in terms of ideal traits for optimal functioning. However, many standards of healthy families are derived from clinical theory and based on inference from disturbed cases seen in clinical practice (see Walsh, Chapter 2, this volume). The pervasiveness of cultural ideals must also be considered. Social norms of the ideal family are culturally sanctioned values that prescribe how families ought to be. Particular family patterns and roles are deemed desirable, proper, or essential for marriage and childrearing, in accord with prevailing standards in the dominant society or particular ethnic or religious values.

It is crucial not to conflate concepts of normal as typical and ideal. In the 1950s, sociologist Talcott Parsons's influential study of "the normal family" made a theoretical leap from description of a sample of "typical" white, middle-class, suburban, nuclear families to the prescription of those patterns, such as "proper" gender roles, as universal and essential for healthy child development (Parsons & Bales, 1955). Leading social scientists and psychiatrists adhered to that model for decades, contending that deviation from those patterns damaged children and even contributed to schizophrenia (Lidz, 1963). Such pathologizing of differences from the norm—either typical or ideal— stigmatizes families that do not conform to the standard, such as working mothers, single-parent households, and gay- or lesbian-headed families (see chapters in Part II, this volume).

Normal Family Processes

The conceptualization of normal family processes, grounded in family systems theory, considers both average and optimal functioning in terms of basic processes in human systems, dependent on an interaction of biopsychosocial variables (von Bertalanffy, 1968; Grinker, 1967). Viewing functioning in sociocultural and developmental contexts, this transactional approach attends to dynamic processes over time and affirms varied coping styles and multiple adaptational pathways. This perspective contrasts sharply from an acontextual approach seeking to define universal or fixed traits of a so-called normal family, thought of as a static, timeless structure or institution.

Normal functioning is conceptualized in terms of basic patterns of inter-action in relational systems (Watzlawick, Beavin, & Jackson, 1967). Such pro-cesses support the integration and maintenance of the family unit and its abil-ity to carry out essential tasks for the growth and well-being of its members, such as the nurturance, care, and protection of children, elders, and other vulnerable members. Unconventional (atypical) family arrangements may be optimal for the functioning of a particular family, fitting its challenges, resources, and context.

Families develop their own internal norms, expressed through explicit and unspoken relationship rules (Jackson, 1965). A set of patterned and pre-dictable rules, conveyed in family stories and ongoing transactions, regulates family processes and provides expectations about roles, actions, and conse-quences. Family belief systems are shared values and assumptions that guide family life, and provide meaning and organize experience in the social world (Reiss, 1981). Societal, ethnic, social class, and spiritual values strongly influ-ence family norms (see McGoldrick & Ashton, Chapter 11; Falicov, Chapter 13; Walsh, Chapter 15, this volume).

A *biopsychosocial systems orientation* takes into account the multiple, recursive influences in individual and family functioning. From an ecosys-temic perspective (Bronfenbrenner, 1979), each family's capabilities and cop-ing style are considered in relation to the needs of individual members and to the larger community and social systems in which the family is embedded. Family functioning is influenced by the *fit*, or compatibility, between indi-viduals, their families, and larger social systems. The bidirectional influences of genetic/biological vulnerabilities and other social influences must be con-sidered (D'Onofrio & Lahey, 2010; Spotts, Chapter 22, this volume). Family distress is viewed in context: It may be generated by internal stressors, such as the strain of coping with an illness, and complicated by external influences, such as inadequate health care (see Rolland, Chapter 19, this volume).

A *family developmental framework* considers processes in the multi-generational system as it moves forward over time (McGoldrick, Carter, & Garcia-Preto, 2011; see McGoldrick & Shibusawa, Chapter 16, this volume). The traditional model of the family life cycle, with normative assumptions of an expectable trajectory and sequence of stages—marriage followed by chil-drearing, launching, retirement, and death/widowhood—tended to stigmatize those whose life course differed. For instance, women who remained single or "childless" were widely judged as having incomplete lives. In contempo-rary life, individuals, couples, and families forge increasingly varied and fluid life passages (Cherlin, 2010). A remarriage family comprised of a 50-year-old husband, his 35-year-old wife, their toddler twins, and his adolescent chil-dren, in shared custody with their mother, cannot be simply classified at a single particular life stage. Still, a flexible family developmental framework can be of value to identify salient issues and challenges that commonly arise with particular phases and transitions, as with parenthood and adolescence, and with divorce and stepfamily formation. Family development can usefully be conceptualized in terms of adaptational processes that involve mastery of challenges and transitional stresses. Optimal family processes may vary with different developmental demands. For instance, families need to shift from high cohesion in rearing small children to more autonomy with adolescents.

Normative stressors are those that are considered common and predictable (Boss, 2001). It is normal to experience disruption with major transitions, such as the birth of the first child (see Cowan & Cowan, Chapter 18, this volume). *Non-normative stressors*, which are uncommon, unexpected, or "off-time" in chronological or social expectations, such as death of a child or early widowhood (Neugarten, 1976), tend to be more difficult (Walsh, 2009a). Intense distress at such times is common (i.e., normal). Strains may be worsened by a pileup or cumulative impact of multiple stressors, both internal and external. How the family deals with stresses as a functional unit is critical. Many adaptational pathways are possible, with more resilient families using a larger variety of coping techniques, more effective problem-solving strategies, and more flexibility in dealing with internal and external life events (Walsh, 2003, 2006; see Walsh, Chapter 17, this volume).

In summary, the integration of systemic and developmental perspectives forms an overarching framework for considering normality. The assessment of average and optimal family processes is contingent on both social and developmental contexts. What is normal—either typical or optimal—varies, with different internal and external demands posing challenges for both continuity and change over the course of the family life cycle (Falicov, 1988). This developmental systems paradigm provides a common foundation for family therapy and family process research, and for the conceptual models by contributors to this volume.

It is important also to clarify the terms "functional" and "dysfunctional," which widely replaced more value-laden labels of "normal" and "pathological," yet have become value-laden themselves. "Functional" essentially means workable. It refers to the utility of family patterns in achieving family goals, including instrumental tasks and the socioemotional well-being of family members. Whether processes are functional is contingent on each family's aims, as well as situational and developmental demands, resources, and sociocultural influences.

"Dysfunctional," in a purely descriptive sense, simply refers to family patterns that are not working and are associated with symptoms of distress— regardless of a problem's source. However, the term "dysfunctional" has come to connote serious disturbance and causal attributions that tend to pathologize families and blame them for individual and social problems. Popular self-help and recovery movements abound for "survivors" of "dysfunctional families." Because individual problems are not necessarily caused by family pathology, caution is urged in labeling families, distinguishing those with serious disturbance, abuse, and neglect from most families that are struggling with ordinary problems in living or impacted by major stressors. It is preferable, and less stigmatizing, to identify particular family processes or relational patterns that are dysfunctional and not to label the family. For families struggling with many persistent life stressors, particularly low-income and minority families, the term "multistressed families" is preferable to the pejorative label "multi-problem families."

Yet what is meant by "functional": functional to what end and for whom? A pattern may be functional at one systems level but dysfunctional at another. As a classic example, interactional rules that stabilize a fragile couple relationship (e.g., conflict avoidance) may have dysfunctional consequences for a child who becomes the go-between. Furthermore, an assessment of family functioning must evaluate available resources and the impact of other systems. For instance, workplace policies deemed necessary for productivity are too often detrimental for families (see Fraenkel & Capstick, Chapter 4, this volume). Dual-earner and single-parent households experience tremendous role strain with the pressures of multiple conflicting demands and inadequate resources (Bianchi & Milkie, 2010). Many parents manage to keep their families intact and their children functional only at a high cost to their couple relationship or personal well-being.

THE CHANGING LANDSCAPE OF FAMILY LIFE: THE BROAD SPECTRUM OF NORMAL FAMILIES

The family has been regarded as the linchpin of the social order. Fears of the demise of the family escalate in periods of social turbulence, as in recent decades when the very survival of the family has been questioned (Coontz, 1997). Many societies have worried about the breakdown of the "traditional family," fitting their own established social, cultural, and religious norms.

Popular images of the typical "normal family" and the ideal "healthy family" both shape and reflect dominant social norms and values for how families are supposed to be. In the United States, two eras have become mythologized: the traditional family of the preindustrial past and the nuclear family of the 1950s. These cherished images of the family have lagged behind emerging social realities, often fueling nostalgia for return to families of the past. Just as storytelling has served in every age and culture to transmit family norms, television and the Internet have become the prime media in depicting family life. For the generation of "baby boomers," TV dramas such as *Little House on the Prairie* transported viewers back to the distant rural past, to a time of large stable families, homespun values, and multigenerational connectedness. Family series, such as *Ozzie and Harriet* and *Leave It to Beaver*, idealized the mid-20th-century white, middle-class, suburban nuclear family, headed by the breadwinner father and supported by the homemaker mother. The lasting popularity of such images expressed longing for not only a romanticized notion of the family but also seemingly simpler, happier, and more secure times. Over recent decades, family sitcoms have gradually portrayed a broader spectrum of family life amid striking social changes. Currently, family sitcoms, such as *Modern Family*, offer less idealized images and more varied and complex patterns in "new normal" family life (Feiler, 2011). They feature loving yet complicated bonds within and across households and generations as members reconfigure and redefine "family" through marriage and cohabiting, divorce, single parenting, and remarriage, and are inclusive of gay couples and interracial adoption. Family members grapple with spousal conflict, childrearing dilemmas, and the intrusion of technology in everyday life; they deal with serious issues, such as substance abuse; and yet they cherish and celebrate their family ties.

With the transformation of norms and structures of societies worldwide, our understanding of family functioning and our approaches to strengthen families must be attuned to our times and social contexts. This chapter and volume focus primarily on patterns in Western societies and statistics in the United States, yet they are relevant to many societies experiencing rapid transformation from traditional to postindustrial, urban contexts. Overall, demographic trends reveal an increasingly diverse and complex family life, and a more ambiguous and fluid set of categories traditionally used to define the family (Cherlin, 2010). A sociohistorical lens offers a valuable perspective on contemporary families, their strengths, and their challenges. At the forefront of current trends are the following:

- Varied family forms
- Varied gender roles and relationships
- Growing cultural diversity: Multicultural society
- Increasing socioeconomic disparity
- Varying and expanded family life course

Varied Family Forms

The idealized American image of intact, multigenerational family households of preindustrial society distorts their actual instability and complexity, with many life uncertainties and unpredictable family transitions. Intact family units were commonly disrupted by early parental death, which led to remarriage and stepfamilies, or to child placements in extended families, foster care, or orphanages. Most families now have greater control over the choice and timing of marriage and parenting, largely related to education, birth control, and medical advances that have increased fertility and childbearing options, and lengthened life expectancy.

American family households before the mid-20th century were actually quite diverse and complex, as they continue to be in many parts of the world. Flexible structures and boundaries with extended kin and community enabled resilience in weathering harsh and unstable life conditions. Households commonly included non-kin boarders, offering surrogate families for individuals on their own, facilitating adaptation of new immigrants, and providing income and companionship for widows and older adults (Aries, 1962). Relatives across households were actively involved in childrearing and care of the infirmed. Aunts, uncles, and godparents played important roles in children's lives, and stepped in as surrogate parents in times of need. In some traditional cultures, a brother-in-law was expected to marry his deceased brother's widow, making their future children both cousins and half-siblings of his own children by another marriage. Actually, the current proliferation of diverse family arrangements and informal support networks continues a long tradition across cultures and over the millennia.

The nuclear family structure arose with the industrial era, peaking in the United States in the 1950s. The household comprised an intact, two-parent family unit headed by a male breadwinner and supported by his full-time homemaker wife, who devoted herself to household management, childrearing, and elder care. Following the Great Depression and World War II, a strong economy and government benefits fueled a broad middle-class prosperity, providing for education, jobs, and home ownership, and enabling most families to live comfortably on one income. After a steady decline in the birth rate, couples married younger and in greater numbers, producing the "baby boom."

In earlier eras, the family fulfilled a broad array of economic, educational, social, and religious functions intertwined with the larger community. Relationships were valued for a variety of contributions to the collective family unit. In contrast, the modern nuclear family, expected to be a self-reliant household, became a rigid, closed system, especially in suburban enclaves, isolated from extended kin and community connections that had been sources of resilience. It also lost the flexibility that had enabled households to reconfigure according to need. Unrealistically high expectations for spouses to fulfill all needs for romantic love, support, and companionship contributed to the fragility of marriage (Coontz, 2005).

Today, the idealized model of the intact nuclear family, with gendered breadwinner–homemaker roles, is only a narrow band on the broad spectrum of normal families. A reshaping of contemporary family life now encompasses multiple, evolving family cultures and structures. Two decades of research have provided solid evidence that families and their children can thrive in a variety of kinship arrangements (Cherlin, 2010; Lansford, Ceballo, Abby, & Stewart, 2001).

Dual-Earner Families

Over two-thirds of all two-parent households in the United States are dual-earner families (see Fraenkel & Capstick, Chapter 4, this volume). Two paychecks have become essential for most families to maintain even a modest standard of living. Women's career aspirations, economic pressures, and divorce have brought the vast majority of wives and mothers into the workforce. Yet flexible work schedules and affordable, quality child care are still difficult to obtain, in contrast to most European societies, which provide generous benefits and services to support families of working parents (Cooke & Baxter, 2010).

Declining Marriage and Birth Rates

Over recent decades, marriage and birth rates have sharply declined in many parts of the world. Just over half of all adults in the United States are currently married, in contrast to 7 in 10 adults in 1960. The average age at marriage has risen to 28 for men and 26 for women, up from ages 22 and 20, respectively, in 1960 (U.S. Bureau of the Census, 2009). Childbearing is also increasingly delayed, especially for women with advanced education and careers. There are striking racial, ethnic, socioeconomic, and educational differentials: Less-educated and lower-income adults are significantly less likely to marry, but those who do tend to marry younger and are more likely to divorce (Cherlin, 2010). Many couples today choose not to have children, defining their relationship as family. Commonly, they decide to raise a pet before, or in lieu of, a child (Walsh, 2009c).

Increasing Cohabitation and Single Living

Cohabitation by unmarried partners continues to be widespread. More than half of all adults cohabit with a partner at some time in their lives. Nearly two-thirds think of their living arrangement as a step toward marriage. Others live together after divorce or widowhood, often preferring not to remarry. Unmarried couples sometimes drift into cohabitation in a gradual process, without a clear decision to live together. Many break up, most commonly within 3 years. For same-sex couples, cohabitation and domestic partnerships remain the only alternatives to marriage outside states where same-sex marriage is legal.

Childbearing and childrearing by cohabiting couples have become more common. While 40% of children are born outside marriage, half of those unmarried women (i.e., legally single parents) are living with the fathers of their children. Also, nearly 40% of unmarried couples have at least one biological child of either partner living in the home (Kennedy & Bumpass, 2008). Instability in these relationships increases the risk of child adjustment problems (Fomby & Cherlin, 2007).

Households are increasingly varied. More people are living on their own at some period in their lives, although the recent economic recession has led more people to share residences with family members or roommates. The number of single adults has nearly doubled over the past two decades. An emerging trend is "living apart together": adults who are in a stable, intimate couple relationship but live separately (Cherlin, 2010).

Single-Parent Households

Single-parent families, headed by an unmarried or divorced parent, now account for over 25% of all households. There are notable differences in births to unmarried women by race: 72% of African American women, 53% of Hispanic women, and 29% of white women (Pew Research Center,

2010b). Nearly half of all children—and over 60% of ethnic/minority children in poverty—are expected to live for at least part of their childhoods in one-parent households (see Anderson, Chapter 6, this volume). Mothers head more than 85% of primary residences. Lack of financial support and inconsistent involvement by many nonresidential fathers have been major factors in child maladjustment. There has been a decline in unwed teen pregnancy, with its high risk for long-term poverty, instability, poor-quality parenting, and a cluster of health and psychosocial problems for mothers and their children. Increasingly, older single women have been choosing to parent on their own when they lack suitable partners for childrearing. Children generally fare well in financially secure single-parent homes where there is strong parental functioning, especially when supported by extended kin networks.

Divorce and Remarriage

Divorce rates, after rising and peaking in 1980, have declined and leveled off at around 45% for first marriages (Amato, 2010). Over 20% of married couples divorce within 5 years. The vast majority of divorced individuals go on to remarry or cohabit, making stepfamilies increasingly common (see Pasley & Garneau, Chapter 7, this volume). Yet the complexity of stepfamily integration contributes to a divorce rate at nearly 60% of remarriages. Claims that divorce inevitably damages children, based on small clinical samples, have not been substantiated in large-scale, carefully controlled research (see Greene, Anderson, Forgatch, De Garmo, & Hetherington, Chapter 5, this volume). Although some studies have found a higher risk of problems for children in divorced families than for those in intact families, fewer than 1 in 4 children from divorced families show serious or lasting difficulties.

Divorce entails a complex set of changing conditions over time. Longitudinal studies have tracked family patterns associated with risk and resilience in the predivorce climate through separation and divorce processes, subsequent reorganization, and, for most, later stepfamily integration (Hetherington & Kelly, 2002). In high-conflict and abusive families, children whose parents divorce do better than those whose families remain intact. Moreover, other factors, particularly economic strain, heighten risk for maladjustment. Above all else, children's healthy adaptation depends on the strong functioning of their residential parents and the quality of relationships with and between parents before and after divorce (Ahrons, 2004).

Adoptive Families

Adoptions have also been increasing for single parents as well as couples (see Rampage et al., Chapter 10, this volume). Most adoptions are now open, based on findings that children benefit developmentally if they know who their birth families are, have the option for contact, and are encouraged to connect with their cultural heritage, especially in biracial and international adoptions (Samuels, 2010). In foster care, permanency in placement is seen as

optimal, keeping siblings together whenever possible, and avoiding the instability and losses in multiple placements.

Kinship Care

Kinship care by extended family members, either legal guardianship or an
informal arrangement, has become the preferred option when parents are
unable to provide adequate care of their children (see Engstrom, Chapter
9, this volume). In the United States one child in 10 lives with a grandparent, with the number increasing steadily over the past decade (Livingston &
Parker, 2010). Kinship care families are disproportionally African American
and Latino, although the sharpest rise during the recent recession has been
among European Americans. In about 40% of cases, grandparents, most
often grandmothers, serve as primary caregivers. Most have been caring for
their grandchildren for a long time: More than half have been the primary
caregiver to at least one grandchild for 3 years or more. Most grandparent
caregivers have very limited financial resources with nearly 1 in 5 living below
the poverty line.

Gender Variance, Same-Sex Couples, and Parenting

Conceptualizations of gender identity and sexual orientation have expanded
to a broader and more fluid understanding of gender variance, and with
greater attention to bisexual and transgender persons (Lev, 2010). The past
decade has seen increasing acceptance of same-sex couples and expanding
legalization of domestic partnerships and marriage. Growing numbers of gay
and lesbian single parents and couples are raising children through adoption
and a variety of reproductive approaches (see Green, Chapter 8, this volume).
Although stigma and controversy persist, particularly among older generations and religious conservatives, public attitudes have been shifting toward
greater acceptance (Pew Research Center, 2010). A large body of research
over two decades has clearly documented that children raised by lesbian and
gay parents fare as well as those reared by heterosexual parents in relationship quality, psychological well-being, and social adjustment (see review by
Biblarz & Savci, 2010). Most studies have focused on co-mother families,
with two lesbian parents (biological, social, or step), finding many strengths,
including high levels of shared responsibility, decision making, and parental
investment.

Lev (2010) encourages researchers, family therapists, and society in general to celebrate the unique qualities that gay and lesbian, bisexual, transgender, and questioning (LGBTQ) parents bring to childrearing. She has raised
concern about underlying heteronormative assumptions in research viewing
as successful LGBTQ parents who raise "normal" heterosexual children who
are no different than those raised in heterosexual families. Being reared in
gender-variant families involves certain "differences," such as unique social

dynamics with two moms or two dads, and they are commonly formed differently than most heterosexual families. A sperm or egg donor, especially a sibling or friend may be quite involved in raising a child. Instead of expecting gay families to be "just like" straight families, both their commonalities and differences need to be acknowledged and honored.

Varied Gender Roles

Over the centuries, and still today in many traditional cultures, marriage has been viewed in functional terms: Matches by families for their children were made on the basis of economic and social position; wives and children were the property of their husbands and fathers. The family patriarch held authority over all members, controlling major decisions and resources. For the husband to be certain of his progeny and (male) heirs, the honor of the family required absolute fidelity of the wife and chastity of marriageable daughters. The valuing of sons over daughters has had devastating consequences for the well-being and survival of girls and women in many parts of the world.

The integration of family and work life in rural settings allowed for intensive sharing of labor, including work by children. Although families had many more children, women invested relatively less parenting time, contributing to the shared family economy in varied ways. Fathers, older children, extended kin, and neighbors all participated actively in childrearing. Industrialization and urbanization brought a redefinition of gender roles and functions. Family work and "productive" paid work became segregated into separate, gendered spheres of home and workplace. Domesticity became glorified, assigning to women exclusively the roles of custodian of the hearth, nurturer of the young, and caretaker of the old. Particularly in North American and British societies, the maternal role became reified, with mothers regarded as the primary, essential, and irreplaceable caregivers responsible for the healthy development of children—and to blame for all problems. Yet women's unpaid domestic work was devalued and rendered invisible, with their total dependency on financial support by male breadwinners. For those in the workforce, their wages and job status were substantially lower than men's, and they remained bound to their primary family obligations—a dual disparity that widely persists.

The belief that "proper gender roles" are essential for healthy family functioning and child development dominated sociological and mental health conceptualization of the normal American family, supported by Parsons's view that the nuclear family structure provided for a healthy complementarity in the division of roles into male instrumental leadership and female socioemotional support (Parsons & Bales, 1955). The breadwinner–homemaker model was highly adaptive to the demands of the industrial economy. However, the rigid gender roles, subordination of wives, and peripheral involvement of most fathers was detrimental to spousal and parent–child relations. The loss of community further isolated men and women from companionship and support. Role expectations came at great personal cost for women, with a disproportionate burden in caring for others while denying their own needs and identities (McGoldrick, Anderson, & Walsh, 1989). Men's self-esteem and value to their families was tied to success as a breadwinner; intimacy with spouses suffered, and fathers barely knew their children.

The feminist movement, in the late 1960s, reacted to the stultifying effects of the modern family model, with its separate and unequal spheres. With reproductive choice and family planning, women sought in the workplace the personal growth and status valued by society. As wives combined jobs and childrearing, they found they were adding on a second shift, since most husbands did not make reciprocal changes toward equal sharing of family responsibilities. Women were made to feel guilty that their outside work was harmful to the family, undermining their husbands' esteem as breadwinners and endangering their children's healthy development. The women's movement then shifted focus in efforts to redefine and rebalance gendered role relations, so that both men and women could seek personal fulfillment, be gainfully employed, and share in the responsibilities and joys of family life. Progress toward equality in recent years has been steady yet uneven. Women have advanced in education and job status, yet they earn roughly 80% of men's salary for comparable jobs (see Fraenkel & Capstick, Chapter 4, this volume). Men are more actively involved in homemaking and parenting, yet working wives still carry a disproportionate share of household and child care obligations. Most young couples today share the desire for a full and equal partnership in family life, yet living out this aim continues to be a work in progress (see Knudson-Martin, Chapter 14, this volume).

Growing Cultural Diversity: Multicultural Society

One of the most striking features of North American families today is the growing cultural diversity. The foreign-born population in the United States has tripled over recent decades, with most coming from Latin America and Asia (McGoldrick, Giordano, & Garcia-Preto, 2005). Over 1 in 5 persons is either a foreign-born or first-generation resident. Through immigration and higher birth rates, ethnic and racial minorities now account for nearly half of the population and are expected to become the majority over coming decades (U.S. Bureau of the Census, 2010). Hispanics are rapidly becoming the largest minority group, currently at 15% of the population, and expected to rise to 25% by 2030. Although immigrants from some regions of the world are often treated as monolithic groups, especially Latinos, Asian Americans, and Africans, there are marked differences in country of origin, racial and ethnic identity, language patterns, religious beliefs, education, and socioeconomic status. Family networks are a complex mix of immigrant and native-born members, including many second- or third-generation Americans. Sadly, recent economic insecurity and fears of terrorism have aggravated racial discrimination and intolerance toward non-European immigrants and minorities, especially Latinos and Muslims, complicating their adaptive challenges.

Contrary to the analogy of the melting pot, American society, with a long tradition of immigration, has always been diverse (McGoldrick et al., 2005). In earlier periods, strong pressure for assimilation into mainstream society led many immigrants to cut off their extended family ties and leave ethnic traditions behind. More recently, scholars find that immigrants, and especially transnationals, are more resilient in navigating the challenges of adaptation when they also maintain continuities in both worlds, essentially becoming bicultural (Falicov, 2007; see Falicov, Chapter 13, this volume). Parents are encouraged to raise their children with knowledge and pride in their kin and community roots, language, ethnic heritage, and religious values.

In our multicultural society, growing numbers of children and families are multiracial (Burton, Bonilla-Silva, Ray, Buckelew, & Freeman, 2010; Samuels, 2010). Interracial and interfaith unions are increasingly common and accepted, blending diversity within families (Rosenfeld, 2007; Walsh, 2010; see Walsh, Chapter 15, this volume). Beyond acknowledgement of diversity, cultivation of cultural pluralism, with mutual understanding and respect for commonalities and differences, can be a source of strength that vitalizes a society.

Increasing Socioeconomic Disparity

Socioeconomic influences must be taken into account in appraising family functioning (Barrett & Turner, 2005; Conger, Conger, & Martin, 2010). Social scientists and public discourse have too often generalized to all families on the basis of white, middle-class values and experience or have compared ethnic and racial groups without adequate consideration of their socioeconomic conditions. Over recent decades, due to economic and political forces, the broad middle class has been shrinking, and the gap of inequality between the rich and poor has widened (Edin & Kissane, 2010). In 2008, 13.2% of the American population and nearly 1 in 5 children were officially poor—rates surpassing those of most Western industrialized countries. Blacks, Hispanics, and female-headed households were most vulnerable to poverty.

Harsh economic conditions and job dislocation have a devastating impact on family formation, stability, and well-being. Independent adulthood is being delayed. The financial prospects of most young families today are lower than those of their parents, with a decline in median income and more families living in poverty. Many are struggling anxiously through uncertain times as businesses downsize, workers lose jobs, and families lose homes to foreclosure. As the economy has shifted from the industrial and manufacturing sectors to technology, those with limited education, job skills, and employment opportunities have been hardest hit. A new "marriage gap" is increasingly aligned with the growing income gap (Cherlin, 2010; Fincham & Beach, 2010). Those with bleak earnings prospects are less likely to get married and more likely to divorce. Persistent unemployment and recurring job transitions can fuel substance abuse, family conflict and violence, and an increase in poor, single-parent households. The impact of homelessness on children and families is devastating (Bassuk, 2010).

Yet it is a mistake to equate poor families with problem families. Data for more than 100,000 families from the National Survey of Children's Health suggest that although families in poverty experience socioeconomic disadvantages, they have many strengths, such as the closeness of relationships, and routines such as shared meals, however meager (Valladares & Moore, 2009). Still, their life chances are worsened by inadequate health care, blighted neighborhood conditions, poor schools, discrimination, and lack of opportunity to succeed. As Aponte (1994) stresses, emotional and relational problems in poor, disproportionately minority families must be understood within the fabric of their socioeconomic and political contexts: They are vulnerable to larger social dislocations and cannot insulate themselves. And in harsh economic times, "when society stumbles, its poorest citizens are tossed about and often crushed" (p. 8). Today's immense structural disparities perpetuate a vast chasm between the rich and the poor, and growing numbers of families struggle to make ends meet. Structural changes in the larger society and its institutional supports are essential if most families are to thrive.

Varying and Extended Family Life Course

As societies worldwide are rapidly aging, four- and five-generation families are increasingly common (Bengston, 2001; Waite, 2009). Yet the importance of the family in later life has been neglected in research and clinical practice (Walsh, 2011). Life expectancy in the United States has increased from 47 years in 1900 to over 78 years today. The booming over-65 age group, now 13% of the population, is expected to double over coming decades. Despite the stigma of ageism, focused on decline and decay, medical advances and neuroscience findings of neuroplasticity support the possibilities for functioning and growth into later years. Most older adults remain healthy and happy well into their 70s finding meaning and fulfillment in new pursuits and active involvement with friends and family, especially with grandchildren. Yet, with advancing age, chronic illnesses and disability pose stressful family caregiving challenges. Adults over age 85, the fastest growing age group, are the most vulnerable, and nearly half are likely to be affected by Alzheimer's disease. A family systems approach broadens the prevalent individual model of caregiving, which overburdens the designated primary caregiver, to involve family members as a caregiving team, each contributing according to abilities and resources. With fewer young people in families to support the growing number of older adults, and with threats to retirement and health care benefits, growing insecurity and intergenerational tensions are more likely in coming years.

Marriage vows "till death do us part" are harder to keep over a lengthening life course. Couples at midlife can anticipate another 20–40 years together. Although the high divorce rate is of concern, perhaps it is more remarkable that over 50% of first marriages do last a lifetime. It is difficult for one relationship to weather the storms and to meet changing needs and priorities. As Margaret Mead (1972) observed, in youth, romance and passion stand out in choosing a partner. In childrearing, relationship satisfaction is linked more to sharing family joys and responsibilities. In later life, needs for companionship and caregiving come to the fore. In view of these shifts, Mead suggested that time-limited, renegotiable contracts and serial monogamy might better fit a long life. In fact, two or three committed long-term relationships, along with periods of cohabitation and single living, have become increasingly common (Cherlin, 2009; Hetherington, 2003; Sassler, 2010). Most adults and their children will move in and out of a variety of family structures as they come together, separate, and recombine. Because instability in relationships and households heightens risk for maladaptation and child problems, families will need to buffer transitions and learn how to live successfully in complex arrangements.

Our conception of the family life cycle must be altered from a normative expectation of orderly progression through predictable life stages to many varied life paths and a wider range of options fitting the diverse preferences and challenges that make each individual, couple, and family unique. Some become first-time parents at the age when others become grandparents. Others start second families in middle age; some who repartner have children as young as their own grandchildren. Many become actively involved with nephews and nieces or with youth or older adults in their communities. Most lives are enriched by forging a variety of intimate relationships and significant kin and social bonds within and beyond households (Roseneil & Budgeon, 2004).

Family Complexities and Lagging Perceptions

Families with varied configurations have different structural constraints and resources for functioning. Two-earner families must organize their households, roles, and family lives quite differently from the breadwinner–homemaker model. Single parents must organize differently from two-parent households. Postdivorce families with joint custody must help children shuttling between two households to feel at home in each and to adapt to different rules and routines. Stepfamily constellations may span two, three, or more households, and the needs for contact between children and grandparents and other extended family members must be considered. With the death of a biological parent or with divorce, a stepparent—or nonbiological coparent—can be legally disenfranchised from rights to continuing contact with children they have been raising. With the intact, self-sufficient nuclear family taken as the norm, there has been insufficient appreciation of strong extended family bonds, especially in African American and immigrant families.

Our language and preconceptions about "the normal family" can pathologize relationship patterns that do not conform to the intact nuclear family model with traditional gender roles. The label "latchkey child" implies *maternal* neglect when parents must work away from home. Despite the growing involvement of fathers and the active contributions to family life by grandparents and other caregivers, there is a lingering presumption that they "help out" or stand in for a working or absent mother. Too often, problems of a child living in a single-parent household are reflexively attributed to "a broken home" or the absence of a father in the house. The term "single-parent family" can blind us to the potential role of a nonresidential parent or the support of the extended kin network. The pejorative label "deadbeat dad" is especially harsh and writes off fathers who do care about their children and could become more involved and responsible than they may have been in the past. A stepparent or adoptive parent may be considered not the "real" or "natural" parent. The belief that stepfamilies are inherently deficient often leads them to emulate the intact nuclear family model—sealing their borders, cutting off ties with nonresidential parents, and feeling they have failed when they don't immediately blend. As family therapy pioneer Carl Whitaker noted (see Walsh, Chapter 2, this volume), the very attempts to fit the social mold of a normal family are often sources of problems and deep pain.

Larger Social Forces and Family Policies

The importance of social and economic contexts for success or breakdown in marriages and families today is increasingly clear (Fincham & Beach, 2010). Many strains in family life today are generated by larger forces in the world around them. Families have experienced multiple dislocations. Job security, health care coverage, and retirement benefits are increasingly uncertain. Workplace demands spill over into family life, generating ongoing stress (Repetti, Wang, & Saxbe, 2009). Conflicting work and family demands create time binds, pressuring lives at an accelerated pace as family members seek elusive "quality time." Many families are exposed to a toxic social environment. Besieged parents are unsure how to raise their children well in a hazardous world, and how to counter pressures of the Internet and popular culture that saturate homes and minds. Geographic mobility, often due to forces in the job market, contributes to the fragmentation of families and communities. Many families must repeatedly expand and contract between two-parent and one-parent households to meet demands of distant jobs or military service.

Seen in context, the stresses in family life are more understandable. Social policies, programs, and services must be geared to help struggling families to manage, with attention to those who are marginalized and underserved, and with safety nets for those most vulnerable (Bogenschneider & Corbett, 2010). Larger system changes and creative strategies are required to insure: workplace security, flexibility, and gender equality; adequate, affordable healthcare and housing; quality care for children and family members with disabilities; educational and job opportunities; and supportive community resources. The rhetoric on behalf of strong families must be matched by family-centered policies—both public and private—to enable families to flourish.

Clinical Implications: A Broad, Inclusive Perspective

With so many changes and challenges in contemporary life, families worry about how well they are doing. They often do not seek help because they fear being judged dysfunctional or deficient. As helping professionals, we also need to examine our implicit assumptions about family normality, health, and dysfunction from our own worldviews, influenced by our cultural standards, personal experience, and clinical theories (see Walsh, Chapter 2, this volume). Through these filtered lenses, we co-construct with clients the problems we "discover" in families and may set therapeutic goals tied to preconceptions about healthy functioning.

As the very definition of "family" can encompass a wide spectrum of relationship options, it is important to explore each family's definition of family and convey our own broad view. Who do they include? Who is significant and what roles do they play? Are there friends they consider their "chosen family?" Legal and blood definitions of "family" or social norms may constrain clients from mentioning important relationships, such as a cohabiting partner. It is crucial not to equate family with household, particularly with divorced, recombined, and transnational families, which have important bonds across household and geographic boundaries. Informal (fictive) kin may be significant. It is also important to ask about the role of pets—considered by most as important family members (Walsh, 2009b, 2009c). Attachment bonds with companion animals can be especially significant for children, singles, and older adults, and can be valued resources through difficult family transitions and adaptation to loss.

In all assessments, it is important to gain a holistic view of the family system and its community linkages. This includes all members of current households, the extended family network, and key relationships that are—or have been—important in the functioning of the family and its members. Clients who presume that "family" is equated with "household" or with legal marriage may not mention a nonresidential parent, children from former marriages, or other relationship that have been, or could become, important resources. Genograms and time lines (McGoldrick, Gerson, & Petry, 2008) are invaluable tools to visualize and bring coherence to a complex network of relationships and residential patterns, noting significant losses and transitions, and identifying existing and potential resources in kin and social networks.

Family time management has become crucial. Work–family strains are particularly important to address, including role functions, financial pressures, and time binds. Inquiring about a typical day and a typical week in family life can reveal fault lines and open discussion about ways to ease pressures. When parents are overburdened, clinicians can explore ways to increase resources and facilitate negotiation of more equitable sharing of responsibilities and joys in family life.

Because transitions such as separation, divorce, and remarriage are evolving processes over time, clinicians need to inquire about previous family units, the timing and nature of events, the current state of relationships, and future anticipated changes in order to understand and address problems in family developmental context. In particular, recent or impending changes in membership or household composition should be noted, as these disruptions may contribute to presenting problems. Clinicians can help families to buffer disruptive transitions and to restabilize family life, creating "new normal" patterns to adapt to new conditions.

Clinicians can usefully draw on family process research demonstrating how a variety of family structures can function well; none is inherently healthy or pathological. As we see in the chapters in Parts II, III, and IV in this volume, a robust body of research is illuminating key variables in risk and resilience, which can usefully inform practice to strengthen family functioning and the well-being of members.

FAMILIES IN TRANSFORMATION: A PLURALISTIC VIEW OF NORMAL FAMILIES

Over recent decades, families have been in transformation, with growing diversity and complexity in structure, gender roles and sexual orientation, multicultural makeup, socioeconomic conditions, and life cycle patterns. As family scholars have concluded (Cherlin, 2010), it no longer makes sense to use the nuclear family as the standard against which various forms of the family are measured. Families in our distant past and in most cultures worldwide have had multiple, varied structures. What remains constant is the centrality, and the fundamental necessity, of relatedness. Our growing diversity requires an inclusive pluralism, beyond tolerance of difference to respect for many different ways to be families, recognizing both their distinctiveness and their commonalities.

Recent surveys find that most Americans today do have an expansive definition of what constitutes a family (Pew Research, 2010a, 2010b). Public response to changing marital norms and family forms reflects a mix of acceptance and unease, with younger generations more inclined to view varied family forms, same-sex marriage, and cohabitation in a positive light. Despite concerns, two-thirds of all adults are optimistic about the future of marriage and family. Most people still view loving, committed bonds—and their own families—as the most important sources of happiness and fulfillment in life. More than 8 in 10 say the family they live in now is as close as or closer than the family in which they grew up.

Yearnings for "family," "home," and "community" are heightened by continuing threats of global instability. As Maya Angelou affirmed, "The ache for home lives in all of us; the safe place where we can go." Life was never more secure in earlier times or distant places, yet families today are in uncharted territory, lacking a map to guide their passage. The many discontinuities and unknowns generate an uncomfortable tension. Myths of the ideal family compound the sense of deficiency and failure for families even though such models don't fit their lives. Yet most families are showing remarkable resilience, making the best of their situations and creatively reconfiguring family life. Constructing a variety of household and kinship arrangements, they are devising new relationship strategies to fit their aspirations and their challenges, and inventing new models of human connectedness. Most are sustaining strong extended family connections across distances and finding kinship with longtime close friends. Many are seeking community and spirituality outside mainstream institutional structures, weaving together meaningful elements of varied traditions to fit their lives and relationships (Walsh, 2010). Particularly impressive are those who reshape the experience of divorce from a painful, bitter schism and loss of resources into a viable kin network—involving new and former partners, multiple sets of children, stepkin, extended families, and friends—into households and support systems collaborating to survive and flourish (Stacey, 1990). It is ironic that today's varied relational configurations are termed "nontraditional families," as their flexibility, diversity, and community recall the resilience found in the varied households and loosely knit kin networks of the past.

In our rapidly changing world, our lives can seem unpredictable and overwhelming. As Mary Catherine Bateson (1994) observed, adaptation emerges out of encounters with novel conditions that may seem chaotic. An intense multiplicity of vision, enhancing insight and creativity, is needed today. Although we can never be fully prepared for new demands, Bateson argues that we can be strengthened to meet uncertainty:

> The quality of improvisation characterizes more and more lives today, lived in uncertainty, full of the inklings of alternatives. In a rapidly changing and interdependent world, single models are less likely to be viable and plans more likely to go awry. The effort to combine multiple models risks the disasters of conflict and runaway misunderstanding, but the effort to adhere blindly to some traditional model for a life risks disaster not only for the person who follows it but for the entire system in which he or she is embedded, indeed for all other living systems with which that life is linked. (p. 8)

If we knew the future of particular families, we might help them gain the necessary skills to succeed. However, today's families need to meet emerging demands of a dynamic society and a changing global environment. As Bateson observes, ambiguity is the warp of life, and cannot be eliminated. In her apt metaphor, "we are called to join in a dance whose steps must be learned along the way" (1994, p. 10).

Thus, we can help families to carry on the process of learning throughout life, to sustain continuities along with change, and to find coherence within complexity. The ability to combine multiple roles and adapt to new challenges can be learned. Encouraging such vision and skills is a core element of strengths-based approaches to family therapy. To enable families to thrive, social and economic policies, as well as clinical and community services, must be attuned to our times. Crisis and challenge are part of the human condition; how we respond can make all the difference for family well-being and successful adaptation.

REFERENCES

Ahrons, C. (2004). *We're still family*. New York: HarperCollins.

Amato, P. (2010). Research on divorce: Continuing trends and new developments. *Journal of Marriage and Family, 72*, 650–666.

Aponte, H. (1994). *Bread and spirit: Therapy with the new poor*. New York: Norton.

Aries, P. (1962). *Centuries of childhood: A social history of family life*. New York: Knopf.

Barrett, A. E., & Turner, R. J. (2005). Family structure and mental health: The mediating effects of socioeconomic status, family process, and social stress. *Journal of Health and Social Behavior, 46*, 156–169.

Bassuk, E. (2010). Ending homelessness in America. *American Journal of Orthopsychiatry, 80*, 496–504.

Bateson, M. C. (1994). *Peripheral visions*. New York: HarperCollins.

Bengston, V. G. (2001). Beyond the nuclear family: The increasing importance of multigenerational bonds. *Journal of Marriage and the Family, 63*, 1–16.

Bianchi, S. B., & Milkie, M. A. (2010). Work and family research in the first decade of the 21st century. *Journal of Marriage and Family, 72*, 705–725.

Biblarz, T., & Savci, E. (2010). Lesbian, gay, bi-sexual, and transgender families. *Journal of Marriage and Family, 72*, 480–497.

Bogenschneider, K., & Corbett, T. (2010). Family policy: Becoming a field of inquiry and subfield of social policy. *Journal of Marriage and Family, 72*, 783–803.

Boss, P. (2001). *Family stress management: A contextual approach*. Thousand Oaks, CA: Sage.

Boyd-Franklin, N. (2003). *Black families in family therapy: Understanding the African American experience* (2nd ed.). New York: Guilford Press.

Bronfenbrenner, U. (1979). *The ecology of human development*. Cambridge, MA: Harvard University Press.

Burton, L. M., Bonilla-Silva, E., Ray, V., Buckelew, R., & Freeman, E. H. (2010). Critical race theories, colorism, and the decade's research on families of color. *Journal of Marriage and Family, 72*, 420–439.

Cherlin, A. (2010). Demographic trends in the United States: A review of research in the 2000s. *Journal of Marriage and Family, 72*, 403–419.

Cherlin, A. J. (2009). *The marriage-go-round: The state of marriage and the family in America today*. New York: Knopf.

Conger, R., Conger, K., & Martin, M. (2010). Socioeconomic status, family process, and individual development. *Journal of Marriage and Family, 72*, 685–704.

Cooke, L. P., & Baxter, J. (2010). "Families" in international context: Comparing institutional effects across Western societies. *Journal of Marriage and Family, 72*, 516–536.

Coontz, S. (1997). *The way we really are: Coming to terms with America's changing families*. New York: Basic Books.

Coontz, S. (2005). *The history of marriage.* New York: Viking.

D'Onofrio, B., & Lahey, B. (2010). Biosocial influences on the family: A decade review. *Journal of Marriage and Family, 72,* 762–782.

Edin, K., & Kissane, R. J. (2010). Poverty and the American family: A decade in review. *Journal of Marriage and Family, 72,* 460–479.

Falicov, C. J. (Ed.). (1988). *Family transitions: Continuity and change over the life cycle.* New York: Guilford Press.

Falicov, C. (2007). Working with transnational immigrants: Expanding meanings of family, community, and culture. *Family Process 46,* 157–172.

Feiler, B. (2011, January 23). What "Modern Family" says about modern families. *New York Times,* pp. 8–9.

Fincham, F. D., & Beach, S. R. (2010). Marriage in the new millennium: A decade in review. *Journal of Marriage and Family, 72,* 630–649.

Fomby, P., & Cherlin, A. J. (2007). Family instability and child well-being. *American Sociological Review, 72,* 181–204.

Foucault, M. (1980). *Power/knowledge: Selected interviews and other writings.* New York: Pantheon.

Grinker, R. R. (1967). Normality viewed as a system. *Archives of General Psychiatry, 17,* 320–324.

Hetherington, E. M. (2003). Intimate pathways: Changing patterns in close personal relationships across time. *Family Relations, 52,* 318–331.

Hetherington, E. M., & Kelly, J. (2002). *For better or for worse: Divorce reconsidered.* New York: Norton.

Hoffman, L. (1990). Constructing realities: An art of lenses. *Family Process, 29,* 1–12.

Jackson, D. D. (1965). The study of the family. *Family Process, 4,* 1–20.

Kennedy, S., & Bumpass, L. (2008). Cohabitation and children's living arrangements: New estimates from the United States. *Demographic Research, 19,* 1663–1692.

Kleinman, A. (1988). *Suffering, healing, and the human condition.* New York: Basic Books.

Lansford, J. E., Ceballo, R., Abby, A., & Stewart, A. J. (2001). Does family structure matter?: A comparison of adoptive, two-parent biological, single-mother, stepfather, and stepmother households. *Journal of Marriage and Family, 63,* 840–851.

Lev, A. (2010). How queer!—The development of gender identity and sexual orientation in LGBTQ-headed families. *Family Process, 49,* 268–290.

Lidz, T. (1963). *The family and human adaptation.* New York: International Universities Press.

Livingston, G., & Parker, K. (2010, September 9). Since the start of the Great Recession, more children raised by grandparents. Retrieved January 3, 2011, from *pewresearch.org/pubs/1724/sharp-increase-children-with-grandparent-caregivers.*

McGoldrick, M., Anderson, C., & Walsh, F. (Eds.). (1989). *Women in families: A framework for family therapy.* New York: Norton.

McGoldrick, M., Carter, B., & Garcia-Preto, N. (2011). *The expanded family life cycle: Individual, family, and social perspectives* (4th ed.). Boston: Pearson.

McGoldrick, M., Gerson, R., & Petry, S. (2008). *Genograms: Assessment and intervention.* New York: Norton.

McGoldrick, M., Giordano, J., & Garcia-Preto, N. (Eds.). (2005). *Ethnicity and family therapy* (3rd ed.). New York: Guilford Press.

Mead, M. (1972). *Blackberry winter.* New York: Morrow.

Minuchin, S. (1974). *Families and family therapy.* Cambridge, MA: Harvard University Press.

Nabokov, V. (1969). *Ada.* New York: McGraw-Hill.

Neugarten, B. (1976). Adaptation and the life cycle. *Counseling Psychologist, 6,* 16–20.

Offer, D., & Sabshin, M. (1974). *Normality: Theoretical and clinical concepts of mental health* (2nd ed.). New York: Basic Books.

Parsons, T., & Bales, R. F. (1955). *Family, socialization, and interaction processes.* Glencoe, IL: Free Press.

Pew Research Center. (2010a, October 6). Gay marriage gains more acceptance. Retrieved January 3, 2011, from *pewresearch.org/pubs/1755/poll-gay-marriage-gains-acceptance-gays-in-the-military.*

Pew Research Center. (2010b, November 18). The decline of marriage and rise of new families. Retrieved January 3, 2011, from *pewresearch.org/pubs/1802/decline-marriage-rise-new-families.*

Reiss, D. (1981). *The family's construction of reality.* Cambridge, MA: Harvard University Press.

Repetti, R., Wang, S., & Saxbe, D. (2009). Bringing it all back home: How outside stressors shape families' everyday lives. *Current Psychological Directions in Science, 18,* 106–111.

Roseneil, S., & Budgeon, S. (2004). Cultures of intimacy and care beyond "the family": Personal life and social change in the early 21st century. *Current Sociology, 52,* 135–159.

Rosenfeld, M. J. (2007). *The age of independence: Interracial unions, same-sex unions and the changing American family.* Cambridge, MA: Harvard University Press.

Samuels, G. M. (2010). Building kinship and community: Relational processes of bicultural identity among adult multiracial adoptees. *Family Process, 49*(1), 26–42.

Sassler, S. (2010). Partnering across the life course: Sex, relationships, and mate selection. *Journal of Marriage and Family, 72,* 557–575.

Stacey, J. (1990). *Brave new families: Stories of domestic upheaval in late twentieth century America.* New York: Basic Books.

Tolstoy, L. (1946). *Anna Karenina.* New York: World.

U.S. Bureau of the Census. (2009). TableMS-2. Estimated median age at first marriage, by sex: 1890 to the present. *Families and living arrangements.* Retrieved May 5, 2009, from *www.census.gov/population/socdemo/hh-fam/ms2.xls.*

Valladares, B. A., & Moore, K. A. (2009). *The strengths of poor families.* Washington, DC: Child Trends Research Brief.

von Bertalanffy, L. (1968). *General system theory and psychiatry: Foundation, developments, applications.* New York: Braziller.

Waite, L. J. (2009). The changing family and aging populations. *Population and Development Review, 35,* 341–346.

Walsh, F. (1982). Conceptualizations of normal family functioning. In F. Walsh (Ed.), *Normal family processes* (pp. 3–42). New York: Guilford Press.

Walsh, F. (1996). The concept of family resilience: Crisis and challenge. *Family Process, 35,* 261–281.

Walsh, F. (2003). Family resilience: A framework for clinical practice. *Family Process,* *42*, 1–18.

Walsh, F. (2006). *Strengthening family resilience* (2nd ed.). New York: Guilford Press.

Walsh, F. (2009a). Family transitions: Challenges and resilience. In M. Dulcan (Ed.), *Textbook of child and adolescent psychiatry* (pp. 675–686). Washington, DC: American Psychiatric Association Press.

Walsh, F. (2009b). Human–animal bonds: I. The relational significance of companion animals. *Family Process, 48*(4), 462–480.

Walsh, F. (2009c). Human–animal bonds: II. The role of pets in family systems and family therapy. *Family Process 48*(4), 481–499.

Walsh, F. (Ed.). (2009d). *Spiritual resources in family therapy* (2nd ed.). New York: Guilford Press.

Walsh, F. (2010). Spiritual diversity: Multifaith perspectives in family therapy. *Family Process, 49*, 330–348.

Walsh, F. (2011). Families in later life: Challenges, opportunities, and resilience. In M. McGoldrick, B. Carter, & N. Garcia-Preto (Eds.), *The expanded family life cycle* (4th ed., pp. 261–277). Boston: Pearson.

Watzlawick, P., Beavin, J., & Jackson, D. (1967). *Pragmatics of human communication*. New York: Norton.

CHAPTER 2

CLINICAL VIEWS OF FAMILY NORMALITY, HEALTH, AND DYSFUNCTION

From a Deficits to a Strengths Perspective

FROMA WALSH

Constructions of family normality, health, and dysfunction, which are embedded in our cultural and professional belief systems, underlie all clinical theory and practice. These assumptions exert a powerful and largely unexamined influence in every family assessment and intervention.

THROUGH A DARK AND NARROW LENS

The field of mental health has long neglected the study and promotion of *health*. In the concentration on mental *illness*, family normality became equated with the absence of symptoms, a situation rarely, if ever, seen in the clinical setting. Assumptions about healthy families were largely speculative and utopian, extrapolated from experience with disturbed clinical cases. Scant attention was given to the stressful challenges and strengths of ordinary families in the community or their larger social context.

Clinical practice and research in the mid-20th century, grounded in medical and psychoanalytic paradigms, focused on the understanding and treatment of psychopathology. The family was viewed darkly in terms of damaging influences in the etiology of individual disturbances. Indeed, throughout much of the clinical literature, families were portrayed as noxious and destructive influences. Focused narrowly on a dyadic view of early childhood attachments, "parenting" was equated with "mothering," with the terms used interchangeably. Maternal deficits were blamed for all problems, as in the following family case analysis in a leading psychiatric journal:

> In this paper, it has been possible to examine minutely a specific family situation. The facts speak rather boldly for themselves. The mother and wife is a domineering, aggressive, and sadistic person with no redeeming good qualities. She crushes individual initiative and independent thinking in her husband, and prevents their inception in her children. (Gralnick, 1943, p. 323)

Such mother-blaming indictments have persisted, deduced from theories of family pathogenesis, often without any direct contact with the mother or assessment of the family system and its social context. "Parent-ectomies" were frequently recommended, keeping families at bay, without "intrusion" in treatment, which offered a corrective relationship with the therapist or therapeutic community. Family assessment, skewed toward identification of deficits and conflicts, has tended to be blind to family strengths and resources to such an extent that—only half jokingly—a normal family might be defined as one that has not yet been clinically assessed!

FAMILY SYSTEMS THEORY AND PRACTICE

The systems paradigm (von Bertalanffy, 1968) advanced conceptualization of the family from a deterministic linear, causal view, focused on parent–child dyadic bonds, to the recognition of multiple, recursive influences within and beyond the family that shape individual and family functioning through ongoing transactions over the life course and across the generations. Yet early family assessment and treatment tended to focus on dysfunctional family processes thought to cause or maintain individual symptoms. Over recent decades, family therapy theory and practice have been reformulated and expanded, with greater recognition of the diversity and complexity of contemporary family life and greater attention to sociocultural and biological influences. Focus has shifted from family deficits and dysfunction to family challenges and resources in community-based collaborative approaches aiming to strengthen family functioning and resilience (Goldenberg & Goldenberg, 2008; Nichols & Schwartz, 2008; Walsh, 2011b).

Although family therapy approaches vary, they share a common conceptual foundation in systems theory, with basic assumptions about the mutual influence of family members. Combining ecological and developmental perspectives, the family is viewed as a transactional system that functions in relation to its broader sociocultural context and evolves over the multigenerational family life cycle (McGoldrick, Carter, & Garcia-Preto, 2011; Minuchin, 1974). Stressful events, environmental conditions, and problems of an individual member affect the whole family as a functional unit, with reverberations for all members and their relationships. In turn, family processes—in relating and handling problems—contribute significantly to positive adaptation or to individual and relational dysfunction.

MAJOR APPROACHES TO FAMILY THERAPY

It is important to examine the views of family normality, health, and dysfunction embedded in major approaches to family therapy because of their critical influence in clinical practice. Earlier editions of this text surveyed the most influential founding models and more recent developments in the field, considering the four perspectives on family normality I outlined in Chapter 1 of this volume. Although generalizations in an evolving field must be made with caution, it is useful to highlight some basic premises about family normality, health, and dysfunction in various approaches. Two questions frame consideration:

1. *Family processes:* What are the explicit and implicit assumptions about normal—typical and optimal—family functioning and views of dysfunction?
2. *Therapeutic goals and processes:* How do these beliefs influence therapeutic objectives, intervention methods, and the stance of the therapist?

As the following overview reveals, various aspects of family and couple functioning receive selective focus in assessment and intervention fitting different views of problem formation/maintenance, therapeutic goals, and change processes (see Table 2.1 on pp. 32–33).

Brief Problem-Solving Approaches

In early models, therapeutic interventions were problem-focused, designed to alter dysfunctional interaction patterns. Since the mid-1980s, approaches have focused increasingly on identifying and expanding strengths, resources, and potential.

Structural Model

Structural family therapy approaches emphasize the importance of organizational processes for family functioning and the well-being of members. Therapy focuses on the patterning of transactions in which symptoms are embedded, viewing problems as an indication of imbalance or rigidity in the family's organization (Minuchin, Nichols, & Lee, 2006).

Minuchin (1974) directly challenged the myth of "placid" normality—the idealized view of the normal family as nonstressful, living in constant harmony and cooperation. Such an image crumbles, he argued, when looking at any family with ordinary problems. Through interviews with effectively functioning families from different cultures, Minuchin described normal (i.e., typical) difficulties of family life transcending cultural differences. In an ordinary family, the parents face many problems in relating, bringing up children, dealing with extended family issues, and coping with the outside world. He noted, "Like all normal families, they are constantly struggling with these problems and negotiating the compromises that make a life in common possible" (p. 16).

Therefore, Minuchin cautioned therapists not to base judgments of family normality or abnormality on the presence or absence of problems. Instead, he proposed a conceptual schema of family functioning to guide family assessment and therapy. This structural model views the family as a social system in transformation, operating within specific social contexts and developing over time, with each stage requiring reorganization. Each system maintains preferred patterns, yet a functional family must be able to adapt to new circumstances, balancing continuity and change to further the psychosocial growth of members. Symptoms are most commonly a sign of a maladaptive reaction to changing environmental or developmental demands. Normal (i.e., common, expectable) transitional strains may be misjudged or mislabeled as pathological. Minuchin advised:

> With this orientation, many more families who enter therapy would be seen and treated as average families in transitional situations, suffering the pains of accommodation to new circumstances. The label of pathology would be reserved for families who in the face of stress increase the rigidity of their transactional patterns and boundaries, and avoid or resist any exploration of alternatives. (1974, p. 60)

These distinctions led to different therapeutic strategies: In average families, the therapist relies more on the motivation of family resources as a pathway to transformation. With greater dysfunction, the therapist becomes more active in order to realign the system.

Minuchin viewed patterns of closeness and separateness as transactional styles or preferences and not as qualitative differences between functional and dysfunctional families, although extremes of enmeshment or disengagement were most often problematic. Structural patterns normally shift over the family life cycle to meet varying needs and challenges, from rearing young children, through adolescence, and launching to caring for ill or disabled members.

Structural family therapists have emphasized the importance of generational hierarchy and the clarity of family rules and boundaries to protect the differentiation of the system and parental/caregiver authority. Minuchin (1974) noted that although the ideal family is often described as a democracy, this does not mean that a family is leaderless or a society of peers. Effective family functioning requires the power to carry out essential functions. The

TABLE 2.1. Major Models of Family Therapy: Normality, Dysfunction, and Therapeutic Goals

Model of family therapy	View of normal/healthy family functioning	View of dysfunction/symptoms	Goals of therapy
Problem-solving approaches			
Structural	Generational hierarchy; strong parental authority Clear boundaries, subsystems Flexibility to fit developmental and environmental demands	Family structural imbalance: Malfunctioning generational hierarchy, boundaries Maladaptive reaction to changing demands	Reorganize family structure: • Strengthen parental/caregiver subsystem • Reinforce clear, flexible boundaries • Mobilize more adaptive patterns
Strategic/systemic	Flexibility Large behavioral repertoire for • Problem solving • Life-cycle passage	Symptom is communicative act • Maintained by misguided problem-solving attempts • Rigidity; lack of alternatives • Serving function for family	Resolve presenting problem; specific objectives Interrupt rigid feedback cycle: symptom-maintaining sequence Shift perspective
Postmodern Solution-focused Narrative	Normality is socially constructed Many options; flexibility	Problem-saturated narratives constrain options Dominant discourse stigmatizes differences from "norm"	Search for exceptions to problem Envision new possibilities Reauthor, thicken life stories Empower clients
Behavioral/ cognitive-behavioral	Adaptive behavior is rewarded More positive exchanges than negative (costs); reciprocity Good communication, problem-solving, conflict management Facilitative beliefs	Maladaptive, symptomatic behavior reinforced by: • Family attention and reward • Deficient exchanges (e.g., coercive, skewed) • Constraining beliefs	Concrete behavior goals: • Reward adaptive, not maladaptive, behavior • Communication, problem-solving skills • Adaptive cognitive restructuring
Psychoeducational	Successful coping and mastery of psychosocial challenges: • Chronic illness demands • Stressful events, transitions	Stress–diathesis in biologically based disorders Normative and non-normative stresses	Multifamily groups provide information, coping skills, and social support to: • Manage demands, master challenges • ↓ Stress and stigma

Multisystemic	Family, social, larger systems promote healthy child development	Multiple systems influence youth conduct disorder, substance abuse	Family-centered, collaborative involvement of peers, schools, courts, community programs; Risk, problem behavior; Youth adaptation, family support

Intergenerational/growth approaches

Psychodynamic	Relationships based on current realities, not past projections; Provide secure base; Trust, nurturance for bonding and individuation	Shared projection process; Unresolved conflicts, losses, loyalty issues in family of origin • Attachment issues • Unconscious role assignment	Gain insight, resolve family of origin issues; ↓Projection processes; Individual and relational growth
Bowen model	Differentiation of self in relation to others; Intellectual/emotional balance	Functioning impaired by family of origin relationships: • Poor differentiation (fusion) • Anxiety (reactivity) • Triangulation • Emotional cutoff/conflicts	Differentiation; ↑Cognitive functioning; ↓Emotional reactivity; Change self in relationships: • Repair conflicts, cutoffs • Gain new perspectives
Experiential	High self-worth; Clear, honest communication; Flexible rules and roles; Open, hopeful social links; Evolutionary growth, change; Playful interaction, humor	Symptoms are nonverbal messages elicited by current communication dysfunction; Old pains are reactivated	Direct, clear communication in immediate experience; Genuine relating; Individual and relational growth

unquestioned authority of the traditional patriarchal model has given way to the importance of flexible, authoritative parenting. A strong parental subsystem is required for childrearing tasks, whether the household is headed by two parents or by a single parent, coordinated with involved nonresidential parents or grandparents. Thus, a primary structural objective in family therapy is to strengthen the leadership subsystem.

In the couple/parental subsystem, spouses are seen to support their partners' better characteristics. At times, spouses in average couples may undermine partners in attempts to improve or rescue them, yet such patterns do not necessarily imply serious pathology. While noting that the spousal subsystem requires complementarity and mutual accommodation, early structural family therapists tended to support the gender-based hierarchy in power and status rooted in patriarchal cultural values (McGoldrick, Anderson, & Walsh, 1987). Therapy was commonly directed to "rebalance" the family by diminishing the mother's influence, while enhancing the father's position of authority (Goldner, 1988). More recent therapists work to empower both partners in a mutually respectful, equal partnership (Knudson-Martin & Mahoney, 2005; see Knudson-Martin, Chapter 14, this volume).

Structural family therapists have shown particular sensitivity to the barrage of external pressures and constraints on poor families that contribute to problems in family organization (Aponte, 1994; Falicov, 1998). Minuchin and his colleagues have also directed efforts to change structural patterns in larger systems, such as child welfare and foster care policies and practices that "dismember" poor families and undermine functioning (Minuchin, Colapinto, & Minuchin, 2006; see Engstrom, Chapter 9, this volume).

In summary, from a structural perspective, no family style is inherently normal or abnormal. Whether organizational patterns are functional or dysfunctional depends largely on their *fit* with the family's developmental and social demands. Many varied styles are potentially workable and may meet ordinary challenges. For optimal functioning, a strong generational hierarchy and clear lines of parental authority are considered essential. The strength of the system requires clear yet flexible boundaries and subsystems for the ability to shift organizational patterns to accommodate needed change.

Strategic/Systemic Approaches

Early strategic and systemic models were developed at the Mental Research Institute (MRI) in Palo Alto (Weakland, Fisch, Watzlawick, & Bodin, 1974), by Haley (1976) and colleagues, and by the Milan team (Selvini Palazzoli, Boscolo, Cecchin, & Prata, 1980). These approaches viewed healthy families as highly flexible, drawing on a large repertoire of behaviors to cope with problems, in contrast to the rigidity and a paucity of alternatives in a dysfunctional family. Beyond this generalization, they deliberately avoided definitions of normality, with a tolerance for differences and ideosyncracies of families and a conviction that each family must define what is normal or healthy for itself in its situation.

Haley (1976) saw descriptions of family interaction as a way of thinking for purposes of therapy when there is a disturbed child but stressed that it would be an error to deduce from that a model for what normal families *should* be like. In observations of over 200 normal—average—families, Haley found patterns so diverse that to talk about a "normal" family seemed to him naive:

> How to raise children properly, as a normal family should, remains a mystery that awaits observational longitudinal studies with large samples. Thinking about the organization of a family to plan therapy is another issue. As an analogy, if a child breaks a leg, one can set it straight and put it in a plaster cast. But one should not conclude from such therapy that the way to bring about the normal development of children's legs is to place them in plaster casts. (p. 108)

Assuming that all families confront problems, the MRI model (Weakland et al., 1974) focused on how families attempt to handle or resolve normal problems in living. Symptoms are seen as a communicative act, appearing when individuals are locked into an unworkable interactional pattern and cannot see a way to change it. Families may *maintain* a problem by the misguided means they are using to handle it. An attempted solution may worsen the problem, or may itself become a problem requiring change. Therapy focuses on problem resolution by altering feedback loops that maintain symptoms. The therapeutic task is to reformulate, or recast, the problem in solvable terms. The therapist's responsibility is limited to initiating change that will get a family "unstuck" from unworkable interactional patterns.

Haley (1976) selectively focused on key family variables involving power and organization that he considered relevant to therapeutic change. Like Minuchin, he thought a variety of arrangements could be functional if the family deals with hierarchical issues (i.e., authority, nurturance, and discipline) and establishes clear rules to govern the differential between generations.

Implicitly, strategic and systemic therapists assumed an asymptomatic perspective on family normality. They limited therapeutic responsibility to symptom reduction, freeing a family from unworkable patterns to define its own functional alternatives. They contended that most families do what they do because members believe it is the right or best way to approach a problem, or because it is the only way they know. The therapeutic task is to interrupt ways of handling a problem that do not work, that is, patterns that are dysfunctional. The Milan approach (Boscolo, Cecchin, Hoffman, & Penn, 1987) emphasized the importance of observation and inquiry to learn the language and beliefs of each family, to see the problem and relational patterns through various members' eyes, and to understand the values and expectations influencing their approach to handling a problem and their inability to change.

Through techniques such as *relabeling* and *reframing*, these approaches strategically redefine a problem situation to cast it in a new light in order to shift a family's rigid view or alter a destructive process. Similarly, circular questioning, positive connotation, and respectful curiosity are used to contextualize symptoms, attribute benign intentions, and generate hope. Therapists also depathologize problems by viewing them as normative life-cycle complications, considering their possible adaptive functions for the family, and acknowledging the helpful, albeit misguided, intentions of caring members trying to help one another. In such reformulations, new solutions can more readily become apparent.

Postmodern Approaches

Solution-focused and narrative approaches are based in constructivist and social constructionist views of reality (Hoffman, 1990). Growing out of strategic/systemic models, yet departing from many earlier tenets, they shift therapeutic focus from problems and the patterns that maintain them to solutions that have worked in the past or might work now, emphasizing future possibilities. They believe that people are constrained by narrow, pessimistic views of problems, limiting the range of alternatives for solution. However, they reject earlier assumptions that problems serve ulterior functions for families. Interventions are oriented toward recognizing and amplifying clients' positive strengths and potential resources (Berg, 1997; deShazer, 1988).

Postmodern therapists believe there is no single "correct" or "proper" way to live one's life. What is unacceptable for some may be desirable or necessary for others. Rather than search for structural or psychic flaws in distressed families, they focus on the ways people describe themselves, their problems, and their aims.

Narrative therapists' avoidance of generalizations about what is normal or abnormal is grounded in Foucault's observations about the abusive power of dominant discourses:

> Too often in human history, judgments made by people in power have been imposed on those who have no voice. Families were judged to be healthy or unhealthy depending on their fit with ideal normative standards. With their bias hidden behind a cloak of science or religion, these conceptions became reified and internalized. One-size-fits-all standards have pathologized differences due to gender, cultural and ethnic background, sexual orientation, and socioeconomic status. (in Nichols & Schwartz, 2008, p. 294)

Postmodern therapists have been especially wary of claims of objectivity, which they regard as unobtainable. They eschew psychiatric labels, family typologies, and evaluation schemas as reductionistic, dehumanizing, and marginalizing of differences from norms. Narrative therapists "situate" themselves with clients and assume a collaborative stance (Freedman & Combs, 1996; White & Epston, 1990). Because clinicians and families are both steeped in the larger cultural discourses, they are adamant that therapists should not impose on clients what they, themselves, think is normal or healthy. In appreciative inquiry, therapists learn from clients about their predicaments and experience (Anderson, 1997). White (1995) challenged therapists to be transparent: to disclose beliefs that inform their therapy and fully own their ideas as their subjective perspective, biased by race, culture, gender, and class. In short, therapists try not to make assumptions or judge clients in ways that objectify them, so as to honor their unique stories, cultural heritage, and visions for their future.

Narrative therapy is guided by a few basic assumptions: that people have good intentions and neither want nor need problems; and that they can develop empowering stories when separated from their problems and constraining cultural beliefs. The therapist redirects focus from family causal assumptions of dysfunction to appreciate the toxic effects of many dominant discourses in the social world. For instance, eating disorders are seen as largely influenced by internalization of cultural obsession with thinness and beauty for women. Contending that therapeutic neutrality is not possible and can perpetuate harmful patterns, clinicians are encouraged to challenge culturally based injustices, such as men over women, rich over poor, and whites over people of color.

Therapeutic goals extend beyond problem solving to a collaborative effort to help people reauthor their life stories and their futures. Through conversation, problematic narratives are thickened and perspectives expanded to incorporate new possibilities for more empowering constructions, problem resolution, and positive growth. Respectful inquiry aims to free clients from constraining or oppressive personal or cultural assumptions, enlarge and enrich their stories, and encourage them to take active charge of their lives.

Behavioral and Cognitive-Behavioral Family Approaches

Behavioral approaches to family therapy, developed from behavior modification and social learning traditions, view families as critical learning contexts, created and responded to by members (Alexander & Sexton, 2002; Patterson, Reid, Jones, & Conger, 1975). Interventions attend to the ongoing interactions and conditions under which social behavior is learned, influenced, and changed, with focus on family rules and communication processes. Therapists specify problems and goals in concrete, observable behavioral terms, guiding family members to learn more effective ways to deal with one another and to enhance positive interactions.

Behavioral approaches view a healthy family in terms of its adaptive, functional transactional processes. Because relationships involve a wide range of possibilities, there are many opportunities for rewarding exchanges. In well-functioning families, adaptive behavior is rewarded through attention, acknowledgment, and approval, whereas maladaptive behavior is not reinforced. Problematic relationship problems tend to have deficient reward exchanges, with reliance on coercive control and punishment (Patterson et al., 1975).

In couples, Gottman (1994; see Driver, Tabares, Shapiro, & Gottman, Chapter 3, this volume) identified specific interactional processes that predict the long-term success or failure of relationships. Of note, happy couples have five positive interactional exchanges for every negative exchange. Couples and families may be helped to change the interpersonal consequences of behavior (contingencies of reinforcement) for more positive acknowledgment and approval of desired behavior. All behavioral researchers emphasize flexibility and adaptability as partners evolve together and cope with the many challenges and external forces in their lives. Also important is long-term reciprocity and trust that the give and take will be balanced out over time. In contrast, dysfunctional relationships are more rigid and skewed, lack mutual accommodation, and are restricted by short-term tit-for-tat exchanges. Communication skills—particularly clear, direct expression of feelings, affection, and opinions; negotiation; and problem solving—are considered key to functional couple and family processes and can be learned. Relationship success is predicted not by the absence of conflict but by acceptance of differences (Jacobson & Christensen, 1996) and conflict management (Halford, Markman, Kling, & Stanley, 2007). For effective problem solving, difficult issues are controlled, escalating conflicts are slowed down, and arguments are kept constructive. Repair of hurts and misunderstandings is crucial.

Cognitive-behavioral couple and family therapy (CBCFT; Dattilio, 2005, 2010) addresses the subjective meanings and emotional experiences of family members that contribute to the persistence of rigid family rules and dysfunctional behavioral patterns. Therapists focus on five types of cognitions influencing relational problems: (1) selective perception of others and the relationship; (2) causal attributions for events in the family; (3) expectancies, or future predictions; (4) assumptions about others and relationships; and (5) standards—beliefs about what characteristics couples and families *should have*. Cultural, religious, or societal norms and ideals are explored as they influence individual and shared family beliefs, or schemas, and related relational patterns. Clinicians coach members in devising their own more benign alternative meanings for distressing events and distorted or constraining cognitions to contribute to enhanced functioning and relational well-being.

Psychoeducational Approaches

The family psychoeducational model, based on solid empirical evidence, was developed for family intervention with schizophrenia and other persistent mental illnesses (e.g., Anderson, Reiss, & Hogarty, 1986; Lefley, 2009). This approach corrects the pathologizing tendency in traditional treatments to blame a "schizophrenogenic mother" or a "toxic" family for causing mental illness. Research has established that mental disorders are influenced by the interaction of a core biological vulnerability and environmental stresses. Families are engaged respectfully as valued and essential collaborators in treatment, serving as vital resources for their loved one's long-term functioning and well-being in the community. Attention is given to their caregiving challenges as they struggle the best they know how in managing severe cognitive, emotional, and behavioral symptoms.

Multifamily group interventions (McFarlane, 2002) are designed to reduce family stress and provide support through practical information and management guidelines for predictably stressful periods in the course of a chronic mental illness. Families are helped to develop coping skills and to plan how to handle future crises. The group format provides social support, sharing of problem-solving experiences, and reduction of stigma and isolation of families. Brief psychoeducational "modules" timed for critical phases of an illness (Rolland, 1994) support families in digesting manageable portions of a long-term coping process and in handling periodic flare-ups.

Psychoeducational multifamily, couple, and single-parent group approaches are finding application in a wide range of problem situations faced by normal (i.e., average) families, such as family psychosocial demands of chronic physical illness (Rolland, 1994; Steinglass, 1998; see Rolland, Chapter 19, this volume), and stressful family transitions, such as job loss (Walsh, 2002, 2006). By identifying common challenges associated with stressful situations, family distress is normalized and contextualized, and therapy is focused on mastering adaptational challenges.

Multisystemic Models

Several evidence-based, multisystemic, and multidimensional models offer highly effective intervention approaches with high-risk and troubled youth by involving families and larger community systems (Henggeler, Clingempeel, Brondino, & Pickrel, 2002; Liddle, Santisteban, Levant, & Bray, 2002; Santisteban et al., 2003; Sexton & Alexander, 2005). These family-centered approaches with adolescent conduct disorder and substance abuse also yield improvements in family functioning, including increased cohesion, communication, and parenting practices, which are significantly linked to more positive youth behavioral outcomes than in standard youth service. Multisystemic interventions adapt structural, strategic, and behavioral approaches; may take a variety of forms; and involve school counselors, teachers, coaches, and peer groups, and may work with the police, probation officers, and judges to address adolescent and family legal issues. They might help a youth and family access vocational services, youth development organizations, social support networks, and religious group resources.

These approaches engage families that are often seen as unready, unwilling, or unmotivated for therapy, in a strengths-oriented collaborative alliance. They develop a shared atmosphere of hope, expectation for change, and a sense of responsibility (active agency) and empowerment. Rather than seeing troubled youth and their families as "resistant" to change, attempts are made to identify and overcome barriers to success in the therapeutic, family, and social contexts. Therapeutic contacts emphasize the positive and draw out systemic strengths and competencies for change. Clinicians maintain and communicate an optimistic perspective throughout assessment and intervention processes.

Intergenerational Approaches

Early in the field of family therapy, several growth-oriented intergenerational approaches to family therapy were developed.

Psychodynamically Influenced Approaches

Several intergenerational approaches bridged psychodynamic, object relations, and family systems theories, broadening focus from early childhood maternal influences to ongoing dynamic processes in the family network of relationships. In core tenets, parents—individually and through couple/parental bonds—promote attachment, separation, and individuation processes considered essential for healthy development. *Attachment theory* was expanded to consider how an optimally functioning family system provides a secure base for members and a context of security, trust, and nurturance (Bowlby, 1988; Byng-Hall, 1995).

Healthy functioning as a spouse or parent is seen as largely influenced by family-of-origin experiences. In theory, a shared projection process, based on complementarity of needs, influences mate choice and ongoing parent–child transactions. In healthy couples, partners are capable of intimacy and commitment, and are relatively well-differentiated, with mutual acceptance despite differences and disappointments. In a healthy family, parents are aware of and free enough from intrapsychic conflicts, projections, and unfulfilled needs to invest in parenting and be responsive to their children's developmental priorities.

Couple and family dysfunction are thought to arise from unresolved past conflicts or losses, interfering with realistic appraisal and response to others. Current situations are interpreted in light of one's inner object world, contributing to distortion, scapegoating, and irrational role assignment. Symptoms can result from attempts to reenact, externalize, or master intrapsychic issues through current relationships. A significant trauma or loss may reverberate through the entire family system, with emotional upheaval fueling distress in other members and relationships.

Assessment and treatment explore the connection of multigenerational family dynamics to disturbances in current functioning and relationships. The therapist facilitates awareness of covert emotional processes, encouraging members to deal directly with each other to work through unresolved issues and to alter negative patterns from the past (Framo, 1992). The conjoint process serves to build mutual empathy in couple and family bonds. Extended family members may be included in sessions, or individuals may work on changing relationships between sessions.

The *contextual approach* of Boszormenyi-Nagy (1987) emphasized the ethical dimension of relationships in intergenerational legacies of accountability and loyalty. Families are thought to be strengthened by actions toward trustworthiness and relational equitability, considering all members' interests for growth, autonomy, and relatedness. Ideally, family members openly negotiate transitions and commitments with flexibility, fairness, and reciprocity. Covert but powerful loyalty issues can fuel conflict and dysfunction. Therapy aims to resolve grievances for reconciliation of relationships.

In summary, these approaches hold a model of ideal, or optimal, functioning toward which therapeutic growth is encouraged. Therapy aims to reduce pathological family dynamics through insight, facilitation of direct communication, and efforts toward relational repair. Assumptions about healthy family processes were extrapolated from clinical theory and dysfunctional cases. Little was said about average families, extrafamilial influences, or family and cultural diversity. The pathological bent has been strong: Consideration of intergenerational dynamics are focused on negative influences to be contained or resolved, with scant attention to positive experiences and relationships in the family of origin or current bonds that might contribute to healthy functioning.

Bowen Model

Bowen (1978) developed a theory of the family emotional system and a method of therapy from observation of a wide range of families, viewing them on a continuum from the most impaired, to normal (i.e., average), to optimally functioning. He accounted for the variability in functioning by the degree of anxiety and differentiation in a family. When anxiety is low, most relationship systems appear normal, or symptom-free. When anxiety increases, tensions develop in the system, blocking differentiation and producing symptoms. Most families were thought to function in the moderate range, with variable cognitive and emotional balance and some reactivity to others in needs for closeness and approval. In families with "moderate to good differentiation of self," couples are able to enjoy a full range of emotional intimacy without losing their individual autonomy. Parents can encourage their children's differentiation without undue anxiety or attempts to mold them. Family members take responsibility for their own behavior and do not blame others. They can function well alone and together. Their lives are more orderly, they can cope with a broad range of situations, and when stressed into dysfunction, they use a variety of adaptive coping mechanisms to recover rapidly.

Bowen related individual and family dysfunction to several processes: (1) high *emotional reactivity* and *poor differentiation* in the family emotional system; (2) *triangles* formed when two members (e.g., parents), avoiding conflict, embroil a vulnerable third person (e.g., child); (3) *family projection processes* focusing parental anxiety on a child; and (4) *emotional cutoff* of highly charged relationships by distancing. Stresses on the family system, especially with death and loss, reduce differentiation and heighten reactivity, commonly producing triangulation or cutoffs. With extreme anxiety and fusion, reactive emotional processes seriously impair functioning and relationships.

The Bowen model values exploration and change beyond symptom reduction. The therapist, as coach, guides client efforts to gather information, gain new perspectives on key family members and patterns, and redevelop relationships by repairing cutoffs, detriangling from conflicts, and changing one's own part in vicious cycles. Carter and McGoldrick (2001) expanded the therapeutic lens to address the impact of larger cultural forces, such as sexism and racism. They clarify that contrary to criticism that Bowen therapy stresses cognitive processes and autonomy (traditional masculine values), the main objective in Bowen therapy is differentiation of self *in relation to others* to achieve richer, deeper relationships not blocked by emotional reactivity, fusion, or distancing.

Experiential Approaches

Innovative experiential approaches developed by Satir and Whitaker were highly intuitive and relatively atheoretical. Yet both held strong views on essential elements of healthy family functioning. Satir (1988) blended a communications approach with a humanistic orientation. She observed a consistent pattern in her experience with optimally functioning families—described as untroubled, vital, and nurturing.

1. Family members have high self-worth.
2. Their communication is direct, clear, specific, and honest.
3. Family rules are flexible, human, and appropriate.
4. Family links to their social world are open and hopeful.

By contrast, in troubled families, self-worth is low; communication is indirect, vague, and dishonest; rules are rigid and non-negotiable; and social interactions are fearful, placating, and blaming. Regardless of the specific problem bringing a family to therapy, Satir believed that changing those key processes relieves family pain and enhances family vitality. She regarded those four aspects of family life as the basic forces operating in all families, whether an intact, one-parent, blended, or institutional family, and in the growing variety and complexity of families. She was ahead of her time in attending to the spiritual dimension of healing and growth.

Whitaker believed that all families are essentially normal but can become abnormal in the process of pain caused by trying to be normal. He distinguished healthy families by attributes similar to those noted by other early systems therapists (Whitaker, 1992). He emphasized the value of humor to diffuse tensions and playfulness for creative fantasy and experimental problem solving. Whitaker also saw healthy families as having an evolutionary sense of time and becoming: a continual process of growth and change across the life cycle and the generations, facilitated by family rituals and a guiding mythology or belief system.

Symptoms are thought to result when old pains from life experience are aroused in current interaction. To change behavior, key elements in family process are addressed; all are believed to be modifiable. Therapists facilitate awareness and mutual appreciation through a shared affective experience, with open communication of feelings and differences. Therapists follow and reflect the immediate experience, catalyzing exploration and spontaneity to stimulate genuine, nondefensive relating. These ideas and methods have been applied in many family and couple enrichment programs.

Summary of Clinical Models

This brief survey of family therapy models reveals varied, yet overlapping, perspectives on family normality, health, and dysfunction. All approaches, grounded in a systemic orientation, view normality in terms of ongoing transactional processes, and most attend to social and developmental contexts. Their differences reflect more a selective emphasis on specific aspects of functioning: structural patterns, communication and problem-solving processes, and meaning systems (Sluzki, 1983). Components of family functioning in each domain are mutually interactive. For example, emotional differentiation facilitates and is facilitated by firm boundaries and clear communication. Family therapists have increasingly integrated elements of various models into practice with a broad range of families, couples, and problem situations (Lebow, 1997; Walsh, 2011b), as in emotionally focused therapy combining attachment theory and behavioral approaches (Johnson, 2004).

In brief therapy approaches that focus on immediate problem solving, therapists should be mindful of contextual influences, such as a recent job loss and financial strains that may not be mentioned by the family focused on child behavior problems. Conflict between a daughter and stepmother may involve interlocking triangles from an unresolved parental divorce. Growth-oriented therapists need to be cautious not to reinforce a family's sense of deficiency by setting unrealistic goals of ideal functioning or value-laden visions of family health reflecting clinician or cultural standards.

FROM A DEFICITS TO A STRENGTHS PERSPECTIVE

Over recent decades, family therapists have rebalanced the skewed perspective that long dominated the clinical field. In the many, varied approaches, therapeutic focus has shifted from deficits, limitations, and pathology to a competency-based, health-oriented paradigm, recognizing and amplifying family strengths and resources (Walsh, 2011b). This positive, future-oriented stance shifts the emphasis of therapy from how families have failed to how they can succeed—envisioning positive goals and options that fit each family's values and situation, and that are reachable through collaborative efforts.

Family therapy approaches have also become more respectful, with awareness that the very language of therapy can pathologize the family. We have become more sensitive to the blame, shame, and guilt implicit in pejorative labels with attributions of family causality. We have turned away from earlier models emphasizing a hierarchical therapist-as-expert stance and adversarial strategies to reduce family pathology. The therapeutic relationship has become more collaborative and empowering of clients, recognizing that effective interventions depend more on drawing out family resources than on therapist change techniques. Interventions aim to reduce stress, enhance positive interactions, support coping efforts, and mobilize kin and community resources to foster loving relationships and effective family functioning.

Strength-oriented approaches are widely used in community settings with "nonclinical" families impacted by acute or chronic stress conditions, such as home- and school-based approaches with low-income underserved families (Boyd-Franklin & Bry, 2000) and collaborative practices with multistressed families (Madsen, 2006) and homeless families (Fraenkel, Hameline, & Shannon, 2009). Family therapists are increasingly addressing the impact of major trauma, such as war-related suffering in military families (MacDermid, Samper, Schwarz, Nishida, & Nyaronga, 2008), and recovery from traumatic loss and community disasters (Rowe & Liddle, 2008; Walsh, 2007).

A family resilience framework has been developed to focus strengths-based practice on highly stressful situations of adversity (Walsh, 2003, 2006; see Walsh, Chapter 17, this volume). Grounded in research on resilience and well-functioning families, this practice approach identifies and facilitates family processes that foster effective coping, adaptation, and positive growth in response to serious life challenges. A family resilience framework has useful application in recovering from crisis, trauma, or loss (e.g., complicated grief, major disasters, refugee experience); in weathering persistent multistress conditions (e.g., chronic illness); in navigating disruptive transitions (e.g., divorce, job loss); in overcoming barriers of poverty or discrimination; in supporting the success of at-risk youth (family–school partnerships); and in enabling vulnerable families to thrive.

Collaborative family health care, a rapidly growing practice area, espouses an interdisciplinary team approach with health care providers, patients, and their families to foster optimal biopsychosocial care based on research showing that preventive and integrative approaches to mental health and health care are most effective when supported by families (McDaniel, Hepworth, & Doherty, 2007; Rolland, 1994). A systems approach expands the customary model of caregiving from one designated, individual caregiver, whose overload can compromise health and well-being, to a mutually supportive *caregiving team* involving siblings and other key family members (Walsh, 2011a).

Current systems approaches include varied intervention formats with individuals, couples, and families, from consultation and brief therapy to multisystemic approaches, multifamily groups, and more intensive family therapy. Families may also be linked with local support groups, online resources, and organizations that advocate for families. A family systems approach is distinguished less by who is in the therapy room and more by the clinician's attention to relationships and systemic patterns in assessment and intervention. Regardless of the source of problems, family therapists involve key family members who can contribute to needed changes. Individuals may be seen separately or brought together for some sessions in different combinations, depending on therapeutic aims. Therapists consider (1) how family members may contribute to and are affected by problem situations; (2) how members can be resources in solving problems; and (3) how family functioning and relational bonds can be strengthened for greater well-being and positive growth.

CHALLENGES AND OPPORTUNITIES FOR CLINICAL PRACTICE, TRAINING, AND RESEARCH

Clinicians' Views of Family Normality and Health

Postmodern perspectives have heightened awareness that clinicians—as well as researchers—co-construct the dysfunctional patterns they "discover" in families, as well as therapeutic goals tied to beliefs about family health. Even unintentionally, one's subjectivity and partiality enter into assessment questions and their framing, the questions not asked, issues considered salient to pursue, and those that are not. Therapists cannot avoid normative thinking at some level. Noticing what we are trained to see, we may be blind to strengths and too readily ascribe pathology. Clinical sensitivity to normative (typical) family challenges and judgments about optimal family functioning reflect therapists' values and beliefs rooted in cultural, professional, and personal orientations. It is essential for clinical training programs to examine social constructions of family normality and explore how such basic premises influence family assessment and intervention.

Beliefs about family normality from clinicians' own cultural backgrounds, life experiences, and professional orientation influence family evaluation and intervention goals. In a survey of family therapists (Walsh, 1987), nearly half viewed their own families of origin as not having been "normal." Yet being "abnormal" held quite different meanings. Some saw their own families as very dysfunctional. Others saw theirs as *atypical*, not conforming to average families in their community. Many felt their families failed to live up to *ideal* family standards in the dominant society or their cultural or religious norms. Clinicians' perceptions were also influenced by their practice models and their own experiences in therapy. Those in systems-oriented approaches were less blaming and more hopeful about change. It is important for clinicians to reflect on their own perspectives on normality and how these influence their views of families in therapy and the goals they set.

Training Experience with "Nonclinical" Families

Clinical training benefits immeasurably from observations and interviews in the community with normal "nonclinical" families, those whose members are not in therapy. The format might include (1) family life narrative interviews (separate and conjoint) to gather different family members' perspectives on their family identity, history, current relationships, and future hopes and dreams; (2) reflection on a problem or crisis faced, and the strategies and resources drawn on for coping and resilience; and (3) direct observation of family interaction on a brief structured task, such as planning a special trip together. A family genogram (McGoldrick, Gerson, & Petry, 2008), as well as a family resilience framework and family functioning assessment tools (see Walsh, Chapter 17, and Lebow & Stroud, Chapter 21, this volume), can be useful to identify strengths and vulnerabilities in family functioning, taking into consideration family members' life challenges, resources, and aspirations.

Interviews with nonclinical families attune students to the diversity of family perspectives and salient issues relative to their life-cycle phase, family form, gender, cultural/religious values, and socioeconomic influences. Discussion of the wide range of "normal" families encountered by classmates provides an opportunity to deconstruct stereotypes, myths, and faulty assumptions. Pathologizing tendencies inherent in the problem focus of clinical training can be examined. In assessing strengths and resources, as well as vulnerabilities, students gain awareness of family competencies and potential. It also becomes apparent that all families are challenged in one way or another over their life course, and most are remarkably resilient.

Multiple-observer perspectives are afforded by having students team up to conduct the interview and later discuss their observations and assessments, and also to note similarities and differences related to their own sociocultural background, gender and sexual orientation, and current developmental phase. Awareness is heightened that each clinician is part of every evaluation and influences what is observed, emerging information, and functional or dysfunctional judgments ascribed to individuals and relational patterns. In expanding perspectives on normality, the experience more importantly can depathologize views of clinical families in distress and humanize the process of therapy.

Normalizing Family Distress

Ordinary families often worry about their own normality: Are they doing well? Are they doing it "right"? Differences from either average or ideal norms are often experienced as stigmatized deviance: deficient and shame-laden. The overwhelming challenges and changes in contemporary life can compound feelings of inadequacy, especially for multistressed families with limited resources. In a culture that readily blames families and touts the virtue of self-reliance, parents often feel doubly deficient: for having a problem, and for being unable to solve it on their own. In my experience, much of what is labeled as family "resistance" to therapy stems from concerns of being judged dysfunctional and blamed for their problems. Nonengagement is often taken as further evidence of their dysfunction or insufficient caring and motivation for change. Many families have felt prejudged and blamed in contacts with schools, mental health or human service providers, welfare agencies, or justice systems. Expecting a therapist to judge them negatively, they may mistake a clinician's neutral stance or well-intentioned silence as confirmation that they are deficient or fail to fit a cultural ideal of the family. It can be helpful to explore families' concerns and the models and myths they hold as ideal. It is crucial to disengage assumptions of pathology from participation in therapy, taking care not to present—or imply—family deficits as the rationale for family therapy. It is essential to understand every family's challenges, affirm members' caring and efforts, and involve them as valued collaborators in therapeutic goals.

The aim of normalizing family members' distress is to *depathologize* and *contextualize* their feelings and experience. For instance, intense emotional reactions are common and understandable in crisis situations and are normal reactions to abnormal conditions, such as war-related trauma. Normalizing is *not* intended to reduce all problems and families to a common denominator; it should neither trivialize clients' suffering, struggle, or plight, nor normalize or condone harmful and destructive behavior patterns.

Errors in Pathologizing Normal Processes

Two types of errors can be made in regard to questions of normality. The first is to overpathologize families by mistakenly judging normal processes as dysfunctional, or difference (deviance) as abnormal (pathological). Clinicians should be aware of their own value-laden assumptions and keep informed by current research on family and couple functioning. Family distress is common and expectable under stressful conditions, such as the challenge of chronic illness or in response to a devastating loss. Members may be coping as well as can be reasonably expected in such adverse situations.

Clinicians may also err in conflating relational style variance with pathology when it reflects personal preferences or cultural differences from dominant North American norms. For instance, the overused label "enmeshment" pathologizes families whose high cohesion is culturally normative, such as Latino families (Falicov, 1998; see Falicov, Chapter 13, this volume). In many cases, high connectedness and caretaking may be both functional and desirable in couples and families, without being intrusive (Green & Werner, 1996).

Clinicians should also be careful not to label a family by an individual member's disorder or substance abuse problem (e.g., an alcoholic family) or by a single family trait or stylistic feature (e.g., "This is a chaotic family"). Given multiple influences, clinicians must not presume a family causal role in individual disturbances. Moreover, the complex texture of family life should not be reduced to a one-dimensional—and pejorative—label. As family systems researchers have documented, individual and family functioning involve multiple family processes intertwined with biological and environmental influences (see Lebow & Stroud, Chapter 21; Spotts, Chapter 22; Fishbane, Chapter 23, this volume).

The structural concept of *parentification* has too often pathologized common patterns as inherently damaging. It is normative in most cultures to expect children to carry a share of family responsibilities, particularly household chores and care of younger siblings. In large families, in situations of parental absence or incapacitation, and in multistressed and underresourced families, such as overburdened single-parent households, delegation of responsibilities to older children may be essential for family functioning. It can work well so long as generational boundaries and lines of authority are clearly drawn. It can also hold benefits for children in gaining competencies, as long as they are not overburdened, abused, or required to sacrifice developmental priorities, such as education and peer relations. What is considered "age-appropriate" is to some extent culture-based, and each family's situation, constraints, and resources must be considered.

Errors in Normalizing Dysfunction

Clinicians may also err by not recognizing and dealing with harmful family processes by assuming them to be normal. Family therapists have recognized that the early systems concept of circular causality, or a therapeutic stance of neutrality, reinforces the status quo and accepted norms and practices. Gender-based, demeaning treatment, violence, or abuse should never be normalized, despite its common occurrence or its rationalization as sanctioned by cultural or religious beliefs. Acceptance of diversity is not the same as "anything goes" when family practices harm any member.

Family Diversity and Complexity: Meeting the Challenges

The cultural ideal of the white, middle-class, intact nuclear family of the mid-20th century long remained an implicit standard in clinical practice, training, and research, lagging behind the changing family structures and challenges of most Americans over recent decades. The generation of family therapists that has come to the forefront has broadened our attention to the multiple ways of being a family, and the impact of larger systems and sociocultural influences on family well-being and dysfunction (e.g., Boyd-Franklin, 2006; Breunlin, Schwartz, & MacKune-Karrer, 1992; Falicov, 2007; Hardy & Laszloffy, 1995; Imber-Black, 1988; McGoldrick & Hardy, 2008).

Family, Social, and Community Connections

Clinical practice can be informed by the burgeoning research and clinical literature addressing the common adaptive challenges and strengths associated with varied family forms and transitions (see Part II, this volume). Research with community samples, especially longitudinal studies, can support efforts to identify predictable strains and facilitate effective family processes. For instance, the research on significant variables in divorce and stepfamily adaptation (see Greene et al., Chapter 5; Pasley & Garneau, Chapter 7, this volume) illuminates key processes that family practitioners can target to help families buffer expectable stresses and facilitate optimal adjustment for children and their parents.

We have moved beyond the myth of the self-reliant nuclear family household to expand attention to the multiple relationships and powerful connections among extended and informal kin living together or separately, and even at great distance. Genograms and time lines (McGoldrick et al., 2008) are valuable tools to diagram complex family structures and note the concurrence of stressful events and transition with symptoms of distress. Postdivorce, remarriage, and adoptive families may need assistance in dealing with normal challenges (i.e., common and expectable in their situation), balancing needs for a cohesive family unit with children's vital connections with noncustodial parents and extended family. Gay communities provide strong bonds in the face of family, cultural, or religious nonacceptance. Close friendships, social networks, faith congregations, and community supports can be invaluable resources. New technologies, from cell phones to the Internet and social networks, offer opportunities for connection and information, as we navigate myriad challenges in today's complex world.

Addressing Varied Life Cycle Challenges

Family therapy training and family process research have tended to focus on couples rearing children and adolescents. With growing diversity in developmental pathways, greater attention is needed to address the full and varied course of individuals and their families (see McGoldrick & Shibusawa, Chapter 16, this volume). We need to recognize the many relational and generative options of those who remain single or without children, whose lives have often been stigmatized as incomplete. With the aging of societies, we need, above all, to attend to family challenges of caregiving and the opportunities for positive change and growth in later life (Walsh, 2011a).

Addressing Culture, Race, Class, Gender, and Spirituality

The intersection of sociocultural influences in family functioning needs to be better integrated into clinical training and research designs, and not marginalized as "special issues." Falicov (1995; Chapter 13, this volume) offers a useful multidimensional framework that views each family as occupying a complex ecological niche, sharing borders and common ground with other families, as well as differing positions (e.g., race/ethnicity, gender, social class, life stage, rural vs. urban). A holistic assessment includes the varied contexts a family inhabits, aiming to understand values, constraints, and resources.

Greater attention is needed to the corrosive effects on couples and families of sexism, racism, heterosexism, ageism, classism, stigma of disabling conditions, and institutionalized forms of discrimination (see McGoldrick & Ashton, Chapter 11, this volume). Systems-oriented therapists have increasingly assumed an affirmative responsibility to advocate for social justice and for changes in larger systems, such as health care disparities, to support strong families and the well-being of all members.

The role of religion and spirituality in couples and families is receiving increasing attention (Walsh, 2009; see Walsh, Chapter 15, this volume). In family therapy, multifaith and multicultural perspectives can guide respectful inquiry to understand spiritual sources of distress and identify potential spiritual resources that fit client belief systems and preferences. Incorporating the spiritual dimension of human experience in theory, research, and practice expands the systemic lens to a biopsychosocial–spiritual orientation.

Progress and Priorities in Family Process Research

Family research and funding priorities must be rebalanced from psychopathology to health and prevention if we are to move beyond the rhetoric of "family strengths" and "healthy families" to clearer understanding of key processes and social supports for families to thrive. Over recent decades, a number of family systems research teams have made important contributions in mapping multidimensional components of well-functioning families (see Lebow & Stroud, Chapter 21, this volume, for a review of major models and assessment tools). Whereas early studies focused on white, middle-class, intact families, researchers have increasingly expanded their studies to a broader diversity.

The contributions of mixed methods, including quantitative and qualitative studies and using observational, interview, and questionnaire approaches, yield valuable *insider perspectives* (by family members) and *outsider perspectives* (by researchers or clinicians) (Sprenkle & Piercy, 2005). Quantitative research has tended to focus on behavioral and communication patterns that can be readily measured through direct observation, rating scales, and self-report questionnaires. Qualitative methods, such as narrative interviews, are especially useful to understand belief systems, perceptions, and other subjectivities of family experience. Advances in biobehavioral research are finding physiological, genetic, and neurological interactions with couple and family processes (see Spotts, Chapter 22, and Fishbane, Chapter 23, this volume). Computerized genogram programs (McGoldrick et al., 2007) hold untapped potential for tracking patterns in multigenerational family research.

Multidisciplinary dialogue and collaboration should be more strongly encouraged in conferences, journals, and research projects. The chasm between clinicians and researchers needs to be bridged through mutual exchange of perspectives: We have much to offer one another toward our common aim to understand and promote healthy family functioning. In future research and theory construction, our challenge is to become more knowledgeable about family functioning *in its diversity*. First, we need to better understand the normal (i.e., typical, expectable) patterns of living, strains, and resilience in families with varying forms, social contexts, and life challenges. Second, we need to identify key processes and mediating variables that foster effective family functioning, adaptation, and the well-being of members. We have much to learn from families that succeed—to inform clinical practice with families in distress and prevention efforts with those who are vulnerable.

CONCLUSION

The diversity and complexity of contemporary family life have heightened recognition that no single model of family functioning should be touted as normal or ideal for all families to emulate or for therapies to promote. It is imperative to examine the social constructions of normality that powerfully influence all clinical theory, research, training, and practice. Therapeutic neutrality is impossible, because we can never be value-free. Thus, it is naive—and ethically questionable—to adopt a neutral position toward normality, dismissing it from consideration, maintaining a stance of "anything goes," or adhering to a "one size fits all" model of intervention. We need to be aware of the implicit assumptions about normality we bring to our work with families from our own worldviews, including cultural standards, clinical/research paradigms, and personal/family experience. We must challenge the stigmatization of differences as pathological and work toward more inclusive social policies and attitudes.

Finally, families today face unprecedented challenges in our highly stressful, rapidly changing society and uncertain world. Many are confused and concerned about how to build and sustain strong, loving relationships; to raise children well; and to care for loved ones in need. Our challenge as therapists is to enable families with diverse values, structures, resources, and life challenges to forge their own varied pathways in coping, adaptation, and resilience. It is important to explore each family's constraining views of normality and support family members' values and preferences for healthy functioning, if we are to be attuned and responsive to the broad spectrum of families in our times.

REFERENCES

Anderson, C. M., Reiss, D., & Hogarty, G. (1986). *Schizophrenia and the family.* New York: Guilford Press.

Anderson, H. (1997). *Conversation, language, and possibilities: A postmodern approach to therapy.* New York: Basic Books.

Aponte, H. (1994). *Bread and spirit: Therapy with the new poor.* New York: Norton.

Berg, I. (1997). *Family-based services: A solution-focused approach.* New York: Norton.

Boscolo, L., Cecchin, G., Hoffman, L., & Penn, P. (1987). *Milan systemic family therapy: Conversations in theory and practice.* New York: Basic Books.

Boszormenyi-Nagy, I. (1987). *Foundations of contextual family therapy.* New York: Brunner/Mazel.

Bowen, M. (1978). *Family therapy in clinical practice.* New York: Aronson.

Bowlby, J. (1988). *A secure base: Parent–child attachment and healthy human development.* New York: Basic Books.

Boyd-Franklin, N. (2006). *Black families in therapy: A multisystems approach* (2nd ed.). New York: Guilford Press.

Boyd-Franklin, N., & Bry, B. H. (2000). *Reaching out in family therapy: Home-based, school, and community interventions.* New York: Guilford Press.

Breunlin, D., Schwartz, R., & MacKune-Karrer, B. (1992). *Metaframeworks: Transcending the models of family therapy.* San Francisco: Jossey-Bass.

Byng-Hall, J. (1995). Creating a secure family base: Some implications of attachment theory for family therapy. *Family Process, 34*(1), 45–58.

Carter, B., & McGoldrick, M. (2001). Advances in coaching: Family therapy with one person. *Journal of Marital and Family Therapy, 27,* 281–300.

Dattilio, F. M. (2005). The restructuring of family schemas: A cognitive-behavioral perspective. *Journal of Marital and Family Therapy, 31*(1), 15–30.

Dattilio, F. M. (2010). *Cognitive-behavioral therapy with couples and families: A comprehensive guide for clinicians.* New York: Guilford Press.

deShazer, S. (1988). *Clues: Investigating solutions in brief therapy.* New York: Norton.

Falicov, C. (1995). Training to think culturally: A multidimensional comparative framework. *Family Process, 34,* 373–388.

Falicov, C. (1998). *Latino families in therapy: A guide to multicultural practice.* New York: Guilford Press.

Falicov, C. (2007). Working with transnational immigrants: Expanding meanings of family, community, and culture. *Family Process, 46,* 157–172.

Fraenkel, P., Hameline, T., & Shannon, M. (2009). Narrative and collaborative practices in work with families that are homeless. *Journal of Marital and Family Therapy, 35,* 1–18.

Framo, J. (1992). *Family-of-origin therapy: An intergenerational approach.* New York: Brunner/Mazel.

Freedman, J., & Combs, G. (1996). *Narrative therapy: The social construction of preferred realities.* New York: Norton.

Goldenberg, I., & Goldenberg, H. (2008). *Family therapy: An overview* (7th ed.). Pacific Grove, CA: Brooks/Cole.

Goldner, V. (1988). Generation and gender: Normative and covert hierarchies. *Family Process, 27,* 17–21.

Gottman, J. (1994). *Why marriages succeed or fail.* New York: Simon & Schuster.

Gralnick, A. (1943). The Carrington family: A psychiatric and social study. *Psychiatric Quarterly, 17,* 294–326.

Green, R.-J., & Werner, P. D. (1996). Intrusiveness and closeness—caregiving: Rethinking the concept of family enmeshment. *Family Process, 33,* 115–136.

Haley, J. (1976). *Problem-solving therapy.* San Francisco: Jossey-Bass.

Halford, K., Markman, H., Kling, G., & Stanley, S. (2007). Best practice in couple relationship education. *Journal of Marital and Family Therapy, 29,* 385–406.

Hardy, K. V., & Laszloffy, T. A. (1995). The cultural genogram: Key to training culturally competent family therapists. *Journal of Marital and Family Therapy, 21,* 227–237.

Henggeler, S. W., Clingempeel, W., Brondino, M. J., & Pickrel, S. G. (2002). Four year follow-up of multisystemic therapy with substance-abusing and substance-dependent juvenile offenders. *Journal of the American Academy of Child and Adolescent Psychiatry, 41*(7), 868–874.

Hoffman, L. (1990). Constructing realities: An art of lenses. *Family Process, 29,* 1–13.

Imber-Black, E. (1988). *Families and larger systems.* New York: Guilford Press.

Jacobson, N., & Christensen, A. (1996). *Integrative couple therapy*. New York: Norton.

Johnson, S. M. (2004). *The practice of emotionally-focused marital therapy: Creating connections* (2nd ed.). New York: Brunner/Mazel.

Knudsen-Martin, C., & Mahoney, A. R. (2005). Moving beyond gender: Processes that create relationship equity. *Journal of Marital and Family Therapy, 31*(2), 235–246.

Lebow, J. (1997). The integrative revolution in couple and family therapy. *Family Process, 36*(1), 1–17.

Lefley, H. (2009). *Family psychoeducation for serious mental illness: Evidence-based practices*. New York: Oxford University Press.

Liddle, H. A., Santisteban, D. A., Levant, R. F., & Bray, J. H. (Eds.). (2002). *Family psychology: Science-based interventions*. Washington, DC: American Psychological Association.

MacDermid, S. M., Samper, R., Schwarz, R., Nishida, J., & Nyaronga, D. (2008). *Understanding and promoting resilience in military families*. West Lafayette, IN: Military Family Research Institute.

Madsen, W. C. (2006). *Collaborative therapy with multi-stressed families* (2nd ed.). New York: Guilford Press.

McDaniel, S., Hepworth, J., & Doherty, H. (2007). *Medical family therapy: Psychosocial treatment of families with health problems* (2nd ed.). New York: Basic Books.

McFarlane, W. (2002). *Multifamily groups in the treatment of severe psychiatric disorders*. New York: Guilford Press.

McGoldrick, M., Anderson, C., & Walsh, F. (Eds.). (1989). *Women in families: A framework for family therapy*. New York: Norton.

McGoldrick, M., Carter, B., & Garcia-Preto, N. (2011). *The expanded family life cycle: Individual, family, and social perspectives* (4th ed.). Boston: Pearson.

McGoldrick, M., Gerson, R., & Petry, S. (2008). *Genograms: Assessment and intervention* (3rd ed.). New York: Norton.

McGoldrick, M., & Hardy, K. (Eds.). (2008). *Re-visioning family therapy: Race, culture, and gender in clinical practice* (2nd ed.). New York: Guilford Press.

Minuchin, S. (1974). *Families and family therapy*. Cambridge, MA: Harvard University Press.

Minuchin, P., Colapinto, J., & Minuchin, S. (2006). *Working with families of the poor* (2nd ed.). New York: Guilford Press.

Minuchin, S., Nichols, M., & Lee, W.-Y. (2006). *Assessing families and couples: From symptom to system*. Boston: Allyn & Bacon.

Nichols, M., & Schwartz, R. (2008). *Essentials of family therapy* (4th ed.). Needham Heights, MA: Allyn & Bacon.

Patterson, G., Reid, J., Jones, R., & Conger, R. (1975). *A social learning approach to family interaction*. Eugene, OR: Castalia.

Rolland, J. (1994). *Families, illness, and disability: An integrative treatment model*. New York: Basic Books.

Rowe, C. L., & Liddle, H. A. (2008). When the levee breaks: Treating adolescents and families in the aftermath of Hurricane Katrina. *Journal of Marital and Family Therapy, 34*, 132–148.

Santisteban, D. A., Coatsworth, J., Perez-Vidal, A., Kurtines, W. M., Schwartz, S. J., LaPerriere, A., et al. (2003). Efficacy of brief strategic family therapy in modifying Hispanic adolescent behavior problems and substance use. *Journal of Family Psychology, 17*(1), 121–133.

Satir, V. (1988). *The new peoplemaking.* Palo Alto, CA: Science and Behavior Books.

Selvini Palazzoli, M., Boscolo, L., Cecchin, G., & Prata, G. (1980). Hypothesizing, circularity, neutrality: Three guidelines for the conductor of sessions. *Family Process, 19*, 3–12.

Sexton, T., & Alexander, J. (2005). Functional family therapy for externalizing disorders in adolescents. In J. Lebow (Ed.), *Handbook of clinical family therapy* (pp. 164–191). Hoboken, NJ: Wiley.

Sluzki, C. (1983). Process, structure, and world views in family therapy: Toward an integration of systemic models. *Family Process, 22*, 469–476.

Sprenkle, D., & Piercy, F. (2005). *Research methods in family therapy* (2nd ed.). New York: Guilford Press.

Steinglass, P. (1998). Multiple family discussion groups for patients with chronic medical illness. *Families, Systems, and Health, 16*(1–2), 55–71.

Stinnett, N., & DeFrain, J. (1985). *Secrets of strong families.* Boston: Little, Brown.

von Bertalanffy, L. (1968). *General system theory and psychiatry: Foundation, developments, applications.* New York: Braziller.

Walsh, F. (1987). The clinical utility of normal family research. *Psychotherapy, 24*, 496–503.

Walsh, F. (2002). A family resilience framework: Innovative practice applications. *Family Relations, 51*(2), 333–355.

Walsh, F. (2003). Family resilience: A framework for clinical practice. *Family Process, 42*(1), 1–18.

Walsh, F. (2006). *Strengthening family resilience* (2nd ed.). New York: Guilford Press.

Walsh, F. (2007). Traumatic loss and major disasters: Strengthening family and community resilience. *Family Process, 46*(2), 207–227.

Walsh, F. (Ed.). (2009). *Spiritual resources in family therapy* (2nd ed.). New York: Guilford Press.

Walsh, F. (2011a). Families in later life: Challenges, opportunities, and resilience. In M. McGoldrick, B. Carter, & N. Garcia-Preto (Eds.), *The expanded family life cycle* (4th ed., pp. 261–277). Boston: Pearson.

Walsh, F. (2011b). Family therapy: Systemic approaches to practice. In J. Brandell (Ed.), *Theory and practice of clinical social work* (pp. 153–178). Thousand Oaks, CA: Sage.

Walsh, F., & McGoldrick, M. (Eds.). (2004). *Living beyond loss: Death in the family* (2nd ed.). New York: Norton.

Weakland, J., Fisch, R., Watzlawick, P., & Bodin, A. (1974). Brief therapy: Focused problem resolution. *Family Process, 13*, 141–168.

Whitaker, C. (1992). Symbolic experiential family therapy: Model and methodology. In J. K. Zeig (Ed.), *The evolution of psychotherapy* (pp. 13–23). Philadelphia: Brunner/Mazel.

White, M. (1995). *Re-authoring lives: Interviews and essays.* Adelaide, Australia: Dulwich Center.

White, M., & Epston, D. (1990). *Narrative means to therapeutic ends.* New York: Norton.

PART II

VARYING FAMILY FORMS AND CHALLENGES

CHAPTER 3

COUPLE INTERACTION IN HAPPY AND UNHAPPY MARRIAGES

Gottman Laboratory Studies

JANICE DRIVER
AMBER TABARES
ALYSON F. SHAPIRO
JOHN M. GOTTMAN

Our research team at the Gottman Laboratory has devoted over three decades to identifying the patterns that distinguish masters of marriage—happy, stable couples—from unhappy couples headed for divorce. Although a great deal of marital research has been based on survey methods such as questionnaires and self-reports, our research also includes detailed, in-depth observations. Our research has focused on marital conflict, which we believe is an important and necessary part of both happy and unhappy marriages. We have found that the success or failure of a marriage depends not on whether there is conflict, but on how conflict is handled when it does occur. This research has enabled us to expose myths about marriage.

Through the years, we have expanded our observational studies to include nonconflict situations of couples during daily interactions and couple interviews. By looking at partners in these three distinct settings, we have identified marked differences between happy and unhappy relationships. We have also learned what factors contribute to the friendship at the foundation of happy marriages. We summarize the major results of these findings in this chapter.

DEMOGRAPHICS

This summary is based on seven different longitudinal studies with a total of 843 married couples. As required by the National Institute of Mental Health, each of these studies matched the major economic, racial, and ethnic groups in the Northwest region where the research was conducted. Approximately 30% of the total sample across all six studies was from nonwhite ethnic groups. Although our sample includes ethnic minorities, we do not make racial distinctions in our summary. This kind of future research would require over-sampling a particular ethnic group to observe differing patterns in couple interactions.

Throughout this summary, we refer to couples as happily married, unhappily married, or divorced. The classification of happy or unhappy was based on marital satisfaction questionnaires given to each of the partners at various time points throughout the study. For a couple to be classified as happy, both partners had to be satisfied with the marriage. To be considered unhappy or distressed, one or both partners had to be dissatisfied with the marriage. If one partner was happy in the marriage and the other was unhappy, we considered the couple to be unhappy or distressed. In all of our studies, we have followed the couples longitudinally to determine whether they remained married. The divorce category includes all couples who went on to divorce.

FOUR HORSEMEN

One consistent characteristic of distressed couples headed for divorce is the expression of specific negative behaviors we call the Four Horsemen of the Apocalypse (Gottman, 1994). Although negativity is part of any marital conflict, these are specific predictors of impending doom to a relationship. The Four Horsemen are criticism, contempt, defensiveness, and stonewalling.

The first of the Four Horsemen, criticism, is very common in distressed relationships. All couples have complaints of some kind during an argument, but criticism goes much further and is more damaging to the relationship than a simple complaint. Criticism is more global and includes character attacks, such as "You didn't take the trash out last night. Why can't you ever remember to do it? You're so lazy!" A complaint, on the other hand, remains specific to a situation, such as "I'm annoyed that you didn't take the trash out last night." The added personality attack of criticism escalates negativity and causes damage to the relationship over time.

In addition to character attacks, criticism includes global complaints, which can be identified by words such as "You always . . . " and "You never . . ., " or it can include a laundry list of complaints that imply "always" or "never." For example, "You didn't clean the bathroom like you said you would. That's so typical! Just like last week when you said you'd organize the shelves and get up early to help make lunch for the kids and you didn't do those things either."

Contempt, the next of the Four Horsemen, is the most corrosive. It is more destructive than criticism, because it conveys disgust and disrespect between spouses. A contemptuous comment might include sarcasm, mockery, insults, eye rolls, scowls, and hostile humor to belittle the partner. The attitude conveyed by contempt is one of disdain or superiority. One spouse may show condescension by taking a higher moral ground: "Did you really think showing up for just one soccer game all season would really be enough? That's an involved parent for you." Contempt is a type of scorn that often hinders any conciliatory attempts by the other spouse and may severely escalate negativity on both sides.

The third of the Four Horsemen is defensiveness. Although defensiveness seems a natural way to protect oneself against a perceived attack, our research shows that it usually becomes a counterattack, which further escalates negativity. Defensiveness is ineffective, because it becomes a way for one spouse to blame the other for his or her own behavior. One person might start with contempt: "Well that was pretty immature to go barhopping with your friends." To which a defensive spouse would respond, "You did the same thing last week." Defensiveness frequently takes on a childish tone, with the partners trying to shield themselves from both attack and personal responsibility.

Stonewalling is the fourth of the Four Horsemen. After many arguments with high levels of contempt, criticism, and defensiveness, it is easy for one spouse to feel overwhelmed by the conflict. At this point, the overwhelmed spouse begins stonewalling by conveying to the speaker that he or she does not want to interact, and appearing not to listen at all. There is no eye contact, no back-channeling, and no verbal response. The speaker is actively ignored. Stonewalling appears after the emergence of what Christensen and Heavey (1990) call the demand–withdraw pattern. This pattern shows clear gender differences, with the wife commonly demanding and the husband withdrawing, each reacting to the other as the couple becomes increasingly polarized. Stonewalling follows this same pattern, with husbands stonewalling more often than wives. Surprisingly, although the stonewaller appears to be hostile, his primary thoughts during this interaction are usually self-protective: "When is she going to quit talking?"; "I can't stand arguing about this anymore"; or "If I'm quiet, she'll leave me alone." This kind of self-protection requires a great deal of energy and makes it impossible to listen, even if the comments are constructive and helpful.

When all of the Four Horsemen are present during a conflict discussion, we are able to predict divorce, even with newlywed couples (Gottman, 1994; Carrère & Gottman, 1999), and to predict decline in marital quality when couples stay married (Gottman, Coan, Carrère, & Swanson, 1998). These truly are danger signals for any relationship. When used habitually during conflict, they erode the marriage and create hostility. Although some happily married couples occasionally use defensiveness, criticism, or even stonewalling, they rarely use contempt. We believe the disrespect that is characteristic of contempt is most harmful to the relationship overall. A high frequency of all the Four Horsemen, however, creates lasting damage and, most likely, the eventual ruin of the marriage.

EMOTIONAL DISENGAGEMENT

Whereas the interactional patterns we call the Four Horsemen are detrimental to a marriage, emotional disengagement is also damaging for a couple (Gottman, 1994). Emotionally disengaged couples do not display extreme levels of negativity and are unlikely to include the Four Horsemen, but they do show a complete lack of positive affect. Characteristically, they demonstrate little of the interest, affection, humor, and concern characteristic of happy couples. Emotional disengagement is an interesting phenomenon because the couples appear fine on the surface but are actually highly distressed. Emotionally disengaged couples are attempting to enclave the problem, so that it does not poison the entire relationship. However, the cost of this avoidance is the erosion of intimacy and the absence of shared positive affect in their interaction. They begin editing out parts of their personality and become hidden from their partners. This further erodes their intimate connection. Couples who appear emotionally disengaged may exhibit higher levels of physiological arousal during conflicts as a result of suppressing negative affect. Gross and Levenson (1997) reported that the suppression of negative affects does increase physiological arousal. In this way, emotionally disengaged couples may also expend tremendous physical effort to act as if everything is OK.

Both emotional disengagement and the Four Horsemen predict divorce, but there is a marked difference in the timing of divorce for each of these negative styles. Gottman and Levenson (2000) found that couples who frequently use contempt, criticism, defensiveness, and stonewalling tend to divorce earlier in the marriage, most within 7 years. Emotionally disengaged couples, however, tend to divorce after 7–14 years. It seems that these relationships slowly atrophy as the partners become more and more distant.

FLOODING

When a conflict is tainted by the Four Horsemen pattern or by emotional disengagement, it is common for one or both partners to become emotionally and physically overwhelmed (Gottman, 1994; Gottman & Levenson, 1983). In our physiological research, we find that at this point of "flooding," palms begin to sweat, heart rate increases to over 90 beats per minute, and breathing becomes shallow or irregular. With these physiological symptoms, the partner is unable to think clearly or participate in constructive conversation. The primary focus of the flooded spouse is reduced to self-preservation, with thoughts such as "I can't stand this anymore" or "Why is she attacking me?" At this point, it is impossible to take in new information. Even positive interactions, such as an apology or a humorous moment, are subdued as the partner tries to protect himself from a perceived attack. Although flooding is more common for men than women, it can happen to either partner during an argument.

Flooding, an emergency state during a conflict, must be treated with respect and concern. The best antidote to flooding is to take a break from the conflict for at least 20 minutes. Taking a break, however, does not mean going to separate rooms and preparing for another attack. The person who feels flooded needs to engage in a soothing activity, such as going for a walk, reading, or listening to music. It is essential during this time to concentrate on thoughts other than the argument. To ruminate on the conflict or brood over being an innocent victim will only maintain a flooded state.

As important as it is to take time out when flooded, it is equally important to return to or reschedule the conflict discussion as soon as possible. If the couple does not return to the argument, a break to relieve flooding becomes a way to stonewall. Thus, the respite, which is intended to improve the marriage, can become a way to damage it.

NEGATIVE RECIPROCITY

Criticism, contempt, defensiveness, and stonewalling are specific types of negative conflict that signal danger, but not all negativity is damaging to the relationship. One pattern of marital conflict we have studied is that of negative reciprocity (Gottman et al., 1998; Gottman, Markman, & Notarius, 1977), in which one spouse responds to the other's negativity with more negativity. There has long been a myth that this pattern is harmful to relationships; but we have found that there are two types of negative reciprocity, only one of which predicts divorce (Gottman et al., 1998).

The more harmful of the two is the pattern of negative escalation, in which negativity is responded to with increased negativity. There is an escalation of the conflict when each partner uses a more hurtful or severe response. In watching these interactions, it is as if each partner is trying to get back at the other by trying to "win." This type of negative escalation is often found in conjunction with the Four Horsemen. A lower level of negative affect, such as anger or sadness, from one spouse will be reciprocated with contempt, criticism, or defensiveness. This specific pattern of combative escalation, along with the Four Horsemen, predicts divorce (Gottman et al., 1998).

The second type of negative reciprocity is characteristic of all marriages, including happy ones. This pattern matches negativity for negativity. One partner will respond to anger with anger, and to sadness with sadness. This does not include, however, those couples that respond to contempt with contempt. We consider this to be escalation of the negativity. When couples are able to match low-level negativity the argument will be negative but not harmful. It is important to understand from this finding that negative emotions are a natural part of conflict and are not all perilous to marriage.

CONFLICT STYLES OF HAPPY COUPLES

As with the myth that all negative reciprocity is destructive, an opposite myth exists regarding happy couples. This is the belief that all happily married couples talk about their problems in a way that validates each other's views. Not all satisfied couples argue in this way, however. We have found three different conflict styles (or couple types) that seem to work well for happy couples: validators, volatiles, and avoiders (Gottman, 1993, 1994).

Validators "talk out" their problems. These partners are very adept at validating their spouse's emotions and opinions. They are very good friends and, when questioned about their relationship, tend to emphasize "we" over "me" or "I." Validators are also noncoercive and tend to have few disagreements. But when disagreements do arise, there is a strong sense of mutual respect between these spouses. Rarely, if ever, would validators raise their voices during conflict. They are very skilled at compromise and use these skills to resolve their differences.

A different approach to dealing with conflict is seen in couples with a volatile style, who have a more explosive approach to handling conflict. Their arguments tend to be higher energy and more heated than disagreements between validators. In volatile couples, both partners are highly involved in the argument, viewing each other as equals. Volatiles give significance to their own individuality and feel marriage should strengthen and accentuate their distinctiveness. During arguments, volatiles express both negative and positive emotions with vigor, though their arguments rarely contain the Four Horsemen. Volatiles tend to be passionate, however, and their displays of warmth and affection counterbalance the negativity. In fact, all stable couple types, including volatiles, exhibit five times more positive interactions than negative ones. For every negative behavior, there are five positive behaviors (Gottman & Levenson, 1992). The key to the success of volatile couples is the overall warm and loving environment they maintain in their marriage despite their negative and explosive moments.

On the opposite end of the conflict scale is the third style, the avoiders. Avoiders minimize their problems and thus avoid conflict. They emphasize any positive aspects of the marriage, while downplaying or completely ignoring any complaints. When ignoring differences is not possible, they often agree to disagree. The marital style of conflict avoiders has been the most difficult for the psychological community to accept, because there is a pervasive myth that "avoiding conflict will ruin your marriage." We have found that some couples prefer to avoid disagreements, but they describe themselves as satisfied with their marriages and share a deep love for each other.

All three conflict styles can be equally effective. Whereas some couples avoid all arguments, others jump into the conflict with shouting, and still others discuss disagreements and find compromise. No one style is better or worse for a marriage, but it is important to understand that it has to work for both spouses. When people of differing styles get married, it can be a difficult situation. For example, if one spouse tends to avoid conflict, he or she is not likely to be happy with someone who argues loudly and vigorously. Thus, an avoider can be happily married to another avoider but would be unhappily married to a volatile. This does not mean that partners are hopeless and destined for divorce if they have differing styles, but the relationship will require tremendous effort and patience on the part of both spouses.

It would be interesting for future research to focus on the cultural differences related to these conflict styles. Each culture may have strong preferences in dealing with interpersonal conflict, but there may also be great variability within each system.

Regardless of the style of handling conflict, it is important to remember that each couple must offset disagreements with positive interactions. As we mentioned earlier, all couples, regardless of style, must counter each negative behavior with five positive behaviors. Maintaining this level of positive interaction is crucial to sustain a happy and stable relationship.

SOLVABLE VERSUS UNSOLVABLE PROBLEMS

Yet another myth about happily married couples is the belief that they are able to resolve all their disagreements. We have found, however, that both happy and unhappy marriages have unsolvable as well as solvable problems. In fact, we have found that all conflict can be reduced to these two categories. Solvable problems have a solution, whereas unsolvable problems are ongoing issues that may never be resolved. Unsolvable or perpetual problems often arise from fundamental personality, cultural, or religious differences, or essential needs of each spouse. One partner may love to hike and camp, while the other enjoys city attractions. Chronic stress may also arise from crisis events or adverse situations beyond the couple's control, such as serious illness and disability, harsh environmental conditions, or prolonged unemployment.

Both successful and unsuccessful marriages have disagreements, but happily married couples seem to understand the distinction between the two types of problems and handle them differently. Satisfied couples deal with perpetual problems much the way aging adults deal with persistent back pain. It may irritate them, but they learn to accept it. The aim in discussing a perpetual problem is to create an atmosphere of acceptance of the partner's viewpoint rather than creating a condition of "gridlock." So the goal is not to solve the problem, but for the couple to find a way to gain some degree of peace around it.

Robert and Anna Maria have opposing views on how to spend their weekends.

> ANNA MARIA: It's just that we have different ideas about what it means to relax. I like to sleep late and take it slow, while you jump out of bed and straight into your running shoes.
>
> ROBERT: No! I usually put on my socks first. (*They both laugh.*)
>
> ANNA MARIA: I do like it when you bring me back some coffee.
>
> ROBERT: That's good. That's my secret to jump-start our day.

Anna Maria may never enjoy getting up early, and Robert may never sleep in, but they are able to live with each other's style. Successful couples try to understand what is at the foundation of the differences that are causing conflicts and use this understanding to communicate amusement and affection while learning to cope with their perpetual issue. The positive affect in these discussions is in direct contrast to gridlocked discussions of perpetual problems.

Greg and Kimberly also discuss how they spend their weekends, but they become gridlocked around the problem.

> GREG: We didn't get a chance to relax all weekend. You're constantly going from one thing to the next.
>
> KIMBERLY: What do you mean? We went on that bike ride on Saturday. That was relaxing.
>
> GREG: Relaxing? That was exhausting! You dragged me half way around the city.
>
> KIMBERLY: Well, I wouldn't have to drag you if you were in better shape.

Partners who are gridlocked are firmly planted in their respective positions. As a result their discussions include very little positive affect and one or more of the Four Horsemen. Over time, these couples feel rejected, overwhelmed, and hopeless about ever reaching any sort of a compromise. Gridlocked couples seem to focus on the unsolvable problem rather than on the underlying meaning that contributes to the opposing views.

ACCEPTING INFLUENCE

One way that masterful couples deal with gridlocked conflict is by accepting "influence" from each other. This is a term we use to describe each partner's willingness to yield during an argument, in order to "win" in the relationship. The best analogy for accepting influence is city driving. You are driving home in traffic when someone stops and illegally parks in your lane. You cannot move unless one of two things happens: Either the other driver moves his car or you change lanes and drive home. It would be a waste of time and energy to park behind the offender, shout threats of traffic violations, and summon a police officer, when simply changing lanes will achieve your greater purpose. Accepting influence is similar to this idea of changing lanes and driving home. By learning to find a point of yielding, even a minor point, the spouse wins the desired purpose of a close and satisfying relationship.

Yielding to win, however, should not be mistakenly translated into a complete surrender of oneself to the other's whims. Instead, accepting influence is the ability to find a point of agreement in the other's position. It is important to note that partner needs to accommodate the other, or the relationship becomes skewed. Often, this agreement is only achieved when each partner tries to understand the meaning of the other's perspective in the conflict.

Vincent and Alicia, for example, often argued about how to spend their vacation. Vincent wanted to visit his family in Virginia, and Alicia preferred that they go somewhere alone as a couple. This problem had been a continuing area of disagreement in their 10-year relationship. Each had decided that his or her position was correct, so the couple considered taking separate vacations. Vincent would go to visit his family, while Alicia would go somewhere with her best friend. To look at this problem from the standpoint of accepting influence, both Vincent and Alicia needed to understand why the other was entrenched (or parked) in his or her position.

Vincent only saw his family once a year and found it easy to relax and enjoy himself in their company. Alicia's family lived nearby, so he saw them often (at least once a week) and felt he deserved to see his family more regularly. Alicia, on the other hand, did not get along with Vincent's mother and found it difficult to spend an entire week with her. She also had a very stressful job and wanted go somewhere more relaxing. Each partner had good reasons for remaining in his or her fixed position. This inflexibility, however, made it impossible to move toward an agreeable solution.

In contrast, if the partners were able to accept influence from each other, they could move from positions that were rigid and unyielding to ones of compromise and collaboration. Vincent would be able to see that Alicia needed a break from her demanding schedule. Alicia would be able to understand Vincent's desire to spend time with his family. If each could acknowledge some part of the other's viewpoint, BOTH could see the problem differently. The issue would no longer be where to go, but how to achieve both goals.

Although accepting influence is difficult at times, it has tremendous power for the marital relationship. When partners learn to yield on certain points of a conflict, they realize that they can cooperate and work together as a couple. The problem itself becomes an issue that they can conquer together as a team. This creates cohesiveness in other areas of their life as well, and they learn to move through time together.

This ability for both partners to accept influence is a skill that discriminates between happily married, unhappily married, and divorced couples in our research. In fact, we found that abusive husbands *never* accepted influence from their wives (Coan, Gottman, Babcock, & Jacobson, 1997). Although these abusive husbands are the extreme, their inability to accept influence highlights its importance for healthy relationships. Gottman et al. (1998) reported that in nonviolent marriages, once again it was the *husband's* rejection of influence from his wife that predicted divorce and not the wife's rejection of influence from her husband. Wives were accepting influence at high rates in all the marriages. This finding speaks to general issues of women's power and powerlessness in heterosexual relationships (Walsh, 1989; see Knudson-Martin, Chapter 14, this volume).

REPAIR ATTEMPTS

In addition to accepting influence, happy couples also manage conflict and miscommunication with what we call "repair attempts." We have defined repair attempts as interactions that prevent or decrease negative escalation. Because disagreements are a natural part of any relationship, even happy relationships, the ability to repair is crucial. This is especially true when couples are engaged in conflict. The actual issue, whether finances, in-laws, or housework, is less important than the way the couple engages in the dispute. Miscommunication during these conflicts often leads to an increase or escalation of negativity and erosion of the relationship; so it is important to repair the miscommunication during the conflict or soon after.

For nearly 3 years we studied repair attempts in an effort to understand their role in preventing and reducing increased negativity. Examples of repair attempts include apologies, humor, affection, and changing the subject. These repair interactions are not necessarily related to the content of the argument but may simply provide a brief reprieve from it. For instance, one husband suddenly stopped in the middle of a heated debate and said, "After this, I need to stop by my sister's house to drop off the DVD we borrowed." The wife went along with his repair by saying, "OK. We can drop it off before we pick up the kids." This seemingly unimportant change of subject gave the couple a brief diversion from the intensity of the conflict. Once they talked about the DVD, both seemed more relaxed and were able to return to the argument. Happy couples tend to give their partners the opportunity to maneuver in the discussion. They allow the conflict to ebb and flow, with occasional unrelated topics interspersed in the conflict. Allowing a change of topic, however, must not be misconstrued as avoiding the topic. Happy couples return to the argument and do not allow the reprieve to derail their discussion, even if the topic is uncomfortable or tense.

Members of unhappy couples, by contrast, frequently respond to these types of repairs with a negative interpretation of their partners' intent. Rather than allowing the change of subject, an unhappy spouse may respond, "You're not listening to me!" or "Who cares about the stupid DVD?" As a result, unhappy couples may remain adamantly fixed on the discussion topic and not allow breaks in the argument. This rigid adherence to the conflict seems to escalate negativity. As a result, unhappy couples are not able to modulate the discussion and thus cannot keep the argument within a tolerable range.

In addition to accepting the repairs, we have seen that couples who use repairs early in the conflict prevent it from becoming too negative. Happily married couples tend to use repairs throughout their discussion, whereas distressed couples wait until the argument is heated and divisive. When the argument is at a point of severe negativity, repair attempts are often less effective and may even backfire. One couple was in the middle of a heated and hostile debate about finances, when the husband tried to lighten the moment with a joke about a stain on his T-shirt. Rather than reducing the negative tone of the conflict, this attempt at humor enraged the wife, who responded with increased anger and contempt. Repairs often have this backlash effect during high negativity, because unhappy spouses tend to ignore or reject a repair when the conflict is too intense. Our research has found that using repairs early and often is more effective than waiting until the conflict is more severe (Driver, Tabares, & Gottman, 2010).

When there is a balance of repair attempts between the spouses, the conflict also tends to maintain a lower level of negativity. If, however, one partner is making repair after repair, while the other plunges on with the conflict, the argument will continue to escalate. This pattern of uneven repair attempts seems characteristic of distressed couples.

Another important component of repair attempts is each partner's ability to respond in a positive way when a repair is made. If one partner recognizes a repair and allows his or her spouse to lighten the moment or gain a reprieve, the overall conflict is more positive. For example, one couple in our laboratory was involved in an intense disagreement about the husband's disappointment with their oldest son. During a brief pause in the argument, the husband commented, "I do admire the fact that you're able to stay calm no matter what he says." The wife smiled and simply said, "Thanks." After this moment of affection (compliment), both the husband and wife returned to the conflict discussion. As this example shows, repairs do not avoid the conflict or demean the partner, but they do interject some positive moments into difficult discussions.

One important finding from our recent study is that all couples attempt to repair during conflict (Driver et al., 2010). This indicates that all couples naturally repair and do not need to be taught how to repair. Instead, partners need to learn to initiate repairs sooner and more often, while also learning to accept and recognize repairs as they occur. This seems encouraging, because it may be easier to enhance and encourage existing repair skills than to teach and build new skills.

In summary, repair attempts are tools that can be used effectively to prevent escalation, to reduce negativity, and to provide a break from intense moments during an argument. The conflict will continue in a more positive manner when repairs are used often and accepted well.

TURNING TOWARD

One of the most important leaps we made in our way of thinking occurred when we started studying marriages in the day-to-day moments outside of conflict. By observing couples' interactions in our apartment laboratory at the University of Washington, and by interviewing couples about the history of their relationship, we have discovered several key factors we attribute to successful marriages.

In couple therapy, there is often an emphasis on the major events in the couple's interactions, such as conflict discussions. However, the minor, everyday moments for a couple may determine how the partners interact when major events unfold. As a foundation for approaching major events, daily interactions are a crucial component for marital success. Imagine, for example, that a husband gives his wife a dozen roses for Valentine's Day. These roses might have a completely different meaning, depending on daily interactions: whether the husband has been aloof, crabby, and absent or attentive, positive, and helpful. In the first instance, the roses would be an inadequate attempt to make up for his neglect; in the second, they would be a loving and romantic gesture. The giving of roses comes with current and ongoing contexts.

To understand these daily interactions, we designed one of our studies to accommodate couples in an apartment laboratory setting. We asked the couples to live in a studio-type apartment and videotaped them for 12 of the 24 hours they stayed there. We allowed them to bring anything from home that would help them feel comfortable, such as groceries, CDs, videos, and work. One couple even brought their cat. The only instruction we gave to each couple was to ask the partners to live as they would at home.

To capture their everyday interactions, we created an observational coding system that categorizes ways in which couples initiate and respond to each other on a moment-to-moment basis. We defined an invitation to interact as a "bid." For each bid, we noted the needs and demands involved, from information exchange to sharing emotional support. The responses to these bids ranged from mere eye movement to playfulness and were categorized as "turning toward," "turning away," and "turning against."

From these data, we found that each time one partner initiates an interaction (or "bids" for attention), the other spouse is given a choice that will improve or erode the marriage. Ignoring the interaction or responding in a negative way fosters distance and separation, whereas even a minor response helps promote emotional connection and friendship. Suppose, for example, that Stephanie and Carl are sitting in the living room reading. Stephanie looks up and comments that there's a sparrow outside their window. At that moment, Carl faces a series of choices for his response. He can ignore the comment and continue reading (turning away); he can comment that he thinks bird watching is a waste of time (turning against); he can momentarily set aside his book to look at the bird (low-level turning toward); or he can look at the bird and comment on its activity (enthusiastic turning toward). If Carl responds by ignoring Stephanie or making a negative comment, it discourages her from making further attempts to interact. Such responses lead to reduced bidding and connection. On the other hand, if Carl responds by looking at the bird and making a comment, he is welcoming her interaction, which will lead to increased interactions and increased marital connection.

We have found that happily married couples rarely ignore their partners. Nearly 85% of their bids were met with some kind of positive response (Driver, 2006). What is interesting about these responses is that they were not always overly attentive or enthusiastic. One partner may simply look up and smile. Acknowledging the bid in some way seemed to play an important role in maintaining a healthy relationship. This does not mean, however, that satisfied couples always made low-level responses. Their responses ranged from low-level to playful. With this variety, spouses expressed their willingness and interest to interact.

Having an eagerness to interact, we believe, creates more interaction and increased friendship. In fact, our happily married couples made up to 77 bids in 10 minutes. Contrast this to some distressed couples that made 10–20 bids in 10 minutes. A positive response to a bid appears to lead to increased bidding and strengthened friendship.

Playful bidding was another characteristic of happy couples. We defined "playfulness" as good-natured teasing with some physical sparring. For example, a husband might throw a crumpled napkin at his wife in a mock snowball fight. Such playful interactions were nonexistent for distressed couples. What is important, however, was that couples who used playfulness and enthusiasm in their daily interactions had better access to humor and affection during their conflict discussions (Driver & Gottman, 2004). In a longitudinal study of middle-aged and senior couples in first marriages, humor and affection during conflict was a characteristic of happily married, stable, older couples (Carstensen, Gottman, & Levenson, 1995). Thus, if daily interactions contribute to more positive affect during conflict, the overall quality of the relationship is affected by these minor moments.

REWRITING THE PAST

Another nonconflict situation we have studied is the way that couples describe their relationship. We have found that a couple's description of the past predicts the future of the marriage (Buehlman, Gottman, & Katz, 1992; Carrère, Buehlman, Coan, Gottman, & Ruckstuhl, 2000; Shapiro, Gottman, & Carrère, 2000). Over and over again, we have seen that partners who are deeply entrenched in a negative view of their spouse and their marriage often revise the past, such that they only remember and talk about the negative things that have happened in their relationship. Happy couples, in contrast, highlight their good memories. This revision of their marital history has allowed us to predict stability in marriage versus divorce with 88–94% accuracy (Buhelman et al., 1992; Carrère et al., 2000). These retrospective descriptions have also allowed us to identify buffers that appear to protect couples from decline in marital satisfaction during the stressful adjustment to parenting (Shapiro et al., 2000).

To engage the partners in a description of their marital history, we use the Oral History Interview (OHI) and related coding system, developed in our laboratory by Buehlman and Gottman (1996). This interview asks couples about the beginnings of their relationship, their philosophy of marriage, how their relationship has changed over time, and what marriage was like in their family of origin. By interviewing the partners in this way, we are able to capture the dynamics of their marital journey and their identity as a couple. Although they may tell us about their past in great detail, our focus is not on content, but rather on how the couples describe their relationship.

Most couples enter marriage with high hopes and great expectations. When a marriage is not going well, however, history gets rewritten for the worst. In a distressed marriage, the wife is more likely to recall that her husband was 30 minutes late to the ceremony. He, in a similar way, may focus on all the time she spent talking to his best man and may even speculate that she was actually flirting with him.

Along with remembering the worst, unhappy couples find the past difficult to remember. It is as though the memory is unimportant or painful, and they have let it fade away. Their lack of appropriate detail, along with their negative perspective, gives us tremendous insight into their marital distress.

In happy marriages, couples tend to look back on their early days with fondness. Even if the wedding was not perfect, they emphasize the highlights rather than the low points, and even joke about the low points and imperfections. This is also true for the way they remember and describe each other. They reminisce about how positive they felt early on, how excited they were when they first met, and how much admiration they had for each other. When they talk about the tough times, they emphasize the strength they drew from each other rather than the specific struggles.

Through categorizing couples' descriptions during the OHI, we have been able to separate the masters of marriage from the disasters. Unhappy spouses headed toward divorce were negative to each other, thought of their lives as chaotic, and expressed disappointment in the marriage. Happy partners used fondness during their interview, used expressions of "we-ness," tended to glorify any hardships, and reflected awareness of each other's worlds through their expansive descriptions. Each of these categories is described in more detail below.

Unhappy Couples

Negativity toward Spouse

Distressed spouses tend to express negativity and criticism toward each other, even when remembering pleasant events such as their wedding or honeymoon. A husband describing the honeymoon might only remember tension and unpleasant experiences: "It seems like all we did was fight; she nagged me all the time. . . . Oh, and the mosquitoes were terrible. I could barely step foot outside." Unhappy partners may also be vague and unclear about what attracted them to their spouse. The husband and wife may wrack their brains to think of a single quality they admired about their spouse before they were married, and sometimes what they remember is not very flattering. One wife's first impression of her husband was "Well, I guess I thought he was cute enough but, boy, was he a bad dresser!"

Chaotic Perceptions

Many couples face struggles such as financial loss or stress at work. When these events occur, however, unhappy couples tend to view their lives as out of control or chaotic. They see themselves as pummeled by outside events: "It's just one thing after another. It seems like one of us is always needed somewhere. If it's not our families, it's the kids or one of our jobs. There's pressure from every angle and there's no way to stop it. We can't do anything about our situation." There is a helpless quality to these chaotic perceptions, with couples feeling unable to overcome stress and hardship. Often these couples are dealing with major stresses, such as sick parents, but the critical thing that defines their relationships is hopelessness. They believe that any solution to their problems is beyond their ability to control.

Disappointment/Disillusionment

One final pattern of unhappy couples is their disappointment and disillusionment with the relationship. Each partner has given up on their marriage and expresses depression about the relationship: "We used to be such good friends and now we don't agree about anything. This is not what I expected." A tone of sadness and resignation often accompanies these statements. Unhappy couples also seem unable to articulate what makes a successful marriage. It is as if personal disappointment alters their general view of marriage, making it difficult to define a happy relationship. During the relationship interviews, negativity and chaos were predictive of divorce, but this tendency toward disappointment was the strongest divorce predictor (Buehlman et al., 1992; Carrère et al., 2000).

Happy Couples

Fondness and Admiration

Happy partners who were still "in love" also showed unique characteristics in the way they described their marital past. Fondness and admiration are two of the most crucial elements in a rewarding and lasting romance. Partners conveyed a fundamental sense that their spouse was worthy of admiration, respect, and love. In a marriage with much fondness and admiration, a wife may recall her first impressions of her husband as being "perfect, like a dream." In a marriage with less fondness, the wife might describe him being "a nice, stable guy." Although even happily married couples have times of frustration with their partners' flaws, partners still remember that the person they married is worthy of honor and respect. When this sense is completely missing from a marriage, we believe the relationship cannot be revived.

Awareness or Love Maps

Along with fondness and admiration, happy spouses usually show an awareness of each other and their relationship. This is clear in the way expansive couples describe the details of their past. They are expressive and descriptive during the interview and often finish each other's sentences.

For example, Marcos and Judy describe their first date:

MARCOS: I remember when I picked her up for the night, she was wearing blue dress that brought out the color of her eyes, and had the brightest smile I had ever seen. I couldn't help thinking how lucky I was to have her going out with me.

JUDY: I kept him waiting for 15 minutes while I was in the bathroom making sure I looked perfect in that blue dress, and he didn't complain at all. He was a perfect gentleman. (*Both laugh and smile.*)

This dimension shows not only each spouse's expressiveness, but also how both respond to and expand on their partner's comments. In contrast, distressed spouses respond to questions with just a few short sentences, seem withdrawn, and do not add to the description. An unhappy spouse would describe the same first date by saying, "We went out to dinner."

Happy spouses are also intimately familiar with their partner's world. They remember the major events in each other's history and keep updating these facts/feelings as their partner's world changes. We call this a richly detailed "love map." When she orders him a salad, she knows to ask for his favorite dressing. We believe that this type of awareness works together with fondness and admiration to create a satisfying relationship. Suppose, for example, that the wife is having a difficult time with her boss at work. If the husband is aware of his wife's distress, he may respond by expressing warmth and emotional support. Thus, the level of awareness is directly related to his ability to express comfort.

Glorifying the Struggle

In contrast to couples who are unhappy in their marriage, happy couples approach hardships as trials to be overcome together and believe that these struggles make their relationship stronger (Walsh, 2006; see Walsh, Chapter 17, this volume). They emphasize how they conquered their difficulties together as a couple: "It was really hard at first when he was laid off, but we managed to support each other and things started to work out." Sometimes the hardships are even about the relationship or adjusting to marriage: "Marriage is the hardest job you'll ever have, but it's worth it." Happy couples emphasize both the difficulty of their experiences and pride in how they managed through it all. Their struggles bring them closer together as they endure challenging outside events and work to prevail.

We-ness

When happy couples describe their marital past, each partner tends to use the words "we" and "us" as opposed to "he or she" or "I." This simple pattern reflects the degree to which couples perceive themselves as a team rather than as individuals: "We oversaw the remodeling of our house. It was difficult at times, but we were able to work it out." If this same couple were low in we-ness, each partner would talk about the remodeling in individual terms: "The remodeling was difficult, but I was able to work with the contractor." Couples who use "we" more often also tend to emphasize the same beliefs, values, and goals.

Although happy couples tend to use the terms "we" and "us," this does not describe their level of differentiation. For example, happy partners may phone each other daily and spend most of their free time together. Other equally happy partners may rarely call during the day, have separate friends, and enjoy different interests. Regardless of their level of independence, happy couples will continue to talk about their relationship in terms of teamwork and collaboration. These couples maintain their desired level of unity or separateness, while referring to themselves as "we" and "us." It is their perception of we-ness that is important.

TRANSITION TO PARENTHOOD

After the arrival of a new baby, for women there is often a dramatic decline in marital satisfaction and increase in hostility during conflict (see Cowan & Cowan, Chapter 18, this volume; Shapiro & Gottman, 2005). In fact, 67% of the wives in our study showed a decline in marital satisfaction (Shapiro et al., 2000). Not all of these couples experienced this decline, however. We again turned to the OHI to understand better why some couples are vulnerable and others are resilient during transition to parenthood. By looking at the way couples talked about their marital past, we were able to predict this decline in marital satisfaction. It is particularly interesting that this prediction was possible from interviews conducted during the early newlywed period.

Our classifications of couples in the OHIs can be seen as reflecting the health of the couples' marital friendship. We have found that this friendship can be seen in the early months of marriage and becomes an important buffer when couples encounter stresses such as the transition to parenthood.

Vulnerable Couples

Based on the newlywed interviews, we have been able to identify two warning signs of couples who are vulnerable to marital decline with the arrival of the first baby: First, the husbands tended to express negativity toward their wives; and second, the partners were likely to view their lives as chaotic. This is valuable information regarding couples at risk for marital decline.

When husbands were critical and negative toward their wives in the newlywed interview, the marital satisfaction of wives plummeted with the arrival of the first baby. Early in their marriage, these husbands tended to express negativity toward their wives and disappointment in the marriage.

Here, again, we see the corrosiveness of criticism and negativity eating away at the quality of the marriage. We found that wives were particularly sensitive and vulnerable to their husbands' negativity and marital disappointment when they became parents. Thus, a habit of negativity seems to have a more damaging impact after the baby is born.

As mentioned earlier, unhappy partners tend to view their lives as chaotic and out of control. This feeling is exacerbated by the disorder that often accompanies life with a new infant. The feelings of chaos expressed by distressed newlywed couples make them particularly vulnerable in coping with the additional stresses and duties necessary for parenting. They are more likely to see parenting challenges as problems beyond their control that throw their lives and their relationship into disarray. Difficulties such as getting up in the middle of the night seem insurmountable and overwhelming.

Resilient Couples

Stable couples, in contrast, use awareness, with fondness and admiration, to buffer the marriage through this stressful period. A husband with a high level of awareness or a detailed love map of his wife's world knows when she is feeling overwhelmed by the challenges she faces as a new mother. He then responds to her stress by expressing his fondness and admiration for her and increasing his level of participation in child care and household tasks. A wife who is highly aware of her husband's world might also sympathize with his frustrations and increasingly support him as well.

The Influence of New Fathers

It is interesting to note that the most important predictor of continuing relationship satisfaction after the first baby is born was the husband's descriptions during the newlywed OHI. Wives are most vulnerable to a decline in marital satisfaction over the transition to parenthood, probably because the wife traditionally bears the bulk of the childrearing responsibilities. They are expected to know naturally how to be good mothers. It is, however, the husband's fondness, awareness, and lack of negativity and disappointment during the newlywed interview that buffers his wife's decline in martial satisfaction when the first baby arrives.

Overall, the OHI provides a dynamic index to the marital relationship. The quality of couples' friendship makes stressful periods, such as the transition to parenthood, either more difficult or smoother. Disappointment in the marriage, negativity toward one's spouse, and the feeling of chaos in couples' lives may reflect vulnerabilities in the relationship and, for some, an overload of stressors that become particularly problematic during stressful periods. On the other hand, qualities such as fondness, admiration, and awareness seem to act as buffers in protecting the relationship during stressful changes.

Transition-to-Parenthood Intervention

Based on the buffers and vulnerabilities for decline in marital satisfaction over the transition to parenthood (Shapiro et al., 2000), we developed a psychoeducational intervention for couples becoming parents (see also Cowan & Cowan, Chapter 18). This intervention, titled Bringing Baby Home, focuses on (1) promoting positive couple relations over the transition to parenthood, (2) promoting positive father involvement, and (3) promoting positive coparenting and sensitive parenting. To date we have found that this psychoeducation has been successful in preventing decline in martial satisfaction, reducing hostility in couple conflict (Shapiro & Gottman, 2005), reducing competition in coparenting during family play with young infants (Shapiro, Nahm, Gottman, & Content, 2011) and increasing father satisfaction with parenting related duties (Shapiro, Pennar, Gottman, & Fink, 2009). This research illustrates that couple relations are amenable to intervention during the transition-to-parenthood period, and that not all marriages need be adversely affected by the birth of a new baby.

CONCLUSIONS

Through careful observational research, we have identified couple interaction patterns that characterize both happy and unhappy marriages. The relationships that end in divorce tend to gravitate toward the Four Horsemen of the Apocalypse and negative reciprocity during conflict discussions. This leads to the dysfunctional coping mechanisms of flooding and eventual emotional disengagement as partners struggle to protect themselves. Likewise, in daily interactions, they reject bid attempts and become more and more distant. These couples also remember and describe their relationships with negativity, disappointment, and feelings of chaos. When stressors such as parenthood come along, these relationships are vulnerable, and the couples become distressed in response to the added pressure.

In contrast, masters of marriage use repair attempts, daily moments of connection, and accepting influence to moderate and counterbalance their negativity. The use of these skills keeps their arguments from escalating out of control and allows them to stay engaged in the conflict. This, in turn, allows them to find possible solutions to their disagreements. If their conflicts are over issues without resolution, they use humor and acceptance to arrive at some peace with the issue. In their daily lives, they encourage interaction and stay emotionally connected. These couples describe their relationship with fondness and expressiveness, reflecting awareness of each other's struggles that leads to support and encouragement over stressful periods such as the transition to parenthood. Later, when the stress has subsided, these couples emphasize their teamwork in conquering the problem.

We believe that finding these clear differences between unhappy and happy couples is the first step toward effecting lasting change for distressed couples. We have not studied cohabiting or same-sex couples to date, but some generalizations have been suggested in other writings (Gottman, & Declair, 2001; Gottman, Levenson, & Swanson, 2003). The next step in our marital research involves further developing and testing interventions aimed at improving couples' marital friendship by increasing positive affect in their daily lives. Our goal is to combine clinical practice with research to create effective, empirically based interventions tailored to each couple's needs and values.

REFERENCES

Buehlman, K. T., & Gottman, J. M. (1996). The Oral History Coding System. In J. Gottman (Ed.), *What predicts divorce: The measures* (pp. OH11–OH118). Hillsdale, NJ: Erlbaum.

Buehlman, K. T., Gottman, J. M., & Katz, L. F. (1992). How a couple views their past predicts their future: Predicting divorce from an oral history interview. *Journal of Family Psychology, 5*, 295–318.

Carrère, S., Buehlman, K. T., Coan, J., Gottman, J. M., & Ruckstuhl, L. (2000). Predicting marital stability and divorce in newlywed couples. *Journal of Family Psychology, 14*(1), 42–58.

Carrère, S., & Gottman, J. M. (1999). Predicting divorce among newlyweds from the first three minutes of a marital conflict discussion. *Family Process, 38*, 293–301.

Carstensen, L. L., Gottman, J. M., & Levenson, R. W. (1995). Emotional behavior in long-term marriage. *Psychology and Aging, 10*(1), 140–149.

Christensen, A., & Heavey, C. C. (1990). Gender and social structure in the demand/withdrawal pattern of marital conflict. *Journal of Personality and Social Psychology, 59*, 73–81.

Coan, J., Gottman, J. M., Babcock, J., & Jacobson, N. (1997). Battering and the male rejection of influence from women. *Aggressive Behavior, 23*(5), 375–388.

Driver, J. L. (2006). *Observations of newlywed interactions in conflict and in everyday life.* Unpublished doctoral dissertation, University of Washington, Seattle.

Driver, J. L., & Gottman, J. M. (2004). Daily marital interactions and positive affect during marital conflict among newlywed couples *Family Process, 43*(3), 301–314.

Driver, J. L., Tabares, A., & Gottman, J. M. (2010). *Repair during marital conflict in newlyweds: Moving from attack–defend to collaboration.* Manuscript submitted for publication.

Gottman, J. M. (1993). The roles of conflict engagement, escalation, and avoidance in marital interaction: A longitudinal view of five types of couples. *Journal of Consulting and Clinical Psychology, 61*(1), 6–15.

Gottman, J. M. (1994). *What predicts divorce?: The relationship between marital processes and marital outcomes.* Hillsdale, NJ: Erlbaum.

Gottman, J. M., Coan, J., Carrère, S., & Swanson, C. (1998). Predicting marital happiness and stability from newlywed interactions. *Journal of Marriage and the Family, 60*, 5–22.

Gottman, J. M., & Declair, J. (2001). *The Relationship Cure: A five-step guide for building better connections with family, friends, and lovers.* New York: Crown.

Gottman, J. M., & Levenson, R. W. (1983). Marital interaction: Physiological linkage and affective exchange. *Journal of Personality and Social Psychology, 45*(3), 587–597.

Gottman, J. M., & Levenson, R. W. (1992). Marital processes predictive of later dissolution: Behavior, physiology, and health. *Journal of Personality and Social Psychology, 63*(2), 221–233.

Gottman, J. M., & Levenson, R. W. (2000). The timing of divorce: Predicting when a couple will divorce over a 14–year period. *Journal of Marriage and the Family, 62*(3), 737–745.

Gottman, J. M., Levenson, R. W., & Swanson, C. (2003). Observing gay, lesbian, and heterosexual couples' relationships: Mathematical modeling of conflict interaction. *Journal of Homosexuality, 45*(1), 65–91.

Gottman, J. M., Markman, H., & Notarius, C. (1977). The topography of marital conflict: A sequential analysis of verbal and nonverbal behavior. *Journal of Marriage and the Family, 39*(3), 461–477.

Gross, J. J., & Levenson, R. W. (1997). Hiding feelings: The acute effects of inhibiting negative and positive emotion. *Journal of Abnormal Psychology, 106*(1), 95–103.

Shapiro, A. F., & Gottman, J. M. (2005). Effects on marriage of a psycho-communicative-educational intervention with couples undergoing the transition to parenthood, evaluation at 1-year post intervention. *Journal of Family Communication, 5*, 1–24.

Shapiro, A. F., Gottman, J. M., & Carrère, S. (2000). The baby and the marriage: Identifying factors that buffer against decline in marital satisfaction after the first baby arrives. *Journal of Family Psychology, 14*(1), 59–70.

Shapiro, A. F., Gottman, J. M., Nahm, E. Y., & Content, K. (2011). Bringing baby home together: Exmining the impact of a couple-focused intervention on the dynamics within family play. *American Journal of Orthopsychiatry, 81*(3), 337–350.

Shapiro, A. F., Pennar, A. L., Gottman, J. M., & Fink, B. (2009, April). *Fathers bringing baby home: Examining a transition to parenthood intervention for promoting father involvement and satisfaction.* Poster session presented at a meeting of the Society for Research in Child Development, Denver, CO.

Walsh, F. (1989). Reconsidering gender in the marital quid pro quo. In M. McGoldrick, C. M. Anderson, & F. Walsh (Eds.), *Women in families: A framework for family therapy* (pp. 267–285). New York: Norton.

Walsh, F. (2006). *Strengthening family resilience* (2nd ed.). New York: Guilford Press.

CHAPTER 4

CONTEMPORARY TWO-PARENT FAMILIES
Navigating Work and Family Challenges

PETER FRAENKEL
CARRIE CAPSTICK

Two-parent families in the 21st century face myriad challenges. As they negotiate developmental issues and transitions in raising children in a more hazardous world, they must address common sources of interspousal, parent–child, sibling, and multigenerational conflicts that arise in family life. Many families cope with additional strains of illness, disability, death and loss; many struggle with unemployment and economic hardship. Those who are oppressed or marginalized on the basis of race, class, ethnicity, immigration status, gender identity, or sexual orientation must overcome societal barriers to thrive. All contemporary families must contend with the impact of the phenomenal growth in communication and information technologies. In this chapter, we focus on the key issues for most contemporary two-parent families; namely, the stressful challenges facing families with both parents in the workforce, so-called "dual-earner" families.

PREVALENCE AND ECONOMIC STATUS OF DUAL-EARNER FAMILIES

Since the 1970s, dual-earner families have become the norm, and most two-parent families in the coming decades will continue this pattern. The steady rise in the rates of dual-earner families largely reflects the increasing representation of women in the workforce and the necessity of two incomes for most families to maintain a moderate standard of living and to send children to college. Concomitant with women's rising level of education and changing workplace policies, the gap between women's and men's salaries has been narrowing. Yet women still, on average, only make 80–85% of male earnings for comparable work and time (Galinsky, Aumann, & Bond, 2009; U.S. Government Accountability Office, 2010).

Of course, social and economic trends are rarely linear, and the rates of dual-earner families fluctuate with changing economic and social circumstances. For instance, a 2010 U.S. Bureau of Labor Statistics report found that 58.9% of married couple families with children under 18 are currently dual earners, a decline from 64.2% nearly a decade earlier, reflecting higher rates of unemployment across most demographics due to the current severe economic downturn. However, despite fluctuations, the majority of couples in the future will continue to be dual earners.

The percentages of dual-earner families are similar across racial/ethnic groups, with lower rates for Latino families, in which the traditional roles of men working and women homemaking continue to prevail for more couples than in other groups. However, similar rates of dual earners across most racial/ethnic groups do not translate into equal employment opportunities. In the current economic crisis, rates of unemployment have been significantly higher in black families (17.4%) and Latino families (16.9%), than in white families (11.1%) (U.S. Bureau of Labor Statistics, 2010).

CHALLENGES AT THE BOUNDARY OF WORK AND FAMILY

Many benefits accrue in a dual-earner family. Foremost are the economic benefits and greater security of income flow. If one partner loses a job and must seek new work, the other's income can sustain the family temporarily, albeit likely with many compromises and constraints (Halpern & Murphy, 2005). Psychologically and relationally, multiple and shared roles for both partners (as parent, partner, and worker), rather than traditional role divisions (men as breadwinners, and women as mothers and homemakers), buffer the impact of negative events in one or the other sphere and increase opportunities for experiencing personal satisfaction and success, as well as increasing positive emotions each partner brings to couple and family relationships. When both partners can avail themselves of social support beyond the dyad, it decreases pressure on the partner to be the sole source of emotional soothing and stress relief. Expanding roles can also enlarge the number of independently accrued experiences and new perspectives on partners' lives and bring new topics to their conversations.

Dual earnership provides the economic basis for challenging partners to confront and take apart constraining, unidimensional gender roles (Barnett

& Hyde, 2001). For instance, couples benefit from the sense of sharing the opportunity and responsibility for earning, potentially reducing gendered power dynamics based on men being the sole source of income. For the increasing number of couples embracing a model of peer marriage in which both partners work and contribute to child care and domestic chores, being a dual-earner couple aligns with core relational values of equality and fairness (Galinsky et al., 2009; Gerson, 2010).

Children are also happier when both parents work. Ellen Galinsky's (1999, 2005) landmark survey of children's perspectives on their parents' work found that children overwhelmingly endorse having both fathers and mothers working. Their main concern is that when the parents are home, they be less stressed and tired and more emotionally available to them.

Despite these many benefits, many, if not most, dual-earner couples struggle to attain a more optimal sense of work–family "balance," "integration," "navigation," or "interaction." Galinsky (1999), a pioneer in this area of research, argues that the term "balancing" work and family posits a zero-sum game in which an increase in time and energy devoted to one domain is viewed as automatically depleting the other domain. She suggests that the notions of work–life "integration" and of "navigating work and family life" better capture the need for flexibility in moving between domains, and emphasizes the goal of maximizing positive—and minimizing negative—mutual influence (positive vs. negative spillover). Halpern and Murphy (2005) argue that the relationship between work and family is better understood by applying the statistical notion of "interaction," examining the effects of two variables in combination for a more accurate (and, in this case, more positive) picture.

Although these points are well taken, we still use the term "balance," because it is endemic to the cultural vernacular and comes up constantly in clinical work with couples and families. However, we view balance not as an ultimately unattainable state of perfect, static equilibrium but as characterized by a dynamic, flexible, and productive tension among one's multiple life involvements—work, couple, family, and community, among others (Fraenkel, 2011). To clarify, we also use the term "work" to mean paid employment, albeit with recognition that those on unpaid home-front duty are also working, and that responsibilities in both spheres are essential family work.

Several recent studies show that most dual-earner couples report significant work–family conflict (Galinsky et al., 2009; Schneider & Waite, 2005). Research has not found racial or ethnic differences in degree of work–nonwork interference, suggesting that this is an issue facing most dual-earner couples (Schieman, Milkie, & Glavin, 2009), although strains are greater for low-income families with fewer resources. Increasingly, attainment of work–life balance and managing conflict between work and family roles has truly become a couple's issue, more equally shared by women and men, rather than a problem shouldered almost entirely by working women (Galinsky et al.,

2009). A study by Williams and Boushey (2010) revealed that 90% of mothers and 95% of fathers report work–family conflict. Social discourse and workplace policy must reframe this from a "woman's problem" to a family issue for both parents and for their children.

To a great extent, the increase in working fathers' involvement in child care is due to the time shifts incurred by dual earnership: As more women are working full time and women's salaries become more essential to the financial well-being of the family (Galinsky et al., 2009), men must contribute more to child care and housework (Wang & Bianchi, 2009). Studies find that employed women do significantly less housework than women who are at home full-time (Kroska, 2004); however, they still do disproportionately more than their husbands. Yet there is evidence that many contemporary fathers across the generations have shifted their beliefs about gender roles in families—both in terms of no longer believing that working compromises women's maternal relationships to children or the children's well-being, and in terms of themselves desiring and actually spending more time as parents than did their fathers (Galinsky et al., 2009; Parke, 2002). And in contrast to the stereotype that men's self-concept is wholly centered on their career success, increasingly men judge themselves and their happiness as much or more by how they function in personal domains, a trend that has been building for over a decade (Levine & Pittinsky, 1997). Thus, for reasons to be described in this chapter, although women continue to shoulder more of the concrete and emotional burdens of balancing work and family life, especially domestic chores, there is a shift more toward a shared desire among heterosexual couples to achieve gender equity in work and family roles (Gerson, 2010). Clearly, aspects of the culture of work and the culture of heterosexual masculinity that keep men from more fully acting on desires to fulfill more equitable roles—for instance, not taking paid parental leave when it is available (Belkin, 2010)—must be addressed if greater work–family balance is to be achieved for both men and women (Williams, 2010). We highlight that the challenge is particularly for *heterosexual* men, because evidence suggests that gay men, as well as lesbian women, distribute responsibility for child care and housework more equitably than typically occurs in heterosexual couples (Bergman, Rubio, Green, & Padrón, 2010; Solomon, Rothblum, & Balsam, 2005).

Despite varied work–life issues that intersect with other aspects of couples' lives, for most if not all couples and families, numerous common factors, from workplace policies to personality styles, may interfere with optimal work–family balance. That said, most research to date has examined the experience of white, middle-class, heterosexual couples.

Work Hours and Schedules

Surveys over the past two decades have consistently found the Unites States among the countries with the longest hours per day and most weeks worked per year (Organisation for Economic Co-Operation and Development, 2010), Overwork generates a time bind, producing individual and family stress (Bellavia & Frone, 2005; Demerouti, Bakker, & Schaufeli, 2005; Galinsky et al., 2005). Work hours have increased for certain occupations, particularly managerial, professional, or technological jobs (Galinsky et al., 2005; Jacobs & Gerson, 2004), but the main reason for the overall greater work hours per family is the increased employment of women (Jacobs & Gerson, 2004). And when working mothers are still expected to handle most of the housework, child care, and care of older adults, as well as coordination of family schedules and activities, conflict commonly occurs between partners about these tacit assumptions and the disproportionate burden of a "second shift" (Hochschild, 1997). It is crucial for couples to rebalance the skew.

Long hours create stress for some families, but for others, stress results from being unable to *increase* work hours or sustain employment needed for the family's well-being (Jacobs & Gerson, 2004). And, certainly, job loss can have a wide range of negative effects on couples and families (Howe, Levy, & Caplan, 2004). Financial insecurity from too little paid work negatively impacts health and family relationships (Ehrenreich, 2001; Probst, 2005). Even at higher socioeconomic levels, reducing work hours can result in challenging trade-offs and may be more predictive of distress than long hours (Barnett & Gareis, 2000a). In their review of studies on men's family involvement, Bianchi and Milkie (2010) reported that insufficient earnings may erode family connections, impairing a husband/father's motivation and ability to interact positively with partners, children, and kin. Thus, for some workers, it is the experienced meaning of reduced work hours, as well as income reductions, that influence overall quality of life (Barnett & Gareis, 2000b). Clearly, both ends of the work-hours spectrum can create difficulties for workers and their families. Although the majority of employees wish for less work hours (Galinsky et al., 2005), job insecurity makes most reluctant to utilize existing work–family balance policies that might provide more time for family.

Indeed, numerous scholars have argued that inadequate American work–family policies cause much of the sense of time crunch and difficulties for dual-earner couples (Gornick & Meyers, 2003; Williams & Boushey, 2010). Additionally, workplace cultures often discourage employees from utilizing existing benefits that would provide more time for family life, such as flextime and compressed workweeks, allowing choice in work schedules (Bond, Galinsky, Kim, & Brownfield, 2005). The Family and Medical Leave Act (FMLA) mandates 12 weeks of unpaid leave for childbirth, adoption, or caring for ill family members (Galinsky, Bond, & Sakai, 2008). However, these policies often do not translate into real options for most workers. For instance, the FMLA is available for less than half of workers, because it does not apply to small businesses (50 or fewer employees) and is not available for fathers (Ray, 2008), part-time, seasonal, or temporary workers, or for families headed by same-sex partners. Because it is *unpaid* leave, most parents cannot afford to utilize this benefit (Han & Waldfogel, 2003). Additionally, many workers are reluctant to do so because of concerns that it will be perceived as lack of job commitment (Eaton, 2003).

Another problematic policy issue is that the United States is the only country among the industrialized nations that has no laws protecting workers' entitlement to a vacation (Gornick & Meyers, 2003). Although 79% of employees have access to paid vacation, the average number of days allotted is a little more than 2 weeks (half of the minimum yearly vacation provided to Europeans), few employees take their full vacation days, 19% use vacation time to attend to family matters or as sick time to make up for lack of sick days or personal leave days provided by the workplace, and almost 25% work while on vacation (Galinsky et al., 2005). Thus, many families cannot count on a once-yearly opportunity to reconnect and immerse together in a few weeks of work-free time.

Problematic policies and workplace cultures place the sense of responsibility for the negative emotional and family effects of overwork on the worker. Employees (and their families) view their overwork as the result of their own (or their partner's) inability to set limits or work efficiently—or, as connoted in the term "workaholic," as the result of an "addiction" to work—rather than an understandable attempt to survive in an unstable, demanding employment culture. This misattribution of blame of the source of overwork from the employment culture to the individual worker can result in increased couple conflict. A vicious cycle may ensue in which the overworked partner then withdraws further from couple and family time and immerses even more intensively into work, either to make more money, get more accumulated work completed (with the usually misguided hope of thereby reducing work demands), or to escape relationship conflict. This withdrawal into work creates further couple or family distress.

Long hours spent on the job and lack of access to flextime, leave, or vacations are not the only temporal risk factors in the equation linking work and family stress. Over 1 in 4 dual-earner couples has one partner doing shift work, such as a night shift. It is more common in families at lower socioeconomic levels (Presser, 2003), suggesting that it is not a sought-after schedule option but one adopted by economic necessity. Shift differences between partners leave less time for the couple relationship and are associated with greater marital distress, including higher depression levels, negative interactions, disagreements, and child-related problems (Ehrenberg, Gearing-Small, Hunter, & Small, 2001; Perry-Jenkins, Goldberg, Pierce, & Sayer, 2007). Yet other studies have documented positive effects of working nonstandard hours for relationships with children, such as increased paternal involvement when mothers work evening hours (Barnett & Gareis, 2007) and more overall time for each parent with the children (Wight, Raley, & Bianchi, 2008).

Temporal dyssynchronies in parents' work schedules need not be as extreme as shift work to create some of the associated challenges. Differences of a few hours in parents' schedules of leaving for and returning from work, when combined with children's wake, bedtime, school, homework, and transportation schedules, can result in significantly less opportunity for partners to have time together (Chenu & Robinson, 2002; Fraenkel, 2011; Fraenkel & Wilson, 2000). On the other hand, depending on their exact timing, partners with differing work schedules can rely on one another to cover different aspects of the children's daily routines, coordinating efforts as a "tag team." For instance, one partner might be able to handle the morning routine and get kids off to school, while the other is there to receive them after school and handle the evening routine. The complexity of synchronizing parents' work schedules with one another, and with children's schedules, and how couples negotiate this process, may be more critical to understanding the experience of work–life imbalance in dual-earner families than long work hours of one or the other parent alone (Gareis, Barnett, & Brennan, 2003).

Technology and the Work–Family Boundary

Whereas some parents struggle with dyssynchronous work shifts, other problems emerge when one or both parents find themselves on one long, endless shift due to virtually unlimited connectivity to the workplace provided by the proliferation of communication and information technologies. Laptops, cell phones, and other devices mean work can take place anywhere, erasing the physical boundary between home and work (Fraenkel, 2001a, 2001b, 2011; Jackson, 2005; Schieman et al., 2009). Certainly, executives and professionals have long taken work home, but contemporary availability of multiple means of highly portable electronic linkages to work has increased this trend dramatically for working parents and has spread it somewhat across classes and occupations.

As a function of this technology, a growing number of workers telecommute, working from home on a regular basis. This increased connectivity to work can bring benefits as well as problems. On the upside, it can save commuting time (and is better for the environment). Depending on the demands and structures of the job, telecommuting can allow some people to work part-time and coordinate work flexibly with child and home care (Fraenkel, 2001b). When a crisis at work might otherwise have resulted in canceling or delaying a vacation or family event, now a few calls or e-mails allow the work problem to be managed from afar.

On the other hand, technology and telecommuting present serious challenges to limiting the encroachment of work on family life (Fraenkel, 2001a, 2001b). An increasing number of families find work invading activities that might otherwise be "work-free zones," such as family dinners, time with kids at the playground, and vacations, as well as time for couple intimacy and for each parent to replenish energies and spirits. Although advertisements for products related to home offices always depict smiling parents working with relaxed concentration while their kids happily look on, many parents working at home report more work–family conflict, increased spillover from work to family, and depression (Chesley, Moen, & Shore, 2003).

Work Stress and Family Stress: A Complex Relationship

With increased hours, little leave or vacation time, more frequent requirements by employers for overtime, more contact with the workplace after hours, the need to assume the responsibilities of colleagues who have been "downsized," and a workplace culture that expects constant multitasking, it is not surprising that one-third of workers report they are chronically overworked and almost 90% experience high levels of job pressure (Galinsky et al., 2005). Employees who feel overworked believe they make more mistakes, feel angrier at employers, harbor more resentment toward colleagues perceived to be slacking off, and are more likely to look for another job; believe they do not take good care of themselves; and report more work-related sleep disruption, poorer health, and higher levels of stress (Galinsky et al., 2005).

Increased job-related stress results in higher likelihood of negative work spillover into personal relationships (Neff & Karney, 2007), especially couple and family relationships. Work stress affects couples by eliciting more negative and less positive couple communication styles; by increasing the likelihood of psychological and physical problems such as sleep disorders, sexual difficulties, and depressed or anxious moods; and by eliciting individual's insecurities, rigidities, and defensiveness (Bodenmann, Ledermann, & Bradbury, 2007).

However, the relationship between the temporal characteristics of work life and stress, and between work stress and family difficulties, is not simple or direct. Studies suggest that it is the *perception* of overwork, not simply the number of hours per se, and the *experience* of stress, rather than number or intensity of job-related stressors, that affect the degree of linkage between work stress and family distress (see Perry-Jenkins, Repetti, & Crouter, 2000, for review). Put differently, "work role quality" (the degree to which a person experiences fulfillment in work) appears to be more related to overall life satisfaction or stress than hours per se (Brett & Stroh, 2003), although at upper limits, long hours appear to induce anxiety and distress for most workers (Galinsky et al., 2005).

A number of variables moderate the relationship between work stressors and family life. In recent studies, variables earlier thought to *reduce* likelihood of job-related stress (e.g., higher status, greater autonomy and decision-making power, and schedule flexibility) have been found to be associated with greater pressure, longer hours, higher expectations of dedication to the company, more interpersonal conflict at work, greater emotional demands, and increased permeability of the border between work and nonwork life (Schieman et al., 2009). In turn, this may increase stress and spillover of work stress to home and conflict with partners and children (Schieman & Reid, 2009). Adding further complexity, personality style has been found to be a mediating variable: For instance, whereas some workers do better with greater job autonomy, others do worse. In one study, control over job responsibilities was associated with better health for persons with high "self-efficacy" (defined as those who felt competent to meet the demands of greater control and autonomy, and did not blame themselves for negative work outcomes), but with *increased* likelihood of poor health for those with low self-efficacy (Schaubroeck, Jones, & Xie, 2001).

Bianchi and Milkie (2010) also emphasize the importance of a life course perspective when evaluating the impact of work stressors on individual and family functioning. There are periods in life when increased work–family conflict is expected, such as having young children in a dual-earner household or caring for a disabled spouse or parent. If couples can increase their threshold for hectic schedules during these life periods, they may do better than those who continue to bemoan lack of a more relaxed and simple life. Many older persons who had expected to retire or at least decrease work pressures now need to stay employed or find a new job to meet costs of living, children's college education, and adequate health care.

Some variables, such as marital quality, are both an outcome of work stress and a moderator between work stress and other outcomes, such as parent–child conflict. Likewise, work–family conflict is both a mediator (in the relationship between time pressure and psychosomatic complaints) and an outcome variable whose relationship to work-related time pressure is affected by other mediating variables (the employee's work-related cognitive and emotional irritation; Höge, 2008).

Table 4.1 presents a list of major moderator variables, along with frequently studied job stressors and family outcomes, summarized from two decades of reviews in the *Journal of Marriage and Family* (Bianchi & Milkie, 2010; Perry-Jenkins et al., 2000).

Although most studies emphasize the impact of work stress on relationships, and find greater negative spillover from work into family than from family to work (Bellavia & Frone, 2005; Roehling, Moen, & Batt, 2003), the link between work and family stress is recursive or bidirectional, and the quality of family relationships and leisure time can affect the quality and productivity of work (Barnett, Gareis, & Brennan, 2009). For instance, a husband's stressful job may decrease his availability or energy to his partner and children, increasing the wife's overburden and sense of resentment. Both partners may then bring that marital distress back to the workplace, decreasing job effectiveness, which in turn contributes to a sense of being overwhelmed with the job, leading to further negative spillover into family relationships.

A number of studies demonstrate relationships between work pressure and increased experience of conflict among multiple family roles (Ransford, Crouter, & McHale, 2008), as well as emotional distress resulting from conflict between work and family (Gonzalez-Morales, Peiro, & Greenglass, 2006). Linkages have been found between work stress and likelihood of parent–child conflict, and poorer child behavioral and emotional outcomes (see review by Perry-Jenkins et al., 2000); between lack of family time and increased risky behaviors for adolescents (Crouter, Head, McHale, & Tucker, 2004); between work stress and decreased parental monitoring and knowledge of children's lives, at least when fathers (but not mothers) had demanding jobs and there

TABLE 4.1. Variables Influencing Work-Related Family Stress

Work variables	Mediators and moderators	Family impact
Work hours	Perception of work–family conflict	Marital distress
Degree of flexibility of hours	Preference for more or less than currently working	Conflict with children and adolescents
Number of roles/ responsibilities/ demands	Perceived role overload/multiple commitments	Child behavior problems
Interestingness of job	Incompatibility of work and children's school schedules	Spouse's depression/ sense of overload
Too much or too little control	Perception of job resources	Decreased shared family time
Quality of social climate/ support at work	Worker emotional distress	
Level of occupational prestige	Worker fatigue	
Hour-to-salary ratio	Commitment to work/career	
Degree of job security	Personality style (negative affectivity, neuroticism, Type A)	
Nonstandard hours	Depression and anxiety in stressed or other spouse	
	Self-efficacy and self-esteem	
	Social support	
	Life stage of family/ages of children	
	Child behavior problems	
	Parenting style	
	Number of children	
	Positive or negative marital quality	
	Perceived fairness of housework and child care distribution	
	Gendered beliefs about emotional expression and partner soothing	
	Gender ideology/partners' beliefs about value and acceptability of mother working	
	Race and class	

was poor marital quality (Bumpus, Crouter, & McHale, 1999); between mothers feeling deprived of time with their children and decreased well-being (Nomaguchi, Milkie, & Bianchi, 2005); and between working more hours than desired and a sense of overwork, reduced sense of coping ability, and emotional distress (Galinsky et al., 2005; Moen & Yu, 2000). Discrimination and lack of support in the work environment based on partners' sexual orientations or other social locations add yet another layer of stress for dual-earner couples (Mor Barak, Findler, & Wind, 2003).

Both high and low marital satisfaction may increase the link between workplace stress and family life. "Crossover," defined as the transmission of stress and strain from one member of a dyad to another (Demerouti et al., 2005), may be more likely between close partners (Lavee & Ben-Ari, 2007), and workers who value their family roles may experience greater conflict between those roles and work. Low marital satisfaction may increase the likelihood that work stress interferes with parenting, possibly by decreasing communication between partners or increasing stress to the point that parents withdraw from their partners and children (Bumpus et al., 1999; Ransford et al., 2008).

The Role of Gender in Dual-Earner Lifestyles

Gender plays a role not only in determining income levels and work hours, but in every aspect of the relationship between work and the family (See Knudson-Martin, Chapter 14, this volume). Continued popular media portrayals of the negative effects on families when two parents (read "when mothers") work (Galinsky, 2005) represent a barely disguised discomfort with the reality that mothers are and will continue to be in the workforce in the years ahead. Mid-20th-century functionalist, psychodynamic, and sociobiological theories assumed men's proper role as the breadwinner and women's supportive role as the homemaker and primary parent. The discomfort with women in the workplace persists despite abundant research documenting that maternal employment is not detrimental to children's development (Gottfried, 2005), as well as the many positive mental and physical health benefits and positive relational correlates for partners when both work (Baltes, Clark, & Chakrabarti, 2010). As noted earlier, paternal participation is often greater when both parents work (Gottfried & Gottfried, 2008), and children demonstrate multiple positive outcomes when fathers are more involved in their lives (e.g., Parke, 2002).

There is abundant research indicating that quality child care provided by a variety of kin and paid caregivers has no deleterious effects on healthy child development (Brooks-Gunn, Wen-Jui, & Waldfogel, 2002). Social and workplace policies that require increased availability of child care across social classes would have an enormous effect on decreasing working parents' anxieties and increasing child well-being (Gornick & Meyers, 2003; Williams & Boushey, 2010).

Despite data showing that men increasingly participate in child care and domestic labor (Sayer, 2005), numerous studies have documented that women actually work more hours than men when paid work, housework, and child care are combined (for reviews, see Coltrane, 2000; Bianchi & Milkie, 2010). In a recent study at the UCLA Center on the Everyday Lives of Families (CELF), through detailed coding and categorizing over 800 hours of video footage of dual-earner families in their homes, researchers found that mothers spent 27% of their time on housework, compared with 18% for fathers. Moreover, mothers spent only 11% of their time on brief periods of leisure compared fathers' 23% (Carey, 2010). Others have found that mothers' leisure time tends to be of lower quality than that experienced by fathers, compromised by unrelenting housework and child care demands (Mattingly & Bianchi, 2003).

In addition to greater demands in the home, women carry more of the burden of attending to extended kin, especially the older generations, including the husband's family (Lockwood, 2003). Increasing pressures for "intensive parenting" (Walla, 2010)—a contemporary childrearing trend emphasizing greater involvement in supporting the child's emotional and cognitive development—coupled with greater demands for caring for older adult relatives make employed women the "sandwiched" generation, weighted with heavy caretaking demands both in early/middle and later adulthood (Lockwood, 2003). Just as mothers are taking on responsibility to contribute to household income, fathers should now be expected to be full partners in coparenting (Harrington, van Deusen, & Ladge, 2010).

Although there are still few studies of racial and ethnic differences in male–female distribution of housework and child care, a recent study found that employed black men do more housework than do employed white men— yet employed black women do at least double the amount of housework their male partners do (Coltrane & Shih, 2010). The findings are mixed with regard to sharing of housework between Latino partners compared to white couples, although division of labor in Latino households is related to practical factors that also influence division of housework in other families, such as time constraints and patterns of employment (Pinto & Coltrane, 2009). Latino partners tend to evaluate distribution of housework less in terms of fairness than do white couples. This difference may be attributable to the tendency of Latino women to consider marriage and family as a source of safety and a buffer against racism and classism in the broader society; to traditional Latino cultural definitions of womanhood that include expectations of suffering, sacrifice, and deference to men (Falicov, 1998); as well as to Latino women, like many other women from ethnic and racial minority groups, regarding household tasks as a highly valued aspect of motherhood (Collins, 2002; Gerstel & Sarkisian, 2006).

A number of studies document the strong relationship between the degree to which women perceive housework as fairly divided with their partners and marital quality, as well as women's rates of depression (Frisco & Williams, 2003; see review by Coltrane, 2000). Despite notable changes in time allocated to housework for men and women over the past decade (Bianchi & Milkie, 2010), normative gender expectations likely contribute to continued disparities. Traditional definitions of masculinity still limit many men's involvement in housekeeping, childrearing, and other tasks perceived as "feminine" (Bittman, England, Sayer, Folbre, & Matheson, 2003). In some cases, a wife's reluctance to forfeit control over the home and childrearing may inhibit greater paternal contribution (Gaunt, 2008). In other cases, women's reluctance to cede control over these tasks results from men ignoring the well-tuned child care and homecare routines and procedures women have crafted through months or years of experience, with men insisting on doing it "their way" (Fraenkel, 2011). Couple therapists can assist men intent on sharing these responsibilities to recognize the importance of adopting and refining, rather than replacing, women's hard-wrought domestic routines.

In couple therapy, men often argue that because of their long work hours, they should not be expected to do more housework. Therapists may find it useful to point out the distinction between the experienced value and rewards of paid work versus housework and child care, as a prelude to suggesting that in the interest of fairness to their female partners (and improving wives' marital satisfaction), men may need to share more household responsibilities. A therapist might cite Coltrane (2000, p. 1225), who writes, "The single most important predictor of a wife's fairness evaluation is what portion of the housework her husband contributes," and that "marital satisfaction increases in relation to the amount of routine housework that is shared by spouses." (Coltrane, 2000, p. 1225). Likewise, studies have found men's housework to be significantly related to future marital satisfaction and lower likelihood of divorce (Sigle-Rushton, 2010).

If one parent leaves the workforce at least temporarily in a work–life balancing strategy called "scaling back" (Becker & Moen, 1999), it is usually the mother (Gornick & Meyers, 2003), who most often does so to care for infants, small children, and older adult family members. Biologically influenced aspects of attachment, still-powerful cultural scripts about proper gender roles, husbands' higher income, and workplace biases influence these decisions (Galinsky, 2005; Gottfried, 2005). Even when the partners initially ascribe to a more equitable sharing of household and child care responsibilities, once women leave their jobs to be home full-time, the couple tends to slide into the traditional male breadwinner–female homemaker roles (Walsh, 1989). Gender construction theory suggests that many women continue to be the primary caretakers, despite their increasing presence in the workforce, because the affective meanings they ascribe to caring for children and the home are associated with gendered norms of accountability for these responsibilities (Kroska, 2003). Of course, men's and women's beliefs about their proper roles derive from the larger set of patriarchal cultural and religious values and mores, especially when reinforced by spouses, extended families, and the media.

A number of studies suggest that dual-earner families do best when adult partners hold flexible gender role assumptions (Barnett & Hyde, 2001; Gerson, 2010; Zimmerman, Haddock, Current, & Ziemba, 2003). Marital quality tends to be negatively affected by wives earning more than their husbands when the men attach great self-definitional value to their earnings and role as breadwinner, as many men still do (Brennan, Barnett, & Gareis, 2001).

By choosing one frequently adopted strategy of avoiding work–family conflicts—delaying pregnancy until well into their 30s or even 40s (Lockwood, 2003)—women potentially incur health problems, and couples commonly experience emotional distress if they encounter fertility difficulties (Peterson, Newton, Rosen, & Schulman, 2006). Given the higher rates of multiple births linked to fertility-enhancing medical procedures, couples who delay having a child may end up with a larger child care load all at once. Accordingly, some couples choose to limit family size or not to have children at all (Altucher & Williams, 2003).

In summary, at many levels, despite evidence of important shifts toward gender equity in work and family roles, this is still a work in progress, and both partners' beliefs about gender are deeply embedded in how they approach and feel about navigating the challenges of blending work and family life. But as Gerson (2010) and Williams (2010) emphasize, gendered beliefs and practices regarding men's and women's appropriate and required workplace and family roles are situated and promulgated in the larger culture, and workplace policies and mores make it difficult for men to step back from job expectations to share more of the responsibilities and joys of childrearing and family life. Yet many couples have found ways to attain better balance, and gender equity and fairness are at the heart of their strategies.

SUCCESSFUL STRATEGIES IN DUAL-EARNER FAMILIES

It is important to examine the recursive pathways linking work stress with individual and family well-being from a positive-coping, family resilience perspective (Walsh, 2006). Recent studies indicate that many dual-earner families cope fairly successfully and even thrive (Greenhaus & Powell, 2006; Halpern & Tan, 2009). We need to identify the variables that enable couples to navigate work and family life, and contribute to the well-being of all family members. Accordingly, the theoretical framework for dual earners has increasingly moved from a perspective of "conflict" (i.e., incompatibility of work–family roles) or "scarcity" (i.e., resources given to one role lead to depletion in another) to one that better captures emerging data showing the physical, mental health, and relational benefits that accrue when men and women inhabit multiple roles (Barnett & Hyde, 2001; Greenhaus & Powell, 2006), as well as the positive spillover and modeling for children when parents enjoy their work lives and share that enjoyment with their children (Galinsky, 1999).

Increasingly, studies of successful coping with dual earnership are examining more ethnically and racially diverse couples (Gerson, 2010), as well as gay and lesbian couples (Bergman et al., 2010; Gartrell, Rodas, Deck, Peyser, & Banks, 2006; Solomon et al., 2005). All echo the main earlier findings of Zimmerman, Haddock, and colleagues (Haddock, Zimmerman, Ziemba, & Current, 2001; Zimmerman et al., 2003), who interviewed 47 mostly white, well-educated, middle-class heterosexual couples that viewed themselves as benefiting from a dual-earner lifestyle, and as having developed means of achieving a successful blend between work and family. The similar strategies found across couples differing in social class demonstrate the fundamental importance of equity, mutual respect, and fairness between partners, and the need to maintain firm temporal boundaries between work time and family time. Specifically, philosophies and practices included the following:

- Prioritizing family time and well-being
- Emphasizing overall equality and partnership, including joint decision making, equal influence over finances, and joint responsibility for housework

- Partners' equal valuing of each other's work and life goals
- Sharing the child care and "emotion work" of family life
- Maximizing play and fun at home
- Concentrating on work while at the workplace
- Taking pride in family and in balancing multiple roles, and believing the family benefits from both parents working (rather than absorbing the dominant cultural narrative of harm)
- Living simply, which includes limiting activities that impede active family engagement
- Adopting high but realistic expectations about household management; employing planning strategies that save time
- Being proactive in decision making and remaining conscious of time's value

One of the most robust predictors of individual wellbeing and lower family–work conflict is a boundary management strategy involving a more fixed work schedule and less permeability between work and family domains (Kossek, Lautsch, & Eaton, 2006).

Drawing on her survey of parents and children, Galinsky (1999) outlined a number of approaches to navigating sometimes the stressful transition from home to work and from work to home. Her suggestions include the following:

- Getting organized the night before
- Setting wake-up times that decrease rushing
- Creating rituals for saying good-bye to children and for reengaging after work
- Expecting such reconnection to include children expressing their daily problems
- Finding trustworthy child care and education; creating backup child care plans
- Creating transitional rituals into and out of work
- Maintaining focused, uninterrupted time with kids just to "hang out"
- Taking some time to decompress after particularly stressful work days

Galinsky (1999) also emphasizes the need for parents to talk "intentionally," not apologetically, about their work, giving them a sense of their enjoyment and excitement.

The vital importance of building in shared, pleasurable leisure time should be underscored. The impact of diminished leisure time for dual-earner families (Jacobs & Gerson, 2004) is compounded by the availability of only small "chunks" of leisure time in the context of a highly regimented schedule, and the feeling that free time is "decompression" time after stressful work experiences rather than time for activities that induce positive feelings (Zvonkovic, Notter, & Peters, 2006).

The changing rhythm in family life must be addressed (Bianchi, Robinson, & Milkie, 2006). Today, children as well as their parents, are overscheduled in school and outside activities, and parents must juggle complex schedules to shuttle their children from place to place and attend sports, music, and other events in which they are involved. Many parents also have long commuting time to and from work. Work and household tasks sometimes trump time for leisure when both parents work. But when families act more intentionally (Doherty, 2002) to engage in rituals of connection, as well as in sustained, active leisure rather than unscheduled "dribbles" in front of the TV (Zvonkovic et al., 2006), this created and protected free time can be an opportunity for reconnection *and* revitalization. Family leisure time is an opportunity to strengthen relationships among members, allowing the family unit to serve as a critical buffer against the stress of a fast-paced work life.

Over the past two decades of working clinically with dual-earner families, Fraenkel has developed a number of attitude shifts and practices that decrease stress and maintain positive connection between partners, thus benefiting interactions with children (Fraenkel, 1994, 1998a, 1998b, 2001a, 2001b, 2011; Fraenkel & Wilson, 2000). In terms of attitudes, he identifies five myths that interfere with realistic coping with time constraints and creation of couple and family time: (1) the myth of "spontaneity," which holds that couple sex and other forms of intimacy, as well as family fun, must occur spontaneously to feel authentic, and so should not be scheduled; (2) the myth of "infinite perfectibility," which holds that the family time crunch is wholly resolvable through better time management, and that no compromises need be made in the number of activities in which families attempt to engage; (3) the myth of "total control," which is the belief that families hold complete autonomy over their time and are to blame if they fail to achieve optimal work–life balance 4) the myth of "quality time," which holds that as long as family members are fully focused on one another during the little "chunks" of leisure time they have, there is no need for longer periods of "quantity time"; and (5) the myth that housework and chores must be sequestered from family fun and couple intimacy.

These myths about how to attain adequate couple and family time translate into two unrealistic beliefs about work–family balance, strongly supported by corporate culture, self-help books, and other popular media. One notion is that by working even harder, multitasking, and implementing more effective time management skills, couples will be able to "find" or "free up" more time for their relationships. Another faulty belief is that attaining optimal work–family balance means arriving at a state of perfect, tensionless equanimity. Rather, the reality of a dynamic balance involves negotiating inevitable tensions and adjustments between time dedicated to career and work, and time dedicated to couple and family time, as well as to other life demands, activities, and relationships. If approached proactively, these tensions among various relationships and endeavors can help to affirm in an ongoing way the couple's fundamental values and choices, lending those choices more meaning and sense of purpose (Fraenkel, 2011).

If families can deconstruct and evade the influence of these myths about couple and family time, and these unattainable standards for work–life balance, they can discover new pathways to work–family balance. Useful work–family balance practices include the following:

1. Creating regular "rhythms" of pleasurable couple and family time together, rather than hoping eventually to "find time."
2. Accepting the need to prioritize certain activities and let others go for the time being.
3. Recognizing the influence on family time of work, school, older family members, health care, and other contexts and relationships, and being less blaming of oneself and one another when the "schedule" does not quite work out.
4. Creating regular periods for quality time that is not necessarily pre-structured, allowing opportunities for spontaneity and serendipity, boredom that leads to creativity, and just for hanging out.
5. Utilizing the natural rhythms of housework and chores as opportunities for connection and fun.

To decrease the transmission of negative affect from work into family interactions, Fraenkel recommends a practice called the decompression chamber (Fraenkel, 1998a, 2011). Each partner makes a list of afterwork activities (solo or conjoint) he or she finds best to relax and to transition into the rest of the evening (e.g., taking a shower, reading the paper, watching a bit of television, exercise, yoga and meditation, playing with the children, talking about the events of the day). The partners then compare their lists and develop a "decompression sequence" that accommodates one another's needs as much as possible and also recognizes the need to accomplish various home and child care tasks. This practice helps resolve the frequent tug-of-war over each partner's needs. It also provides an opening for partners to talk about their longings for soothing and care from one another—an aspect of interaction found highly predictive of relationship satisfaction and stability (Gottman, Coan, Carrère, & Swanson, 1998)—and to reveal their needs for "alone time." In many cases, it is also a useful entree into conversations about each partner's beliefs and expectations, borne from both past experience and family and culture of origin, about how to handle difficult emotions emerging from work.

To increase the sense of connection between partners with long hours apart, Fraenkel (1998b, 2011) recommends a practice called the "60-second pleasure point." Partners engage in fun, pleasurable, and sensual activities they can do together that each last 60 seconds or less, such as short massages, a hug or kiss, leaving notes in each other's wallets, sending loving messages, and planning what to do when they have more time. Couples who utilize this technique typically report an enhanced sense of connection across the day, which in turn decreases their anxiety about reconnecting at day's end, taking pressure off this transition. Although research has yet to be conducted on this technique, it is supported by the Gottman et al. (1998) findings about the positive, long-term effects on marital satisfaction and stability of partners' initiating and responding to each other's bids for often-short periods of attention.

More important than any specific technique or practice, it is critical for adult partners to maintain an open and ongoing dialogue about the challenges they face. This includes recognition of the influences on their experience of personal finances, a pile-up of stress events, and cultural beliefs about work, gender roles, and the good life, some of which they may bring from their families of origin. Recognizing the power of these conditions to shape individual and family experience can allow partners to sustain a nonjudgmental attitude that engenders mutual support. Finally, recognizing that they are not alone in the struggle to balance work and home may lead to new dialogues and action within workplaces, communities, and political arenas that promote more widespread, family-friendly policies. For healthy family functioning, changes in the mores of the work culture and broader culture are essential in order for employees to avail themselves of these policies. Ultimately, the domains of work and family life should not be set in competition with one another, but rather should interact in a dynamic balance that contributes to every family member's well-being.

REFERENCES

Altucher, K. A., & Williams, L. B. (2003). Family clocks: Timing parenthood. In P. Moen (Ed.), *It's about time: Couples and careers* (pp. 49–59). Ithaca, NY: Cornell University Press.

Baltes, B. B., Clark, M., & Chakrabarti, M. (2010). Work–life balance: The roles of work–family conflict and work–family facilitation. In A. P. Linley, S. Harrington, & N. Garcea (Eds.), *Oxford handbook of positive psychology and work* (pp. 201–212). New York: Oxford University Press.

Barnett, R. C., & Gareis, K. C. (2000a). Reduced-hours employment: The relationship between difficulty of trade-offs and quality of life. *Work and Occupations, 27,* 168–187.

Barnett, R. C., & Gareis, K. C. (2000b). Reduced-hours, job-role quality and life satisfaction among married women physicians with children. *Psychology of Women Quarterly, 24,* 358–364.

Barnett, R. C., & Gareis, K. C. (2007). Shift work, parenting behaviors, and children's socioemotional well-being: A within-family study. *Journal of Family Issues, 28,* 727–748.

Barnett, R. C., Gareis, K.C., & Brennan, R. T. (2009). Reconsidering work time: A multivariate longitudinal within-couple analysis. *Community, Work and Family, 12,* 105–133.

Barnett, R. C., & Hyde, J. S. (2001). Women, men, work, and family. *American Psychologist, 56,* 781–796.

Becker, P. E., & Moen, P. (1999). Scaling back: Dual-earner couples' work–family strategies. *Journal of Marriage and the Family, 61,* 995–1007.

Belkin, L. (2010). Calling Mr. Mom? *New York Times Magazine.* Retrieved October 21, 2010, from *www.nytimes.com/2010/10/24/magazine/24fob-wwln-t.html?_r=1&emc=eta1.*

Bellavia, G. M., & Frone, M. R. (2005). Work–family conflict. In J. Barling, E. K. Kelloway, & M. R. Frone (Eds.), *Handbook of work stress* (pp. 113–148). Thousand Oaks, CA: Sage.

Bergman, K., Rubio, R. J., Green, R. J., & Padrón, E. (2010). Gay men who become fathers via surrogacy: The transition to parenthood. *Journal of GLBT Family Studies, 6,* 111–141.

Bianchi, S. M., & Milkie, M. A. (2010). Work and family research in the first decade of the 21st century. *Journal of Marriage and Family, 72,* 705–725.

Bianchi, S. M., Robinson, J. P., & Milkie, M. (2006). *Changing rhythms of American family life.* New York: Russell Sage Foundation.

Bittman, M., England, P., Sayer, L., Folbre, N., & Matheson, G. (2003). When does gender trump money?: Bargaining and time in household work. *American Journal of Sociology, 109,* 186–214.

Bodenmann, G., Ledermann, T., & Bradbury, T. N. (2007). Stress, sex, and satisfaction in marriage. *Personal Relationships, 14,* 551–569.

Bond, J. T., Galinsky, E., Kim, S. S., & Brownfield, E. (2005). *The 2005 National Study of Employers.* New York: Families & Work Institute.

Brennan, R. T., Barnett, R. C., & Gareis, K. C. (2001). When she earns more than he does: A longitudinal study of dual-earner couples. *Journal of Marriage and Family, 63,* 168–182.

Brett, J., & Stroh, L. (2003). Working 61-plus hours a week: Why do managers do it? *Journal of Applied Psychology, 88,* 67–78.

Brooks-Gunn, J., Wen-Jui, H., & Waldfogel, J. (2002). Maternal employment and child cognitive outcomes in the first three years of life: The NICHD study of early child care. *Child Development, 73,* 1052–1072.

Bumpus, M. F., Crouter, A. C., & McHale, S. M. (1999). Work demands of dual-earner couples: Implications for parents' knowledge about children's daily lives in middle childhood. *Journal of Marriage and the Family, 61,* 465–475.

Carey, B. (May 23, 2010). Families' every fuss, archived and analyzed. *The New York Times,* p. A1. Retrieved October 30, 2010, from *www.nytimes.com/2010/05/23/science/23family.html?_r=1&scp=1&sq=benedict%20carey%20may%20 23%202010&st=cse.*

Chenu, A., & Robinson, J. P. (2002). Synchronicity in the work schedules of working couples. *Monthly Labor Review, 125,* 55–63.

Chesley, N., Moen, P., & Shore, R. P. (2003). The new technology climate. In P. Moen (Ed.), *It's about time: Couples and careers* (pp. 220–241). Ithaca, NY: Cornell University Press.

Collins, P. H. (2002). Work, family and black women's oppression. In B. R. Hare (Ed.), *2001 Race odyssey: African Americans and sociology* (pp. 114–139). Syracuse, NY: Syracuse University Press.

Coltrane, S. (2000). Research on household labor: Modeling and measuring the social embeddedness of routine family work. *Journal of Marriage and the Family, 62,* 1208–1233.

Coltrane, S., & Shih, K. Y. (2010). Gender and the division of labor. In J. C. Chrisler & D. R. McCreary (Eds.), *Handbook of gender research in psychology* (pp. 401–422). New York: Springer.

Crouter, A. C., Head, M. R., McHale, S. M., & Tucker, C. J. (2004). Family time and the psychosocial adjustment of adolescent siblings and their parents. *Journal of Marriage and Family, 66*, 147–162.

Demerouti, E., Bakker, A. B., & Schaufeli, W. B. (2005). Spillover and crossover of exhaustion and life satisfaction among dual-earner parents. *Journal of Vocational Behavior, 67*, 266–289.

Doherty, W. J. (2002). *The intentional family: Simple rituals to strengthen family ties.* New York: Quill/HarperCollins.

Eaton, S. C. (2003). If you can use them: Flexible policies, organizational commitment, and perceived performance. *Industrial Relations, 42*, 145–167.

Ehrenberg, M. F., Gearing-Small, M., Hunter, M. A., & Small, B. J. (2001). Childcare task division and shared parenting attitudes in dual-earner families with young children. *Family Relations, 50*, 143–154.

Ehrenreich, B. (2001). *Nickel and dimed: On (not) getting by in America.* New York: Metropolitan Books.

Falicov, C. J. (1998). *Latino families in therapy: A guide to multicultural practice.* New York: Guilford Press.

Fraenkel, P. (1994). Time and rhythm in couples. *Family Process, 33*, 37–51.

Fraenkel, P. (1998a). Time and couples: Part I. The decompression chamber. In T. Nelson & T. Trepper (Eds.), *101 interventions in family therapy* (Vol. 2, pp. 140–144). West Hazleton, PA: Haworth.

Fraenkel, P. (1998b). Time and couples: Part II. The sixty second pleasure point. In T. Nelson & T. Trepper (Eds.), *101 interventions in family therapy* (Vol. II, pp. 145–149). West Hazleton, PA: Haworth.

Fraenkel, P. (2001a). The beeper in the bedroom: Technology has become a therapeutic issue. *Psychotherapy Networker, 25*, 22–65.

Fraenkel, P. (2001b). The place of time in couple and family therapy. In K. Daly (Ed.), *Minding the time in family experience: Emerging perspectives and issues* (pp. 283–310). London: JAI.

Fraenkel, P. (2011). *Sync your relationship, save your marriage: Four steps to getting back on track.* New York: Palgrave-Macmillan.

Fraenkel, P., & Wilson, S. (2000). Clocks, calendars, and couples: Time and the rhythms of relationships. In P. Papp (Ed.), *Couples on the fault line: New directions for therapists* (pp. 63–103). New York: Guilford Press.

Frisco, M. L., & Williams, K. (2003). Perceived housework equity, marital happiness, and divorce in dual-earner households. *Journal of Family Issues, 24*, 51–73.

Galinsky, E. (1999). *Ask the children: What America's children really think about working parents.* New York: Morrow.

Galinsky, E. (2005). Children's perspectives of employed mothers and fathers: Closing the gap between public debates and research findings. In D. F. Halpern & S. E. Murphy (Eds.), *From work–family balance to work–family interaction: Changing the metaphor* (pp. 219–236). Mahwah, NJ: Erlbaum.

Galinsky, E., Aumann, K., & Bond, J. T. (2009). *Times are changing: Gender and generation at work and at home: The 2008 National Study of the Changing Workforce.* New York: Families & Work Institute.

Galinsky, E., Bond, J. T., Kim, S. S., Backon, L., Brownfield, E., & Sakai, K. (2005). *Overwork in America: When the way we work becomes too much*. New York: Families & Work Institute.

Galinsky, E., Bond, J. T., & Sakai, K. (2008). *The 2008 National Study of Employers*. New York: Families & Work Institute.

Galinsky, E., Kim, S. S., & Bond, J. T. (2001). *Feeling overworked: When work becomes too much*. New York: Families & Work Institute.

Gareis, K. C., Barnett, R. C., & Brennan, R. T. (2003). Individual and crossover effects of work schedule fit: A within-couples analysis. *Journal of Marriage and Family, 65,* 1041–1054.

Gartrell, N., Rodas, C., Deck, A., Peyser, H., & Banks, A. (2006). The USA National Lesbian Family Study: Interviews with mothers of 10-year-olds. *Feminism and Psychology, 16,* 175–192.

Gaunt, R. (2008). Maternal gatekeeping: Antecedents and consequences. *Journal of Family Issues, 29,* 373–395.

Gerson, K. (2010). *The unfinished revolution: How a new generation is reshaping family, work, and gender in America*. New York: Oxford University Press.

Gerstel, N., & Sarkisian, N. (2006). Sociological perspectives on families and work: The import of gender, class and race. In M. Pitt-Catsouphes, E. E. Kossek, & S. Sweet (Eds.), *The work and family handbook* (pp. 237–265). New York: Erlbaum.

Gonzalez-Morales, M., Peiro, J., & Greenglass, E. (2006). Coping and distress in organizations: The role of gender in work stress. *International Journal of Stress Management, 13,* 228–248.

Gornick, J. C., & Meyers, M. K. (2003). *Families that work: Policies for reconciling parenthood and employment*. New York: Russell Sage Foundation.

Gottfried, A. E. (2005). Maternal and dual-earner employment and children's development: Redefining the research agenda. In D. F. Halpern & S. E. Murphy (Eds.), *From work–family balance to work–family interaction: Changing the metaphor* (pp. 197–217). Mahwah, NJ: Erlbaum.

Gottfried, A. E., & Gottfried, A. W. (2008). The upside of maternal and dual-earner employment: A focus on positive family adaptations, home environments, and child development in the Fullerton Longitudinal Study. In A. Marcus-Newhall, D. F. Halpern, & S. J. Tan (Eds.), *The changing realities of work and families: An interdisciplinary approach* (pp. 25–42). New York: Blackwell.

Gottman, J. M., Coan, J., Carrère, S., & Swanson, C. (1998). Predicting marital happiness and stability from newlywed interactions. *Journal of Marriage and Family, 60,* 5–22.

Greenhaus, J. H., & Powell, G. N. (2006). When work and family are allies: A theory of work–family enrichment. *Academy of Management Review, 10,* 72–92.

Haddock, S. A., Zimmerman, T. S., Ziemba, S. J., & Current, L. R. (2001). Ten adaptive strategies for family and work balance: Advice from successful families. *Journal of Marital and Family Therapy, 27,* 445–458.

Halpern, D. F., & Murphy, S. E. (2005). From balance to integration: Why the metaphor is important. In D. F. Halpern & S. E. Murphy (Eds.), *From work–family balance to work–family interaction: Changing the metaphor* (pp. 3–9). Mahwah, NJ: Erlbaum.

Halpern, D. F., & Tan, S. J. (2009). Combining work and family: From conflict to compatible. In J. H. Bray & M. Stanton (Eds.), *The Wiley–Blackwell handbook of family psychology* (pp. 564–575). New York: Blackwell.

Han, W., & Waldfogel, J. (2003). Parental leave: The impact of recent legislation on parents' leave taking. *Demography, 40,* 191–200.

Harrington, B., van Deusen, F., & Ladge, J. (2010). *The new dad: Exploring fatherhood within a career context.* Boston: Boston College Center for Work & Family.

Hochschild, A. (1997). *The time bind: When work becomes home and home becomes work.* New York: Holt.

Höge, T. (2008). When work strain transcends psychological boundaries: An inquiry into the relationship between time pressure, irritation, work–family conflict, and psychosomatic complaints. *Stress and Health, 25,* 41–51.

Howe, G., Levy, M., & Caplan, R. (2004). Job loss and depressive symptoms in couples: Common stressors, stress transmission, or relationship disruption? *Journal of Family Psychology, 18,* 639–650.

Jackson, M. (2005). The limits of connectivity: Technology and 21st-century life. In D. F. Halpern & S. E. Murphy (Eds.), *From work–family balance to work–family interaction: Changing the metaphor* (pp. 135–150). Mahwah, NJ: Erlbaum.

Jacobs, J. A., & Gerson, K. (2004). *The time divide: Work, family and gender inequality.* Cambridge, MA: Harvard University Press.

Kossek, E. E., Lautsch, B. A., & Eaton, S. C. (2006). Telecommuting, control and boundary management: Correlates of policy use and practice, job control, and work–family effectiveness. *Journal of Vocational Behavior, 68,* 347–367.

Kroska, A. (2003). Investigating gender differences in the meaning of household chores and child care. *Journal of Marriage and Family, 65,* 456–473.

Kroska, A. (2004). Divisions of domestic work: Revising and expanding the theoretical explanations. *Journal of Family Issues, 25*(7), 900–932.

Lavee, Y., & Ben-Ari, A. (2007). Relationship of dyadic closeness with work-related stress: A daily diary study. *Journal of Marriage and Family, 69,* 1021–1035.

Levine, J. A., & Pittinsky, T. L. (1997). *Working fathers: New strategies for balancing work and family.* New York: Harcourt Brace.

Lockwood, N. (2003). Work/life balance: Challenges and solutions. *Society for Human Resource Management Research Quarterly, June.* Retrieved November 7, 2010, from *www.allbusiness.com/specialty-businesses/home-based-businesses-work/567760-1.html.*

Mattingly, M. J., & Bianchi, S. M. (2003). Gender differences in the quantity and quality of free time: The U.S. experience. *Social Forces, 81,* 999–1030.

Moen, P., & Yu, Y. (2000). Effective work/life strategies: Working couples, work conditions, gender, and life quality. *Social Problems, 47,* 291–326.

Mor Barak, M. E., Findler, L., & Wind, L. H. (2003). Cross-cultural aspects of diversity and well-being in the workplace: An international perspective. *Journal of Social Work Research and Evaluation, 4,* 145–169.

Neff, L. A., & Karney, B. R. (2007). Stress crossover in newlywed marriage: A longitudinal and dyadic perspective. *Journal of Marriage and Family, 69,* 594–607.

Nomaguchi, K. M., Milkie, M. A., & Bianchi, S. M. (2005). Time strains and psychological well-being: Do dual-earner mothers and fathers differ? *Journal of Family Issues, 26,* 756–792.

OECD (Organization for Economic Co-operation and Development), OECD stat extracts, average annual hours actually worked per worker. Retrieved May 12, 2010, from *stats.oecd.org/index.aspx?datasetcode=anhrs.*

Parke, R. D. (2002). Fathers and families. In M. H. Bornstein (Ed.), *Handbook of parenting: Vol. 3. Being and becoming a parent* (2nd ed., pp. 27–73). Mahwah, NJ: Erlbaum.

Perry-Jenkins, M., Goldberg, A. E., Pierce, C. P., & Sayer, A. G. (2007). Shift work, role overload and transition into parenthood. *Journal of Marriage and Family, 69,* 123–138.

Perry-Jenkins, M., Repetti, R. L., & Crouter, A. C. (2000). Work and family in the 1990s. *Journal of Marriage and the Family, 62,* 981–998.

Peterson, B. D., Newton, C. R., Rosen, K. H., & Schulman, R. S. (2006). Coping processes of couples experiencing infertility. *Family Relations, 55,* 227–239.

Pinto, K. M., & Coltrane, S. (2009). Divisions of labor in Mexican origin and Anglo families: Structure and culture. *Sex Roles, 60,* 482–495.

Presser, H. B. (2003). *Working in a 24/7 economy.* New York: Russell Sage Foundation.

Probst, T. M. (2005). Economic stressors. In J. Barling, E. K. Kelloway, & M. R. Frone (Eds.), *Handbook of work stress* (pp. 267–297). Thousand Oaks, CA: Sage.

Ransford, C. R., Crouter, A. C., & McHale, S. M. (2008). Implications of work pressure and supervisor support for fathers', mothers', and adolescents' relationships and well-being in dual-earner families. *Community, Work, and Family, 11,* 37–60.

Ray, R. (2008, September). *A detailed look at parental leave policies in 21 OECD countries.* Washington, DC: Center for Economic and Policy Research. Retrieved May 22, 2010, from *www.emplaw.co.uk/content/index?startpage=data/20033221. htm.*

Roehling, P. V., Moen, P., & Batt, R. (2003). Spillover. In P. Moen (Ed.), *It's about time: Couples and careers* (pp. 101–121). Ithaca, NY: Cornell University Press.

Sayer, L. C. (2005). Gender, time, and inequality: Trends in women's and men's paid work, unpaid work, and free time. *Social Forces, 84,* 285–303.

Schaubroeck, J., Jones, J. R., & Xie, J. L. (2001). Individual differences in utilizing control to cope with job demands: Effects on susceptibility to infectious disease. *Journal of Applied Psychology, 86,* 265–278.

Schieman, S., Milkie, M. A., & Glavin, P. (2009). When work interferes with life: The social distribution of work–nonwork interference and the influence of work-related demands and resources. *American Sociological Review, 74,* 966–988.

Schieman, S., & Reid, S. (2009). Job authority and health: Unraveling the competing suppression and explanatory influences. *Social Science and Medicine, 69,* 1616–1624.

Schneider, B., & Waite, L. J. (2005). Why study working families? In B. Schneider & L. J. Waite (Eds.), *Being together, working apart: Dual career families and the work–life balance* (pp. 3–17). Cambridge, UK: Cambridge University Press.

Sigle-Rushton, W. (2010). Men's unpaid work and divorce: Reassessing specialization and trade in British families. *Journal Feminist Economics, 16,* 1–26.

Solomon, S. E., Rothblum, E. D., & Balsam, K. F. (2005). Money, housework, sex, and conflict: Same-sex couples and heterosexual married siblings. *Sex Roles, 52,* 561–575.

U.S. Bureau of Labor Statistics. (2010). *Employment characteristics of families in 2009.* Available online at *www.bls.gov/news.release/famee.nr0.htm.*

U.S. Government Accountability Office. (2010). *Women in management: Analysis of female managers' representation, characteristics, and pay* (GAO-10–892R). Retrieved October 20, 2010, from *www.gao.gov/new.items/d10892r.pdf.*

Walla, G. (2010). Mothers' experiences with intensive parenting and brain development discourse. *Women's Studies International Forum, 33,* 253–263.

Walsh, F. (1989). Reconsidering gender in the "marital quid pro quo." In M. McGoldrick, C. Anderson, & F. Walsh (Eds.), *Women in families: A framework for family therapy* (pp. 267–285). New York: Norton.

Walsh, F. (2006). *Strengthening family resilience* (2nd ed.). New York: Guilford Press.

Wang, R., & Bianchi, S. M. (2009). ATUS fathers' involvement in childcare. *Social Indicators Research, 93,* 141–145.

Wight, V. R., Raley, S. B., & Bianchi, S. M. (2008). Time for children, one's spouse, and oneself among parents who work nonstandard hours. *Social Forces, 87,* 243–274.

Williams, J. C. (2010). *Reshaping the work–family debate: Why men and class matter.* Cambridge, MA: Harvard University Press.

Williams, J. C., & Boushey, H. (2010, January). *The three faces of work–family conflict: The poor, the professionals, and the missing middle.* Washington, DC: Center for American Progress.

Zimmerman, T. S., Haddock, S. A., Current, L. R., & Ziemba, S. (2003). Intimate partnership: Foundation to the successful balance of family and work. *American Journal of Family Therapy, 31,* 107–124.

Zvonkovic, A. M., Notter, M. L., & Peters, C. L. (2006). Family studies: Situating everyday family life at work, in time and across contexts. In M. Pitt-Catsouphes, E. E. Kossek, & S. Sweet (Eds.), *The work and family handbook* (pp. 141–164). New York: Erlbaum.

CHAPTER 5

RISK AND RESILIENCE AFTER DIVORCE

Shannon M. Greene
Edward R. Anderson
Marion S. Forgatch
David S. DeGarmo
E. Mavis Hetherington

Divorce and life in a single-parent household have become common experiences for parents and children in contemporary American society. The purpose of this chapter is to provide an overview of the kinds of stresses and adaptive challenges that adults and children face when confronting transitions that surround divorce. We start by discussing the prevailing model of divorce as part of a continuous process of family reorganization, before examining the prevalence of divorce and subsequent transitions. Following a review of the consequences of divorce on physical and mental health outcomes, we explore concomitant changes in family processes, relationships, and life experiences. We conclude with a brief focus on two emerging areas in the literature: (1) how courtship and nonmarital cohabitation affect family processes and the well-being of individual family members, and (2) how families navigate the legal system in addressing initial and ongoing parenting concerns.

A PROCESS MODEL OF DIVORCE

The most commonly accepted theoretical model of divorce involves a process perspective that addresses stress, risk, and resilience. In this model, divorce is viewed as a cascade of potentially stressful changes and disruptions in the social and physical environments of adults and children, rather than as reactions to a single negative event (e.g., Amato, 2010; Hetherington, 2006; Strohschein, 2005). Thus, marital instability and divorce introduce a complex chain of marital transitions and family reorganizations that alter roles and relationships, and affect individual adjustment. Each transition presents new adaptive challenges, and the response to these challenges is influenced by previous family functioning and experiences.

The success with which individuals cope with these stressors depends on the presence of protective and vulnerability factors. Protective factors buffer the person or promote resilience in coping with the challenges of divorce; vulnerability factors complicate adjustment, increasing the likelihood of adverse consequences. Examples include personal characteristics of the individual; family processes and relationships; and ecological systems external to the family, such as friends, extended family, school, the workplace, and the larger neighborhood. Additionally, developmental factors play a central role in the adjustment of children and adults to marital transitions. Individuals may be more sensitive to stresses and opportunities presented by marital transitions at specific developmental periods; some challenges may trigger delayed adjustment effects to divorce (i.e., so-called "sleeper" effects). In addition to the normative challenges associated with changes in age, family members must confront non-normative challenges associated with the event of divorce (e.g., adjusting to life in a single-parent household, parental dating, remarriage). Thus, this model underscores the importance of studying the postdivorce adjustment of parents and children over time, as marital transitions and family reorganizations unfold. In some cases, divorce may offer parents and children potential benefits: an escape from an unhappy, conflictual family situation; the opportunity to build more fulfilling relationships; and the potential for personal development. In other words, what is perhaps most striking about this model is not the inevitability but the *diversity* of responses for parents and children who face the challenges of divorce. We turn next to a consideration of the prevalence of divorce and related transitions.

PREVALENCE OF DIVORCE AND RELATED TRANSITIONS

The divorce rate for the United States peaked in 1981, the culmination of a dramatic increase that began in the 1960s (Krieder, 2005). The rate has declined since, with most recent reports showing a lower rate in 2009 compared to earlier in the decade (Tejada-Vera & Sutton, 2010).[1] Lifetime probability of a first marriage ending in divorce still approaches 50% (Amato, 2010; Raley & Bumpass, 2003; Schoen & Canudas-Romo, 2006) but may be lower for more recent marriages (Cherlin, 2010). By the 5-year anniversary, 20% of marriages have been disrupted due to separation or divorce. This proportion increases to 33% and 43% by 10 and 15 years, respectively (Bramlett & Mosher, 2002).

About half of all dissolving marital unions consist of families with children (Amato, 2000; Krieder, 2005; Raley & Bumpass, 2003), with the majority of children (84%) residing primarily with their mothers (Grall, 2009). Even prior to the actual divorce decree, many families already may be in transition: A mixed sample of mothers and fathers showed that half had some experience with dating new partners within 60 days of the filing, rising to 79% by 1-year postfiling (Anderson et al., 2004). Moreover, 27% of parents in this study had experienced a "serious" dating relationship at the time of filing, increasing to 53% by 1 year. By 2 years, a sample of residential mothers showed that 89% reported experience with dating (Anderson, Hurley, Greene, Sullivan, & Webb, 2009).

As repartnering progresses, family life continues to be transformed. By 2 years after filing for divorce, two-thirds of residential mothers report having a new romantic partner spending the night while the children are present (Anderson et al., 2009). Many families go on to experience full-time cohabitation; the proportion of mothers and fathers who cohabit full-time with a new partner increases from 8% by 60 days after divorce filing, to 24% by 1 year after filing (Anderson et al., 2004). Families also may experience breakups, with 32% of mothers and fathers reporting having dated three or more partners by 1-year after filing for divorce (Anderson et al., 2004).

Collectively, these events have important potential implications for adjustment, because multiple transitions increase the adaptive challenges that confront parents and children (Anderson & Greene, 2005; Anderson et al., 2004; Capaldi & Patterson, 1991; Cavanagh & Huston, 2008; Fomby & Cherlin, 2007; Martinez & Forgatch, 2002; Osborne & McLanahan, 2007; Raley & Wildsmith, 2004). Thus, the process perspective on divorce is being extended to include more microaspects of changes in family formation.

RISK FACTORS THAT CONTRIBUTE TO DIVORCE

Relative risk for experiencing divorce depends on a variety of factors, including age at marriage, education, household income, race/ethnicity, religiosity, parents' marital history, and community characteristics (e.g., the crime rate, the community unemployment rate, and the percent of families in poverty; Bramlett & Mosher, 2002). Some of these relations are relatively straightforward. For example, 48% of women first married before age 18 have divorced within 10 years, compared to 24% of women who married after 25. Other factors may interact with one another in complex ways. Among non-Hispanic white women, for instance, education is inversely related to risk of divorce: 48% of non-Hispanic white women without a high school degree have divorced after 10 years of marriage, compared with 27% of those with more than a high school education. Among Hispanic women, however, there is a positive relation between education and divorce risk: Only 29% of Hispanic women without a high school degree have divorced after 10 years, compared with

39% of those with more than a high school education. Thus, an examination of risk for divorce must be tempered by the possibility of complex interactions with other variables (see Vaaler, Ellison, & Powers, 2009, for an example with regard to the impact of religiosity on risk of divorce).

With regard to race/ethnicity, by 10 years after marriage, the likelihood of divorce is 20% for Asian American women, 32% for non-Hispanic white women, 34% for Hispanic women, and 47% for African American women (Bramlett & Mosher, 2002). Hispanic and African American women are more likely than non-Hispanic white women to remain separated without divorcing. Ninety-seven percent of non-Hispanic white women have completed legal divorce within 5 years after separation, whereas the comparable rate is 77% and 67% for Hispanic and African American women, respectively. Rates of cohabitation and remarriage also differ across race/ethnicity. By 5 years after separation, 58% of non-Hispanic white women, 50% of Hispanic women, and 31% of African American women have cohabited with a new partner. Rates of remarriage 5 years after divorce are 58%, 44%, and 32% for non-Hispanic white, Hispanic, and African American women, respectively. Risk for divorce also is associated with a wide array of factors reflecting socioeconomic disadvantage (e.g., community male unemployment rate, percent receiving public assistance, median family income, percent below poverty line; Bramlett & Mosher, 2001). It is unclear to what extent racial and ethnic differences in risk for divorce are proxy indicators for long-standing economic and educational disparities (Amato, 2010; Bratter & King, 2008).

The likelihood of divorce also is associated with patterns of interaction and personal characteristics of married adults. Couples are at higher risk for divorce if their interaction involves escalation or reciprocation of negative affect, disengagement, stonewalling, contempt, denial, and blaming (Gottman & Notarius, 2001; Hetherington, 1999b; Hetherington & Kelly, 2002). Relatedly, risk increases if couples differ on their views of family life, if they share few interests or friends (Hetherington, 1999b; Notarius & Vanzetti, 1983), and if there is little spousal interdependence (Rogers, 2004). There is some evidence that participation in premarital education can be beneficial in reducing conflict and divorce (Stanley, Amato, Johnson, & Markman, 2006). Sexual dissatisfaction contributes more to risk of instability for men than for women (Hetherington & Kelly, 2002), although the finding is stronger for white than for black men (Orbuch, Veroff, & Hunter, 1999). Additionally, risk is associated with preexisting levels of personal maladjustment, such as antisocial behavior, depression, alcohol/substance abuse, and impulsivity. Individuals with a history of these kinds of problems are more likely to encounter stressful life events, to experience relationship distress that ends in divorce, and to be deficient in parenting skills (Capaldi & Patterson, 1991; Hetherington, 1999b; Kitson & Holmes, 1992; Kurdek, 1990). Antisocial individuals also are more likely to select an antisocial partner (Amato, 2000; Hetherington & Kelly, 2002), thereby compounding any relationship problems.

EFFECTS OF DIVORCE ON ADJUSTMENT

Adult Adjustment

Divorce is one of the most stressful experiences adults may face; not surprisingly, many individuals exhibit a variety of problematic outcomes. Although not all postdivorce changes are negative (see Hetherington & Kelly, 2002, for a review), a substantial body of work documents the increased risk of psychopathology, higher incidence of motor vehicle accidents, elevated drinking and drug use, alcoholism, suicide, and even death for those who separate or divorce, as compared to the continuously married (see Amato, 2000, for a review of this earlier work).

More recent research supports and extends these earlier findings toward providing a more nuanced understanding of potential factors that moderate the effects of divorce on physical health outcomes. For example, increases in depression, dysthymia, alcohol abuse, and lowered global happiness depend upon particular factors such as gender, economic resources, the quality of the marriage, and the presence of young children (Overbeek et al., 2006; Williams & Dunne-Bryant, 2006). Alcohol abuse and dysthymia increased after divorce, but not for those who left lower quality marriages (Overbeek et al., 2006). The presence of preschool-age children increases risk of depression for men and women after divorce (Williams & Dunne-Bryant, 2006). Divorce also is associated with increased alcohol abuse for men regardless of the presence of children; for women, increased alcohol abuse is only seen when preschool-age children are present, in part because of concomitant increases in parenting strain and frequency of contact with the former spouse.

Strain also comes from inadequate levels of income. Divorce typically leads to a dramatic reduction in the residential parent's household income, with per capita declines averaging 13–35% in national populations (Cherlin, 1998; Peterson, 1996). Women with children under the age of 6 may be at special risk for strain, with over half of this group below the poverty line (Teachman & Paasch, 1994). Reduced income contributes to other potentially stressful circumstances, such as changes in employment, education, and residence (DeGarmo & Forgatch, 1999; Forgatch, Patterson, & Ray, 1996; Lorenz et al., 1997; McLanahan, 1999; Patterson & Forgatch, 1990). Stress usually dissipates with time (DeGarmo & Forgatch, 1997; Forgatch et al., 1996; Hetherington, 1993; Lorenz et al., 1997), although those with lower incomes generally experience a greater number of disruptive events. If income remains low, stress often persists. Correlations between income and happiness/life satisfaction are generally small; however, it is notable that social relationships and emotional support largely moderate adverse effects of economic distress on family relations and adjustment following divorce (Hetherington & Kelly, 2002; Simons & Associates, 1996).

An emerging literature also addresses the underlying processes and diseases by which long-term health may be affected after divorce, such as changes in blood pressure (Sbarra, Law, Lee, & Mason, 2009), immune functioning (Kiecolt-Glaser, McGuire, Robles, & Glaser, 2002), cardiovascular disease markers (Zhang & Hayward, 2006), and chronic illnesses and mobility limitations (Hughes & Waite, 2009). Moreover, there is evidence that family disruption is related to the community homicide rate (Schwartz, 2006).

Child Adjustment

The relation between divorce and child adjustment is well established, although controversy arises over how best to integrate the findings. Readers may encounter, for example, the following seemingly incongruent statements:

1. Children of divorce are at serious risk for maladaptation.
2. Most children display no serious difficulties after their parents' divorce.
3. Substantial numbers of children of divorce are better adjusted than those from nondivorced households.
4. Some children's lives are enhanced by their parents' divorce.
5. Negative effects of divorce on children generally resolve soon afterward.
6. Children may be adversely affected even into adulthood by parental divorce.
7. Many of the negative effects associated with divorce exist well before the marriage ends.

Interestingly, each statement correctly summarizes a part of the literature relating to children of divorce. These statements further comprise two broad domains: (1) descriptions of the overall risk associated with divorce (Statements 1–4); and (2) changes in adjustment over time (Statements 5–7).

Overall Risk

Studies of divorce generally find that approximately 25% of children in divorced families experience high levels of problem behaviors versus 10% of children from nondivorced households (e.g., Forgatch et al., 1996; Hetherington et al., 1992; McLanahan & Sandefur, 1994; Simons & Associates, 1996; Zill, Morrison, & Coiro, 1993). Although select studies have found larger differences, meta-analyses approach these figures (Amato, 2000). We can correctly conclude that the experience of parental divorce doubles the risk of serious problems for children (support for Statement 1). However, we also can correctly conclude that the overwhelming majority of children (i.e., the 80% without behavioral problems) show no serious difficulties in relation to their parent's divorce (support for Statement 2). Both statements are supported by the data, although the former emphasizes the risk for some individuals, whereas the latter emphasizes the resilience demonstrated by most. Furthermore, with substantial overlap in the distribution of adjustment between the children from divorced versus nondivorced families, we also can correctly conclude that a substantial number of children of divorce (i.e., about 40%), are better adjusted than their nondivorced counterparts (support for Statement 3).

Some researchers have argued that the divorce itself is but a marker for other factors that create problematic adjustment in children, such as parental conflict. Children appear to be better off in cases in which the divorce substantially reduces levels of parental conflict or when there was ongoing violence in the marriage (support for Statement 4; Amato, Loomis, & Booth, 1995; Booth & Amato, 2001; Emery, 2009; Jekielek, 1998; Strohschein, 2005). Children from the most conflicted homes also are more likely to report feeling relieved that their parents divorced, although those from less conflicted homes are more likely to report distress after their parents' divorce (Amato & Booth, 1997). Many children, in fact, initially respond to divorce with confusion, anxiety, and anger, but over time are able to adjust, with the support and involvement of a caring, competent adult.

Adjustment Over Time

Evidence suggests that for children of divorce, some adjustment problems may be transitory, others may persist, and still others may be present long before the actual dissolution occurs. Longitudinal studies (e.g., Guidubaldi, Perry, & Nastasi, 1987; Hetherington, Cox, & Cox, 1982) find, for example, that many problems dissipate within the 1–2 years following a divorce, as families adjust to their new life situation (support for Statement 5). In other cases, effects of divorce persist over time. Across reporter (boys, mothers, teachers, peers, trained observers), Hetherington (1993) found that boys who experience parental divorce while in preschool continue to show more significant elevations in externalizing behavior than their nondivorce counterparts, with differences maintained into adolescence. With respect to early adolescence, Hetherington et al. (1992) reported that regardless of gender, children demonstrated difficulties in school and home settings even 4–6 years after the divorce. In a meta-analysis of 37 studies linking parental divorce in childhood with eventual adjustment in adulthood, Amato and Keith (1991) found moderate-size negative effects for depression, diminished life satisfaction, and lower marital quality, educational attainment, income, occupational prestige, and physical health (support for Statement 6). There is evidence that parental divorce impacts womens' expectations for their own marriages, so that women who experienced their parents' divorce have lower relationship commitment and relationship confidence, controlling for prior parental conflict and current relationship adjustment (Whitton, Rhoades, Stanley, & Markman, 2008). Selection of a stable, supportive spouse from a nondivorced family, however, can essentially eliminate the risk of marital instability associated with having divorced parents (Hetherington, 1999b; Hetherington & Kelly, 2002).

In part, long-term effects may persist because of disruptions in normal developmental trajectories during the period of adolescence (e.g., Chase-Lansdale, Cherlin, & Kiernan, 1995). In addition, a confluence of risk factors may occur in adolescent girls from divorced families. Girls from divorced and remarried families achieve physical signs of puberty earlier, which, when combined with association with older male peers, poor parental monitoring and control, and an overtly sexually active divorced mother, lead to early initiation of sexual activities, more sexual partners, and higher rates of sexually transmitted diseases and pregnancy (Hetherington, 1993; Hetherington & Kelly, 2002).

Despite evidence for long-term difficulties, some problems stem not from the divorce itself but from earlier deteriorating conditions in the family (support for Statement 7). Strohschein (2005) found, for example, that children whose parents later divorce exhibited higher levels of antisocial behavior and anxiety/depression even before the divorce. Sun and Li (2002) found that children whose parents divorced had lower test scores 3 years prior to divorce, with additional declines after the divorce. These studies echo earlier work by Block, Block, and Gjerde (1986), Chase-Lansdale et al. (1995), and others.

In an effort to synthesize the existing literature on divorce, researchers increasingly are adopting a perspective that emphasizes diversity in children's responses (Amato, 2000; Hetherington, Bridges, & Insabella, 1998; Hetherington & Kelly, 2002; Strohschein, 2005). Relatedly, there is growing interest in identifying the conditions that influence risk versus resilience, such as the child's own temperament (e.g., Hetherington, 1991), although resilience does not mean that children are invulnerable to effects of divorce (Emery, 1999). Although divorce generally exerts only a moderately negative—and in many cases temporary—effect on children, the differences are far from trivial for the families involved. Most families avoid the more calamitous outcomes, such as school dropout and unwed pregnancy. But avoiding calamity is not the equivalent of having achieved success. Emery describes the concerns of many parents who worry that their children, while not necessarily demonstrating clinically significant levels of problems, still show some level of behavioral problems or emotional distress from having experienced the divorce. The children themselves as young adults report more distress over recalling their childhood experiences around divorce (Laumann-Billings & Emery, 2000). Many families seek help in addressing these concerns. Some of what they may seek is help for psychological pain of a more subtle nature (Amato, 2010; Laumann-Billings & Emery, 2000), or to repair or bolster key family relationships. Thus, the diversity of postdivorce outcomes for children reflects various unique qualities of the family.

Finally, it is important to determine how results of the substantial body of existing literature on divorce will track with emerging demographic shifts in marriage that are now taking place, such as delays in age at marriage, and more educated individuals selecting marriage (see Schoen & Cheng, 2006, for discussion), combined with increased rates of child support compliance and noncustodial contact that are occurring (see a later section for discussion). These and other shifts ultimately may moderate risk for problems associated with divorce for future cohorts of children produced from these marriages.

EFFECTS OF DIVORCE ON FAMILY RELATIONSHIPS

Relationships between Divorced Spouses

After a divorce, overall levels of physical contact, conflict, and emotional attachment between spouses typically diminish rapidly. Men are more likely, however, to have lingering emotional attachment to the ex-spouse and to entertain thoughts of reconciliation, although, ironically, men also are quicker to remarry. In cases where the ex-spouse remarries, women commonly report sustained anger, resentment, and competitiveness toward the new wife (Hetherington & Kelly, 2002). If violence arises, it is most likely to occur toward wives in the time during the decision to divorce and immediately after the separation, with highest risk when wives have initiated the divorce. By 6 years postdivorce, most adults have moved on to build reasonably satisfying lives, and intense emotions associated with the breakup have faded.

Some studies find evidence that conflicts linger on, especially when former spouses are tied to one another through mutual children or other factors (Fischer, De Graaf, & Kalmijn, 2005; Kalmijn & Monden, 2006). About 25% of divorced parents exhibit sustained or even increased conflict that usually concerns finances and relations with the children (Buchanan, Maccoby, & Dornbusch, 1996; Maccoby & Mnookin, 1992; Tschann, Johnson, Kline, & Wallerstein, 1990). Some children report feeling "caught" between parental loyalties or think that they are to blame for these arguments; in such situations, boys are more likely to engage in noncompliant, angry, acting-out behaviors, whereas girls are more likely to respond with guilt and anxiety (Hetherington, 1999a).

Ideally, postdivorce family life would involve minimal conflict between parents, who are able to engage in a cooperative, supportive role with regard to each other's involvement with the child. Such a situation characterizes only about one-fourth of divorced households. Instead, most ex-spouses become disengaged or resort to parallel parenting, characterized by little collaboration or communication but, fortunately, with few instances of actively undermining the other parent (Ahrons, 2011; Buchanan et al., 1996; Hetherington, 1999a; Hetherington & Kelly, 2002).

Relationships between Residential Parents and Children

In the early years after divorce, residential mothers and fathers often struggle with task overload and question their adequacy as parents; they also experience health problems associated with a lowered immune system and report psychological distress, such as anxiety, depression, and loneliness (Hetherington,

1993; Hetherington & Kelly, 2002; Kiecolt-Glaser et al., 1988; Simons & Associates, 1996). Residential parents often are preoccupied with their own adjustment problems, and demonstrate irritability and a lack of emotional support toward the children. Discipline may be erratic and punitive, while monitoring of children's whereabouts and behaviors typically diminishes (Forgatch et al., 1996; Hetherington, 1993). As a consequence, children generally display increased noncompliance, anger, and dependence during this time. Relationships involving residential mothers and their sons may be especially disturbed, as demonstrated by the presence of escalating, mutually coercive interactions (DeGarmo & Forgatch, 1999; Hetherington, 1993; Hetherington et al., 1992). By 2 years postdivorce, many of these problems have diminished, although the residential mother–son relationship continues to be more distressed than those in nondivorced families. In contrast, after an initial period of perturbation, relationships involving residential mothers and their daughters often are characterized as warm, close, and companionate.

Additional problems may surface during adolescence. As daughters reach puberty, their relationships with mothers may become strained, particularly in cases where early-maturing daughters demonstrate precocious sexual or acting-out behaviors (Hetherington, 1993; Hetherington et al., 1992). Maternal attempts to correct for these problems by increasing parental monitoring and control of the adolescent daughter generally are unsuccessful. About one-third of children of divorce also disengage from their families earlier than counterparts in nondivorced families. If familial influence is replaced with involvement in an antisocial peer group, risk for delinquent behavior may increase; alternatively, development of a supportive relationship with a competent adult (e.g., a grandparent, teacher, or neighbor) may buffer negative effects of this early familial disengagement (Hetherington, 1993).

Although residential mothers and fathers demonstrate similarities in the pattern of deterioration and recovery of competent parenting, some differences remain. Residential mothers communicate and self-disclose more openly with their children and are more active in monitoring children's activities and knowing their friends. Residential fathers report less childrearing stress than do mothers and tend to have fewer problems with discipline or control. Additionally, divorce appears to undermine opposite-gender relationships more than same-gender relationships, such that mothers and daughters are considerably more affectionate and close than daughters and fathers, or mothers and sons. Sons in divorced families have less contact with fathers and feel less affectionate toward them than sons in nondivorced families, although the differences are relatively small (Amato & Booth, 1997).

Consistent with findings for nondivorced households, the parenting style that works well in divorced households is authoritative, characterized by warmth, support, responsiveness, and consistent control and monitoring. In contrast to disengaged, authoritarian, or permissive parenting styles, children raised with an authoritative parenting style have higher levels of social and academic competence, and lower levels of psychopathology (Anderson,

Lindner, & Bennion, 1992; Avenoli, Sessa, & Steinberg, 1999; Hetherington, 1993; Hetherington & Kelly, 2002; Martinez & Forgatch, 2002). Divorced parents are less likely than those in nondivorced households to use an authoritative parenting style, however (Hetherington, 1993; Hetherington & Kelly, 2002; Martinez & Forgatch, 2002; Simons & Associates, 1996; Thomson, McLanahan, & Curtin, 1992), and mean levels of problem behaviors are still higher in divorced versus nondivorced families, even when authoritative parenting is used (Anderson et al., 1992).

Relationships between Nonresidential Parents and Children

Nonresidential divorced fathers report a strong desire to stay involved with their children (Braver, Ellman, & Fabricius, 2003), and children themselves report similar desires to be involved with their nonresidential fathers (Fabricius & Hall, 2000; Schwartz & Finley, 2009). Although negative stereotypes of nonresidential fathers still persist (Troilo & Coleman, 2007), more recent cohorts show that, at least in the short term, there is little or no decline in contact between nonresidential fathers and their children (DeGarmo, 2010). With respect to maintaining weekly contact over time, results of nationally representative data pooled from the 1970s to the 2000s show a substantial increase, from 8% in 1976 to 31% in 2002; 37% rates of no contact in 1976 decreased to 29% in 2002 (Amato, Meyers, & Emery, 2009).

Contact is more likely to be maintained in situations in which mediation is used, when there is low parental conflict, when the nonresidential parent believes he or she has some control in decisions affecting the child, and when the child is a boy (Amato, 2000; Amato & Gilbreth, 1999; Braver et al., 1993; Maccoby & Mnookin, 1992). The presence of a cooperative coparenting relationship also is associated with increases in contact (Sobolewski & King, 2005). Contact is associated with compliance with paying child support in a consistent and timely fashion (Juby, Billette, Laplante, & Le Bourdais, 2007). It is of concern, therefore, that child support payments continue to lag, with 2004 data indicating that less than half pay the full amount (Grall, 2006).

Frequent contact with nonresidential fathers during childhood is associated with a number of positive child outcomes, including better feelings toward both parents (Fabricius, 2003; Fabricius & Luecken, 2006) and less blame of fathers as the cause of the divorce (Laumann-Billings & Emery, 2000). Additionally, quality involvement has direct benefits for children (Amato & Sobolewski, 2004; Aquilino, 2006; Fabricius & Luecken, 2007; King, 2006; King & Sobolewski, 2006) and for father–child relationship quality and responsive fathering (Sobolewski & King, 2005). For boys, close relationships with fathers reduce feelings that they will themselves divorce as adults (Risch, Jodl, & Eccles, 2004).

Most studies have shown that nonresidential mothers have greater contact and closeness with their children (e.g., Hawkins, Amato, & King, 2006).

For example, in a comparison of nonresidential fathers and nonresidential mothers, Gunnoe and Hetherington (2004) found that adolescents reported more contact and social support from nonresidential mothers than from non-residential fathers. In addition, the relation between perceived social support and adolescent adjustment was greater for those with nonresidential mothers. Although they are less authoritative than residential mothers or mothers in nondivorced families, nonresidential mothers are more likely to make efforts at monitoring and controlling their children's behavior, and to be more supportive and sensitive to their needs. Nonresidential mothers, however, are less likely to pay child support than nonresidential fathers (Sousa & Sorenson, 2006), although child support orders do improve rates of compliance (Braver et al., 1993; Grall, 2009). Finally, the greater involvement and closeness of nonresidential mothers may interfere with the formation of close bonds with a stepmother (Hetherington & Kelly, 2002).

Relationships between Siblings

In contrast to the postdivorce research on parent–child relationships, studies of siblings are rare. The few studies in this area show that sibling relationships following parental divorce are generally distressed, marked by patterns of conflict and negativity, as well as disengagement and avoidance (Conger & Conger, 1996; Hetherington, 1993; Hetherington & Kelly, 2002). Within 4 to 6 years after divorce, many of these differences have abated, although, consistent with the research on parent–child relationships, sibling relationships in divorced families continue to be more negative compared to those in nondivorced families (Anderson & Rice, 1992). Patterns of disengagement and avoidance may explain why child adjustment is less strongly related to sibling relationship quality in divorced versus nondivorced families (Anderson et al., 1992). In contentious divorces, siblings may be drawn into opposite sides of parental disputes, aligning with one parent against the other (McGoldrick & Carter, 2011).

Research in this area provides evidence for a spillover effect with other family relationships. More negative sibling relationships are related to higher levels of conflict between divorced spouses, and between parents and children (Conger & Conger, 1996; Hetherington, 1993; Hetherington & Kelly, 2002; MacKinnon, 1989). Over time, the presence of a sibling may introduce the potential for differential treatment by parents, and differential involvement in parental disputes (Greene & Anderson, 1999). When sibling relationships are positive, they may buffer the effects of a conflictual relationship with a parent (Hetherington, 1993), although boys appear to receive less sibling support than do girls (Anderson & Rice, 1992; Conger & Conger, 1996; Hetherington, 1993). Even in adulthood, it is mothers and female siblings who promote more family cohesion through phone calls, organizing joint activities or celebrations, and coming together at vacations (Hetherington, 1999a).

Relationships with Grandparents

Following divorce, a strengthening of ties with blood relatives often occurs (Gongla & Thomson, 1987). Many divorced mothers turn to their own parents for economic assistance; about one-fourth of divorced women live with their parents at some point after the divorce (Hetherington & Kelly, 2002). Many residential mothers and fathers also rely on their family of origin for child care and emotional support. Reflective of economic disadvantage, help in African American families is more likely to take the form of providing services, in contrast to the monetary support provided in white families (Cherlin & Furstenberg, 1994).

Divorce also increases the risk of lost contact between grandparents and grandchildren (Drew & Smith, 2002; Drew & Silverstein, 2007; Lussier, Deater-Deckard, Dunn, & Davies, 2002). Grandparents who had lost contact with their grandchildren due to separation, divorce, or other events were found to have adverse emotional health, including greater increases in depression up to 15 years later (Drew & Silverstein, 2007).

Related research findings on the role of grandparents in protecting children from the adverse effects of parental divorce have been mixed. Some have found that children, especially African Americans in mother-headed homes, may benefit from the presence of a grandmother in the home (Kellam, Adams, Brown, & Ensminger, 1982; Lussier et al., 2002); however, family stress may increase in situations where residential grandmothers and divorced mothers have conflict over views of control and discipline of children, the divorced mother's social life, and level of independence (Hetherington, 1989). Moreover, support from grandparents that comes with unwanted advice, costs, and restrictions is unhelpful to parents or children (Amato, 2000; Cherlin & Furstenberg, 1994; Hetherington, 1989; Kitson & Holmes, 1992; Miller, Smerglia, Gaudet, & Kitson, 1998). When the presence of a grandparent has advantageous effects on children, it is because the grandmother's support leads to improved maternal parenting (Hetherington, 1989). Although there is little research on the impact of grandfathers on children's postdivorce adjustment, some evidence indicates that the presence of an involved, competent, residential grandfather in a divorced family can decrease antisocial behavior and increase achievement in grandsons (Hetherington, 1989).

EXTRAFAMILIAL RELATIONSHIPS AND DIVORCE

In addition to family ties, relationships external to the family have the potential to exert influence on adjustment after divorce. In fact, this influence may occur even before the actual breakup: Of note, about 75% of those who initiate a divorce report that either an adult confidant (e.g., a friend, or family member) or new romantic partner played a major role in their decision to leave the marriage (Hetherington & Kelly, 2002). In the aftermath of divorce, parents seem likely to continue seeking contact from these adults for support and assistance.

Relationships with Romantic Partners

Along with the divorce comes the legally and socially sanctioned potential to form new romantic attachments with other adults. In fact, the strongest contributor to a divorced adult's well-being and happiness is the eventual formation of a supportive, mutually caring, intimate relationship (Hetherington, 1993; Hetherington & Kelly, 2002). Moreover, situations in which the romantic partner is residential may provide more immediate support than nonresidential partners, or nonresidential friends and relatives (DeGarmo & Forgatch, 1997; Simons & Johnson, 1996). Unlike a live-in partner, who is available to offer encouragement, advice, and actual help with childrearing, nonresidential partners, friends, and relatives, even if supportive, may not be present to assist with everyday duties, and may exert little influence on the quality of parenting.

Ironically, the potential for a new partner to offer emotional and social support to the family is not always reflected in improved child outcomes. The adjustment of children in cohabiting families may be worse than that in divorced, single-parent households (Buchanan et al., 1996; Cherlin & Furstenberg, 1994; Seltzer, 2000). It may be that the stresses and challenges in forming successful cohabiting relationships (e.g., ambiguity of the new partner's parental role, uncertainty of a long-term commitment) at times outweigh the benefits of possible support, or that the adverse effects of divorce are pervasive and long-lasting (Anderson, Greene, Hetherington, & Clingempeel, 1999; Buchanan et al., 1996; Cherlin & Furstenberg, 1994). Furthermore, families continue to confront emerging challenges related to postdivorce life and repartnering, with potential reverberations felt across the coparent households (see later sections). Yet many postdivorce families over time are able to establish gratifying relationships and a salutary environment in which competent children can develop (Hetherington et al., 1998; Seltzer, 2000; Thomson et al., 1992). Given that cohabitation is such a common experience for postdivorce families, we turn next to a consideration of the available literature.

REPARTNERING AND NONMARITAL COHABITATING RELATIONSHIPS

Nonmarital cohabitation appears to be a difficult transition for many families. Buchanan et al. (1996) have found, for example, that boys in cohabitating postdivorce households scored higher on almost every problem measured, including substance use, school deviance, antisocial behavior, poor grades, and problem peer relations, compared to boys in remarried families. Girls in cohabitating families were more likely than those whose parents were remarried or romantically noninvolved to have strained relations with the residential parent. Additionally, parenting was more problematic in dating and cohabitating families than in remarried families. Nonmarital cohabitation has adverse potential effects for adult adjustment as well; the risk of physical abuse to adults in cohabitating relationships is three times greater than that for married couples, 15% versus 5%, respectively (Waite, 2000). Perhaps because of uncertainty in the cohabitating state, couples are less likely to pool income, although income sharing increases when a child is born into the union. When cohabitation occurs after engagement, such relationships may be more successful (Stanley, Rhoades, & Markman, 2006; Xu, Hudspeth, & Bartkowski, 2006).

Compared to stepfathers or nondivorced fathers with biological children, the cohabiting romantic partner is likely to be less financially and emotionally invested in any residential children (King, 2009). The cohabiting romantic partner's relationships and parenting style with residential children are more problematic, with the partner typically devoting less time to youth-oriented activities at school or in community or religious organizations (Ryan, Franzetta, Schelar, & Manlove, 2009; Thomson et al., 1992). In cohabitating families, strain between the romantic partner and child can spill over into distressed relations between the residential parent and child, particularly daughters (Buchanan et al., 1996).

Given the challenges inherent in adjusting to divorce, along with the likelihood that many of these families eventually will remarry, which factors contribute to successful repartnering? Although literature on the topic of postdivorce repartnering at present is limited, it seems likely that the period prior to actual legal remarriage comprises a time of potentially dramatic levels of change as the parent, the new romantic partner, and children meet one another and begin to form the basis for new relationships and attempt to forge a new family system. Specifically, repartnering success may be dependent on how well parents handle three central challenges in the repartnering process: (1) developing effective decision-making strategies for dating others; (2) serving as gatekeepers or regulators of information to children concerning their own repartnering and their ex-spouse's repartnering; and (3) acting as managers of emerging relationships in repartnered families.

As part of the first challenge, developing decision-making strategies in dating, parents must evaluate their personal readiness to begin the dating process; some already have begun the process of repartnering even as the marriage dissolved, whereas others may not be ready for months or even years after the divorce. Parents also must decide on their selection criteria for the new romantic partner, including the strategies used to meet others, such as the dating arena or specific setting that they select as a way to access a potential source of eligible partners (e.g., work, bars and clubs, religious organizations, personal ads, the Internet, contact with friends or relatives). Finally, parents must determine the extent to which considerations about the child affect the process of dating, including the child's own level of readiness and individual adjustment. The presence of residential children appears to increase the chance of forming a union with a new partner who also has children (Goldscheider & Sassler, 2006), and there is some research to suggest that positive child adjustment may accelerate the repartnering process (Forgatch et al., 1996; Montgomery, Anderson, Hetherington, & Clingempeel, 1992).

With respect to the second challenge, parents must serve in the role as gatekeeper by orchestrating whether, when, and how to disclose information relating to the romantic relationship itself (e.g., the extent of this disclosure, its timing and level of developmental appropriateness). For example, they must decide how to handle the child's exposure to any implied sexual involvement between the parent and partner, such as the frequency and timing of overnight stays (Anderson et al., 2009). The success with which the parent is able to manage such situations has important potential implications for children. Inappropriate levels of exposure and knowledge may lead to precocious sexual knowledge (Hetherington, Cox, & Cox, 1978; Wallerstein & Kelly, 1980), and increase distress and acting-out behaviors in adolescents (Koerner, Wallace, Lehman, Lee, & Escalante, 2004).

With the third challenge, managing emerging relationships, parents must incorporate the new romantic partner into the existing system with the children, such as deciding on the level of the partner's involvement in discipline. There also must be opportunities for joint activities between children and the new romantic partner. Shared activities may influence how well families adapt over the long term to the new romantic partner (Montgomery et al., 1992). Relatedly, the adjustment of families to postdivorce events such as parental repartnering takes place against a backdrop of mutual and recursive influence among family members. The ways in which the parent responds to the interaction between the new romantic partner and the child provides, for example, a signal to the child as to how to interpret and further react to the partner's behavior. The child's response to overtures made by the new romantic partner may provide the parent with a means to gauge the successful integration of the partner into the family and, thus, an indirect assessment of the long-term prospects for the repartnered relationship. Moreover, whereas much of this discussion on postdivorce parental repartnering has concerned the residential parent, the little available research demonstrates that even changes in the *non*-residential parent's romantic life exert effects on child development (Anderson et al., 1999). In summary, the negotiation of family transitions around postdivorce repartnering has important implications for adult and child adjustment and parental functioning. Further research is needed to identify the mechanisms involved in successful repartnering and to inform theory, as well as interventions, with divorced populations.

THE LEGAL SYSTEM AND DIVORCING FAMILIES

Divorce has become a major focus for social policy (Amato, 2004). The Federal Government created a major initiative to support marriage, and three states have instituted covenant marriage laws as a way to discourage divorce. In the past two decades, many U.S. jurisdictions have adopted statutes that promote joint legal custody, shared parental responsibility, and continued contact with both parents. Moreover, nearly half of all U.S. counties have some sort of parenting education program in place for divorcing parents (Arbuthnot, 2002).

About 10% of divorcing families are not able to reach even a minimal level of agreement to allow for coparenting their children (Grych & Fincham, 1999; Maccoby, Depner, &Mnookin, 1990). Such high-conflict domestic relations cases are recognized as recidivists, since these families repeatedly resort to court processes because of ongoing disagreements. High-conflict family cases consume a disproportionate amount of court resources and contribute to burnout among family court practitioners. High conflict has long been associated with poor child outcomes; thus, these families pose special risks and challenges for social scientists, policymakers, and the courts.

Consequently, there is an evolving concern that adversarial procedures may entrench families in litigation, giving rise to alternative efforts to foster nonadversarial means of deciding issues of legal and physical custody, visitation schedules, and parenting plans (e.g., Atwood, 2007; Warshak, 2007a, 2007b). Alternative efforts include mediation and collaborative divorce (Emery, 2007). Results from interventions that employ collaborative law approaches show promise (Ebling, Pruett, & Kline Pruett, 2009). Use of collaborative law attorneys, for example, was associated with better psychological functioning for mothers, which yielded indirect positive effects for child outcomes (Pruett, Williams, Insabella, & Little, 2003). Moreover, use of divorce mediation has been demonstrated to lower trial rates and enhance coparenting (Emery, Laumann-Billings, Waldron, Sbarra, & Dillon, 2001; Emery, Sbarra, & Grover, 2005).

High-conflict families that become entrenched in the legal system are essentially allowing for judicial determination of custody. Judge Judith Kreeger (2003) raises a concern that most family court judges, while experienced in family law, have little formal training in family systems, mental health, and child development issues. In such cases, judges may rely on custody evaluators to assist in decision making, a practice that has been criticized (Emery, 2007; O'Connell, 2007; Tippins & Wittmann, 2005).

In response to a demand from practitioners for clearer custody guidelines (Emery, 2007), the American Law Institute has recommended inclusion of an approximation rule to guide contested custody cases. This approach involves determining physical custody on the basis of the proportion of time the child has spent with each parent in the past. The goal of approximation is to anchor custody decisions in "lived" experience (Atwood, 2007), extrapolating from past parenting behavior to anticipate what may likely be future parenting behavior (Emery, 2007). In contrast, disputed custody arrangements have historically been determined using the best-interest-of-the-child standard, an approach that has been criticized because of a lack of consensus on what actually constitutes the best interest of the child (e.g., Emery, Otto, & O'Donohue, 2005; O'Connell, 2007). A debate over the relative merits of the two approaches appeared recently in *Child Development Perspectives* (Atwood, 2007; Emery, 2007; Lamb, 2007; O'Connell, 2007; Warshak, 2007a, 2007b). Even among authors with differing views on this debate, however, there is strong consensus that parenting with minimal conflict is optimal for children, with an agreed-upon parenting plan determined by the parents themselves (Atwood, 2007;

Emery, 2007; Lamb, 2007; O'Connell, 2007; Warshak, 2007a, 2007b). Emery (2007) states that "parental self-determination should be parents' first priority and our legal system's overriding goal" (p. 133). Thus, practitioners should be concerned with identifying alternatives to relitigation and promoting children's meaningful contact with both parents (Emery et al., 2005). Psychological interventions for high-conflict divorcing families exist but have yet to be empirically tested in the field. Promising approaches include Lebow's (2003) integrative multilevel family therapy, and Benjamin and Gollan's (2005) controlled communication model.

SUMMARY

The breakdown of a marriage initiates a series of notable changes in the lives of parents and children. As emerging challenges are met, with new relationships formed, and family roles and processes altered, most adults and children experience considerable stress. Whereas about one-fourth experience lasting problems in adjustment, it should be underscored that most are resilient, able to move on and lead satisfying new lives. Postdivorce resilience largely depends on the ability of parents and children to build close, constructive, mutually supportive relationships that play a profound role in buffering families from effects of related adversity.

NOTE

1. It should be noted that prior to January 1996, the National Center for Health Statistics (NCHS) compiled its annual marriage and divorce statistics from actual counts provided by all of the individual states. Since that time, six states no longer collect actual counts of divorce (California, Georgia, Hawaii, Indiana, Louisiana, and Minnesota). Thus, the annual divorce rate is now derived from actual counts from the states that continue to participate, supplemented with estimates of the rates for the missing states from nationally representative surveys, such as the National Survey of Family Growth.

REFERENCES

Ahrons, C. R. (2011). Divorce: An unscheduled family transition. In M. McGoldrick, B. Carter, & N. Garcia-Preto (Eds.), *The expanded family life cycle: Individual, family, and social perspectives* (4th ed., pp. 292–306). Boston: Allyn & Bacon.

Amato, P. R. (2000). The consequences of divorce for adults and children. *Journal of Marriage and Family, 62,* 1269–1287.

Amato, P. R. (2004). Tension between individual and institutional views of marriage. *Journal of Marriage and Family, 66,* 959–965.

Amato, P. R. (2010). Research on divorce: Continuing trends and new developments. *Journal of Marriage and Family, 72,* 650–666.

Amato, P. R., & Booth, A. (1997). *A generation at risk: Growing up in an era of family upheaval.* Cambridge, MA: Harvard University Press.

Amato, P. R., & Gilbreth, J. G. (1999). Nonresident fathers and children's wellbeing: A meta-analysis. *Journal of Marriage and Family, 61,* 557–575.

Amato, P. R., & Keith, B. (1991). Parental divorce and adult well-being: A metaanalysis. *Journal of Marriage and Family, 53,* 43–58.

Amato, P. R., Loomis, L. S., & Booth, A. (1995). Parental divorce, marital conflict, and offspring well-being in early adulthood. *Social Forces, 73,* 895–916.

Amato, P., Meyers, C., & Emery, R. (2009). Changes in nonresident father–child contact from 1976 to 2002. *Family Relations, 58*(1), 41–53.

Amato, P.R., & Sobolewski, J.M. (2001). The effects of divorce and marital discord on adult chidren's psychological well-being. *American Sociological Review, 66,* 900–921.

Anderson, E. R., & Greene, S. M. (2005). Transitions in parental repartnering after divorce. *Journal of Divorce and Remarriage, 43,* 47–62.

Anderson, E. R., Greene, S. M., Walker, L., Malerba, C. A., Forgatch, M. S., & DeGarmo, D. S. (2004). Ready to take a chance again: Transitions into dating among divorced parents. *Journal of Divorce and Remarriage, 40,* 61–75.

Anderson, E. R., Greene, S. M., Hetherington, E. M., & Clingempeel, W. G. (1999). The dynamics of parental remarriage: Adolescent, parent, and sibling influences. In E. M. Hetherington (Ed.), *Coping with divorce, single parenting, and remarriage: A risk and resiliency perspective* (pp. 295–319). Mahwah, NJ: Erlbaum.

Anderson, E. R., Hurley, K., Greene, S. M., Sullivan, K., & Webb, A. P. (2009, April). *When Mom's boyfriend spends the night: Children's reactions to post-divorce overnight stays with parents' new romantic partners.* Presented at the biennial meetings of the Society for Research in Child Development, Denver, CO.

Anderson, E. R., Lindner, M. S., & Bennion, L. D. (1992). The effect of family relationships on adolescent development during family reorganization. *Monographs of the Society for Research in Child Development, 57*(2–3, Serial No. 227), 178–200.

Anderson, E. R., & Rice, A. M. (1992). Sibling relationships during remarriage. *Monographs of the Society for Research in Child Development, 57*(2–3, Serial No. 227), 149–177.

Aquilino, W. S. (2006). The noncustodial father–child relationship from adolescence into young adulthood. *Journal of Marriage and Family, 68,* 929–946.

Arbuthnot, J. (2002). A call unheeded: Courts' perceived obstacles to establishing divorce education programs. *Family Court Review, 40,* 371–382.

Atwood, B. A. (2007). Comment on Warshak: The approximation rule as a work in progress. *Child Development Perspectives, 1,* 126–128.

Avenoli, S., Sessa, F. M., & Steinberg, L. (1999). Family structure, parenting practices, and adolescent adjustment: An ecological examination. In E. M. Hetherington (Ed.), *Coping with divorce, single parenting and remarriage: A risk and resiliency perspective* (pp. 65–90). Mahwah, NJ: Erlbaum.

Benjamin, G. A. H., & Gollan, J. K. (2005). *Family evaluation in custody litigation: Reducing risks of ethical infractions and malpractice.* Washington, DC: American Psychological Association.

Block, J. H., Block, J., & Gjerde, P. F. (1986). The personality of children prior to divorce: A prospective study. *Child Development, 57,* 827–840.

Booth, A., & Amato, P. R. (2001). Parental divorce relations and offspring postdivorce well-being. *Journal of Marriage and the Family, 63,* 197–212.

Bramlett, M. D., & Mosher, W. D. (2001). *First marriage dissolution, divorce, and remarriage in the United States: Advance data from vital and health statistics.* Hyattsville, MD: National Center for Health Statistics.

Bramlett, M.D., & Mosher, W. D. (2002). Cohabitation, marriage, divorce, and remarriage in the United States. *Vital and Health Statistics, Series 23.* Washington, DC: U.S. Government Printing Office.

Bratter, J., & King, R. B. (2008). But will it last?: Marital instability among interracial and same-race couples. *Family Relations, 57,* 160–171.

Braver, S. L., Ellman, I. M., & Fabricius, W. V. (2003). Relocation of children after divorce and children's best interests: New evidence and legal considerations. *Journal of Family Psychology, 17,* 206–219.

Braver, S. L., Wolchick, S. A., Sandler, I. N., Sheets, V. L., Fogas, B., & Bay, R. C. (1993). A longitudinal study of nonresidential parents: Parents without children. *Journal of Family Psychology, 7*(1), 9–23.

Buchanan, C. M., Maccoby, E. E., & Dornbusch, S. M. (1996). *Adolescents after divorce.* Cambridge, MA: Harvard University Press.

Capaldi, D. M., & Patterson, G. R. (1991). Relation of parental transitions to boys' adjustment problems: I. A linear hypothesis. II. Mothers at risk for transitions and unskilled parenting. *Developmental Psychology, 27,* 489–504.

Cavanagh, S. E., & Huston, A. C. (2008). The timing of family instability and children's social development. *Journal of Marriage and Family, 70,* 1258–1269.

Chase-Lansdale, P. L., Cherlin, A. J., & Kiernan, K. E. (1995). The long-term effects of parental divorce on the mental health of young adults: A developmental perspective. *Child Development, 66,* 1614–1634.

Cherlin, A. J. (1998). Marriage and marital dissolution among black Americans. *Journal of Comparative Family Studies, 29,* 147–158.

Cherlin, A. J. (2010). Demographic trends in the United States: A review of research in the 2000s. *Journal of Marriage and Family, 72,* 403–419.

Cherlin, A. J., & Furstenberg, F. F. (1994). Stepfamilies in the United States. *Review of Sociology, 20,* 359–381.

Conger, R. D., & Conger, K. J. (1996). Sibling relationships. In R. L. Simons & Associates (Eds.), *Understanding differences between divorced and intact families* (pp. 104–121). Thousand Oaks, CA: Sage.

DeGarmo, D. S. (2010). Coercive and prosocial fathering, antisocial personality, and growth in children's postdivorce noncompliance. *Child Development, 81,* 503–516.

DeGarmo, D. S., & Forgatch, M. S. (1997). Determinants of observed confidant support. *Journal of Personality and Social Psychology, 72,* 336–345.

DeGarmo, D. S., & Forgatch, M. S. (1999). Contexts as predictors of changing maternal parenting practices in diverse family structures: A social interactional perspective of risk and resilience. In E. M. Hetherington (Ed.), *Coping with divorce, single parenting and remarriage: A risk and resiliency perspective* (pp. 227–252). Mahwah, NJ: Erlbaum.

Drew, L. M., & Silverstein, M. (2007). Grandparents' psychological well-being after loss of contact with their grandchildren. *Journal of Family Psychology, 21,* 372–379.

Drew, L. M., & Smith, P. K. (2002). Implications for grandparents when they lose contact with their grandchildren: Divorce, family feud, and geographical separation. *Journal of Mental Health and Aging, 8,* 95–119.

Ebling, R., Pruett, K. D., & Kline Pruett, M. (2009). "Get over it": Perspectives on divorce for young children. *Family Court Review, 47,* 665–681.

Emery, C. R. (2009). Stay for the children?: Husband violence, marital stability, and children's behavior problems. *Journal of Marriage and Family, 71*, 905–916.

Emery, R. E. (1999). Postdivorce family life for children: An overview of research and some implications for policy. In R. A. Thompson & P. R. Amato (Eds.), *The postdivorce family: Children, parenting, and society* (pp. 3–27). Thousand Oaks, CA: Sage.

Emery, R. E. (2007). Rule of Rorschach?: Approximating children's best interests. *Child Development Perspectives, 1*, 132–134.

Emery, R. E., Laumann-Billings, L., Waldron, M., Sbarra, D. A., & Dillon, P. (2001). Child custody mediation and litigation: Custody, contact, and coparenting 12 years after initial dispute resolution. *Journal of Consulting and Clinical Psychology, 69*, 323–332.

Emery, R., Otto, R., & O'Donohue, W. (2005). A critical assessment of child custody evaluations: Limited science and a flawed system. *Psychological Science in the Public Interest, 6*(1), 1–29.

Emery, R. E., Sbarra, D. A., & Grover, T. (2005). Divorce mediation: Research and reflections. *Family and Conciliation Courts Review, 43*, 22–37.

Fabricius, W. V. (2003). Listening to children of divorce: New findings that diverge from Wallerstein, Lewis, and Blakeleee. *Family Relations, 52*, 385–396.

Fabricius, W. V., & Hall, J. (2000). Young adults' perspectives on divorce: Living arrangements. *Family and Concilliation Courts Review, 38*, 446–461.

Fabricius, W. V., & Luecken, L. J. (2007). Postdivorce living arrangements, parent conflict, and long-term physical health correlates for children of divorce. *Journal of Family Psychology, 21*, 195–205.

Fischer, T., De Graaf, P. M., & Kalmijn, M. (2005). Friendly and antagonistic contact between former spouses after divorce: Patterns and determinants. *Journal of Family Issues, 26*, 1131–1163.

Fomby, P., & Cherlin, A. J. (2007). Family instability and child well-being. *American Sociological Review, 72*, 181–204.

Forgatch, M. S., Patterson, G. R., & Ray, J. A. (1996). Divorce and boys' adjustment problems: Two paths with a single model. In E. M. Hetherington & E. A. Blechman (Eds.), *Stress, coping, and resiliency in children and the family* (pp. 67–105). Mahwah, NJ: Erlbaum.

Goldscheider, F., & Sassler, S. (2006). Creating stepfamilies: Integrating children into the study of union formation. *Journal of Marriage and Family, 68*, 275–291.

Gongla, P. A., & Thomson, E. H. (1987). Single-parent families. In M. B. Sussman & S. K. Steinmetz (Eds.), *Handbook of marriage and the family* (pp. 297–418). New York: Plenum.

Gottman, J. M., & Notarius, C. T. (2001). Decade review: Observing marital interaction. *Journal of Marriage and Family, 62*, 146–166.

Grall, T. (2009). *Custodial mothers and fathers and their child support: 2007* (Current population reports, 60-237). Washington, DC: U.S. Bureau of the Census.

Greene, S. M., & Anderson, E. R. (1999). Observed negativity in large family systems: Incidents and reactions. *Journal of Family Psychology, 13*, 372–392.

Grych, J. H., & Fincham, F. D. (1999). The adjustment of children from divorced families: Implications of empirical research for clinical intervention. In R. M. Galatzer-Levy & L. Kraus (Eds.), *The scientific basis of child custody decisions* (pp. 96–119). Hoboken, NJ: Wiley.

Guidubaldi, J., Perry, J. D., & Nastasi, B. K. (1987). Assessment and intervention for children of divorce: Implications of the NASP-KSU nationwide survey. In J. Vincent (Ed.), *Advances in family intervention, assessment, and theory* (Vol. 4, pp. 109–151). New York: Plenum.

Gunnoe, M., & Heatherington, E. (2004). Stepchildren's perceptions and noncustodial mothers and noncustodial fathers: Differences in sociemotional involvement and associations with adolescent adjustment problems. *Journal of Family Psychology, 18*(4), 555–563.

Hawkins, D., Amato, P., & King, V. (2006). Parent–adolescent involvement: The relative influence of parent gender and residence. *Journal of Marriage and Family, 68*(1), 125–136.

Hetherington, E. M. (1989). Coping with family transitions: Winners, losers, and survivors. *Child Development, 60,* 1–14.

Hetherington, E. M. (1991). The role of individual differences and family relationships in children coping with divorce and remarriage. In P. Cowan & E. M. Hetherington (Eds.), *Family transitions* (pp. 165–174). Hillsdale, NJ: Erlbaum.

Hetherington, E. M. (1993). An overview of the Virginia longitudinal study of divorce and remarriage with a focus on early adolescence. *Journal of Family Psychology, 7*(1), 39–56.

Hetherington, E. M. (1999a). Should we stay together for the sake of our children? In E. M. Hetherington (Ed.), *Coping with divorce, single parenting and remarriage: A risk and resiliency perspective* (pp. 93–116). Mahwah, NJ: Erlbaum.

Hetherington, E. M. (1999b). Social capital and the development of youth from nondivorced, divorced, and remarried families. In A. Collins (Ed.), *Relationships as developmental contexts: The 29th Minnesota Symposium on Child Psychology* (pp. 177–209). Hillsdale, NJ: Erlbaum.

Hetherington, E. M. (2006). The influence of conflict, marital problem solving and parenting on children's adjustment in nondivorced, divorced, and remarried families. In A. Clarke-Stewart & J. Dunn (Eds.), *Families count: Effect on child and adolescent development* (pp. 203–237). New York: Cambridge University Press.

Hetherington, E. M., Bridges, M., & Insabella, B. M. (1998). What matters? What does not?: Five perspectives on the association between marital transitions and children's adjustment. *American Psychologist, 53,* 167–184.

Hetherington, E. M., & Clingempeel, W. G., in collaboration with Anderson, E. R., Deal, J. E., Stanley Hagan, M., Hollier, E. A., & Lindner, M. S. (1992). Coping with marital transitions: A family systems perspective. *Monographs of the Society for Research in Child Development, 57*(2–3, Serial No. 227).

Hetherington, E. M., Cox, M., & Cox, R. (1978). The aftermath of divorce. In J. H. Stevens, Jr., & M. Mathews (Eds.), *Mother–child, father–child relations* (pp. 148–176). Washington, DC: National Association for the Education of Young Children.

Hetherington, E. M., Cox, M., & Cox, R. (1982). Effects of divorce on parents and children. In M. Lamb (Ed.), *Nontraditional families* (pp. 233–288). Hillsdale, NJ: Erlbaum.

Hetherington, E. M., & Jodl, K. (1994). Stepfamilies as settings for development. In A. Booth & J. Dunn (Eds.), *Stepfamilies* (pp. 55–80). Cambridge, MA: Harvard University Press.

Hetherington, E. M., & Kelly, J. (2002). *For better or for worse: Divorce reconsidered.* New York: Norton.

Hughes, M., & Waite, L. (2009). Marital biography and health at mid-life. *Journal of Health and Social Behavior, 50*(3), 344–358.

Jekielek, S. (1998). Parental conflict, marital disruption and children's emotional well-being. *Social Forces, 76*, 905–936.

Juby, H., Billette, J., Laplante, B., & Le Bourdais, C.L. (2007). Nonresident fathers and chidren: Parents' new unions and frequency of contact. *Journal of Family Issues, 28*, 1220–1245.

Kalmijn, M., & Monden, W. S. (2006). Are the negative effects of divorce on well-being dependent on marital quality? *Journal of Marriage and Family, 68*, 1197–1213.

Kellam, S. G., Adams, R. G., Brown, C. H., & Ensminger, M. A. (1982). The long-term evolution of the family structure of teenage and older mothers. *Journal of Marriage and Family, 4*, 539–554.

Kiecolt-Glaser, J. K., Kennedy, S., Malkoff, S., Fisher, L. D., Speicher, C. E., & Glaser, R. (1988). Marital discord and immunity in males. *Psychosomatic Medicine, 50*, 213–229.

Kiecolt-Glaser, J. K., McGuire, L., Robles, T. F., & Glaser, R. (2002). Psychoneuroimmunology and psychosomatic medicine: Back to the future. *Psychosomatic Medicine, 64*(1), 15–28.

King, V. (2006). The antecedents and consequences of adolescents' relationships with stepfathers and nonresident fathers. *Journal of Marriage and Family, 68*, 910–928.

King, V. (2009). Stepfamily formation: Implications for adolescent ties to mothers, nonresident fathers, and stepfathers. *Journal of Marriage and Family, 71*, 954–968.

King, V., & Soboloewski, J. M. (2006). Nonresident fathers' contributions to adolescent well-being. *Journal of Marriage and Family, 68*, 537–557.

Kitson, G. C., & Holmes, W. M. (1992). *Portrait of divorce: Adjustment to marital breakdown.* New York: Guilford Press.

Koerner, S. S., Wallace, S., Lehman, S. J., Lee, S.-A., & Escalante, K. A. (2004). Sensitive mother-to-adolescent disclosures after divorce: Is the experience of sons different from that of daughters? *Journal of Family Psychology, 18*, 46–57.

Kreeger, J. L. (2003). Family psychology and family law—a family court judge's perspective: Comment on the Special Issue. *Journal of Family Psychology, 17*, 260–262.

Krieder, R. M. (2005). *Number, timing, and duration of marriages and divorces: 2001.* Washington, DC: U.S. Bureau of the Census.

Kurdek, L. A. (1990). Divorce history and self-reported psychological distress in husbands and wives. *Journal of Marriage and the Family, 52*, 701–708.

Lamb, M. E. (2007). The "approximation rule": Another proposed reform that misses the target. *Child Development Perspectives, 1*, 135–136.

Laumann-Billings, L., & Emery, R. E. (2000). Distress among young adults from divorced families. *Journal of Family Psychology, 14*, 671–687.

Lebow, J. (2003). Integrative family therapy for disputes involving child custody and visitation: When, whether, and how? *Journal of Family Psychology, 17*, 193–205.

Lorenz, F. O., Simons, R. L., Conger, R. D., Elder, G. H. J., Johnson, C., & Chao, W. (1997). Married and recently divorced mothers' stressful events and distress: Tracing change across time. *Journal of Marriage and Family, 59*, 219–232.

Lussier, G., Deater-Deckard, K., Dunn, J., & Davies, L. (2002). Support across two generations: Children's closeness to grandparents following parental divorce and remarriage. *Journal of Family Psychology, 16,* 363–376.

Maccoby, E. E., Depner, C. E., & Mnookin, R. H. (1990). Coparenting in the second year after divorce. *Journal of Marriage and Family, 52,* 141–155.

Maccoby, E. E., & Mnookin, R. H. (1992). *Dividing the child: Social and legal dilemmas of custody.* Cambridge, MA: Harvard University Press.

MacKinnon, C. E. (1989). An observational investigation of sibling interactions in married and divorced families. *Developmental Psychology, 25,* 36–44.

Martinez, C. R., Jr., & Forgatch, M. S. (2002). Adjusting to change: Linking family structure transitions with parenting and boys' adjustment. *Journal of Family Psychology, 16,* 107–117.

McGoldrick, M., & Carter, B. (2011). Families transformed by the divorce cycle. In M. McGoldrick, B. Carter, & N. Garcia-Preto (Eds.), *The expanded family life cycle* (4th ed., pp. 317–345). Boston: Allyn & Bacon.

McLanahan, S. (1999). Father absence and the welfare of children. In E. M. Hetherington (Ed.), *Coping with divorce, single parenting and remarriage: A risk and resiliency perspective* (pp. 117–146). Mahwah, NJ: Erlbaum.

McLanahan, S., & Sandefur, G. (1994). *Growing up with a single parent: What hurts, what helps?* Cambridge, MA: Harvard University Press.

Miller, N. B., Smerglia, V. L., Gaudet, D. S., & Kitson, G. C. (1998). Stressful life events, social support, and the distress of widowed and divorced women. *Journal of Family Issues, 19,* 181–203.

Montgomery, M. J., Anderson, E. R., Hetherington, E. M., & Clingempeel, W. G. (1992). Patterns of courtship for remarriage: Implications for child adjustment and parent–child relationships. *Journal of Marriage and Family, 54,* 686–698.

Notarius, C. I., & Vanzetti, N. A. (1983). The marital agenda as protocol. In E. E. Filsinger (Ed.), *Marriage and family assessment* (pp. 209–227). Beverly Hills, CA: Sage.

O'Connell, M. E. (2007). When noble aspirations fail: Why we need the approximation rule. *Child Development Perspectives, 1,* 129–131.

Orbuch, T. L., Veroff, J., & Hunter, A. G. (1999). Black couples, white couples: The early years of marriage. In E. M. Hetherington (Ed.), *Coping with divorce, single parenting and remarriage: A risk and resiliency perspective* (pp. 23–46). Mahwah, NJ: Erlbaum.

Osborne, C., & McLanahan, S. (2007). Partnership instability and child well-being. *Journal of Marriage and Family, 69,* 1065–1083.

Overbeek, G., Vollebergh, W., de Graaf, R., Scholte, R., de Kemp, R., & Engels, R. (2006). Longitudinal associations of marital quality and marital dissolution with the incidence of DSM-III-R disorders. *Journal of Family Psychology, 20,* 284–291.

Patterson, G. R., & Forgatch, M. S. (1990). Initiation and maintenance of process disrupting single-mother families. In G. R. Patterson (Ed.), *Depression and aggression in family interaction* (pp. 209–245). Hillsdale, NJ: Erlbaum.

Peterson, R. R. (1996). A re-evaluation of the economic consequences of divorce. *American Sociological Review, 61,* 528–536.

Pruett, M. K., Williams, T. Y., Insabella, G., & Little, T. D. (2003). Family and legal indicators of child adjustment to divorce among families with young children. *Journal of Family Psychology, 17,* 169–180.

Raley, R. K., & Bumpass, L. L. (2003). The topography of the divorce plateau: Levels and trends in union stability after 1980. *Demographic Research, 8*, 246–258.

Raley, R. K., & Wildsmith, E. (2004). Cohabitation and children's family instability. *Journal of Marriage and Family, 66*, 210–219.

Risch, S. C., Jodl, K. M., & Eccles, J. S. (2004). Role of the father–adolescent relationship in shaping adolescents' attitudes toward divorce. *Journal of Marriage and Family, 66*, 46–58.

Rogers, S. J. (2004). Dollars, dependency, and divorce: Four perspectives on the role of wives' income. *Journal of Marriage and Family, 66*, 59–74.

Ryan, S., Franzetta, K., Schelar, E., & Manlove, J. (2009). Family structure history: Links to relationship formation behaviors in young adulthood. *Journal of Marriage and Family, 71*, 935–953.

Sbarra, D. A., & Emery, R. E. (2008). Deeper into divorce: Using actor–partner analyses to explore systemic differences in coparenting conflict following custody dispute resolution. *Journal of Family Psychology, 22*, 144–152.

Sbarra, D. A., Law, R. W., Lee, L. A., & Mason, A. E. (2009). Marital dissolution and blood pressure reactivity: Evidence for the specificity of emotional intrusion-hyperarousal and task-related emotional difficulty. *Psychosomatic Medicine, 71*(5), 532–540.

Schoen, R., & Canudas-Romo, V. (2006). Timing effect on divorce: 20th century experience in the United States. *Journal of Marriage and Family, 68*, 749–758.

Schoen, R., & Cheng, Y. A. (2006). Partner choice and the differential retreat from marriage. *Journal of Marriage and Family, 68*, 1–10.

Schwartz, J. (2006). Effects of diverse forms of family structure on female and male homicide. *Journal of Marriage and Family, 68*, 1291–1312.

Schwartz, S. J., & Finley, G. E. (2009). Mothering, fathering, and divorce: The influence of divorce and reports of and desires for maternal and parental involvement. *Family Court Review, 47*, 506–522.

Seltzer, J. A. (2000). Families formed outside of marriage. *Journal of Marriage and Family, 62*, 1247–1268.

Simons, R. L., & Associates. (1996). *Understanding differences between divorced and intact families: Stress, interaction, and child outcome.* Thousand Oaks, CA: Sage.

Simons, R. L., & Johnson, C. (1996). The impact of marital and social network support on quality of parenting. In G. R. Pierce, B. R. Sarason, & I. G. Sarason (Eds.), *Handbook of social support and the family* (pp. 269–288). New York: Plenum.

Sobolewski, J. M., & King, V. (2005). The importance of the coparental relationship for nonresident fathers' ties to children. *Journal of Marriage and Family, 67*, 1196–1212.

Sousa, L., & Sorensen, E. (2006). *The economic reality of nonresident mothers and their children: Assessing the New Federalism, Series B, No. B-69.* Washington, DC: The Urban Institute.

Stanley, S. M., Amato, P. R., Johnson, C. A., & Markman, H. J. (2006). Premarital education, marital quality, and marital stability: Findings from a large, random household survey. *Journal of Family Psychology, 20*, 117–126.

Stanley, S. M., Rhoades, G. K., & Markman, H. J. (2006). Sliding versus deciding: Inertia and the premarital cohabitation effect. *Family Relations, 55*, 499–509.

Strohschein, L. (2005). Parental divorce and child mental health trajectories. *Journal of Marriage and Family, 67,* 1286–1300.

Sun, Y., & Li, Y. (2002). Children's well-being during parents' marital disruption process: A pooled time-series analysis. *Journal of Marriage and Family, 64*(2), 472–488.

Teachman, J. D., & Paasch, K. M. (1994). Financial impact of divorce on children and their families. *The Future of Children, 4,* 63–83.

Tejada-Vera, B., & Sutton, P. D. (2010). *Births, marriages, divorces, and deaths: Provisional data for October 2009.* (National Vital Statistics Reports, 58, No. 22). Hyattsville, MD: National Center for Health Statistics.

Thomson, E., McLanahan, S. S., & Curtin, R. B. (1992). Family structure, gender, and parental socialization. *Journal of Marriage and Family, 54,* 368–378.

Tippins, T., & Wittmann, J. (2005). Empirical and Ethical Problems With Custody Recommendations: A Call for Clinical Humility and Judicial Vigilance. *Family Court Review, 43*(2), 193–222.

Troilo, J., & Coleman, M. (2007). College student perceptions of the content of father stereotypes. *Journal of Marriage and Family, 70,* 218–227.

Tschann, J. M., Johnston, J. R., Kline, M., & Wallerstein, J. (1990). Conflict, loss, change, and parent–child relationships: Predicting children's adjustment during divorce. *Journal of Divorce and Remarriage, 13,* 1–22.

Vaaler, M. L., Ellison, C. G., & Powers, D. A. (2009). Religious influences on the risk of marital dissolution. *Journal of Marriage and Family, 71,* 917–934.

Waite, L. J. (2000). Trends in men's and women's well-being in marriage. In L. J. Waite (Ed.), *The ties that bind: Perspectives on marriage and cohabitation* (pp. 268–392). New York: Aldine de Gruyter.

Wallerstein, J. S., & Kelly, J. B. (1980). *Surviving the breakup: How children and parents cope with divorce.* New York: Basic Books.

Warshak, R. A. (2007a). The approximation rule, child development research, and children's best interest after divorce. *Child Development Perspectives, 1,* 119–125.

Warshak, R. A. (2007b). Best interests and the fulfillment of noble aspirations: A call for humbition. *Child Development Perspectives, 1,* 137–139.

Whitton, S. W., Rhoades, G. K., Stanley, S. M., & Markman, H. J. (2008). Effects of parental divorce on marital commitment and confidence. *Journal of Family Psychology, 22,* 789–793.

Williams, K., & Dunne-Bryant, A. (2006). Divorce and adult psychological well-being: Clarifying the role of gender and child age. *Journal of Marriage and Family, 68,* 1178–1196.

Xu, X., Hudspeth, C. D., & Bartkowski, J. P. (2006). The role of cohabitation in remarriage. *Journal of Marriage and Family, 68,* 261–274.

Zhang, Z., & Hayward, M. D. (2006). Gender, the marital life course, and cardiovascular disease in late midlife. *Journal of Marriage and Family, 68,* 639–657.

Zill, N., Morrison, D. R., & Coiro, M. J. (1993). Long-term effects of parental divorce on parent–child relationships, adjustment, and achievement in young adulthood. *Journal of Family Psychology, 7,* 91–103.

CHAPTER 6

The Diversity, Strengths, and Challenges of Single-Parent Households

Carol M. Anderson

The number of single-parent households has dramatically increased in the past few decades, now constituting over one-fourth of all American families with children under the age of 18 (Kreider & Elliott, 2009). An understanding of the challenges and resources in these families is a complex task, because they are quite diverse. Some single parents are financially secure and/or employed; others are not. Some have material and child care support from another parent; others do not. Some have always been single; others are separated, divorced, or widowed. Some have an extensive network of supportive family and friends; others are relatively isolated. Some choose to be single parents, with the additional challenges associated with adoption, donor insemination, or surrogacy. Others are single parents as the result of a lost relationship or at least the lost dream of a relationship. Some live alone with their children; others live with parents, and still others have another adult in the home. Some became single parents as mature adults in their 30s or 40s with stable networks; others are teen parents coping with financial and relationship instability. Single parenthood is also growing across socioeconomic groups, including a significant increase among the affluent and well educated. Today, there are career women and never-married celebrities with high incomes who can afford private schools and full-time child care; there are gay and lesbian single parents with biological or adopted children; and a small but increasing number of fathers are assuming primary parenting responsibility for their children (Brown, 2000; McLanahan & Percheski, 2008; Wolfe, 2009). All of these groups have some issues in common, but at least as many issues are unique to their particular version of single-parent family, each representing a particular family structure or composition with a range of interacting individual, familial, and community factors of risk and resilience. Their status also changes over time as parents move in and out of relationships and change the composition of their household (Park, 2005).

PATHWAYS TO SINGLE PARENTHOOD

Single parenthood status most often evolves by default: A partnership has been terminated through separation, divorce, death, or a desired intimate partnership for childrearing never developed. Thus, most single-parent families are built on a foundation of loss of a relationship or loss of a dream. The impact of the personal and social experiences individuals accumulate on their pathway to single parenthood becomes a backdrop for both unmarried and divorced parents as they take on primary responsibility for rearing children alone.

Additionally, those who become single-parent mothers often feel that they have failed at what traditionally has been seen as women's prime mandate: to secure a husband or maintain the nuclear family unit, a perception often reinforced by negative feedback from family, religious groups, and society. Those who have children outside marriage (including cohabiting couples) also bear the negative judgment of a societal context that has become more tolerant of divorce but less so of nonmarital childbearing (Usdansky, 2009). All of these factors—parental socioeconomic and psychological characteristics, reasons and pathways to single parenthood, the amount of social and cultural support—contribute to the level of life satisfaction of single parents, the quality of their parenting, and the psychological health and development of their children.

COMMON CHALLENGES
FOR SINGLE-PARENT FAMILIES

Going it alone, coping with the loss of a relationship, and enduring financial hardship are common tasks that can make single parents and their children more psychologically vulnerable (Crosier, Butterworth, & Rogers, 2007). Compared to their married counterparts, single parents as a group also work longer hours, have more economic problems, face more stressful life changes, are more frequently depressed, and have less emotional support in performing their parental role (Barrett & Turner, 2005; Mistry, Vandewater, Huston, & McLoyd, 2002).

Although they may be more physically and psychologically vulnerable, it is inaccurate to say that single-parent households are inherently deficient.

Most single parents provide the structure, values, and nurturance that their children need, while they simultaneously manage a household, a job, and at least a marginal social life, without the assistance of a partner. Many single parents, especially those with limited income, competently keep all these balls in the air while they live on the edge of crisis, acutely aware that some emergency need for increased funds, some break in the routine, could push a carefully organized but marginal system over the edge. Nevertheless, their homes are not "broken," their lives are not miserable, and although their children may have problems, most eventually thrive.

What is known about the well-being of children raised in single-parent families is complex, with considerable disagreement as to the immediate and long-term impact. Certainly, as a group, the children of single parents have more than their fair share of behavioral or emotional problems, as well as poorer academic performance and lower self-esteem (Cherlin, 2010; Potter, 2010). Some researchers contend that children who grow up in a household with only one biological parent are worse off, on average, than children who grow up in a household with two parents, regardless of race or educational background (McLanahan & Sandefur, 1994).

However, much of the research stressing the negative impact of single parenthood on both parents and children is compromised by the fact that it does not address the relative impact of poverty, the possible history of living in a dysfunctional or abusive nuclear family, the stage of adjustment to divorce, or differences generated by having become a single-parent household by choice, divorce, or unwed and/or teen parenthood (Afifi, Coz, & Enns, 2006; Berger, 2007; Cain & Combs-Orme, 2005; Crosier, Butterworth, & Rodgers, 2007; Wen, 2008). Although growing up in a single-parent household may have some long-term impact, it is not all negative. For instance, in the aftermath of divorce, initial distress most often subsides, unless there are ongoing multiple transitions or disruptions causing instability (Anderson et al., 2004; Cavanaugh & Huston, 2006; Cherlin, 2010; Fomby & Cherlin, 2007). When marriages have involved high parental conflict, those children whose parents divorce do better than those whose parents stay together (Hetherington & Kelley, 2002; see Greene, Anderson, Forgatch, DeGarmo, & Hetherington, Chapter 5, this volume).

It is also difficult to draw conclusions about the impact of single parenthood without considering that many households are single in name only and perhaps for relatively brief periods of time. A single parent may reside with extended family, friends, or a long-term, intimate partner who is positively involved in helping with household tasks and childrearing (Bzostek, 2008). In addition, many noncustodial parents are actively involved with their child and may provide the custodial parent with financial and emotional support. These relationships, often invisible to researchers and clinicians, require consideration in assessing the challenges, resources, and relevant interventions for single-parent families.

THE INFLUENCE OF POVERTY AND STRESS ON PARENTAL AND CHILD MENTAL HEALTH

Although numerous studies show an association between single parenthood and financial strain, maternal psychological problems, child development, and family functioning, it is difficult to disentangle the substantial contributions of poverty, class, and racial discrimination on child or parent well-being. Poverty itself is a known influence on parental psychological functioning, child functioning, and family relationships. Female-headed households have a 28.7% poverty rate (Edin & Kissane, 2010), with nearly 1 in 5 children living in poverty (DeNavas et al., 2009), many dependent on rapidly evaporating public assistance for support. For parents, financial strain is associated with higher levels of depressive symptoms, which directly and negatively influence the quality of their childrearing (DeGarmo & Forgatch, 2005; Feder et al., 2009). For children, poverty is correlated with lower school achievement and a higher incidence of behavior problems, even when factors such as family structure and community disadvantage are taken into account (Leventhal & Brooks-Gunn, 2000; Nievar & Luster, 2006). In fact, studies suggest that poverty accounts for more of the variance in both child outcomes and parental functioning than does single parenthood per se (Berger, 2007; Crosier et al., 2007; Edin & Kissane, 2010; Zahn & Pandy, 2004).

LOW-INCOME MINORITY SINGLE PARENTS

The most common form of single parenthood (75%) involves low-income minority mothers, many of whom become parents as teens (Kreider & Elliott, 2009; Ventura, 2009). These young parents are disproportionally exposed to stressful life events that put them at increased risk for psychological distress. They assume parenthood with less education, fewer resources, and less helpful support networks, while living in more troubled communities—all factors that influence parental stress, disempowerment, dissatisfaction, and child development (Barrett & Turner, 2005; Edin & Kissane, 2010; Zahn & Pandy, 2004).

Low income and lack of resources leave these single parents vulnerable to greater disrespect from schools and landlords, and to intrusions of external authorities into their lives and decisions. Without the assurance that they can survive financially on their own, they more frequently tolerate abuse or neglect in relationships with partners they otherwise might reject, impacting their mental health, family functioning, childrearing practices, and their children's development. On a more positive note, some low-income, minority single parents have supportive extended family and friendship networks that provide them with at least some of the resources and child care they need for survival, even when these networks also have some disadvantages

(Goldscheider & Kaufman, 2006; Hawkins, 2010; Hilton & Kopera-Frye, 2008; Jones, Zalot, Foster, Sterrett, & Chester, 2007).

Many teen mothers live with their parents or receive support from extended family, allowing them to finish high school, work, or have a social life. Three-generation households, however, have their own strains, difficulties, and complicated relationship and generational boundary issues. The addition of another generation to an existing family household requires fundamental changes in family structure and the way roles are defined, producing an ongoing need to sort out who is responsible for child care tasks and adult household chores. The time when a teen naturally seeks more independence becomes a time when she needs increased support from her family to help with her child: She must defer authority in some areas, usually to her parents, while taking charge of her child and maintaining her own credibility as the child's parent. At the same time, the young mother's middle-aged parents must put their own needs on hold to provide continued financial and emotional support to a daughter they may see as irresponsible. When grandparents or the wider kinship network do accept some childrearing responsibilities, the well-being of young parents and their children benefits. Unfortunately such support is not always available to those who need it the most—those with the most psychological difficulties, the least income and education, and the smallest support networks (Ceballo & McLoyd, 2002; Crosier et al., 2007).

Because many children of teen parents are the product of relatively short-term relationships, young fathers are less likely to remain involved with either mother or child. Whether they do stay in contact depends on many factors, including their own experience of being fathered, and whether they are employed, whether they have a history of drug use, antisocial behavior, or incarceration (Dyer, 2005). It also depends on whether they have ongoing contact with the child's mother, or whether either parent has developed a new relationship (Devault et al., 2008; Dudley, 2007; Guzzo, 2009; Swiss & Le Bourdais, 2009). Facilitating a young father's involvement with his child can be beneficial for both, but it is often difficult, particularly when a teen mother's parents do not approve of him (Johnson, 2001). His support, however, can reinforce the father–child bond and contribute to the financial and psychological well-being of the teenage mother and child.

Rather than writing off fathers based on their past lack of involvement, it is worthwhile to assess their current prospects for becoming more responsible and connected to their children. Many have matured, turned their lives around, and want to develop a relationship that would contribute to their children's well-being. When ongoing substance use or child endangerment is not an issue, children and their mothers can benefit from positive father involvement over the years. Since 40% of African American women never marry and many have children, this invisible source of potential support could be a particularly valuable resource.

Therapists can facilitate attempts to repair relationships and forge new ones. Indeed, Johnson's (2001) study of uninvolved African American fathers in a low-income urban neighborhood found that many fathers desired involvement with their children but did not know how to overcome the barriers, such as the negative feelings of the child's mother and her family about their earlier irresponsibility or misconduct.

POSTDIVORCE SINGLE PARENTHOOD

The second most common pathway to single parenthood is divorce. These households are predominantly headed by mothers, in cases of either sole custody or as the primary residence for children in joint custody. Frequently these single parents and their children request help as they attempt to deal with the loss of one family structure and the formation of a new one, a time when they are grappling with issues of loss, decreased financial viability, changed relationships with friends and family, and how to manage the ongoing involvement of the nonresidential parent (see Greene et al., Chapter 5, this volume). At these disruptive times, children need supportive adults who function well enough to provide consistent nurturance, limits, and values, and who communicate clearly with them about their new living arrangements and their contact with the nonresidential parent. They become distressed if they experience their families as unpredictable, but they can and do adjust to their circumstances. If they have irregular contact with their nonresidential parent and his or her network, or have parents who cannot agree on visitation arrangements, they at greater risk for mental health problems over the long haul (Cherlin, 1998). Effective postdivorce single parenthood requires a reorganization of the family system, delegating greater age-appropriate responsibilities to older children while the custodial parent provides financial and emotional support, nurturing, and negotiates a workable relationship with the ex-spouse for the sake of the child.

Therapists can also help single parents by challenging the unrealistic belief that they must be both mother and father to their children, when in fact their only realistic option is to be the best mother or father they can be.

SINGLE PARENTS BY CHOICE

Increasingly, single adults make a choice to become parents through adoption, donor insemination, or surrogacy. The majority of individuals who make this choice are in their 30s and 40s, college educated, and well-established in their careers. Most report they would have preferred to raise a child with a loving life partner, but they do not see marriage or a committed relationship on the horizon, or see it as essential to their well-being. When they realize it is increasingly unlikely that they will find a partner as they become older, they also realize that they are unwilling to forgo experiencing the joys of parenthood and family.

Most prospective single parents by choice give considerable thought and time to the advantages and challenges in making this decision. The process of obtaining a child through adoption, insemination, or surrogacy is expensive, lengthy, and does not always work out. The choice involves a lifetime commitment to being a child's sole parent, requiring that these parents consider whether they have adequate financial and emotional resources, and whether they are willing to make the necessary sacrifices of freedom that will allow them to raise a child successfully. The majority of parents by choice are women, but this population now includes a rapidly increasing number of men, mostly gay, who are choosing to be fathers through surrogacy or adoption.

Like all single-parent families, those that are created by choice have their own specific advantages and disadvantages. Without an ex-spouse in the picture, there is less ongoing baggage from a failed past relationship to deal with, and less chance of future conflicts about childrearing and custody, even if the parent later takes on a partner. However, both male and female single parents by choice frequently report that their social lives suffer. They cite the importance of developing a satisfying balance between work and home, learning to nurture a network that involves child-oriented friends and family, and, for those with less child experience, learning child management strategies (Anderson et al., 2004). An increasing number of support groups that target this population have become available through community agencies and can help these parents to cope and feel less alone.

OTHER COMMON ISSUES IN SINGLE-PARENT FAMILIES

Living in Extended Family Households

When single parents live with their family of origin there are significant benefits, especially if intergenerational conflicts can be minimized. These arrangements can provide financial help, respite from child care stresses, and stronger connections for children with grandparents, and with aunts, uncles, and cousins in the extended family. In fact, in many cultures, and for many single parents, such expanded networks can provide a sense of belonging that transcends what is provided by many intact nuclear families.

However, the benefits accrued can be at the cost of the single parent's independence. In particular, once-autonomous, older single parents commonly find it frustrating to defer to their parents' authority when living in their household, oftentimes their own childhood home. Both generations can slide back into the earlier parent–child adolescent conflicts as the single parent struggles to maintain a sense of him- or herself as a competent adult who wants to be in charge of his or her children in the face of increased grandparental involvement. A teenage single parent, invested in adolescent freedoms and never having been independent, may surrender so much authority that his or her child is unclear about who the parent is.

The Role of Nonresidential Fathers

Many nonresidential fathers are actively involved with their children or would prefer to be, which makes the term "single-parent family" (rather than single-parent household) a misnomer. Other nonresidential fathers, whether never married or divorced from the child's mother, tend to be uninvolved and to become even less so over time. There are multiple reasons. A father's involvement in his child's life sometimes drops off if either he or the child's mother has moved on to another relationship. A divorced father is likely to diminish his financial support and contact with his children if there is a continuing bitter struggle with the child's mother (Guzzo, 2009).

Despite these challenges, these fathers are a potential resource for their children and the single-parent household. Their active involvement should be recognized and encouraged, if possible. For instance, never-married single-parent fathers may live in the neighborhood and regularly see their children even if they have children with other mothers and provide no support to this single-parent household. Divorced fathers may share joint legal custody or have visitation rights, actually resulting in two single-parent households with children shuttling between them. In either case, therapists involved with single mothers should maintain a focus beyond the single-parent household, assessing potential stresses, exploiting opportunities to facilitate the father's involvement, and acknowledging how difficult this process can be for the single-parent mother. Even teen fathers can be helped to spend time with their children, contribute at least some financial support, and even serve as partial role models. Apparently unavailable divorced fathers may be helped to take on more responsibility for their children, if stressed and ambivalent mothers can be helped to accept their participation. As long as there are not concerns about substance abuse, extreme conflict, or child maltreatment, it helps if a therapist can make it clear that children tend to do better if both parents remain actively involved, providing reliable and cooperative parenting to children and welcome periods of respite to themselves. Therapists should be prepared to help single parents negotiate the multiple challenges involved in maintaining father involvement, and to use their strengths and their network of family and friends to manage the issues effectively (Ahrons, 2004; Forgatch, Beldavs, Patterson, & DeGarmo, 2008; Guzzo, 2009).

Custodial Single-Parent Fathers

Single-parent father households, a growing subgroup of one-parent families, currently constitute approximately 17% of all single-parent families (Kreider

& Elliott, 2009). Single-parent fathers, whether created by divorce, adoption, or surrogacy, cope differently than single-parent mothers and are seen differently by their communities. They are more likely to be employed and reasonably financially secure (Fagan, Palkovitz, Roy, & Farrie, 2009). Compared to single mothers, they are less likely to be criticized and more likely to be seen as noble. Yet many single fathers are more emotionally isolated than single mothers, without an available network to provide psychological support. Fortunately custodial fathers more readily draw on extended family members (usually their mothers) or female partners to provide practical support and child care, and the noncustodial mother tends to stay involved with the children and carry some parenting responsibilities. Still, some single fathers complain about having few role models to normalize their experiences, not feeling welcome in mother-oriented child care groups or school activities, or even being regarded with suspicion as potential sexual predators by other parents, some of whom may resist allowing their children to play or have sleepover parties in male-headed homes.

The Role of Live-In Partners

Both postdivorce and never-married single parents often expand their households to include a new partner, reducing some stresses while increasing others. Under the best of circumstances, these relationships can meet some important needs for both single parent and child, and many even develop supportive and lasting ties. Having a romantic partner in the home may provide a single parent with intimacy and emotional support, help with household tasks, and extra income to mitigate financial strain.

On the negative side, single parents often have difficulty balancing the need to meet the needs of their children and those of a new partner. They struggle with conflicting loyalties, conflicts over childrearing practices, and ongoing competition for their attention. These struggles can be even more pronounced if the new partner the single parent brings into the household is inappropriate or unwilling to make a genuine commitment. While this partner may temporarily meet some financial, sexual, or psychological needs, the result, especially for the single-parent mother, may mean increased stress as she ensures appropriate discipline and confronts the threat of household instability. For instance, men who do not have a biological/genetic bond or long-term commitment to a child are more likely to be physically and sexually abusive (Margolin, 1992), and it is often difficult for mothers to protect their children when they fear alienating the new partner and being left without his companionship and support. Even when there is not the risk of abuse or worries about a new partner leaving, live-in partners, especially males, often expect to establish or enforce family rules before they have the mandate or the credibility to make them. Therapists can help by working to negotiate an appropriate role for the new partner in the household, not of taking charge but of supporting the single parent in his or her child care efforts. Therapists can also help to provide a greater sense of comfort and stability by encouraging these single parents to expand their adult support network.

CLINICAL IMPLICATIONS/INTERVENTIONS

The presence of problems in single-parent families is not necessarily evidence of pathology or parental inadequacies, and most single parents manage without therapy. Nevertheless, the job of single parenting is difficult, and clinicians may find that their practices contain a disproportionate number of single parents requesting help with very real problems, whether their children's or their own. Fortunately they also tend to have considerable resilience and strengths that can be mobilized to deal with these problems effectively (Levine, 2009). A strengths-based approach helps to provide the support they need to be responsible and loving with their children. It also helps therapists to avoid the mistake of implicitly blaming single parents for their children's problems. However, a focus on strengths must begin by first acknowledging the very real challenges of single parenthood, avoiding the premature reassurance that can close down the possibility of discussing topics about which parents do not feel good, competent, or wise. For instance, one single mother who dropped out of therapy with a very supportive therapist said that she felt the pressure to be "constantly wonderful." Her therapist's attempts to affirm her strengths, in fact, made her feel that it was not acceptable to have problems. Discussing hardships or frustrations first means acknowledging the resilience and courage single parents generate on a daily basis in the face of those challenges (Walsh, 2006).

Engaging single parents in therapy requires special attention to the experiences they have had on the journey to their single-parent status, and appreciation of their current efforts to succeed at raising children without the sanction of marriage or in the wake of a relationship that was not viable. A cultural and historical perspective can provide a lens to frame their current problems in a developmental context that includes satisfactions and achievements, as well as struggles and disappointments. Affirming past successes and noting that many of their current struggles are a result of society's failure to provide support can lay the groundwork for single parents to build their self-esteem and help them cope more effectively.

Single-parent families are most likely to seek help at four points in time: (1) when they are trying to manage reactions to loss and create a new structure following a breakup or divorce; (2) when parental coping has been compromised by depression or overwork; (3) when a new partner enters the household; and, most frequently, (4) when their children encounter academic and behavioral difficulties. Each of these times can push a functional system over the edge. It is in this context that therapists can work on the four primary tasks that contribute to successful single parenthood: (1) improving parental well-being; (2) promoting a predictable family structure that provides nurturance and limits; (3) mitigating the impact of bitter divorce, and (4) strengthening network supports.

The Importance of Attending to Parental Well-Being

The single most important contribution therapists can make to the functioning of single-parent households is to promote parental well-being. Mobilizing parental strengths requires that therapists address the issue of the single parent's sense of self-worth. Attention to parental needs is crucial, because when parents are stressed, depressed, or overwhelmed, they are less able to provide the nurturance, limits, and structure that children need. Working to improve self-esteem is particularly important for young, low-income single parents who have yet to develop an independent sense of self-worth, or for those exiting a troubled marriage who have lost their sense of self in a neglectful or abusive relationship.

Increasing the self-esteem of very young, single mothers may require both affirmation that their ambivalence about the loss of their teenage freedoms is normal, and support of their responsibilities and ability to care for their child. For newly divorced single mothers, increasing self-esteem sometimes involves helping them to feel less responsible for the failure of their marriage and cultivating a view of themselves as capable of "flying solo" or reconnecting, whichever they desire (Anderson, Stewart, & Dimidjian, 1994). Discussion of the problems, and especially the benefits, of single parenthood can improve self-esteem as they gain perspective that many of the things they are being forced to learn will in time become valued strengths. Therapists should acknowledge the difficulties of "going it alone" but reinforce the message, supported by research, that they can be happy and fulfilled without a partner, and should take pride in their accomplishments in raising their children. The benefits for children are considerable as they learn to cope with issues that would challenge many adults, and make important contributions to the family's well-being. Specific benefits include increased closeness between parent and child; accelerated development and early acquisition of independence by functioning in responsible helping roles; acquisition of a wide range of survival skills, including the ability to cope with loss and adapt to change; and increased appreciation of the importance of links to a rich, diverse, and flexible network of friends, neighbors, extended family, and religious groups.

Because single parents tend to put the needs of their children first, it is crucial for them to hear that what their children need most is a parent who is not overstressed. Parents frequently do not seek or accept help for themselves, so therapists should attend to their well-being as a major target of assessment and intervention, even when the presenting complaint is focused entirely on the child (Anderson et al., 2006). In the context of busy schedules and task overload, parents may view therapy as just one more time-consuming burden, believe that they would not be so stressed if only their children were better behaved, and fear losing their children if they acknowledge having any needs at all. However, like a game of dominos, a parent's coping influences the child's adjustment, and if a parent's needs are not addressed, there is a negative impact on the child's mental health and response to therapy (Rishel et al., 2006; Swartz et al., 2005). It is important to emphasize that confronting the negative impact of unmet parental needs is not to blame them but to emphasize the importance of encouraging them to focus some of their energies on self-nurturance, even when their initiative is low.

Parental well-being and self-esteem can also be improved by promoting employment and adequate child care arrangements. Paid employment contributes to the well-being of both single parents and their children despite conflicts with parenting tasks. It significantly increases available household resources; contributes to a stable, predictable family structure; and offers the single parent time with other adults, a sense of job competence, and respite from constant child care, all key factors in the ability of single parents to accomplish the tasks they face (Park, 2005; Wen, 2008; Zabkiewicz, 2010). Although employment takes away some time that parents might otherwise have for their children or their own leisure, the resultant benefits to self-esteem and mood probably contribute more by improving parenting in the long run.

Promoting Parental Authority and a Strong, Predictable Family Structure

A strong family organization with clear generational boundaries creates a more predictable environment. All children, especially distressed children who have experienced traumatic life transitions, need the security of this structure and predictability. Also, at least for boys (who appear more vulnerable to the impact of marital dissolution), the maintenance of family routines buffers stress and contributes to a sense of control and security in the family (Jackson & Huang, 2000). Forming a new family, or reorganizing from a two-parent family, requires that the newly single parent develop credibility and assume the role of sole executive of the family system. Because this new family structure must be created at a time when the parent may be distressed, a significant amount of support may be necessary. The limit setting that is crucial for single-parent executive functioning may be constrained for parents who have never lived independently, who have tended to rely on their spouses to provide discipline, or have been temporarily immobilized by depression or loss. Divorced single parents may be overly permissive about a child's negative behaviors in an attempt to make up for the traumas suffered during the dissolution of the marriage, so they may find themselves exhausted by unproductive standoffs with their children. Those who live in multigenerational homes may be unclear about whether the parent or the grandparents are in charge, leaving children either confused or able to play one adult against another. A therapist's support to reinforce parental authority will not only help to maintain parental sanity but also provide children with a greater sense of security. Boundaries that define who has the right to make household rules are useful, whether single parents are living with new or temporary partners, or with their own parents.

Ongoing negative family interaction can be avoided by helping single parents work out an equitable division of labor among family members that provides help and respite by sorting out which tasks can be reasonably delegated to children, depending on their age. For example, it is important to validate the need to set reasonable limits that help keep child care demands manageable. Appropriate bedtimes for children or delegation of child care responsibilities to older children for short periods of time can provide parents with occasional quiet time for themselves. Parents who worry that it may be damaging to require older children to assume some increased responsibility for the household or their siblings can be reassured that chores are good for children, unless they are totally deprived of a childhood. However, care must be taken to ensure that chores be delegated, not abdicated, rather than comprising the parent's ultimate authority or ability to be in charge of the family. Therapists also can help parents to retain their authority by encouraging a direct line to each child even when family circumstances dictate that an older child be given more than the usual responsibilities for younger siblings. In family therapy, if single mothers or fathers appear to have problems establishing themselves as the ultimate family executive, therapists can serve as role models by effectively limiting children and repeatedly reinforcing parental authority in front of the children. Particular care must be taken by therapists to avoid exacerbating any parental sense of deficiency by ingratiating themselves with children at parental expense or getting caught in a struggle between the parent and child, or even between the parent and the family of origin. Although specific tasks such as chore charts and token economies can be helpful in providing children with structure, care must be taken to design tasks and interventions that do not require an unrealistic amount of monitoring that taxes already overburdened parents.

Establishing predictability in family life is not just a matter of creating rules and enforcing them. Family stability, connectedness, and parental authority also can be reinforced by maintaining traditional family routines and rituals, and creating new ones (see Imber-Black, Chapter 20, this volume). Some single parents become so overwhelmed with day-to-day survival issues that they neglect the need for routines and rituals, forgetting the comfort and sense of continuity they provide. In fact, after a death or a divorce, some families avoid even the most basic rituals, from regular family dinners to birthday parties or holiday celebrations. Some parents admit to feeling that rituals are no longer relevant, because there is no longer a "real" family. The cultural reification of the intact family makes it essential that therapists challenge views that single-parent families are abnormal or inherently deficient. Reestablishing rituals and routines can reassure children that theirs is also a normal family.

To combat the natural tendency for depressed or overwhelmed parents to neglect routine household maintenance, therapists may need to support single parents to keep daily routines alive, stressing the value of family dinners and age-appropriate bedtimes for children. Without these daily rituals, a sense of family is diminished, and exhausted parents are left with ongoing struggles and less time for themselves. Reinforcing bedtime, making it an opportunity for close and quiet times together is particularly important to prevent exhausted parents from having to deal with overtired and emotionally overloaded children, who then experience an increased likelihood of concentration difficulties in school.

Mitigating the Impact of a Bitter Divorce

Divorce can have long-term repercussions, in which each parent participates in a vicious cycle of withholding what the other needs, leaving the children caught in the middle. Ambivalence about arranging the noncustodial parent's (usually a father's) contact with children often contributes to a lack of follow through with promised plans and visits, and stirs children's feelings of abandonment and anger at their noncustodial parent's unreliability, often leading them to take out this anger on their custodial parent. For example, to protect the child from these repeated disappointments, the custodial mother understandably may decide to withhold the father's visitation, which in turn reinforces an unhealthy cutoff between father and child. The result is that both parents and children become caught in an unproductive cycle of stressful and harmful interactions. Therapists should use a wide-angle lens to assess how the residue of the divorce may be impacting the single-parent household's current reality, then work to involve each parent in creating a better coparenting relationship in the child's best interests. This often requires supporting the custodial parent in allowing the father access to the child, not always an easy step. However, the result may be that both single parent and child receive greater emotional and financial support (Fagan et al., 2009). If the father has not remarried, he too is a single parent, one who can certainly be helped to assume significant parenting tasks, albeit with fewer daily responsibilities. If he has remarried, therapy may help him balance the needs of the children from his first family with those of his new one.

Strengthening Existing Networks and Creating New Connections

Many single-parent families are well connected outside the home, but others live an isolated existence in a judgmental community. In either case, these families are profoundly influenced by the social context in which they spend their lives, and single-parent families are less vulnerable if they are embedded in a fabric of social and instrumental support (Kaplan, McLoyd, & Toyokawa, 2008). This makes attention to networks a cornerstone of all therapeutic work. Networks of both parent and child should be assessed, then strengthened and expanded as needed. Because single-parent family connections can be complex, sometimes involving multiple fathers and extended kinship systems, it may help to use a genogram to diagram complex family patterns to assess available and potential supports. These diagrams should include nuclear and extended family members, informal kin, chosen family and friends, spiritual resources, and even neighbors and community contacts. It is essential to determine the quality of these contacts, because stress-laden social networks can be associated with increased conflict, maternal depression, and parenting problems (Hawkins, 2010).

There are times when a single parent's network cannot provide the right kind of help or support: Ties have been weakened or disrupted by divorce or relocation; existing network members are insensitive to the challenges of single parents and their children. Those single parents who most need support may not have the skills to develop and maintain the kind of relationships they need. Many single parents find it exceedingly difficult to ask available extended family or friends to pitch in with practical, financial, or emotional support. They may also be aware that frequent contact with some family members may be a mixed blessing. This makes it important to assess which family members potentially are helpful resources, and to facilitate their involvement. Other family members may be the source of increased stress through their disapproval of the single parent's behavior, inappropriate alignments with children, split loyalties postdivorce, or requests for help that drain the single parent's limited resources. Helping single parents to redefine relationships with their families of origin may be especially important for family members who have difficulty accepting or understanding divorce or the choice to become a single parent. For some, it is important to explore religious or cultural taboos against divorce or single parenthood.

Therapists can help single parents explore whether estranged relationships or destructive patterns of interaction can be mitigated, or whether these efforts must be temporarily put on a back burner. For instance, one young mother who worked hard to support her 9-month-old daughter in a community day care program turned to her "family" of friends rather than her crack-addicted sister and alcoholic mother, both of whom regularly asked for money and criticized her for neglecting her child by taking a job instead of seeking public assistance. In families involving extreme dysfunction or even abuse, it may be more sensible to help the parent cultivate friendship networks or connections to extrafamilial resources and support groups.

The assessment of existing and potential networks lays the groundwork for broadening the sense of connectedness for both parent and child. Therapists can help single parents begin to mobilize their networks by first attending to people already actively involved in important aspects of family life, moving next to those who might be available if asked (e.g., a somewhat distant nonresident coparent), then seeking ways to use community contacts. It is not always easy for single parents to ask for help, however, especially from outside the family, because of their pride and fear of becoming a burden, fear of rejection, or loss of custody of their child. Developing new strands of support can also seem like just one more chore. Many overextended single parents would rather collapse on the couch after a trying day than take the initiative to con-nect, especially with people they do not yet know well. It may take a thera-pist's encouragement and coaching to get network development off the ground and alleviate the intensity of problems in single-parent households by carefully weaving a web of support beyond the household. This includes encouraging a range of positive connections for both parent and child, including an inter-related network of individuals and groups that provide a context of reciprocal support and mutual responsibility.

Network interventions for single parents should be planned with a wide-angle lens, meeting the needs of each family member for both a sense of belonging and concrete assistance. For instance, child care exchanges can be arranged with other parents; godparents can take a more active role. In post-divorce single-parent families, predivorce networks sometimes assume that the single parent would be uncomfortable in gatherings of couples or intact families, while others may be uneasy about seeming to choose one partner's side over the other in the divorce. Single parents may also be seen as a threat to intact marriages. Thus, friends that single parents had when they were mar-ried may no longer be available, unless they work to keep these contacts. It is possible, with effort, to sort out, maintain, and strengthen most of these ties, yet single parents may need to be strongly encouraged to tolerate the risk of rejection or the discomfort of going alone to social gatherings.

When previously existing networks are unavailable or insufficient, thera-pists should help single parents to build new connections for companionship, support, and practical help. In addition, these contacts can provide opportuni-ties for parental respite through trade-off of child care responsibilities, trans-portation to children's activities, or information about community resources. A number of community resources can be tapped, including workplace con-tacts, established community groups, or religious congregations. Single-parent groups, such as "Parents without Partners," can provide opportunities for sharing common challenges and coping strategies in discussions and activi-ties that can make single parents feel less isolated and stigmatized. Needs for diversion and renewal can be met through exercise, sports, crafts, or other structured group activities. Those parents whose mobility is compromised by limited child care or community contacts can find support and connection through Internet websites and social networks.

Children's Networks: Connecting with Noncustodial Fathers and Beyond

Many children of single-parent mothers have little contact with their fathers. If there is a chance for a father to become more involved, it is important to try to make an absent father an ongoing part of the child's network (Amato & Gilbreth, 1999; Cowan, Cowan, Pruett, Pruett, & Wong, 2009). Ongoing contact between father and child can be facilitated by helping the mother and her family to see that it is in the child's best interests. A good percentage of these efforts succeed. However, if a mother's relationship with him is poor, or the risk of abuse precludes contact with the child, the therapist should explore the possibility of the child's continued involvement with the father's family, including grandparents, aunts, uncles, and cousins (Fagan et al., 2009).

The child's network can also be augmented by facilitating relationships with supportive adults and groups in the community. Teachers, sports coaches, Big Brothers and Sisters, and activity group leaders can be positive role models and mentors for children. These connections may be particularly useful in balancing the intensity of the single-parent–child relationship for an only child, or can serve as additional resources for siblings competing for limited parental energies. Positive involvement in interest groups and teams can also foster a sense of belonging and competence. Each resource can mitigate the impact of familial loss and stress, filling the gaps in what any one parent, however competent, can provide, and offering valuable bonds that support each child's positive growth and resilience.

SUMMARY AND CONCLUSIONS

The increased number of single-parent households has been regarded by some as evidence that the future of marriage, the very foundation of our culture, is endangered. Yet despite an increased decoupling of marriage and childrearing in recent decades, the desire to raise children well in a family context continues to be strong, even when those family forms vary considerably. Although single parents can and do create satisfying lives on their own, most continue to prefer to share the burdens and joys of parenting within a good marriage or a long-term, loving relationship. This is not surprising, since parenting and providing financial support can be overwhelming for a sole parent. It is even more challenging for low-income or divorced families, especially in times of economic downturns, when jobs are scarce and the safety net for families becomes less available. During these times, single parents must function without adequate funds or child care, heightening the risks for family problems. The failure of society to provide single-parent families with financial, social, or psychological support requires each individual family to address and conquer problems that could be better addressed collectively, even though the problems are usually less the result of personal deficits than of inadequacy of the service systems that should be supporting them.

When single parents and/or their children are seen in therapy, they are most often struggling to find ways to deal with an overload of child care and household chores, limited time and energy for their own interests, and, frequently, insufficient financial resources to cover their basic essentials. What they need from therapists is understanding, support, and help in mobilizing their strengths and networks to create and manage a workable life in the face of multiple competing and complex challenges. Clinical work requires that therapists facilitate their ability to use and expand the strengths and resources of single parents and their children to survive and thrive by increasing their self-esteem, reinforcing a strong family structure, and helping parents and their children to be involved in webs of kin and social support beyond the nuclear family.

Three guidelines allow therapists to maintain a helpful perspective in working with these single parents.

1. It is important to remember that single-parent families differ dramatically based on their route to single parenthood and their unique problems and needs. For some, becoming a single parent is traumatic; for others, it is a choice and a blessing.
2. Like most families, there are particular times when single parents are most likely to encounter difficulties that can exceed their ability to manage solo, such as when they first become a single-parent household, when finances are strained, and when the parent or child experiences emotional or behavioral problems.
3. In assessing both the needs and resources of single-parent households, it is important to remember that the family unit involves not only those who live together but also a noncustodial parent whose relationship with the child should be nurtured in the child's best interests. While at times stressful, such a relationship can also provide respite for the custodial parent and better child adjustment. The family's potential network may also include a range of extended family members and close friends, and wider community groupings. Attention to all of these contacts beyond the parent–child dyad will expand the family's resources and strengthen potential lifelines to the larger system.

REFERENCES

Afifi, T. O., Coz, B. J., & Enns, M. W. (2006). Mental health profiles among married, never-married and separated/divorced mothers in a nationally representative sample, *Social Psychiatry and Psychiatric Epidemiology, 41*, 122–129.

Ahrons, C. (2004). *We're still family.* New York: HarperCollins.

Amato, P. R., & Gilbreth, J. G. (1999). Nonresident fathers and children's wellbeing: A meta-analysis. *Journal of Marriage and the Family, 61*, 557–573.

Anderson, C. M., Robins, C. S., Greeno, C. G., Cahalane, H., Copeland V., & Andrews, R. M. (2006). Why low-income mothers do not engage with the formal mental health care system: Preliminary findings from an ethnographic study. *Qualitative Health Research, 16*(7), 926–943.

Anderson, C. M., Stewart, S., & Dimidjian, S. (1994). *Flying solo: Single women in midlife.* New York: Norton.

Anderson, E. R., Greene, S. M., Walker, L., Malerba, C., Forgatch, M. S., & DeGarmo, D. S. (2004). Ready to take a chance again: Transitions into dating among divorced parents. *Journal of Divorce and Remarriage, 40*(3–4), 61–75.

Barrett, A. E., & Turner, R. J. (2005). Family structure and mental health: The mediating effects of socioeconomic status, family process, and social stress. *Journal of Health and Social Behavior. 46*(2), 156–169.

Berger, L. M. (2007). Socioeconomic factors and substandard parenting. *Social Service Review, 81*(3), 485–522.

Brown, B. (2000). The single father family: Demographic, economic, and public transfer use characteristics. *Marriage and Family Review, 29*(2–3), 203–220.

Bzostek, S. H. (2008). Social fathers and child well-being. *Journal of Marriage and Family, 70*, 950–961.

Cain, D. S., & Combs-Orme, T. (2005). Family structure effects on parenting stress and practices in the African American family. *Journal of Sociology and Social Welfare, 32*(2), 19–40.

Cavanaugh, S. E., & Huston, A. C. (2006). Family instability and children's early problem behavior. *Social Forces, 85*, 551–581.

Ceballo, R., & McLoyd, V. C. (2002). Social support and parenting in poor, dangerous neighborhoods, *Child Development, 73*(4), 1310–1321.

Cherlin, A. J. (2010). Demographic trends in the United States: A review of research in the 2000s. *Journal of Marriage and Family, 72*, 403–419.

Cowan, P. A., Cowan, C. P., Pruett, M. K., Pruett, K., & Wong, J. J. (2009). Promoting fathers' engagement with children: Preventive interventions for low-income families. *Journal of Marriage and Family, 71*(3), 663–679.

Crosier, T., Butterworth, P., & Rodgers, B. (2007). Mental health problems among single and partnered mothers: The role of financial hardship and social support. *Social Psychiatry and Psychiatric Epidemiology, 42*(1), 6–13.

DeGarmo, D. S., & Forgatch, M. S. (2005). Early development of delinquency within divorced families: Evaluating a randomized preventive intervention trial. *Developmental Science, 3*(3), 229–239.

DeNavas, C., Welniak, E. J., Proctor, B. E., Smith, J. C., Stern, S., & Nelson, C. T. (2009). *Income, poverty, and health insurance coverage in the United States.* Washington, DC: U.S. Bureau of the Census.

Devault, A., Milcent, M., Ouellet, F., Laurin, I., Jauron, M., & Lacharite, C. (2008). Life stories of young fathers in contexts of vulnerability. *Fathering, 6*(3), 226–248.

Dudley, J. R. (2007). Helping nonresidential fathers: The case for teen and adult unmarried fathers. *Families in Society, 88*(2), 171–181.

Dyer, W. J. (2005). Prison, fathers, and identity: A theory of how incarceration affects men's paternal identity. *Fathering, 3*(3), 201–219.

Edin, K., & Kissane, R. J. (2010). Poverty and the American family: A decade in review. *Journal of Marriage and Family, 72*, 460–479.

Fagan, J., Palkovitz, R., Roy, K., & Farrie, D. (2009). Pathways to paternal engagement: Longitudinal effects of risk and resilience on nonresident fathers. *Developmental Psychology, 45*(5), 1389–1405.

Feder, A., Alonso, A., Tang, M., Liriano, W., Warner, V., Pilowsky, D., et al. (2009). Children of low-income depressed mothers: Psychiatric disorders and social adjustment. *Depression and Anxiety, 26*(6), 513–520.

Fomby, P., & Cherlin, A. J. (2007). Family instability and child well-being. *American Sociological Review, 72*, 181–204.

Forgatch, M. S., Beldavs, Z. G., Patterson, G. R., & DeGarmo, D. S. (2008). From coercion to positive parenting: Putting divorced mothers in charge of change. In M. Kerr, H. Stattin & R. C. M. E. Engles (Eds.), *What can parents do?: New* insights into the role of parents in adolescent problem behavior (pp. 191–209). London: Wiley.

Goldscheider, F., & Kaufman, G. (2006). Single parenthood and the double standard. *Fathering, 4*(2), 191–208.

Guzzo, K. B. (2009). Maternal relationships and nonresidential father visitation of children born outside of marriage. *Journal of Marriage and Family, 71*(3), 632–649.

Hawkins, R. L. (2010). Fickle families and the kindness of strangers: Social capital in the lives of low-income single mothers. *Journal of Human Behavior in the Social Environment, 20*(1), 38–55.

Hetherington, E. M., & Kelly, J. (2002). *For better or for worse: Divorce reconsidered*. New York: Norton.

Hilton, J. M., & Kopera-Frye, K. (2007). Gendered expectations?: Reconsidering single fathers' childcare time. *Journal of Marriage and Family, 70*(4), 978–990.

Jackson, A. P., & Huang, C. C. (2000). Parenting stress and behavior among single mothers of preschoolers: The mediating role of self-efficacy. *Journal of Social Service Research, 26*, 29–42.

Johnson, W. E. (2001). Paternal involvement among unwed fathers. *Children and Youth Services Review, 23*(6–7), 513–536.

Jones, D. J., Zalot, A. A., Foster, S. E., Sterrett, E., & Chester, C. (2007). A review of childrearing in African American single mother families: The relevance of a coparenting framework. *Journal of Child and Family Studies, 16*(5), 671–683.

Kaplan, R., McLoyd, V. C., & Toyokawa, T. (2008). Work demands, work–family conflict, and child adjustment in African American families: The mediating role of family routines *Journal of Family Issues, 29*(10), 1247–1267.

Kreider, R. M., & Elliott, D. B. (2009). America's families and living arrangements: 2007 (Current Population Reports 20-561). Washington, DC: U.S. Bureau of the Census.

Lehr, R., & MacMillan, P. (2001). The psychological and emotional impact of divorce: The noncustodial fathers' perspective. *Families in Society, 82*(4), 373–382.

Leventhal, T., & Brooks-Gunn, J. (2000). The neighborhood they live in: Effects of neighborhood residence on child and adolescent outcomes. *Psychological Bulletin, 126*, 309–337.

Levine, K. A. (2009). Against all odds: Resilience in single mothers of children with disabilities. *Social Work in Health Care, 48*(4), 402–419.

Margolin, L. (1992). Child abuse by mothers' boyfriends: Why the overrepresentation? *Child Abuse and Neglect, 16*(4), 541–551.

McLanahan, S., & Percheski, C. (2008). Family structure and the reproduction of inequalities, *Annual Review of Sociology, 34*, 257–276.

McLanahan, S., & Sanderfur, M. J. (1994). *Growing up with a single parent: What hurts and what helps*. Cambridge, MA: Harvard University Press.

Mistry, R. S., Vandewater, E. A., Huston, A. C., & McLoyd, V. C. (2002). Economic well-being and children's social adjustment: The role of family process in an ethnically diverse low-income sample. *Child Development. 73*(3), 935–951.

Nievar, M. A., & Luster, T. (2006). Developmental processes in African American families: An application of McLoyd's theoretical model. *Journal of Marriage and Family, 68*, 320–331.

Park, J. M. (2005). The roles of living arrangements and household resources in single mothers' employment. *Journal of Social Service Research, 31*(3), 46–67.

Potter, D. (2010). Psychosocial well-being and the relationship between divorce and children's academic achievement. *Journal of Marriage and Family, 72*(4), 933–946.

Rishel, C. W., Greeno, C. G., Marcus, S. C., Sales, E., Shear, M. K., Swartz, H. A., et al. (2006). Impact of maternal mental health status on child mental health treatment outcome. *Community Mental Health Journal, 42*(1), 1–12.

Swartz, H. A., Shear, M. K., Wren, F. J., Greeno, C. G., Sales, E., Sullivan, B. K., et al. (2005). Depression and anxiety among mothers who bring their children to a pediatric mental health clinic. *Psychiatric Services, 56*(9), 1077–1083.

Swiss, L., & Le Bourdais, C. (2009). Father–child contact after separation: The influence of living arrangements. *Journal of Family Issues, 30*(5), 623–652.

Usdansky, M. L. (2009). A weak embrace: Popular and scholarly depictions of single-parent families. *Journal of Marriage and Family, 71*(2), 209–225.

Ventura, S. J. (2009). Changing patterns of nonmarital childbearing in the United States. *NCH 8 Data Brief, 18*, 1–8.

Walsh, F. (2006). *Strengthening family resilience* (2nd ed.). New York: Guilford Press.

Wen, M. (2008). Family structure and children's health and behavior. *Journal of Family Issues, 29*(11), 1492–1519.

Wolfe, D. L. (2009). Review of single by chance, mothers by choice: How women are choosing parenthood without marriage and creating the new American family. *American Journal of Sociology, 114*(5), 1568–1570.

Zabkiewicz, D. (2010). The mental health benefits of work: Do they apply to poor single mothers? *Social Psychiatry and Psychiatric Epidemiology, 45*(1), 77–87.

Zahn, M., & Pandy, S. (2004). Economic well-being of single mothers: Work first or postsecondary education? *Journal of Sociology and Social Welfare, 31*(3), 87–112.

CHAPTER 7

Remarriage and Stepfamily Life

Kay Pasley
Chelsea Garneau

Because divorce remains common and individuals maintain interest in marriage, remarriage and stepfamilies continue to be part of American family life. Estimates show that between 40 and 50% of first-married couples ultimately divorce (Bramlett & Mosher, 2002; Cherlin, 2010; Teachman & Tedrow, 2008), and these divorced individuals typically go on to remarry or repartner. When those remarriages include children from a prior union, stepfamilies are formed. Also, an increasing number of cohabiting couples dissolve their relationships and go on to either legally marry or form a repartnership (Teachman, 2008; Teachman & Tedrow, 2008). In many cases, these couples also include children from prior unions, so scholars acknowledge them as stepfamilies as well (Pasley & Lee, 2010; Sweeney, 2010).

Our best estimates suggest that about 9% of married couples and 12% of cohabiting couples have a stepchild residing in the household (Kreider, 2008; Teachman & Tedrow, 2008). Importantly, these estimates are based on the census definition of children being younger than 18 years and residing in the household. Excluded from these estimates are (1) children who reside with a resident single parent (usually the mother), and whose nonresident parent (usually the father) has remarried or repartnered; (2) children who are 18 years and older and continue to reside at home; and (3) children who reside with same-sex couples, where one adult is their biological parent and the other serves a stepparent role (Pasley & Lee, 2010).

Although divorce and dissolution of other relationships are common, we know that most individuals continue to couple and recouple, and that children often are involved in these relationship transitions. Whether the adults

---

We dedicate this chapter to the memory of Drs. Emily and John Visher, pioneers in bringing stepfamilies to the attention of clinicians and advocating for research-informed therapy.

are legally married or not, the child experiences these transitions as parental divorce and remarriage. Of concern to those interested in prevention and intervention, a good deal of research shows that poor child outcomes are associated with changes in family structure (Bulanda & Manning, 2008) and the number of accompanying transitions (e.g., changing homes, schools, friendship groups; Amato, 2010).

Our purpose here is to review briefly the extant literature on remarriage and stepfamily life to address the common life challenges these families face early on. We also describe the processes that are important for both individual and family adjustment and well-being. Although much has been written from a deficit perspective, our focus is on inherent strategies and strengths developed in these complicated families, including those formed through both marriage and cohabitation. We end with a discussion of the relevance of this research for those involved in psychoeducation and clinical work. Of note, we include citations as example throughout the chapter; however, we have made no attempt to be inclusive.

WHO REMARRIES AND FORMS STEPFAMILIES?

Kreider (2005) reported that 30.2% of all marriages in 2001 were remarriages for at least one member of the couple, which is a significant reduction from earlier estimates of 45%. This reduction likely reflects the overall decrease in marriage and the concomitant increase in cohabitation (Cherlin, 2010). Our best estimates suggest that about 65% of remarriages form stepfamilies, with either stepfather-only or stepfather–stepmother families being the most common; stepmother-only families remain least common (Kreider, 2008). Other data from an urban cohort showed that almost 60% of unmarried couples had at least one child from a prior union, constituting nonlegal stepfamilies (Carlson & Furstenberg, 2006). Thus, remarriages or repartnerships remain common, although overall we see a decrease in remarriages and an increase in repartnerships (Cherlin, 2010).

Regarding stability, remarriages end slightly more frequently than do first marriages, a consistent finding over time (Coleman & Ganong, 1990; Coleman, Ganong, & Fine, 2000; Sweeney, 2010). What has changed is that the median amount of time from first marriage to divorce and remarriage to divorce is now about 8 years (Kreider, 2005). Earlier estimates were 7.5 years from first marriage to divorce and 4.5 years from remarriage to divorce (Kreider, 2005). This suggests similar stability now among those who marry for the first time and those who remarry. Least stable are cohabiting unions following divorce, many of which include children, as these repartnerships dissolve more frequently than do actual remarriages (Poortman & Lyngstad, 2007; Xu, Hudspeth, & Bartkowski, 2006).

Studies of the demographic characteristics of those who remarry or repartner typically focus on the presence and number of children, gender, prior marital status, age, race, level of education, and prior experience with cohabitation. Specifically, having children from a prior marriage or union reduces the likelihood of remarriage for women but increases the likelihood for men (e.g., Brown, Lee, & Bulanda, 2006). Furthermore, women with children tend to marry men who also have children, thereby forming complex stepfamilies (i.e., his and her family combination; Goldscheider & Sassler, 2006). Single men who marry divorced women do so more frequently when these women are not parents (Golscheider, Kaufman, & Sassler, 2009), and men with nonresident children are more likely to cohabit than to marry or remarry (Stewart, Manning, & Smock, 2003).

Choosing to remarry is a more common phenomenon among younger, white women with lower levels of education (Kreider, 2005), many of whom have prior experience with cohabitation (Xu et al., 2006). Repartnering is more common among African American women with lower levels of education (Kreider, 2005). Unlike women, men with higher levels of education are more likely to remarry or repartner, and the presence of children from a prior union does not diminish this probability (Brown et al., 2006).

WHAT THE LITERATURE REVEALS

The Couple Relationship

Although there is a good deal written about changes in family structure and some of the demographic characteristics associated with these changes, much less in known about the nature of the relationships formed (van Eeden-Moorefield & Pasley, 2008). There is some research showing that those who remarry have better physical and emotional health than those who are single (Hughes & Waite, 2009). Also, evidence suggest that those who remarry expect these relationships to operate like first marriages, and that such expectations are associated with adjustment difficulties (Bray & Kelly, 1998). However, little is known about how couples go about creating positive relationships (Coleman et al., 2000).

Other evidence suggests that, for many, cohabitation (often more than one such partnership) is the first step toward remarriage (Ganong & Coleman, 2004), and this can delay remarriage (Xu et al., 2006). Stewart and associates (2003) found that cohabitation is preferred to remarriage for men, a finding that may be related to other research showing that men are slower to make a commitment to relationships in general (see Rhoades, Stanley, & Markman, 2006).

The Role of Conflict

Pasley and Lee (2010) argue that remarriages and stepfamilies are likely to experience more conflict and greater challenges in adjusting to family life than are first-marriage couples. They noted that this is likely due to the increased complexity of relationships within the newly formed family, the brevity of shared history among members, and the existence of "interested outsiders" (e.g., former spouses and nonresident parents). Frequent conflict situations may be one explanation for reports of lower levels of cohesion (Bray & Kelly, 1998), more equal power in decision making between spouses (Ganong, Coleman, & Hans, 2006), and endorsement of greater autonomy regarding finances and children (Allen, Baucom, Burnett, Epstein, & Rankin-Esquer, 2001). Examples of conflict situations include dealing with nonresident parents, which can spillover to mother–child and stepfather–stepchild conflict (Dunn, Cheng, O'Connor, & Bridges, 2004); working out issues of parenting/stepparenting (Hetherington & Kelly, 2002; Shelton, Walters, & Harold, 2008), especially in stepfamilies with stepdaughters (Feinberg, Kan, & Hetherington, 2007); and setting rules and determining boundaries early on (Afifi, 2008).

Beyond these realities, other evidence shows that the quality of the stepparent–stepchild relationships is more predictive of marital adjustment and outcomes than is the quality of the marriage itself, which does not hold true for first marriages. Importantly, the stepparent–stepchild relationship provides fertile ground for conflict, and research shows that child-related issues rank first as a source of marital conflict in remarriages, with finances ranking second; in first marriages, these sources also rank first and second, but the order is reversed (see Stanley, Markman, & Whitton, 2002).

Conflict is reflective of communication processes in families, and remarried couples report being both less positive and less negative in communication compared with reports from first marriages/couples (Halford, Nicholson, & Sanders, 2007). Also, research shows that those in stepfamilies more frequently use avoidance strategies (e.g., withdrawal) than do members of first-marriage families in dealing with conflict, and such strategies are linked with poorer adjustment (Halford et al., 2007). Furthermore, use of avoidance strategies is common among adolescents and young adults in stepfamilies (Golish & Caughlin, 2002). Stepfathers and stepchildren engage more frequently conflict than do mothers and children, and when children are involved in stepfamily arguments, they commonly side with their mothers (Dunn, O'Connor, & Cheng, 2005). Greater success in stepfamilies has been attributed to open communication and flexibility (Golish, 2003).

Marital Quality

Both conflict and cohesion are linked with marital quality in general. Thus, it follows that those in stepfamilies would report lower martial quality. However, there is contradictory evidence about marital quality in remarriages, with some studies suggesting no difference between that in first marriages and in remarriages, and others suggesting that remarriages have lower quality (Coleman et al., 2000; Sweeney, 2010). Certain factors are linked with lower marital adjustment and satisfaction: complex stepfamilies (his *and* hers;

Hobart, 1991), stepfather-only rather than stepmother-only (Kurdek, 1991), greater financial hardship (Higginbotham & Felix, 2009) poorer spousal communication skills, and older children (Beaudry, Boisvert, Simard, Parent, & Blais, 2004).

Marital Stability

Findings regarding the link between relationship quality and stability make intuitive sense: Poorer relationship quality is associated with more instability (Sweeney, 2010)—a finding that also holds for first marriages (Amato, 2010). Additional correlates of relationship instability and later redivorce include less perceived fairness and more relationship conflict, findings that varied by family complexity. For example, in a study using longitudinal data, perceived fairness predicted later marital quality for couples in stepfamilies and explained almost twice the variance in relationship stability over time compared with those in remarriages without children (van Eeden-Moorefield & Pasley, 2008).

Taken together, the extant literature suggests that the presence of children from a prior union influences the nature of the new marital relationship. As noted, this is a consistent finding over time (Coleman & Ganong, 1990; Coleman et al., 2000; Sweeney, 2010). Children potentially complicate communication through increased conflict, less effective problem solving, and more financial strain. Adding new members to any social system disrupts existing patterns of interaction, and much of literature suggests that the nature of the stepparent–stepchild relationship is the strongest predictor of both the quality and the stability of the new family (Coleman et al., 2000).

Taking on the Role of Stepparent

Without reservation, ample evidence shows that stepparenting is more difficult than parenting one's own child (see Pasley & Moorefield, 2004, for a summary). Scholars agree that much of this difficulty is the result of greater conflict and ambiguity associated with the stepparent role (Ganong & Coleman, 2004; Hetherington & Kelly, 2002). Also, more ambiguity is associated with poorer stepfamily adjustment (Coleman et al., 2000; Sweeney, 2010), more complicated relationships across multiple households, and when unmarried parents cohabit (Brown & Manning, 2009; Stewart, 2005).

Influential Factors

Several factors influence stepparenting, including sex of stepparent–stepchild and residence of stepchild, support for adopting the stepparent role, disengagement behaviors, birth of a common child, and marital status of parents. For example, recent research shows that same-sex stepparents and stepchildren (e.g., stepfather and stepson) residing together facilitate the development of effective stepparenting behaviors (Schmeeckle, 2007). Others show that when there is little spousal support for adopting a stepparenting role (Gosselin & David, 2007), or when the stepparent remains disengaged from the parenting process over time (Fisher, Leve, O'Leary, & Leve, 2003), developing effective stepparenting is less possible. Having a common child does not diminish the stepparent–stepchild involvement (Stewart, 2005), although the quality of parenting behaviors in married stepfamilies is higher than that of cohabiting stepfamilies (Berger, Carlson, Bzostek, & Osborne, 2008).

Stepfathering

We know more about the experience of stepfathers in general, because much of the research has focused on them: They are the most common resident stepparent (Kreider, 2008), even when they are also fathers to children residing elsewhere. Research shows that stepfathers have greater latitude than stepmothers in adopting parental behaviors (Coleman et al., 2000; Hetherington & Kelly, 2002). The quality of this involvement and parenting does not differ dramatically from that of a biological father (Adamsons, O'Brien, & Pasley, 2007), although stepfathers engage in fewer monitoring behaviors (Fisher et al., 2003). Also, recent findings from a large study of at-risk families (Berger et al., 2008) showed that relationship status makes a difference, such that cohabiting fathers and stepfathers exhibited poorer parenting than did married fathers and stepfathers. Stepfathers were perceived as less trustworthy but, compared with fathers, were more engaged in cooperative parenting.

Other research has identified a variety of factors influencing stepfather involvement with stepchildren. Specifically, when a stepfather reports lower marital quality and fewer concerns over the adjustment of the stepchild, his involvement is less frequent (Adamsons et al., 2007; Flouri, Buchanan, & Bream, 2002). Also, the nature of his parenting of stepchildren is influenced by his involvement with the nonresident father (MacDonald & DeMaris, 2002), where alliance building facilitate greater involvement. His involvement is also affected by the age and sex of the stepchild, such that when stepchildren are older and female, involvement is diminished. This may be because conflict between stepparents and stepdaughters is more intense than that with stepsons (Bray & Kelly, 1998), and these relationships are less close over time (Falci, 2006). Interestingly, stepchildren expect stepfathers to be less involved and secondary to the mother (Moore & Cartwright, 2005), and some of the conflict may result when this expectation is not met.

Some parents' preference to control decisions about their children (Coleman, Fine, Ganong, Downs, & Pauk, 2001) can serve as another source of conflict between stepparent and parent that spills over into the stepparent–stepchild relationship. Interestingly, there is some evidence that stepparenting is perceived by all members of the family as positive when stepparents, parents, and stepchildren can find and share common ground, or what Papernow

(1996) called "thickening the middle ground" (see also Marsiglio, 2004; Robertson, 2008).

Nonresident Stepfathers

Mothers are least likely to be nonresident parents (Kreider, 2008); however, nonresident stepfathers remain understudied (Coleman et al., 2000; Sweeney, 2010). We know that nonresident mothers typically have more contact with children than do nonresident fathers (Gunnoe & Hetherington, 2004; Stewart, 1999). If the nonresident mother is repartnered, this nonresident stepfather has more opportunity to influence the newly formed stepfamily in which the child resides. As expected with the maturation of children, the level of contact between nonresident parents decreases more for children in stepfamilies, and reduced conflict between parents is linked to the quick repartnering of a nonresident parent, especially the father (Amato, Meyers, & Emery, 2009).

Stepmothers

Given the gendered expectations that women as stepmothers assume more involvement in parenting, they are crippled by negative stereotypes (Coleman, Troilo, & Jamison, 2008). Thus, stepmothering is more complicated for both resident and nonresident stepmothers, although little is known about these women. Resident stepmothers report slightly higher levels of conflict with their spouses regarding parenting compared with biological mothers in first-marriage families (Feinberg et al., 2007). Some findings show that about 67% of adolescents residing with stepmothers report feeling close to them (King, 2007), although the results are mixed about the effects of stepmothering on children (Coleman et al., 2000; Sweeney, 2010).

Nonresident Stepmothers

Most findings are from qualitative studies and offer limited insight into the roles these women play. For example, Weaver and Coleman (2005) identified four roles: adult friend, supporter of father, liaison between father and mother, and outsider (remained uninvolved). A similar study (Henry & McCue, 2009) showed that when stepmothers were reluctant to take on the liaison role, higher marital conflict was reported between them and their spouses, the fathers of their stepchildren. The inability to take on an active role in the stepfamily was linked with reports of nonresident stepmothers having more depressed mood and feeling more anxious and stressed (Henry & McCue, 2009; Johnson et al., 2008).

Overall, the relationship between stepparents and nonresident parents remains understudied (Coleman et al., 2000; Sweeney, 2010). Past recommendations from scholars often emphasized the value of building positive relationships between these adults (Clapp, 2000). Research shows that involving the nonresident father and building parenting alliances between fathers and stepfathers is linked with higher quality stepfathering (King, 2007; Marsiglio & Hinojosa, 2007). Other research shows that the quality of parenting in stepfamilies is influenced by the level and nature of involvement of the nonresident father (MacDonald & DeMaris, 2002). Because many fathers maintain frequent contact with their children following divorce and relationship dissolution (Amato et al., 2009), their repartnering, especially when done quickly, is associated with a decrease in involvement (Ahrons, 2007; Juby, Billette, Laplante, & Le Bourdais, 2007).

Children's Experiences in Stepfamilies

Much of the research on stepfamilies has focused on children's experiences and is summarized in several comprehensive review articles (see Coleman & Ganong, 1990; Coleman et al., 2000; Pasley & Moorefield, 2004; Sweeney, 2010), as well as two meta-analyses (Amato, 1994; Jeynes, 2006). Primarily the research addresses two outcomes: academic achievement and behavior problems (both externalizing and internalizing). Overall, the results show that children in stepfamilies fare worse than those in intact first-marriage families, but similar to or better than children in single-parent households. Such differences are typically noted by small effect sizes and are of little practical importance. However, when meaningful differences are noted, more internalizing (e.g., depression) is common in children in stepfamilies compared with those with a single mother, although health-related and some other behaviors were better in children in stepfamilies (e.g., Hawkins, Amato, & King, 2007; Sweeney, Wang, & Videon, 2009). Comparisons between children in married and cohabiting stepfamilies show mixed results (Sweeney, 2010).

Specific to children's academic achievement, results show a similar pattern of achievement among stepchildren and children with a single parent, and worse performance compared with children in first-marriage families. Those in cohabiting stepfamilies fared worst of all groups (Heard, 2007; Tillman, 2008). More important than family structure in explaining differences in academic achievement were the number and recency of family transitions (e.g., changing parental figures, moving to another residence, changing schools; Jeynes, 2006; Tillman, 2008).

Earlier research on children's behavior problems and the effects of living in a stepfamily revealed that the children were at greater risk for experiencing higher levels of externalizing problems (Coleman et al., 2000). However, recent finding show reductions in the level of externalizing problems (Collishaw, Goodman, Pickles, & Maughan, 2007), although children in stepmother families and those in complex stepfamilies (with half-siblings and or stepsiblings) are at greatest risk (Tillman, 2008) for these behaviors. As noted, research shows that "cumulative family instability" (Sweeney, 2010, p. 674) is linked with behavior problems and early sexual involvement, early childbearing, and poorer academic outcomes (e.g., Bulanda & Manning, 2008; Fomby & Cherlin, 2007; Wu & Thomson, 2001); that is, those experiencing more transitions and other indicators of instability (e.g., low resources, homelessness) have the most problems.

Some evidence shows that positive stepparenting and being male (girls are at 2.5 times greater risk) can serve to buffer some of these negative outcomes (Hoffman, 2006; Rodgers & Rose, 2002; Willetts & Maroules, 2005). Research also shows that a high-quality relationship with both resident stepfathers and nonresident fathers is associated with better youth outcomes (King, 2006). The quality of the relationship with the stepparent is most influential and has the greatest effect when the stepfamily members have been together longer and the child's relationship with his or her mother is also of high quality (Yuan & Hamilton, 2006).

Regarding internalizing behavior problems, results from studies are mixed. Although earlier studies often showed that children in stepfamilies experience more internalizing problems than do children in other family structures (Coleman et al., 2000), more recent research shows that this negative outcome increases with more transitions, and more frequent transitions; greater sibling conflict and perception of unequal treatment; being in a stepfather versus stepmother family; and experiencing negative stepparenting (Saint-Jacques et al., 2006; Sweeney, 2007; Yuan, 2009).

Some of these negative outcomes may be explained by growing evidence that children in stepfamilies, who are exposed to and engage in higher levels of conflict with parents, stepparents, siblings, and stepsiblings, fare more poorly than those in families where conflict is controlled (Greeff & Du Toit, 2009; Yuan & Hamilton, 2006). Unlike children in first-marriage families in which threat and self-blame mediate the effects of parental conflict on child outcomes, children in stepfamilies are more affected by mother–stepfather conflict that results in rejecting and hostile parenting and stepparenting (Shelton et al., 2008).

EQUATING ADJUSTMENT WITH THE EXPERIENCE OF MOVING TO A FOREIGN COUNTRY

We draw from Pasley and Lee (2010) and liken the experience of adjusting to stepfamily life to moving to a foreign country; that is, having lived in a home country for some time (first family), knowledge of what is expected and how to follow rules is ingrained. There are specific roles to be filled and rules to guide actions and interactions with others on a daily basis. Becoming a member of a new stepfamily is similar to taking up residence in a new country, where people speak a different language, or the nuances of a shared language have different meanings, and a new set of rules, roles, laws, and customs must be learned. Even something as simple as food preference, scheduled mealtimes, and mealtime etiquette may be different. Commonly, breaking rules or showing insensitivity to customs out of ignorance can be problematic as newcomers attempt to thrive in the new environment.

Depending on the country and the prior preparations, the transition can be more or less challenging. For example, families moving from the United States to Canada might be expected to experience fewer challenges than families moving from the United States to China. Similarly, stepfamilies whose members have greater divides in family cultures would be expected to struggle more; however, we suggest that when stepfamilies are more meticulous and intentional about their preparation for and navigation of the transition and have strong communication and problem-solving skills, much of the struggle can be ameliorated.

Commonly, stepfamily members have unrealistic expectations regarding how their new life will be (Papernow, 2008), and the more unrealistic these expectations are, the more likely they are to experience "culture shock," a term used to describe the disorientation, anxiety, and feelings of loss that accompany the loss of one's customary culture and social rules (Winkleman, 1994). Members often lack knowledge about stepfamily life, expecting their experiences to be similar to those of their first-marriage families (Visher & Visher, 1996). Misguided expectations and lack of awareness of what is "normal" can be a source of conflict early on and may be perceived as a unique failure of their family rather than an expected part of the processes associated with making such huge cultural shifts. Not all members of new stepfamilies have the necessary foresight to know what to expect or how to prepare for change. Thus, information about strategies for easing the adjustment of these new stepfamilies follows.

STRATEGIES FOR EASING ADJUSTMENT

Importance of Research-Based Knowledge

From both quantitative and qualitative research on stepfamily life, it is clear that stepfamilies differ fundamentally from first-marriage families. Scholars have compiled lists of characteristics that are unique to stepfamilies (Ganong & Coleman, 2004). Examples include greater structural complexity, lack of common history among family members, incongruent family life cycles among members, and development of parent–child bonds prior to spousal bonds. Because working with stepfamilies requires an understanding of these key differences, it is essential that professionals have a solid background in the extant research as their foundation, especially within a therapeutic context. If professionals apply the same guiding principles with which they work with first-marriage families, they are likely to increase the stress and frustration noted by those seeking assistance. In fact, in findings from a study of 267 adults in stepfamilies' experiences in therapy, 13% reported that therapy had been unhelpful; of these, almost 74% commented that this was due to their therapist's lack of knowledge and skill for treating stepfamily issues or engendering trust and empathy (Pasley, Rhoden, Visher, & Visher, 1996). Furthermore, 73% sought therapy within the first 3 years of their marriage, when Papernow (2008) suggests harsh realities and unfulfilled fantasies and expectations are prominent.

The Value of Psychoeducation

We believe that psychoeducation is the best starting place for stepfamilies struggling primarily with challenges of normal transitional issues, such as exploring unrealistic or misguided expectations. A focus on normalizing the stepfamily experience, understanding the unique challenges and common themes in emerging stepfamily households, and/or having the opportunity to share these experiences with other members of stepfamilies can be beneficial for those who lack serious family problems. One of the most useful outcomes of psychoeducation is the relief that stepfamilies experience when they understand that their struggles are common and they are not alone. Without knowledge of such commonalities from the extant literature, professionals can set first-marriage family expectations as the standard. This can result in feelings of failure when stepfamily members' experiences do not measure up. Learning that some expectations do not fit for stepfamilies can depersonalize struggles and reduce the demoralization that many experience, giving stepfamily members a boost in self-esteem and confidence—all requisites for moving forward to meet other challenges.

Whether psychoeducation occurs within couple or family therapy sessions, group therapy intervention (Michaels, 2000), or as part of relationship education programs (see Adler-Baeder & Higginbotham, 2004), the primary foci should include normalizing, addressing common parenting and stepparenting issues, and exploring best ways to handle issues associated with "interested outsiders." We now discuss these foci and strategies for their implementation.

The Importance of Normalizing

Normalizing stepfamily experience gives members realistic expectations to replace their first-marriage family expectations. Exposure to how stepfamilies develop over time is a good place to start. For example, commonly stepfamily members have fantasies about a quick and easy adjustment early on, thinking that such an adjustment will help them to become indistinguishable from a first-marriage family. Resulting stress from unrealistic expectations often becomes apparent as children participate in two households and feel less accepting of a new stepparent who attempts to take charge or divert attention away from them.

Understanding that these are common experiences and common feelings can ease some of the associated stress for the couple and help to reduce blame and enhance empathy for one another. Visher and Visher (1996) suggested that genograms, an often used tool in therapy, are helpful to illustrate clearly the differences in family structure between first-time families and stepfamilies, thus influencing stepfamily expectations. Although discussions of expectations are best initiated early, and well before cohabitating, Bray and Kelly (1998) have suggested that spouses who continue to discuss expectations of stepfamily life and learn to share openly their disappointments are able to strengthen their couple bond and approach their challenges as a team.

As stepfamilies challenge unrealistic expectations, focus can be directed toward assisting members to understand the needs and perspective of each person. In part, understanding comes through shared experiences in which revised or newly negotiated values, rules, and cultural norms develop, or what Papernow (1996) calls the "middle ground." When there is thin middle ground between members, making decisions requires more negotiation, resolution of differences, or even "translation" before agreement is reached. The difference between first-marriage families and stepfamilies is the location of the thickest middle ground. In first-marriage families, the couple likely has had time to build and deepen their relationship prior to the birth of children. In stepfamilies, the parent–child relationship has the longest and richest shared history and, thus, thickest middle ground. Many of the common issues that stepfamilies inherently encounter develop due to this significant difference in structure. Again, normalizing this can help members to prepare better for handling the associated issues and find creative ways to thicken the middle ground for all.

Addressing Parenting and Stepparenting

Some stepchildren may never like being in a stepfamily, but establishing agreed-upon ground rules is necessary, so that daily family life is more harmonious and less stressful for everyone. This is especially important to emphasize when working with stepfamilies with adolescents. Some problems between adolescent stepchildren and stepparents may be stepfamily issues. Other problems that can be attributed to stepfamily dynamics are actually the result of common and expected adolescent developmental issues (Ganong & Coleman, 1994). For example, it is developmentally appropriate for adolescents to seek more autonomy, withdraw from their families, and even exhibit mild rebellious behaviors. Yet these behaviors may be viewed as pulling away from the new stepfamily and rebelling against the stepparent. Distinguishing between expected struggles in parenting adolescents and stepfamily adjustment is important and requires knowledge of both.

Relationships between stepparents and stepchildren significantly impact satisfaction of all family members and may carry the heaviest burden of unrealistic expectations. Whether coming from the parent, child, or stepparent, an expectation of instant love between stepparent and stepchild often leads to initial disappointment (Visher & Visher, 1996). When these fantasies do not materialize, the frustration and hurt can run deep, and normalizing this experience can help members understand their experiences. In fact, they may need help letting go of their old expectations before they are able to move onto building relationships that are more realistic and make sense based on what we know about stepfamily life.

Another source of stress from expectations is the extent of the disciplinarian role or limit-setting behaviors adopted by the stepparent. These expectations may differ among stepfamily members. Typically stepparents' attempts to assume some parental control are challenged by stepchildren, who are unwilling to accept the validity of their authority (Bray, 1999). These attempts are often undermined by the parent who wants to protect his or her child from undue stress. Building more middle ground between stepparents and stepchildren through befriending behaviors is a common recommendation before engaging in limit-setting behaviors (Pasley, Dollahite, & Ihinger-Tallman, 1993). Papernow (2008) argued that activities focusing on one-to-one time rather than "family" bonding time are also key, especially when these activities are of interest to the stepchild rather than something the stepparent wants to share (Ganong, Coleman, Fine, & Martin, 1999). The recommendation is that befriending should begin early during courtship and prior to cohabitation or remarriage (Visher & Visher, 1996), and this opportunity can be reduced when couples move quickly to cohabitation. Others suggest the importance of befriending adolescent stepchildren, because resistance to accepting the authority of a new stepparent is common (Ganong & Coleman, 1994; Hetherington & Kelly, 2002). However, it is clear that significant bonding between possible future stepparents and children takes a good deal of time (Ganong et al., 1999).

Coupled with befriending, stepparents can assume a monitoring role (Bray & Kelly, 1998; Hetherington & Kelly, 2002) and take a more active role in parenting decisions behind the scenes, so the couple presents a growing united front to the children. Pasley and associates (1993) discussed adopting a "sitter posture," in which the stepparent "monitors or supervises the child's behavior" and "directs disciplinary action to the parent" (p. 319). For example, a stepparent might be coached to say, "Your mother wants your room picked up, and I'm here to make sure her wishes are followed." Such behaviors allow for the gradual introduction of the stepparent into the parenting process, especially when limit setting is necessary and often a source of conflict.

Communication about parenting issues can be an especially sensitive topic for some couples, who can benefit from practicing skills to address this respectfully and with compassion and empathy for the other's position. Some of this sensitivity stems from the tension associated with discrepancies between the needs and expectations of the parent regarding appropriate parenting behaviors and the actual comfort level and skills of the stepparent (Svare, Jay, & Mason, 2004). When adults are not parents and lack significant exposure to children, they can be unaware of what to expect of children at different developmental stages. Unnecessary frustration results when stepparenting or discipline is unsuccessful for these reasons. These stepparents may benefit from parenting classes, groups, or books on child development (Ganong, Coleman, & Weaver, 2002).

Because stepparent–stepchild relationship quality has a considerable impact on the quality of stepfamily life overall and the martial relationship specifically, it remains important to build the couple relationship (Papernow, 2008). Uncommonly, the couple relationship competes with the strength of the parent–child relationship, so couples are encouraged early on to carve out time for their relationship to thicken their middle ground and form a solid unit to better withstand the challenges of stepfamily life. Suggestions vary on how best to accomplished this, but they often include initiating a "date night" ritual in which the couple routinely sets aside a specific and regular time to spend alone. Separate time to discuss important family or other issues can also be established to focus the couple's energy on handling difficult issues and working on problem solving. Also, because of the challenges in resolving conflict and communicating effectively, interventions with stepfamily couples that focus on effective communication skills to decrease negativity without increasing avoidance may be beneficial (Whitton, Nicholson, & Markman, 2008). Techniques (e.g., learning to approach difficult subjects with a "soft start-up"; Gottman, 1999; Papernow, 2008) can help couples in stepfamilies feel less overwhelmed by the idea of attempting to resolve conflict.

Handling Multiple "Interested Outsiders"

Initially stepparents report feeling like an "outsider"—an experience often associated with loneliness and isolation in the family. Parents also struggle with their experience of being an "insider," overwhelmed by loyalty conflicts as they address the needs of their children and those of their new spouse or partner (Pasley & Lee, 2010). Early in stepfamily formation, relationship building is best done primarily within dyads, or one-on-one between members of dyads. However, as the connection between new family members grows and the middle ground thickens, building a sense of "we-ness" or stepfamily identity is important.

Coaching stepfamily members to create new rituals or family traditions is an effective strategy to foster family identity (Bray & Kelly, 1998; Visher & Visher, 1996). Some rituals may begin effortlessly and stem from family members' one-on-one time. For example, a stepparent may start by assisting the stepchild to build model cars, with the intent to learn about one another; this then becomes something they continue to do regularly. Other rituals, such as a family meetings or game nights, might be initiated. Encouraging members to think creatively and to reconsider related rules (e.g., "We always celebrate birthdays with a cake") can assist them in being less rigid with new rituals. Creating shared rituals in a gradual manner that includes parent, children, and stepparent can help to ease the feelings associated with being in the insider/outsider position.

Part of the stress associated with being an outsider results from coparenting by stepparents (a symbolic outsider) and nonresident biological parent (an actual outsider to the residential household). Stepfamilies are often influenced by the "other household" to which stepchildren belong (Visher & Visher, 1996). Even stepfamilies with amicable arrangements and friendly coparenting relationships may feel frustrated by the loss of control over their family life. Thus, children's nonresident parent inevitably exerts some influence on stepfamily life, even if he or she is deceased, increasing a sense of helplessness and discouragement among members of the new family. These feelings are exacerbated when relationships across households are volatile, making even simple tasks feel impossible (e.g., deciding on a drop-off time and location). When such relationships are strained, a good strategy is restricting contact between the adults to necessary communications about the logistics of visits and schedules. In fact, Papernow (2008) used the metaphor of a "Dutch door," in which the bottom half of the door remains closed to establish a firm boundary between families, and the top half remains open only for these essential communications about children.

Issues with the other household can cause immense strain for stepfamilies. When the formation of a stepfamily follows a hurtful divorce or breakup, interactions with the former partner and his or her household can be especially difficult due to unresolved feelings of loss, hurt, and betrayal. There is ample evidence that relationships between former spouses that remain volatile negatively affect children (Ahrons, 2007) and their stepfamily adjustment by intensifying loyalty conflicts. It is sometimes possible to improve these relationships by eliminating unnecessary contact and coming to an agreement about how coparenting will occur. Both of these approaches require parents' participation, if these changes are to be successful. Sometimes such issues escalate, and therapy or mediation becomes essential as family members work toward accepting the difficulty of the situation and learning how to cope better within their own household rather than continue their attempts to change the other household.

WHEN TO MOVE FROM PSYCHOEDUCATION TO THERAPY

Competent interpersonal communication is necessary to meet common stepfamily challenges and successfully navigate the adjustment process. When stepfamilies become stuck or mired in repetitive negative interactions, this often indicates a need to move from psychoeducation to therapy (Ganong et al., 2002). When underdeveloped interpersonal skills are not the culprit, intrapsychic issues may halt progress in adjustment, and therapy is warranted (Papernow, 2008). Moreover, stepfamily members who have a difficult time within a particular issue or specific interpersonal communication skill often struggle with deeper feelings of hurt, isolation, or fear that go beyond the scope of basic psychoeducation and skills training. Depending on the depth of the intrapsychic issues, it can be helpful to work in individual sessions so a spouse can explore the issues without fear of saying something hurtful in front of his or her partner or children. Once the individual who is struggling with an intrapsychic issue better understands the source and the associated behavior pattern, the therapist can guide the sharing of any new insights with the partner in a couple session.

The Value of Subsystems Therapy

Key to assessing stepfamilies is clinicians' ability to distinguish between normal issues of stepfamily dynamics and underlying clinical issues that exist within the family or individuals in the family. Much of what is often done in therapy is psychoeducation rather than treatment of serious intrapersonal issues. However, we believe, as do others (Browning & Artelt, in press; Papernow, 2008; Visher & Visher, 1996), that successful therapy with stepfamilies differs not only in *what* is done during sessions but also *how* the process is structured. As such, the overall structure of therapy must take into account differences between stepfamilies and first families.

Many therapists who work with families are trained in systems theory (Ackerman, 1970), in which a first tenet is to do therapy with all members of the system so as to view the entire system and increase the intensity of therapy (Minuchin, 1974). Browning (1994) convincingly argued that adhering to this traditional model of family therapy and assessment with stepfamilies is problematic in two ways. First, it further reinforces the myth that stepfamilies are not different than first-marriage families. Second, because stepfamilies seeking professional help often experience intense conflict, likely lack requisite skills, and have weak emotional bonds, they are less able to withstand increased intensity or the associated potent emotional experience.

Fundamentally, stepfamilies are made up of subgroups, with relationships that often rely on the boundaries defining them to manage early stepfamily life. Beginning with the smallest possible subsystem (preferably the couple) and addressing its specific concerns is needed before adding others (Browning & Artelt, in press; Visher & Visher, 1996). Contrary to suggestions found in early writings on therapy with remarried families (e.g., Sager et al., 1983), we now understand that couple therapy is a necessary first step, even during the initial evaluation sessions, because once comments are shared in therapy, they cannot be taken back, and stepfamilies entering therapy can be fragile.

The idea of seeing subsystems and purposefully completing the evaluation of a stepfamily without all family members present may seem contrary to what many therapists are trained to do. In part, systems therapy is based on the idea that therapists will not be able understand the overall dynamics of a family and its problems without seeing therapy unfold with all members in attendance. Further, the assumption is that there is no way of knowing how and when change needs to happen without this group process. However,

Visher and Visher (1996) pointed out that a couple is often unable or unwilling to discuss certain issues with stepchildren present, so seeing the partners alone can actually benefit the evaluation process by allowing them to speak freely, perhaps for the first time, about their stepfamily issues without children hearing.

CONCLUSIONS

Remarriage and stepfamilies are not new to family structures, although some recent variations are (e.g., cohabiting stepfamilies). The extant literature about the nature of these families has grown considerably since first appearing in the 1980s decade reviews published in the *Journal of Marriage and Family* (see Macklin, 1980; Price-Bonham & Balswick, 1980). Furthermore, the quality of the empirical literature has improved greatly, so we have more confidence in the findings.

Much of the stress and the feelings of frustration and helplessness that bring stepfamilies into therapy can be ameliorated through the psychoeducation described here. Part of that reeducation, however, also includes helping families prioritize their issues and differentiate what can be changed from what cannot. Although identified as common stressors and experiences, not all stepfamily issues necessarily need to change for family members to feel satisfied and fulfilled.

For those interesting in working with these families in professional settings where psychoeducation and family therapy occur, there is limited evidence regarding best practices (see Nicholson, Sanders, Halford, Phillips, & Whitton, 2008; Whitton et al., 2008). Yet those noted for their successful work with these families offer valuable recommendations, many of which are noted here. As we move forward, we encourage testing their recommendations in systematic ways so that best practices become a reality for stepfamilies in their various forms.

REFERENCES

Ackerman, N. W. (1970). *Family process*. New York: Basic Books.

Adamsons, K., O'Brien, M., & Pasley, K. (2007). An ecological approach to father involvement in biological and stepfather families. *Fathering, 5*, 129–147.

Adler-Baeder, F., & Higginbotham, B. (2004). Implications of remarriage and stepfamily formation for marriage education. *Family Relations, 53*, 448–459.

Afifi, T. D. (2008). Communication in stepfamilies. In J. Pryor (Ed.), *The international handbook of stepfamilies: Policy and practice in legal, research, and clinical environments* (pp. 299–322). Hoboken, NJ: Wiley.

Ahrons, C. R. (2007). Family ties after divorce: Long-term implications for children. *Family Process, 46*, 53–65.

Allen, E. S., Baucom, D. H., Burnett, C. K., Epstein, N., & Rankin-Esquer, L. A.

(2001). Decision-making power, autonomy, and communication in remarried spouses compared with first-married spouses. *Family Relations, 50,* 326–334.

Amato, P. R. (1994). The implication of research findings on children in stepfamilies. In A. Booth & J. Dunn (Eds.), *Stepfamilies: Who benefits? Who does not?* (pp. 81–88). Hillsdale, NJ: Erlbaum.

Amato, P. R. (2010). Research on divorce: Continuing trends and new developments. *Journal of Marriage and Family, 72,* 650–666.

Amato, P. R., Meyers, C. E., & Emery, R. E. (2009). Changes in nonresident father–child contact from 1976 to 2002. *Family Relations, 58,* 41–53.

Beaudry, M., Boisvert, J. M., Simard, M., Parent, C., & Blais, M. C. (2004). Communication: A key component to meeting the challenges of stepfamilies. *Journal of Divorce & Remarriage, 42*(1–2), 85–104.

Berger, L. M., Carlson, M. J., Bzostek, S. H., & Osborne, C. (2008). Parenting practices of resident fathers: The role of marital and biological ties. *Journal of Marriage and Family, 70,* 625–639.

Bramlett, M. D., & Mosher, W. D. (2002). *Cohabitation, marriage, divorce, and remarriage in the United States* [Vital and Health Statistics, 23(22)]. Washington, DC: National Center for Health Statistics.

Bray, J. (1999). From marriage to remarriage and beyond. In E.M. Hetherington (Ed.), *Coping with divorce, single parenting, and remarriage* (pp. 253–271). Mahwah, NJ: Erlbaum.

Bray, J. H., & Kelly, J. (1998). *Stepfamilies: Love, marriage, and parenting in the first decade.* New York: Broadway.

Brown, S. L., Lee, G. R., & Bulanda, J. R. (2006). Cohabitation among older adults: A national portrait. *Journals of Gerontology B: Psychological Sciences and Social Sciences, 61,* S71–S79.

Brown, S. L., & Manning, W. D. (2009). Family boundary ambiguity and the measurement of family structure. *Demography, 46,* 85–101.

Browning, S. (1994). Treating stepfamilies: Alternatives to traditional family therapy. In K. Pasley & M. Ihinger-Tallman (Eds.), *Steppareting: Issues in theory, research, and practice* (pp. 175–197). Westport, CT: Praeger.

Browning, S., & Artelt, E. (in press). *Stepfamily therapy: A 10-step clinical approach.* Washington, DC: American Psychological Association.

Bulanda, R. E., & Manning, W. D. (2008). Parental cohabitation experiences and adolescent behavioral outcomes. *Population Research and Policy Review, 27,* 593–618.

Carlson, M. J., & Furstenberg, F. (2006). The prevalence and correlates of multipartnered fertility among urban U.S. parents. *Journal of Marriage and Family, 68,* 718–732.

Cherlin, A. J. (2010). Demographic trends in the United States: A review of research in the 2000s. *Journal of Marriage and Family, 72,* 403–419.

Clapp, G. (2000). Divorce and new beginnings: *A complete guide to recovery, solo parenting, co-parenting and stepfamilies* (2nd ed., pp. 307–343). New York: Wiley.

Coleman, M., Fine, M. A., Ganong, L. H., Downs, K. J. M., & Pauk, N. (2001). When you're not the Brady Bunch: Identifying perceived conflicts and resolution strategies in stepfamilies. *Personal Relationships, 8,* 55–73.

Coleman, M., & Ganong, L. H. (1990). The uses of juvenile fiction and selfhelp books with stepfamilies. *Journal of Counseling and Development, 68,* 327–331.

Coleman, M., Ganong, L., & Fine, M. (2000). Reinvestigating remarriage: Another decade of progress. *Journal of Marriage and the Family, 62,* 1288–1307.

Coleman, M., Troilo, J., & Jamison, T. (2008). The diversity of stepmothers: The influences of stigma, gender, and context on stepmother identities. In J. Pryor (Eds.), *The international handbook of stepfamilies: Policy and practice in legal, research, and clinical environments* (pp. 369–393). Hoboken, NJ: Wiley.

Collishaw, S., Goodman, R., Pickles, A., & Maughan, B. (2007). Modeling the contribution of changes in family life to time trends in adolescent conduct problems. *Social Science & Medicine, 65,* 252–287.

Dunn, J., Cheng, H., O'Connor, T. G., & Bridges, L. (2004). Children's perspectives on their relationships with their nonresident fathers: Influences, outcomes, and implications. *Journal of Child Psychology and Psychiatry, 4,* 553–566.

Dunn, J., O'Connor, T. G., & Cheng, H. (2005). Children's responses to conflict between their different parents: Mothers, stepfathers, nonresident fathers, and nonresident stepmothers. *Journal of Clinical Child and Adolescent Psychology, 34,* 223–234.

Falci, C. (2006). Family structure, closeness to residential and nonresidential parents, and psychological distress in early and middle adolescence. *Sociological Quarterly, 47,* 123–146.

Feinberg, M. E., Kan, M. L., & Hetherington, E. M. (2007). The longitudinal influence of coparenting conflict on parental negativity and adolescent maladjustment. *Journal of Marriage and Family, 69,* 687–702.

Fisher, P., Leve, L., O'Leary, C., & Leve, C. (2003). Parental monitoring of children's behavior: Variations across stepmother, stepfather, and two-parent biological families. *Family Relations, 52,* 45–52.

Flouri, E., Buchanan, A., & Bream, V. (2002). Adolescents' perceptions of their fathers' involvement: Significance to school attitudes. *Psychology in the Schools, 39,* 575–582.

Fomby, P., & Cherlin, A. J. (2007). Family instability and child well-being. *American Sociological Review, 72,* 181–204.

Ganong, L, H., & Coleman, M. (1994). Adolescent stepchild–stepparent relationships: Changes over time. In K. Pasley & M. Ihinger-Tallman (Eds.), *Stepparenting: Issues in theory, research, and practice* (pp. 87–104).Westport, CT: Praeger.

Ganong, L. H., & Coleman, M. (2004). *Stepfamily relationships: Development, dynamics, and interventions.* New York: Kluwer Academic/Plenum.

Ganong, L., Coleman, M., Fine, M., & Martin, P. (1999). Stepparent's affinity-seeking and affinity-maintaining strategies with stepchildren. *Journal of Family Issues, 20,* 299–327.

Ganong, L., Coleman, M., & Hans, J. D. (2006). Divorce as prelude to stepfamily living and the consequences of redivorce. In M. A. Fine & J. H. Harvey (Eds.), *Handbook of divorce and relationship dissolution* (pp. 409–434). Mahwah, NJ: Erlbaum.

Ganong, L. H., Coleman, M., & Weaver, S. (2002). Relationship maintenance and enhancement in stepfamilies: Clinical applications. In J. H. Harvey & A. Wenzel (Eds.), *A clinician's guide to maintaining and enhancing close relationships* (pp. 105–129). Mahwah, NJ: Erlbaum.

Goldscheider, F., Kaufman, G., & Sassler, S. (2009). Navigating the "new" marriage market: How attitudes toward partner characteristics shape union formation. *Journal of Family Issues, 30,* 719–737.

Goldscheider, F., & Sassler, S. (2006). Creating stepfamilies: Integrating children into the study of union formation. *Journal of Marriage and Family, 68*, 275–291.

Golish, T. (2003). Stepfamily communication strengths: Understanding the ties that bind. *Human Communication Research, 29*, 41–80.

Golish, T., & Caughlin, J. (2002). "I'd rather not talk about it": Adolescents' and young adults' use of topic avoidance in stepfamilies. *Journal of Applied Communication Research, 30*, 78–106.

Gosselin, J., & David, H. (2007). Risk and resilience factors linked with the psychosocial adjustment of adolescents, stepparents, and biological parents. *Journal of Divorce & Remarriage, 48*(1–2), 29–53.

Gottman, J. M. (1999). *The marriage clinic: A scientifically based marital therapy.* New York: Norton.

Greeff, A. P., & Du Toit, C. D. (2009). Resilience in remarried families. *American Journal of Family Therapy, 37*, 114–126.

Gunnoe, M. L., & Hetherington, E. M. (2004). Stepchildren's perceptions of noncustodial mothers and noncustodial fathers: Differences in socioemotional involvement and associations with adolescent adjustment problems. *Journal of Family Psychology, 18*, 555–563.

Halford, K., Nicholson, J., & Sanders, M. (2007). Couple communication in stepfamilies. *Family Process, 46*, 471–483.

Hawkins, D. N., Amato, P. R., & King, V. (2007). Nonresident father involvement and adolescent well-being: Father effects of child effects? *American Sociological Review, 72*, 990–1010.

Heard, H. E. (2007). Fathers, mothers, and family structure: Family trajectories, parent gender, and adolescent schooling. *Journal of Marriage and Family, 69*, 435–450.

Henry, P. J., & McCue, J. (2009). The experience of nonresidential stepmothers. *Journal of Divorce & Remarriage, 50*, 185–205.

Hetherington, E. M., & Kelly, J. (2002). *For better or worse: Divorce reconsidered.* New York: Norton.

Higginbotham, B. J., & Felix, D. (2009). Economic predictors of marital quality among newly remarried rural and urban couples. *Family Science Review, 14*, 18–30.

Hobart, C. W. (1991). Conflict in remarriages. *Journal of Divorce & Remarriage, 15*(3–4), 69–86.

Hoffmann, J. P. (2006). Family structure, community context, and adolescent problem behaviors. *Journal of Youth and Adolescence, 35*, 867–880.

Hughes, M. H., & Waite, L. J. (2009). Marital biography and health at mid-life. *Journal of Health and Social Behavior, 50*, 344–358.

Jeynes, W. H. (2006). The impact of parental remarriage on children: A meta-analysis. *Marriage & Family Review, 40*, 75–98.

Johnson, A. J., Wright, K. B., Craig, E. A., Gilchrist, E. S., Lane, L. T., & Haigh, M. M. (2008). A model for predicting stress levels and marital satisfaction for stepmothers utilizing a stress and coping approach. *Journal of Social and Personal Relationships, 25*, 119–142.

Juby, H., Billette, J. M., Laplante, B., & Le Bourdais, C. (2007). Nonresident fathers and children: Parents' new unions and frequency of contact. *Journal of Family Issues, 28*, 1120–1245.

King, V. (2006). The antecedents and consequences of adolescents' relationships with stepfathers and nonresident fathers. *Journal of Marriage and Family, 68*, 910–928.

King, V. (2007). When children have two mothers: Relationships with nonresident mothers, stepmothers, and fathers. *Journal of Marriage and the Family, 69*, 1178–1193.

Kreider, R. M. (2005). *Numbering, timing, and duration of marriages and divorces: 2001* (Current Population Reports, P70-97). Washington, DC: U.S. Bureau of the Census.

Kreider, R. M. (2008). *Living arrangements of children: 2004* (Current Population Reports, P70-114). Washington, DC: U.S. Bureau of the Census.

Kurdek, L. A. (1991). The relations between reported wellbeing and divorce history, availability of a proximate adult, and gender. *Journal of Marriage and the Family, 52*, 81–85.

MacDonald, W., & DeMaris, A. (2002). Stepfather–stepchild relationship quality: The stepfather's demand for conformity and the biological father's involvement. *Journal of Family Issues, 23*, 121–137.

Macklin, E. D. (1980). Nontraditional family forms: A decade of research. *Journal of Marriage and the Family, 42*, 905–922.

Marsiglio, W. (2004). When stepfathers claim stepchildren: A conceptual analysis. *Journal of Marriage and Family, 66*, 22–39.

Marsiglio, W., & Hinojosa, R. (2008). Managing the multifather family: Stepfathers as father allies. *Journal of Marriage and Family, 69*, 845–862.

Michaels, M. L. (2000). The stepfamily enrichment program: A preliminary evaluation using focus groups. *American Journal of Family Therapy, 28*, 61–73.

Minuchin, S. (1974). *Families and family therapy.* Cambridge, MA: Harvard University Press.

Moore, S., & Cartwright, C. (2005). Adolescents' and young adults' expectations of parental responsibilities in stepfamilies. *Journal of Divorce & Remarriage, 43*(3–4), 109–127.

Nicholson, J. M., Sanders, M. R., Halford, W. K., Phillips, M., & Whitton, S. W. (2008). The prevention and treatment of children's adjustment problems in stepfamilies. In J. Pryor (Ed.), *The international handbook of stepfamilies: Policy and practice in legal, research, and clinical environments* (pp. 485–521). Hoboken, NJ: Wiley.

Papernow, P. (1996). *Becoming a stepfamily: Patterns of development in remarried families.* Hillsdale, NJ: Analytic Press.

Papernow, P. L. (2008). A clinician's view of "stepfamily architecture": Strategies for meeting the challenges. In J. Pryor (Ed.), *The international handbook of stepfamilies* (pp. 423–454). Hoboken, NJ: Wiley.

Pasley, K., Dollahite, D., & Ihinger-Tallman, M. (1993). Bridging the gap: Clinical applications of research findings on the spouse and stepparent roles in remarriage. *Family Relations, 42*, 315–322.

Pasley, K., & Lee, M. (2010). Stress and coping within the context of stepfamily life. In S. J. Price, C. A. Price, & P. C. McKenry (Eds.), *Families and change: Coping with stressful events and transitions* (4th ed., pp. 235–261). Thousand Oaks, CA: Sage.

Pasley, K., & Moorefield, B. (2004). Stepfamilies: Changes and challenges. In M. Coleman & L. Ganong (Eds.), *Handbook of contemporary families: Considering the past, contemplating the future* (pp. 317–330). Thousand Oaks, CA; Sage.

Pasley, K., Rhoden, L., Visher, E. J., & Visher, J. S. (1996). Successful stepfamily therapy: Clients' perspectives. *Journal of Marital and Family Therapy, 22,* 343–357.

Poortman, A. R., & Lyngstad, T. H. (2007). Dissolution risks in first and higher order marital and cohabiting unions. *Social Science Research, 36,* 1431–1446.

PriceBonham, S., & Balswick, J. O. (1980). The noninstitutions: Divorce, desertion, and remarriage. *Journal of Marriage and the Family, 42,* 959–972.

Rhoades, G. K., Stanley, S. M., & Markman, H. J. (2006). Pre-engagement cohabitation and gender asymmetry in marital commitment. *Journal of Family Psychology, 20,* 553–560.

Robertson, J. (2008). Stepfathers in families. In J. Pryor (Ed.), *The international handbook of stepfamilies: Policy and practice in legal, research, and clinical environments* (pp. 125–150). Hoboken, NJ: Wiley.

Rodgers, K., & Rose, H. (2002). Risk and resiliency factors among adolescents who experience marital transitions. *Journal of Marriage and Family, 64,* 1024–1037.

Sager, C. J., Brown, H. S., Crohn, H., Engel, T., Rodestein, E., & Walker, L. (1983). *Treating the remarried family.* New York: Brunner/Mazel.

Saint-Jacques, M. C., Cloutier, R., Pauzé, R., Sinard, M., Gagné, M., & Poulin, A. (2006). The impact of serial transitions on behavioral and psychological problems among children in child protection services. *Child Welfare, 85,* 941–964.

Schmeeckle, M. (2007). Gender dynamics in stepfamilies: Adult stepchildren's views. *Journal of Marriage and Family, 69,* 174–189.

Shelton, K. H., Walters, S. L., & Harold, G. T. (2008). Children's appraisals of relationships in stepfamilies and first families. In J. Pryor (Ed.), *The international handbook of stepfamilies: Policy and practice in legal, research, and clinical environments* (pp. 250–276). Hoboken, NJ: Wiley.

Stanley, S. M., Markman, H. J., & Whitton, S. (2002). Communication, conflict, and commitment: Insights on the foundation for relationships success from a national survey. *Family Process, 41,* 659–675.

Stewart, S. D. (1999). Nonresident mothers' and fathers' social contact with children. *Journal of Marriage and the Family, 61,* 894–907.

Stewart, S. D. (2005). How the birth of a child affects involvement with stepchildren. *Journal of Marriage and Family, 67,* 461–473.

Stewart, S., Manning, W., & Smock, P. (2003). Union formation among men in the U.S.: Does having prior children matter? *Journal of Marriage and Family, 65,* 90–104.

Svare, G. M., Jay, S., & Mason, M. A. (2004). Stepparents on stepparenting: An exploratory study of stepparenting approaches. *Journal of Divorce & Remarriage, 41*(3–4), 81–97.

Sweeney, M. M. (2007). Stepfather families and the emotional well-being of adolescents. *Journal of Health and Social Behavior, 48,* 33–49.

Sweeney, M. M. (2010). Remarriage and stepfamilies: Strategic sites for family scholarship in the 21st century. *Journal of Marriage and Family, 72,* 667–684.

Sweeney, M. M., Wang, H., & Videon, T. M. (2009). Reconsidering the association between stepfather families and adolescent well-being. In H. E. Peters & C. M. Dush (Eds.), *Marriage and family: Perspectives and complexities* (pp. 177–225). New York: Columbia University Press.

Teachman, T. (2008). The living arrangements of children and their educational well-being. *Journal of Family Issues, 29,* 734–761.

Teachman, J., & Tedrow, L. (2008). The demography of stepfamilies in the United States. In J. Pryor (Ed.), *The international handbook of stepfamilies: Policy and practice in legal, research, and clinical environments* (pp. 3–29). Hoboken, NJ: Wiley.

Tillman, K. H. (2008). "Non-traditional" siblings and the academic outcomes of adolescents. *Social Science Research, 37,* 88–108.

van Eeden-Moorefield, B., & Pasley, K. (2008). A longitudinal examination of marital processes leading to instability in remarriages and stepfamilies. In J. Pryor (Ed.), *The international handbook of stepfamilies: Policy and practice in legal, research, and clinical environments* (pp. 231–249). Hoboken, NJ: Wiley.

Visher, E. B., & Visher, J. S. (1996). *Therapy with stepfamilies.* New York: Brunner/ Mazel.

Weaver, S. E., & Coleman, M. (2005). A mothering but not a mother role: A grounded theory study of the nonresidential stepmother role. *Journal of Social and Personal Relationships, 22,* 477–497.

Whitton, S. W., Nicholson, J. M., & Markman, H. J. (2008). Research on interventions with stepfamily couples. In J. Pryor (Ed.), *The international handbook of stepfamilies: Policy and practice in legal, research, and clinical environments* (pp. 455–484). Hoboken, NJ: Wiley.

Willetts, M. C., & Maroules, N. G. (2005). Parental reports of adolescent well-being: Does marital status matter? *Journal of Divorce & Remarriage, 43*(1–2), 129–148.

Winkelman, M. (1994). Culture shock and adaptation. *Journal of Counseling and Development, 73,* 121–126.

Wu, L. L., & Thomson, E. (2001). Race differences in family experience and early sexual initiation: Dynamic models of family structure and family change. *Journal of Marriage and Family, 63,* 682–696.

Xu, X., Hudspeth, C. D., & Bartkowski, J. P. (2006). The role of cohabitation in remarriage. *Journal of Marriage and Family, 68,* 261–274.

Yuan, A. S. V. (2009). Sibling relationships and adolescents' mental health. *Journal of Family Issues, 30,* 1221–1244.

Yuan, A. S. V., & Hamilton, H. A. (2006). Stepfather involvement in adolescent well-being: Do mothers and nonresidential fathers matter? *Journal of Family Issues, 27,* 1191–1213.

CHAPTER 8

GAY AND LESBIAN FAMILY LIFE
Risk, Resilience, and Rising Expectations

ROBERT-JAY GREEN

I magine a society in which for over 200 years:

- Heterosexuals were forbidden from having any kind of romantic love relationships and prohibited from getting married.
- Their sexual relationships were illegal and punishable by incarceration or death.
- They were denied employment or fired merely for being heterosexual.
- They were ostracized from their families, peer groups, and religious communities if their heterosexuality became known.

Given the above scenario, in what shape would heterosexuals' relationships be now? In what shape would the entire society be now?

I offer this analogy to help readers understand that much of what is unique about gay and lesbian family life is an outgrowth of the historical context in which the majority of lesbian, gay, bisexual, and transgender (LGBT) people were born and came of age in American society.[1] These social constraints dominated the lives and relationships of gay and lesbian people throughout recorded history in most societies worldwide, and laws codifying them remained in force in various parts of the United States until as recently as 2003, when the Supreme Court finally decriminalized homosexuality. In fact, with that decriminalization and the advent of same-sex marriage in several states since 2004, large numbers of gay and lesbian people in the United States have literally gone from being "outlaws" to "in-laws" in their lifetimes.

Despite recent signs of equal treatment as this chapter is being written (June, 2011), major obstacles threatening the success of lesbian and gay family relationships still remain:

• *Employment discrimination.* In most states and under the federal statutes governing employment, gay and lesbian people still are not protected from arbitrary discrimination in employment, housing, public accommodations, and credit. Thus, the majority of gays and lesbians in the United States have no legal recourse if they are denied loans, jobs, or housing, or are summarily fired by their employers simply for being gay or lesbian. Many social scientists and mental health professionals mistakenly seem to think gay and lesbian people are somehow protected from such discrimination under the federal Civil Rights Act in the same way that people are protected from discrimination based on race, gender, national origin, and religion. However, as of this writing, gays and lesbians have no legal protections against these forms of discrimination under federal law or in most states.

• *Bullying of gay and lesbian youth.* The vast majority of states still do not have laws protecting gay and lesbian youth from harassment and bullying in schools. The small group of states that do have such laws generally have very weak implementation and resort mainly to sending copies of the law to school superintendents, who may or may not do anything more with the information than send it on to school principals, who in turn may only file it away. The majority of self-identified gay and lesbian youth report significant levels of verbal harassment or physical bullying, with most of it occurring at school (D'Augelli, Grossman, & Starks, 2006).

• *Same-sex marriage and other legalized couple statuses in the United States.* As of June, 2011, only 6 states (Connecticut, Iowa, Massachusetts, New Hampshire, New York, and Vermont) and the District of Columbia have laws permitting same-sex marriages, whereas 44 states do not. Eight states provide broad recognition of same-sex relationships, affording them the same legal rights as marriages within the state. These include Delaware, Hawaii, Illinois, and New Jersey, which permit "civil unions" for same-sex couples as well as California, Nevada, Oregon, and Washington, which allow comprehensive "domestic partnerships" for same-sex couples. Another 4 states (Colorado, Maine, Wisconsin, and Maryland) provide more limited relationship recognition to same-sex couples. Of the 44 states that do not perform same-sex marriage, 41 expressly prohibit it either through state constitutional amendments or statutes defining marriage as being only between one man and one woman. Of 31 states that have held a public referendum on this issue, all have rejected same-sex marriage.

At the national level, the 1996 Defense of Marriage Act (DOMA) prevents the federal government of the United States from recognizing same-sex marriages performed anywhere. Among the most serious consequences of DOMA, surviving same-sex spouses or partners are denied the federal social security benefits and inheritance tax benefits (and for federal employees, pension benefits) that are granted to surviving heterosexual spouses. These exclusions place a large segment of the older gay and lesbian population at a disadvantage. The impact can be especially severe because many of them were "disowned" by their families of origin after coming out, and most do not have adult children who can help support them financially.

- *Parental custody rights.* The majority of states do not allow same-sex partners to adopt one another's biological children (so called "second-parent adoptions") regardless of how involved the nonbiological parents have been in planning for or raising their shared children since birth. In these states, the nonbiological parent and child are legal strangers to one another in the eyes of the law. This leaves the child in jeopardy of being taken into permanent state custody or of custody being given to family members other than the nonbiological parent if the child's biological parent dies or becomes incapacitated. Also in these families—even if the nonbiological parent has been functioning as the child's primary caregiver since birth—the nonbiological parent and child can legally be denied access to each other by the biological parent if the couple separates.

Our society is just now beginning to understand the psychological toll this context of discrimination has taken on gay and lesbian people and on their couple and family relationships. The impact can be seen not only in the most overt forms of persecution, such as social rejection, bullying, blackmail, firings, arrests, assaults, involuntary psychiatric placements to change sexual orientations, or murder. The long history of discrimination also has had an insidious effect in terms of unconscious repression of the self and of aspirations for the future. Older generations of gay and lesbian adults who internalized society's negative stereotypes felt unworthy of, and were unable even to imagine having, what society considered "normal" lives. Until only relatively recently, living as gay or lesbian meant having to enter a secret society that existed mostly at night, apart from the rest of society, and it remains that way in many rural and conservative communities.

The core of this chapter concerns the unique existential position of gay and lesbian people in American society and how that position influences child, couple, and family functioning. In the sections below, I first consider the concept of "normality" in a society characterized by discrimination from some quarters and acceptance from others. Then I describe gay and lesbian issues in the major "vectors" of family life: families of origin, same-sex couples, and lesbian and gay parents and their children. I conclude with some thoughts about "relational ambiguity" in the lives of gay and lesbian people, and the psychological impact of recent political events around same-sex marriage.

"NORMAL" IN SOCIOCULTURAL CONTEXT

"Normal" is in the eye of the beholder, and all beholders are in the grip of larger sociopolitical, religious, and cultural narratives that influence what they can see and how they interpret it (see Walsh, Chapter 1, and McGoldrick & Ashton, Chapter 11, this volume). As illustrated by the following real-world exchange between a mother and her gay son in the process of coming out, invoking the "normal" may also be a control strategy, a means of demanding compliance with heterocentric conceptions of the "good" and "true" way to be:

MOTHER: Don't you want to be *normal* like other people?

GAY SON: I don't really care about being "normal" like other people. My goal was never to be normal. I just want to be happy!

MOTHER: Well then how can you possibly be happy if you're not normal like other people? I just want you to be happy.

The term "normal" is thus a historically loaded one for many gay and lesbian people. Too often, it has been used against them by their families, workplaces, the courts, the health care system, organized religions, and mental health professionals. From the perspective of the social sciences and family systems theory, criteria for "normality" of a gay or lesbian individual or a same-sex relationship have to be defined in terms of effective coping or adaptation in a specific sociocultural niche at a particular point in history.

Since the early 1970s, the major American professional organizations in psychiatry, psychology, and social work have viewed being gay or lesbian as *a normal human variation*. Most of the national psychiatric associations in the Western hemisphere have followed suit. More recently, in 2001, the Chinese Psychiatric Association also removed homosexuality as a category of mental illness. The prevailing view of the psychiatric establishments in these countries is that homosexuality is an expectable variation in human populations, much like left-handedness, which characterizes a minority of the population. Just as left-handedness was regarded over the centuries as a sign of evil and possession by the devil (from Latin *sinestre* for left) and children were forced by parents and teachers to become right-handed, homosexuality is increasingly regarded not as an evil or an illness but as being within the normal range of human diversity.

There also is evidence that homosexual behavior exists throughout the animal kingdom, in species as varied as flocks of birds *and* flocks of human parishioners (Roselli & Balthazart, 2011). From an ethological perspective, being "opposed" to homosexuality (as some social commentators proudly proclaim themselves to be) is a little like being "opposed" to the migration of birds. Homosexuality and bisexuality have characterized a portion of the population in all human societies for all recorded time, and they always will. A degree of sexual orientation diversity is built into the species.

Most important is that having a same-sex relational orientation is not problematic in and of itself. It is "instinctive" and thus "normal" for the individuals who have such orientations, and ordinarily it is experienced as an integral, "natural" part of the self. Gay and lesbian people do not "decide" or "choose" their sexual orientations any more than heterosexuals "decide" to be heterosexual. People either intrinsically know or discover their sexual orientations through experience and reflection. Other people's intrusive reactions to this expectable human variation complicate the lives of gay and lesbian people.

In fact, the single common thread in the experience of gay and lesbian people is that they all are subject to some amount of antigay prejudice and discrimination in their environments. To the extent there is such a thing as a gay and lesbian "community" with its own cultural norms and behavior patterns, it evolved over many decades as part of a secret society that protected its members against physical, economic, legal, and social threats to survival and well-being. However, other than this shared vulnerability to discrimination, any two individuals within the gay and lesbian population may have no more in common with each other than any two heterosexual or left-handed individuals have in common with one another.

Most important to bear in mind is that there is enormous variability now in the exposure of gay and lesbian people to prejudice and discrimination depending on *when* the individuals were born (generational cohort), *where* they reside, and their *cultural group memberships* (including intersections of ethnic, racial, religious, and social class factors within a given society). It therefore has become much harder to make generalizations about the lives and relationships of gay and lesbian people, especially in a multicultural, pluralistic nation like the United States.

Over the last 10–15 years, most countries in Western Europe and many metropolitan areas of North America have become increasingly accepting of gay and lesbian people. Most other nations are still in great flux over their views of sexual orientation and gender identity (Smith, 2011). Some outcomes of these shifting attitudes have been unexpected, such as the introduction of legalized same-sex marriage in Spain, Portugal, and Mexico City, and of civil unions in Ireland and Colombia, all of whose populations are almost entirely Catholic (a religion whose hierarchical leadership denounces homosexual behavior as a sin).

Still, many gay and lesbian people in rural and immigrant communities in North America—and most gay and lesbian people throughout all of Asia, the Middle East, most of Latin America, most of Eastern Europe, and almost all of Africa—continue to lead entirely hidden lives, posing as heterosexual in public in order to *survive* physically and economically in their countries. In nations ruled by authoritarian governments (especially those with fundamentalist religious ideologies), gay and lesbian people often live in terror of state-sponsored executions officially mandated by laws and are vulnerable to uninvestigated "extrajudicial killings" and "disappearances" by government security forces, vigilante groups, and sometimes even family members who seek to remove the source of the family's "shame" by murdering a gay and lesbian offspring or sibling—so-called "honor" killings.

Over 76 countries worldwide officially continue to criminalize homosexuality.[2] In five countries, homosexuality is still a crime punishable by execution—Iran, Mauritania, Saudi Arabia, Sudan, and Yemen, plus some parts of Nigeria and Somalia. In many countries, the predominant coping strategy among gay and lesbian people is to get married to a person of the other sex and to remain completely closeted from one's family members and people in all other contexts except, perhaps, other trusted gay and lesbian individuals in very clandestine situations.

Thus, unlike certain Western European and North American middle-class contexts, where coming-out to family members and at work is frequently considered a sign of mental health, maturity, assertiveness, and "differentiation of self," coming out publicly in other countries is tantamount to committing physical or social suicide. It still is the case that most gay and lesbian people in the world are vulnerable to severe forms of discrimination throughout their entire lives, and only a minority of the world's gay and lesbian population is enjoying relative safety and acceptance. In this sense, the forms of persecution versus protection in an individual's social environment greatly influence what can be considered adaptive or "normal." One must guard against assuming that successful coping in one cultural niche can be generalized to others, even across subcultures within a given city.

RISING EXPECTATIONS

The American Community Survey of 2005 revealed approximately 776,943 same-sex couple households in the United States (Romero, Baumle, Badgett, & Gates, 2007). Among these cohabiting couples, approximately 20% were raising children, and the percentage of same-sex couples of color raising children was even higher (about one-third). In fact, most observers suspect that the number of same-sex couples in the United States may be much higher that the 2005 count, because respondents (especially those in more conservative areas of the country) may still have been reluctant at that time to reveal information about their sexual orientations to the U.S. Bureau of the Census. The recent 2010 U.S. Census counted same-sex marriages for the first time, and demographers are eagerly awaiting the results. Preliminary figures suggest a 50% increase in self-identified same sex couples between the 2000 and 2010 census (CNN, 2011).

What do gay and lesbian people want now in terms of public policies and their couple and family relationships for the future? In a survey of the legal and political priorities of 768 gay, lesbian, and bisexual people, Egan, Edelman, and Sherrill (2008) found interesting generational differences. For adults age 65 and older, highest priorities were *laws against hate crimes*, followed by *workplace discrimination protections*. However, for those ages 18–25, highest priorities were *marriage rights*, followed by *parental and adoption rights*. These findings seem to reflect the two age groups' different experiences historically.

When gay and lesbian people who are over age 65 first came out, it was inconceivable that marriage or parenting would be available to them, and their major concerns revolved around being physically harmed or fired from their jobs for being gay or lesbian. The younger generation, by contrast, seems to have taken a giant leap forward in terms of rising expectations for equality, striving for same-sex marriage rights and for the same opportunities to adopt or conceive children (via alternative insemination or surrogacy) that hetero-sexual married couples enjoy.

For example, in a study of gay and lesbian youth, D'Augelli, Rendina, Sinclaire, and Grossman (2007) interviewed 133 self-identified urban and suburban young people in the New York Metropolitan area (50 females, 83 males, ages 16–22; 42% Hispanic, 39% people of color). In this sample, 92% of the lesbian youth and 82% of gay male youth reported that they expected to be in a long-term monogamous relationship within 10 years. Furthermore, 78% of the lesbian youth and 61% of gay male youth said it was "very" or "extremely" likely they would marry a same-sex partner, if legally possible. In terms of parenting, 66% of the lesbian youth and 52% of the gay male youth said it was "very" or "extremely" likely they would be raising children in the future. These high percentages of youth anticipating marriage and parent-hood would have been unthinkable to older generations of gays and lesbians, who could not in their wildest dreams have imagined a time when such oppor-tunities would be available.

In this regard, despite indications of continuing prejudice and discrimi-nation against lesbian and gay people, there is abundant evidence of change in the direction of greater acceptance by Americans. For example, in a recent ABC News/Washington Post public opinion poll (Langer, 2011), 53% of the American public said that it should be legal for gay and lesbian couples to marry, and the trend in favor is rapidly accelerating for all demographic groups. Moreover, the recent polls are showing a strong effect of age, with about two-thirds of people younger than age 40 in favor of same-sex marriage and about two-thirds of those older than 50 opposed to same-sex marriage.

Despite a majority of Americans now saying that same-sex marriage should be legal, it is important to keep in mind that residents in the largest met-ropolitan areas of the United States tend to be more accepting of same-sex mar-riage than the rest of the country. The 53% majority of all Americans in favor of same-sex marriage is not reflected by similar majorities in any but a handful of states. Given that marriage laws are state-based, we are not likely to see same-sex marriage permitted in most states anytime soon, unless the Supreme Court of the United States rules that prohibitions on same-sex marriage violate the equal protection clause of the U.S. Constitution. In other opinion polling, there is recent evidence that most Americans (68%) now say their definition of "family" includes same-sex couples raising children (Crary, 2010).

Overall, it is clear that we are witnessing a gradual acceptance of gay and lesbian couple and family relations in the United States. This trend is likely to accelerate in the next 10–20 years as today's youth come of age. In light of these changes, we must ask, "If what one came out *to* as a gay or lesbian person in the past was a secret society of mostly single, childless adults liv-ing socially in the shadows of society, how will it shape the lives of American youth today to come out in a gay and lesbian community that is more integrated with the mainstream institutions of society, such as the public schools and the military?" How might an individual youth's expectations that she or he probably will marry a same-sex partner someday and raise children affect her or his self-image, career choices, risk-taking, and the gay and lesbian community's patterns of dating, "courtship," mate selection, relationship stability, and monogamy? What will the "new normal" look like for the relationships of gay and lesbian people in the United States?

FAMILIES OF ORIGIN

Unlike members of racial, ethnic, and religious minority groups, children who eventually self-identify as gay or lesbian rarely have parents or siblings who share their same sexual minority status. Being different from other family members in this fundamental way has a profound impact on the development of almost every gay and lesbian person. For example, because heterosexual parents have not suffered sexual orientation discrimination themselves, even the most well-meaning among them are unable to provide the level of insight and anticipatory socialization that would prepare their child to cope specifically with antigay prejudice or to resist internalizing that prejudice.

By contrast, when children and parents both identify as members of the same minority group (e.g., African Americans, Jews, Muslims), the children are directly taught—and parents model—ways to counter society's antipathy toward their group. Usually, minority parents and children are involved together in community institutions (often religious) that are instrumental in supporting children's development of a positive minority racial/ethnic identity, and parents take a very protective stance regarding their children's experiences of discrimination.

However, the parents of future gay or lesbian children ordinarily are not even aware of their child's sexual orientation and therefore are not likely to seek out community groups that would support the development of their child's positive gay or lesbian identity. In some cases, rather than protecting their child against antigay prejudice, parents and siblings become the main perpetrators of aggressive discrimination against a gay or lesbian youth. Instead of taking their child's side against prejudicial forces in the community and society at large, family members' own antigay attitudes and behavior can become the greatest threats leading to physical or sexual abuse or ejection of the child from the home. It is estimated, for example, that 40% of all homeless youth in the United States are LGBT, with many of them having been thrown out of their families' homes or leaving after suffering family harassment or abuse because of their different sexual orientations or gender identities.

In addition, large numbers of gay and lesbian adults in the United States, especially members of conservative religious families or immigrant families living in ethnic enclaves in the United States, still remain closeted from parents and other relatives with strong antigay attitudes. They often feel they must either distance from family members to maintain secret couple relationships or relinquish couple commitments in order to stay closely connected with their families.

As one illustration, a Mexican American lesbian born in the United States was not "out" to any of her family members, all of whom were born in rural Mexico. She was having serious problems in her couple relationship because of the large amount of time she was spending with these family members, and away from her partner. Just when she was strengthening her resolve to come out to her family, a 15-year-old male cousin remarked (in reaction to a television episode about gay people): "It's a good thing there are no gay Chicanos. They would be such a disgrace to our race!" This seemingly casual remark by a 15-year-old boy crushed her intent to come out to her family. The resulting loss of hope by her partner quickly led to dissolution of their relationship.

Similarly, most first-generation and many second-generation Asian American gays and lesbians do not come out to their parents, usually because they fear disappointing their parents and bringing shame to the family's reputation in the community. By the third generation after immigration, however, most Latino and Asian American offspring come out to their parents.

Although, in fact, the majority of parents in the United States do not completely reject their children after disclosure of sexual orientation, the level of acceptance offspring receive after coming out is highly variable and usually somewhat qualified (Herdt & Koff, 2000; Lasala, 2010; Savin-Williams, 2001; Stone-Fish & Harvey, 2005). Siblings tend to be told first, then mothers, and lastly fathers, which parallels the degree of acceptance gay and lesbian people tend to receive from these family members. Initially, family members tend to be more rejecting than accepting, and the longer term outcome tends to be more akin to "tolerance" rather than affirmative "acceptance." Fathers, in particular, tend to have difficulty accepting gay sons' sexual orientations, and mothers often find themselves in a go-between role. Ryan, Huebner, Diaz, and Sanchez (2009) found that even modest increases in family acceptance had a large positive impact on the mental health and substance use of gay and lesbian adolescents.

Against this backdrop of mixed reactions from family members, gay and lesbian people frequently turn to their friends for greater levels of mutual support and identification. Ideally, these friends and selected family members are woven together into a so-called "family of choice"—an interconnected system of emotional and instrumental support over time (Weston, 1991). However, because of the higher likelihood of discrimination from various segments of their social networks, gay and lesbian people risk having less cohesive social support systems than heterosexuals. They have to be much more deliberate in their efforts to build an integrated system of social support and a sense of "community" in their lives, which many heterosexuals find in their religious congregations and their extended families (Green & Mitchell, 2008). This is especially true for gay and lesbian immigrants from traditional cultures, gay and lesbian people of color, gay and lesbian interracial couples, and bisexual or transgender people. Members of these minority groups within the LGBT population often are subject to much higher levels of discrimination from their families and original communities, as well as from the majority white gay and lesbian community (Firestein, 2007; Fox, 2006; Laird & Green, 1996; and Lev, 2004, 2010).

SAME-SEX COUPLES

There is as much demographic and psychological diversity *within* the population of same-sex couples as there is within the population of heterosexual couples. In fact, knowing a couple's sexual orientation conveys much less information than is often assumed. In many respects, same-sex couples may be more like heterosexual couples of their same social class, religious, racial/ethnic, or occupational group than they are like same-sex couples from markedly different demographic groups, except for their common vulnerability to antigay prejudice.

Heterosexuality and homosexuality are *not* logical opposites. Counterposing one against the other inevitably exaggerates their differences and minimizes their commonalities. Both same-sex and other-sex orientations are most accurately viewed as variations on a continuum of attractions and potential for love relationships. Furthermore, regardless of their sexual orientation, nobody is attracted to "all males" or "all females." Thus, the term "sexual orientation" itself should rightfully be described as much more complex and fluid rather than reduced only to the biological sex of a desired partner or only to sexual as opposed to affiliative components of attraction. In fact, a more accurate term would be "sociosexual orientation" to connote closeness beyond purely sexual motivations.

Research directly comparing same-sex and heterosexual couples reveals they are remarkably similar to each other on most dimensions (Kurdek, 2004; Peplau & Fingerhut, 2007; Roisman, Clausell, Holland, Fortuna, & Elief, 2008; Rothblum, Balsam, & Solomon, 2008; Solomon, Rothblum, & Balsam, 2004, 2005). For example, regardless of the partners' sexual orientations, the same set of factors tends to predict relationship quality and relationship longevity across all types of couples: (1) placing more value on security, permanence, shared activities, and togetherness; (2) placing lower value on having separate activities and on personal autonomy; (3) higher expressiveness; (4) more perceived intrinsic rewards for being in the relationship; (5) fewer perceived attractive alternatives to the relationship; (6) more perceived barriers to ending the relationship; (7) less belief that disagreement is destructive; (8) higher trust in the partner—viewing the partner as dependable; (9) greater closeness and flexibility; (10) better problem-solving and conflict-negotiation skills; (11) higher shared/egalitarian decision making; and (12) greater perceived social support from sources outside the relationship.

However, group comparison studies also suggest that same-sex couples (especially lesbian couples) have an advantage in escaping the traditional gender role divisions that make for power imbalances and dissatisfaction in many heterosexual relationships. Although not perfectly equal, same-sex couples tend to be markedly more equal in division of household labor and decision-making power than are heterosexual couples (Gotta et al., 2011). Furthermore, in research by Green, Bettinger, and Zacks (1996), lesbian couples described themselves as emotionally closer than gay male couples who, in turn, described themselves as emotionally closer than heterosexual married couples. Lesbian couples also reported the most flexibility in the way they handled rules and roles in the relationship, whereas heterosexual couples reported the least flexibility. Overall, high levels of closeness and flexibility were reported by 79% of lesbian couples and 56% of gay male couples, but by only 8% of heterosexual married couples. In contrast to old clinical stereotypes based on traditional gender role theory, lesbian couples were not characterized by dysfunctional fusion nor were gay male couples characterized by disengagement.

Same-sex couples' greater equality also was confirmed in studies by Gottman, Levinson, Gross, et al. (2003; Gottman, Levenson, Swanson, et al., 2003). Based on observations of couples interacting in conflict situations, these scientists found that same-sex couples were better at resolving disagreements. They approached problems from a position of peer equality, using "softer" (less aggressive and accusatorial) initiation of conflict discussions and more humor during the discussion to avoid escalation of hostilities. With married heterosexual couples, the researchers observed much more of a power struggle, with one partner being invalidated by the other.

Other differences between lesbian, gay, and heterosexual couples have emerged in the research. Despite the evidence that same-sex couples may be functioning better than heterosexual couples in terms of closeness and equality within the relationship, same-sex relationships tend not to last as long as heterosexual marriages. For example, Green et al. (1996) found that even slightly lower levels of closeness, flexibility, and satisfaction in lesbian couples are likely to lead to separations over a 2-year period, whereas heterosexual couples may simply "tough it out" despite more substantial decreases in closeness, flexibility, and satisfaction over longer periods of time. One explanation for this difference may be that because same-sex couples are less likely to be raising children together and to have a legalized status as a couple, they face fewer legal, financial, religious, and social barriers to ending their relationships. Thus, same-sex partners can more easily walk away from their relationships during inevitable periods of conflict or emotional distance. In contrast, heterosexual partners are more likely to feel locked into and remain in dissatisfying couple relationships because of external social, legal, financial, religious, and childrearing constraints and responsibilities.

In the area of sexual behavior, gay male couples have reported much higher rates of nonmonogamous behavior and higher rates of having explicit nonmonogamous agreements than lesbian and heterosexual couples (Gotta et al., 2011). Authors have speculated that these higher rates of reported nonmonogamy are the result of several factors:

1. Men are more likely to engage in nonmonogamy than women, and the composition of the gay couple (two males) doubles the likelihood that they have experienced nonmonogamy as a couple.
2. The legal and social penalties and lack of supports historically for ongoing gay male relationships promoted brief, anonymous sexual encounters rather than ongoing relationships, thus establishing norms favoring single status and a recreational view of sex in the gay male community.
3. In research studies, gay men may be much more willing than lesbians, heterosexual men, or heterosexual women to admit to nonmonogamous behavior.

Several studies have shown that most of the nonmonogamy in gay male couples is by prior mutual agreement. Such extrarelational sex typically adheres to specifically agreed-upon parameters by the couple as to where, when, with whom, what activities, what frequency, and so on. This kind of "negotiated nonmonogamy" (Shernoff, 2006) does not involve lying, nor does it carry the implications of "betrayal" or "cheating" that the same behavior tends to have for heterosexual partners, who are more likely to hide and lie about their extrarelational affairs. One research project (Kurdek, 1988) that looked carefully into behavioral patterns among gay couples with nonmonogamy agreements found that these male partners actually had sex outside the relationship only rarely (80%) or never (9%). In contrast to findings about heterosexual couples' affairs, several studies have shown that there is no association between gay male partners' nonmonogamy and their overall satisfaction or the duration of their relationships (Kurdek, 2004; Peplau, Fingerhut, & Beals, 2004; Peplau & Fingerhut, 2007).

Recent research also shows that monogamy among gay male couples has increased markedly over the last 25 years (Gotta et al., 2011). About half of gay male couples report now that they have been monogamous, with the other half reporting one or more episodes of nonmonogamy by at least one of the partners since they met (Campbell, 2000). Also, in the area of sexuality, lesbian couples are reporting lower frequency of having sex than heterosexual or gay male couples (Gotta et al., in press; Peplau et al., 2004). Lack of sex is a common presenting problem of lesbian couples in therapy (Hall, 2004).

Despite these notable differences pertaining to greater equality in same-sex couples, less monogamy among gay male couples, and less frequent sex in lesbian couples, the dynamics *within* lesbian, gay male, and heterosexual couples are remarkably similar. Regardless of couple type, the very same kinds of interactional patterns of closeness, equality of power, conflict resolution, openness of communication, and social support are associated with partners' psychological well-being, couple satisfaction, and relationship stability.

LESBIAN AND GAY PARENTS AND THEIR CHILDREN

The U.S. Census 2000 reported that 22% of gay male couples and 33% of lesbian couples were living with their children under 18 years of age (Simmons & O'Connell, 2003). Some of these children are progeny from former heterosexual marriages that ended in divorce or from heterosexual nonmarital liaisons that otherwise led to pregnancy. However, there has been a dramatic rise in recent years of children being adopted (Brodzinsky, Green, & Katuzny, 2011) or being conceived through alternative reproductive technologies by intended parents who are openly lesbian or gay from the outset (Goldberg, 2009; Mitchell & Green, 2007).

All such families must deal with issues inherent in the psychological (as opposed to merely biological) conception of a baby; establishing parental legitimacy; gaining validation and support from families of origin and the greater community; and answering questions about the family's structure with their children and other individuals in their social networks (Mitchell & Green, 2007). For openly gay and lesbian people, achieving parenthood requires a great deal of planning and intentionality. In addition, the legal fees and other expenses for adoption, alternative insemination for lesbians, or surrogacy for gay men always necessitate a level of organization and a financial commitment to becoming parents that is not usually required for heterosexual parents except for the minority who adopt or undergo fertility treatments. Thus, these children of openly lesbian and gay parents are always deeply wanted and never born by "accident."

Despite the increasing social visibility of gay and lesbian families, there are very few studies that deal with the experiences of gay fathers and their children. Most of the statistically controlled, quantitative research has focused on the experiences of lesbian-headed families (Goldberg, 2009). A few studies have explored the transition to parenthood and other variables for gay male parents (e.g., Bergman, Rubio, Green, & Padron, 2010; Mallon, 2004; Lewin, 2009), but most have focused on lesbian mothers because of their greater prevalence.

The longest research study to date of children conceived by lesbian couples through donor insemination is the 25-year National Longitudinal Lesbian Family Study (NLLFS; Gartrell & Bos, 2010). These families were studied before the children were born (N = 154 lesbian parents) and again when the target children were 2-, 5-, 10-, and 17-years-old (with a 93% retention rate of participants). Below I present findings across these five data-gathering points, because the results are so representative of what other researchers of lesbian and gay parenting have discovered.

In terms of work and domestic responsibilities before the children were born, the couples established flexible work schedules in anticipation of child care demands. After having children, most mothers reduced their work hours or made other changes in their career commitments. When the children were 10 years old, most of the mothers managed their parenting and career responsibilities satisfactorily. Most mothers sought legal protections for their children, including establishment of wills, powers of attorney for their children's medical care, and second-parent adoption by the lesbian mother who had no genetic link to the child.

Compared to traditional heterosexual families, the lesbian mothers valued having two equally active, equally involved parents raising their children. This advantage continued throughout childhood and adolescence. Childrearing responsibilities, domestic chores, and income earning consistently remained equitably shared between the partners. They took turns engaging in full- or part-time employment to accommodate child care needs. This evidence of "degendered parenting" is consistent with findings in other studies that compared gay fathers or lesbian mothers to heterosexual parents. Same-sex couples are more likely to divide the breadwinning, household chore, and childrearing responsibilities equitably in the family than are heterosexual couples. In another study, gay male parents noted that this egalitarian division of parental responsibilities was decided by mutual agreement as opposed to defaulting to prescribed gender roles (Schacher, Auerbach, & Silverstein, 2005). Additionally, a study of gay fathers by McPherson (2003) indicated that fathers were more satisfied with their division of child care tasks than were their heterosexual counterparts.

Before having children, most of the lesbian couples were worried about a decline in time and energy for their partners once the children were born. After having children, as the mothers' lives became more child-focused, most reported that childrearing was stressful for their relationships with their partners, and they had less time and energy for their relationships. This was accompanied by reports of sexual infrequency and greater relationship conflict. When the children were 5 years old, almost one-third of the original participants had separated (a divorce rate comparable to heterosexual marriages), with 15% of the divorces occurring when the children were between 2 and 5 years old. In the McPherson (2003) study, gay fathers reported greater satisfaction with their couple relationships compared to heterosexual fathers.

Regarding relationships with their families of origin before the child was born, most expectant mothers reported strong social support from their parents and families. Having a child enhanced the lesbian mothers' relationships with their parents and increased their contact with them. Most grandparents were delighted with their grandchildren. It is noteworthy that the grandparents' openness about their daughter's lesbian family steadily rose over time. Similarly, a study of gay fathers via surrogacy (Bergman et al., 2010) also reported this increase in familial support from both partners' families of origin across the transition to parenthood. Parents of gay fathers often were more supportive and approving than had been expected (Mallon, 2004; Schacher et al., 2005).

An interesting finding about lesbians who became parents via alternative insemination is that even though the two mothers tended to share childrearing and household responsibilities much more equally than heterosexual parents, the biological mother still tended to be significantly more involved in child care than the nonbiological mother (sometimes referred to as the "co-mother"). In this regard, it is difficult to disentangle the influence of the symbolic importance that lesbian mothers, families of origin, and society in general put on genetic relations versus the influence of pregnancy and breastfeeding by the biological mother on the parent–child relationships. Some observers of lesbian coparenting believe that breastfeeding demands in particular may establish patterns of greater biological mother–child closeness that may extend over time into other areas of parent–infant and then parent–toddler interaction.

Despite the statistically greater involvement in child care of biological compared with nonbiological lesbian mothers, both female partners are still dramatically more equal than heterosexual couples in their division of child care responsibilities, primarily because most heterosexual fathers play a much less central role than heterosexual mothers in child care. Moreover, unlike in stepfamilies following divorce—where the stepparent is clearly considered an addition to a preexisting "procreative" family—lesbian coparents typically define themselves to each other and the child as the equally responsible, legitimate, "co-creative" parents. Co-mothers typically do not occupy the kind of secondary status that heterosexual stepparents sometimes do when it comes to making decisions concerning the child. In fact, many co-mothers are the primary caregiving parent for the child.

After having children, most lesbian mothers and gay fathers report a decline in socializing with their friends, and many report losing friendships with others who are not parents (a pattern also common for heterosexual parents). In fact, lesbian and gay parents say that most of their current friends are heterosexual parents with children the same age. For example, the NLLFS found that the lesbian mothers' social network when the children were age 10 included more straight parents compared to before the children born or when the children were age 5, because of their children's choices of peers. As the children grow older, their friendships determine who the focal family socializes with, and the same tends to be true for families headed by heterosexual parents. Most lesbian parents also continued to be involved in lesbian support groups and social activities.

Changes in social network composition associated with being parents also were evident among the gay fathers in Mallon's (2004) study of adoptive gay male parents and in Bergman et al.'s (2010) study of gay fathers via surrogacy. Gay fathers reported that their friendships ceased to be mainly among other gay and lesbian people, and became progressively more inclusive of heterosexual parents over time as their children's school friendships played a greater role in the whole family's socializing.

In terms of psychological well-being, identity, and stigmatization, the NLLFS reported that prospective mothers were concerned about raising their children in an all-female household and a homophobic world. Before the child's birth, most of the mothers were planning to be open about their lesbian identity to their children. The participants had been increasingly coming "out" at work (e.g., 93% were "out" at work when the child was 2 years old). In an effort to reduce homophobia in their communities, the mothers also had been more active politically (e.g., 75% at child's age 5) in educational initiatives to increase awareness and acceptance of diversity in human relationships. Almost all of the mothers made intentional efforts to connect their children with adult male relatives and friends, so that their children would have relationships with male adult figures throughout childhood and adolescence.

With regard to the overall impact of having a child, most of the mothers expressed that having children was the most enjoyable and best thing that ever happened to them, and they noted that participating in their children's growth and development was the most gratifying aspect of parenting. Similarly, gay fathers also spoke of a sense of personal fulfillment and pride in having children, and a new sense of commonality with heterosexual parents (Schacher et al., 2005). Bergman et al. (2010) found that gay fathers via surrogacy became significantly closer to their families of origin after the children were born and reported significantly increased self-esteem as a result of becoming parents. Other aspects of transition to parenthood paralleled the experiences of both lesbian and heterosexual parents. Across all types of families with young children, the children's needs, friendships, and school lives tend to organize and direct the whole family's social and recreational life, and there seems to be no differences in this regard among families headed by lesbian, gay male, or heterosexual parents.

Parenting Practices and Child Outcomes

Myriad studies have explored developmental outcomes of children raised by gay and lesbian parents. The research literature from the United States (e.g., Gartrell & Bos, 2010; Patterson, 2005; Wainright & Patterson, 2006, 2008; Wainright, Russell, & Patterson, 2004), Great Britain (e.g., Tasker & Golombok, 1997), and Scandinavia (e.g., Bos, van Balen, & van den Boom, 2007) consistently shows that children and adolescents raised by gay and lesbian parents function as well as those raised by heterosexual parents in terms of mental health outcomes and peer relations. For comprehensive reviews of this research see Biblarz & Savci, 2010; Biblarz & Stacey, 2010; Crowl, Ahn, & Baker, 2008; Goldberg, 2009; Patterson, 2005, 2006; Tasker & Patterson, 2007).

In contrast to the oft-repeated false claim by antigay groups that children do better when raised by a heterosexual man and woman who are married to each other, there exists not a shred of credible social science evidence that children raised by married heterosexual mothers and fathers do better on any measure of well-being than children raised by lesbian or gay couples. All of the social science studies on this question actually converge on the conclusion that there are extremely few statistically significant differences in mental health outcomes, peer relations, academic achievement, gender conformity, or substance use between children and adolescents raised by lesbian parents compared with those raised by heterosexual parents.

In the few instances in which significant differences have been obtained, the more desirable outcomes have occurred among children of lesbian parents

(Gartrell & Bos, 2010). For example, daughters of lesbian mothers seem to be somewhat more career-oriented; sons of lesbian mothers seem to be less objectifying in their approach to romantic partners; and lesbian parents report being closer to their children and using less physical punishment (Biblarz & Savci, 2010; Biblarz & Stacey, 2010; Tasker & Patterson, 2007).

By late adolescence, the children in the Gartrell and Bos (2010) longitudinal study actually showed more overall psychosocial competence and fewer behavior problems than children raised by heterosexual parents. Although the children of lesbian parents do experience stigmatization (e.g., teasing) because of their parents' sexual orientation, the negative effects of such experiences are mitigated by positive aspects of family functioning (Bos & Gartrell, 2010).

Although one might expect that there would be fewer problems integrating lesbian and gay parent identities among more recent lesbian and gay parents, current research has documented continuing difficulties, especially for gay male parents. Several studies have described *heterosexist gender role strain* among gay men (e.g., Schacher et al., 2005). Gay fathers' competence is fairly routinely doubted by a society that believes in the primacy of women in childrearing roles. Similarly, most gay men in previous generations grew up believing that they would never become parents. Many authors describe how gay fathers must negotiate a triple minority status by being both *gay* and *male* in the heterosexual parenting community (which is largely organized around heterosexual and female parents as primary caregivers) and by being *fathers* in the gay community (which is organized around being single or coupled without children).

Just to give a local example, even in San Francisco, where one might expect the greatest level of support for gay fathers, the largest socializing and support group for middle-class parents of infants and toddlers is called "Golden Gate *Mothers* Group" (Stevens, 2011). It has over 4,000 members, and membership requires that the parent reside in San Francisco, have children younger than kindergarten age, and be women. Fathers are forbidden from joining the group or going to any of its daily, very well-attended events or playgroups throughout the year. For gay fathers, many of whom are co-equal or primary caregivers for their children, there really are no groups of nearly comparable range and frequency of events in San Francisco.

In sum, despite all the expressed concern among social conservatives about lesbian and gay parenting, and despite some of the challenges of dealing with stigmatization from outside the family, there are few differences between children raised by same-sex parents compared to those raised by heterosexual parents. The few differences that have been found slightly favor children of lesbian parents. The parent–child interactional processes that produce positive child and adolescent functioning are exactly the same in all types of families. Gay and lesbian parents appear to be as capable as heterosexual parents in providing nurturing, responsible, stable, and organized homes. Children's psychological outcomes are related only to processes of family interaction (emotional support and appropriate guidance), not to the gender or sexual orientation of the parents.

RELATIONAL AMBIGUITY AND THE POLITICS
OF SAME-SEX MARRIAGE

Elsewhere, I have suggested that a central task for gay and lesbian people is to resolve "relational ambiguity" in their couple and family relationships (Green & Mitchell, 2008). Most fundamentally, every couple or family relationship in the world is based on an underlying definition of what constitutes membership in the relationship and an implicit "contract" (often unconscious or implicit rather than explicit) consisting of mutual expectations and responsibilities over time. The challenge for gay and lesbian people is that their membership in and expectations for their family relationships are often less clear than is the case for the families of heterosexuals, whose relationships are defined to a greater extent by preexisting traditions, current norms, and law.

For example, being lesbian or gay and coming out to one's heterosexual family members almost always carries some risk of being "disowned" and losing ties to relatives. The universal gay or lesbian dilemma about whether to come out to parents leaves gay and lesbian people with a heightened awareness that continuation of family-of-origin relations in adulthood is entirely voluntary on both sides. The *possibility* of being completely cut off and losing emotional membership in their families is a consequence that most gay and lesbian persons must contemplate seriously before choosing to disclose to their family members. As Weston observed:

> Of course, heterosexuals can also be disowned. But when straight people encounter rejection by relatives, that rejection arises on a case-by-case basis, generally in response to something done rather than something fundamental to their sense of self. Self-identified lesbians and gay men, in contrast, experience rejection as an ever-present possibility structured by claiming a stigmatized sexual identity. (1991, p. 74)

Although most parents do not actually reject their lesbian or gay children after disclosure, the experience of being marginalized or having love relationships rendered invisible or less valuable by family members is actually quite common. Thus, many gay and lesbian people feel like "swans in duck families" and are uncertain about the extent to which they are and will remain full-fledged members of their families compared to the way most heterosexuals (including their own heterosexual siblings) ordinarily take family membership for granted.

Similarly when it comes to couple relationships, the absence of normative templates and public models for being a same-sex couple, and the lack of legal statuses and protections leave many same-sex partners unsure about whether their "coupleness" is indeed valid or "real" like heterosexual couple relationships, which are legitimized by families, social networks, and organized religion, and by the government through legal marriage. In fact, for many same-sex partners who are unable to marry, the transition from "noncouple" to "couple" status itself remains murky (Greenan & Tunnell, 2002). How do same-sex partners and their social networks know when the partners have become a couple *"from this day forward, for better, for worse, for richer, for poorer, in sickness or in health, to love and to cherish 'till death do us part"* if there is no legally sanctioned marriage to demarcate a transition to a full couple status? When the government will not recognize the existence of the partners' relationship or any claims to mutual responsibilities, each partner is extremely vulnerable to financial mistreatment by the other in the event of separation, or vulnerable to financial mistreatment by the other partner's next of kin in the event of a partner's death, unless legal wills and trust documents have been drawn up in advance to prevent that outcome.

Furthermore, in the many jurisdictions where second-parent adoption of children by same-sex partners is not permitted, the nonbiological or nonadoptive parent and child in a family have no legal claim to a relationship with one another. They may be members of one another's "families" psychologically but not legally. Being a "nonlegal parent" is a precarious status, especially if the parents' relationship dissolves, or if the legal parent dies unexpectedly while the family is traveling abroad. Many protracted custody battles have followed couple breakups or the deaths of biological parents of children being raised by same-sex couples. Sometimes the biological parent attempts to cut off the child's contact with the nonbiological parent after a couple breaks up; and sometimes a child's biological grandparents attempt to terminate the nonbiological parent's contact with and custody of a child after the biological parent dies.

In addition, the equal validity of same-sex couple and family relationships has been constantly under attack during the many media campaigns, state ballot initiatives, legislative votes, and court decisions concerning same-sex marriage in the United States in recent years. Gay and lesbian people are bombarded almost daily with messages from media commentators and politicians debating whether same-sex relationships are worthy of equal marriage and parenting rights. The denial of marriage rights through voter initiatives has had a significant demoralizing effect on gay and lesbian citizens and their families in many states.

For example, researchers found that an anti-same-sex marriage initiative in Tennessee created greater psychological distress among the family-of-origin members of gay and lesbian residents (Arm, Horne, & Levitt, 2009). The campaign for the initiative provided omnipresent reminders that gay and lesbian people were seen as little more than objects in debates by their government and the public. These relatives felt that their gay and lesbian family members' lives had been constantly misrepresented to advance hostile political agendas. The increased stress was reflected in greater fears of rejection and hypervigilance to protect themselves against random acts of prejudice. Some chose to isolate themselves. Others chose to become political activists in an attempt to gain some sense of control under the circumstances. In a broader survey of gay and lesbian citizens across many states, researchers found increased minority stress, depression, and anxiety following passage of constitutional amendments to prohibit same-sex marriage in participants' states of residence (Rostosky, Riggle, Horne, & Miller, 2009).

The greatest challenge for gay and lesbian people in their couple and family relationships is to maintain a sense of dignity, legitimacy, and responsible commitment in the face of such undermining messages from both proximal and distal sources. There is every reason to believe that marriage rights would reduce relational ambiguity and convey greater legitimacy to gay and lesbian couple and family relationships in the minds of heterosexuals and gay and lesbian people alike. There already is evidence that same-sex couples who obtain civil unions are more likely to stay together over a 3-year period than comparable same-sex partners without civil unions (Balsam, Beauchaine, Rothblum, & Solomon, 2008). Same-sex marriage also would provide important legal protections, such as health care benefits and immigration rights for same-sex spouses and their children, as well as social security benefits and inheritance tax benefits for surviving spouses. Same-sex marriage would make it safer for the partners to invest more psychologically and financially in their future as a couple together (Green & Mitchell, 2008).

However, just as the advent of legal interracial marriage has not provided full equality of opportunity for historically oppressed racial minority groups, same-sex marriage will be no cureall for the discrimination that gay and lesbian families face. As Ettelbrick (1997) commented:

> We must not fool ourselves into believing that marriage will make it acceptable to be gay or lesbian. We will be liberated only when we are respected and accepted for our differences and the diversity we provide to this society. (p. 124)

It is to that larger mission that readers of this chapter can contribute—by conveying to members of our own communities, the media, and public policymakers what we, as professionals, have learned about gay and lesbian family life.

NOTES

1. Throughout this chapter, I use the terms "gay" and "lesbian" to refer to people who self-identify as having primary love and sexual orientations toward people of the same sex. However, many people who engage in such relationships do not identify with these labels. Some of them would more accurately be referred to simply as "men who have sex with men," "women who have sex with women," "same-gender-loving men or women," or "bisexuals," and others prefer terms such as "queer," "questioning," or "fluid."

Although it is common to refer to the LGBT community as a unitary group, I did not feel that I could do justice to bisexual and transgender family relations given the lack of family systems research on these topics and the page limitations of the current chapter. For more about bisexual and transgender people's family relations, see the clinical writings of Bigner and Wetchler (in press), Firestein (2007), Fox (2006), Lev (2004, 2010), and McGoldrick and Ashton (Chapter 11, this volume).

2. Current information about the country-by-country status of LGBT human rights can be obtained from the website of the International Gay and Lesbian Human Rights Commission (IGLHRC), *www.iglhrc.org*.

REFERENCES

Arm, J., Horne, S. G., & Levitt, H. (2009). Negotiating connection to GLBT experience: Family members' experience of anti-GLBT movements and policies. *Journal of Counseling Psychology, 56,* 82–96.

Balsam, K., Beauchaine, T., Rothblum, E., & Solomon, S. (2008). Three-year follow-up of same-sex couples who had civil unions in Vermont, same-sex couples not in civil unions, and heterosexual married couples. *Developmental Psychology, 44,* 102–116.

Bergman, K., Rubio, R.-J., Green, R.-J., & Padron, E. (2010). Gay men who become fathers via surrogacy: The transition to parenthood. *Journal of GLBT Family Studies, 6,* 111–141.

Biblarz, T. J., & Savci, E. (2010). Lesbian, gay, bisexual, and transgender families. *Journal of Marriage and Family, 72,* 480–497.

Biblarz, T. J., & Stacey, J. (2010). How does the gender of parents matter? *Journal of Marriage and Family, 72,* 3–22.

Bigner, J. J., & Wetchler, J. L. (Eds.). (in press). *Handbook of LGBT-affirmative couple and family therapy.* New York: Taylor & Francis.

Bos, H., & Gartrell, N. (2010). Adolescents of the U.S. National Longitudinal Lesbian Family Study: Can family characteristics counteract the negative effects of stigmatization? *Family Process, 49,* 559–572.

Bos, H. M. W., van Balen, F., & van den Boom, D. C. (2007). Child adjustment and parenting in planned lesbian-parent families. *American Journal of Orthopsychiatry, 77,* 38–45.

Brodzinsky, D. M., Green, R.-J., & Katuzny, K. (2011). Adoption by lesbians and gay men: What we know, need to know, and ought to do. In D. M. Brodzinsky & A. Pertman (Eds.), *Adoption by lesbians and gay men: Research and practice issues* (pp. 233–253). New York: Oxford University Press.

Campbell, K. M. (2000). *Relationship characteristics, social support, masculine ideologies and psychological functioning of gay men in couples.* Unpublished doctoral dissertation, California School of Professional Psychology, Alameda.

CNN (2011). Census: More same-sex couples in more places. Retrieved September 8, 2011, from *www.cnn.com/2011/us/08/24/same.sex.census/index. html?&hpt=hp-c2%20*.

Crary, D. (2010, September 15). Who's a family?: New study tracks shifting US views. *ABC News.com.* Retrieved September 15, 2010, from *abcnews.go.com/US/wireStory?id=11640416*.

Crowl, A., Ahn, S., & Baker, J. (2008). A meta-analysis of developmental outcomes for children of same-sex and heterosexual parents. *Journal of GLBT Family Studies, 4,* 385–407.

D'Augelli, A. R., Rendina, H. J., Sinclaire, K. O., & Grossman, A. H. (2007). Lesbian and gay youth's aspirations for marriage and raising children. *Journal of LGBT Issues in Counseling, 1,* 77–98.

D'Augelli, R. D., Grossman, A. H., & Starks, M. T. (2006). Childhood gender atypicality, victimization and PTSD among gay, lesbian and bisexual youth. *Journal of Interpersonal Violence, 21,* 1462–1482.

Egan, P. J., Edelman, M. S., & Sherrill, K. (2008, November 10). *Findings from the Hunter College poll of lesbians, gays, and bisexuals: New discoveries about identity, political attitudes and civic engagement.* Retrieved from *www.hrc.org/documents/hunter_college_report.pdf.*

Ettelbrick, P. (1997). Since when is marriage a path to liberation? In A. Sullivan (Ed.), *Same-sex marriage: Pro and con* (pp. 118–124). New York: Vintage Books.

Firestein, B. (Ed.). (2007). *Becoming visible: Counseling bisexuals across the lifespan.* New York: Columbia University Press.

Fox, R. (Ed.). (2006). *Affirmative psychotherapy with bisexual women and bisexual men.* Binghamton, NY: Haworth.

Gartrell, N., & Bos, H. (2010). U.S. National Longitudinal Lesbian Family Study: Psychological adjustment of 17-year-old adolescents. *Pediatrics, 10,* 1–9.

Goldberg, A. E. (2009). *Lesbian and gay parents and their children: Research on the family life cycle.* Washington, DC: American Psychological Association.

Gotta, G., Green, R.-J., Rothblum, E., Solomon, S., Balsam, K., & Schwartz, P. (2011). Lesbian, gay male, and heterosexual relationships: A comparison of couples in 1975 and 2000. *Family Process, 50,* 353–376.

Gottman, J. M., Levenson, R. W., Gross, J., Frederickson, B. L., McCoy, K., Rosenthal, L., et al. (2003). Correlates of gay and lesbian couples' relationship satisfaction and relationship dissolution. *Journal of Homosexuality, 45,* 23–43.

Gottman, J. M., Levenson, R. W., Swanson, C., Swanson, K., Tyson, R., & Yoshimoto, D. (2003). Observing gay, lesbian, and heterosexual couples' relationships: Mathematical modeling of conflict interaction. *Journal of Homosexuality, 45,* 65–91.

Green, R.-J., Bettinger, M., & Zacks, E. (1996). Are lesbian couples "fused" and gay male couples "disengaged?": Questioning gender straightjackets. In J. Laird & R.-J. Green (Eds.), *Lesbians and gays in couples and families: A handbook for therapists* (pp. 185–230). San Francisco: Jossey-Bass/Wiley.

Green, R.-J., & Mitchell, V. (2008). Gay and lesbian couples in therapy: Minority stress, relational ambiguity, and families of choice. In A. S. Gurman (Ed.), *Clinical handbook of couple therapy* (4th ed., pp. 662–680). New York: Guilford Press.

Greenan, D., & Tunnell, G. (2002). *Couple therapy with gay men.* New York: Guilford Press.

Hall, M. (2004). Resolving the curious paradox of the (a)sexual lesbian. In J. Bigner & J. L. Wetchler (Eds.), *Relationship therapy with same-sex couples* (pp. 75–84). New York: Routledge.

Herdt, G., & Koff, B. (2000). *Something to tell you: The road families travel when a child is gay.* New York: Columbia University Press.

Kurdek, L. A. (1988). Relationship quality of gay and lesbian cohabitating couples. *Journal of Homosexuality, 25,* 93–118.

Kurdek, L. A. (2004). Are gay and lesbian cohabitating couples really that different from heterosexual married couples? *Journal of Marriage and Family, 66,* 880–900.

Laird, J., & Green, R.-J. (Eds.). (1996). *Lesbians and gays in couples and families: A handbook for therapists.* San Francisco: Jossey-Bass/Wiley.

Langer, G. (2011). *Support for gay marriage reaches a milestone: More than half of Americans say gay marriage should be legal.* Retrieved March 18, 2011, from *abcnews.go.com/politics/support-gay-marriage-reaches-milestone/story?id= 13159608.*

LaSala, M. C. (2010). *Coming out, coming home: Helping families adjust to a gay or lesbian child.* New York: Colombia University Press.

Lev, A. I. (2004). *Transgender emergence: Therapeutic guidelines for working with gender-variant people and their families.* Binghamton, NY: Haworth.

Lev, A. I. (2010). How queer!—The development of gender identity and sexual orientation in LGBTQ-headed families. *Family Process, 49,* 268–290.

Lewin, E. (2009). *Gay fatherhood: Narratives of family and citizenship in America.* Chicago: University of Chicago Press.

Mallon, G. P. (2004). *Gay men choosing parenthood.* New York: Columbia University Press.

McPherson, D. (1993). *Gay parenting couples: Parenting arrangements, arrangement satisfaction, and relationship satisfaction.* Unpublished doctoral dissertation, Pacific Graduate School of Psychology, Palo Alto, CA.

Mitchell, V., & Green, R.-J. (2007). Different storks for different folks: Gay and lesbian parents' experiences with alternative insemination and surrogacy. *Journal of GLBT Family Studies, 3*(2/3), 81–104.

Mooallem, J. (2010). Can animals be gay? *New York Times.* Retrieved March 29, 2010, from *www.nytimes.com/2010/04/04/magazine/04animals-t.html?emc=eta1.*

Patterson, C. J. (2005). *Lesbian and gay parenting: Summary of research findings.* Washington, DC: American Psychological Association. Retrieved June 18, 2011, from *www.apa.org/pi/parent.html.*

Patterson, C. J. (2006). Children of lesbian and gay parents. *Current Directions in Psychological Science, 15,* 241–244.

Peplau, L. A., & Fingerhut, A. W. (2007). The close relationships of lesbians and gay men. *Annual Review of Psychology, 58,* 405–424.

Peplau, L. A., Fingerhut, A. W., & Beals, K. P. (2004). Sexuality in the relationships of lesbians and gay men. In J. Harvey, A. Wenzel, & S. Sprecher (Eds.), *The handbook of sexuality in close relationships* (pp. 349–269). Mahwah, NJ: Erlbaum.

Roisman, G. I., Clausell, E., Holland, A., Fortuna, K., & Elief, C. (2008). Multimethod comparision of same-sex couples with opposite-sex dating, engaged, and married dyads. *Developmental Psychology, 44,* 91–101.

Romero, A. P., Baumle, A., Badgett, M. V. L., & Gates, G. J. (2007). *Williams Institute Census snapshot: December 2007.* Retrieved December 10, 2010, from *www.law.ucla.edu/williamsinstitute/publications/uscensussnapshot.pdf.*

Roselli, C., & Balthazart, J. (Eds.). (2011). Sexual differentiation of sexual behavior and its orientation. *Frontiers in Neuroendocrinology, 32,* 109–264.

Rostosky, S. S., Riggle, E. D. B., Horne, S. G., & Miller, A. D. (2009). Marriage amendments and psychological distress in lesbian, gay, and bisexual (LGB) adults. *Journal of Counseling Psychology, 56,* 56–66.

Rothblum, E. D., Balsam, K. F., & Solomon, S. E. (2008). Comparison of same-sex couples who were married in Massachusetts, had domestic partnerships in California, or had civil unions in Vermont. *Journal of Family Issues, 29,* 48–78.

Ryan, C., Huebner, D., Diaz, R. M., & Sanchez, J. (2009). Family rejection as a predictor of negative health outcomes in white and Latino lesbian, gay, and bisexual young adults. *Pediatrics, 123,* 346–352.

Savin-Williams, R. C. (2001). *"Mom, dad. I'm gay:" How families negotiate coming out.* Washington, DC: American Psychological Association.

Schacher, S. J., Auerbach, C. F., & Silverstein, L. B. (2005). Gay fathers expanding the possibilities for us all. *Journal of GLBT Family Studies, 1,* 31–52.

Shernoff, M. (2006). Negotiated nonmonogamy and male couples. *Family Process, 45,* 407–418.

Simmons, T., & O'Connell, M. (2003). *Married-couple and unmarried-partner households: 2000.* Washington, DC: U.S. Department of Commerce, Economics and Statistics Administration, Bureau of the Census.

Smith, T. W. (2011). *Cross-national differences in attitudes toward homosexuality. GSS cross-national report number 31.* Chicago: National Opinion Research Center, University of Chicago. Retrieved July 31, 2011, from *www3.law.ucla. edu/Williamsinstitute/pdf/Smith-CrossNational-NORC-May2011.pdf.*

Solomon, S. E., Rothblum, E. D., & Balsam, K. F. (2004). Pioneers in partnership: Lesbian and gay male couples in civil unions compated with those not in civil unions and married heterosexual siblings. *Journal of Family Psychology, 18,* 275–286.

Solomon, S. E., Rothblum, E. D., & Balsam, K. F. (2005). Money, housework, sex, and conflict: Same-sex couples in civil unions, those not in civil unions, and heterosexual married siblings. *Sex Roles, 52,* 561–575.

Stevens, E. L. (2011). In a clubby world of San Francisco mothers, men needn't apply. *New York Times.* Retrieved April 2, 2011, from *www.nytimes.com/2011/04/03/ us/03bcstevens.html?src=twrhp.*

Stone Fish, L., & Harvey, R. G. (2005). *Nurturing queer youth: Family therapy transformed.* New York: Norton.

Tasker, F., & Golombok, S. (1997). *Growing up in a lesbian family: Effects on child development.* New York: Guilford Press.

Tasker, F., & Patterson, C. J. (2007). Research on gay and lesbian parenting: Retrospect and prospect. *Journal of GLBT Family Studies, 3*(2/3), 9–34.

Wainright, J. L., & Patterson, C. J. (2006). Delinquency, victimization, and subtance use among adolescents with female same-sex parents. *Journal of Family Psychology, 20,* 526–530.

Wainright, J. L., & Patterson, C. J. (2008). Peer relations among adolescents with female same-sex parents. *Developmental Psychology, 44,* 117–126.

Wainright, J. L., Russell, S. T., & Patterson, C. J. (2004). Psychosocial adjustment, school outcomes, and romantic relationships of adolescents with same-sex parents. *Child Development, 75,* 1886–1898.

Weston, K. (1991). *Families we choose: Lesbians, gays, kinship.* New York: Columbia University Press.

CHAPTER 9

FAMILY PROCESSES IN KINSHIP CARE

MALITTA ENGSTROM

Over thousands of years and across diverse cultures and contexts, extended families have provided care for children. When children cannot be cared for by their parents, care provided by other relatives and close nonrelatives, known as "kinship care," is increasingly recognized as the favored alternative for children in need of foster care. "Formal" arrangements involve the child welfare system; "informal" arrangements, without child welfare involvement, may still involve formal procedures, including legal custody and decision-making power. Informal kinship care is also referred to as "private kinship care," and formal kinship care is also referred to as "kinship foster care," when the state assumes custody of the child, and "voluntary kinship care," when the state does not assume custody (Geen, 2003b). Unless noted, this chapter uses the term "kinship care" to refer to both formal and informal arrangements.

In 2009, 423,773 children were in formal foster care in the United States. Nearly 1 in 4 resided with relatives (U.S. Department of Health and Human Services [DHHS], 2010). Precise estimates of the number of children in informal foster care are difficult to obtain; however, recent data (U.S. Census Bureau, 2008) indicate that more than 2.3 million children reside with relatives other than their parents. Of this group, an estimated 69% live with a grandparent. The majority of grandparent caregivers are women. Caregiving grandparents, and kinship caregivers in general, are more likely to be African American, to be single, to live in poverty, and to have more people living in their homes than noncaregiving grandparents or nonkin caregivers (for review see Cuddeback, 2004; Fuller-Thomson & Minkler, 2007; Minkler & Fuller-Thomson, 2005).

CONTEXT OF KINSHIP CARE

A wide range of circumstances prompt kinship care arrangements, including military deployment; long-distance employment; parental physical, mental health, or substance use problems; parental death; lack of material resources; young parenthood; neglect, abuse, or abandonment of children; and parental incarceration (Beeman, Kim, & Bullerdick, 2000; Bunch, Eastman, & Moore, 2007; Gleeson et al., 2009). In the midst of such challenges, families often demonstrate profound commitments to each other and to the children in their care. For example, expressions of love, efforts to keep the children out of nonkin foster care, and instances of caring for children despite their own physical or financial hardships are common among kinship caregivers (Minkler & Roe, 1993; O'Brien, Massat, & Gleeson, 2001).

When compared to nonkin foster care, formal kinship care is associated with many positive gains for children. In addition to supporting familial, cultural, and community ties (Hegar, 1999), studies document more regular contact with birth parents (Berrick, Barth, & Needell, 1994), greater stability in placement (Koh, 2010), high rates of placement with siblings (Testa & Rolock, 1999), high rates feeling consistently loved (Wilson & Conroy, 1999), reduced risk of running away (Courtney & Zinn, 2009), and lower risk of developing depression and substance use disorders once in placement (Keller, Salazar, & Courtney, 2010).

Gains for kinship caregivers include rewards related to supporting the children's well-being and watching them grow, experiencing joy and pride in relation to the children, feeling blessed by the children's presence, helping their own adult children, keeping their families together, and fulfilling a sense of duty (Burton, 1992; Gleeson et al., 2009; Minkler & Roe, 1993; O'Brien et al., 2001; Ruiz, 2004). Gains for birth parents include more regular contact with their children in kinship care, as well as gratitude for the love, safety, and care their children receive and the caregiver's role in keeping the child out of nonkin foster care (Gleeson & Seryak, 2010; Smith, Krisman, Strozier, & Marley, 2004). Further, multigenerational bonds often associated with kinship care can strengthen families' resilience in the midst of difficult life experiences (Bengtson, 2001).

INTERACTING, MULTIFACETED CHALLENGES

While kinship care can yield important gains for children, caregivers, birth parents, and families, it is not without its challenges, including complex relational processes, financial strains, physical and mental health problems, and cumbersome service systems. These challenges interact in dynamic ways, often exacerbating each other. This chapter offers an integrative, multisystemic framework to consider these complex, interacting challenges and to strengthen families' inherent resilience (Walsh, 2006). While recognizing and building upon families' bonds, strengths, and resources, this multisystemic framework provides a road map for understanding and addressing key challenges families face when engaged in kinship care. It can complement an array of family therapies employed in kinship care, including structural (Minuchin, Colapinto, & Minuchin, 2007), intergenerational, contextual (Brown-Standridge & Floyd, 2000), parent–child interaction (Timmer, Sedlar, & Urquiza, 2004), attachment-based (Strong, Bean, & Feinauer, 2010), and integrative approaches (for discussion see Ziminski, 2007). Other family therapies that do not target, but nonetheless assist families engaged in kinship care may be augmented with the kinship-care-specific information addressed in this chapter.

This framework can also complement family-oriented individual and group interventions in kinship care that address parenting, health issues, stress and coping, and navigating complex service systems (Kelley, Yorker, Whitley, & Sipe, 2001). Of particular note, caregiver support groups, often highly regarded by participants, have shown capacity to reduce depressive symptoms and to improve coping, social support, self- and child care, caregiver–parent relationships, and resource access (Burnette, 1998; Dressel & Barnhill, 1994; King et al., 2009; O'Brien et al., 2001). Multifamily groups also hold potential to effect positive systemic changes and to strengthen social support (Crumbley & Little, 1997; Engstrom, 2008). This multisystemic framework begins with consideration of families' relational processes in kinship care and broadens to consider salient contextual factors that interact with families' kinship care experiences (e.g., permanency and legal concerns; poverty; physical and mental health problems; and obstacles to service engagement). It concludes with multisystemic practice principles to support thriving among families engaged in kinship care.

COMPLEX RELATIONAL PROCESSES

Defining Family Inclusively in the Context of Kinship Care

Although there have long been calls for systemic, family-centered approaches in kinship care (Bartram, 1996; McLean & Thomas, 1996), practice and scholarship in this area often focus on individuals, dyads, or subsystems of the family, typically the children and caregivers who coreside. A systemic perspective recognizes that the well-being of the children, caregivers, birth parents, and other family members is intricately interwoven and interdependent. A multisystemic perspective moves thinking beyond the individual or dyadic level to a recognition that there is a dynamic, mutually influencing interplay among all members of the family system and, simultaneously, between the family and the sociocultural contexts with which the members interact. This perspective enables us to move flexibly between close-up views of family interactions and wide-angle views of interactions between families and broader systems.

An inclusive, systemic approach to the family is required to adequately understand and address the ways in which individuals' and subsystems' experiences reverberate in mutually influencing ways throughout the relational network. For example, a grandmother's decision to become her grandchildren's primary caregiver influences relational processes beyond the kin caregiving triad (i.e., grandmother, birth parents, and children), including those with her partner, adult children, other residential and nonresidential grandchildren, and extended family members. These relational adjustments, in turn, influence the family's kinship care experiences. For example, a partner who is supportive of the kinship care arrangement may be counted on to contribute to a warm, mutually supportive tenor within the family, while one who does not support the arrangement may repeatedly express dissatisfaction, fueling stress and conflict for the couple and the family. An inclusive assessment of the family involves exploration of all family members' perspectives about and adjustment to the kinship care arrangement, and their mutual influence. This important information might otherwise be overlooked in a narrow focus on individuals, dyads, or triads.

Additionally, attention to the broader family system can identify overlooked sources of support (Engstrom, 2008; Minuchin et al., 2007; Walsh, 2006). Families frequently develop and maintain caregiving patterns that rely on specific members, typically women, to assume primary caregiving responsibilities (McGoldrick, 2011). Particularly when caregiving arrangements are made in crisis situations, established patterns are often readily relied upon, with limited attention to alternative possibilities or additional sources of support. The potential role of a grandfather may be overlooked. Those who may have been less involved in childrearing in the past may now have the ability to be actively involved in caring for their grandchildren and helping their adult children. Efforts to support family well-being and kinship care stability require consideration of the ways in which families establish caregiving arrangements and how members can create a collaborative, team approach to caregiving. Although one person may assume primary caregiving responsibility, other members can offer valuable additional assistance. An aunt may regularly take the children to the park both to strengthen their relationship and to provide the caregiver respite. A grandfather may cook his specialty on Sundays, bringing the extended family together. A pastor may provide a supportive ear and spiritual encouragement for the caregiver; a parish youth group may be a valuable connection for teens. It is important to involve extended family and community members, including "non-blood" relatives and others who are considered "family" to "widen the circle of caring" within the family (American Humane Association [AHA], 2010, p. 25; see Boyd-Franklin & Karger, Chapter 12, this volume).

Genograms to Facilitate an Inclusive Definition of Family

Genograms facilitate exploration of family structural patterns, relationships, and sociocultural contexts to inform family assessment and intervention in rich and meaningful ways (McGoldrick, Gerson, & Petry, 2008). They are particularly useful in gaining a broadly inclusive view of the family and identifying potential resources in a wide circle of caring. They can draw explicit attention to nonresidential family members with important roles; those who could be sources of support; and those who may be missed in conversations about the family, including fathers' and partners' families. Questions that inquire about who is considered part of the family, who attends significant events, and who is sought out in times of need may also assist with developing an inclusive understanding of the family (AHA, 2010). Exploring family interactions, communication, and supports across relational networks, as well as members' satisfaction with current relational processes, can highlight key points of intervention to expand emotional and practical resources and to support the well-being of the entire family system.

Additionally, a genogram and timeline enable clinicians to explicitly address multigenerational caregiving and cumulative strains associated with multiple caregiving responsibilities. It is not uncommon for kinship caregivers to be caring for multiple generations of family members, as well as for neighbors or friends (Burton, 1992; Minkler & Roe, 1993). Extensive caregiving responsibilities, especially with limited resources, can fuel distress within the family (Hughes, Waite, LaPierre, & Luo, 2007), which makes it crucial to assess and improve the fit between caregiving demands and available resources.

Interactions with Broader Systems

Strengthening a family's capacity to manage the complex challenges that often accompany kinship care requires consistent attention to the broader systems with which the family interacts. Of critical importance in culturally competent practice is consideration and flexible integration of the family's multiple sociocultural locations (Falicov, 1995). Relatedly, kinship care arrangements occur within or against the backdrop of the child welfare system, within which children of color are disproportionately represented. For example, children from African American and Alaska Native/American Indian backgrounds comprise approximately 14% and 0.9% of children in the United States (U.S. Census Bureau, 2005–2009), yet they represent 50% and 2% of children in formal foster care, respectively (DHHS, 2010). Explanations of this disproportionality include intersections between poverty, race, and gender that result in higher rates of maltreatment reports; racial bias in assessment and protective actions related to parenting and child behavior; and race-related differences in the quality and quantity of services that families involved in the child welfare system receive (Berger, McDaniel, & Paxson, 2005; Courtney et al., 1996). This disproportionality and contributing factors necessitate a therapeutic climate in which the role of racism in the problems families face and in the services they receive can be openly discussed and can be addressed by actions that improve their immediate situations and challenge racism across broader systems (Engstrom, 2008; see McGoldrick & Ashton, Chapter 11, this volume).

Families engaged in kinship care are likely to be involved with multiple systems in addition to the child welfare system. These systems, including workplaces, schools, religious organizations, social networks, neighborhoods, community groups, physical and mental health services, public welfare agencies, and correctional settings, may be sources of support, comfort, frustration, and depletion. Routine inquiry regarding interactions with broader systems and ways they can be strengthened can facilitate empowerment, enhanced community connections, greater collaboration in solving problems, improved access to supportive resources, and reduced stress in the family system (Boyd-Franklin & Karger, Chapter 12, this volume; Engstrom, 2008).

Routes to Kinship Care

The ways in which kinship caregiving arrangements develop can affect families' adaptation and coping. Some relatives may have been providing care since very early in the child's life (O'Reilly & Morrison, 1993). In this context, the birth parents' presence may have varied over time. Their intermittent involvement with the children and family system can present multifaceted challenges as families continually adjust to their presence and absence (Gibson, 2002; Russell & Malm, 2003). In other cases, birth parents may have had limited or no involvement with the children and family system over a long period of time. The family's challenges may include strains associated with long-standing caregiving responsibilities, grief related to ambiguous parental loss, and hopes and frustrations regarding the parents' ability to care for the children (Boss, 2006; O'Brien et al., 2001).

Some kinship caregivers assume their roles in response to sudden events, such as parental incarceration, death, substance misuse, illness, or neglect of a child. An abrupt, unanticipated call to action may prompt their caregiving (O'Brien et al., 2001). In these circumstances, families may have to adjust roles and responsibilities very quickly, with little time for emotional or practical preparation.

Other kinship caregivers may assume their roles based on their observations of family circumstances over time (Russell & Malm, 2003). While there may be complex issues regarding the situations observed, the initiation of care, and interactions with birth parents regarding the caregiving arrangements, time allows caregivers, birth parents, and others to prepare for role and residential shifts. Further, child and family adjustment may be facilitated by gradual increases in caregivers' involvement. Finally, some kinship care arrangements emerge through "complex pathways," in which children have lived in numerous previous settings (Gleeson et al., 2009, p. 308). These situations pose challenges related to multiple losses, attachment, and predictability.

Inquiry about pathways to kinship care and their associated challenges and achievements can facilitate contextual understanding of a family's kinship caregiving arrangement and potential points of intervention. For example, families who describe long-standing challenges with parents' intermittent presence due to military involvement, employment obligations, or health problems may benefit from discussion of ways in which the family can anticipate and shift organization to accommodate this pattern, clarify expectations and roles, and maximize their coping with this situation.

Family Decision Making and Support

Kinship care arrangements emerge from and are sustained through multiple decisions. These decisions are often based on assessments of parents' ability to care for their children, children's safety in their parents' home, qualities of alternative caregiving arrangements, capacities of kinship caregivers, and available supports within the family and community. While child welfare agencies frequently drive these decision-making processes as they seek to uphold children's safety, the recognition that children's well-being is best supported in the context of family connections and that involving families in decision making can facilitate family empowerment, fuels their growing use of family group decision making (FGDM). FGDM is based on family group conferences that emerged from New Zealand more than 20 years ago in response to disproportionate representation of indigenous children in out-of-home placement (Weigensberg, Barth, & Guo, 2009). Central aims of FGDM include correcting power imbalances between staff and families, supporting families' identification of needs and strategies to address them, honoring families' cultural and community connections, building on families' strengths, and enhancing outcomes for children and families (AHA, 2010; Rauktis, McCarthy, Krackhardt, & Cahalane, 2010).

These aims are achieved by partnering with families to make key decisions. Efforts are made to define family inclusively, to include all family members and important others in the decision-making process, to provide opportunity for facilitated and independent family meetings, and to pursue the family's chosen plan to the greatest extent possible (see AHA, 2010). Although research findings are not unanimous (Center for Social Services Research, 2004; Sundell & Vinnerljung, 2004), several studies have found FGDM to be associated with improved child welfare outcomes, including reduced child maltreatment and family violence; greater stability of placements; quicker exits from care; higher ratings by families on measures of empowerment and clarity of expectations; and improved engagement in parenting services, mental health treatment for parents, and counseling for children (Crampton & Jackson, 2007; Pennell & Burford, 2000; Rauktis et al., 2010; Sheets et al., 2009; Weigensberg et al., 2009). With its recognition of the family as a resource and the power of collaborative decision making, FGDM is also likely to be helpful with families engaged in kinship care outside of the child welfare system.

Transitions

Transitional times are generally marked by uncertainty as families shift from one state of being to another. It is normal for families to experience stress as they adapt to changing circumstances and develop modified ways of interacting and coping to meet the demands of the new situation. Transitions occur in multiple ways, including those involving births, deaths, relationship commitments, separations, developmental changes, illness, and changes in daily routines (see McGoldrick & Shibusawa, Chapter 16, this volume). In the context of kinship care, it is important to consider major transitions, such as changes in caregiving arrangements, household membership, legal custody, and schools, as well as smaller-scale transitions, such as the family's adjustment to parental visits and contacts.

Transitions associated with changes in caregiving arrangements and visits require caregivers and parents to share and shift responsibilities for the children's care. Like a pilot and copilot flying a plane, caregivers and parents need to collaborate as they make these adjustments in pursuit of their shared mission to support the children's well-being. Just as unplanned, abrupt transfer of control between the pilot and copilot may jolt the plane, so, too, can children and families be jolted. Collaborative planning, including clear communication about roles, boundaries, and expectations, can facilitate smoother processes as responsibilities and roles shift. Additional core strategies to enhance families' adaptation involve the following:

- Identifying transitions, including the ways they may require evolving adaptation over time.
- Normalizing associated stresses.
- Taking steps to make changes less abrupt and disruptive.
- Facilitating adaptive interpretations of changes.
- Developing ways of coping with the new circumstances (Cowan, 1991; Minuchin et al., 2007).

Navigating Evolving Relationships

As the family's organization, roles, and responsibilities shift, caregivers, birth parents, children, and extended family must navigate evolving relationships with each other. Family members may experience conflicted loyalties, strained relationships, and challenges with attachment (Engstrom, 2008; Poehlmann, Dallaire, Loper, & Shear, 2010). They may also experience problematic relational triangles across generations and subsystems (Minuchin et al., 2007). The intensity of these experiences is likely to be influenced by preexisting relationships and the circumstances prompting the kinship care arrangement. More specifically, preexisting collaborative family relationships, in which challenges are approached with teamwork and conflicts are resolved effectively, position families well for adapting to their evolving relationships, organization, and roles. Alternatively, families experiencing long-standing relational strains, communication difficulties, unresolved conflict, and hostility are likely to be more vulnerable to the relational challenges associated with kinship care arrangements. Additionally, vulnerability to these challenges is likely to increase when stigmatized circumstances, such as substance use problems, incarceration, and child maltreatment, prompt the kinship care arrangement.

For example, a child residing with his maternal grandmother due to parental substance abuse may experience deep love for her; however, this affection may be complicated with feelings that the attachment makes him disloyal to his parents, discounts his relationship with them, and reflects negatively upon them as parents. Additionally, while the child maintains his love for his parents, he may at the same time feel hurt, confused, and frustrated by their difficulties. The grandmother in this situation may also experience conflicting loyalties as she balances her love for her daughter and son-in-law, her belief in the importance of the child's relationships with them, her efforts to support their roles as parents, and her commitment to ensure her grandson's well-being and safety by monitoring parental visits. The birth mother in this situation may simultaneously feel grateful for her mother's assistance, critical of rules her mother sets for her son, and upset by monitored visits. The extended family members may also experience conflicting loyalties based on their love and concern for each member of the caregiving triad, their own involvement in the caregiving arrangement, and the challenge of supporting each family member's well-being.

As noted earlier, the complex relational processes may fuel problematic relational triangles as the family members seek to manage uncomfortable feelings and reduce stress in the system. The child may join with his mother in critiquing his grandmother's rules and visitation monitoring. The mother may experience this alliance with her son as an opportunity for connection with him and as an avenue to support her parenting role. This relational process could risk undermining consistent limits for the child, destabilizing the grandmother's daily interactions with him, and fueling stress within the family. However, in a family whose approach to solving problems is to talk directly about them until a solution is achieved, the grandmother can readily initiate conversation with her daughter. They can collaborate about how they will support the child's well-being, come to an agreement about appropriate rules and limits, and identify ways in which each of their vital roles can be supported as they care for the child.

Supporting the approach of systemically oriented clinicians, research documents the importance of close relationships between caregivers, birth parents, and children. In fact, in a study with 459 grandmothers raising grandchildren, triple bonding, meaning close relationships between the grandmother, birth parent, and child, was associated with the highest rates of well-being for the grandmother and child. As bonding decreased, so too did measures of well-being (Goodman, 2007). Similarly, research regarding parental incarceration suggests that strong parent–caregiver relationships are associated with increased parent–child contact, which, in the majority of studies, is associated with diverse gains for parents who are incarcerated. Contact through letters has consistent benefits for children, while the effects of visits appear to vary by context for children. Most notably, visitation that is part of an intervention is more likely to yield benefits for children. Several factors may influence the effects of visits, including the prior relationship with the parent, the child-friendliness of the facility, and the preparation of the entire family for visits. Audio and video technologies, such as video conferencing and recordings of books or messages from parents, as well as pictures, cards, journals, scrap-books, and phone calls, are also recommended ways to support contact and relationships during parental incarceration (Poehlmann et al., 2010).

Given the critical intersections between family relationships and well-being, it is important that clinicians explore and build upon the family's bonds. Such exploration can be facilitated by inquiring about specific domains of relationships across generations, including affection, love, communication, involvement, supportiveness, conflict, and satisfaction (Goodman, 2007). Relationships may be enhanced with clinical interventions that

- Focus on the strengths of the family's connections.
- Facilitate open communication.
- Clarify key expectations, including those related to daily routines, parenting, coparenting, and visits with birth parents.
- Improve conflict resolution processes.
- Identify and support stress management strategies, including respite.
- Foster collaboration across triangular connections.
- Enhance family members' involvements with each other.
- Support opportunities for the family to have fun together (Engstrom, 2008; Houck & Loper, 2002; King et al., 2009; McKay, Gonzales, Quintana, Kim, & Abdul-Adil, 1999; Minuchin et al., 2007; Poehl-mann et al., 2010).

Where relational disconnects and ambiguous loss persist, families can benefit from opportunities to label and grieve this experience, as well as from efforts that support living well in the midst of ambiguity (Boss, 2006).

Changing Roles, Expectations, and Limits

Changes in roles and expectations associated with kinship care can challenge families in many ways. Family members who assume a caregiving role may struggle to balance elements of their prior relationships with increased responsibility for the children's well-being. Common challenges include integrating the children into the current household, supporting harmonious relationships between all children and others in the household, establishing family routines, clarifying expectations, coparenting with birth parents, responding to the daily rigors of childrearing, and setting limits (Gibson, 2002).

Depending upon the children's age, the caregiver's prior role, and the interactions with birth parents, effective limit setting may be among the greatest challenges the family experiences (Russell & Malm, 2003), and these difficulties can disrupt the stability of the placement (Goodman, 2007). Some caregivers may be reluctant to set limits as they assume their new roles or as they seek to diminish any additional upset or disappointment for the children. Other caregivers may struggle with inconsistent, overly protective, or harsh limit setting (De Robertis & Litrownik, 2004; Harden, Clyman, Kriebel, & Lyons, 2004), which can exacerbate problematic behaviors and contribute to a negative cycle within the family. Finally, some may manage limit setting with birth parents and children effectively, but may not enjoy how they are perceived. As described by one kinship caregiver, "You become the heavy" (O'Brien et al., 2001, p. 731).

Interactions around limit setting are likely to reflect complex feelings about the kinship care arrangement. Children may test limits with the hope that if their behavior is too problematic, they will be able to return to their parents (O'Brien et al., 2001). Some may test limits to understand the boundaries and expectations in the caregivers' home and to confirm the predictability and security of the arrangement. Some children may chafe against limits in reaction to expectations that differ from those they have known. For example, a young adolescent whose parents were disengaged may have had considerable autonomy prior to the kinship care arrangement. The change in expectations may involve a sense of loss of that autonomy and difficulty understanding the rationale for structures she does not feel she needs. However, consistent structure, expectations, and limits, even when they differ from those that children have previously known, together with warmth and affection, positively influence children's experiences in kinship care (Altshuler, 1999). Finally, caregivers' love, commitment, protectiveness, strain, and fatigue may be manifested in their limit setting, and birth parents' multifaceted feelings about the kinship caregiving arrangement are likely to influence the degree to which they support the caregivers' limits (Russell & Malm, 2003).

Exploring how limits are set, how positive behavior is acknowledged, how children respond to both limits and praise, how these processes may reflect feelings about the kinship care arrangement, and how the family feels these processes are working provides valuable inroads to understanding and addressing interactions and emotions that may be particularly challenging. Further, family stress can be alleviated and well-being can be supported throughout the family system with the following clinical strategies:

- Normalizing the challenges families face in this area.
- Facilitating direct communication regarding the feelings reflected in these processes.
- Anticipating ways in which transitions, including visits with birth parents, may affect these processes.
- Strengthening the family's effectiveness in setting limits and offering praise.

Developmental Considerations

Multiple developmental considerations influence kinship care experiences for families. Birth parents' youth and developmental capacity may have precipitated the kinship care arrangement. Older birth parents may have had repeated challenges raising their children. Such varied developmental circumstances intersect with the family's adjustment to and coping in the kinship care arrangement, as does variation in children's needs related to their age and developmental processes. Although infants and younger children have particularly high needs for care, as children age, concerns arise regarding peer relationships, academic functioning, preparation for independent living, and engagement in high-risk behaviors and contexts.

While grandparents are frequent kinship caregivers, it is important to recognize that kinship caregivers encompass a wide range of developmental phases. They may be young adults, including aunts, uncles, and older siblings, whose own preparation to launch independent living coincides with their assumption of caregiving responsibilities. In other situations, they may be middle-aged adults managing multiple caregiving and work responsibilities, or older adults preparing for time of their own. Additionally, health, well-being, and the degree to which caregiving is experienced as "off-time" are likely to vary across diverse developmental contexts and to affect adjustment to and maintenance of caregiving activities (Solomon & Marx, 2000).

Adapting to and maintaining caregiving activities are also influenced by the family's developmental phase. Kinship caregiving responsibilities may complement or challenge a family's life-cycle expectations (McGoldrick, Carter, & Garcia-Preto, 2011). For example, an individual or couple with unfulfilled hopes of rearing children may welcome caregiving as a way to meet this developmental expectation. Likewise, families who are already in the midst of raising young children may find kinship caregiving consistent with and enriching for this phase in their family's life. Alternatively, assumption of caregiving responsibilities may hasten the accommodation to children for newly committed partners and may delay or eclipse prior childbearing or adoption plans. For example, a couple who previously planned to have children may find that caring for their nephews causes them to put these plans on hold and to reconsider whether their current emotional and financial resources can support a larger family. Finally, families in later life may find caregiving to be a generative way to contribute to younger generations, to be an unanticipated activity at this phase of life, particularly after fulfilling earlier childrearing and employment responsibilities, or both (Burton, 1992; Minkler & Roe, 1993; O'Brien et al., 2001).

Inquiring about expectations for this phase in the individuals' and family's development provides families the opportunity to reflect upon and maximize the fit between kinship care arrangements, expectations, and aspirations. This process can be facilitated with questions regarding the ways in which plans or activities have been altered, postponed, or relinquished with kinship caring

(Rolland, 1994). Identifying steps to support individual and family developmental goals in the context of kinship care can enhance adjustment, growth, and resilience throughout the family system.

PERMANENCY, REUNIFICATION, AND LEGAL CONCERNS

When children are in foster care situations, there are well-founded concerns about the permanence of these situations and the potential for reunification with their parents. "Permanency" generally refers to legally binding arrangements, including adoption, guardianship, and parental custody (see Rampage et al., Chapter 10, this volume). Although kinship care arrangements may involve lasting relationships and commitments, in the absence of legal binding, they do not reflect permanency as it is typically defined (Testa, 2001). The 1997 Adoption and Safe Families Act (ASFA) aimed to quicken the time to permanency for children by requiring movement toward termination of parental rights once a child reaches 15 of 22 consecutive months in foster care, unless family is providing the child's care. ASFA allows for kinship care to become the permanent plan (Geen, 2003b). In this context, numerous studies have examined permanency and reunification in kinship care. A recent meta-analytic review found that although children in nonkinship foster care were somewhat more likely to be reunified with parents, the finding was not statistically significant; however, that group was more likely to be adopted, less likely to have a relative assume guardianship, and less likely to continue in care than children in formal kinship care (Winokur, Holtan, & Valentine, 2009).

While a permanent, caring arrangement that supports a child's growth and well-being into adulthood is of critical importance, families engaged in kinship care may favor lasting arrangements over binding ones, and permanency may be defined differently by family and child welfare systems (Geen, 2003a; Testa, 2001). It is important to explore family members' expectations regarding the permanence of their kinship care arrangement, their permanency goals, obstacles to these goals, and resources needed to support these goals. Steps to support relational permanence and a lasting sense of belonging can contribute to well-being for children and families (Samuels, 2008).

POVERTY

Poverty is one of the most potent challenges for many families engaged in kinship care. A recent U.S. Census Bureau report (Kreider, 2008) illustrates the heightened risk of poverty among children living with relatives other than their parents: Approximately 17% of children living with at least one parent experienced poverty in 2004. This number jumped to 34% for children living with other relatives, and was highest, 45%, for children living with grand-mothers. Nationally representative comparisons between kinship and nonkin-ship formal foster care also demonstrate significantly greater risk of poverty and food insecurity among those in kinship care (Ehrle & Geen, 2002; Main, Ehrle Macomber, & Geen, 2006).

In addition to daily challenges to get by with limited income, poverty is associated with numerous biopsychosocial risks for families. Low socioeco-nomic status in childhood, lack of resources to buffer against stressful life experiences, and cumulative social disadvantage are particularly problematic and increase the risk of physical and mental health problems across the life course (Adler & Stewart, 2010; Cohen, Janicki-Deverts, Chen, & Matthews, 2010; Engstrom, 2011). Poverty and related deprivation can also stress family relational processes, complicate other challenges accompanying kinship care, and eclipse clinical work with families. Further, a family's financial and mate-rial needs may risk the stability of the kinship care arrangement (Simpson & Lawrence-Webb, 2009).

Despite the high risk of poverty and its negative effects, kinship caregiv-ers often do not receive financial assistance and other services for which they are eligible (Geen, 2004). Several factors contribute to this problem. First, eli-gibility for benefits is complicated and differs by state. Benefit eligibility typi-cally depends on the kinship caregiving arrangement, the child's Title IV-E status, the kinship caregiver's fulfillment of foster care licensing requirements, the receipt of competing benefits and, for some benefits, current income level. Second, some families are not informed about available benefits either due to workers' unawareness of them or to efforts to reduce public spending. Third, other considerations may keep kinship caregivers from accessing benefits, including lack of awareness of resources, reluctance to ask for help or engage with welfare agencies, and intrusive, unhelpful experiences with service pro-viders (Simpson & Lawrence-Webb, 2009). While there is variation across states, resources for kinship caregivers to explore include foster care pay-ments, Temporary Assistance for Needy Families (TANF) child-only grants or Income Assistance Grants, food stamps, Medicaid, State Children's Health Insurance Program (SCHIP), Supplemental Security Income (SSI), Social Security survivors benefits, child care subsidies and other child care assistance programs, preschool and Head Start programs, and supportive services from child welfare agencies (Ehrle, Geen, & Clark, 2001).

Given the profound impact of poverty on families' well-being, it is imper-ative for clinicians to know about the resources available in their communi-ties and to link families to them. Rather than viewing resource linkage as a case management activity separate from clinical work, a more integrated clinical approach incorporates this activity and recognizes that helping fami-lies access and navigate service systems can facilitate family problem solv-ing and empowerment. Working with families to identify problems, generate possible solutions, select a solution, take action, and evaluate those actions can strengthen their active coping, their efficacy in accessing resources, and their management of other challenges (Walsh, 2006). Clinicians' advocacy in broader systems may be required in some instances; however, it is important that families take action to improve their situations to the greatest extent possible (Boyd-Franklin, 2003). Clinicians are also in a unique position to advocate for collective responses from broader systems. This advocacy may involve participating in efforts to improve public policies and programs that serve families engaged in kinship care, advocating for change through letters and calls to legislators, and developing more responsive services in their own agencies.

PHYSICAL AND MENTAL HEALTH CONCERNS

In the context of kinship care, physical and mental health concerns are typically multidimensional and multigenerational. Parents' physical and mental health problems, including problematic substance use and co-occurring concerns, often prompt kinship care arrangements (Beeman et al., 2000; Gleeson et al., 2009) and may have early-onset, long-term effects on children's well-being (Balsa, Homer, & French, 2009; Fechter-Leggett & O'Brien, 2010; Fergusson, Boden, & Horwood, 2008; Osborne & Berger, 2009). When abuse, neglect, and abandonment precipitate kinship care, children may experience psychological trauma, other mental health problems, behavioral difficulties, cognitive impairments, academic difficulties, and increased risk of involvement in the juvenile justice system (Margolin & Gordis, 2000; McMillen et al., 2005; Ryan & Testa, 2005).

Psychiatric and alcohol use disorders are prevalent among youth in kinship care. For example, among older youth preparing to exit formal kinship care, an estimated 12% have experienced posttraumatic stress disorder (PTSD) in their lifetimes. This rate far exceeds the 1–6% lifetime prevalence found in community samples (Keller et al., 2010). An estimated 13% of older youth in formal kinship care experience conduct disorder or oppositional defiant disorder (McMillen et al., 2005). Such estimates illustrate the high potential for serious emotional and behavioral difficulties among children in formal kinship care. Further, among older youth in formal kinship care, we see lifetime rates of alcohol use disorders (8.5%) that are at the high end of rates found in comparable community samples (American Academy of Child and Adolescent Psychiatry, 2005; Keller et al., 2010).

Parental difficulties, such as substance misuse, mental health problems, and physical illness, may involve long-standing strain for kinship caregivers, particularly grandparents and other close relatives. Kinship caregivers may also experience stigma, embarrassment, and disappointment related to the birth parents' struggles, and such feelings may inhibit help seeking (Hungerford, 1996; O'Brien et al., 2001). The challenges associated with caring for a child experiencing complex biopsychosocial needs can add to this cumulative strain for kinship caregivers (Burnette, 1999; Hayslip, Shore, Henderson,

& Lambert, 1998). High levels of caregiver strain, together with limited resources, may contribute to the increased risk of placement disruption that children with behavioral and other health problems experience in their formal kinship care arrangements (Chang & Liles, 2007; Kelley, Whitley, Sipe, & Yorker, 2000).

While demands and resources influence well-being among kinship caregivers, several studies indicate that kinship caregivers experience rates of physical and mental health problems, particularly depression and stress, that exceed those of nonkinship caregivers and noncaregiving grandparents (Berrick et al., 1994; Blustein, Chan, & Guanais, 2004; Ehrle & Geen, 2002; Minkler & Fuller-Thomson, 2005). Research with grandmothers finds the negative effects on health particularly pronounced when caregiving begins or increases (e.g., Hughes et al., 2007). However, research also finds declining health over time among this group, consistent with age-related progression of health problems (Musil et al., 2011).

The complex psychosocial concerns and high risk of physical and mental health problems among families engaged in kinship care are likely to interact with and exacerbate other difficulties. In addition to routine inquiry about physical and mental health problems, including substance abuse, and their impact on the family, key practices include the following:

- Recognizing and addressing the impact of caregiving transitions on health.
- Linking families to appropriate specialized health services.
- Providing psychoeducation regarding health conditions.
- Facilitating family processes that are associated with better health outcomes, including close, mutually supportive interactions, effective resolution of conflicts, open communication regarding health conditions and treatment, clarity in family organization, and effective coping skills.
- Improving access to material and social resources to strengthen the family's capacity to manage physical and mental health concerns in the context of kinship care (Kelley et al., 2000; Weihs, Fisher, & Baird, 2002).

OVERCOMING OBSTACLES TO SERVICES

Families engaged in kinship care often face numerous barriers to accessing services, particularly mental health services. Potential barriers include the following:

- Lack of information regarding resources.
- Lack of transportation or insurance.
- Lack of child care.

- Cost.
- Stigma.
- Perceptions regarding the need for assistance and the potential usefulness of services.
- Multiple demands on the family's time.
- Physical limits on caregiver mobility.
- A history of negative experiences with service providers.
- Agency factors that impede access, including long waiting lists for services and the absence of culturally competent services (Corrigan, 2007; Geen, 2004; Grote, Zuckoff, Swartz, Bledsoe, & Geibel, 2007; King et al., 2009; Simpson & Lawrence-Webb, 2009).

In addition to addressing agency barriers, numerous studies indicate that intensive engagement approaches that commence with initial family contact improve service engagement. For example, the Strategic Structural Systems Engagement model draws upon principles of brief strategic family therapy to diagnose, join, and restructure the family from the beginning of contact through the first session (Coatsworth, Santisteban, McBride, & Szapocznik, 2001). Similarly, several other approaches begin clinical work and attend to family engagement with services from the point of initial contact. Central elements include active attention to caregiver perceptions of and concerns about services and problem solving to reduce obstacles to services. In particular, engagement is improved with clarification of the need for services, support for the caregiver's commitment and capacity to participate in services, and problem solving to address barriers to engagement (e.g., expectations of services, previous service experiences, transportation, multiple time demands, and child care) in the initial contact. Engagement is also furthered by actions that address immediate concerns. Experiencing a gain in the first session can positively influence family members' perceptions regarding the usefulness of services and inclination to continue with them. Additionally, clarifying the nature of the helping process, including roles of the clinician and family, service options, expected outcomes, and timelines, can facilitate engagement and continued participation in services (McKay & Bannon, 2004; McKay et al., 2004). Providing services in families' homes or convenient locations, accommodating scheduling needs, offering crisis assistance, and maintaining a flexible stance may also strengthen families' engagement and ongoing involvement in services.

Finally, while these intensive engagement strategies offer specific clinical tools to reduce service barriers, it is critically important that clinicians use their professional selves effectively to fortify these efforts. More specifically, multisystemic practices can be strengthened by clinicians' attention to their own reactions to the family and to each member. Particularly when birth parents' struggles have impaired their ability to care for their children and caused pain for their children and other family members, there may be an inclination to overlook the importance of their roles within the family and the potential for mutually supportive interactions with other members. Not uncommonly, service providers harbor strong negative feelings toward birth parents as they attempt to engage and facilitate change with the family. They may inaccurately presume that the other family members share their negative feelings and that birth parents' relationships with their families are damaged beyond repair. However, it is crucial for clinicians to support the potential for positive change and to involve parents with empathy for their life struggles.

The enduring relational connections of many families involved in kinship care arrangements are reflected across generations in multiple ways. For example, children in kinship care often experience regular contact and special bonds with their parents, even while recognizing the reasons they cannot live with them (Altshuler, 1999). Parents whose children are in kinship care arrangements commonly express attention to and interest in supporting their children's well-being, hopes for their children's future, and aspirations to improve their lives in order to be helpful to their children (Gleeson & Seryak, 2010; Smith et al., 2004). Additionally, caregiving grandparents often take steps to support the birth parents. These efforts include not only caring for their grandchildren as a way to help their own children, but also providing them with emotional and practical supports, such as food, money, and housing (Minkler & Roe, 1993). A caregiving grandfather offers a vivid description of this support in the midst of multiple caregiving responsibilities: "I take care of my wife who has cancer and my two grandbabies. I chase around after my daughter on the street trying to make sure she eats, at least" (Burton, 1992, p. 748). While attending to the safety of children and all members of the family, it is critical to honor and build upon families' enduring bonds in the context of kinship care.

Clinicians' negative reactions limit both their understanding of the family's enduring bonds and their capacity for empathy with each family member. Empathy, genuineness, and acceptance, widely recognized as core ingredients that facilitate change, are especially important in the context of kinship care. First, empathy facilitates openness to change. Attuned empathy can reduce defensiveness, improve engagement in the helping process, enhance motivation for change, and facilitate achievement of meaningful individual and family goals (Miller & Rollnick, 2002). Second, a lack of empathic attunement or negative reactions to an individual member may be off-putting to others in the family, hindering effective work with the family system. As described by one caregiving grandmother in my research with families affected by maternal substance use problems and incarceration, "I didn't like it [the agency]. . . She [the case manager] gave her [the grandmother's daughter] a hard time. . . I went and I seen how it was, so I got her in another counseling program. . . . They need sensitivity training. . . They need to get out here and see what is really going on, especially when kids come from the ghetto. They don't know what they've been through to get on that stuff" (Engstrom, 2010, unpublished data). As reflected in this grandmother's statement, insensitivity can negatively influence families' perceptions of a program, undermine their confidence in the service provider's qualifications, and hinder their engagement in services. Third, modeling empathy can enhance mutual empathy among family members and strengthen their relationships. Finally, empathy is essential to counter the stigma, shame, and disempowerment that families too often experience in the child welfare system (Wells, 2010).

CONCLUSION: MULTISYSTEMIC ASSISTANCE FOR FAMILIES TO THRIVE

While families engaged in kinship care often draw upon profound strengths in the midst of difficult situations, the daunting challenges they face may prompt attention to services that help them get by or manage just a bit better. However, such a stance limits the potential gains a family can experience. Drawing upon the idea of family resilience, that a family can experience growth and become stronger in the face of adversity, it is critical that clinicians orient their work in kinship care with resilience-supporting attitudes and practices, including hopefulness, collaboration, recognition of strengths, and possibility (Minuchin et al., 2007; Walsh, 2006). This aim may be realized, in part, with attention to the supports needed for families to thrive. Although challenges must not be minimized and problems must be addressed, attention to thriving, rather than getting by, can orient interactions with families to support possibility and potential. Explicit conversations with families about what it would take for them to thrive can guide clinical work in ways that enlarge the field of what seems possible, honor families' interests, and expand the range of gains they experience.

The multisystemic framework presented in this chapter involves several core practice principles to support thriving among families engaged in kinship care. Most notably, practice in this framework

- Defines and engages families inclusively.
- Values and integrates families' sociocultural connections.
- Honors and builds upon families' bonds and strengths.
- Empowers families in decision-making processes.
- Recognizes that it is normal for families to experience distress during disruptive transitions, and when demands are great and resources are limited.
- Fosters collaborative, mutually supportive family processes.
- Facilitates structural clarity, open communication, and effective conflict resolution.
- Considers and addresses multidimensional interactions between relational, legal, financial, health, and service access challenges.
- Orients helping efforts toward resilience and thriving.

Together, these principles guide practices that build on families' resources and aspirations to address complex, interacting challenges and to support thriving of children and families in the context of kinship care.

ACKNOWLEDGMENTS

The author's collection of unpublished data cited in this chapter was made possible by funding from the John A. Hartford Foundation and the National Institute on Drug Abuse (R03DA27940). The author is solely responsible for the content of this chapter, which does not necessarily represent the official views of these organizations.

REFERENCES

Adler, N. E., & Stewart, J. (2010). Health disparities across the lifespan: Meaning, methods, and mechanisms. *Annals of the New York Academy of Sciences, 1186*(1), 5–23.

Altshuler, S. J. (1999). Children in kinship foster care speak out: "We think we're doing fine." *Child & Adolescent Social Work Journal, 16*(3), 215–235.

American Academy of Child & Adolescent Psychiatry. (2005). Practice parameter for the assessment and treatment of children and adolescents with substance use disorders. *Journal of the American Academy of Child & Adolescent Psychiatry, 44*(6), 609–621.

American Humane Association (AHA). (2010). *Guidelines for family group decision making in child welfare.* Retrieved November 21, 2010, from *americanhumane. org/assets/docs/protecting-children/pc-fgdm-guidelines.pdf.*

Balsa, A. I., Homer, J. F., & French, M. T. (2009). The health effects of parental problem drinking on adult children. *Journal of Mental Health Policy and Economics, 12*(2), 55–66.

Bartram, M. (1996). Clarifying subsystem boundaries in grandfamilies. *Contemporary Family Therapy, 18*(2), 267–277.

Beeman, S. K., Kim, H., & Bullerdick, S. K. (2000). Factors affecting placement of children in kinship and nonkinship foster care. *Children and Youth Services Review, 22*(1), 37–54.

Bengtson, V. L. (2001). Beyond the nuclear family: The increasing importance of multigenerational bonds. *Journal of Marriage & Family, 63*(1), 1–16.

Berger, L. M., McDaniel, M., & Paxson, C. (2005). Assessing parenting behaviors across racial groups: Implications for the child welfare system. *Social Service Review, 79*(4), 653–688.

Berrick, J. D., Barth, R. P., & Needell, B. (1994). A comparison of kinship foster homes and foster family homes: Implications for kinship foster care as family preservation. *Children and Youth Services Review, 16*(1–2), 33–63.

Blustein, J., Chan, S., & Guanais, F. C. (2004). Elevated depressive symptoms among caregiving grandparents. *Health Services Research, 39,* 1671–1699.

Boss, P. (2006). *Loss, trauma, and resilience: Therapeutic work with ambiguous loss.* New York: Norton.

Boyd-Franklin, N. (2003). *Black families in therapy: Understanding the African American experience* (2nd ed.). New York: Guilford Press.

Brown-Standridge, M. D., & Floyd, C. W. (2000). Healing bittersweet legacies: Revisiting contextual therapy for grandparents raising grandchildren in crisis. *Journal of Marital and Family Therapy, 26*(2), 185–197.

Bunch, S. G., Eastman, B. J., & Moore, R. R. (2007). A profile of grandparents raising grandchildren as a result of parental military deployment. *Journal of Human Behavior in the Social Environment, 15*(4), 1–12.

Burnette, D. (1998). Grandparents rearing grandchildren: A school-based small group intervention. *Research on Social Work Practice, 8*(1), 10–27.

Burnette, D. (1999). Physical and emotional well-being of custodial grandparents in Latino families. *American Journal of Orthopsychiatry, 69*(3), 305–318.

Burton, L. M. (1992). Black grandparents rearing children of drug-addicted parents: Stressors, outcomes, and social service needs. *The Gerontologist, 32*(6), 744–751.

Center for Social Services Research. (2004). Title IV-E Child Welfare Waiver Demonstration Project. Retrieved December 1, 2010, from *cssr.berkeley.edu/research_units/cwrc/project_details.html#waiver*.

Chang, J., & Liles, R. (2007). Characteristics of four kinship placement outcome groups and variables associated with these kinship placement outcome groups. *Child & Adolescent Social Work Journal, 24*(6), 509–522.

Coatsworth, J. D., Santisteban, D. A., McBride, C. K., & Szapocznik, J. (2001). Brief strategic family therapy versus community control: Engagement, retention, and an exploration of the moderating role of adolescent symptom severity. *Family Process, 40*(3), 313–332.

Cohen, S., Janicki-Deverts, D., Chen, E., & Matthews, K. A. (2010). Childhood socioeconomic status and adult health. *Annals of the New York Academy of Sciences, 1186*(1), 37–55.

Corrigan, P. W. (2007). How clinical diagnosis might exacerbate the stigma of mental illness. *Social Work, 52*, 31–39.

Courtney, M. E., Barth, R. P., Berrick, J. D., Brooks, D., Needell, B., & Park, L. (1996). Race and child welfare services: Past research and future directions. *Child Welfare, 75*(2), 99–137.

Courtney, M. E., & Zinn, A. (2009). Predictors of running away from out-of-home care. *Children and Youth Services Review, 31*(12), 1298–1306.

Cowan, P. A. (1991). Individual and family life transitions: A proposal for a new definition. In P. A. Cowan & M. Hetherington (Eds.), *Family transitions* (pp. 3–30). Hillsdale, NJ: Erlbaum.

Crampton, D., & Jackson, W. L. (2007). Family group decision making and disproportionality in foster care: A case study. *Child Welfare: Journal of Policy, Practice, and Program, 86*(3), 51–69.

Crumbley, J., & Little, R. L. (1997). *Relatives raising children: An overview of kinship care.* Washington, DC: CWLA Press.

Cuddeback, G. S. (2004). Kinship family foster care: A methodological and substantive synthesis of research. *Children and Youth Services Review, 26*(7), 623–639.

De Robertis, M. T., & Litrownik, A. J. (2004). The experience of foster care: Relationship between foster parent disciplinary approaches and aggression in a sample of young foster children. *Child Maltreatment, 9*(1), 92–102.

Dressel, P. L., & Barnhill, S. K. (1994). Reframing gerontological thought and practice:

The case of grandmothers with daughters in prison. *The Gerontologist, 34*(5), 685–691.

Ehrle, J., & Geen, R. (2002). Kin and non-kin foster care: Findings from a national survey. *Children and Youth Services Review, 24*(1–2), 15–35.

Ehrle, J., Geen, R., & Clark, R. (2001). *Children cared for by relatives: Who are they and how are they faring?* Washington, DC: Urban Institute Press.

Engstrom, M. (2008). Involving caregiving grandmothers in family interventions when mothers with substance use problems are incarcerated. *Family Process, 47*, 357–371.

Engstrom, M. (2010). *Families affected by maternal substance use problems and incarceration.* Unpublished raw data.

Engstrom, M. (2011). Physical and mental health: Interactions, assessment, and interventions. In S. Gehlert & T. A. Browne (Eds.), *Handbook of health social work* (2nd ed., pp. 164–218). Hoboken, NJ: Wiley.

Falicov, C. (1995). Training to think culturally: A multidimensional comparative framework. *Family Process, 34*(4), 373–388.

Fechter-Leggett, M. O., & O'Brien, K. (2010). The effects of kinship care on adult mental health outcomes of alumni of foster care. *Children and Youth Services Review, 32*(2), 206–213.

Fergusson, D. M., Boden, J. M., & Horwood, L. J. (2008). The developmental antecedents of illicit drug use: Evidence from a 25-year longitudinal study. *Drug and Alcohol Dependence, 96*(1–2), 165–177.

Fuller-Thomson, E., & Minkler, M. (2007). Mexican American grandparents raising grandchildren: Findings from the Census 2000 American Community Survey. *Families in Society, 88*(4), 567–574.

Geen, R. (2003a). Kinship care: Paradigm shift or just another magic bullet. In R. Geen (Ed.), *Kinship care: Making the most of a valuable resource* (pp. 231–260). Washington, DC: Urban Institute Press.

Geen, R. (2003b). Kinship foster care: An ongoing, yet largely uninformed debate. In R. Geen (Ed.), *Kinship care: Making the most of a valuable resource* (pp. 1–23). Washington, DC: Urban Institute Press.

Geen, R. (2004). The evolution of kinship care: Policy and practice. *Children, Families and Foster Care, 14*(1), 131–149.

Gibson, P. A. (2002). Caregiving role affects family relationships of African American grandmothers as new mothers again: A phenomenological perspective. *Journal of Marital and Family Therapy, 28*(3), 341–353.

Gleeson, J. P., & Seryak, C. M. (2010). "I made some mistakes . . . But I love them dearly": The views of parents of children in informal kinship care. *Child and Family Social Work, 15*(1), 87–96.

Gleeson, J. P., Wesley, J. M., Ellis, R., Seryak, C., Talley, G. W., & Robinson, J. (2009). Becoming involved in raising a relative's child: Reasons, caregiver motivations and pathways to informal kinship care. *Child and Family Social Work, 14*(3), 300–310.

Goodman, C. C. (2007). Intergenerational triads in skipped-generation grandfamilies. *International Journal of Aging and Human Development, 65*(3), 231–258.

Grote, N. K., Zuckoff, A., Swartz, H., Bledsoe, S. E., & Geibel, S. (2007). Engaging women who are depressed and economically disadvantaged in mental health treatment. *Social Work, 52*(4), 295–308.

Harden, B. J., Clyman, R. B., Kriebel, D. K., & Lyons, M. E. (2004). Kith and kin care: Parental attitudes and resources of foster and relative caregivers. *Children and Youth Services Review, 26*(7), 657–671.

Hayslip, B., Jr., Shore, R. J., Henderson, C. E., & Lambert, P. L. (1998). Custodial grandparenting and the impact of grandchildren with problems on role satisfaction and role meaning. *The Journals of Gerontology: Series B: Psychological Sciences and Social Sciences, 53B*(3), S164–S173.

Hegar, R. L. (1999). The cultural roots of kinship care. In R. L. Hegar & M. Scannapieco (Eds.), *Kinship foster care: Policy, practice, and research* (pp. 17–27). New York: Oxford University Press.

Houck, K. D. F., & Loper, A. B. (2002). The relationship of parenting stress to adjustment among mothers in prison. *American Journal of Orthopsychiatry, 72*(4), 548–558.

Hughes, M. E., Waite, L. J., LaPierre, T. A., & Luo, Y. (2007). All in the family: The impact of caring for grandchildren on grandparents' health. *The Journals of Gerontology: Series B: Psychological Sciences and Social Sciences, 62*(2), S108–S119.

Hungerford, G. P. (1996). Caregivers of children whose mothers are incarcerated: A study of the kinship placement system. *Children Today, 24,* 23–27.

Keller, T. E., Salazar, A. M., & Courtney, M. E. (2010). Prevalence and timing of diagnosable mental health, alcohol, and substance use problems among older adolescents in the child welfare system. *Children and Youth Services Review, 32*(4), 626–634.

Kelley, S. J., Whitley, D., Sipe, T. A., & Yorker, B. C. (2000). Psychological distress in grandmother kinship care providers: The role of resources, social support, and physical health. *Child Abuse and Neglect, 24*(3), 311–321.

Kelley, S. J., Yorker, B. C., Whitley, D. M., & Sipe, T. A. (2001). A multimodal intervention for grandparents raising grandchildren: Results of exploratory study. *Child Welfare: Journal of Policy, Practice, and Program, 80*(1), 27–50.

King, S., Kropf, N. P., Perkins, M., Sessley, L., Burt, C., & Lepore, M. (2009). Kinship care in rural Georgia communities: Responding to needs and challenges of grandparent caregivers. *Journal of Intergenerational Relationships, 7*(2), 225–242.

Koh, E. (2010). Permanency outcomes of children in kinship and non-kinship foster care: Testing the external validity of kinship effects. *Children and Youth Services Review, 32*(3), 389–398.

Kreider, R. M. (2008). *Living arrangements of children: 2004.* Retrieved September 16, 2010, from *www.census.gov/prod/2008pubs/p70–114.pdf.*

Main, R., Ehrle Macomber, J., & Geen, R. (2006). *Trends in service receipt: Children in kinship care gaining ground.* Washington, DC: Urban Institute Press.

Margolin, G., & Gordis, E. B. (2000). The effects of family and community violence on children. *Annual Review of Psychology, 51*(1), 445–479.

McGoldrick, M. (2011). Women and the family life cycle. In M. McGoldrick, B. Carter, & N. Garcia-Preto (Eds.), *The expanded family life cycle: Individual, family and social perspectives* (4th ed., pp. 42–58). Boston: Allyn & Bacon.

McGoldrick, M., Carter, B., & Garcia-Preto, N. (2011). Overview: The life cycle in its changing context: Individual, family and social perspectives. In *The expanded family life cycle: Individual, family, and social perspectives* (pp. 1–19). Boston: Pearson.

McGoldrick, M., Gerson, R., & Petry, S. (2008). *Genograms: Assessment and intervention* (3rd ed.). New York: Norton.

McKay, M. M., & Bannon, W. M., Jr. (2004). Engaging families in child mental health services. *Child and Adolescent Psychiatric Clinics of North America, 13*(4), 905–921.

McKay, M. M., Gonzales, J., Quintana, E., Kim, L., & Abdul-Adil, J. (1999). Multiple family groups: An alternative for reducing disruptive behavioral difficulties of urban children. *Research on Social Work Practice, 9*(5), 593–607.

McKay, M. M., Hibbert, R., Hoagwood, K., Rodriguez, J., Murray, L., Legerski, J., et al. (2004). Integrating evidence-based engagement interventions into "real world" child mental health settings. *Brief Treatment and Crisis Intervention, 4*(2), 177–186.

McLean, B., & Thomas, R. (1996). Informal and formal kinship care populations: A study in contrasts. *Child Welfare, 75*(5), 489–505.

McMillen, J. C., Zima, B. T., Scott, L. D., Jr., Auslander, W. F., Munson, M. R., Ollie, M. T., et al. (2005). Prevalence of psychiatric disorders among older youths in the foster care system. *Journal of the American Academy of Child & Adolescent Psychiatry, 44*(1), 88–95.

Miller, W. R., & Rollnick, S. (2002). *Motivational interviewing: Preparing people for change* (2nd ed.). New York: Guilford Press.

Minkler, M., & Fuller-Thomson, E. (2005). African American grandparents raising grandchildren: A national study using the Census 2000 American Community Survey. *The Journals of Gerontology: Series B: Psychological Sciences and Social Sciences, 60*(2), S82–S92.

Minkler, M., & Roe, K. M. (1993). *Grandmothers as caregivers: Raising children of the crack cocaine epidemic.* Thousand Oaks, CA: Sage.

Minuchin, P., Colapinto, J., & Minuchin, S. (2007). *Working with families of the poor* (2nd ed.). New York: Guilford Press.

Musil, C. M., Gordon, N. L., Warner, C. B., Zauszniewski, J. A., Standing, T., & Wykle, M. (2011). Grandmothers and caregiving to grandchildren: Continuity, change, and outcomes over 24 months. *The Gerontologist, 51*(1), 86–100.

O'Brien, P., Massat, C. R., & Gleeson, J. P. (2001). Upping the ante: Relative caregivers' perceptions of changes in child welfare policies. *Child Welfare: Journal of Policy, Practice, and Program, 80*(6), 719–748.

O'Reilly, E., & Morrison, M. L. (1993). Grandparent-headed families: New therapeutic challenges. *Child Psychiatry and Human Development, 23*(3), 147–159.

Osborne, C., & Berger, L. M. (2009). Parental substance abuse and child well-being: A consideration of parents' gender and coresidence. *Journal of Family Issues, 30*(3), 341–370.

Pennell, J., & Burford, G. (2000). Family group decision making: Protecting children and women. *Child Welfare: Journal of Policy, Practice, and Program, 79*(2), 131–158.

Poehlmann, J., Dallaire, D., Loper, A. B., & Shear, L. D. (2010). Children's contact with their incarcerated parents: Research findings and recommendations. *American Psychologist, 65*(6), 575–598.

Rauktis, M. E., McCarthy, S., Krackhardt, D., & Cahalane, H. (2010). Innovation in child welfare: The adoption and implementation of family group decision making in Pennsylvania. *Children and Youth Services Review, 32*(5), 732–739.

Rolland, J. S. (1994). *Families, illness, and disability: An integrative treatment model.* New York: Basic Books.

Ruiz, D. S. (2004). Custodian African American grandmothers: Reasons for caregiving and assumption of the caregiver role. *African American Perspectives, 10,* 152–159.

Russell, V., & Malm, K. (2003). In their own words: Kin speak out about their caregiving experiences. In R. Geen (Ed.), *Kinship care: Making the most of a valuable resource* (pp. 201–230). Washington, DC: Urban Institute Press.

Ryan, J. P., & Testa, M. F. (2005). Child maltreatment and juvenile delinquency: Investigating the role of placement and placement instability. *Children and Youth Services Review, 27*(3), 227–249.

Samuels, G. M. (2008). *A reason, a season, or a lifetime: Relational permanence among young adults with foster care backgrounds.* Chicago: Chapin Hall Center for Children at the University of Chicago.

Sheets, J., Wittenstrom, K., Fong, R., James, J., Tecci, M., Baumann, D. J., et al. (2009). Evidence-based practice in family group decision-making for Anglo, African American and Hispanic families. *Children and Youth Services Review, 31*(11), 1187–1191.

Simpson, G. M., & Lawrence-Webb, C. (2009). Responsibility without community resources: Informal kinship care among low-income, African American grandmother caregivers. *Journal of Black Studies, 39*(6), 825–847.

Smith, A., Krisman, K., Strozier, A. L., & Marley, M. A. (2004). Breaking through the bars: Exploring the experiences of addicted incarcerated parents whose children are cared for by relatives. *Families in Society, 85*(2), 187–195.

Solomon, J. C., & Marx, J. (2000). The physical, mental, and social health of custodial grandparents. In B. Hayslip & R. Goldberg-Glen (Eds.), *Grandparents raising grandchildren: Theoretical, empirical, and clinical perspectives* (pp. 183–219). New York: Springer.

Strong, D. D., Bean, R. A., & Feinauer, L. L. (2010). Trauma, attachment, and family therapy with grandfamilies: A model for treatment. *Children and Youth Services Review, 32*(1), 44–50.

Sundell, K., & Vinnerljung, B. (2004). Outcomes of family group conferencing in Sweden: A 3-year follow-up. *Child Abuse & Neglect, 28*(3), 267–287.

Testa, M. F. (2001). Kinship care and permanency. *Journal of Social Service Research, 28*(1), 25–43.

Testa, M. F., & Rolock, N. (1999). Professional foster care: A future worth pursuing? *Child Welfare, 78*(1), 108–124.

Timmer, S. G., Sedlar, G., & Urquiza, A. J. (2004). Challenging children in kin versus nonkin foster care: Perceived costs and benefits to caregivers. *Child Maltreatment, 9*(3), 251–262.

U.S. Census Bureau. (2005–2009). American Community Survey: Children Characteristics S0901. Retrieved July 14, 2011, from *factfinder.census.gov/servlet/sttable?_bm=y&-geo_id=01000us&-qr_name=acs_2009_3yr_g00_s0901&-ds_name=acs_2009_5yr_g00_.*

U.S. Census Bureau. (2008). Survey of Income and Program Participation, 2004 Panel, Wave 2: Detailed living arrangements of children by race, Hispanic origin, and age: 2004. Retrieved September 15, 2010, from *www.census.gov/population/www/socdemo/children.html.*

U.S. Department of Health and Human Services (DHHS). (2010). *The AFCARS Report: Preliminary FY 2009 Estimates as of July 2010.* Retrieved September 15, 2010, from *www.acf.hhs.gov/programs/cb/stats_research/afcars/tar/report17.htm.*

Walsh, F. (2006). *Strengthening family resilience* (2nd ed.). New York: Guilford Press.

Weigensberg, E. C., Barth, R. P., & Guo, S. (2009). Family group decision making: A propensity score analysis to evaluate child and family services at baseline and after 36 months. *Children and Youth Services Review, 31*(3), 383–390.

Weihs, K., Fisher, L., & Baird, M. (2002). Families, health, and behavior: A section of the commissioned report by the Committee on Health and Behavior: Research, Practice, and Policy Division of Neuroscience and Behavioral Health and Division of Health Promotion and Disease Prevention Institute of Medicine, National Academy of Sciences. *Families, Systems, and Health, 20*(1), 7–46.

Wells, K. (2011). A narrative analysis of one mother's story of child custody loss and regain. *Children and Youth Services Review, 33*(3), 439–447.

Wilson, L., & Conroy, J. (1999). Satisfaction of children in out-of-home care. *Child Welfare, 78*(1), 53–69.

Winokur, M., Holtan, A., & Valentine, D. (2009). Kinship care for the safety, permanency, and well-being of children removed from the home for maltreatment. *Cochrane Database of Systematic Reviews, 1*, CD006546.

Ziminski, J. (2007). Systemic practice with kinship care families. *Journal of Social Work Practice, 21*(2), 239–250.

CHAPTER 10

ADOPTIVE FAMILIES

CHERYL RAMPAGE
MARINA EOVALDI
CASSANDRA MA
CATHERINE WEIGEL FOY
GINA MIRANDA SAMUELS
LEAH BLOOM

Adoption begins with a decision to parent a child not born or conceived of one's own body. Adoptive families are thus intentional families, bound together by belief, will, practice, and most of all, love. Taken as a whole, adoption is a highly successful solution to the problem of providing permanent care and family relationships to children whose biological parents are unavailable (Fisher, 2003; Nickman et al., 2005). There are currently approximately 1.5 million adopted children under the age of 18 years living in the United States (Nickman et al., 2005).

All families face numerous challenges as they move through their life course. Adoptive families face almost all of the challenges of nonadoptive families and several more that arise as a function of the unique circumstances of adoption, including the fact that every adopted child has two families. These circumstances make adopted families complex. There remain biases in society that view this complexity as deficiency. Language referring to "natural" or "real" parents is but one way this bias is revealed. The premise of this chapter, however, is that adoptive families are an expression of the diverse forms that human relations can take and are eminently capable of meeting children's needs for family and parents. Although historically, formal adoptive parenthood in the United States was almost entirely limited to heterosexual married couples, changes in law and custom over the past few decades have resulted in a considerable number of single people, as well as lesbian and gay couples, forming their families through adoption.

CURRENT ADOPTION PRACTICES
IN THE UNITED STATES

"Open adoption" has today become more the norm than the exception in domestic adoptions. Openness describes a continuum; it may mean a onetime exchange of pictures and letters between birth parents and adoptive parents, a series of letters and picture exchanges over the years, or a face-to-face, ongoing relationship in which the birth parent is incorporated into the adoptive family on a permanent basis.

The trend toward openness has been met with ambivalence by some adoptive parents, who worry about whether their child will feel divided loyalty between the birth family and the adoptive family. Most birth mothers, however, feel much more satisfied with the experience of making an adoption plan when they have more information about the adoptive family and at least the opportunity for ongoing contact of some sort (Brodzinsky & Schecter, 1990). The first large cohort of children to experience open adoption is just entering young adulthood, so it will be some time before the long-term effects of openness can be clearly assessed. However, anecdotal evidence suggests that adoptees value openness, and that it may actually facilitate the development of a fully integrated and coherent sense of self.

Another trend impacting contemporary adoption practices is the increasing number of children being adopted from abroad. As the number of healthy domestic infants available for adoption plummeted during the decade after abortion became legal, parents and adoption agencies looked to various parts of the world, where social upheaval or dire economic circumstances made governments receptive to the idea of foreign adoption as an alternative to institutional care for their orphaned or abandoned children.

The process of adopting from a foreign country creates several layers of complexity for American parents. First, the adequacy of care varies considerably from country to country, and even from one orphanage to another within the same country. Records vary in completeness and even accuracy. The amount of paperwork and bureaucracy results in the children being older at the time of placement than is the case in most domestic adoptions, which means that there is a higher risk of a disrupted attachment or no attachment at all. Particularly if the child is from a different ethnic or racial group than the parents, the physical dissimilarity among family members means that the fact of the adoption will always be public, open to comment and interpretation from strangers as well as friends.

Another social trend affecting current adoption practice is a preference for adoption over long-term foster care placement for children whose parents are alive, but whose function is compromised by addiction, criminal activity, mental illness, or some other disability (see also, discussion of kinship care, Engstrom, Chapter 9, this volume). Increasingly, during the past two decades, child welfare departments of state governments have pressed for either speedy reunification of birth parents and children or prompt termination of parental rights, followed by placement in a permanent adoptive home. This policy, relatively new in most states, has created a pool of especially challenging adoption situations. Most of the children in this group are older; most have suffered some degree of neglect, and many have been abused. Many of the children who have had multiple placements have experienced multiple losses. Some of them have severe attachment disorders. Child welfare agencies are attempting to help families cope with the variety of challenges that parenting such children creates (Smith & Howard, 1999).

The Decision to Adopt

Although many couples think positively about adoption as a method of family formation, most only seriously pursue adoption if they are unable to conceive or carry a pregnancy to term. Indeed, most adoption agencies require proof of infertility as a prerequisite to beginning the adoption process, unless the parents are willing to adopt an older or "special needs" child. Thus, loss is an issue from the very beginning of adoption. Most adoption professionals believe it is important that the prospective adoptive parents resolve the loss that infertility has created before entering the adoption process. Resolving this loss means, in part, letting go of the idealized child that was hoped for, mourning that loss, and coming to accept it. Support groups such as RESOLVE attempt to assist couples in this process.

An alternative route to adoption is based on social or religious beliefs. In such cases, adoption is seen as the fulfillment of an obligation to do good and to care for those less fortunate than oneself. Parents who come to adoption in this manner often express an interest in adopting an older child or a child with a significant disability.

Yet another path to adoption may begin with the decision of a single person, or a gay or lesbian couple, to raise a child, and to choose adoption over various reproductive technologies as a way to become parents. Some adoption agencies will work with single parents; few are yet willing to accept applications by lesbian and gay couples.

The Adoption Process

When parents decide to adopt, they face the considerable challenge of determining whether to adopt through an agency or privately (usually facilitated by an attorney), whether to adopt domestically or internationally, and whether to accept an older child (in the adoption field, this generally means a child 2 years or older), a child with identified problems, or a child of mixed racial heritage.

Because the vast majority of potential adoptive parents are white and their number greatly exceeds the number of healthy, white infants available for adoption, agencies have established stringent criteria for adoptive parents seeking to adopt these children. These criteria include maximum ages for parents (often 40 or 45 for a first child), a minimum number of years married (3–5), proof of infertility, and, in some cases, religious affiliation. Couples who meet agency requirements then undergo a "home study," in which complete medical and social histories are collected. Many agencies also ask potential parents to participate in preparatory seminars and/or support groups. Once parents have been approved and are licensed as foster parents, they begin the waiting process. This is a period of indeterminate length, sometimes as much as 2 years, during which prospective parents live with the stress of knowing that they may get a call telling them that they will receive their baby in 2 or 3 days. When the placement has been made, there is a waiting period of 6 months to 1 year before the family can go to court and finalize the adoption.

This process applies only to the domestic adoption of healthy, white infants, the only category of adoptable children in short supply. The entire approval process is expedited if parents are interested in adopting an older child, a mixed-race child, or a child with some significant disability. Similarly, African American couples who wish to adopt are liable to have their approval process expedited, because there are far fewer of them than there are African American children waiting to be adopted (Smith & Howard, 1999).

If their ages, marital status, gender orientation, mixed religious affiliations, or any other factors prevent couples from seeking the help of an agency in adopting, they may choose to adopt privately. Private adoptions, generally conducted with the assistance of an attorney, may involve the adoptive parents' direct solicitations through newspaper advertisements, letters to physicians, and requests of family and friends to seek a birth mother who is considering an adoption plan for her child. There is little regulation of this type of adoption. Parents must contract with an agency to do a home study, but the amount of psychological preparation or counseling is minimal.

NORMAL PROCESSES IN ADOPTIVE FAMILIES

Attachment

Attachment, a process of relationship formation, is central to the social development of human beings (Ainsworth, 1989; Bowlby, 1960, 1973, 1980). It is an affectional bond that develops through positive, needs-satisfying, and pleasurable interaction. Attachment grows slowly, first between parents and child, eventually becoming the template for all future emotional relationships. Not an all-or-nothing phenomenon, attachment falls on a continuum that includes many variations, with solid, secure attachment on one end, and severe difficulties, such as reactive attachment disorder, on the other (O'Connor, Rutter, & the English and Romanian Adoptees Study Team, 2000). The majority of children fall somewhere in between the extremes (Melina, 1998).

Children placed for adoption within the first 12 months of life tend not to differ from nonadopted infants in developing healthy attachment relationships (Groze & Rosenberg, 2001). The important task of attachment formation in

adoptive families may be more complicated if the child has suffered neglect/
deprivation or disrupted attachments from earlier caregivers, if the parents
are unusually anxious, or if there is a poor match between parental expectations and the child's characteristics and behavior. Children placed after 12
months may be at risk for attachment problems and developmental difficulties
(Bowlby, 1973; Groze & Rosenberg, 2001). These children are likely to experience acute separation distress as a result of the severing of previous attachment relationships. Furthermore, in cases in which children have experienced
multiple placements or suffered early maltreatment, the formation of healthy
attachments in the adoptive family may be compromised.

Children adopted after infancy may lose relationships with birth parent,
siblings, and extended family members. They may suffer secondary losses of
friends, pets, toys, foods, customs, and familiar surroundings. These children
may also lose access to information about themselves (Chasnoff, Schwartz,
Pratt, & Neuberger, 2006). Adoptive parents may also experience secondary
losses, such as the loss of an earlier relationship with a birth or hoped-for birth
child. They may have experienced loss of status in the eyes of some people,
and loss of biological continuity. These losses may constrain both parents and
child in their willingness to risk developing subsequent attachments.

Research confirms that children placed in adoptive homes soon after
birth develop attachments to caregivers in the same way birth children do
and, subsequently, do not perceive the loss connected to adoption until around
age 8 (Brodzinsky & Brodzinsky, 1992). Cognitive development that occurs
between ages 8 and 11 enables them to have a deeper understanding of adoption. The normal process of adaptive grieving by adopted children usually
begins during this period.

The implications of attachment theory for the study of adoption are profound. Many adoption professionals believe that learning to cope with the
inevitable losses associated with adoption is critical for the development of
healthy attachments in the adoptive family. Yet, for some adoptive parents,
the existence of previous attachment figures, such as birth parents or foster
parents, is often experienced as a threat. Consequently, the parents may tend
to minimize the importance of these figures in their child's life and provide
little opportunity for the youngster to discuss feelings about these individuals. In such cases, the chance of coping effectively with adoption-related loss
is compromised, leading to increased risk for problems in the adoptive family (Belsky & Fearon, 2002; Reitz & Watson, 1992; Smith & Brodzinsky,
2002).

Attachment is an interactional process influenced by aspects of both the
child's and the parents' experiences. Difficulties sometimes arise even in the
attachment of birth children to their biological parents because of temperament differences or a mismatch in personality styles. For a child entering the
family at age 5 or 8, with a lot of emotional baggage and unmet needs, developing an attachment is even more complex. Furthermore, just as the effect of
past losses is a consideration for the child, resolution of past losses is also a

challenge for adoptive parents. Some families adopt a child who is the same age as a biological child of theirs who died. Others grieve for the "normal" child their adopted child might have been if he or she had not suffered so many blows before coming into their lives (Groze & Rosenberg, 2001). Adoptive parents grieve the damage done to their child and the pain the child is still experiencing.

A feeling of entitlement and the capacity emotionally to claim the adoptive child as their own also affect parents' development of attachments to the adopted child. The sense of being entitled to be parents of the child may be compromised by having to answer to agency workers or agency policies, such as having to get permission to take a child out of state. Claiming a child as one's own is a feeling and a commitment. Parents may need encouragement and support that underscore their unique role as adoptive parents in order to make this commitment. In addition to being claimed by parents, adopted children need to be claimed as belonging members of the extended family.

An added dimension of attachment formation in a family adopting an older child is the sibling connection. Some of the strongest, most positive attachments that children coming through the child welfare system have experienced are to siblings. Siblings in maltreating families often nurture each other and form strong bonds of dependence and loyalty. For many years after adoption, children may sustain feelings of responsibility or longing for siblings with whom they have lost contact.

Siblings already in the adoptive family are also affected by the arrival of an adopted child. Biological children of the adoptive parents may feel both an internal sense of privilege and unconscious guilt in their entitlement. Biological or previously adopted children in the family, when they learn about the adoption of a new sibling, may wonder about the circumstances of that sibling's birth, then develop uncertainty or questions about their own origins.

Developing a Livable, Coherent Family Story

All families develop stories to describe events and convey the meaning of those events to others. Because adoptive families are formed differently than biological families, this activity takes on greater significance. The family story has been called by various names, including the "life story" or the "adoption story." As family therapists, we prefer to refer to it as the "family story," because it is inclusive of individual development and places emphasis on the story as a vehicle for family development.

The family members' story about how their child came to live with them can provide a concrete link to the child's past and support his or her growing curiosity about origins. How the story is told is key. When told while the child, curled up on a parent's lap, basks in the concentrated attention from that parent, the message received is likely to encourage further exploration about adoption issues. This kind of telling promotes attachment and contributes to the development of an environment ripe for reinforcing positive views about self and one's heritage. If, on the other hand, no story is developed, the child is likely to sense the barrier being set between the biological and adoptive families, and open exploration of adoption issues is constrained.

Knowledge of developmental issues is essential both to crafting of the evolving family story and to the process and purpose of the telling. A child's ability to articulate and integrate the family story emerges over time. Between 1 and 2 years of age, a child develops a sense of "me" and often talks about "things that happened to me." "I was adopted" might be readily expressed without any understanding of adoption. Around 3 years of age, a child acquires the capacity for narratives that highlight the desires and beliefs that motivate actions. "I wanted ice cream, so I pulled the chair to the freezer, and . . . " Or "Anna was mean to me so I hid her doll." By 5 years old, children know that stories occur in a specific place and time, and involve characters who act on their beliefs and desires. Elementary school experiences (ages 5–10 years) teach children that good stories have a structure, and they learn what should be included, applying it to single personal events. It is not until adolescence that causal coherence emerges, allowing the adoptee to explain how one event caused or was related to other events in life. "My birth mom was only 17 years old when she got pregnant with me; she couldn't hold a job, finish school and take care of me. Her father had lost his job and couldn't take care of me either." In late adolescence/young adulthood, the thematic coherence of the family story emerges when the adoptee identifies values, themes, or principles that integrate various aspects in his or her life. "My birth father loved biology in high school and wanted to be a scientist. My (adoptive) parents taught me the value of 'giving back' to others; we went on service trips as a family throughout my childhood and adolescence. This all influenced me to go to med school, to prepare myself to work in communities in need" (Habermas & Bluck, 2000; McAdams, 2001).

With the development of the child's cognitive skills at about age 8 comes the dawning awareness that the family came together out of experiences of loss. Smith and Howard refer to this as the assumption that "somebody loves you and somebody doesn't" (1999, p. 90). Some believe they were given away because they were too much trouble or unlovable. Depending on how the context around telling the family story has developed, as well as on other child and parent specific variables (e.g., temperament and personality characteristics), the family story can become a vehicle through which loss can be addressed. Children's developing cognitive abilities allow them to comprehend more details regarding birth parents and their decision to make an adoption plan, as well as what led the adoptive parents to adopt. In this way, the family story becomes richer and more nuanced, and can be returned to again and again to understand life in a meaningful way. By developing a satisfactory account for the cause of the losses, the child is helped to make sense of the loss and recover from it (Melina, 1998). Even if the child does not talk about adoption, it is important to assume that he or she is thinking about it. As with any story, there is always the public or official family story. But just as significant is the private version that each family member holds and often does not share.

Most adoption professionals endorse an "early telling" theory about when to begin to talk with children about adoption. Through telling the family story when their child is very young, parents encourage openness about discussing adoption. It also gives them more time to practice the telling. Even when the child is too young to grasp the meaning of adoption, the "early telling" sets the stage for an honest, fuller exchange at a later time (Melina, 1998). Although parents should decide when and what to tell their child about adoption, it can become problematic if the child first learns about his or her adoption from someone other than a parent. Clinical wisdom supports telling the story even before the child can really comprehend its significance, in order to avoid even a semblance of secrecy or shame about the issue of adoption.

What to tell a child about his or her past is dependent on his or her age and developmental stage. In general, sharing accurate facts about the child's history is a good starting place. Of particular importance is information about transitions (i.e., where he or she was born, how he or she got to the adoptive home). With maturity, the child needs to hear about the interpretations of these facts. Telling the child that his or her birth parents probably did not consider the possibility of a pregnancy helps the child begin the struggle to see the complexity of human behavior rather than just label the birth parents as irresponsible or uncaring people. With difficult information, it is particularly important to be sensitive to the child's developmental stage, to strive for a balance between honoring the birth parent and acknowledging hardships and limitations (Melina, 1989). Sometimes the most painful details are the very things that give coherence to the story. If there are knowledge gaps in what is known, acknowledging this is a first step. Suggesting what might have been the case can also be helpful. For example, if the birth mother's age is not known, the parent can suggest that she might have been in her 20s, because most mothers who place their children are that age.

Early on, adoptive parents make the decision about what, when, and how to disclose information. By adolescence, parents' role in the developing narrative becomes more facilitative, as some children press for more information about or contact with their birth family. With the current milieu supporting more openness in the adoption process, some adopted children learn to deal with the presence of the biological family in their lives from an early age.

Telling the family's adoption story to the extended family and community requires parents to be prepared to meet the larger society's biases about adoption. Comments about how fortunate the child is or how wonderful the adoptive parents are for taking in another's child can bespeak an underlying belief that adoption is a less desirable way to create a family. In sharing their decision to adopt with extended family members, adoptive parents prepare the way for the arrival and welcoming of the child into the family. It is important to allow extended family members to give voice to their thoughts as they struggle with their own understanding of adoption, as well as their own sense of loss of a biological grandchild, niece, nephew, or cousin. However, the decision to talk about a child's adoptive status with people outside the immediate social circle of the family might best be done on a "need to know" basis. It makes sense to inform the child's teacher, because some school projects will undoubtedly include identifying family roots. But a parent responding to a stranger's comment about whom the child looks like might not include information about the child's adoptive status. The process need not become an exercise in converting the world to a better understanding of adoption; working with one's own family, close friends, and professionals that touch a child's life is likely to be enough.

THE ADOPTIVE FAMILY LIFE CYCLE

In a sense, adoption is a diversity issue, making it one of the many dimensions that are important to consider when trying to understand the uniqueness of any family system and family development. Just as race or ethnicity influence the tasks of family development, so, too, adoption is a dynamic affecting the stages through which families traverse.

Families with Infants and Toddlers

In contrast to most of the past century, in which non-relative adoptions were mostly of infants, an increasing number of adoptions today are of toddler-age children. The modal number of finalized adoptions is for children between the ages of 1 to 5 years (U.S. Department of Health and Human Services, 2006). Therefore, adoption often begins with the remarkable challenge for a child to adapt to a new "family environment" and for the family to adapt to a child who is already in the midst of rapid developmental leaps in cognition, language, and rudimentary personality features.

Compared to infant adoptions, in which parents have the freedom to consider when and how to disclose adoption as a part of the family story, conversations between parents and children adopted as toddlers or older children are an immediate and urgent necessity. With toddler adoptions there is a discontinuity in "family" that is readily apparent to the child. Depending upon age and linguistic abilities, the child may begin asking questions about the changes in family from the moment of meeting the adoptive parents.

The task of integrating the conversation about genesis of the family is central to the early stages of family development, whether the child was adopted as an infant or toddler. Research indicates that the family's ability to converse openly about adoption is directly correlated with the child's future adjustment (Brodzinsky & Palacios, 2005). The natural question of toddlerhood—"Where did I come from?"—lends itself to beginning a conversation. Preschoolers often process adoption at the level of how babies are made and how they became a part of the adoptive family. Young children develop a sense of belonging by examining similarities between themselves and adoptive parents. "Gotcha Day" is one form of ritual, used by many adoptive families, to celebrate the day the child became a part of the current family.

Families with School-Age Children

Two shifts occur as children transition out of toddlerhood: increasing abilities to understand the movement from the birth family to the adoptive family, and the entrance into school. The transition from the seemingly more "positive" atmosphere of the previous stage into another marked by more complexity can be difficult for children and their families. Both processes involve the incorporation of adoption as a part of identity.

"Adaptive grieving" is an important and healthy task for children at this stage of development. With realization of the loss of the birth family, feelings of rejection, loss, and grief associated with the relinquishment by the birth parent become a part of the reworking process. With an environment of openness to discussion about adoption, children can process questions about why birth parents relinquished them and how adoptive parents decided to adopt.

School, for most families, involves exposure to a greater diversity of families than ever before. Through school and/or extracurricular activities, the process of learning that there are many different types of families provides the context for social comparison. This developmental process, for children of adoptive families, may be more or less monumental depending upon the degree of difference between their family and other families in the environment. For example, a child growing up in a community in which intercultural parent–child relationships are common would likely have an easier time adapting to the transition than if that same family lived in a culturally homogeneous environment.

School also carries with it the task of handling school projects related to the definition of "family." With increasing sensitivity in the school systems to the diverse definitions of "family," school activities have become more inclusive for children from adoptive families than in previous decades. The Center for Adoption Studies and Education (CASE; 2010), for example, is an organization that provides support and advocacy for adoptive families in helping children negotiate the educational system.

Families with Adolescents

The individuation process, inherent in the socialization of American teenagers, is especially complex for the adoptee. Included in the separation process is the heightening of differences between adolescent and parents. For the adoptee, the perceived differences between him or herself and the adoptive parents may be attributed to not only an emerging difference in values and ideals but also the biological connection with another family, the birth family, even if that family is not known to the adoptee. The intensity of the separation between the adult and adolescent can trigger, for many adoptive families, anxieties about the potential loss of relationship. Research has found that there is more conflict in families with adopted adolescents than in similar, nonadoptive families (Rueter, Keyes, Iacono, & McGue, 2009). Working through the differences in developing a cohesive identity means integrating the parts of self from both the birth and adoptive families. The task of connecting to different parts of oneself while sorting through differences is an internal expression of integrating self, the biological family, and the adoptive family.

The question "What if?" underlies the additional task of developing a continuous narrative for the adolescent adoptee. Fantasies of how life might have proceeded with one's birth family, juxtaposed with the reality of the life in the current family system and social context, necessitate the weaving together of two stories into one. While this process is very much an individual struggle for the adolescent, adoptive parents provide a crucial context for exploration of identities by increasing freedom yet providing adequate safety and boundaries.

Adult Adoptees

Identity formation continues as the teenager becomes an adult. The constant reintegration process develops as the young adult adoptee learns more about self through vocational and/or educational pursuits. The task of gaining self-efficacy through work and the development of life skills aids in the process of moving past what may be perceived limitations from the past or predefined life courses.

In late adolescence and young adulthood many adoptees consider pursuing a search for biological parents and relatives. The continuing question "Who am I?" becomes central to the task of identity development. Embedded within this question, for the adoptee, are questions about biological/genetic history and birth family. Questions about one's past, for the young adult, facilitate the project of integrating the past, present, and future. For the adoptee, the search for information about biological predispositions, medical history, and other birth family-of-origin issues can be triggered by nodal life events, such as marriage, contemplation of becoming a parent, or the death of a family member. For many adoptees, little information may be available. For children from closed adoption situations or children adopted internationally, when birth parents are not known, identity formation may more heavily rely upon the adolescent's beliefs about what missing information might entail.

For parents, it is important to understand that the need of their child to gain knowledge about his or her past and birth family is a part of identity development and not a rejection of the adoptive family. For most families, the search process results in more intimate attachment between the adoptee and adoptive family. As the young adult makes progress in the task of integrating the adoption story into the larger narrative of his or her life, adoption itself moves from foreground to background.

"SPECIAL-NEEDS" ADOPTION

The federal government uses the term "special needs" to describe adoptable children who are either (1) over the age of 5 years; (2) from a minority background; (3) physically, emotionally, or developmentally disabled; or (4) part of a sibling group, all of whom are eligible for adoption (Public Law 96-272, Federal Register, 1980). Individual states can expand their definition of the term to include other categories of children, such as those in foster care (Brodzinsky, Smith, & Brodzinsky, 1998; Glidden, 1990).

Historically, children who fall into the category of "special needs" have been difficult to place into adoptive homes, and many have languished in institutional or foster care until "aging out." However, the dearth of healthy infants available for adoption since the widespread use of birth control and legalization of abortion in the 1970s has led to an increased number of special-needs adoptions in the past several decades (Smith & Howard, 1999). Each year more than 50,000 families in the United States adopt an older/special-needs child, usually from the ranks of children in foster care (Adoption and Foster Care Analysis and Reporting Systems, 2005). Although the majority of these adoptions are reported to be satisfying and/or successful by the families, there is a significant risk of disruption, in which the adoptive placement fails before it has been legally finalized. The rates of disruption in these adoptions are generally in the range of 10–25% but increase with the age of the child at the time of the adoptive placement (National Adoption Information Clearinghouse, 2004).

The greater risk of disruption is not surprising, given the life experiences of many older/special-needs adoptees. The majority of these children have been physically or sexually abused and/or had basic needs neglected for extended periods throughout infancy and early childhood (Grotevant, Dunbar, Kohler, & Lash, 2000). Many present with a variety of clinical issues, including post-traumatic stress, and behavioral problems (Smith & Howard, 1999). They often have attachment issues, ranging from mild to full-blown attachment disorders. Particularly challenging are cases in which the extent of the child's impairment is not immediately obvious (e.g., a prenatal environment that included drug or alcohol exposure sufficient to cause cognitive impairment; problems with executive functioning and impulse control, but not so severe that the child would be diagnosed with fetal alcohol syndrome). In such situations the child may seem to function fairly well at the time of placement, only to have difficulties become apparent over time, suffering academic failures, behavior problems, and difficulty learning from experience. Parents in these situations suffer along with their child, and often turn to one "expert" after another trying to discover a solution to their child's difficulty. Some parents who adopt older, "special needs" children feel that they were unprepared for the enormity of the child's needs and the paucity of real solutions. Parents who began the adoptive process equally committed and enthusiastic may diverge in their capacity to stay empathically connected to the child, placing a strain on the marriage, and leaving the more committed parent laboring under an even greater strain.

Children with Physical Disabilities

In comparison to parents who adopt children with psychological impairments, parents who adopt children with known physical disabilities generally report feeling pleased with their decision to adopt, and disruption rates of such adoptions are quite low (Rosenthal, Groze, & Aguilar, 1992), perhaps because the parents in such cases clearly understand from the outset of the adoption process the limitations of their child and accept the demands created by the child's physical disability. These parents often feel "called" by a spiritual desire to love and care for children whom other parents may not want, and they often find tremendous support in their families and religious communities (see Walsh, Chapter 15, this volume).

Successful Families

While a considerable literature documents the hazards and risks associated with older child and special-needs adoption, some families report successful outcomes with these children. These families tend to have an open communication style and the ability to provide warmth, empathy, and security (Triseliotis, 1991). Successful outcomes are also associated with families that display high levels of family closeness and flexibility (Clark, Thigpen, & Yates, 2006; Rosenthal & Groze, 1992). Couples who report marital stability and equal commitment to the adoption by both partners also report higher success rates. Furthermore, parental attitudes, such as confidence in their ability to handle aggressive impulses (Kagan & Reid, 1986), acceptance of their child's vulnerabilities, and the perception of the child's legitimate membership in the family (Kadushin, 1970; Triseliotis, 1991) have also been found to be associated with successful outcomes. In contrast, within 12 to 15 months, parents tend to give up on adoption if they are unable to detect an attachment with the child and/or an improvement in the child's behavior. Relative to this point, Clark et al. (2006), found that families who reported successful outcomes in adopting older and special-needs children describe a recursive process of experiencing a connection to the child and perceiving a reciprocal connection of the child to them as parents. The authors hypothesized that this connection process was facilitated by the parents' perceived affirmations of their competency.

A central implication of the research on successful older child and special-needs adoption is that some child management problems may be corrected through teaching more effective parenting technique and attitudes, and that children's actual functioning may have less impact on successful adoption outcomes than parental perceptions of those behaviors. This conclusion is consistent with that of Rushton, Dance, and Quinton (2000), who found that behavioral difficulties per se do not present a major risk for disruption provided the family can develop a structure in which the behaviors can be managed. Techniques the successful families used included reframing of the child's behavior and viewing behavior in context. These families view improvements in behavior as evidence of positive responses to nurturing. For adoption workers and family therapists these findings give hope for the placement of children displaying difficult behaviors, and offer families an alternative to what has been referred to as the deficit adoption discourse (Gorman, 2004).

INTERNATIONAL ADOPTION

International adoptions in substantial numbers began to occur in the United States after World War II, and the United States is currently one of the leading supporters, receiving just over half of all such adoptions (United Nations Children's Fund [UNICEF], 2003). Recent trends include an increase in the number of countries allowing international adoptions and an emphasis on the importance of supporting exploration of the adoptee's ethnic identity. Asia and Southeast Asia are the most common homelands of internationally adopted children in the United States, but there are currently programs open throughout Eastern Europe, South America, and Ethiopia (U.S. Department of State, 2009), creating a highly diverse community of families formed through international adoption. Which countries are willing to allow their youngest and most vulnerable citizens to be adopted internationally is a complex issue, dependent on the country's sociopolitical climate and stability, as well as on environmental conditions.

The Hague Convention of 1993, which originally sought to provide a core framework of policy, practice, and agreement between countries in the best interest of the child, was amended in 2008 in a further effort to streamline uniform practices across adoption agencies, thereby increasing quality of care and ethical practice (Bailey, 2009). Still, international adoption is a more complex process in general than domestic adoption. Procedures and rules vary widely from country to country; parents sometimes have to travel multiple times to the country of origin to complete the process, and information about birth parents is frequently very sparse.

Health and Development

Cognitive, communication, health, and language delays are some of the challenges commonly associated with international adoption, in addition to concerns about general health care and attachment experiences prior to the placement. There is a wide range of quality in the care infants and children receive in the preadoptive placement, varying from country to country and even between orphanages in the same country. Concern about the extent of developmental delays sometimes leads potential parents to seek out advice and opinion from U.S. pediatricians, a few of whom offer screenings based on video and photographic images, as well as the available health documentation from the orphanage.

Implications for Identity Development

The trend toward international adoption in the United States has vastly increased the number of multiracial and multiethnic families in this country (Pertman, 2000). The importance of providing resources, open dialogue, and opportunities to immerse not only the child but also the *entire* family into the various cultures and ethnicities is the core of the term "cultural socialization" (Lee, Grotevant, Hellerstedt, Gunnar, & the Minnesota International Adoption Project Team, 2006). Many families of internationally adopted children each year attend culture camps organized around celebrating the culture of the child's country of origin. As an added benefit, the families get to share their experiences with other families who have made the same journey and faced similar challenges.

The legal and political complexities associated with the permanent removal of a child from his or her country of origin result in adopted children usually being placed during toddlerhood or early childhood rather than infancy. Many internationally adopted children arrive in this country speaking the language of their original country, with memories of a life before adoption, and having already absorbed some of their original culture in such forms as music, games, food, and toys. The culture shock they experience can be profound and difficult for them to articulate. Adoption agencies often specialize in adoptions emanating from one particular country. These agencies encourage American parents to learn some simple phrases in the child's original language, hear music sung in that language, prepare foods that are familiar, and ultimately see themselves as a bicultural family. Relationships with other such families are encouraged, so that the child sees multiple families in which homogeneity of skin color or ethnic identity is not the norm within the family.

However well the adoptive family handles issues of multiculturalism during early years, the child's adolescence is likely to intensify feelings of differentness, perhaps accompanied by wishes to reconnect with members of the birth family, or to visit the country of origin. Rapid changes in the physiology of adolescents lead most of them to look into the mirror occasionally and not recognize the person staring back at them. The teen being raised by biological parents has the implicit awareness of becoming more physically like the adult relatives in the family. In most cases of international adoption, the teen has no image of related adults to use as some forecast of how he or she will look as an adult, and may not even have any ethnically similar adults in the community to serve as role models. The sense of differentness can be compounded by peer groups' pressures for conformity. Some make every effort to fit in, even attempting to lighten hair or skin, or change the shape of their eyes; others withdraw to the margins. Open parent–child communication and understanding of these dilemmas can support efforts to navigate the teenage social world.

Transnational adoptees' efforts to find their place in the larger world ("Where do I belong?"; "Where is my true home?") are similar to the challenges of transnational migrants. Immigrants who adapt best avoid the extreme of assimilation and cutoff from their roots, and attemp to hold "two hearts" in an expanded bicultural identity and connection (see Falicov, Chapter 13, this volume).

Some adult adoptees have addressed their struggle through the modality of film, providing powerful and poignant opportunities to see life through their eyes. A notable example of this genre is Deann Borshay Liem's autobiographical documentary, *First Person Plural* (1999). In her journey to find herself and her Korean identity, the filmmaker discovers her true name and the fact that she was not an orphan, then reconnects with her biological family in Korea. Wanting to integrate her two families and her own identity, she makes a second visit to Korea with her adoptive parents. The film captures the moment when her adoptive parents meet her biological family for the first time. The adoptive mother brings a wonderful gift to the birth mother: an album of photos of Deann as she was growing up. This scene also reveals how caring adoptive parents can provide unconditional love and support and yet be unable to completely empathize with their child's experience. As Deann's adoptive mother asks to be reminded of her daughter's Korean name, Deann replies: "Cha Jung Hee." Because it is not her native language, the mother has difficulty pronouncing it and simply says it does not matter, she'll always be "Deann" to her. Unintentionally invalidating the daughter's Korean identity, it poignantly exemplifies the complexities of the adoptee's experience in even the most supportive family environment. After the visit, Deann asks her parents why they never asked her about her experience of adoption. They reply, "We were waiting for you to ask us." The mother adds, "I suppose we were also afraid of what we might hear and that we might lose you." This common fear of rejection and loss often silences important conversations about adoption in families. Parents are urged to take the initiative in opening communication, and to approach it as an evolving process over time.

The documentary *Not a Svensson Anymore* (Olsson & Hanslep, 2009) tracks the journey of Emilio, adopted in Sweden, in search of his birth father in Columbia. Emilio's adoptive father Bengt accompanies him on the journey and gives voice to the often underrepresented perspective of the male experience in adoption—from both the adoptee and the paternal perspective. Raised by Swedish parents, Emilio describes having a continual desire to connect with his birth family to discover who he looks like. Emilio's thrust toward wanting to connect with his culture and biological family is in essence a desire to connect with sameness. Taken against the backdrop of feeling different in a homogeneous society such as Sweden, this film highlights the universal challenge for international adoptees: that the search for identity is not only an emotional journey but also a geographical one. Successful adoptive parents do not interpret these longings as rejection or signs of their failure as parents; rather they empathize with their child's desires and collaborate to meet the adoptee's needs as well as they can. It is therefore relevant to apply the term "first-person plural" to the international adoption narrative—the collective voice of all parties touched by adoption and lending their support as the adoptee traverses the complex road of self-discovery toward an expanded bicultural sense of identity and connection.

TRANSRACIAL ADOPTIONS

Transracial adoptions may be either domestic or international. They involve parents of one race adopting a child of another. While no reliable statistics exist to track transracial adoption in the United States, estimates suggest anywhere from 24 to 40% of all adoptions are transracial (Samuels, 2009; Vandivere, Malm, & Radel, 2009).

All international adoptions are transnational and cross-cultural, because they involve parents adopting children from another country or nation. In this case, parents and children differ in culture of origin and nationality. Many international adoptions are also transracial, because parents who adopt internationally are predominantly white and the children available for adoption are often from non-European countries.

In the United States and globally, debates have persisted over the importance of racial similarity between parents and children. At one end of the continuum are color-blind ideals expressed as "love is enough," which often risk diminishing the salience of race and racism. At the other end, predictions of severe identity problems and cultural loss risk pathologizing all transracial adoptees as inherently doomed to these negative outcomes. Today, with the exception of Native American children, adoption policy outlaws the use of race or culture to delay or deny any potential adopter from adopting any child (Interethnic Adoption Provisions, 1996). Despite protransracial adoption laws, and increases in multiracial families across the United States, multiracial adoptive families continue to navigate a litany of public opinions and politics attached to their family system (Trenka, Oparah, & Shin, 2006). These societal stigmas require multiracial adoptive families to develop coping skills and, together, to foster resilience.

Contemporary research, including scholarship authored by adult adoptees, generally finds that color-blind or "child choice" approaches to racial socialization can be developmentally detrimental into adulthood (Lee, 2003; Samuels, 2009, 2010; Shiao & Tuan, 2008; Smith, McRoy, Freundlich, & Kroll, 2008; Trenka et al., 2006). This approach to parenting ignores or downplays the role of race, or the presence of racial and ethnic "difference" in the family. Among adoptees whose parents overemphasize "sameness," research suggests that this can leave children feeling racially isolated and unsupported in dealing with racism and their obvious racial difference both in and outside of their families. Color blindness can facilitate disconnections between parents and child when the child's experience of a highly racialized world does not correspond to parental philosophies of a color-blind one. Consequently, the "search" process, a hallmark developmental task among many adult adoptees, often holds increased importance for racial identity work among this group. In general, many report that key aspects of their racial identity work occurred in adulthood, when they were able to establish, often for the first time, the meaningful racial–ethnic and cultural connections that were desired but often missing during childhood (Lee, 2003; Samuels, 2009; Trenka et al., 2006).

White families are still not perceived as the "normative" context in which children of color grow up. Despite changes in the U.S. Census and expanding definitions of "family," the normative expectation of all persons is that they come from families where all members share a racial heritage and identity. Similar to nonadoptive multiracial families, many transracial adoptees find themselves in social situations where they are expected to have familially grounded cultural experiences, relationships, and racial–ethnic affiliations and identities that they may not possess. Many transracial adoptees also continue to grow up in suburban and rural settings, contexts in which they are perpetual minorities in both their families and communities. While many persons of color experience communities in which they too are racial–ethnic minorities, most persons are not also racial–ethnic minorities in their families. This familial difference (lacking at least one parent of color) marks transracial adoptees as "different" within their ethnic communities of origin.

Yet despite a lack of access to these relationships and experiences, transracial adoptees are still socially expected to retain strong ties to their cultures of origin. In the long term, in developing skills to navigate these social expectations successfully, familial differences serve as strengths into adulthood for negotiating complex multicultural contexts (e.g., biculturalism). In childhood, without parental support, acknowledgment, or guidance for their bicultural development, many transracial adoptees can experience the litany of questions seeking to resolve the confusion of others around their "true" racial identities and allegiances (e.g., "Is that your mother? Where are you from?"). This can be experienced as isolating and stigmatizing, only adding to the racial stigma any person of color may experience due to his or her racial appearance. Thus, adoptive parents share the same parenting task as parents of color, to socialize their children racially and culturally to navigate racism and discrimination. However, they have the unique, added task of preparing their children for the racial politics and bias (in both minority and majority communities) toward multiracial family systems headed by white parents, including transracially adoptive ones (Samuels, 2009).

Increasingly, research suggests that resilient identities among transracial adoptees and families can be fostered by (1) parents maintaining positive relational ties to their child's cultural and racial communities of origin prior to adopting; (2) creating a multicultural and a multiracial identity and daily lifestyle that is shared among all family members; (3) connecting to other multiracial families and transracially adopted children as additionally supportive communities; and (4) openly discussing and acknowledging racism, prejudice, and bias, including that toward transracial adoption, as it manifests uniquely in white communities and in communities of color. The tendency to rely on culture camp, festivals, ethnic dolls and books, or use of a specific racial label as primary socialization strategies is increasingly viewed as insufficient to support a child's enduring sense of belonging or connection to a cultural or ethnic community (Lee, 2003; Samuels, 2010). Rather, parents are encouraged to actively consider their own racial and cultural identities and origins, and those of their children, in order to forge a unique family culture and identity that is inclusive and affirming to all its members across the life course.

CLINICAL ISSUES

The clinical issues faced by adoptive families vary over the course of their life cycle, and also as a function of unique intrapersonal and interpersonal factors in the family. Careful assessment of these factors allows clinicians to be of greatest assistance to an adoptive family seeking professional help. This section reviews both issues and solutions at various life stages, with special attention to the qualities and experiences that promote resilience in adoptive families.

The Child and Family at Preplacement

For parents, possibly the most important predictor of success that can be assessed at this stage is how realistic their expectations are. If adoption is being considered because biological reproduction is not an option, grieving that loss is an essential task to protect the adopted child from being seen as the far less satisfactory solution to having a child. This turning to an adopted child to serve as a substitute for the ungrieved loss is not necessarily within parents' conscious awareness, so they may not recognize its role as it manifests later on. Since adoption practices vary widely, and some families adopt without any significant contact with an adoption agency, it is important to assess how prepared the parents are to manage the difference between becoming a family through adoption versus birth. For family resilience, parents should be encouraged to be open to education about adoption, and not to expect that their love alone can overcome any preplacement deficits or challenges their child has faced. They should be able to openly discuss their concerns or fears about dealing with a birth parent in an open adoption, raising a child who is culturally or racially different from themselves, or accepting the fact that someday their child may wish to search for a birth parent.

Helpful steps for clinicians to recommend at this point include the following:

- Reaching out to other families who have adopted, both for education and support.
- Reading books and Internet-based material about the adoption experience from the perspective of the adopted child, the birth parent, and the adoptive parent.
- Making decisions about how to respond to the inevitable questions from the extended family and larger community about their child and their decision.
- In cases where the adopted child is from a different racial or ethnic group than the adoptive family, preparing to embrace a bicultural or biracial family identity.

For the child at preplacement, the situation is clearer, and choice is hardly a consideration. Children are most likely to reach their maximum potential when raised in a loving family. No matter how good an institution is, it is a poor substitute for an adequate family. Little can be done to prepare a preverbal child for an adoptive placement, but older children benefit from having a predictable transition plan, including visits and letters from the adoptive parents.

Early Postplacement

Families who seek help during this period have usually spent time anticipating that it would be challenging. Thus, few families who adopt infants immediately seek clinical services. On the other hand, it is not uncommon for families who adopt older children to arrange for professional help even before placement. In addition to the range of physical needs these children might have, often requiring medical intervention, they also often demonstrate some degree of difficulty with attachment. This may range from something as relatively simple as clinging behavior or shyness of strangers to full-blown reactive attachment disorder. Regarding the child's tantrums, indifference or rejection as a personal attack may result in parental withdrawal, or failure to fully bond with the child. Resilience is served when parents regard the child's behavior as a problem to be solved, not as a sign that the adoption is failing. Viewed through that lens, parents can patiently accept the child's problems as part of the process of becoming part of the family, and begin to develop a viable story about the adoption with the child. Members of the parents' family or community often are aware of the fact of adoption prior to the adoptee being told. How the parents want family and friends to handle this information is something that parents ought to think about, and perhaps discuss with family and friends, prior to the adoptee reaching the age when he or she can understand such facts. At the same time, a child's readiness to disclose the fact of his or her adoption status to the peer group may not always reflect the parents' desire for such openness. A child may hesitate to disclose the adoption identity for a period of time after learning about said status. Families may need help recognizing the importance of honoring the child's tempo, and understanding the challenges to the child in coming to terms with his or her identity as an adoptee.

Community values and mores may also impact the ability of the adoptive parents to integrate a child smoothly into the family. Such attitudes can be conveyed by friends and neighbors, as well as by the pediatrician and other professionals. The expression of unsupportive attitudes in the community about international or mixed-race adoption—whether in subtle or direct forms—can negatively impact the adoptive parents' ability to transition smoothly into their new family status, and can compound for them any postplacement questions with which they might be struggling about the wisdom of having adopted at all. This is especially true when adoptees, whether infants or older children, are presenting serious behavioral challenges and causing unexpectedly high levels of distress in the home.

Clinical intervention at this stage might focus on the following:

- Educating the family about the challenges to the child in transitioning into a new family.
- Normalizing the child's behavior as a response to his or her increased vulnerability.
- Assisting the adoptive family members in developing their preferred responses to questions and comments ranging from "Do you know who his real parents were?" to "She's so lucky to have the two of you."
- Helping family members notice and appreciate small gains in their process of truly becoming family to each other.
- Helping two-parent families negotiate parental differences about how to answer their adopted child's questions, or manage the child's openness with the outside world about the fact of adoption. Differences in partners' perceptions around issues of safety (if the child discloses his or her status to others), and how they may perceive (and value) the identity of an adoptive family can create tensions in the parental relationship that easily trickle down to the child. Professional guidance can help.
- Encouraging the family to develop ongoing relationships with other adoptive families.
- Referral to a therapist who specializes in helping children with attachment disorders, if indicated.

Later Challenges

For many adoptees, adoption starts out as just a neutral fact about themselves, not much different than their hair color or where they live. The psychological meaning of adoption evolves over a period of years. Parents who have reached the conclusion that their child has fully integrated the adoption experience before adulthood are often surprised to find that their 10-year-old is wishing he were like everyone he knows who is being raised by biological parents, or that their 16-year-old wants to do a search for her birth mother. People raised in biologically related families take for granted the contributions to identity that their relatives provide, just by sharing so many genes and a common history threaded through the family tree. Adoptees must form their identities from the customs, habits, and preferences to which they have been exposed in their adopted family, *and* from the biological predispositions of a family they may not know. At this stage, resilient parents are empathic to the adopted child's potential need to understand his or her biological heritage, perhaps even to establish contact with the birth parents. Openness and an unswerving commitment to love the child are the foundation of the relationship. Clinical issues that may emerge in this stage include the following:

- Exploring the adoptee's fantasy of the birth family, and possibly to recruit the adoptive parent(s) to facilitate a search process. Consultation with a family therapist around the search (and possible reunion) process can be very helpful in allowing adoptive parents to develop a supportive, nondefensive response to their child's wish to know more about the birth family. In addition, therapy can assist the adoptee in fully considering the possible outcomes of a search, which may range from total rejection to an offer for full inclusion in the birth family.

- Increased conflict between the adoptive parents and their teen (O'Brien & Zamostny, 2003), possibly due to a less than optimal fit between the personalities and/or behavioral tendencies of the parents and the teen. A family therapist might be able to help family members work around or otherwise minimize the potential difficulties of such a misfit.

- Encouraging the adoptee to develop an identity that incorporates *both* the learning and experience from the adoptive family *and* elements whose origins are not clear, or which are clearly associated with the birth family.

CONCLUSIONS

Families formed by adoption are necessarily complex. Their stories always include loss, intervention by legal and social service professionals, and an awareness that they are different from most other families. When this complexity is accepted, when the losses are acknowledged and resolved; when parents and their children feel satisfied with adoption as a legitimate route to becoming a family; and when the community of family, friends, and professionals who surround them is affirming, then the outcomes for adoptive families are very positive.

REFERENCES

Adoption and Foster Care Analysis and Reporting System. (2005). The AFCARS Report: Current estimates as of August 2004. Retrieved February 14, 2005, from *www.acf.hhs.gov/programs/cb.*

Ainsworth, M. D. S. (1989). Attachment beyond infancy. *American Psychologist, 44*(4), 709–716.

Bailey, J. D. (2009). Expectations of the consequences of new international adoption policy in the U.S. *Journal of Sociology and Social Welfare, 36*(2), 169–184.

Belsky, J., & Fearon, R. M. P. (2002). Early attachment security, subsequent maternal sensitivity, and later child development: Does continuity in development depend on continuity in caregiving? *Attachment and Human Development, 4*(3), 361–387.

Bowlby, J. (1960). Grief and mourning in infancy and early childhood. *Psychological Study of the Child, 15,* 9–52.

Bowlby, J. (1973). *Attachment and loss: Separation.* New York: Basic Books.

Bowlby, J. (1980). *Attachment and loss: Loss, sadness and dependency.* New York: Basic Books.

Brodzinsky, D. M., & Brodzinsky, A. B. (1992). The impact of family structure on the adjustment of adopted children. *Child Welfare, 71,* 69–75.

Brodzinsky, D. M., & Palacios, J. (2005). *Psychological issues in adoption: Theory, research and practice.* Westport, CT: Greenwood.

Brodzinsky, D. M., & Schecter, M. D. (1990). *The psychology of adoption.* New York: Oxford University Press.

Brodzinsky, D. M., Smith, D. W., & Brodzinsky, A. (1998). *Children's adjustment to adoption: Developmental and clinical issues.* Thousand Oaks, CA: Sage.

Center for Adoption Studies and Education (CASE). (2010). Retrieved June 28, 2010, from *www.adoptionsupport.org.*

Chasnoff, I. J., Schwartz, L. D., Pratt, C. L., & Neuberger, G. J. (2006). *Risk and promise—a handbook for parents adopting a child from overseas.* Chicago: NTI Publications.

Clark, P., Thigpen, S., & Yates, A. M. (2006). Integrating the older/special needs adoptive child into the family. *Journal of Marital and Family Therapy, 32*(2), 181–194.

Federal Register. (1980, February 22). Public Law No. 96-272: *The Adoption Assistance and Child Welfare Act of 1980.* Retrieved December 8, 2010, from *www.acf.hhs.gov/programs/cb/laws_policies/policy/pgm/pgm8101.htm.*

Fisher, A. P. (2003). Still, "Not quite as good as having your own"?: Towards a sociology of adoption. *Annual Review of Sociology, 29,* 335–361.

Glidden, L. M. (Ed.). (1990). *Formed families: Adoption of children with handicaps.* Binghamton, NY: Haworth.

Gorman, P. (2004, May–June). Resisting the deficit view. *Family Therapy Magazine,* pp. 22–25.

Grotevant, H., Dunbar, N., Kohler, J., & Lash, E. A. (2000). Adoptive identity: How contexts within and beyond the family shape developmental pathways. In R. Javier, L. Baden, F. A. Biafora, & A. Camcho-Gingerich (Eds.), *Handbook of adoption: Implications for researchers, practitioners and families* (pp. 77–89). Thousand Oaks, CA: Sage.

Groze, V., & Rosenberg, K. (2001). *Clinical and practice issues in adoption: Bridging the gap between adoptees placed as infants and as older children*. Westport, CT: Bergin & Garvey.

Habermas, T., & Bluck, S. (2000). Getting a life: The emergence of the life story in adolescence. *Psychological Bulletin, 126*, 748–769.

Interethnic Adoption Provisions [IEAP], Public Law No. 104-1888, 3448, (1996).

Kadushin, A. (1970). *Adopting older children*. New York: Columbia University Press.

Kagan, R. M., & Reid, W. J. (1986). Critical factors in the adoption of emotionally disturbed youth. *Child Welfare, 65*, 63–73.

Lee, R. M. (2003). The transracial adoption paradox: History, research, and counseling implications of cultural socialization. *Counseling Psychologist, 31*(6), 711–744.

Lee, R. M., Grotevant, H. D., Hellerstedt, W. L., Gunnar, M. R., & the Minnesota International Adoption Project Team. (2006). Cultural socialization in families with internationally adopted children. *Journal of Family Psychology, 20*(4), 571–580.

Liem, D. B. (Producer/Director). (1999). *First person plural* [Documentary film]. Berkeley, CA: MU Films.

McAdams, D. (2001). The psychology of life stories. *Review of General Psychology, 5*, 100–122.

Melina, L. (1998). *Raising adopted children* (rev. ed.). New York: Harper & Row.

National Adoption Information Clearinghouse. (2004). Adoption disruption and dissolution: Numbers and trends. Retrieved February 14, 2005, from *naic.acf.hhs. gov.pubs/s-disrup.cfm*.

Nickman, S. L., Rosenfeld, A. A., Fine, P., MacIntyre, J. C., Pilowsky, D. J., Howe, R. J. D., et al. (2005). Children in adoptive families: Overview and update. *Journal of the American Academy of Child and Adolescent Psychiatry, 44*, 987–995.

O'Brien, K. M., & Zamostny, K. P. (2003). Understanding adoptive families: An integrative review of empirical research and future directions for counseling psychology. *Counseling Psychologist, 31*, 679–710.

O'Connor, T. G., Rutter, M., & the English and Romanian Adoptees Study Team. (2000). Attachment disorder behavior following early severe deprivation: Extension and longitudinal follow-up. *Journal of American Academy of Child and Adolescent Psychiatry, 39*(6), 703–712.

Olsson, M. (Producer), & Hanslep, T. (Director). (2009). *Not a Svensson anymore* [Motion picture]. Sweden: Mattias Olsson Film och Bild.

Pertman, A. (2000). *Adoption nation: How the adoption revolution is transforming America*. New York: Basic Books.

Reitz, M., & Watson, K. W. (1992). *Adoption and the family system*. New York: Guilford Press.

Rosenthal, J. A., & Groze, V. K., (1992). *Special-needs adoption: A study of intact families*. New York: Praeger.

Rosenthal, J. A., Groze, V. K., & Aguilar, G. D. (1992). Adoption outcomes for children with handicaps. *Child Welfare, 70*(6), 623–636.

Rueter, M. A., Keyes, M. A., Iacono, W., & McGue, M. (2009). Family interactions in adoptive compared to nonadoptive families. *Journal of Family Psychology, 23*(1), 58–66.

Rushton, A., Dance, C., & Quinton, D. (2000). Findings from a UK based study of late permanent placements. *Adoptive Quarterly, 3*, 51–73.

Samuels, G. M. (2009). "Being raised by white people": Navigating racial difference among adopted multiracial adults. *Journal of Marriage and Family, 71*, 80–94.

Samuels, G. M. (2010). Building kinship and community: Relational processes of bicultural identity among adult multiracial adoptees. *Family Process, 49*(1), 26–42.

Shiao, J. L., & Tuan, M. H. (2008). Korean adoptees and the social context of ethnic exploration. *American Journal of Sociology, 113*(4), 1023–1066.

Smith, D. W., & Brodzinsky, D. M. (2002). Coping with birthparent loss in adopted children. *Journal of Child Psychology and Psychiatry, 43*, 213–223.

Smith, S. L., & Howard, J. A. (1999). *Promoting successful adoptions: Practice with troubled families.* Thousand Oaks, CA: Sage.

Smith, S. L., McRoy, R., Freundlich, M., & Kroll, J. (2008). *Finding families for African American children: The role of race and law in adoption from foster care.* New York: Evan B. Donaldson Institute.

Trenka, J. J., Oparah, J. C., & Shin, S. Y. (2006). *Outsiders within: Writing on transracial adoption.* Cambridge, MA: South End Press.

Triseliotis, J. (1991). Adoption outcomes: A review. In E. E. Hibbs (Ed.), *Adoption: International perspective* (pp. 291–310). Madison, CT: International Universities Press.

United Nations Children's Fund (UNICEF). (2003). *Innocenti social monitors.* Florence, Italy: UNICEF Innocenti Research Centre. Retrieved May 20, 2010, from *www.unicefcdc.org/publications/pdf/monitor03/monitor2003.pdf.*

U.S. Department of Health and Human Services, Administration for Children and Families, Administration on Children, Youth and Families, Children's Bureau. (2006). *AFCARS Report.* Retrieved December 8, 2010, from *www.acf.hhs.gov/programs/cb/stats_research/index.htm.*

U.S. Department of State. (2009). *Total adoptions to the United States* [Bar graph and accompanying table illustrating total adoptions, 1999–2009 and FY 2005–FY 2009, respectively]. Retrieved May 20, 2010, from *adoption.state.gov/news/total_chart.htm.*

Vandivere, S., Malm, K., & Radel, L. (2009). *Adoption USA: A chartbook based on the 2007 national survey of adoptive parents.* Washington, DC: U.S. Department of Health and Human Services, Office of the Assistant Secretary for Planning and Evaluation.

PART III

CULTURAL DIMENSIONS IN FAMILY FUNCTIONING

CHAPTER 11

CULTURE

A Challenge to Concepts of Normality

MONICA MCGOLDRICK
DEIDRE ASHTON

> No one goes anywhere alone, least of all into exile—not even
> those who arrive physically alone, unaccompanied by family,
> spouse, children, parents, or siblings. No one leaves his or her
> world without having been transfixed by its roots, or with
> a vacuum for a soul. We carry with us the memory of many
> fabrics, a self soaked in our history, our culture; a memory,
> sometimes scattered, sometimes sharp and clear, of the streets
> of our childhood.
>
> —FRIERE (1994, p. 32)

In psychotherapy and the provision of social service assistance to individuals, couples, and families, culture matters. Culture is primary, essential, and integral to the healing process (McGoldrick & Hardy, 2008; Smith, 2010; Sue & Sue, 2008). It is significantly correlated with our worldview, how we see ourselves in relationship to our world and others, how we define and understand reality, and how we think (Sue & Sue, 2008). All of our theories of psychology, human development, family systems, wellness, pathology, and healing are informed by cultural values, beliefs, and norms (Carter, 2003; Ponterotto, Casas, Suzuki, & Alexander, 2010). For example, traditional Eastern cultures tend to define the person as a social being and categorize development by growth in the human capacity for empathy and connection. Many Western cultures, by contrast, begin by positing the individual as a psychological being and defining development as growth in the capacity for autonomous functioning. African Americans (Boyd-Franklin, 2006; Hines & Boyd-Franklin, 2005) have a very different foundation for their sense of identity, expressed as a communal sense of "We are, therefore I am" contrasting starkly with the individualistic European ideal: "I think, therefore I am." In the United States, the dominant cultural assumptions have generally been derived from a few

Northern European cultures and, above all, British assumptions, which are taken to be the universal standard. Those values have tended to be viewed as "normal," and values derived from other cultures have tended to be viewed as "ethnic." These other values have tended to be marginalized, even though they reflect the traditional values of the majority of the population.

Historically, throughout the mental health field, therapeutic models have generally been presented as if they were free of cultural bias rather than reflections of the social assumptions out of which they arise. For example, although human behavior results from an interplay of individual, interpersonal, familial, socioeconomic, and cultural forces, the mental health field has paid greatest attention to the personality factors that shape life experiences and behavior. Family therapists have recognized that individual behavior is mediated through family rules and patterns, but we have not sufficiently appreciated how deeply these rules are rooted in cultural norms. The study of cultural influences on human emotional functioning has been left primarily to cultural anthropologists. And even they have more often explored these influences in distant non-European cultures rather than studying the tremendous ethnic diversity within our own society.

Currently, many of our mental health, counseling, social work, and family therapy professional associations and credentialing bodies acknowledge the relevance of culture in their ethical codes and standards of practice (American Association of Marriage and Family Therapy, 2004; American Counseling Association, 2005; American Psychological Association, 2010; Council on Social Work Education, 2010; National Association of Social Workers, 2008) by mandating that practitioners become culturally competent. Griner and Smith (2006) have demonstrated that interventions congruent with the cultural values and beliefs of clients increase retention, client satisfaction, and improve intervention outcomes. Over recent decades, the field of family therapy has increasingly expanded from a universalist perspective to include an awareness of the structural impact of gender in families and the relevance of culture (McGoldrick & Hardy, 2008). Under the universal perspective, patriarchal, white, middle-class, heterosexual families were held as the standard for normal development and health family functioning (see Walsh, Chapter 1, this volume). Gender perspectives challenged the patriarchal values underlying family systems theories and the ways in which women held less power in the world and were held more responsible for family functioning. Cultural perspectives have recognized minority cultures, but culture still tends to be thought of as something that non-Americans and people of color possess. When discussion of ethnicity has occurred, it has often focused on groups' "otherness" in ways that emphasize their deficits rather than their adaptive strengths or their place in the larger society. The emphasis has also been on how so-called "minorities" relate to the "dominant" societal values of "normality." Since the 1990s, family therapy has moved toward the understanding that for all people, including white people of European ancestry, culture organizes family patterns, structure, values, beliefs, norms, and practices, and is central for our thinking with every family with whom we work (McGoldrick, Giordano, & Garcia-Preto, 2005). Thus, everyone's assumptions must be examined, not just those kept at the periphery of society. Despite the growing awareness that culture is ubiquitous, and that each cultural group has its own particular worldview (Sue & Sue, 2008), we still find ourselves in the position of having to convince many of our colleagues, trainees, and students of the dominant culture that culture matters for everyone. In many mental health and social service agencies data about cultural identity are routinely collected as part of the assessment process, but little, if anything, is ever done with this information. Dominant cultural assumptions are too often used to define normality, to conceptualize the presenting problem and to formulate interventions. In reviewing many introductory family therapy texts we find culture discussed as if it is relevant only for those who are not white or of European ancestry, and relegated to one page, or one chapter in the text, under the category of special issues or the treatment of special populations. We still find that many trainees and practicing clinicians resist focusing on culture. Eyes glaze over and they tell us they want to focus on the "real" clinical issues or that they "did" culture already in their undergraduate or graduate programs. Some note clients' ethnicity, social class, religion, or race on assessment forms or genograms but do not attend to culture in a substantive way.

ADDRESSING CULTURE: DIVERSITY AND COMPLEXITY

To address culture in a meaningful way, it is important to define what it is, how cultural identity is determined and by whom, and how meaningfully to integrate culture into therapy and counseling.

Culture refers to the ongoing social context within which our lives have evolved. It patterns our thinking, feeling, and behavior in both obvious and subtle ways, although generally we are not aware of it. Culture plays a major role in determining how we live our lives—how we eat, work, love, raise our families, celebrate, grieve, and die. Cultural identity has a profound impact on our sense of well-being, our mental, physical, and spiritual health. We are defining "culture" as including ethnicity, race, class, gender, sexual identity or orientation, generational status, religion, and migration experience. "Ethnicity" is a complex construct that refers to a group's common ancestry through which they have evolved shared values, beliefs, and customs that are transmitted over generations through the family, providing a sense of belonging and historical continuity, and shaping identity. For example, "Jewish ethnicity" is a meaningful term to millions of people (Rosen & Weltman, 2005), yet immigrants come from all parts of the world, with different migration patterns, and speak many languages. They may have Ashkenazi cultural roots from Northern and Eastern Europe, or Sephardic traditions from North Africa or Spain, They also vary in religious beliefs and practices from orthodox, conservative, and reform movements to secular humanists. Similar complexity applies to definitions of Arabs (Abudabbeh, 2005), who may be Eastern Orthodox Syrians, Roman Catholic Lebanese, or Jordanian or Egyptian Muslims. Yet there is some sense of cultural connection among these groups. To name one's ethnicity as a single ethnic group (e.g., Irish, Anglo, African American) is to oversimplify, since we all have multiple cultural roots and are in the process of transforming our ethnic identities throughout our lives, influenced by the changing contexts in which we live.

Our Evolving Ethnicities

We are all always in the process of ongoing cultural evolution. Our ethnic identity is ever-changing—incorporating ancestral influences, while forging new and emerging group identities. Group identities emerge in a complex interplay of members' relationships with each other, and with outsiders. We may feel negative or proud and appreciative of our cultural heritage, or we may not know thre cultural groups to which we belong. But our relationship to our cultural heritage will in any case influence our well being, as will our sense of relationship to the dominant culture. Do we feel we belong to it? Are we "passing" as members? Do we feel like marginalized outsiders? Or are we outsiders who have so absorbed the dominant culture's norms and values we do not even recognize that our internalized values reflect their prejudices and attempts to suppress cultural difference?

Our society's dominant definitions of cultural groups have shifted over time. In the 1700s only those of British and Dutch ancestry were thought to be "white." As Ben Franklin put it:

> All Africa is black or tawny. Asia chiefly tawny. America (exclusive of the new Comers) wholly so. And in Europe the Spaniards, Italians, French, Russians and Swedes are generally of what we call a swarthy Complexion; as are the Germans also, the Saxons only excepted, who with the English make up the principal body of White People on the face of the Earth. I could only wish their numbers were increased. (quoted in Hitchcock, 2001, p. 18)

Over the centuries we have greatly expanded the category of "white" cultures to include Europeans previously considered "ethnic," such as Poles, Italians, Irish, and Jews. People of mixed heritage are often pressed to identify with a single cultural group rather than being able to claim the true complexity of their cultural heritage (Root, 1992, 1996). The 2000 Census was the first to allow people to acknowledge any mixed heritage. However, many believe that white majorities are seeking to increase their count through distinctions for Latinos between those who are white and those who are of color, out of concern that whites are expected to become less than half of the population by 2050.

Ethnic intermarriage also plays an enormous role in the evolution of cultural patterns (Crohn, 1995; McGoldrick & Garcia-Preto, 1984; Root, 2001).

Although, as a nation, we have a long history of intercultural relationships, until 1967 our society explicitly forbade racial intermarriage, and discouraged cultural intermarriage as well, because it challenged white supremacy. But traditional ethnic and racial categories are now increasingly being challenged by the cultural and racial mixing that has been a long submerged part of our history. Maria Root (1996, 2001), one of the prime researchers on this area, has defined a special bill of rights for people of mixed race, asserting their right to define themselves for themselves, and not be limited by society's racial and ethnic stereotypes and caricatures.

The consciousness of ethnic identity varies greatly both between and within groups. Indigenous people of this land, and many immigrants, have been forced to assimilate and to give up their names, their language, and their cultural connections. Because of the pressure within our society to conform to dominant cultural norms that deny the existence of bias, others may ignore or deny their ethnicity by changing their names, and rejecting their families and social backgrounds. Whether by choice or force, the surrender of cultural connections creates a loss of historical and cultural continuity and identity. Intrafamily conflicts over the level of accommodation should be viewed not just as family conflicts, but also as reflecting explicit or implicit pressure from the dominant culture regarding which characteristics are more highly valued.

Individuals should not have to suppress parts of themselves in order to "pass" for what the dominant group defines as "normal." People function best when they are at peace with the multiple aspects of who they are and are not forced into rigidly defined group identities that cause strains in loyalties. Those who try to assimilate at the price of forgetting their connections to their heritage are likely to have more problems than those who maintain a positive sense of connection with their heritage. As family therapists we believe in helping clients understand their ethnicity as a fluid, ever-changing aspect of who they are, not something to be defined for them by others. The character Vivian Twostar in *The Crown of Columbus* (Erdrich & Dorris, 1991) describes the complexity this cultural self-definition always entails:

> I belong to the lost tribe of mixed bloods, that hodgepodge amalgam of hue and cry that defies easy placement. When the DNA of my various ancestors Irish and Coeur d'Alene and Spanish and Navajo and God knows what else combined to form me, the result was not some genteel indecipherable puree that comes from a Cuisinart. You know what they say on the side of the Bisquick box, under instructions for pancakes? Mix with fork. Leave lumps. That was me. There are advantages to not being this or that. You have a million stories, one for every occasion, and in a way they're all lies and in another way they're all true. When Indians say to me, "What are you?" I know exactly what they're asking and answer Coeur D'Alene. I don't add, "Between a quarter and a half," because that's information they don't require, first off though it may come later if I screw up and they're looking for reasons why. If one of my Dartmouth colleagues wonders, "Where did you study?" I pick the best place, the hardest one to get into, in order

to establish that I belong. If a stranger on the street questions where (my daughter) gets her light brown hair and dark skin, I say the Olde Sodde and let them figure it out. There are times when I control who I'll be, and times when I let other people decide. I'm not all anything, but I'm a little bit of a lot. My roots spread in every direction, and if I water one set of them more often than others, it's because they need it more. . . . I've read anthropological papers written about people like me. We're called marginal, as if we exist anywhere but on the center of the page. We're parked on the bleachers looking into the arena, never the main players, but there are bonuses to peripheral vision. Out beyond the normal bounds, you at least know where you're not. You escape the claustrophobia of belonging, and what you lack in security you gain by realizing—as those insiders never do—that security is an illusion. . . . "Caught between two worlds," is the way we're often characterized, but I'd put it differently. We are the catch. (pp. 166–167)

Twostar's brilliant expression of a multifaceted cultural identity comprised of complex heritages reflects the experiences of many. It illustrates the ways in which context and the projection of others determine which aspect of identity we highlight, and emphasizes what those who belong have to learn from those who are marginalized.

If we look carefully enough, everyone is a "hodgepodge." Those who were born white, who conform to the dominant societal norms, probably grew up believing that "ethnicity" referred to others who were different from themselves and that they were "regular." As Tataki (1993) has pointed out, we have always tended to view Americans as European in ancestry. Many students, trainees, and professionals of European ancestry have made such assertions. Those of African, Latin, Asian, Arab, Aboriginal, or Indigenous ancestry are more likely to affirm that they have a culture and know what it is and what it is not. Cultural awareness is often born out of experiences of oppression and marginalization as cultural identity becomes a source of strength, resilience, and survival. Those who assert that they do not have a culture are often members of the dominant group whose way of being in the world is taken for granted, rarely challenged, and seen as universal truth. And those of us in mental health have been specifically trained by the official diagnostic manual (DSM) to define problems as if they exist in some universal vacuum, without reference to culture. The current edition of the manual specifically disallows discussion that asserted diagnoses are influenced by cultural factors. If we study our individual, family, and collective subjugated histories, we will learn or be reminded that many of us who claim one cultural identity or no cultural identity are "mixed blood," and our context has determined how we name and claim ourselves as well as the way in which others view us.

When asked about my cultural identity, today my (Deidre Ashton) quick response is Black (United States of) American or African American. As a child in the 1960s and 1970s I simply saw myself as Black, a member of a group who began in slavery. This limiting conceptualization was based on an education that did not discuss the history of Black people in the world prior to slavery. World history included primarily North America and Europe, and to a much lesser degree Asia, South America, and Central America. I did not see myself as American as I was aware that even following the civil rights movement, Black people held second-class status in the United States. I thought that only white people were American, because everything outside of my family reflected whiteness—my toys, television programs, music played on most radio stations, textbooks, and most of the literature presented in educational settings, including my children's Bible. When I entered college I was introduced to an Afrocentric worldview, and learned that I was of African descent and that, like many Black people born and raised in the United States, I could not specify a country of origin because my ancestors were forcibly taken from their homes. When African American became the seemingly self-selected name for ourselves, I was pleased to claim the African roots already integrated into my identity, but I had white colleagues who were born in South Africa and naturalized in the United States, so were they too African American? Because being Black in the United States means being connected to a particular history, sociopolitical experience, values, and beliefs that have been shaped by African cosmology, racism, the maafa, enslavement, and liberation movements, I came to see Black/African as my racial/cultural identity. Finally, when I traveled outside the United States, I came to see myself as an (United States of) American, based on my language, beliefs and practices, and the unearned privilege I was granted by people of other nations. I am a Black/African (United States of) American.

However, there are other aspects of my ancestry that I do not name when I am asked to name my racial/ethnic identity. I am also of Shinnecock, Irish, and Scottish descent. These are the roots that I believe Twostar would describe as less watered. The color of my skin, and that of my parents, and their parents in migration between northern Virginia and Long Island, New York, and the system of racial stratification organizing the United States, determined that my Black, now African roots would be watered regularly and come to dominate my sense of ethnic identity. I do not claim that the Shinnecock, Scottish, and Irish do not have influence over my identity. For now, that influence is out of my awareness, gone on a conscious level but perhaps not forgotten on a metaphysical level.

I (Monica McGoldrick), born in 1943 in Brooklyn, New York, one of the most diverse cities on the planet, and raised there and in Bucks County Pennsylvania, grew up thinking I was "regular" and that the concept of ethnicity did not apply to me. Nowhere in all my education was this concept challenged. I learned basically only white history, educated in the 1950s eastern United States in relatively affluent communities and schools (virtually all white all the way from kindergarten through graduate school). I am of Irish heritage, the fourth generation born in the United States, so by the time I came along we knew we were Irish in name only. No reference was ever made in my family to any influence of Irish heritage, and such a concept had no meaning to me. Having studied Russian culture in college and graduate school before moving to social work and family therapy in the mid-1960s, I still had no idea that culture pertained to me. Even when I married my Greek immigrant husband in 1970 I thought I was still "regular" but had just married into ethnicity! It was not until I was 32 and went to Ireland for the first time that I was transformed by the realization that I had been Irish all the time and never knew it. I think now my family felt so much shame and pain in their migration to this country that they saw their salvation in giving up their culture and trying to pass for the dominant group. So I grew up with a real emptiness about who I was, but without any awareness of the cultural mystification in which I was raised. I think often now of the questions I never thought to ask about my own history and about the history of others around me. I grew up in a multiracial household, where the person closest to me was African American, but the servant in the household. Yet I never asked why this racial arrangement existed, why my schools and neighborhoods were so segregated, why the history I learned was only about white people. It amazes me now how few cultural questions I ever asked. What happened to suppress my curiosity about the cultural context in which I grew up, and what has it cost me in obliviousness to the pernicious cultural structures in which all our lives are still embedded?

Developing cultural respectful practice requires us to question the dominant culture values, to explore the complexities of cultural identity, and to develop culturally informed healing practices that are liberating (Sue & Sue, 2008). Our healing work may often entail helping clients locate themselves culturally so they can overcome their sense of mystification, invalidation, or alienation that comes from not being able to feel culturally at home in one's society. It becomes imperative for every clinician, researcher, and educator in the field to examine his or her cultural identity. How do you define yourself culturally? Do you see yourself as of mixed blood? Of one cultural group? Of no cultural group? What experiences shape how you see and define yourself or how others see you? When asked to define yourself, what feelings emerge: pride, shame, confusion, anger? As a member of your cultural group(s) do you feel seen and understood, or are you, as the character Twostar says, at the margins? Is your response to these questions "It depends," meaning that culture is fluid, unfolding, evolving, complex, and embedded in history and context? We view "cultural genograms" as axiomatic for all work with trainees and clients (Hardy & Laszloffy, 1995; McGoldrick, Gerson, & Petry, 2008). Genograms should help us contextualize our kinship network in terms of culture, class, race, gender, religion, and migration history. When we ask people to identify themselves ethnically, we are asking them to make explicit themes of cultural continuity and identity.

We need to develop an open social system with flexible boundaries so that people can define themselves by the groupings that relate to their heritages and practices, and go beyond labels such as "minorities," "Blacks," "Latinos," "Asians," or "Americans." Our limiting language reflects the biases embedded in our society's dominant beliefs. The term "Latino," for example, refers simultaneously to Native Americans of hundreds of different groups through Latin and South America, as well as to immigrants from numerous other cultures, including Cubans of Spanish origin; Chinese who settled in Puerto Rico; families from Africa, whose enslaved ancestors were brought to Latin and South America; and Argentinian Jews, whose ancestors fled European ghettoes, pogroms, and the Nazi Holocaust (Bernal & Shapiro, 2005; Falicov, 2005; Garcia-Preto, 2005a, 2005b). The term "minority" peripheralizes groups whose heritage is different from the dominant groups. The term "Black" obliterates the ancestral heritage of Americans of African heritage altogether and defines people only by their color. The term "Asian" lumps together separate cultural groups from India, Japan, Vietnam, Korea, China, Laos, and other countries that had thousands of years of separate history and even enmity toward each other. The fact that there is no term to describe people of the United States, such as "United Statesan," but only the inaccurate term "American," which makes invisible Canadians, Mexicans, and other Americans, is extremely limiting in our discussion of these issues.

Factors Interacting with Ethnicity

Understanding the intersection of ethnicity, race, class, gender, sexual orientation, class, religion, migration, and politics, as well as age and generation, and urban or rural background (Falicov, 1995) is essential to understanding culture. These factors influence every person's social location in our society, access to resources, inclusion in dominant culture's definitions of "belonging," and how family members relate to their cultural heritage, to others of their cultural group, and to preserving cultural traditions. Systems of oppression based on these socially constructed categories are interdependent and powerful forces as people who are marginalized may develop distinct worldviews, values, beliefs, and survival practices in order to live under the weight of impoverished circumstances and contemptible treatment by individuals and institutions of the dominant, privileged cultural group (Liu, Soleck, Hopps, Dunston, & Pickett, 2004). Although two individuals may belong to the same ethnic group, their experiences may vary dramatically based on variation in membership in the socially constructed categories upon which society is stratified. In recognizing and working through a cultural lens, the challenge is to recognize the intersectionality of these multiple aspects of identity in an integrative and holistic manner rather than as additive statuses.

However, for discussion purposes, we present each factor individually and ask the reader to think about the meaning of race, class, gender, sexual orientation, religion, migration status, and ethnicity as they interact with one another, and not as individual, competing components of culture. For example, when we discuss gender, let us not presume that we are focused on white, heterosexual, middle-class, natal women of European ancestry. We intend to focus on all women of varying ethnicities, classes, sexualities, gender expressions, races, and religions. We also attend to the interactive effects of the multiple forms of oppression that shape cultural evolution, family processes, and lived experience for both the privileged and the marginalized.

Race and Racism

Race is a sociopolitical issue, not a biological or genetic one. Despite our variation in the ethnic identities, we all share a common ancestry tracing back to Africa (Cann, Stoneking, & Wilson, 1987). Race has been shown to be only skin deep and not correlated with any other meaningful attributes or abilities, such as intelligence. Racial groups differ in only about 6% of their genetic makeup, meaning that 94% of genetic variation is found to be within group variation (American Anthropological Association, 1998; Brown & Armelagos, 2001; Goodman, 2006; Lewinton, 1972). As Ignatiev (1995) puts it: "No biologist has ever been able to provide a satisfactory definition of 'race'—that is, a definition that includes all members of a given race and excludes all others." Race is a biological expression of physical appearance that is socially and politically constructed to privilege certain people at the expense of others. It is a construct that imposes judgment on us from the outside, based on nothing more than our physical features. Racism operates like sexism, a similar system of privilege and oppression, justified within the dominant society as a biological or cultural phenomenon, which functions systematically to advantage certain members of society at the expense of others (Burton, Bonilla-Silva, Ray, Buckelew, & Freeman, 2010; Hardy & Laszloffy, 1992; Hitchcock, 2001; Katz, 1978; Mahmoud, 1998). Racism and poverty have always dominated the lives of ethnic minorities in the United States. Race has always been a major cultural definer and divider in our society, since those whose skin color marked them as different always suffered more discrimination than others. They could not "pass," as other immigrants might, leaving them with an "obligatory" ethnic and racial identification.

Although racism may be more subtle and covert today, the politics of race continue to be complex and divisive, and, unfortunately, whites remain generally unaware of the problems our society creates for people of color. In a similar way that patriarchy, class hierarchies, and heterosexist ideologies have been invisible structural definers of all European groups' ethnicity, race and racism have also been invisible definers of European groups' cultural values. The invisible knapsack of privilege (McIntosh, 2008) that benefits all white Americans because of the color of their skin is something that most white ethnics do not acknowledge. Although conditions have improved from a generation ago, when Blacks were not permitted to drink from the same water fountains as whites or to attend integrated schools, we still live in an essentially segregated society. The racial divide continues to be a painful chasm creating profoundly different consciousness for people of color than for whites.

Most people find it more difficult to talk to each other about race and racism than about ethnicity. Each new racial incident ignites feelings and expressions of anger and rage, helplessness and frustration. Exploring our own ethnicity and racial identity is vital to overcoming our prejudices and expanding understanding of ourselves in context. But we must also take care in our pursuit of multicultural understanding not to diminish our efforts to overcome racism (Katz, 1978). All therapists must be concerned about undoing racism to eradicate this pernicious force in our society. The judgments about self or family that reflect these false categorizations are almost impossible to avoid making in therapy (see Boyd-Franklin & Karger, Chapter 12, this volume).

Social Class and Classism

"Social class" is a complex construct that intertwines income, education, occupation, wealth, and access to resources, and reflects our social location and status (Laszloffy, 2008; Liu et al., 2004). Individuals of the same ethnic or racial group may have vastly different lives based on their social class. Those living in poverty have to deal with the stresses of survival; blighted and unsafe neighborhoods; and lack of access to quality education, jobs, and health care, as well as public scrutiny. All profoundly impact their way of being in the world, as well as the values and beliefs that they come to hold. In contrast, the worldview of the wealthy is informed by their experience of privacy and autonomy; getting their needs met is likely to be taken for granted, affording them time and energy to focus on fulfillment of their desires, without fear for their family's support. The privileges of wealth may transform a worldview rooted in shared ethnic background and community interdependence and lead to an insensitivity to cultural context.

The United States, always stratified along class lines, has become increasingly stratified in recent years, with the top 1% controlling 34% of our nation's wealth, while the bottom 70% of our population controls just 29% (Kristof, 2010). This has led to a serious disconnect between those at the top, who control resources, and those below, who have less and less access or control over their lives and the values and direction of our nation. The dominant culture tends to blame people for being poor, for failing to pull themselves up by their bootstraps, while ignoring the systems of oppression and inequality that deny access to the resources that support and enable the affluent to maintain and enhance their status (Laszloffy, 2008). When individuals and families of lower classes present for mental health or social service treatment, they are often objectified and treated as pathological because they are poor (Liu et al., 2004).

Gender, Sexism, and Gender Oppression

The dominant cultures of the United States, and many other societies hold the belief that biological sex determines gender, gender determines gender role, and gender role determines sexual orientation (Lev, 2004). While biological sex may be a genetic fact, gender is a social construct that reflects the individual's sense of self as man, woman, gender-variant or fluid, or transcendent of binary gender (Catalano, McCarthy, & Shlasko, 2007). Gender roles are socially constructed to reflect the ways in which society defines and determines the customs, behaviors, and practices deemed appropriate for people based on their biological sex and assumed gender identity (see Knudson-Martin, Chapter 14, this volume).

Historically, when discussing the construct of gender we have thought of two categories: men and women. A binary gender system is a cornerstone in the construction of sexism, a system of oppression that privileges men over women (Botkin, Jones, & Kachwaha, 2007). The early feminist movement and gender perspectives in family therapy examined and challenged power differentials experienced by women in families and in society at large, and sought equality and justice in both private and public spheres. While they challenged patriarchal assumptions embedded in theories of normal family functioning, most did not name or challenge binary gender assumptions, As lesbian, gay, bisexual, and transgender (LGBT) professionals in our field advanced clinical awareness and attention to LGBT issues in clinical training and practice, there has more recently been greater consideration of gender-variant individuals and wider recognition of gender fluidity and gender oppression (Lev, 2004; McGoldrick & Hardy, 2008).

The relationship among culture, gender, and gender roles is multidirectional, as gender is embedded in cultural values and beliefs, and gender and gender roles shape the evolution of culture over time as the less empowered and marginalized groups develop counter worldviews to transcend the limitations of traditional cultural imperatives. Additionally, there is variation in the construction of gender identity and gender role performance cross culturally. For example, some of the indigenous peoples of the Americas do not subscribe to binary gender but to a continuum of multiple gender possibilities (Griffin, 2007). African American and Jewish cultures reflect more gender role flexibility. Thus, as clinicians working through a cultural lens, we must investigate our gender assumptions, and those of the theories we use, those embedded in the specific culture of those presenting for service, and the ways in which conformance to gender definitions and gender norms feels oppressive and restrictive or empowering and adaptive.

Sexual Orientation and Identity, Heterosexism, and Heteronormativity

Sexual identity and orientation are social constructs of the 20th century that are embedded in culture, and like race, class, and gender, deeply impact our experiences and the evolution of cultural practices (Griffin, D'Errico, Harro, & Schiff, 2007). "Sexual identity" consists of the integration of one's sexual orientation, gender identity, and gender role (Stonefish & Harvey, 2005). "Sexual orientation" reflects the direction of sexual, affectional, and emotional attraction, may evolve and shift over time, and is not determined by biological sex, gender identity, or gender role (Griffin, 2007; Lev, 2004; Stonefish & Harvey,

2005). Heterosexism has evolved along with sexism and gender oppression to privilege straight, natal men, with racism to privilege white straight, natal men, and classism to privilege white, middle-class, straight natal men. Much like the feminist movement at the outset, the gay and lesbian civil rights movements were begun by white, middle-class men and women, with early activism sparked by the 1969 Stonewall uprising (that included white gay men and lesbians, working class and LGBT people of color; Griffin et al., 2007) and the AIDS epidemic in the 1980s. Gradually, focus has expanded to address concerns of LGBT persons of color, across cultures, and across class. However, it is still mostly white voices that are being heard (Catalano et al., 2007).

A recent study focused on urban African American and Latino LGBT communities highlights the ways in which cultural groups that occupy multiple marginalized statuses develop alternative kinship structures. One structure that provides a protective, safe, accepting, and nurturing home for queer, urban African American and sometimes Latino/a LGBT people is known as the "ballroom" or "house culture" (Arnold & Bailey, 2009). The houses consist of fictive kin networks that join together to produce performance art shows. On the surface, show production may appear to be *raison d'être* for the ballroom community. However the houses feature a national kinship network in which queer African American and Latino youth and adults can feel culturally at home, and create norms and customs that promote authentic gender and sexual identity expression and protect against the insidious effects of racism, sexism, classism, gender oppression, and heterosexism. Ballroom culture illustrates the way race, ethnicity, gender, and sexual orientation interact to generate adaptive cultural practices that build on the African American and Latino/a traditions of creating family that is inclusive of fictive kin.

Spirituality, Religion, Religious Oppression

"Religion" is a socially constructed institution, organized by a set of values, beliefs, norms, practices, and ritual behaviors that joins people together and creates a spiritual community (Fukuyama & Sevig, 1999; Schlosser, Foley, Potrock Stein, & Holmwood, 2010; see Walsh, Chapter 15, this volume). Because religious institutions and dogma strongly influence individual and family beliefs and practices, religion has been a powerful force that shapes culture and reinforces certain cultural norms, such as patriarchy. Ethnicity and religion are inextricably intertwined. People who practice Islam may be seen as an ethnic group despite variation in race, ethnicity, and nationality. Among many African Americans and other ethnic groups, religious tradition is an essential element of culture as it has been a powerful influence in organizing the community, and in resisting and overcoming oppression (Boyd-Franklin, 2006; Falicov, 2005; Kamya, 2008; Sue & Sue, 2008). Accordingly, attention to the potential of religion and spirituality for harm, as well as for healing and resilience, becomes critical in assessing strengths, resources, and organizing beliefs of families that present for therapy (Walsh, 2009, 2010).

Migration Experience

Because of the historical practices of eminent domain and the fact that this country consists mostly of immigrants who migrated in the both the distant and recent past, migration experience is a critical aspect of culture. Families' migration experience may have a major influence on their cultural values (see Falicov, Chapter 13, this volume). To understand them, it is essential to know the reasons for migration, the length of time since migration, the group's historical experience, and the degree of discrimination experienced. A family's dreams and fears when immigrating become part of its heritage. Parents' attitudes toward what came before and what lies ahead will have a profound impact on the expressed or tacit messages they transmit to their children. Families that have experienced trauma and devastation within their own society, before even beginning the process of immigration, will have a monumentally more difficult time adjusting to a new life than those who migrated for economic betterment. The hidden effects of this history, especially where it goes unacknowledged, may linger for many generations, as illustrated by the history of the Irish (Hayden, 2001; McGoldrick et al., 2005), Armenians (Dagirmanjian, 1996), African Americans (Hines & Boyd-Franklin 2005), Latinos (Garcia-Preto, 2005b), and Jews (Cowan, 1982; Rosen & Weltman, 2005), among others.

Adaptation to the new situation is also affected by whether one family member migrated alone or whether a large portion of the family or community came together. Those who migrate alone usually have a greater need to adapt, and their losses are often more hidden. Families who migrate together, such as the Scandinavians who settled in the Midwest, are often able to preserve much of their traditional heritage. When a large part of the population or nation comes together, as happened in the waves of Irish, Polish, Italian, and Jewish migration, discrimination against the group may be especially intense, as the newest immigrants are often regarded as a threat to those who came just before, who fear losing their tenuous social status and economic security. Collective migration may also create opportunity for an ethnic enclave to emerge. These neighborhoods can provide a cushion against the stresses of migration and help to sustain cultural links through the preservation of language and availability of familiar foods and local religious congregations. Families who remain within an ethnic neighborhood, who work and socialize with members of their group, and those whose religion reinforces ethnic values, will probably maintain their ethnicity longer than those who live in heterogeneous settings.

Therapists need to be as attuned to migration stresses and ethnic identity conflicts as they are to other stresses of a family's history (Falicov, 2011). They should learn about the family's ethnic network and encourage the rebuilding of social and informal connections through family visits or letters, or creating new networks. Assessing such factors is crucial for determining whether a family's dysfunction is a "normal" reaction to a high degree of cultural stress, or whether it goes beyond the bounds of transitional stress and requires greater intervention.

Not Romanticizing Culture

It is essential to remember that because values or beliefs are cultural does not mean they are sacrosanct. Some cultural practices are unethical. Mistreatment of women or children through disrespect, physical abuse, or sexual abuse is a human rights issue, no matter the cultural context in which it occurs. Every intervention is value laden. We must not use notions of neutrality or "deconstruction" to shy away from committing ourselves to the values we believe in. We must have the courage of our convictions, even while realizing that we can never be too certain that our perspective is the "correct" one. It means we must learn to tolerate ambiguities and continue to question our stance in relation to the position and values of our clients. And we must be especially careful about the power differential if we are part of the dominant group, since the voices of those who are marginalized are harder to hear. The disenfranchised need more support to have their position heard than do those who feel they are entitled because theirs are the dominant values.

We must address all forms of oppression and discrimination. We must work for the right of every person to have a voice and a sense of safety and belonging. When cultural groups are encouraged to "speak for themselves," we must consider the process by which the spokesperson has been selected. Helping families define what is "normal" in the sense of healthy may require supporting marginalized voices within the cultural group that express liberating possibilities for family adaptation.

Stereotypes

While generalizing about groups has often been used to reinforce prejudices, one cannot discuss ethnic cultures without generalizing. In fact, we perpetuate covert negative stereotyping by failure to address culture explicitly in our everyday work. Many avoid discussion of group characteristics altogether, in favor of individual family patterns, maintaining, "I prefer to think of each family as unique," or "I prefer to think of family members as human beings rather than pigeonholing them in categories." But the values, beliefs, status, and privileges of families in our society are profoundly influenced by their sociocultural location, which is deeply embedded in their cultural background; thus, these issues are essential to our clinical assessment and intervention, and the failure to acknowledge and discuss group characteristics is a failure to acknowledge culture.

Our openness to making a space for cultural diversity is the key to expanding our cultural understanding. We learn about culture primarily not by learning the "facts" of another's culture but by changing our own attitudes about cultural difference (Fadiman, 1998). Cultural paradigms are useful to the extent that they help us challenge our long-held beliefs about "the way things are or are supposed to be." But we cannot learn about culture cookbook fashion through memorizing recipes for relating to other ethnic groups. Information we learn about cultural variation will, we hope, expand our understanding and cultivate humility and respectful curiosity about those who are different from us. The best cultural training for family therapists might be to experience what it is like not to be part of the dominant culture by traveling to a foreign country or participating in community experiences other than their own, such as attending a church in a Black or Latino community. It could help us gain the humility for respectful cultural interactions, based on more than a one-way hierarchy of normality, truth, and wisdom.

CLINICAL PRACTICE GUIDELINES

Appreciation of cultural variability and transparency about the cultural foundation of our working theories leads to a radically new conceptual model of clinical intervention. It is important to remember that variability exists not only between groups but within groups based on race, class, gender, sexual orientation, religious affiliation, and migration experience. Helping a person achieve a stronger sense of self may require resolving internalized negative cultural attitudes, and cultural conflicts within the family or between the family and the community, or in the wider context in which the family is embedded. It may also include helping individuals and families identify and consciously select which cultural values they wish to retain and which they wish to discontinue. Families may benefit from coaching to distinguish deeply held cultural beliefs and practices asserted for emotional reasons.

It is almost impossible to understand the meaning of behavior unless one is first aware one's own cultural assumptions, and knows something of the cultural values of a family. Even the definition of "family" differs greatly from group to group. For example, the dominant American (Anglo) definition focuses on the intact nuclear family, whereas family for Italians means a strong, tightly knit three- or four-generational family, African American families often include an even wider network of kin and community, and Chinese definitions of family generally reflect a very much longer time frame, including all male ancestors and descendents. Other obvious and essential variables are the family's attitude toward help seeking and therapy, how they define problems, and how they understand their resolution. The dominant assumption is that formal institutions can be trusted and are resources, and that talk is good and can heal a person. Therapy has even been referred to as "the talking cure." Talking to the therapist or to other family members is seen as the path to healing. Clients may not talk openly or seek therapy for many different reasons related to their cultural background or values. Consider the different value various cultures place on help seeking, the source of help, and talk therapy. For instance, in Sioux Indian culture, talking is actually proscribed in certain family relationships. A wife does not to talk directly to her father-in-law, for example, yet she may experience closeness to him. The reduced emphasis on verbal expression seems to free Native American families for other kinds of experiences of each other, of nature, and of the spiritual realm.

There may be variation in what ethnic groups define as problematic behavior. First, culturally based strengths may become problematic as the context changes. Second, based on their worldview, groups may value some practices over others. Third, cultural groups vary in how they understand problem formation and conceptualize useful responses to problems. However, we cannot make assumptions about how families define problem formation or possible solutions simply because we know how they identify culturally. We must bring respectful curiosity to our work and awareness of our own worldview.

As we seek to join families in facilitating healing, in addition to listening for the various ways in which problems may emerge, be defined, or responded to, we must also listen for the ways families define and organize themselves, socialize their members, define and demarcate life-cycle transitions, and draw boundaries between themselves and the rest of the world (McGoldrick et al., 2005).

What is adaptive in a given situation? Answering this requires appreciation of the total context in which behavior occurs. The following case may help to illustrate this.

> Syreeta, a 36-year-old African American, middle-class, female therapist, working in a school-based counseling program in an urban, low-income community of color, presented a family in clinical supervision. Syreeta began working with the family when Mona, a 17-year-old Mexican American high school senior who was a stellar student, began to decline in her grades. Syreeta learned that Mona was pregnant and experiencing conflict with her parents because of the pregnancy. Mona wanted to graduate and then get a job in order to provide for her child, while Mona's parents wanted her to drop out and join her mother on the factory assembly line in order to prepare for the birth of her child. Syreeta met with Mona, her parents, and paternal grandmother in their home. She listened for the family's description of the problem, their strengths, attempted solutions, and preferred outcome. Syreeta also informed the family that Mona needed a high school education and joined with Mona in attempting to shift the position of the parents. When presenting the family in supervision, Syreeta described the family as multigenerational, working class, and Mexican American. She expressed her limited knowledge of Mexican American culture, and described the way in which she interviewed the family to elicit their cultural values, beliefs, and practices. Syreeta stated that she was deeply troubled by the family's insistence that Mona drop out of school. In her hypothesis, Syreeta

indicated that the parents seemed to conform to traditional Mexican gender roles, characterizing the father as a distant, uninvolved protector and provider, and the mother as a caretaker who was enmeshed with her daughter. Syreeta thought that the work of the therapy was to help the family acculturate, so that the parents would allow Mona to complete high school.

Syreeta seemed to use her previous training about culture to explore cultural influence, to acknowledge her own knowledge gap, and to defer to the family's expertise about their culture. However, she then erroneously interacted with the family in a way that was culturally incongruent and assessed the family according to culturally bound theories of normative development and healthy family functioning, the programmatic goal of increasing student retention, and her own middle-class African American values in which education is valued as the key to liberation. Her conceptualization of the presenting problem pathologized the family and resulted in formulation of a solution that required the family to devalue its culture and conform to the dominant norms. Through the lens of dominant culture theories, the supervisee did not acknowledge the ways in which a caring, cohesive family was attempting to keep the family together and prepare for the next generation. She potentially undermined the therapeutic relationship and the possibility of co-constructing a culturally respectful solution to address the needs of the student as an individual, and as a family member.

Rather than seeing the family's solution to a challenging situation as dysfunctional or wrong, the family was better served once the clinician was able to use supervision to recognize the cultural values and assumptions that informed her assessment and intervention. Syreeta was then able to recognize and respect the values of the family members, and their culture, and build on adaptive cultural strengths. She was able to ask questions about the family's belief system, relationship history, migration story, level of acculturation, community relatedness, hopes, dreams, fears, and concerns without measuring them against dominant culture standards. Collaboratively, they were able to develop a plan for Mona to remain in school while working and preparing for the birth of her child, and using her family as a resource. The therapist's role in such situations may become one of a cultural broker, helping family members to recognize their own ethnic values and to resolve the conflicts that evolve out of different perceptions and experiences.

CONCLUSION

Clinicians must conduct culturally grounded assessments that enhance the likelihood of engagement in culturally respectful, congruent, and competent healing practices. We need to inquire about the family's cultural identity and listen for the way family members conceptualize their identity, and how that identity informs their lived experiences. We must listen for the worldview of the family members and the primary beliefs and rules that organize them as a system. Our inquiry must elicit culturally embedded strengths, resources, and limitations, and experiences of oppression as they relate to reasons that a family is presenting for treatment.

Clinicians must also be aware of the difficulties related to cultural difference that we may experience in engaging families. We must be aware of the ways in which our cultural beliefs may be an asset or a liability in engagement, assessment, and intervention processes.

The following questions may be helpful in helping both clinician and client understand the client's cultural background (McGoldrick et al., 2005). They can be useful in guiding the clinician and family in locating the family's sources of resilience, the values of its heritage, and family members' ability to transform their lives and work toward long-range goals that fit with their cultural values. Basically, we recommend use of questions that help to locate families in their cultural context and help them access their strengths in the midst of the stress of their current situation.

- What ethnic groups, religious traditions, nations, racial groups, trades, professions, communities, and other groups do you consider yourself a part of?
- When and why did you or your family come to the United States? To this community? How old were family members at the time? Did they and do you feel secure about your status in the United States? Did they (Do you) have a green card?
- What language did they (do you) speak at home? In the community? In your family of origin?
- What burdening wounds has your cultural/racial/ethnic group experienced? What burden does your group carry for injuries to other groups? How have you been affected by the wounds your group has committed, or that have been committed against your group?
- How have you been wounded by the wrongs done to your ancestors? How have you been complicit in the wrongs done by your ancestors? How can you give voice to your group's guilt, your own sorrow, or your own complicity in the harm done by your ancestors? What would reparations entail?
- What experiences have been most stressful for family members in the United States?
- To whom do family members in your culture turn when in need of help?
- What are your culture's values regarding male and female roles? Gender identity? Sexual orientation? Education? Work and success? Family

connectedness? Family caretaking? Religious practices? Have these values changed in your family over time?

- Do you still have contact with family members in your country of origin?
- Has immigration changed family members' education or social status?
- What do you feel about your culture(s) of origin? Do you feel you belong to the dominant U.S. culture?

Culturally respectful clinical work involves helping people clarify their cultural and self-identity in relation to family, community, and their history, while also adapting to changing circumstances as they move through life. The following guiding assumptions are meant to suggest the kind of inclusive thinking that is necessary for judging family problems and normal adaptation in cultural context.

- Assume that all theories of psychology, family therapy, human development, pathology, wellness, intervention models, and definitions of normality reflect specific worldviews, and values (including this chapter).
- Assume that all clinicians bring their particular worldviews and cultural values to the therapy process.
- Assume that awareness of and transparency about the values and worldview of the clinician enhance the therapeutic interaction.
- Assume that family members' cultural background influences how they view their problems and possible solutions, until you have evidence to the contrary.
- Assume that language matters, and that working in the preferred language of the client is best. Understand that language conveys culture, and that the language of origin may be far more expressive.
- Assume that no one can ever fully understand another's culture, but that curiosity, humility, awareness of one's own cultural values and of history will contribute to sensitive interviewing.
- Assume that having a positive awareness of one's cultural heritage, just like a positive connection to one's family of origin, contributes to one's sense of mental health and well-being.
- Assume that a negative feeling or lack of awareness of one's cultural heritage might be reflective of cutoffs, oppression, or traumatic experiences that have led to suppression of history.
- Assume that clients from marginalized cultures have probably internalized society's prejudices about them, and that those from dominant cultural groups have probably internalized assumptions about their own superiority and right to be privileged within our society.

Last, as a field, we must broaden our theories of development and models of intervention to take into account multiple cultural worldviews.

REFERENCES

Abudabbeh, N. (2005). Arab families. In M. McGoldrick, J. Giordano, & N. Garcia-Preto (Eds.), *Ethnicity and family therapy* (3rd ed.). New York: Guilford Press.

American Anthropological Association. (1998). Statement on race. Retrieved September 3, 2010, from *www.aaanet.org/stmts/racepp.htm*.

American Association of Marriage and Family Therapy. (2004). Marriage and family therapy core competencies. Retrieved August 28, 2010, from *www.aamft. org/about/coamfte/version%2011%20standards/mft%20core%20competencies%20(december%202004).doc*.

American Counseling Association. (2005). ACA Code of Ethics. Retrieved August 28, 2010, from *www.counseling.org/resources/codeofethics/tp/home/ct2.aspx*.

American Psychological Association. (2010). Ethical principles of psychologists and code of conduct. Retrieved on August 28, 2010, from *www.apa.org/ethics/code/index.aspx*.

Arnold, E. A., & Bailey, M. M. (2009). Constructing home and family: How the ballroom community supports African American GLBTQ youth in the face of HIV/AIDS. *Journal of Gay and Lesbian Social Services, 21*(2), 171–188.

Bernal, G., & Shapiro, E. (2005). Cuban families. In M. McGoldrick, J. Giordano, & N. Garcia-Preto (Eds.), *Ethnicity and family therapy* (3rd ed.). New York: Guilford Press.

Botkin, S., Jones, J., & Kachwaha, T. (2007). Sexism curriculum design. In M. Adams, L. A. Bell, & P. Griffin (Eds.), *Teaching for diversity and social justice* (2nd ed.). New York: Routledge.

Boyd-Franklin, N. (2006). *Black families in therapy: Understanding the African American experience*. New York: Guilford Press.

Brown, R. A., & Armelagos, G. J. (2001). Apportionment of racial diversity: A review. *Evolutionary Anthtropolgy, 10*, 34–40.

Burton, L. M., Bonilla-Silva, E., Ray, V., Buckelew, R., Freeman, E. H. (2010). Critical race theories, colorism, and the decade's research on families of color. *Journal of Marriage and Family, 72*(3), 440–459.

Cann, R. L., Stoneking, M., & Wilson, A. C. (1987). Mitochondrial DNA and human evolution. *Nature, 325*, 31–36.

Carter, R. (2003). Becoming racially and culturally competent: The racial–cultural counseling laboratory. *Journal of Multicultural Counseling and Development, 31*(1), 20–30.

Catalano, C., McCarthy, L., & Shlasko, D. (2007). Transgender oppression curriculum. In M. Adams, L. A. Bell, & P. Griffin (Eds.), *Teaching for diversity and social justice* (2nd ed.). New York: Routledge.

Council on Social Work Education. (2010). Educational policy and accreditation standards. Retrieved July 15, 2010, from *www.cswe.org/accreditation/41865.aspx*.

Cowan, P. (1982). *An orphan in history: Retrieving a Jewish legacy*. New York: Doubleday.

Crohn, J. (1995). *Mixed matches*. New York: Fawcett Columbine.

Dagirmanjian, S. (2005). Armenian families. In M. McGoldrick, J. Giordano, & J. K. Pearce (Eds.), *Ethnicity and family therapy* (2nd ed.). New York: Guilford Press.

Erdrich, L., & Dorris, M. (1991). *The crown of Columbus*. New York: Harper.

Fadiman, A. (1998). *The spirit catches you and you fall down: A Hmong child, her American doctors and the collision of two cultures.* New York: Farrar, Straus & Giroux.

Falicov, C. J. (1995). Training to think culturally: A multidimensional framework. *Family Process, 34,* 373–388.

Falicov, C. J. (2005). Mexican families. In M. McGoldrick, J. Giordano, & N. Garcia-Preto (Eds.), *Ethnicity and family therapy* (3rd ed.). New York: Guilford Press.

Falicov, C. J. (2011). Migration and the family life cycle. In M. McGoldrick, B. Carter, & N. Garcia-Preto (Eds.), *The expanded family life cycle: Individual, family, and social perspectives* (4th ed.). Boston: Allyn & Bacon.

Friere, P. (1994). *The pedagogy of hope.* New York: Continuum.

Fukuyama, M. A., & Sevig, T. D. (1999). *Integrating spirituality into multicultural counseling.* Thousand Oaks, CA: Sage.

Garcia-Preto, N. (2005a). Latino families: An overview. In M. McGoldrick, J. Giordano, & N. Garcia-Preto (Eds.), *Ethnicity and family therapy* (3rd ed.). New York: Guilford Press.

Garcia-Preto, N. (2005b). Puerto Rican families. In M. McGoldrick, J. Giordano, & N. Garcia Preto (Eds.), *Ethnicity and family therapy* (3rd ed.). New York: Guilford Press.

Goodman, A. (2006). Two questions about race. Retrieved on September 3, 2010, from *raceandgenomics.ssrc.org/goodman.*

Griffin, P. (2007). Overview: Sexism, heterosexism, and transgender oppression. In M. Adams, L. A. Bell, & P. Griffin (Eds.), *Teaching for diversity and social justice* (2nd ed.). New York: Routledge.

Griffin, P., D'Errico, H. H., Harro, B., & Schiff, T. (2007). Heterosexism curriculum design. In M. Adams, L. A. Bell, & P. Griffin (Eds.), *Teaching for diversity and social justice* (2nd ed.). New York: Routledge.

Griner, D., & Smith, T. (2006). Culturally adapted mental health interventions: A meta-analytic review. *Psychotherapy: Theory, Research, Practice, and Training, 43,* 531–548.

Hardy, K. V., & Laszloffy, T. A. (1992). Training racially sensitive family therapists: Context, content and contact. *Families in Society, 73*(6), 363–370.

Hardy, K. V., & Laszloffy, T. A. (1995). The cultural genogram: Key to training culturally competent family therapists. *Journal of Marital and Family Therapy, 21*(3), 227–237.

Hayden, T. (2001). *Irish on the inside: In search of the soul of Irish America.* New York: Verso.

Hines, P. M., & Boyd-Franklin, N. (2005). African American families. In M. McGoldrick, J. Giordano, & N. Garcia Preto (Eds.), *Ethnicity and family therapy* (3rd ed.). New York: Guilford Press.

Hitchcock, J. (2001). *Unraveling the white cocoon.* Dubuque, IA: Kendall/Hunt.

Ignatiev, N. (1995). *How the Irish became white.* New York: Routledge.

Kamya, H. (2008). Healing from refugee trauma: The significance of spiritual beliefs, faith community, and faith-based services. In F. Walsh (Ed.), *Spiritual resources in family therapy* (2nd ed., pp. 286–300). New York: Guilford Press.

Katz, J. H. (1978). *White awareness: Handbook for anti-racism training.* Norman: University of Oklahoma Press.

Kristof, N. D. (2010, November 18). A hedge fund republic? *New York Times,* p. A37.

Laszloffy, T. (2008). Social class: Implications for family therapy. In M. McGoldrick & K. V. Hardy (Eds.), *Revisioning family therapy: Race, culture, and gender in clinical practice* (2nd ed.). New York: Guilford Press.

Lev, A. I. (2004). *Transgender emergence: Therapeutic guidelines for working with gender-variant people and their families.* Binghamton, NY: Haworth.

Lewinton, R. C. (1972). The apportionment of human diversity. *Evolutionary Biology, 6*, 381–398.

Liu, W. M., Soleck, G., Hopps, J., Dunston, K., & Pickett T., Jr. (2004). A new framework to understand social class in counseling: The social class worldview model and modern classism theory. *Journal of Multicultural Counseling and Development, 32*(2), 95–122.

Mahmoud, V. (1998). The double bind dynamics of racism. In M. McGoldrick (Ed.), *Re-visioning family therapy: Race, culture, and gender in clinical practice.* New York: Guilford Press.

McGoldrick, M., & Garcia-Preto, N. (1984). Ethnic intermarriage. *Family Process, 23*(3), 347–362.

McGoldrick, M., Gerson, R., & Petry, S. (2008). *Genograms: Assessment and intervention* (3rd ed.). New York: Norton.

McGoldrick, M., Giordano, J., & Garcia-Preto, N. (2005). Overview. In M. McGoldrick, J. Giordano, & N. Garcia-Preto (Eds.), *Ethnicity and family therapy* (3rd ed.). New York: Guilford Press.

McGoldrick, M., & Hardy, K. (2008). Introduction: Re-visioning family therapy from a multicultural perspective. In M. McGoldrick & K. V. Hardy (Eds.), *Re-visioning family therapy: Race, culture, and gender in clinical practice* (2nd ed.). New York: Guilford Press.

McIntosh, P. (2008). White privilege and male privilege: A personal account. In M. McGoldrick & K. V. Hardy (Eds.), *Re-visioning family therapy: Race, culture, and gender in clinical practice* (2nd ed.). New York: Guilford Press.

National Association of Social Workers. (2008). Code of Ethics. Retrieved August 28, 2010, from *www.naswdc.org/pubs/code/code.asp.*

Ponterotto, J., Casas, J., Suzuki, L., & Alexander, C. (2010). *Handbook of multicultural counseling* (3rd ed.). Thousand Oaks, CA: Sage.

Root, M. P. P. (Ed.). (1992). *Racially mixed people in America.* Thousand Oaks, CA: Sage.

Root, M. P. P. (Ed.). (1996). *The multiracial experience: Racial borders as the new frontier.* Thousand Oaks, CA: Sage.

Root, M. P. P. (2001). *Love's revolution: Interracial marriage.* Philadelphia: Temple University Press.

Rosen, E., & Weltman, S. (2005). Jewish families: An overview. In M. McGoldrick, J. Giordano, & N. Garcia-Preto (Eds.), *Ethnicity and family therapy* (3rd ed.). New York: Guilford Press.

Schlosser, L. Z., Foley, P. F., Potrock Stein, E., & Holmwood, J. R. (2010). Why does counseling psychology exclude religion?: A content analysis and methodological critique. In J. Ponterotto, J. Casas, L. Suzuki, & C. Alexander (Eds.), *Handbook of multicultural counseling* (3rd ed.). Thousand Oaks, CA: Sage.

Smith, T. (2010). Culturally congruent practices in counseling and psychotherapy: A review of research. In J. Ponterotto, J. Casas, L. Suzuki, & C. Alexander (Eds.), *Handbook of multicultural counseling* (3rd ed.). Thousand Oaks, CA: Sage.

Stonefish, L., & Harvey, R. (2005). *Nurturing queer youth: Family therapy transformed*. New York: Norton.

Sue, D. W., & Sue, D. (2008). *Counseling the culturally diverse: Theory and practice* (5th ed.). Hoboken, NJ: Wiley.

Tataki, R. (1993). *A different mirror: A history of multicultural America*. Boston: Little, Brown.

Walsh, F. (Ed.). (2008). *Spiritual resources in family therapy* (2nd ed.). New York: Guilford Press.

Walsh, F. (2011). Spiritual diversity: Multifaith perspectives in family therapy. *Family Process, 49*, 330–348.

CHAPTER 12

INTERSECTIONS OF RACE, CLASS, AND POVERTY

Challenges and Resilience in African American Families

NANCY BOYD-FRANKLIN
MELANIE KARGER

I n order to evaluate what is "normal" in the development of any family, clinicians and researchers must explore the larger social context in which the family lives (Hines & Boyd-Franklin, 2005; Pinderhughes, 2002; Walsh, Chapter 1, this volume). Race and class are two of the most complex and emotionally loaded issues in the United States. For poor, inner-city African American families, the day-to-day realities of racism, discrimination, classism, poverty, homelessness, violence, crime, and drugs create forces that continually threaten the family's survival (Sampson & Wilson, 2005). The election of President Obama, despite its historic nature, has not eased these challenges. In the report, *The State of Black America 2009*, published by the National Urban League, Jones (2009) indicated, "Ironically, even as an African American man holds the highest office in this country, African Americans remain twice as likely as whites to be unemployed; three times more likely to live in poverty, and more than six times as likely to be incarcerated" (p. 1). The purpose of this chapter is to provide a framework that will be helpful for clinicians in understanding and working with African American families. Many clinicians who have no framework with which to view these complex realities may become overwhelmed (Boyd-Franklin, 2003; Pinderhughes, 1989; Sue, 2003). The first part of the chapter explores these issues in depth, and the second part utilizes a multisystems model (Boyd-Franklin, 2003) in order to empower families and the clinicians who work with them.

Two cautions are in order. First, discussing race, class, and poverty in one chapter necessitates a less thorough treatment of each than is warranted. A second caveat is that race, class, and poverty are not monolithic constructs that apply unilaterally. Race, for example, has many different levels of meaning for African American individuals and families in the United States. Class as an issue is equally complex and not merely a socioeconomic distinction. For many African Americans, class or socioeconomic level does not foreordain value system: For example, a family classified as "poor" because of income may have "middle-class" values (Billingsley, 1992; Hill, 2003). Also, a "culture of poverty"—coping mechanisms necessary for survival "on the streets"—may persist even as families achieve greater economic success. Finally, the societal realities of racism, oppression, and classism contribute to the challenges that many African American families experience irrespective of financial status (Hajnal, 2007; Hill, 1999, 2003).

RACE, RACISM, AND OPPRESSION

It is important to explore the societal context of life for African American families. Historically, they share both a common African heritage and the degradation of slavery in the United States. In order for Americans of European ancestry to have justified slavery, persons of African American descent had to be viewed as subhuman (Jones, 1997; Sue, 2003). The oppression of slavery—and later segregation and discrimination—contributed to a sense of rage that persists to this day in many African Americans (Hardy & Laszloffy, 1995).

Slavery created a legacy for white people as well. Grier and Cobbs (1968) and Hines and Boyd-Franklin (2005) have indicated that the consequences of slavery were as evident in the children of slavemasters as they were in the children of slaves. Race continues to be an extremely conflicted issue for many white Americans. For some, the issue elicits emotions of guilt, rage, or fear. The increasing number of bias-related incidents in this country (U.S. Department of Justice, 2008) reveals that these old wounds remain an indelible part of the American psyche (Jones, 1997; Sue, 2003).

Although this chapter focuses primarily on the experiences of African American families, it is important to note that the entire discourse on race in this country is compounded by the fact that the term "Black" in America today does not just refer to African Americans. Burton, Bonilla-Silva, Ray, Buckelew, and Freeman (2010) in their careful review of the evolution of critical race theories over the last decade, have documented that "Black" also applies to families that have immigrated (or whose ancestors have come) from the Caribbean or Africa. Some of these families did not experience the same U.S. history of slavery as African Americans, but they may be affected by experiences of racism in this country. Similarly, they note that the increase in biracial and multiracial couples and families has also broadened the dialogue on race. The 2000 Census was the first to document these complex identities. Burton et al. (2010) and Samuels (2006) also discuss the challenges facing biracial and multiracial children, who may be labeled in America as "Black" but may have more complex personal identities.

For many African Americans, however, the concept of race has many levels of meaning (Franklin, Boyd-Franklin, & Kelly, 2006). On one level, it identifies those persons of African ancestry and implies a shared origin. Often, it applies to shared physical characteristics, such as skin color, hair texture, and appearance (Boyd-Franklin, 2003). African Americans commonly may have various mixtures of ancestry, including Native American and European elements; thus, as a race, they present in a wide range of skin colors and appearances. There are also important distinctions in terms of racial identity within African Americans as a group (Carter, 1995; Helms & Cook, 1999).

Jones (1997) and Pinderhughes (1989, p. 71) have shown that "over time, race has acquired a social meaning . . . via the mechanism of stereotyping. . . . Status assignment based on skin color identity has evolved into complex social structures that promote a power differential between Whites and various people of color." Hopps (1982) has stated that "although many forms of exclusion and discrimination exist in this country, none is so deeply rooted, persistent or intractable as that based on color" (p. 3). For this reason, many African American families' perceptions of the world—including self-identity, racial pride, childrearing, educational and school-related experiences; job or employment opportunities or the lack of them; financial security or the lack of it; as well as treatment in interpersonal encounters and male–female relationships—are screened through the lens of the racial experience (Boyd-Franklin, 2003; Boyd-Franklin, Kelly, & Durham, 2008; Franklin, Boyd-Franklin, & Draper, 2002; Kelly, 2003).

IMPACT OF RACE ON CHILDREARING

Many African American parents, aware of the degrading messages their children may receive from society, particularly through the school systems, make a conscious effort to instill a sense of racial pride and strong positive identity in their children (Franklin et al., 2002; McAdoo, 2002; White-Johnson, Ford, & Sellers, 2010). A further challenge in childrearing for African Americans is combating pervasive negative images, particularly in the media (Jenkins, 2006; Martin, 2008; Stevenson & Davis, 2004).

Thus, within such a context, "normal family development" requires many African American parents to practice racial socialization, to educate their children to the realities of racism and discrimination, and to prepare them for the negative messages they may encounter (Franklin et al., 2002; McAdoo, 2002; Stevenson & Davis, 2004; Stevenson, Davis, & Abdul-Kabir, 2001). African American parents, interviewed for the book *Boys Into Men: Raising Our African American Teenage Sons* (Boyd-Franklin, Franklin, & Toussaint,

2000), frequently stated that they felt that they had to be more vigilant in order to raise an African American child today, particularly a male child. However, parents must walk a fine line between giving children the tools to understand racism, so that they do not internalize the process, and instilling in them a belief that they can achieve despite the odds and overcome racism, without becoming consumed with rage and bitterness. This is a complex task and a difficult developmental journey for a family or an individual to navigate (Stevenson & Davis, 2004; Stevenson et al., 2001).

RACISM, THE INVISIBILITY SYNDROME, AND GENDER ISSUES

There are many levels of complications of racism with which African Americans must contend in the process of family development. The legacy of slavery and oppression has contributed to a fear in American society of African American males that begins at a very early age. Franklin (1999, 2004) and Franklin and Boyd-Franklin (2000) referred to an "invisibility syndrome," a paradoxical process by which the high skin color visibility of African American men causes society to view them with fear and, as a consequence, to treat them as if they are "invisible."

African American male children, who may begin school being perceived as "cute" by teachers, at a very young age (7, 8, or 9) are viewed as a threat. Kunjufu (1985), in his book *Countering the Conspiracy to Destroy Black Boys*, discusses the "fourth-grade failure syndrome," in which teachers (and therapists) often become intimidated by African American male children and begin to label them as aggressive and hyperactive, and as failures (Boyd-Franklin et al., 2000; Stevenson & Davis, 2004).

African American families are thus in a double bind, particularly when raising sons. Although racism clearly exists for both male and female African American children, society tends to be more punitive toward and restrictive of male children (Boyd-Franklin et al., 2000). The risk in raising sons to be assertive is that society will see them as aggressive. The consequences of this have many levels of impact, including labeling within the school system; high dropout and unemployment rates; overrepresentation in the prison system; and, most tragically, early death on the streets (Boyd-Franklin et al., 2000; Stevenson & Davis, 2004).

CLASS AND RACE

Social class is extremely complicated in the United States, particularly when coupled with issues of race. Many African American families find that their experiences of class distinctions within their own communities are very different from the class categories applied in the broader American society (Hill, 1999, 2003). For example, on the one hand, many poor, working-class African American families are considered "middle class" within their own communities because of their values, aspirations, and expectations for their children. On the other hand, enhanced class status is very precarious for many African Americans to maintain. In troubled economic times, African Americans are particularly vulnerable to layoffs and often fall victim to "last hired, first fired" policies (Borjas, 2006; Couch & Fairlie, 2010).

In addition, there has been a long debate about the relative importance of race and class variables in the lives of African Americans. Thirty years ago, a prominent sociologist, William Julius Wilson, in his book *The Declining Significance of Race* (1980), argued that whereas race and racism dictated the poverty of African Americans in the past, the legislation and policies of the late 1960s and 1970s created opportunities to achieve middle-class status. Wilson contended that class replaced race as the salient distinction, thus relegating the vast numbers of African American families trapped in the vicious cycle of poverty to an "underclass." Wilson's work had a major impact on public policy; however, he has since modified his view of the complex interplay of variables such as race, class, and poverty in more recent publications (Sampson & Wilson, 2005; Wilson, 1987, 1996).

The continuing significance of race must be explored in assessing the normal family processes of African Americans. It is important to acknowledge class and race together with oppressive poverty in working with inner-city families. Similarly, it is also relevant to explore the ways in which race continues to impact the lives of middle-class Black families.

MIDDLE-CLASS AFRICAN AMERICAN FAMILIES

Although this chapter primarily focuses on the experience of African American families living in poverty, it is important to explore briefly the growth of the Black middle class and the unique issues facing such families. Within the last several decades, there has been an increase in the number of middle-class Black families. Yet most require two incomes to achieve an affluent status and have considerably less wealth and assets than comparable white families (Hill, 2003).

The severe and repeated economic crises afflicting the early 21st century have served to challenge the aspirations of the Black middle class (Hill, 2003). Bias-related incidents in cities and on college campuses have increased. Many African Americans began to experience a "white backlash" from those who felt their own opportunities threatened, and the "blaming the victim" philosophy of an earlier era has since returned.

The enduring yet more subtle and covert racism that has emerged in the 21st century can be even more damaging to the emerging Black middle class than the overt racism that preceded it (Hill, 2003; McAdoo, 2002; Stevenson & Davis, 2004). An empirical study by Merritt, Bennett, Williams, Edwards, and Sollers (2006) reported higher levels of cardiovascular response in African Americans shown more subtle forms of racism than those shown more blatant forms of racism. This finding is quite notable "given the observations that older, blatant forms of racism are increasingly being supplanted by more subtle forms of racism" (p. 367).

Ellis Cose (1993), in his book *The Rage of the Privileged Class*, describes the anger and rage felt by many middle- and upper-class African Americans when their high educational and socioeconomic level does nothing to prevent continuing encounters with overt racial assaults and more subtle "microaggressions" (Franklin, 2004; Sue, 2010). Middle-class, educated African Americans are rudely reminded of the existence of institutionalized racism in this country as they confront a "glass ceiling" when anticipated promotions in their professions do not materialize. Tokenism persists, with the hiring and promotion of relatively few African Americans to high-level positions. Hajnal (2007) argues that "for Blacks, class gains are likely to be associated with increasing contact with an often unwelcoming and seldom race blind white world—an environment that may reinforce rather than erode race" (p. 583). Furthermore, Hajal found that middle-class Blacks continue to support an African American agenda despite their elevated economic status, suggesting that, for these individuals, "race is not being replaced by class as a primary social identity" (p. 583).

POVERTY AND THE "VICTIM SYSTEM"

Many African American communities remain mired in multigenerational poverty (Hill, 1999, 2003) despite the number of African Americans who have benefited from job and educational opportunities. These communities are rife with drug and alcohol abuse, gangs, crime, homelessness or increasingly dangerous public housing, violence and death, teenage pregnancy, high unemployment and school dropout rates, poor educational systems, and ongoing issues with the police and the justice system (Bolland, Liam, & Formichella, 2005; Thompson & Massat, 2005). Families see few options for their children, and many feel trapped, which leads to what Pinderhughes (1989) has termed "the victim system."

A victim system is a circular feedback process that

> threatens self-esteem and reinforces problematic responses in communities, families and individuals. The feedback works as follows: Barriers to opportunity and education limit the chance for achievement, employment, and attainment of skills. This limitation can, in turn, lead to poverty or stress in relationships, which interferes with adequate performance of family roles. (Pinderhughes, 1982, p. 109)

As Boyd-Franklin et al. (2000) have shown, adolescence begins early within poor, inner-city communities. At a very young age, children are expected to assume household responsibilities and are exposed to pressures related to sexuality, drugs, and alcohol use. Random violence, particularly drug-related violence, has become a major concern for poor, inner-city families. Many parents live in fear for themselves and their children, and struggle with helplessness as they view the prospect of "the streets" claiming their children. This sense of futility and disempowerment is a potent issue for many poor African American families (Bolland et al., 2005), particularly when their economic conditions have worsened.

CHRONIC POSTTRAUMATIC STRESS DISORDER

Inner-city children and families commonly experience chronic trauma and stress (Thompson & Massat, 2005). Children and adults living in low-income housing projects or housing shelters often report intense fear as they walk through darkened halls, or past deserted buildings and crack houses. It is not unusual for children to have to walk through a "needle park" to get to school, or to confront crack vials and discarded syringes in the playground. Many are acquainted from an early age with violence in their homes in the forms of spousal and child abuse or sexual abuse. They may have seen family members experience a drug overdose and/or AIDS. Traumatic deaths and painful losses reverberate through family networks.

Children often begin to exhibit behavior problems after witnessing traumatic events, such as violent deaths in their communities (Thompson & Massat, 2005). In addition to acting-out behaviors manifested in oppositional or conduct disorders, these children often experience anxiety or depressive symptoms. However, the classic features of posttraumatic stress disorder (PTSD)—nightmares, flashbacks of the traumatic event, generalized fear and anxiety, and fears of entering areas where traumatic events occurred—are often overlooked by clinicians (Schwartz, Bradley, Sexton, Sherry, & Ressler, 2005).

In an empirical study, Schwartz et al. (2005) examined PTSD among 184 African Americans in an inner-city outpatient mental health clinic. Of this sample, 43% showed symptoms of PTSD, yet only 11% had PTSD listed in their charts. Schwartz et al. went on to state, "It appears that PTSD is an under treated and under reported source of psychiatric morbidity in this urban community of African Americans with low socioeconomic status" (p. 214). In a study of 110 African American sixth graders attending an inner-city Chicago public school, Thompson and Massat (2005) examined the frequency of witnessing violence. They found that the level of exposure to violence was significantly related to levels of behavior problems and negatively related to school achievement. Furthermore, Thompson and Massat emphasized the correlation among community, family, and witnessing violence, suggesting that the parents of the children may also be suffering from PTSD due to past exposure to violence. Given these realities, further research is also needed on high rates of diagnosis of attention deficit disorder (Tucker & Dixon, 2009), as well as low treatment rates (Miller, Nigg, & Miller, 2009). These realities require more attention to contextual sources of child distress.

RACISM AND POVERTY, ANGER, AND RAGE

Although there are significant numbers of poor families in this country who are not African American, and many have lived for generations in poverty, poor African Americans experience a dual oppression based on race and class (Boyd-Franklin, 2003; Hill, 2003). Unlike immigrants who often arrived in the United States poor but experienced upward mobility within a generation or two, high dropout rates for African American youth and chronic unemployment, particularly for men ages 15–25, have left many families with pessimistic views of their future options (Hill, 2003).

The combination of discrimination and oppression, augmented by racism and poverty, has produced a fierce anger in many African Americans (Cose, 1993; Franklin, 2004; Hardy & Laszloffy, 1995; Jones, 1997). For African American families trapped in poverty and assaulted by unemployment, high dropout rates, drugs, violence, crime, and homelessness (at times, the result of urban gentrification), anger and rage have been growing for decades. Often, rage is turned on those living in the community, as can be seen in incidents of "Black on Black" crime (Franklin, 2004). It can be acted out through conduct disordered or delinquent behavior, or in the family, by stealing, child abuse, or domestic violence. Finally, rage can be internalized and manifested as depression, or self-destructive drug or alcohol abuse.

Service providers must be aware that anger and rage may be directed against them, irrespective of their race or ethnic status. This anger and rage frequently paralyzes well-meaning clinicians. Training programs must address this issue and prepare clinicians for work in these communities by helping them learn not to personalize it, and by teaching them effective strategies for joining and building trust with these families (Boyd-Franklin, 2003; Boyd-Franklin & Bry, 2000).

ATTITUDES OF MENTAL HEALTH WORKERS TOWARD POOR AFRICAN AMERICAN FAMILIES

In the mental health field prior to the 1970s, poor African Americans were often pathologized and labeled (Moynihan, 1965), too often leading clinicians to "blame the victim" and dismiss these families as untreatable (Boyd-

Franklin, 2003). Intervention models often offer a limited focus on "individuals" or "families," without considering social context. Mental health workers may thus be overwhelmed and ill-equipped to cope with the reality of inner-city poverty, for example, homelessness, teenage pregnancy, unemployment, crime, appalling living conditions, hunger, poor health care, and maltreatment of the poor by public agencies (e.g., schools, police, juvenile justice, courts, and child welfare systems). As a consequence, mental health workers and family therapists may find themselves mirroring the lack of empowerment that these families feel.

RESPONSES OF POOR AFRICAN AMERICAN FAMILIES TO MENTAL HEALTH SERVICES

For many families, poverty has led to a greater likelihood of intrusion by outside agencies. Often, inner-city families live with the fear of removal of their children by child welfare or child protective services. Many African Americans have a long memory for the policies of the past, such as the Aid to Dependent Children program in which assistance would often be denied if a man was contributing to the support of a family. This policy set a disincentive for past generations of couples to marry when pregnancy occurred (Boyd-Franklin et al., 2008; Pinderhughes, 2002), relegating men to a peripheral status within their families, a factor that contributed significantly to the "invisibility" of African American men (Franklin, 1999, 2004; Franklin & Boyd-Franklin, 2000; Franklin, Boyd-Franklin, & Kelly, 2006). Even though the laws have now changed, and women are not pressured to claim that they head "single-parent" households, generations of African Americans were impacted by those policies.

The legacy of intrusion by social and child protective services, police, and legal and criminal justice systems is endemic to impoverished communities. It is far more intense with the added variable of racism and has resulted in a "healthy cultural suspicion" (Boyd-Franklin, 2003; Grier & Cobbs, 1968) that extends toward helping institutions and helping professions as well. Thus, schools and teachers; social service agencies and social workers; mental health clinics and therapists of all disciplines; and hospitals and medical, nursing, and other health care professionals may be faced with families who are suspicious of their efforts. Service providers who are unaware of the legacy of racism and classism may personalize this initial response and erroneously presume that these families do not want their services or cannot be treated.

Another complication is that many African American families, particularly those living in the inner city, may not be self-referred and may feel coerced to enter treatment. There is also a very widely held stigma in this community that therapy is "for crazy, sick, or weak people" or for "white folks" (Boyd-Franklin, 2003). Several authors have drawn attention to the significance of shame and denial as barriers to care seeking among African Americans (Cruz, Pincus, Harman, Reynolds, & Post, 2008; Holden, 2009). In addition, because of healthy cultural suspicion, poor African Americans may tell their children that family business is "nobody's business but our own," and may caution against "airing the dirty laundry outside the family." Therefore, mental health service providers may find it necessary to address these issues first, thus establishing trust with families before any intervention can take place (Boyd-Franklin, 2003).

FAMILY STRENGTHS AND SURVIVAL SKILLS

Some social scientists and service providers have focused on the deficiencies in inner-city African American families (Moynihan, 1965). Viewing families through a deficit lens blinds one to their inherent strengths and survival skills. It is extremely important that public policy and clinical training programs focus on the strengths that must be mobilized to produce change.

Bell-Tolliver, Burgess, and Brock (2009) examined the perspective of African American psychotherapists' identification of strengths in African American families, and how they view and use these strengths in therapy. The study affirmed Hill's (1999) earlier findings that identified kinship bonds, strong work orientation, adaptability of family roles, strong achievement orientation, and strong religious orientation as significant strengths of African American families. A sixth strength has since emerged: their willingness to seek counseling, or as one participant stated, "The fact that they are willing to seek help, that they are willing to look at themselves, and that they are open to changing whatever the issue might be within the family" (Bell-Tolliver et al., 2009, p. 298). Additionally, several therapists mentioned seeing an increasing number of families that, after being involuntarily referred for therapy by various legal institutions, make the decision to utilize the therapy setting to address the reason they were referred. This commitment to change was seen as another important strength.

Another theme emerged in the same study: the value of having a strong family hierarchy, respect within the family system, and respect for other authority figures. The therapists spoke about the value of utilizing the bond or the connection with previous generations to help the family to resolve current problems. "There is a more respectful bond between the children and the parents and the grandparents or down through the generations than in a lot of other races. Respect is still there, but has deteriorated some through the generations; but, it's still there" (Bell-Tolliver et al., 2009, p. 299).

A further strength of African American families is an extensive kinship network that comprises "blood" and "nonblood" family members (Billingsley, 1992, 1994; Boyd-Franklin, 2003; Hill, 2003; Logan, 2001; McAdoo, 2002) who provide support, encouragement, and "reciprocity" in terms of sharing goods, money, and services. This network might include older relatives such as great-grandparents, grandmothers, grandfathers, aunts, uncles, cousins, and older brothers and sisters, all of whom may participate in childrearing, as well as "nonblood relatives" such as godparents, babysitters, neighbors, friends, church family members, ministers, ministers' wives, and so forth.

Because it is "normal" for many African American families to be connected to such a network (Billingsley, 1992, 1994; Boyd-Franklin, 2003; Hill, 2003; Logan, 2001; McAdoo, 2002), those families who come to the attention of mental health services may have become isolated or disconnected from their traditional support network (Boyd-Franklin, 2010a). Families may become disconnected when the key "switchboard" family members of the older generation begin to die. These older family members were often the ones who brought the family together on Thanksgiving, Christmas, and other holidays and special occasions. They organized family reunions and disseminated "family news," such as births, deaths, and marriages. Disconnection may also arise from behavioral causes. For example, a family member who engages in substance abuse may steal from the family in order to support a drug habit and become "cut off" from the family network by anger. Additionally, a "cut-off" may become homeless, commonly as a result of eviction or being "burnt out." In some inner-city areas, entire neighborhoods have been dispossessed through arson or efforts of gentrification. Another possibility is that networks may have become so overwhelmed that they are unable to take on additional responsibilities.

Establishing trust may be difficult at first, particularly if the therapist is of a different race, class, or culture. However, once trust has been established after a number of contacts, families are often more willing to share vital information and their genograms, family trees, or "real family" networks. The task for therapists is often to search for persons who represent "islands of strength" within the family (Billingsley, 1992; Logan, 2001). Unfortunately, these family members often do not come in to agencies or clinics. Therefore, in order to identify and/or meet the individuals who really hold the power in African American families, the worker may have to obtain the family's permission to visit the home (Boyd-Franklin & Bry, 2000).

It is not unusual for poor African American mothers to present with their children at mental health centers as overwhelmed single parents. In traditional clinical settings, the distress presented by such women has been overpathologized by locating the source of their problems within them as individuals. It is crucial to appreciate the context of their sense of being overwhelmed, or their disorganization and lack of resources to manage situations that are, in fact, overwhelming (Aponte, 1994). Therapists should avoid making snap judgments on the basis of first impressions and instead broaden their lens and familiarize themselves with the formal and informal networks to which the family may be connected. For families who are "cut off" from these support systems, a part of the therapy must focus on helping them to resolve conflictual issues in order to reconnect with their families of origin or to form new support networks within their communities. Such an approach might prove particularly empowering for poor families who experience a sense of isolation and fear within their own communities.

RELIGION, SPIRITUALITY, AND OTHER SURVIVAL SKILLS

Many African American families have gained strength from their spiritual and/or religious orientation (Bell-Tolliver et al., 2009, Billingsley, 1994; Boyd-Franklin, 2010a; Boyd-Franklin & Lockwood, 2009; Hill, 2003; Walsh, Chapter 15, this volume). Particularly for the older generation (Armstrong & Crowther, 2002; Johnson, Elbert-Avila, & Tulsky, 2005; Taylor, Chatters, Bullard, Wallace, & Jackson, 2009; Taylor, Chatters, & Jackson, 2007; Taylor, Chatters, & Levin, 2004), this may translate into church membership and a feeling of community or connectedness with a "church family" (Billingsley, 1994; Boyd-Franklin, 2003). Many poor families have used their church family to provide role models and support with childrearing. For families who fight a constant battle to "save their children from the streets," churches often provide an alternative network for friends. The organizational nature of churches also provides very visible and active male and female adult role models. Figures who have achieved stature and distinction may include the minister, the minister's wife, deacons, deaconesses, elders, and trustee boards. Church organizations are also very conscious of their function in the upbringing of children within the community and offer education programs either after school or during the summer, child care, and camp and opportunities for children to become involved in services such as choir and junior usher programs (Nye, 1993).

Despite the life enhancement that is offered by the church, many younger African American families in inner-city areas have either rebelled against this support system or become disconnected and dispirited (Aponte, 1994). It is essential that we learn from the functional, poor families in African American communities who identify these supports for themselves and their children. Service providers should be aware of the "church families" and become acquainted with the ministers in African American communities. Such religious leaders often have a great deal of influence and can sometimes provide help and support for a family that is homeless, for a mother who is struggling to raise her children alone and searching for afterschool activities, or for a chronically mentally ill adult who has become "cut off" from his or her extended family after the death of the main caregiver.

It is also important to note a distinction between "spirituality" and "religious orientation" in African Americans (see Walsh, Chapter 15, this volume). Family members who may not have a "church home" or formal membership in a church community may still have a deep, abiding "spirituality." In the Afrocentric tradition and view of the world, the psyche and the spirit are one (Mbiti, 1990; Nobles, 2004). Therefore, for African American families spirituality is often a strength and a survival mechanism that can be tapped, particularly in times of death and dying, illness, loss, and bereavement (Boyd-Franklin, 2010a; Dass-Brailsford, 2010). Thus, family members who do not go to church may still "pray to the Lord" when times are hard. Additionally, a growing number of African Americans draw on the Islamic faith for their spiritual sustenance (McAdams-Mahmoud, 2005).

LOVE OF CHILDREN: ANOTHER LOOK AT EXTENDED FAMILY CHILDREARING PRACTICES

Because of the harshness of their lives and the skills necessary for survival in a racist society, many African American inner-city families have adopted the strict discipline known as "spare the rod, spoil the child" (Boyd-Franklin et al., 2000). Therapists working with such families may find themselves making judgments about values regarding childrearing and see this concept of discipline as abusive treatment of children. It is important, however, for clinicians to recognize that this parenting practice is often rooted in feelings of love and concern in families who fear for their children's well-being, particularly that of their male children. Reframes with these families that focus on caring intentions, such as "You love him (or her) so much that you are trying to teach him right and protect him from harm," are very powerful. Once this respect has been given, parental family members will be more receptive to hearing about more constructive alternatives, such as "But I have the sense that all of your efforts do not seem to be working. Are you open to learning new techniques for discipline that may lead to different results for you and your children?"

Some families preach a "tough" philosophy but are very inconsistent in their parenting. Once the underlying love has been recognized, these parents can hear the need for consistency. Another variable related to consistency has to do with extended family involvement in childrearing. Researchers have documented the widespread pattern of "multiple mothering or fathering," in which parenting responsibilities are often shared by grandmothers, grandfathers, aunts, uncles, cousins, older brothers and sisters, and "nonblood relatives" such as ministers, church family members, neighbors, friends, and babysitters (Billingsley, 1992; Boyd-Franklin, 2003; Hill, 1999; Hines & Boyd-Franklin, 2005; Logan, 2001; McAdoo, 2002). These supports often provide aid and strength to overburdened parents; however, the negotiation of these relationships can be complex, and inconsistencies in parenting may develop because so many individuals are involved. In family assessments, practitioners need to look beyond the household to identify important kin. Alas, overvaluing the "nuclear family" in the dominant culture may blind workers to rich multigenerational ties. The clinician's task in working with such family networks is to open communication between the "parental" figures and reach consensus on boundaries, rules, and disciplinary practices.

SINGLE-PARENT FAMILIES

There is a tendency in the social science literature to treat single-parent families as if they represent a homogeneous group. In fact, there are many different kinds of single-parent families, whose circumstances vary according to family functioning, capabilities of the parent, socioeconomic and income level, employment, and degree of extended family support (see Anderson, Chapter 6, this volume).

Service workers are cautioned about the tendency to mislabel automatically all single-parent families as dysfunctional. *The fact of single parenthood does not make a family dysfunctional* (Boyd-Franklin, 2003; McAdoo, 2002; Murray & Brody, 2002). Lindblad-Goldberg, Dukes, and Lasley (1988) compared functional and dysfunctional low-income, African American, single-parent families living in Philadelphia. The functional families predictably had clear boundaries and role responsibilities. They were not isolated, and they drew readily on the support of their extended family kinship network.

There are also differences in the ways in which families become single-parent entities (see Anderson, Chapter 6, this volume). Subsequent to the birth of their children, increasing numbers of African American parents become single through divorce or separation, or they are widowed (a trend that mirrors a similar pattern in American society as a whole) (Boyd-Franklin, 2003; Pinderhughes, 2002). Some women choose single parenthood as they reach their 30s and 40s, and do not want to remain childless. Although these trends are important, the largest number of African American single parents initially attain that status through unwed, teenage pregnancy.

TEENAGE PREGNANCY

One of the most complicated phenomena in African American communities is the issue of teenage pregnancy. There has been an ongoing tendency in social science literature to "blame the victim" and to label these young women as irresponsible (McAdoo, 2002; Tatum, Moseley, Boyd-Franklin, & Herzog, 1995). This phenomenon must be viewed within the context of poverty, unemployment, racism, and the general sense of hopelessness that frequently pervades inner-city urban communities (Edin & Kefalas, 2005). For many young women living in these conditions, having a child becomes a "rite of passage" to womanhood. Edin and Kefalas, in their 2½-year field study of 162 young, unmarried mothers living in Philadelphia's poorest inner-city neighborhoods, observed that poor single women often have children in the absence of better opportunities and that, for these women, "children offer a tangible source of meaning, while other avenues for gaining social esteem and personal satisfaction appear vague and tenuous" (p. 49). The role of male partners' persuasion of vulnerable teenage girls to have unprotected sex must also be addressed, with similar consideration of their life situation.

Unemployment and lack of opportunity affect both young women and men in inner-city African American neighborhoods. Wilson (1987) has clearly shown that when men had jobs or believed they had prospects as breadwinner/provider, they were significantly more likely to marry. Unfortunately, the realities of a declining economy and the results of racism and discrimination leave them with few options. For some African American men who feel disenfranchised, having a child becomes a way to demonstrate manhood. Because they lack the sense of a future, immediate pleasure and the potency involved in creating a life become part of a more present-oriented way of life. Furthermore, for many fathers, access to their children is determined by their ability to provide financially (Burton et al., 2010; Gavin et al., 2003).

In 1996, the Personal Responsibility and Work Opportunity Reconciliation Act (PRWORA) replaced Aid to Families with Dependent Children (AFDC). Temporary Assistance for Needy Families (TANF) is part of this welfare reform. This system further reinforces the exclusion or "invisibility" of the man by decreasing a family's financial support if he is present (Franklin, 2004; Gavin et al., 2003; Kirshnakumar & Black, 2003). Furthermore, because girls become pregnant as young as age 13, 14, or 15, older women in the family are usually actively involved in child care. This creates complex family and parenting dynamics (Kirshnakumar & Black, 2003; see Engstrom, Chapter 9, this volume).

MULTIGENERATIONAL ISSUES

For many young women, teenage pregnancy and single parenthood is a multigenerational family pattern—both the mother and the grandmother may also have become pregnant during their adolescent years. Often, as a daughter approaches puberty, there is increased anxiety within the family system (Tatum et al., 1995). Families react in a variety of ways, the most common of which are (1) to become overly rigid, restrictive, and punitive with the child in an attempt to protect her from pregnancy or (2) to feel overwhelmed with this multigenerational family transmission process (Bowen, 1976; Nichols, 2009) and to "throw up their hands," leaving the child with the responsibility of raising herself. These adolescents often appear very much out of control, and parents often feel helpless to make a difference. It is paradoxical that either of these extreme responses increases the risk that the girl will carry out the family script of multigenerational teenage pregnancy. Family sessions that explore these issues openly between the generations in a family can help to break this cycle (Boyd-Franklin, 2003). Connecting young people and their families with their multigenerational history is also empowering, as they gain new knowledge of their ancestors, an understanding of the legacies of slavery, and an appreciation of their resilience (Pinderhughes, 2008).

EMPOWERMENT

Confronting the obstacles of racism, classism, poverty, and the "victim system" has left many inner-city African American families feeling disenfranchised and powerless. Therefore, a key focus in any treatment approach must beon empowerment (Boyd-Franklin, 2003; Boyd-Franklin & Bry, 2000). This concept of empowerment is multifaceted, consisting of the empowerment of both the "executive" or parental system in the family (Minuchin, 1974) and the family members to intervene in the multiple systems that impact and intrude on their lives.

Structural family therapy, which encourages clinicians to put parental figures in charge of their children, is a very powerful approach (Aponte, 1994; Minuchin, 1974). When families feel that they are "losing their children to the streets," it is very empowering to pull extended family members together to fight and "take their children back" (Boyd-Franklin et al., 2000).

Empowerment through Multiple-Family Groups

Social isolation (homelessness and lack of support networks) exacerbates mental health problems. One approach that is extremely empowering to family members, as well as to the clinicians who work with them, is the multiple-family group therapy intervention. Families who lack support systems are brought grouped together with other families struggling to overcome similar problems in their community. Together they become a support system for each other and often form relationships that continue beyond the life of the group (Boyd-Franklin & Bry, 2000). This approach is especially valuable for single parents who face myriad challenges on their own.

African American families traditionally search out and create social supports when moving to a new community. However, because of the fear of violence, crime, and drugs, many inner-city African American families today find themselves isolated, virtually held hostage within their own homes and apartments (Boyd-Franklin & Bry, 2000). Therefore, it is truly empowering to introduce these families to one another and bring them together around their common concerns for their children, as the enhanced sense of community destigmatizes common dilemmas. It is both comforting and personally empowering to know that one is not alone and that there exists support for change. An example of such a support situation would be for families to be able to go together to meet with the principal at their children's school to discuss their concerns related to drugs, crime, and so forth.

Empowerment through a Multisystems Model

Treatment must take into consideration the fact that, as discussed earlier, poor, inner-city African American families cope with the intrusiveness of many organizations, such as agencies, schools, hospitals, police, courts, juvenile justice systems, welfare, child protective services, and housing and mental health services on a daily basis (Boyd-Franklin, 2003; Boyd-Franklin & Bry, 2000; Henggeler, Schoenwald, Borduin, Rowland, & Cunningham, 2009). Empowerment within this context means identifying the various agencies or institutions that affect a family's life. An eco map (Boyd-Franklin, 2003; Hartman & Laird, 1983) can be helpful in diagramming these systems. The family members can then be empowered to intervene in the following ways: (1) calling meetings of various agencies that have the power to make decisions for their families; (2) writing letters, and getting letters from therapists, doctors, and so forth, in support of their families; and (3) obtaining a therapist's support to be empowered to ask for conferences with supervisors of resistant workers. The key here is that family members must be empowered to take charge of these issues. Clinicians must resist the urge to do the work themselves.

Empowerment of Clinicians

Many training programs in all disciplines in the mental health field have not adequately prepared clinicians for working with poor, African American families (Holden, 2009). Well-meaning, eager clinicians may be unprepared for the racial tension, anger, and "healthy cultural suspicion" they encounter. They also may well be overwhelmed by the realities of poverty, or be unprepared to cope with the myriad multisystems levels and agencies that are factors in these families' lives. There are also difficulties in outreach, because families may not have phones, or they may live in dangerous neighborhoods. Practitioners may find it helpful to work through natural community bases in schools, churches, and health care clinics.

The process of training clinicians to work effectively with families who are dealing with racism, classism, and poverty is also one of empowerment. It is not surprising that this process must begin by helping therapists to look at themselves—at their own values, upbringing, and attitudes about race, class, and poverty. There are now a number of excellent training tools available. Pinderhughes's (1989) book *Understanding Race, Ethnicity and Power* describes in detail a training program designed to help therapists explore these issues. Aponte (1994) has long been a pioneer in helping therapists explore their own use of self with poor families.

Boyd-Franklin (2003) devotes a chapter to the therapist's use of self with relevant countertransference issues for African American clients and white clinicians. The last chapter explores the role of training and supervision in the process of empowering clinicians. The multisystems model (Boyd-Franklin, 2003; Boyd-Franklin & Bry, 2000) addresses and helps prepare clinicians to deal more effectively with the complex issues of race, culture, class, and poverty, to look at African American families within the context of their history and culture, and to recognize the strengths that can be utilized to produce empowerment.

Work with African American inner-city families requires a therapist who is prepared to be "active" and committed to facilitating families in their own empowerment. It also requires supervisors who are committed to being "on the front lines" and empowering their trainees to look at the complex and difficult questions of race, class, poverty, and to examine their own values and responses to these issues. Beyond didactic teaching, this model produces empowerment by focusing on the process of supervision and training as an opportunity to develop the "person of the therapist" (Aponte & Carlsen, 2009; Aponte et al., 2009). Only through a very personal process can therapists be trained to recognize the complex issues discussed in this chapter, to be true to themselves, and to allow their own humanity to be communicated to the families with whom they work.

Empowerment through Social Policy Intervention

Strong social policy programs must address this issue of empowerment of families and communities by incentives that encourage self-determination. These programs should provide housing to counteract homelessness, affordable and accessible health care, and better and more responsive educational systems and work incentives. Those in the mental health field, including family therapists, social workers, psychologists, and psychiatrists, must unite to advance these key issues on the national agenda.

Researchers (Kirshnakumar & Black, 2003; Hill, 1999; Weil & Finegold, 2002) have discussed the ways in which "welfare reform" legislation in this past decade ended federally guaranteed, long-term entitlements for poor families with dependent children and gave states the responsibility for administering welfare programs through "block grants." One block grant to states for Temporary Assistance for Needy Families (TANF), was designed to help welfare recipients leave the rolls within specified time limits: 2 years to obtain jobs, and a maximum length of 5 years to receive welfare benefits before they are terminated. Although a second block grant was designed to provide subsidized child care for welfare recipients who are able to obtain jobs, funds are inadequate for the large number of recipients who will need child care assistance.

Hill (1999) regards this legislation as inconsistent with the goal of helping welfare recipients to become self-sufficient and find their way out of poverty. His critique of welfare reform focuses on six major weaknesses:

> (1) It has fixed amounts that will not be responsive to economic downturns and periodic recessions; (2) it has inadequate resources for providing extended training and education to enhance the capabilities of "long-term" recipients with few marketable skills; (3) it will place most recipients into short-term, low-wage jobs with no health benefits; (4) it has inadequate funds to provide subsidized child care for the large numbers of recipients who are expected to find jobs; (5) it relies on churches and other nonprofit

institutions to provide increased assistance to the poor with limited government resources; and (6) it is likely to increase the number of persons who are homeless, poor, and in foster care. (p. 155)

Another policy area that must be addressed is kinship care (see Engstrom, Chapter 9, this volume). Historically, African American families have "informally adopted" children into the homes of extended family members. Unfortunately, prior to 1980, many African American children were removed from their homes and placed in foster care, although viable kinship placements were available. In 1980, however, with the passage of the Adoption Assistance and Child Welfare Act (Public Law 96-272), a number of changes began to occur (Hill, 1999). This legislation strongly encouraged family preservation services. Many states began to implement procedures for locating viable extended family caregivers. Major discrepancies remain, however. Even though kinship care is more likely to be utilized for placement (Berrick & Barth, 1994; Wilson & Chipungu, 1996), kin caregivers are usually not given adequate funding to provide for these children (Boyd-Franklin, 2003; Hill, 2003). As a result, many of these caregivers, often older adult relatives, incur a large financial burden. There is a need for major federal and state legislation to provide funding to support viable kinship care for African American families (Boyd-Franklin, 2003).

CHANGE IN SOCIETAL ATTITUDES THAT FOSTER RACISM, CLASSISM, AND POVERTY

Ultimately, mental health providers must accept a personal sense of social responsibility for changing those attitudes that foster racism, classism, and poverty. The first step is honestly acknowledging the existence of these phenomena and learning about their complex interplay. On the microcosm level, we can begin with ourselves and the families with whom we work. Many mental health clinicians, however, like the families they serve, become overwhelmed when asked to move to a "macro" level. If these issues are ever to be resolved fully in any society, we must be willing to speak out for and advocate change in our own agencies and clinics, communities, and local, state, and national governments.

REFERENCES

Aponte, H. (1994). *Bread and spirit: Therapy with the new poor.* New York: Morton Press.

Aponte, H. J., & Carlsen, J. C. (2009). An instrument for person-of-the-therapist supervision. *Journal of Marital and Family Therapy, 35*(4), 395–405.

Aponte, H. J., Powell, F. D., Brooks, S., Watson, M. F., Litzke, C., Lawless, J., et al.

(2009). Training the person of the therapist in an academic setting. *Journal of Marital and Family Therapy, 35*(4), 381–394.

Armstrong, T. D., & Crowther, M. R. (2002). Spirituality among older African Americans. *Journal of Adult Development, 9*, 3–12.

Bell-Tolliver, L., Burgess, R., & Brock, L. J. (2009). African American therapists working with African American families: An exploration of the strengths perspective in treatment. *Journal of Marital and Family Therapy, 35*(3), 293–307.

Berrick, J., & Barth, R. P. (Eds.). (1994). Kinship foster care. *Children and Youth Service Review, 16*(1–2), 107

Billingsley, A. (1992). *Climbing Jacob's ladder: The enduring legacy of African-American families.* New York: Simon & Schuster.

Billingsley, A. (Ed.). (1994). The Black church. *National Journal of Sociology, 8*(1–2). (Double issue.)

Bolland, J. M., Liam, B. E., & Formichella, C. M. (2005). The origins of hopelessness among inner-city African-American adolescents. *American Journal of Community Psychology, 36*(3–4), 293–305.

Borjas, G. (2006). Wage trends among disadvantaged minorities. In R. M. Blank, S. H. Danzinger, & R. F. Schoeni (Eds.), *Economic challenges, policy changes, and poverty* (pp. 59–86). New York: Russell Sage Foundation.

Bowen, M. (1976). Theory in the practice of psychotherapy. In P. J. Guerin (Ed.), *Family therapy: Theory and practice* (pp. 42–90). New York: Gardner.

Boyd-Franklin, N. (2003). *Black families in therapy: Understanding the African American experience* (2nd ed.). New York: Guilford Press.

Boyd-Franklin, N. (2010). Incorporating spirituality and religion into the treatment of African American clients. *Counseling Psychologist, 38*(7), 1–25.

Boyd-Franklin, N., & Bry, B. H. (2000). *Reaching out in family therapy: Home-based, school, and community interventions.* New York: Guilford Press.

Boyd-Franklin, N., Franklin, A. J., & Toussaint, P. (2000). *Boys into men: Raising our African American teenage sons.* New York: Plume.

Boyd-Franklin, N., Kelly, S., & Durham, J. (2008). African American couples in therapy. In A. Gurman (Ed.), *The clinical handbook of couples therapy* (pp. 681–697). New York: Guilford Press.

Boyd-Franklin, N., & Lockwood, T. W. (2009). Spirituality and religion: Implications for psychotherapy with African American families. In F. Walsh (Ed.), *Spiritual resources in family therapy* (2nd ed., pp. 141–155). New York: Guilford Press.

Burton, L. M., Bonilla-Silva, E., Ray, V., Buckelew, R., & Freeman, E. H. (2010). Critical race theories, colorism, and the decade's research on families of color. *Journal of Marriage and Family, 72*(3), 440–459.

Carter, R. T. (1995). *The influence of race and racial identity in psychotherapy: Toward a racially inclusive model.* New York: Wiley.

Cose, E. (1993). *The rage of the privileged class.* New York: HarperCollins.

Couch, K. A., & Fairlie, R. (2010). Last hired, first fired?: Black–white unemployment and the business cycle. *Demography, 47*(1), 227–247.

Cruz, M., Pincus, H. A., Harman, J. S., Reynolds, F., & Post, E. P. (2008). Barriers to care-seeking for depressed African Americans. *International Journal of Psychiatry in Medicine, 38*(1), 71–80.

Dass-Brailsford, P. (Ed.). (2010). *Crisis and disaster counseling: Lessons learned from Huricane Katrina and other disasters.* Thousand Oaks, CA: Sage.

Edin, K., & Kefalas, M. (2005). *Promises I can keep: Why poor women put motherhood before marriage.* Berkeley, CA: University of California Press.

Franklin, A. J. (1999). The invisibility syndrome and racial identity development in psychotherapy and counseling of African American men. *Counseling Psychologist, 27*(6), 761–693.

Franklin, A. J. (2004). *From brotherhood to manhood: How black men rescue their relationships and dreams from the invisibility syndrome.* Hoboken, NJ: Wiley.

Franklin, A. J., & Boyd-Franklin, N. (2000). Invisibility syndrome: A clinical model of the effects of racism on African-American males. *American Journal of Orthopsychiatric Association, 70*(1), 33–41.

Franklin, A. J., Boyd-Franklin, N., & Draper, C. (2002). A psychological and educational perspective on Black parenting. In H. McAdoo (Ed.), *Black children: Social, educational and parental environments* (2nd ed., pp. 119–140). Thousand Oaks, CA: Sage.

Franklin, A. J., Boyd-Franklin, N., & Kelly, S. (2006). Racism and invisibility: Race-related stress, emotional abuse and psychological trauma for people of color. *Journal of Emotional Abuse, 6*(2/3), 9–30.

Gavin, L. E., Black, M. M., Minor, S., Abel, Y., Papas, M. A., & Bentley, M. E. (2003). Young, disadvantaged fathers' involvement with their infants: An ecological perspective. *Journal of Adolescent Health, 31,* 266–276.

Grier, W., & Cobbs, P. (1968). *Black rage.* New York: Basic Books.

Hajnal, Z. L. (2007). Black class exceptionalism insights from direct democracy on the race versus class debate. *Public Opinion Quarterly, 71*(4), 560–587.

Hardy, K. V., & Laszloffy, T. A. (1995). Therapy with African Americans and the phenomenon of rage. *In session: Psychotherapy in Practice, 1*(4), 57–70.

Hartman, A., & Laird, J. (1983). *Family-centered social work practice.* New York: Free Press.

Helms, J., & Cook, D. (1999). *Using race and culture in counseling and psychotherapy.* Boston: Allyn & Bacon.

Henggeler, S. W., Schoenwald, S. K., Borduin, C. M., Rowland, M. D., & Cunningham, P. B. (2009). *Multisystemic therapy for antisocial behavior in children and adolescents* (2nd ed.). New York: Guilford Press.

Hill, R. (1999). *The strengths of African American families: Twenty-five years later.* Lanham, MD: University Press of America.

Hill, R. (2003). *The strengths of black families* (2nd ed.). Maryland: University Press of America.

Hines, P. M., & Boyd-Franklin, N. (2005). African American families. In M. McGoldrick, J. Giordano, & N. Garcia-Preto (Eds.), *Ethnicity and family therapy* (3rd ed., pp. 66–84). New York: Guilford Press.

Holden, K. B. (2009). Disadvantages in mental health care among African Americans. *Journal of Health Care for the Poor and Underserved, 20*(2A), 17–23.

Hopps, J. (1982). Oppression based on color [Editorial]. *Social Work, 27*(1), 3–5.

Jenkins, T. S. (2006). Mr. Nigger: Challenges of educating black males. *Journal of Black Studies, 37*(1), 127–155.

Jones, J. M. (1997). *Prejudice and racism* (2nd ed.). New York: McGraw-Hill.

Jones, S. J. (Ed.). (2009). *The state of black America 2009: Message to the President.* New York: National Urban League.

Johnson, K. S., Elbert-Avila, K. I., & Tulsky, J. A. (2005). The influence of spiritual beliefs and practices on the treatment preferences of African Americans: A review of the literature. *Journal of the American Geriatric Society, 53,* 711–719.

Kelly, S. (2003). African American couples: Their importance to the stability of African American families and their mental health issues. In J. S. Mio & G. Y. Iwamasa (Eds.), *Culturally diverse mental health: The challenges of research and resistance* (pp. 141–157). New York: Brunner/Routledge.

Kirshnakumar, A., & Black, M. M. (2003). Family processes within three-generation households and adolescent mothers' satisfaction with father involvement. *Journal of Family Psychology, 17*(4), 488–498.

Kunjufu, J. (1985). *Countering the conspiracy to destroy black boys* (Vol. 1). Chicago: African-American Images.

Lindblad-Goldberg, M., Dukes, J., & Lasley, J. (1988). Stress in black, low-income, single-parent families: Normative and dysfunctional patterns. *American Journal of Orthopsychiatry, 58*(1), 104–120.

Logan, S. L. M. (Ed.). (2001). *The Black family: Strengths, self-help, and positive change* (2nd ed.). Boulder, CO: Westview Press.

Martin, A. C. (2008). Television media as a potential negative factor in the racial identity development of African American youth. *Academic Psychiatry, 32,* 338–342.

Mbiti, J. S. (1990). *African religions and philosophy* (2nd ed.). Portsmouth, NH: Heinemann.

McAdams-Mahmoud, V. (2005). African American Muslim families. In M. McGoldrick, J. Giordano, & N. Garcia-Preto (Eds.), *Ethnicity and family therapy* (3rd ed., pp. 138–150). New York: Guilford Press.

McAdoo, H. (Ed.). (2002). *Black children: Social, educational and parental environments* (2nd ed.). Thousand Oaks, CA: Sage.

Merritt, M. M., Bennett, G. G., Williams, R. B., Edwards, C. L., & Sollers, J. J. (2006). Perceived racism and cardiovascular reactivity and recovery to personally relevant stress. *Health Psychology, 25*(3), 364–369.

Miller, T. W., Nigg, J. T., & Miller, R. L. (2009). Attention deficit hyperactivity disorder in African American children: What can be concluded from the past ten years? *Clinical Psychology Review, 29,* 77–86.

Minuchin, S. (1974). *Families and family therapy.* Cambridge, MA: Harvard University Press.

Moynihan, D. P. (1965). *The Negro family: The case for national action.* Washington, DC: U.S. Department of Labor.

Murray, V. M., & Brody, G. H. (2002). Racial socialization processes in single-mother families: Linking maternal racial identity, parenting, and racial socialization in rural, single-mother families with child self-worth and self-regulation. In H. McAdoo (Ed.), *Black children: Social, educational and parental environments* (2nd ed., pp. 97–118). Thousand Oaks, CA: Sage.

Nichols, M. (2009). *The essentials of family therapy* (4th ed.). Boston: Pearson Education.

Nobles, W. (2004). African philosophy: Foundation of Black psychology. In R. Jones (Ed.), *Black psychology* (4th ed., pp. 57–72). Hampton, VA: Cobb & Henry.

Nye, W. (1993). Amazing grace: Religion and identity among elderly Black individuals. *International Journal of Aging and Human Development, 36,* 103–114.

Pinderhughes, E. (1982). Afro-American families and the victim system. In M.

McGoldrick, J. K. Pearce, & J. Giordano (Eds.), *Ethnicity and family therapy* (pp. 108–122). New York: Guilford Press.

Pinderhughes, E. (1989). *Understanding race, ethnicity and power: The key to efficacy in clinical practice.* New York: Free Press.

Pinderhughes, E. (2002). African American marriage in the 20th century. *Family Process, 41*(2), 269–282.

Pinderhughes, E. (2008). Black genealogy revisited: Restorying an African American family. In M. McGoldrick & K. Hardy (Eds.), *Re-visioning family therapy: Race, culture, and gender in clinical practice* (2nd ed., pp. 114–134). New York: Guilford Press.

Sampson, R. J., & Wilson, W. J. (2005). Race, crime, and justice: A reader. In S. L. Gabbider & H. T. Greene (Eds.), *Toward a theory of race, crime and urban inequality* (pp. 177–191). New York: Routledge.

Samuels, G. M. (2006). Beyond the rainbow: Multi-raciality in the 21st century. In D. Engstrom & L. Piedra (Eds.), *Our diverse society: Race, ethnicity and class-Implications for the 21st century America.* Washington, DC: NASW Press.

Schwartz, A. C., Bradley, R. L., Sexton, M., Sherry, A., & Ressler, K. J. (2005). Post-traumatic stress disorder among African Americans in an inner city mental health clinic. *Psychiatric Services, 56*(2), 212–215.

Stevenson, H. C., & Davis, G. Y. (2004). Racial socialization. In R. Jones (Ed.), *Black psychology* (4th ed., pp. 176–189). Hampton, VA: Cobb & Henry.

Stevenson, H. C., Davis, G., & Abdul-Kabir, S. (2001). *Stickin' to, watchin' over, and gettin' with: An African American parent's guide to discipline.* San Francisco: Jossey-Bass.

Sue, D. W. (2003). *Overcoming our racism: The journey to liberation.* San Francisco: Jossey-Bass.

Sue, D. W. (2010). *Microaggressions in everyday life: Race, gender, and sexual orientation.* New York: Wiley.

Tatum, J., Moseley, S., Boyd-Franklin, N., & Herzog, E. (1995, February–March). A home based family systems approach to the treatment of African American teenage parents and their families. *Zero to Three: Journal of the National Center for Clinical Infant Programs, 15*(4), 18–25.

Taylor, R. J., Chatters, L. M., Bullard, K. M., Wallace, J. M., & Jackson, J. S. (2009). Organizational religious behavior among older African Americans: Findings from the National Survey of American Life. *Research on Aging, 31,* 440–462.

Taylor, R. J., Chatters, L., & Jackson, J. S. (2007). Religious and spiritual involvement among older African Americans, Caribbean Blacks, and Whites: Findings from the National Survey of American Life. *Journals of Gerontology B: Psychological Sciences and Social Sciences, 62,* S238–S250.

Taylor, R. J., Chatters, L. M., & Levin, J. (2004). *Religion in the lives of African Americans: Social, psychological, and health perspectives.* Thousand Oaks, CA: Sage.

Thompson, T., & Massat, C. R. (2005). Experiences of violence, post-traumatic stress, academic achievement and behavior problems of urban African American children. *Child and Adolescent Social Work Journal, 22*(5–6), 367–393.

Tucker, C., & Dixon, A. L. (2009). Low-income African American male youth with ADHD symptoms in the United States: Recommendations for clinical mental health counselors. *Journal of Mental Health Counseling. 31*(4), 309–322.

U.S. Department of Justice. (2008). *FBI hate crime statistics* (Criminal Justice Information Services Division). Retrieved September 20, 2010, from *www.fbi.gov/ucr/ucr.htm*.

Weil, A., & Finegold, K. (Eds.). (2002). *Welfare reform: The next act*. Washington, DC: Urban Institute Press.

White-Johnson, R. L., Ford, K. R., & Sellers, R. M. (2010). Parental racial socialization profiles: Association with demographic factors, racial discrimination, childhood socialization, and racial identity. *Cultural Diversity and Ethnic Minority Psychology, 16*(2), 237–247.

Wilson, D., & Chipungu, S. (Eds.). (1996). Kinship care [Special issue]. *Child Welfare, 75*(5).

Wilson, W. J. (1980). *The declining significance of race* (2nd ed.). Chicago: University of Chicago Press.

Wilson, W. J. (1987). *The truly disadvantaged: The inner city, the underclass and public policy*. Chicago: University of Chicago Press.

Wilson, W. J. (1996). *When work disappears: The world of the new urban poor*. New York: Knopf.

CHAPTER 13

IMMIGRANT FAMILY PROCESSES
A Multidimensional Framework

CELIA JAES FALICOV

The experience of migration is in constant flux. Today's migration contexts differ significantly from those of the past. Moving within a globalized world impacts processes of risk and resilience in families. The changes imposed by migration on family processes deserve our careful study to inform better delivery of social, medical, and educational services attuned to the special needs of immigrants. Concepts from family systems theory and family therapy, supplemented with concepts from studies on migration, can be used to deepen our understanding of the family transformations brought about by migration.

This chapter expands on my earlier writings about the dilemmas of personal, family, and social transformation faced by immigrants and their capacity to find "both/and" solutions rather than forcing "either/or" choices regarding cultural change (Falicov, 1998a, 2002). This position differs from the common deficit-oriented description of immigrants living "*between* two worlds" and not fitting in either one. It is also different from classical acculturation theory, in which the immigrant gradually assimilates to mainstream culture. Rather, many families are able to live "*in* two worlds" by alternating their everyday practices, rituals, and cultural codes depending on the context in which they find themselves, or by finding new hybrid cultural mixes.

A most dramatic contemporary example of this dual vision is the lived experience of many of today's immigrants. In a global world, the nature of migration has changed from abrupt or gradual disengagement from family and culture to the possibility of maintaining intense family connections at long distance through the use of modern communication technologies. Many contemporary immigrants and their children could be described as transnationals who live with "two hearts" as opposed to a "broken heart," as it was said about the immigrants that arrived in the past (Falicov, 2005, 2007, 2008).

I also discuss in this chapter the emergence of immigrant resilient practices that I label as *spontaneous rituals*, because they encapsulate in ritualized ways various family, social, and cultural restitutive attempts following migration. In addition, I address situations in which migration risks test families' capacity for blending continuity and change, and may result in clinical symptoms.

A MULTIDIMENSIONAL MODEL OF MIGRATION AND ACCULTURATION PROCESSES

The MECA model (multidimensional, ecosystemic, comparative approach; Falicov, 1995, 1998, 2003) provides a framework for understanding the experiences of migration and acculturation, the changed ecological context, and issues related to the family life cycle and family organization. Each immigrant family participates in multiple contexts of insertion and exclusion, and acquires shared meanings and partial perspectives imparted by dimensions of similarity and difference within its own group and within the host culture, such as ethnicity, race, language, social class, education, geography, climate, religion, nationality, occupation and political ideology. The combination of these variables comprises each individual family's own *ecological niche* (Falicov, 1998b, 2003, in press). Families and individuals derive their meanings from their particular ecological niches and unique personal histories. The process of adaptation and acculturation is also intricately tied to each immigrant's ecological niche. A newly arrived immigrant who fits well with the dominant aspects of the adoptive culture in terms of language, religion, education, or race is more likely to assimilate, integrate, or develop biculturality than a new immigrant whose characteristics vary from those of the dominant culture and class. Where the family arrives and locates itself, and what the family members bring with them, such as their life cycle views and timings, as well as how the family is organized, will have implications for how immigrant family processes unfold.

The dimensions encompassed by MECA, summarized in Figure 13.1, provide a framework to conceptualize the processes immigrant families undergo and, at the level of clinical practice it, articulate assessments and interventions related to social justice and cultural diversity.

VARIATIONS IN THE EXPERIENCE OF MIGRATION AND ACCULTURATION

Many aspects of migration are contingent on a number of premigration experiences, such as the type of migration, or the gender or age of the immigrant, that shape, constrain, and have long-lasting influences on how postmigration adaptations unfold.

Transformations: Continuity and Change	**Migration and Acculturation**	• Type of migration (e.g., undocumented) • Composition of separations (e.g., father alone) • Trauma pre-, during, postmigration • Losses and gains • Uprooting of Meanings • Transnationalism • Psychological or virtual family • Complex acculturation (e.g., alternation) • Spontaneous rituals • Second-generation transnational exposure • Adolescent–parent biculturalism
	Ecological Context	• Poverty • Work/school • Neighborhood • Isolation • Ethnic community • Virtual community • Church and religion • Racism/anti-immigrant reception • Contextual dangers (drugs, violence, gangs) • Contextual protections (language, social network)
	Family Life Cycle	• Cultural ideals • Meanings • Timings • Transitions • Rituals • Sociocentric childrearing practices • Developmental dilemmas (autonomy/family loyalty) • Suicide attempts and parent–adolescent conflicts • Pile-up of transitions • Absences at crucial life-cycle markers

	Family Organization	• Separations and reunifications
		• Long-distance connections
		• Kin care: transnational triangles
		• Remittances
		• Relational stresses
		   o Gender evolutions
		   o Polarizations about migration
		   o Boundary ambiguity

*(Right column spanning: **Social Justice** aligns with Migration and Acculturation and Ecological Context; **Cultural Diversity** aligns with Family Life Cycle and Family Organization.)*

FIGURE 13.1. Multidimensional, ecological, comparative framework: Continuities and changes in immigrant family processes.

- *Voluntary and involuntary types of migrations.* Voluntary and involuntary migrations differ significantly. Refugees forced to leave beloved homelands for religious, political, or war-related reasons often have experienced trauma and feel intensely ambivalent about their longing to return and the necessity of departure. Such anguish may be ameliorated in those who left willingly in search of a more prosperous life. Asylum seekers live with the painful ambiguity of having escaped a terrible situation but having no assurance of a safe future. Their fate is uncertain, and they always await a decision as to whether they will be granted legal status to stay or be sent back to their old country, where their lives will be at risk or their freedom curtailed.

- *Documented or undocumented status.* Immigration status creates vastly different physical, social, emotional, and cultural contexts for immigrants. Unlike the fairly predictable, albeit lengthy, situation that accrues for the immigrant who can arrive in the United States and obtain a legal visa, a green card, or a work permit and trust the process of becoming a permanent resident or U.S. citizen, the undocumented immigrant often risks many potential harms. These dangers range from a perilous border passage that can result in death by dehydration, robbery, or rape by the smuggler, to slavery or prostitution inflicted by an employer after entering the United States. Many psychological stresses also result from living "in the dark" because of fear of detention accompanied by brutality, only to culminate in deportation. Families are often split up when an undocumented parent is deported, even after many years in the United States, forced apart from a grieving spouse and children.

- *Proximity between homeland and new land.* Proximity between homeland and new land also mediates the intensity of the loss and the possibility of a gain. The ability to make frequent visits or even reside in both countries is dubbed a "two-home," transnational lifestyle. This binational arrangement alleviates immigrants' pain by maintaining their sense of belonging and participation, a much less feasible option for those whose homelands are far away and unreachable for political or economic reasons.

- *Gender and generation.* Migration is vastly different for women and men; infants, children, or adolescents; and young adults or older adults. Developmental issues such as language acquisition, socialization, internalization of cultural codes, and a formed or unformed sense of national identity, figure into the ease or difficulty of adaptation.

- *Family composition at migration.* Whether members of the family unit migrate together as a couple, family, or extended group, or in sequential stages, the family composition before and after migration (from extended three- and four-generation families to two-generation nuclear arrangements, single-parent or individual alone) has important implications for family connections and disconnections that affect outcomes and coping with the stresses of separation, reunification, or adaptation to the host culture.

• *Host country receptions and community insertions.* Negative or ambivalent receptions and shortage of adequate economic and social opportunities because of race and/or class discrimination alter radically the ability to absorb the losses involved in migration. Community social supports also vary widely depending on the opportunities for reconstructing ruptured social networks and re-creating cultural spaces in ethnic neighborhoods or in work settings. Without such connections, isolation may contribute to a host of biopsychosocial consequences.

All of these factors make up specific configurations for each family's resources and constraints, as well as the meaning of the migration experience. The local knowledge and experiences described by each immigrant are always infinitely more complex, complete, and nuanced than any attempts at generalization. Nevertheless, some generalizations are important insofar as these allow clinicians and researchers to address common issues and challenges.

THE EXPERIENCE OF MIGRATION LOSS AND GAIN

Despite their myriad differences, immigrants in the United States encounter to one degree or another the loss, grief, and mourning that are characteristic of the migration experience (Falicov, 1998a, in press; Potocky-Tripodi, 2000). These losses have been compared with the processes of grief and mourning precipitated by the death of loved ones. Yet migration loss has special characteristics that distinguish it from other kinds of loss (Falicov, 2002). Compared with death, for example, migration is both larger and more complex. It is larger because migration brings with it losses of all kinds. For the immigrants, gone are the family members and friends who stayed behind; gone is the community, the familiar language, the customs and rituals, the food and music, and the comforting identification with the land itself. The losses of migration also touch the family back home and reach forward to shape future generations born in the new land.

Migration loss also is more complicated than death, because despite the grief and mourning occasioned by physical, social, and cultural uprooting, the losses are not absolutely clear, complete, and irretrievable. An exception is the case of refugees and asylum seekers who have had loved ones tortured, sexually assaulted, killed, or disappeared, or when whole communities have been destroyed; some have been the victims of ethnic cleansing/genocide. They may not ever be able to return without endangering their lives, and they may not find a large supportive community of ethnic compatriots that resembles the original cultures. For refugees and asylum seekers the losses may be more total and less ambiguous than for economic immigrants. In most cases, loved ones are still alive but just not immediately reachable or present. Unlike coping with the finality of death, after migration, it is always possible to fantasize an eventual return or forthcoming reunion. Like Janus, one face is turned to the new shore, the other toward the familiar harbor. Furthermore, immigrants seldom migrate toward a social vacuum. A relative, friend, or acquaintance usually waits on the other side to help with work, housing, and guidelines for life in the new country. A social community and ethnic neighborhood reproduces in pockets of remembrance the sights, sounds, smells, and tastes of one's village or country (Falicov, 1998a). For most immigrants, all of these elements create a remarkable mix of emotions—sadness and elation, loss and restitution, and absence and presence—that make grieving incomplete, postponed, ambiguous.

The Ambiguity of Losses and Gains

The concept of ambiguous loss proposed by Pauline Boss (1999, 2006; Falicov, 2002) describes situations in which loss is unclear, incomplete, or partial. Basing her thesis on stress theory, Boss describes two types of ambiguous loss. In one type, family members are physically absent but psychologically present such as a soldier missing in action, a disappeared relative (as in Kosovo or Argentina), a nonresidential parent in divorce, or a migrating relative seeking a better future. In the second type, family members are physically present, but psychologically absent (as with the deterioration of Alzheimer's disease or the parent who is emotionally unavailable due to stress or depression).

Migration represents what Boss (1999) calls a "crossover," in that it has elements of both types of ambiguous loss. Although beloved people and places are left behind, they remain keenly present in the psyche of the immigrant; at the same time, homesickness and the multiple stresses of adaptation may leave some family members emotionally unavailable to support and encourage others. The very decision to migrate has at its core two ambivalent poles. For many immigrants, frustrations with dire economic or political conditions compel the move and result in new opportunities and gains, but love of family and surroundings pull in another direction.

Not all aspects of migration challenges are sad and bleak, as there are gains to be enjoyed. The experience can bring a sense of adventure and excitement, of hope and new dreams, possibly greater economic stability and prosperity over time, better education, and in some cases, increased human and civil rights. Over time there is higher parental involvement (Martinez, DeGarmo, & Eddy, 2004), better academic achievement (Kao & Tienda, 1995), and, for some ethnic groups, less tolerance for domestic violence (Harris, Firestone, & Vega, 2005) and greater safety precautions, such as wearing safety belts and helmets (Romano, Tippetts, Blackman, & Voas, 2005). Immigrant families also demonstrate increased openness to seek professional counseling (Harris et al., 2005; Miville & Constantine, 2006). Labor opportunities for women immigrants increase their wish to settle in the United States, and they appear to adjust faster than men, citing not only economic gains but also more personal and relational freedoms than in their countries (González-López, 2005; Hirsch, 2003).

Lack of Transitional Rituals

It is perhaps because of its ambiguous, inconclusive, impermanent quality that migration as a life transition is devoid of clear rituals or rites of passage. The preparations that precede the actual departure may bear some similarities to rituals, but practices such as packing symbolic, meaningful objects (e.g., photographs or other mementos, including a small cache of native soil) are random and idiosyncratic, and do not involve family members or friends. There is no formal structure, no designated place or time, no cultural collective celebration that allows people to come together to mark the transition, try to transcend it, and provide a container for the strong emotions everybody is feeling. Thus, migration is similar to other transitions that lack cultural rituals: A miscarriage or perinatal loss represents a future life that was cut off; a divorce leaves partners feeling that what could have been is no longer possible. Even the term "adopted country," like an adopted child not raised by its biological parents, suggests that there was a "homeland," a map of a possible territory that could have been inhabited but is not now accessible.

Uprooting of Meanings

In comparison with other ambiguous losses, what is distinctive and most dramatic about migration is the uprooting of entire systems of meanings: physical, social, and cultural. Urban ecologist Peter Marris (1980) suggests that the closest human counterpart to the root structure that nourishes a plant is the systems of meaning that provide familiarity with a physical, social, and cultural reality. If we take the uprooting metaphor further, we can see that when a plant is plucked from the earth, some residue of soil always remains attached to the roots. Good gardeners know that when replanting in the new soil, they must not wash away this little bit of residue of the old soil, in order to minimize shock and ensure the success of the transplantation.

Although immigrants no longer have the depth and expanse of the native soil to nourish their roots, the little bit of original native soil they bring with them is represented in the type of households they recreate, the traditions they pass on to their children, the language they speak, the foods they cook, the friendships they form, the connections they keep with their country of origin, and the family and social rituals that evolve over time. Therefore, it seems plausible that as in the case of plants, migrant families that hold onto and recreate parts of the old context, while adapting to new ecologies, are able to develop firmer family and cultural foundations in the new context. This may contribute to the healthy growth of future generations.

THE IMPACT OF RACISM
AND ANTI-IMMIGRANT RECEPTION

The adaptation to a life of uncertainty and ambivalent feelings depends to a large extent on the number and type of contextual stresses families face in the new country. Striving for economic stability and psychological equilibrium in the new land is riddled with pressure to assimilate the dominant culture's negative judgment of dark-skinned, poor immigrants and to cope with oppressive institutional treatment and derogatory stereotypes.

Racial, ethnic, and economic discrimination shape the individual stories of most immigrants, particularly those from disadvantaged classes and poor countries, who are almost always perceived as the "other," not as us. The concept of "double consciousness," which Du Bois (1903) first used to describe the social situations of African Americans, is useful to understand the situation of many immigrants, because it encompasses a perception of who one really is as a person within one's own group, as contrasted with the attributions of the larger society's story regarding that group.

When immigrant children from various ethnic groups (Chinese, Haitian, Central American, Dominican, and Mexican) were asked what was most difficult about immigration, discrimination and racism were recurrent themes in the research data. Researchers Suárez-Orozco and Suárez-Orozco (2000), observed that immigrant children develop a keen eye for their reception and incorporate these socially negative reflections in the image of themselves and their ethnic identity, a phenomenon these authors call "social mirroring." Parents' positive mirroring often cannot compensate for the distorted reflections children encounter in daily life, but hope is essential for positive outcomes. In fact, hope and confidence that social marginalization is a temporary rather than permanent price to pay, and a belief that the family will triumph over the odds, are elements that keep alive immigrants' dreams of a better life for themselves and their children.

DUAL VISIONS: CONTINUITY AND CHANGE

Migration disrupts family stability and poses struggles to regain continuity in the midst of new challenges and opportunities. From a family systems viewpoint, for a family to be both flexible and stable during crucial family transitions the tendencies toward both change and continuity need to occur simultaneously. To cope with life challenges these two processes must be integrated, so that a sense of continuity, identity, and stability can be maintained while new patterns of behavior, interactions, or beliefs evolve.

Today the notion of continuity is not circumscribed to ritual re-creation of the old culture in the midst of cultural change experienced within the new culture. Rather, original cultures and relationships can be both maintained and transformed through a form of mutual "co-presence" of people and places

(Baldassar, 2008). The flow of people and information between cultures, and the increasing globalization of the world allow immigrant families to find connectedness through new technologies of communication that help continuity and allow for change and renewal within their culture of origin and with family members left behind (Abrego, 2009; Falicov, 2007; Levitt & Waters, 2002; Vertovec, 2004; Wilding, 2006).

Rethinking Linear Acculturation Models

Undoubtedly, migration experiences require a complex blend of cultural continuity and cultural change. For the past two decades, new acculturation theories have questioned the simplistic cultural assimilation theory that postulated a gradual, steady shedding of the original language and culture in favor of the adoptive language and culture. New concepts reflect a much more complex and dynamic balance of continuity and change. Terms such as "binationalism," "bilingualism," "biculturalism," and "cultural bifocality" describe dual visions, ways of continuing familiar cultural practices while acquiring new behaviors to fit the new physical and social contexts. Unlike linear models of assimilation, new constructs of alternation, hybridization, segmented or selective acculturation, or syncretism provide frameworks for describing continuous family, community, and cultural connections in this country and also the country of origin, along with discontinuous changes or adaptations to the new cultural settings.

Among these newer acculturation frameworks, alternation theory proposes that individuals can alternate or switch language and cultural codes according to the social context at hand. Those social contexts, so variable in our multicultural society, comprise "cultural borderlands" in which people move and live, and where behavior is flexibly alternated according to the need at hand. The result is a sense of fit or partial belonging in more than one cultural and linguistic context.

Multidimensional models of acculturation (Schwartz, Unger, Zamboanga, & Szapocznik, 2010) and integrative models that include multiple influences, opportunities, and constraints for immigrant families (Glick, 2010; Piedra & Engstrom, 2009; Portes & Rumbaut, 2001) bear similarities to MECA and to the idea of *ecological niche*. These new models consider specific dimensions of immigrants' ethnic, socioeconomic, and cultural backgrounds, such as language or country of origin, that result in various degrees of similarity and difference, and complex acculturation processes between the culture of origin and the adoptive culture.

Sense of Coherence and Family Resilience

The theme of ambiguous loss, gain, and integration is not limited to the first stages of migration. Choices about affirming cultural meaning systems or adapting to change are made throughout a family's initial transplantation and for other generations to come. There are compelling psychological reasons for retention of cultural and family identities, among them the family's attempt at preserving a *sense of family coherence.*

A family's sense of coherence refers to the perceived coherence of family life in coping with specific crises. The concept addresses meaning and purpose in life, and a larger and deeper existential confidence than is implied in concepts such as *mastery* or *locus of control,* which focus more narrowly on self-reliance and specific coping strategies. According to Walsh (2003, 2006), this sense of coherence and hope are key ingredients in *family or relational resilience,* those processes by which families surmount persistent stress.

In the next section, I describe a number of practices that appear with regularity in the lives of immigrants, reflecting not only a spirit of pride and respect for continuity of their language and cultural background but also demonstrating that awareness of social location and flexibility to transform family life to the present requirements can facilitate success and adaptation.

THE EMERGENCE OF SPONTANEOUS RITUALS

Immigrants deal with the massive uprooting of meanings and migration loss, with attempts at physical, social, and cultural restitution through a number of practices that create makeshift physical, social, and cultural bridges across the absences. These actions have a number of characteristics that bear many similarities with *rituals:* They are catalysts for feeling, thinking, and action; they validate ties between past, present, and future; and they contain both sides of the ambiguity—presence and absence, connection and disconnection, gain and loss, ideal and real. Such actions tend to be repetitive and incorporate continuity in the midst of change and familiarity in the midst of strangeness. In fact, immigrants find themselves almost magnetically drawn to the following situations, when nobody really instructs them to do so. It may be tempting to speculate that these rituals have psychological and social "functions." However, it seems preferable simply to assume that these activities have psychological, cognitive, and emotional *effects* in the way all rituals do.

Visits Home, Communications, and Money Remittances: Rituals of Connection

Longing for one's country makes visits home a priority. Visits close the gap between that which is psychologically present and physically absent. When economically possible, trips to the country of origin serve to revive, renew, and reinforce personal and cultural connections, and not allow such connections to stagnate or wither away. Some immigrants make it a ritual to go home for special holidays or family reunions. The actual experience is rife with paradoxes, sweet interpersonal nourishment, and bitterness at what has changed or is no longer accessible. The return to the country of adoption may be full of not only regret but also relief at the newfound freedom or opportunity.

Historically, most voluntary immigrants, and even refugees, often have managed to maintain connections through letters, messages, and packages. Ease of transportation and global telecommunications have increased the possibilities of staying in contact and have made modern-day migrations a transnational experience. Today, many immigrants from poor countries worldwide send money home as soon as they are able. These remittances contribute significantly to the economic sustenance of their families and even their countries, maintaining both their social continuity and long-distance presence.

The actions of visiting, communicating, and sending money home are filled with planning and caring. These may amount to carrying out *rituals of connection* involving ritualized practices, such as contacting intermediaries at a specific time of the month, purchasing money orders, going to the post office, setting up joint transnational bank accounts, and getting an acknowledgment from the people receiving the remittance.

Re-Creating Ethnic and Social Spaces: Re-Creation Rituals

In most cities where immigrants live, one can find distinct ethnic neighborhoods. These urban landscapes reproduce in public environments the sights, smells, sounds, flavors, and tastes of the native country. Open markets and Sunday flea markets reproduce with uncanny fidelity the meeting places of the past, such as grocery stores, restaurants, the church, all using the original language. This collective cultural revival meeting may be thought as a psychological return, in a cultural representational form (Ainslie, 1998). These makeshift, "as if " environments, where cultural memories remain alive, become *rituals of re-creation* that allow for routines in which people feel at home in a foreign land, which is clearly much better than not being home at all. These powerful actions help not only to reestablish links with the lost land but also to transform the receiving cultures into more familiar places. No doubt, they reflect continuity. Yet the ethnic and social spaces have elements of difference, the dominant culture being ever-present through the money, the products, the mix of languages.

The vicissitudes of the disruption of lifelong networks, and the attempts at reconstructing them, attest to immigrants' constructive attempts to make present the absent—ways of saying "hello again" in the midst of the many good-byes. Most immigrants seem to be able to reconstruct networks of co-nationals in the urban environments toward which they gravitate. Again, we can observe that these transformational phenomena synthesize both/and solutions, the old and the new.

Reminiscing about the Past: Memory Rituals

In popular media depictions, immigrants are portrayed as telling stories about their countries, recounting the details of their migration saga, repeating old proverbs, and pining away for the special foods or customs of their country. They are also known to make either idealized or denigrating judgments about the differences between their country of origin and the country of adoption. These practices have the effect of promoting personal and cultural continuity by building connections with those in the new land, mostly the immigrant's own children (Falicov, 2005; Levitt & Waters, 2002; Stone, Gomez, Hotzoglu, & Lipnitsky, 2005). It is a mistake to think of this storytelling as merely a quaintly nostalgic or sentimental self-indulgence. Much of it serves to create a coherent narrative past and to make meaning out of inevitable transition into the present circumstances, as well as hopes for the future. Rather than feeling bored or tired about the parents' reminiscing, a good number of young people become attached to their parents' land (Levitt & Waters, 2002; Stone et al., 2005).

The perpetual ambiguities of the migration story may create a powerful cognitive and emotional magnet within a family system (Troya & Rosenberg, 1999). The migration story may become the family's dominant story—the way it makes sense of all other aspects of life, the magnet that provides meaning and *narrative coherence*. Experiences of failure, success, sadness, resignation, heroism, marital conflict, the wife's newfound assertiveness, the ungrateful adult children, and the nascent freedom to be oneself all can be contained within an explanation: "This is happening to us because we came here."

The gap between physical absence and psychological presence may be particularly intense for immigrants and refugees who maintain the dream of permanent return. For them, ambiguous loss may translate into a frozen grief, as is often the case for refugees who cannot return home and for whom; unrealistic reunion fantasies block the development of new attachments and commitments. A family may remain unable to mobilize its resources, make settlement decisions, or take full advantage of existing opportunities.

Preserving Culturally Patterned Rituals

Processes of continuity and change in an immigrant family over the generations can be studied through the transmission of family and cultural rituals. Family systems theorists and practitioners have long known about the power of rituals (Imber-Black, Roberts, & Whiting, 2003; see Imber-Black, Chapter 20, this volume) to restore continuities with a family's heritage and reaffirm a sense of cultural identity.

The preservation of traditional life-cycle rituals and celebrations (weddings, baptisms, funerals, etc.) may represent an immigrant family's balance between continuity and change. Even when original cultural contents have shifted or faded, rituals continue to have the inherent power to strengthen families by reinforcing old bonds and reaffirming blended social identities. Interviews of immigrant families and therapist's evaluations should include a close look at both persistent and newly evolving cultural family rituals, from routine family interactions (dinners or prayers) to celebrations of birthdays, holidays, and rites of passage, as well as the old and new meanings family members associate with them.

An immigrant's *daily family rituals*, such as meal preparation, home decoration, forms of daily greeting, and dress, may not only mimic the local customs of the original culture but also mix in the new elements of language and customs of the adoptive culture.

Even when immigrants cannot transport the physical and social land-scapes, belief systems reflected in *religious* and *traditional medicine rituals* have transportability. Perhaps the most transportable ritual is the practice of prayer or meditation. Indigenous beliefs and rituals about health, illness, and cures also persist, along with the growing acceptance of current medical practices; for example, a family may consult an indigenous healer for a case of "fright," while also turning to a mainstream physician to deal with the same symptoms of nervousness (Falicov, 2009). It is important for therapists to learn to work collaboratively with practitioners of other systems of healing, such as religion and traditional medicine.

The emergence of spontaneous rituals of connection, re-creation of social and ethnic spaces, memory rituals, and the preservation of cultural rituals illustrate the immigrants' attachments and losses. Embedded in these spontaneous rituals are healthy "both/and" responses or "solutions," which demonstrate that people learn to live with the ambiguity of never achieving final closure of the migration experience. Therapists' work with immigrant families could greatly profit from an exploration of the place of rituals in their lives. It is possible that the abandonment of meaningful rituals or, alternatively, excessive reliance on the performance of these cultural and religious rituals at the expense of adaptations to the new culture, could contribute to problematic adaptations.

FAMILY TRANSFORMATIONS

Extended Families

In spite of national and class variations, many immigrants come from countries that favor collectivistic narratives stemming from three-generational and extended family lifestyles (Falicov, 1998a; Triandis, 1995). A primary component of the collectivistic narrative is an internalized obligation to help extended family members throughout life, regardless of how good, or not so good, those relationships might be (Falicov, 2001; Organista, 2007; Santiago-Rivera, Arredondo, & Gallardo-Cooper, 2002). At least in some large populations of immigrants, family obligations and supports seem to withstand migration and persist in some form for one, two, or more generations. New technologies of communication aid in the persistence of these relationships at long distance (Baldassar, 2008; Falicov, 2007, 2008; Wilding, 2006). Furthermore, the emphasis on family relationships appears to be an enduring psychosocial feature of family life and not just a marshaling of family forces in reaction to migration (Suárez Orozco & Suárez Orozco, 1995). Nevertheless, the realities of migration frequently involve temporary or permanent separation or disconnection between the nuclear and the extended family. Transnational lives involving nuclear family members' separations, such as those between couples and their children, or mothers and children, are possible only because of the kinship care provided by extended family members. The care is reciprocal because the immigrant supports the economic survival of many family members at long distance via remittances (Abrego, 2009; Schmalzbauer, 2005).

The Psychological Presence of Extended Family

Today's immigrants often construct a psychologically present family of origin and, to some extent, a "virtual" family by continuing to express family connectedness through long-distance phone calls, remittances, concerns and preoccupations, and occasional visits. It is possible to speak of a psychological family or a virtual family in a global world (Falicov, 2007).

Studies show that as families of Mexican descent acculturate, they become increasingly involved and competent in dealing with the norms of outside social systems, but their basic internal family system allegiances remain unchanged (Rueschenberg & Buriel, 1989). Acculturated Latinos often live in small nuclear family households and learn how to behave in a dominant individualistic culture that values assertiveness, independence, and achievement. But they do not tend to acquire mainstream internal patterns of family interaction, keeping instead the values and meanings of collectivistic families in terms of their cohesion, visiting patterns, interdependence or interpersonal reliance, and controls. They live dual lives, functioning as mainstream Americans in the affairs of the community at large but continuing their ethnically patterned lives within their own closed circle.

The Physical Presence of Extended Family

From a family systems viewpoint, the presence of a collectivistic group generates complexity, affectional attachments, options for fulfilling instrumental or expressive functions, and alternatives for resolving problems and modeling behaviors. Because models of family life have been based predominately on the prevailing cultural form in the United States, the small nuclear family, as we attempt to understand the role of extended family members in immigrant families, we have few guidelines about the complexities of these family arrangements before and after migration.

Extended family members who are physically present play a significant role in shoring up the family as it struggles for continuity and copes with change. Their collectivistic sense drives a concern for one another's lives, a pulling together to weather crises, and sociocentric values that teach children to care about others (Harwood, Miller, & Irizarry, 1995). These patterns yield support among adult siblings through pooling of money and resources, or closeness between adult children and their parents (Falicov, 2001). Family members who are able to access public resources or programs become important resources for those in their extended families who do not have access (Gilbertson, 2009).

The presence of extended family members does not, however, guarantee that all is well for the immigrant family. The depiction of family closeness is sometimes taken to such extremes that images of picturesque family life dominate, while tensions and disconnections among extended family members simmer below, discounted or ignored. Migration may exacerbate preexisting family problems. Large families generate different problems than small families. For examples, triangles involving husband, wife, and mother-in-law, or coalitions involving mother, grandmother, and child, may be more common in three-generational households. Thus, closely tied, richly joined networks may generate their own problematic triangular patterns that need to be looked at both culturally and contextually (Falicov, 1998b). Transnational triangles reflecting tensions between the mother who migrated alone, the child who was left behind, and the caretaker to whom she entrusted the child are common and often reveal themselves in full force at the time of reunification (Falicov, 2007).

Gender and Generational Conflict: Impact on the Second Generation

Children of immigrants do not experience migration loss with the same poignancy as their parents, but they are often exposed to their parents' emotions about their ambiguous losses, gains, risks, and hardships. Thus, children and adolescents are central participants in the family's evolving cultural narratives and the homegrown cultural spaces that re-create a subjective, altered past in the present. Children help mix continuity with change in their language, values, and identities. Thus, they co-construct with the parents and with society the family's transformations.

Immigrant parents, as they re-create familiar patterns and perpetuate customs, may help instill a sense of cohesion and connectedness that binds together even distant generations and may promote attachment with the parents' countries of origin, a form of emotional transnationalism (Falicov, 2005; Levitt & Waters, 2002; Stone et al., 2005). When immigrant parents ensure the psychological presence (e.g., through photos, stories, or e-mail) of absent relatives, they may expand for their children the meaning of family to broader ethnic and national identifications with their country of origin (Troya & Rosenberg, 1999).

Generational Tensions:
Continuity and Change

Traditional depictions of immigrant parents' relationships with their preadolescent, adolescent, or adult children almost invariably include eruptions of conflict. This conflict is said to be based primarily on the fact that children, who learn to speak English and understand American ways much faster than their parents, become translators of the culture and the language. They often act as helpers to their parents, and the hierarchical reversal that ensues strips authority from the parent. This pattern has been observed many times, yet new studies reveal a much greater variety of outcomes (Morales & Hanson, 2005; Orellana, Dorner, & Pulido, 2003).

Suárez Orozco and Suárez Orozco (1995) found much less parent–child conflict in the stories told by Mexican and Mexican American adolescents than in those of white American adolescents. These authors tie their findings to the familistic tendencies of Mexicans, whose sense of self is deeply embedded in social others rather than being defined "against" others, as is more typical of individualistic cultures. Their recent research findings (Suárez-Orozco & Suárez-Orozco, 2008) also point to the strong positive role that family connectedness and ethnic affiliation play in the motivation for school achievement in children and adolescents of various cultures, who identify with their immigrant parents' dreams and sacrifices.

These observations coincide with recent findings (Santisteban & Mena, 2009) that acculturation per se does not create conflict and loss of parental authority so long as a strong cultural family orientation is maintained in the home. Only when parents and children do not share languages at all does the acculturation gap become so large that the family may not have the resources to resolve cultural conflicts (Choi, He, & Harachi, 2008; Portes & Rumbaut, 2001).

Importance of Reciprocal Parent–Child Biculturalism
for Adolescents

Although studies have shown that Latino youth face numerous risk factors when integrating into U.S. culture, from increased alcohol and substance abuse to higher suicide and school dropout rates, a recent longitudinal study (Smokowski, David-Ferdon, & Stroupe, 2009) indicates that adolescents who actively embrace their parents' native culture—and whose parents, in turn, become more involved in U.S. culture—stand a greater chance of avoiding those risks and developing healthy behaviors overall. The study showed that parents who construct a strong bicultural perspective have teen children who are less likely to feel anxiety, and who face fewer social problems. It appears that parents who were more involved in U.S. culture were in a better position proactively to help their adolescents with peer relations, forming friendships and staying engaged in school.

Similarly, Portes and Rumbaut's (2001) research with several Asian and Latino groups demonstrated important variations in generational conflict between situations of "dissonant acculturation," which separate children and parents along language and cultural lines, and "selective acculturation," in which both parents and children are able to retain language and culture to some extent and in some areas of life. The latter is more common when a community of the same ethnicity, sufficient size, and institutional diversity surrounds the family and helps to buffer the cultural shift. This *selective style* preserves parental authority and provides a strong bulwark against the deleterious effects of racial and ethnic discrimination. A third type of acculturation found in Portes and Rumbaut's study is "consonant acculturation," whereby both parents and children abandon language and culture at about the same pace, a situation most often found when parents are educated professionals, who are quickly incorporated in mainstream institutional settings.

It seems possible that unacculturated parents, isolated and fearful of the mainstream world, exert an authoritarian style of control as opposed to a nurturant and authoritative style, and thus unwittingly alienate or antagonize their adolescent children. The developmental process of striving toward greater personal autonomy and testing parental limits can be difficult in the face of multiple contextual stressors and high-risk conditions brought about by migration, poverty, and neighborhood dangers such as drugs, sex and crime. Many immigrant parents exert their authority to protect their children from these contextual dangers. The cultural demand that parental hierarchies be respected may be at play, but the very real dangers for adolescents exacerbate the need for controls and authoritarian intervention.

Cultural Assimilation and Violence in Adolescence

The perils of rapid assimilation and rejection of parents' cultures are demonstrated in recent studies. In a review, Gonzales, Knight, Morgan-López, Sáenz, and Sirolli (2002) found that higher adolescent U.S. cultural involvement or "assimilation" by youth in immigrant families was associated with increased delinquency and strong relationships with antisocial peers. More recently, Smokowski, David-Ferdon, et al. (2009) reported that in 9 out of 13 empirical investigations, higher adolescent cultural assimilation to U.S. culture and relationships was associated with increased youth violence.

Conversely, researchers have consistently found a positive relationship between culture-of-origin involvement, in the form of ethnic identity, and self-esteem for Latinos (Santisteban & Mena, 2009; Schwartz, Zamboanga, & Jarvis, 2007). In fact, Gonzales et al. (2002) found culture-of-origin involvement to have a moderately strong, positive relationship with self-esteem across ethnicities, genders, and age groups.

The implications of these findings need to be taken into account by therapists through bolstering of families' own inclinations toward selective acculturation and biculturalism.

Gender-Based Conflicts: New Perspectives

Gender also enters into the equation of migration in complex ways. In search of a better economic or political future, historically, men took the lead on the migration journey. They left wife and children behind, sent remittances, and reunited with the family later, typically in the United States. Sometimes, men acquired a second wife and children, thus having one family in each country. In the 21st century, increasingly, women from many developing countries take up the journey by themselves and leave their children with family caretakers; they send remittances and work to be reunited later. Sometimes many years pass before reunification, and much family reorganization may take place, such as having more children in the country of adoption.

Both men and women experience emotional difficulties following individual or solo migration. They use a variety of coping mechanisms that appears to follow their gender socialization, such as women seeking help for depression or psychosomatic problems, and men becoming alcohol dependent or exhibiting violent behaviors. Gender ideologies regarding performance in parental roles continue to be highly durable in transnational contexts. Fathers who succeed as economic providers can maintain stable relationships with their children. Mothers' relationships with their children depend on their ability to demonstrate emotional intimacy from a distance (Abrego, 2009; Artico, 2003; Dreby, 2006).

Over time, the presence of community networks helps to ameliorate the symptoms of isolation and disenfranchisement, especially in women (González-López, 2005). When men and women migrate together, particularly when both leave the children behind, sometimes polarizations take place that reflect the ambiguities about leaving and staying, with one supporting the decisions to return, while the other opposes it. When the nuclear family is together, other polarizations focus on one parent supporting language and cultural continuity in the home, while the other sponsors language and cultural change (Falicov, 1998a, 2010).

The positions that men and women assume in these polarizations seem to depend at least in part on the historical moment and the encounter of cultures and social contexts that may create different ambiguities, gains, or losses for the two genders in the country of adoption compared to the country of origin. Immigrant men from traditional patriarchal cultures and ecological niches may feel threatened and disempowered by the more Western, egalitarian values influencing their wives and children in American mainstream culture. Nevertheless, it is also important for therapists to raise critical issues relative to *machismo* stereotypes, as men from patriarchal cultures present a variety of conceptions and manifestations of masculinity, and respond to cultural change in their countries and in the country of adoption (Falicov, 2010).

These changes are likely to be tied to the increased participation of women in the workforce. Thus, many immigrant women feel torn by the dual vision and double shift of maintaining ethnic traditional lifestyles within the home, while becoming modernized in their outside work settings (Gil & Vazquez, 1996). Some women manage to integrate the old and new roles by articulating their wish for greater equality in decisions about sex, intimacy, and fertility, through invoking benefits to children and family, since framing the requests in this fashion is more culturally acceptable to their men (Hirsch, 2003).

Gender and Adolescence in Immigrant Families

Gender also interacts with migration processes in adolescents. Gender rules differ significantly for boys and girls within the same immigrant family. Parents have biological rationales that designate girls as the "weaker sex" that need protection from street dangers, such as getting pregnant. The traditional imperative that a daughter must be pure and virginal to be marriageable also plays a role in exerting higher controls (Smith, 2006; Zayas, Lester, Cabassa, & Fortuna, 2005).

A family in therapy for depression in their 19-year-old daughter, Consuelo, related that both the mother and the father controlled her behavior by having her boyfriend visit her in the home and sit to watch TV without touching even the side of their arms, because in their estimation, the most minimal physical contact would stimulate the boyfriend's temptations. In contrast, Consuelo's 18-year-old brother was allowed to come home late at night after drinking, going to dances, and spending time in the backseat of cars with girls. To add to the controls, this younger brother was supposed to supervise Consuelo's activities in the street when boys were around. When Consuelo would express her frustration to her parents over the obvious "double standard" she would get a few slaps in the face for her disobedience, along with intimations that she was on the brink of becoming a woman of ill repute for wanting to go out alone with her boyfriend. Her depression needed to be seen in the context of immutable parental positions that were blocking her desires for greater autonomy.

"Lockdown" is an expression commonly used by second-generation adolescent girls, referring to their parents' insistence that they stay home (Smith, 2006). Most likely parents exercise very high controls on girls because of their perception that the dangers and costs on the street are much greater for girls than for boys, even though boys are exposed to other dangers, such as drug abuse and gangs.

Zayas et al. (2005) and Zayas (2011) have constructed a clinically useful model to understand why so many Latina teens attempt suicide, a model based on the notion that different cultural ideals create internal conflicts for the immigrant family. The suicide attempt is seen as representing a major developmental dilemma between the adolescent's need for autonomy (in her identity and her sexuality) and her deep respect for the value of family unity that originated in her family's cultural socialization. Culture plays a role, too, in that family honor is linked to chastity of wife and daughter. In many traditional cultures today (e.g., Kurdish, some Arab groups) teen girls and young women who are seen alone with a boy/man dishonor the family and are pressured to commit suicide (commonly dousing themselves with kerosene and setting on fire).

In other ethnic groups, such as Asian Americans, a similar generational dynamic between need for autonomy and respect for family values takes place between adolescent boys and girls and their parents. Strong cultural conflict with parents who exert their old cultural ideals rigidly and shelter offspring against external dangers correlates with suicidal attempts in youth following a disciplinary crisis (Lau, Jernewall, Zane, & Myers, 2002).

Therapists must be cognizant of these dilemmas between the old and new ways, and the force of contextual risks. However, therapists need to be mindful not to condone threatened harm or self-harm as either respecting or defying a family's culture. Rather, therapists need to help families move beyond either/or positions and help adolescents and parents find both/and solutions to honor traditions and build a bridge toward modern cultural norms, so as not to inflict harm on loved ones.

New studies strongly suggest that families that embrace biculturalism; that is, adolescents who attempt to maintain strong ties to their parents' cultures, and have parents who reach out to learn the skills of the new culture, perform better academically, face less anxiety, and adjust more easily socially (Santisteban & Mena, 2009; Smokowski, Buchanan, & Bacallao, 2009).

The Transnationalization of Adolescence. Recent developments brought about by global communication technologies allow for transnational exposures in the lives of immigrants that create a new cultural scenario for the second generation. A comparative study of adolescence in New York and in Ticuani, Mexico (Smith, 2006) uncovers many interesting aspects of adolescence in transnational contexts. In New York, adolescent girls are locked down, parental controls are intense, and adolescence is experienced as a very constraining life stage. However, when the adolescent girls and boys go to Ticuani, their parents' hometown in Puebla, Mexico, it is like going to live in a better neighborhood. In Ticuani, parents and grandparents grant a lot more freedom to girls and boys during their summer visits, because they experience a much greater sense of safety and familiarity there than in New York. Thus, second-generation adolescents have to find a way to integrate these two sets of experiences and parental directives, complicating their life-cycle predicaments between dependency and autonomy.

Contextual protections also play a role, in that adolescents have more caring people around them in Ticuani than they do in New York, where their immigrant parents work more hours farther away and there is a less rich community of relatives and acquaintances around to keep an eye on youth. So paradoxically, in their parents' country, they have both more personal freedoms and more caring involvement from adults than in the United States, where they could presumably have more material resources.

IMMIGRANT FAMILIES' RISKS: RELATIONAL STRESSES

Sometimes families' brave and complex attempts at integrating continuity and change, and restoring a sense of narrative coherence, falter in the face of intense loss or unbearable ambiguity. Among several categories of disruptive outcomes, I discuss three types of situations to illustrate how the ambiguous losses in migration are compounded by a confusing family context, a lack of clarity as to who is in and who is out of the family system or subsystems. Boss (2006) labeled this phenomenon "boundary ambiguity." In my clinical experience, situations that heighten the risks of boundary ambiguity for immigrant families often include reluctant or unprepared migrations, separations and reunions in the nuclear family, and family life-cycle transitions.

Reluctant and Unprepared Migrations

In family migrations, not all family members have equal say over the decision to migrate. There may be subtle power lines and asymmetries that involve gender and generation. Among those coaxed into migration somewhat against their will are children and adolescents, wives who reluctantly follow their husbands, and older parents, who are hastily convinced by their adult children to take on the journey, often after losing a spouse (Falicov, 1998a; Falicov, in press). In such situations, migration loss is further compounded by the lack of readiness to migrate and the constant ambivalence about the decision The reluctant immigrant may feel torn by family loyalties, inconclusive good-byes, and lingering ties and obligations to family members left behind. It is not surprising, therefore, that coaxed or reluctant individuals experience more ambivalence and difficulties of adaptation than those who actively elect to migrate. They often present with clinical symptoms of depression, anxiety, or psychosomatic problems.

Separations and Reunions among Nuclear Family Members

When a father or a mother migrates first, leaving family or children behind to be reunited at a later time, the family membership confusion that ensues may be mild and temporary or prolonged and intense. Even when a parent remains connected through monetary remittances and occasional contact, if lengthy time passes, the family left behind may feel abandoned, or find internal or external substitutes to supplement the functions left vacant. At the time of reunification, boundaries and relationships need to change again to allow for reentry of the absent member into the family system. Meanwhile, confusion may reign as to whether an absent mother or father is truly a part of the system and can be reincorporated again (Artico, 2003; Falicov, 2007; Hondagneu-Sotelo & Avila, 1997; Suárez-Orozco, Todorova, & Louie, 2002).

Among the motivations for leaving children behind is to avoid exposing them to the dangers of illegal passage, the economic hardships, the instability

of parental employment, and the lack of adequate caretaking in the new country. Sometimes a child may be left behind with a grandparent to assuage the
immigrant's guilt about leaving, and to symbolize that migration is provisional and experimental rather than permanent. However, these separations
and subsequent reunifications complicate the experiences of loss and reconnection, and raise issues of inclusion and exclusion for members of the three
generations, heightening the possibility of family conflict after reunification
(Falicov, 1998a, 2007; Hondagneu-Sotelo & Avila, 1997).

Recent data on separations in preadolescents, adolescents, and young
adult children whose parents have migrated away show that not only are
they deeply affected by their parents' absences, but they also acquire considerable influence over time to affect their parents' decisions to stay or to
return (Dreby, 2007). Although these stresses present significant risks, many
families cope successfully with separations and reunifications, and are able
to maintain a healthy family life that may include multiple caretakers for
the same child (Suárez-Orozco et al., 2002). For those who suffer negative
effects, family therapists are developing models of intervention with behavior problems in adolescents who have experienced immigration-related separations (Falicov, 2007; Mitrani, Santisteban, & Muir, 2004; Santisteban &
Mena, 2009).

Life-Cycle Transitions

Like all families, immigrant families undergo major life-cycle changes, such
as birth, leaving home, illness, and death. These transitions involve stressful reorganizations of the family. When nonambiguous, irretrievable losses
occur in the life of an immigrant family—perhaps the death of a relative back
home—the uncertainty of old good-byes accentuates migration loss. The
immigrant family may even experience the appearance of other ambiguous
losses (e.g., a teenager leaving home or a spouse separating and divorcing)
as more stressful than if they had occurred in a context that did not involve
migrations (Falicov, 2002).

Family transitions that involve members of the family who have stayed
behind in the country of origin may be particularly stressful. Many immigrants postpone visiting an aging parent for lack of money or time; sometimes
they avoid thinking about the topic, because they may feel overwhelmed by
guilt at not being able to do as much as expected for their loved ones at a distance. When a death occurs, they may feel profound regret and sadness at not
having made the effort to see more frequently their parent, sibling, or friend.
They may worry about not being present to help other family members with
the loss, and endure unbearable loneliness at not participating in communal
grieving. Renewed questions about the wisdom of the decision to migrate and
where one really belongs—with the family back home or the present one—
further complicate the feelings of emptiness and despair.

CONCLUSIONS

Many immigrant families deal in flexible and creative ways with the losses, risks, and gains of migration. They are able to restore a sense of coherence to their lives by developing dual visions and lifestyles that preserve central themes of a cultural family life, while incorporating new ideas and skills. They are also able to make positive existential meaning out of the experience of migration, while being aware of obstacles and social injustices. The emergence of new rituals that re-create cultural and social spaces, rekindle the past, and maintain long-held spiritual beliefs and religious or health practices, actions that in the past had been regarded as deficits or rigidities, can be interpreted in a "both/and" frame as active attempts at restitution that bolster rather than constrain family adaptations.

Immigrant families face a number of possible relational risks tied to the difficulties of integrating culturally different gender and generational expectations, an integration made much more difficult by contextual stressors of poverty, racism, and discrimination. While separations have always been at the core of migrations, transnational scenarios have changed the players and processes of the migration discourse. Consistently, studies show that biculturality has significant health and mental health advantages for the first and the second generation. Achieving biculturality appears as potentially more possible in a globalized world that facilitates greater contact between the generations of the immigrant family and the country of origin.

REFERENCES

Abrego, L. (2009). Economic well-being in Salvadoran transnational families: How gender affects remittance practices. *Journal of Marriage and Family, 71,* 1070–1085.

Ainslie, R. C. (1998). Cultural mourning, immigration, and engagement: Vignettes from the Mexican experience. In M. M. Suárez-Orozco (Ed.), *Crossings* (pp. 285–305). Cambridge, MA: Harvard University Press.

Artico, C. (2003). *Latino families broken by immigration: The adolescents' perceptions.* New York: LFB Scholarly Publishing LLC.

Baldassar, L. (2008). Missing kin and longing to be together: Emotions and the construction of co-presence in transnational relationships. *Journal of Intercultural Studies, 29*(3), 247–266.

Boss, P. (1999). *Ambiguous loss: Learning to live with unresolved grief.* Cambridge, MA: Harvard University Press.

Boss, P. (2006). *Loss, trauma, and resilience: Therapeutic work with ambiguous loss.* New York: Norton.

Choi, Y., He, M., & Harachi, T. (2008). Intergenerational cultural dissonance, parent–child conflict and bonding, and youth problem behaviors among Vietnamese and Cambodian immigrant families. *Journal of Youth and Adolescence, 37,* 85–96.

Dreby, J. (2006). Honor and virtue: Mexican parenting in the transnational context. *Gender and Society, 20*(1), 32–59.

Dreby, J. (2007). Children and power in Mexican transnational families. *Journal of Marriage and Family, 69,* 1050–1064.

Du Bois, W. E. B. (1903). *The souls of black folk.* Chicago: McClurg.

Falicov, C. J. (1995). Training to think culturally: A multidimensional comparative framework. *Family Process, 34,* 373–388.

Falicov, C. J. (1998a). *Latino families in therapy: A guide to multicultural practice.* New York: Guilford Press.

Falicov, C. J. (1998b). The cultural meaning of family triangles. In M. McGoldrick et al. (Eds.), *Re-visioning family therapy: Race, culture, and gender in clinical practice* (pp. 37–49). New York: Guilford Press.

Falicov, C. J. (2001). The cultural meaning of money: The case of Latinos and Anglo-Americans. *American Behavioral Scientist, 45*(2), 313–328.

Falicov, C. J. (2002). Ambiguous loss: Risk and resilience in Latino immigrant families. In M. Suárez-Orozco (Ed.), *Latinos: Remaking America* (pp. 274–288). Berkeley: University of California Press.

Falicov, C. J. (2003). Culture in family therapy: New variations on a fundamental theme. In T. Sexton, G. Weeks, & M. Robbins (Eds.), *Handbook of family therapy: Theory, research and practice* (pp. 37–55). New York: Brunner/Routledge.

Falicov, C. J. (2005). Emotional transnationalism and family identities: Commentary to Stone et al. *Family Process, 44,* 399–406.

Falicov, C. J. (2007). Working with transnational immigrants: Expanding meanings of family, community, and culture. *Family Process, 46,* 157–171.

Falicov, C. J. (2008). Transnational journeys. In M. McGoldrick & K. Hardy (Eds.), *Re-visioning culture, race, and class in family therapy* (2nd ed., pp. 25–38). New York: Guilford Press.

Falicov, C. J. (2009). Religion and spiritual traditions in immigrant families: Significance for Latino health and mental health. In F. Walsh (Ed.), *Spiritual resources in family therapy* (2nd ed., pp. 156–173). New York: Guilford Press.

Falicov, C. J. (2010). Changing constructions of machismo for Latino men in therapy: "The devil never sleeps." *Family Process, 49*(3), 309–329.

Falicov, C. J. (in press). *Latino families in therapy: A guide to multicultural practice* (2nd ed.). New York: Guilford Press.

Gil, R. M., & Vazquez, C. I. (1996). *The Maria Paradox: How Latinas can merge old world traditions with new world self-esteem.* New York: Putnam.

Gilbertson, G. (2009). Caregiving across generations: Aging, state assistance, and multigenerational ties among immigrants from the Dominican Republic. In N. Foner (Ed.), *Across generations: Immigrant families in America* (pp. 135–159). New York: New York University Press.

Glick, J. E. (2010). Connecting complex processes: A decade of research on immigrant families. *Journal of Marriage and Family, 72,* 498–515.

Gonzales, N. A., Knight, G. P., Morgan-López, A., Saenz, D., & Sirolli, A. (2002). Acculturation and the mental health of Latino youths: An integration and critique of the literature. In J. M. Contreras, K. A. Kerns, & A. M. Neal-Barnett (Eds.), *Latino children and families in the United States* (pp. 45–74). Westport, CT: Greenwood.

González-López, G. (2005). *Erotic journeys: Mexican immigrants and their sex lives.* Berkeley/Los Angeles: University of California Press.

Harris, R. J., Firestone, J. M., & Vega, W. A. (2005). The interaction of country of origin, acculturation, and gender role ideology on wife abuse. *Social Science Quarterly, 86,* 463–483.

Harwood, R. L., Miller, J. G., & Irizarry, N. L. (1995). *Culture and attachment: Perceptions of the child in context.* New York: Guilford Press.

Hirsch, J. (2003). *A courtship after marriage: Sexuality and love in Mexican transnational families.* Berkeley: University of California Press.

Hondagneu-Sotelo, P., & Avila, E. (1997). "I'm here, but I'm there": The meanings of Latina transnational motherhood. *Gender and Society, 11*(5), 548–571.

Imber-Black, E., Roberts, J., & Whiting, R. (Eds.). (2003). *Rituals in families and family therapy* (2nd ed.). New York: Norton.

Kao, G., & Tienda, M. (1995). Optimism and achievement: The educational performance of immigrant youth. *Social Science Quarterly, 76*(1), 1–19.

Lau, A. S., Jernewall, N. M., Zane, N., & Myers, H. F. (2002). Correlates of suicidal behaviors among Asian-American outpatient youths. *Cultural Diversity and Ethnic Minority Psychology, 8,* 199–213.

Levitt, P., & Waters, M. C. (2002). *The changing face of home: The transnational lives of the second generation.* New York: Russell Sage Foundation.

Marris, P. (1980). The uprooting of meaning. In G. V. Coelho & P. I. Ahmed (Eds.), *Uprooting and development: Dilemmas of coping with modernization* (pp. 101–116). New York: Plenum.

Martinez, C. R., Jr. (2006). Effects of differential family acculturation on Latino adolescent substance use. *Family Relations, 55,* 306–317.

Martinez, C. R. Jr., DeGarmo, D. S., & Eddy, J. M. (2004). Promoting academic success among Latino youth. *Hispanic Journal of Behavioral Sciences, 26*(2), 128–151.

Mitrani, V. B., Santisteban, D. A., & Muir, J. A. (2004). Addressing immigration-related separations in Hispanic families with a behavior-problem adolescent. *American Journal of Orthopsychiatry, 74,* 219–229.

Miville, M. L., & Constantine, M. G. (2006). Sociocultural predictors of psychological help-seeking attitudes and behavior among Mexican American college students. *Cultural Diversity and Ethnic Minority Psychology, 12*(3), 420–432.

Morales, A., & Hanson, W. E. (2005). Language brokering: An integrative review of the literature. *Hispanic Journal of Behavioral Sciences, 27,* 471–503.

Organista, K. C. (2007). *Solving Latino psychosocial and health problems: Theory, practice, and populations.* Hoboken, NJ: Wiley.

Orellana, M. F., Dorner, L., & Pulido, L. (2003). Accessing assets: Immigrant youth's work as family translators or "para-phrasers." *Social Problems, 50,* 505–524.

Piedra, L. M., & Engstrom, D. W. (2009). Segmented assimilation theory and the life model: An integrated approach to understanding immigrants and their children. *Social Work, 54,* 270–277.

Portes, A., & Rumbaut, R. G. (2001). *Legacies: The story of the immigrant second generation.* Berkeley: University of California Press.

Potocky-Tripodi, M. (2000). *Where is my home?: A refugee journey.* Lincoln, NE: Writer's Showcase Press.

Romano, E., Tippetts, S., Blackman, K., & Voas, R. (2005). Acculturation, income, education, safety belt use, and fatal motor vehicle crashes in California. *Prevention Science, 6*(2), 139–148.

Rueschenberg, E., & Buriel, R. (1989). Mexican American family functioning and acculturation: A family systems perspective. *Hispanic Journal of Behavioral Sciences, 11*(3), 232–244.

Santiago-Rivera, A. L., Arredondo, P., & Gallardo-Cooper, M. (2002). *Counseling Latinos and la familia: A practical guide.* Thousand Oaks, CA: Sage.

Santisteban, D. A., & Mena, M. P. (2009). Culturally informed and flexible family-based treatment for adolescents: A tailored and integrative treatment for Hispanic youth. *Family Process, 48,* 253–268.

Schmalzbauer, L. (2005). *Striving and surviving: A daily life analysis of Honduran transnational families.* New York: Routledge.

Schwartz, S. J., Unger, J. B., Zamboanga, B. L., & Szapocznik, J. (2010). Rethinking the concept of acculturation: Implications for theory and research. *American Psychologist, 65*(4), 237–251.

Schwartz, S. J., Zamboanga, B. L., & Jarvis, L. H. (2007). Ethnic identity and acculturation in Hispanic early adolescents: Mediated relationships to academic grades, prosocial behaviors, and externalizing symptoms. *Cultural Diversity and Ethnic Minority Psychology, 13,* 364–372.

Smith, R. (2006). *Mexican New York: Transnational lives of new immigrants.* Berkeley/Los Angeles: University of California Press.

Smokowski, P., Buchanan, R. L., & Bacallao, M. L. (2009). Acculturation and adjustment in Latino adolescents: How cultural risk factors and assets influence multiple domains of adolescent mental health. *Journal of Primary Prevention, 30*(3–4), 371–393.

Smokowski, P. R., David-Ferdon, C., & Stroupe, N. (2009). Acculturation and violence in minority adolescents: A review of the empirical literature. *Journal of Primary Prevention, 30*(3–4), 215–263.

Stone, E., Gomez, E., Hotzoglou, D., & Lipnitsky, J. Y. (2005). Transnationalism as a motif in family stories. *Family Process, 44,* 381–398.

Suárez-Orozco, C., & Suárez-Orozco, M. (1995). *Transformations: Migration, family life, and achievement motivation among Latino adolescents.* Stanford, CA: Stanford University Press.

Suárez-Orozco, C., & Suárez-Orozco, M. (2000). *Children of immigration.* Cambridge, MA: Harvard University Press.

Suárez-Orozco, C., & Suárez-Orozco, M. (2008). *Learning a new land: Immigrant students in American society* Cambridge, MA: Harvard University Press.

Suárez-Orozco, C., Todorova, I., & Louie, J. (2002). Making up for lost time: The experience of separation and reunification among immigrant families. *Family Process, 41,* 625–641.

Triandis, H. C. (1995). *Individualism and collectivism.* Boulder, CO: Westview Press.

Troya, E., & Rosenberg, F. (1999). "Nos fueron a México": Qué nos pasó a los jóvenes exiliados consureños? *Sistemas Familiares, 15*(3), 79–92.

Vertovec, S. (2004). Cheap calls: The social glue of migrant transnationalism. *Global Networks, 4,* 219–224.

Walsh, F. (2003). Clinical views of family normality, health, and dysfunction: From deficit to strengths perspective. In F. Walsh (Ed.), *Normal family processes* (3rd ed., pp. 27–57). New York: Guilford Press.

Walsh, F. (2006). *Strengthening family resilience* (2nd ed.). New York: Guilford Press.

Wilding, R. (2006). "Virtual" intimacies?: Families communicating across transnational contexts. *Global Networks, 6,* 125–142.

Zayas, L. H. (2011). *Latinas attempting suicide: When cultures, families, and daughters collide.* New York: Oxford University Press.

Zayas, L. H., Lester, R. J., Cabassa, L. J., & Fortuna, L. R. (2005). Why do so many Latina teens attempt suicide?: A conceptual model for research. *American Journal of Orthopsychiatry, 75,* 275–287.

CHAPTER 14

CHANGING GENDER NORMS IN FAMILIES AND SOCIETY
Toward Equality amid Complexities

CARMEN KNUDSON-MARTIN

A male client from a conservative Christian faith declares that he is going to stay home and raise the children; that his wife will be the economic provider. He does not consult her in making this decision.

A Muslim professor in the United States considers herself a feminist yet chooses to wear the *hijab*; her husband objects and worries that this will cause others to view him as her oppressor (Daneshpour, 2009).

A father is a primary caregiver for his 4-year-old son. When he picks the son up from preschool, his son is delighted with the Valentine cards he received. The boy holds up a pink one with a dancing fairy on it and throws it aside, announcing, "I don't like fairies! None of the boys at school do."

These are but a few of the gender complexities and contradictions that contemporary families face. Across the globe there are substantial efforts to advance gender equality (United Nations, 2008). Most women and men in the industrialized West express egalitarian attitudes (Sullivan, 2006). There is also evidence of shifts toward gender equality among many couples in collectivist cultures such as Singapore and Iran (Moghadam, Knudson-Martin, & Mahoney, 2009; Quek, 2009). Yet despite these changes, gender inequality persists and continues to organize many aspects of family life in ways that are often subtle and beyond conscious awareness (Ferree, 2010; Knudson-Martin & Mahoney, 2009).

Families are where "the rubber hits the road" as societal transformation intersects with day-to-day life. This chapter provides a framework to address changing gender norms, social structures, interpersonal processes, and individual development as they converge in family life. The chapter begins with an overview of why it is important to address gender issues in clinical practice. Then I examine five areas that are particularly problematic as therapists consider how to position their work in relation to larger sociocultural gender patterns. I conclude with a model of equality to guide families and their clinicians, and a summary of key practice implications.

GENDER ORGANIZES FAMILY

"Gender" is a socially created construct that consists of expectations, characteristics, and behaviors that members of a culture consider appropriate for males or females (Mahoney & Knudson-Martin, 2009a, p. 17). Although ideas about appropriate gender behavior change over time and vary from one culture to another, contemporary societal scripts still do not convey the full range of gender diversity that exists within families. An increasing number of persons consciously step out of societal expectations for gender identity and sexual orientation to live in ways that fit better for them (Lev, 2010; see Green, Chapter 8, and McGoldrick & Ashton, Chapter 11, this volume). Despite the considerable variation, societal messages regarding gender are pervasive and suggest that everyone *should* conform to the stereotypical gender expectations associated with their natal sex whether or not they fit one's own experience and preferences (Lev, 2010). Because gender also defines the worth and value of individual family members and their power in relation to each other and the larger society (McGoldrick, Anderson, & Walsh, 1989), pressures to conform to gender expectations can be intense.

Rather than an issue that is sometimes relevant in certain cases, gender is a central construct around which family processes organize (Goldner, 1989; Walters, Carter, Papp, & Silverstein, 1988). It is important to address in all clinical practice, no matter what the family structure or presenting issue. As Goldner (1994) so well articulated,

> Given that we are born into a symbolic and material work that is *already* gendered in every possible way, it is impossible to overstate its effects. . . . We cannot "see through" gender to the person "inside." . . . all of us are swept up into these narratives, performing gender in compliance with, or in resistance to them. I will always be my son's *mother*, not simply his parent. (p. 46)

Paradoxically, dealing with gender in therapy is often overlooked because it is so pervasive. It is as though gender norms and expectations are in the air we breathe; they are central to who we are but invisible to the eye and often are taken for granted (Mahoney & Knudson-Martin, 2009a; Walsh & Scheinkman, 1989). But without attention to gender and the other larger systems and life-cycle contexts within which it intersects (race, class, ethnicity, sexual orientation, religion, age, marital status, etc.), it is impossible truly to practice systemic therapy.

Gender organizes families via its influence in three aspects of family life (Knudson-Martin, 2009a):

- *Structure.* Gender organizes how decisions are made, whose interests take priority, and whose version of reality prevails. In ways that are often not intentional, gender determines who does what in families and how children are socialized.

- *Emotion and meaning.* People's individual feelings and emotional reactions to each other are framed by gender discourses and structures in the larger society. The same behavior or symptom takes on different meaning depending on the gender context.

- *Skills.* Stereotypical gender constructions limit both male and female development. "Personal" traits such as "nurturing" or "assertive" are influenced by cultural constructions of gender. To maintain changes in the structure of their relationships and parenting practices, many women and men need to expand their skills and develop new competencies.

What happens in therapy either replicates existing sociocultural gender patterns and inequities or is part of transforming them. As Hare-Mustin (1978) noted nearly 35 years ago, therapists reproduce existing gender constructions by either ignoring gender or by exaggerating gender differences. An important challenge for therapists today continues to be how to recognize and identify the influence of sociocultural gender discourses and structures, while also developing strategies and interventions that help families transform constricting, harmful, or unjust patterns in their lives. Five areas are particularly problematic: (1) gender binaries; (2) gendered power; (3) cultural discourse; (4) personal choice; and (5) relational responsibility.

THE PROBLEM OF GENDER BINARIES

Families live in societal contexts that exaggerate gender differences despite considerable evidence that meaningful differences between sexes are minimal (Eliot, 2009; Hyde, 2005). Furthermore, binary gender constructions typically presume heteronormativity, linking definitions of masculinity and femininity to heterosexual behavior. A recent ethnographic study of gender practices among high school adolescents found that boys gained approval of masculinity by "lobbing homophobic epithets at one another" and "engaging in heterosexist discussions of girls bodies and their own sexual experiences" (Pascoe, 2007, p. 5). Students who did not conform to ritualized expressions of heterosexist gender dichotomies were marginalized.

In recent decades the popularuzed binary view of gender has been to think of women and men as representing two different cultural worlds (i.e., men are from Mars and women are from Venus; Gray, 2004). These distinctions in how genders think and behave are sometimes described as "hardwired," as though gendered differences in brain functioning are inborn, and men and women are innately different. There are two problems with this approach:

- Differences *within* sexes are much greater than differences between sexes.
- Social experience shapes the brain.

Eliot (2009), a neurobiologist who specializes in children's brains, has done an extensive review of the findings on differences between male and female brains. She characterizes conclusions that women and men are hardwired differently as a misuse of neuroscience. Because nearly all such studies have been done on adults, differences such as women averaging more connections between the two sides of the brain do not take into account the role of experience in creating observed differences. For example, the biggest predictor of verbal pathways in the brain is experience with language. Some men have more verbal pathways than the average woman. Rather than being from different planets, Eliot says it is as though "men are from North Dakota and women are from South Dakota" (p. 13).

According to Eliot (2009), there are some differences between boy and girl babies; however, the magnitude of the differences is small. Boys are somewhat more excitable. Girls have a slightly more mature brain. Boys prefer more active kinds of toys. Eliot emphasizes, however, that these minor differences are exaggerated by the ways people respond, with the result that boys and girls are discouraged from developing their full capacities. She suggests that parents help children compensate for minor initial differences, for example, by encouraging boys to read more.

Gender is thus inherently relational. Gender differences are reproduced or resisted as family members relate with each other and the larger society (Walters et al., 1988). Maccoby and Jacklin's (1974) classic study revealed little evidence of gender differences. Yet when children interacted with each other, they enacted stereotypical gender patterns. Similarly, Hyde (2005), who reviewed 46 meta-analyses of gender differences studies, found that males and females are statistically comparable on nearly all the psychological variables studied. Her analysis also emphasized the importance of the social context in creating, erasing, or even reversing gendered psychological differences.

Parents who want to encourage the full range of their children's capacities must do so intentionally. Children learn what it means to be boys or girls "through the routine daily events of family life and it is through these same events that gender inequality is reproduced between grown-up women and men" (Kimmel, 2011, p. 159). Children learn early on that being labeled a girl (i.e., a "sissy") is not as good as being classified as a boy (i.e., "tomboy"). The pressures associated with exaggerated gender binaries grow as children move into adolescence and toward intimate relationships.

There is tremendous variation in how contemporary families do or do not live out gender binaries. However, families that enact stereotypical gender patterns are less able to respond flexibly to life's ups and downs (Gerson, 2010). A socially constructed, process view of gender, which suggests a recursive interaction among biology, family, and the environment (Knudson-Martin, 2003), helps clinicians identify the personal and relational consequences of gender binaries and makes visible more potential options. Doing so requires attention to gendered power disparities.

THE PROBLEM OF POWER DISPARITIES

Each society establishes of a set of social power positions based on gender, socioeconomic status, skin color, age, language, and a host of other perceived categorizations (McGoldrick & Hardy, 2008). These societal positions carry with them taken-for-granted rights, privileges, and obligations. The values and ways of knowing of the dominant groups drive what is prized in society and influence how individuals in all strata experience themselves and others. Interpersonal gender processes must be understood in the context of these societal systems of privilege and domination (Almeida, Dolan-Del Vecchio, & Parker, 2008; McDowell & Fang, 2007; Silverstein & Goodrich, 2003).

Invisible Male Privilege

Privilege associated with male status organizes family processes. In most traditional contexts, a father or grandfather is accorded special status as head of the household; however, gendered power differences are often much less intentional and beyond conscious awareness of the persons involved (Knudson-Martin & Mahoney, 2009). In these cases, male power comes not from outright acts of domination but from an unacknowledged preeminence of men's priorities, needs, and desires in ways that seem unquestionable or natural (Walsh, 1989).

Our research on a diverse sample of heterosexual couples (Knudson-Martin & Mahoney, 2005) revealed that many couples continue to organize around a "gender legacy" of invisible male power. These women and men *say* that they do not use gender to determine roles and responsibilities, but women end up listening to and accommodating their partners much more than do the men. A smaller number of couples, which we labeled "postgender," made conscious efforts to resist stereotypical gender patterns and demonstrated relatively equal accommodation, attending, and status in their relationships. Men in these relationships described intentionally learning to attend to their partners and taking initiative in child care and household responsibilities (i.e., they resisted male privilege).

The impact of gender and gendered power on heterosexual families is made more visible when we observe the relatively equal relationships of committed same-sex couples (e.g., Connolly, 2005; Jonathan, 2009; see Green, Chapter 8, this volume). Jonathan found that like the postgender couples mentioned earlier, most same-sex partners took active steps to maintain "equal weight" in workload, decisions, and attending emotionally to each other. When circumstances such as perceived discrepancies in workplace demands or child care issues resulted in inequality, most of the same-sex couples appeared aware of these power differences and acknowledged them, and the benefiting partner tried to compensate in some way. In contrast, the heterosexual gender legacy couples fell into unequal relationship patterns, with little discussion or conscious negotiation. Gendered power differences tended to be accepted because they felt "natural" or were attributed to personal characteristics of the partners.

Power in Relational and Social Context

To understand the working of gendered power discrepancies in any particular family can be complex, because gender intersects with other sources of power and discrimination. For example, the struggle for racial justice is a backdrop for African American family life (Hill, 2005; see Boyd-Franklin & Karger, Chapter 12, this volume). Gender equality can be a practical outcome as African American women and men pull together for survival (Cowdery, Scarborough, Lewis, & Seshadri, 2009; Marks et al., 2008). On the other hand, demonstrations of male control and dominance at home may be an attempt to compensate for lack of societal power (Hill, 2005). Female partners may also attempt to protect black men from societal humiliation, and both may view a male head of the household as a sign of attaining success according to standards of the dominant culture internalized within their own subculture.

In the larger society, white women may have more power than men of color. Higher education and socioeconomic status may also grant women power. Gay men hold less societal power than straight men. People may have power in some societal positions and not in others. Nonetheless, gendered power can be surprisingly tenacious. The give and take in a couple is based on the resources each partner brings to the relationship, both material and positional, and is highly influenced by gender norms regarding what is expected (Sullivan, 2006). What is considered "fair" must be understood in this context.

For example, though money is generally a source of power, a study of heterosexual couples in which the women earned more money than the men found that men still felt entitled to privilege in the household, and women went out of their way to help their husbands maintain their gendered power positions (Tichenor, 2005). Power disparities such as these contribute to marital unhappiness and thus increase the risk of divorce, especially when women have the financial resources to leave (Amato, 2010).

Lower status in the larger society means that women frequently carry an unequal burden in the home. Women still do the bulk of the housework and child care despite also holding workplace roles (Bianchi & Milkie, 2010; see Fraenkel & Capstick, Chapter 4, this volume). Even couples who "equally share" childcare and household tasks typically leave organization of these tasks (arranging carpools, keeping the family calendar, identifying household tasks to be done, etc.) to women (Zimmerman, Haddock, Ziemba, & Rust, 2001).

Consequences of Gendered Power

Although women derive satisfaction from giving care, they often pay a high price for the care they provide their families. For example, wives of veterans with posttraumatic stress disorder (PTSD) who were actively engaged in managing the disorder and their relationships suffered emotional distress as a result (Dekel, Goldblatt, Keidar, Solomon, & Polliack, 2005). In another study (Knudson-Martin, 2009b), when men had diabetes, their wives took on or shared responsibility for their partner's care, but when women had diabetes, their husbands described diabetes management as her own responsibility.

In the United States, and in most places across the globe, female depression is connected to gender inequality and a lack of relational reciprocity (Jack & Ali, 2010). Female single parents and grandmothers who carry primary responsibility for their grandchildren suffer particularly high levels of stress (Umberson, Pudrovska, & Reczek, 2010; see Engstrom, Chapter 9, this volume). When ill or disabled children and older adult family members require extensive care, female family members (including daughters-in-law) are assigned the role of primary caregiver in most families. Gendered discrepancies in giving and receiving care have health consequences but tend to be masked and taken for granted as part of gender norms.

Another frequently overlooked consequence of gendered power is the disparate impact on feelings of entitlement and how family members validate each other's worth (Greenberg & Goldman, 2008). When one person is dominant, he becomes the focus in the family. The less powerful are made responsible to soothe his emotions and attend to his or her needs (Silverstein, Bass, Tuttle, Knudson-Martin, & Huenergardt, 2006).

Power disparities affect communication processes. If power is equal, people are likely to use direct strategies to influence each other; when it is not, the less powerful use indirect strategies (Steil, 1997). In equal relationships, no one feels compelled to "silence the self" (Jack & Eli, 2010). That there are multiple voices means there will also sometimes be conflict. Stereotypical gender patterns limit conflict, because women and children are expected to stifle their thoughts and automatically accommodate or defer when interests differ. The ability to deal with conflict is a key finding that distinguishes couples who successfully create equal relationships (Knudson-Martin & Mahoney, 2005;

2009). Direct expression of conflict—even fighting—is a sign that partners have not given up on mutual influence.

Unequal power positions and stereotypical gender socialization also make the vulnerability inherent in intimacy difficult (Rampage, 2003). In skewed relationships, the more powerful may fear appearing weak or letting his guard down. The less powerful may hold back out of a need for self-protection and fear that their needs will not be acknowledged. Intimacy is fostered when the most powerful person takes a more vulnerable stance that begins to equalize power positions rather than maintain power over the other (Goodrich, 1991; Knudson-Martin & Huenergardt, 2010).

The payoff for resisting gendered power disparities was especially evident in our analyses of parenting practices in an ethnically diverse sample of working- and middle-class parents of young children (Cowdery & Knudson-Martin, 2005; Matta, 2009). Postgender fathers, those in relationships based on equal power, developed emotional connections with their children that were similar to those of the mothers. They noticed their children's needs and responded directly to them. In contrast, gender legacy and traditional fathers described feeling that the mothers were more connected to their children and, in some cases, more loved by them. They said they wanted to be involved parents but did not tune into their children's moment-by-moment needs. Male privilege allowed fathers to focus less on their children. The cost was a limited relational bond.

Gendered Power and Social Justice

The power disparity between women and men is a social justice issue. If therapists focus only on behaviors, without attending to the gendered power context in which they occur, or if they do exactly the same interventions with each partner in the interests of being "neutral," they are likely to perpetuate gendered power disparities. For example, men's violence leads to more negative outcomes than does women's. Women are more likely to be seriously injured by a male partner by 9 to 1, and 20–30% of all girls now 12 years old will experience a violent sexual attack during their lives (Kimmel, 2011). Women who have been abused are more likely to suffer low self-esteem and to receive a diagnosis of depression or anxiety (Anderson, 2010; Woods, 2010). Gendered power encourages men to feel entitled to sex and to use violence to maintain their power over women, children, and other men. Spousal abuse tends to occur when female partners challenge the perpetrator's authority and control—or attempt to leave the abusive relationship. Men often use violence to incite fear; women tend to resort to violence to express frustration or defend themselves (Kimmel, 2011).

Equal support of women and men in a "not neutral world" requires practices that intentionally counteract gender inequality (Knudson-Martin & Huenergardt, 2010; McGoldrick et al., 1989). Understanding the sociocultural discourses that perpetuate or challenge gendered power differences is thus important to provide a culturally sensitive foundation from which to confront gender and power issues.

THE PROBLEM OF CULTURAL DISCOURSE

Gender is a major way that culture is expressed in families. Some therapists are therefore reluctant to challenge gender inequality, because they want to respect culture. Yet there is tremendous variation within cultures, and cultures are continually changing. Working with gender requires a way to consider the fluid nature of culture and to make sociocultural influences visible and open to discussion and change (Laird, 1999).

Discourses are shared ways that members of a social community talk and think. Because what is expected of women and men is in transition in virtually every culture, gender discourses reflect sociocultural contradictions and tensions (Falicov, 1995). At any given time, members of a society have available to them a whole palate of sociocultural discourses and draw on many—often contradictory—societal narratives to guide and inform experience (Winslade, 2009). In addition to discourses that support gender inequality, most cultures and religions also hold values that support mutual respect and reciprocity. The question is not *whether* people will follow cultural models; it is *which* ones foster their mutual well-being and how they will enact them (Knudson-Martin & Huenergardt, 2010).

For example, a study in Iran found that Muslim couples draw on diverse cultural and religious legacies that include both a history of strong women and a contemporary male-dominant social order (Moghadam et al., 2009). Islamic values of mutuality and respect for women were a part of the narratives of nearly all study participants; at the same time, Iranian laws give men authority over women. There was considerable diversity in how couples responded to these conflicting sociocultural messages. A number of the educated women and some men appeared to be actively challenging gender inequality in their families. Others appeared to accept male dominance and female accommodation with little question or ability to confront it. Moreover, gender was experienced differently in different settings.

The fluid nature of gender discourse is made visible to immigrants as they observe gender differences from one culture to another (Maciel, van Putten, & Knudson-Martin, 2009): As one woman related: "Here in the United States, I learned to confront conflict by speaking up. In my native country I am not supposed to speak up" (p. 17). In this study couples evolved a personal gender culture as they adopted some parts of the new culture and retained others by choice, necessity, or automatic default to traditional gender norms. But this is not an easy process. Poor and working-class families are likely to shift gender role patterns before ideology, because families need women's income, and tensions can fuel relationship distress or violence (Inclan, 2003), especially if working mothers challenge expectations that they should also carry all traditional household and childcare responsibilities (see Fraenkel & Capstick, Chapter 4, this volume). Also, intergenerational differences can spark conflict in families, with children likely to push for more gender freedom, especially in immigrant families (see Falicov, Chapter 13, this volume).

It is important to explore unique personal experiences around societal narratives. It is especially helpful to identify discourses that guide how people orient themselves to others (Silverstein et al., 2006). These include messages about independence and connection, position and hierarchy, sources of personal worth and value, expectations about roles and decision making, and the meaning of accommodating and attending to others. It is also important to notice what is taken for granted in peoples' descriptions of their relationships and what other possibilities are absent but implicit (Carey, Walther, & Russell, 2009). For example, the idea of gender equality is a common, unrealized sociocultural ideal. In one couple, implicit in the husband's statement, "I was attracted to Ellie because she could think for herself," was a model of women and men as equally competent, autonomous, and able to make decisions. Similarly, when Ellie said, "I get upset when Damon leaves dealing with family members to me," there was an implicit expectation that men, as well as women, *should* be responsible for maintaining family relationships. These implicit discourses offer alternatives to gender inequality.

Other implicit discourses legitimate male power. In another case, Wes became upset when Kathy was busy getting ready to leave for a meeting and did not appear interested in hearing about his day. Implicit in his anger was a cultural message that privileges male time and says "women should be available." Challenging this taken-for-granted gender norm, the therapist made this implicit gender expectation visible: "Do you expect to drop what you are doing when Kathy interrupts you?" Wes was momentarily caught off guard. "Hmmm . . . I can't think of a time when she interrupted me like that." Naming this power difference enabled Wes to reconsider his expectations.

When gendered relationship patterns are recognized as sociocultural, people feel less blame and are more receptive to change. In the following exchange, therapist Jill Freedman helps Hollie, a female client, recognize cultural discourses that limit women's voices. In this example, Hollie has just described an incident from her childhood, when her father threw over the entire family dinner table, sending everything crashing to the floor:

HOLLIE: My mother just stood there and didn't say a word . . .

JILL: Do you think there are ideas in the world that would keep her quiet that way?

HOLLIE: I do. She probably thought she was supposed to calm everything down, protect us kids.

JILL: So you think there are dictates in our culture for women not to take a stand, to put other people first?

HOLLIE: I do.

They discuss how this gender model for relationships has affected Hollie's marriage:

> HOLLIE: When I think back to my relationship with Robert there were some situations where I never said a word, when I should have. I'd say to myself, "No, don't say anything because he's entitled to this."

> JILL: Do you think that model of the woman always giving and the man having the say tricks people into not behaving in ways that suit them?

> HOLLIE: Yeah. I guess. I didn't think of it before, but it looks like it.

> JILL: So you said that model of relationship sort of left you without a voice. . . . does any particular incident come to mind when you've been able to break out of this model? (Freedman & Combs, 1996, pp. 159–161)

Freedman helped Hollie recognize the sociocultural gender discourses at work in her family relationships and then began to help her resist them by identifying an alternative gender model. However, choice is not as simple as picking this possibility or that (Winslade, 2009). Current sociocultural discourses reflect a convergence of male and female aspirations, and there is more gender flexibility and crossing of gender boundaries (Coontz, 2005; Gerson, 2010); yet some research finds persistent pressures to conform to gender stereotypes (Kimmel, 2008), such as constraining gendered workplace policies (see Fraenkel & Capstick, Chapter 4, this volume). How do families make choices? How much choice do they really have?

THE PROBLEM OF CHOICE

When my colleague and I (Knudson-Martin & Mahoney, 1998) studied a sample of well-educated, newly married couples over a decade ago, most described unequal relationship patterns at the same time that they reported egalitarian ideals. Many participants used the language of "choice" to explain unequal relationship patterns. For example, one wife in a relationship with several indicators of inequality said, "Today people do what they feel like doing . . . we don't have duties" (p. 86). Implicit in participants' narratives was the idea that people make decisions independently, of their own free will. Yet over and over again "personal" decisions end up reinforcing inequitable institutional patterns (Winslade, 2009).

For example, though most professional women remain in the workforce, a provocative study of highly trained professional women who "chose" to step out of their jobs found that underneath the rhetoric of personal choice these women experienced a punishing workplace context and gendered expectations in homemaking and child care that made continued engagement in high-status professions too stressful to continue (Stone, 2010). Their husbands, equally involved in high pressure jobs, did not face the same kind of bind—they "got a pass" at home (p. 71). Their workloads and love for their work were accepted as normal. As a result, these fathers often were simply "not around" and "not able" to participate in child care, and the mothers gave up careers that were important to them. Similarly, in a longitudinal study of dual-career parents of young children in Singapore, husbands and wives agreed that whether the mother remained in full-time employment was *her* choice (Quek, Knudson-Martin, Orpen, & Victor, 2011). Implicit in their narratives was that parenting decisions and responsibilities were primarily the women's problem.

Resisting sociocultural gender patterns, as some couples do, requires conscious discussion and ongoing monitoring of the partners' shared process (Knudson-Martin & Mahoney, 2005; Risman & Johnson-Summerford, 1998; Vachon & Vachon, 2010). When gender differences do not organize relationship decisions, as in same-sex couples, partners engage in considerable direct decision making and evaluation of how their relationship decisions are working (Jonathan, 2009).

Choices regarding whether to conform to gender stereotypes can be especially difficult for adolescents. Boys who do not fit the model of masculinity based on power and dominance tend to avoid drawing attention to themselves so as not to suffer bullying or humiliation (Kimmel, 2008). Young men are often torn between proving their masculinity and expressing their humanity. Those who choose humanity (a false choice, of course) describe the important role of parents. Kimmel encourages mothers and fathers to resist messages that they are "feminizing" their sons and instead "stay connected" with them, in order to help boys to resist the destructive mores of hypermasculinity.

Teenage girls are confronted with dilemmas posed by pressures to define themselves through the eyes and approval of boys and masculine models of success. Each girl has to decide what to go along with and what to resist. As girls increasingly strive to construct their own models for positive development, they still experience what Brown and Gilligan (1992) called the "relational paradox": Do I sacrifice being myself to maintain relationship?

THE PROBLEM OF RELATIONAL RESPONSIBILITY

"Relational responsibility" refers to the efforts people make to maintain their family connections and build relationship bonds. It includes willingness to be influenced by others, to be responsive to their needs, interests, and perspectives (Knudson-Martin & Huenergardt, 2010). This openness to being changed by others runs counter to stereotypical masculine socialization. Yet validating others by accepting influence is critical to building relationships (Greenberg & Goldman, 2008). No wonder willingness of men to accept influence (and share housework!) has been found to be so highly predictive of relationship stability and success (Gottman, Coan, Carrère, & Swanson, 1998; see Driver, Tabares, Shapiro, & Gottman, Chapter 3, this volume).

Relational responsibility also involves attunement to others. According to Siegel (2007), attunement happens only when we *intentionally* open ourselves to resonate with another. This experiential awareness invites us to make changes to advance our partners' well-being and promotes parent–child attachment bonds and emotional development of the child (Siegel & Hartzell, 2003). Gender inequality skews this important relational activity (Jonathan & Knudson-Martin, 2012). In the earlier case example of Damon and Ellie, Damon simply left the room when his aunt (with whom they were living) said something he did not like. He never considered what it was like for Ellie to have to smooth things over, or how his aunt felt. When he opened himself to empathically take on their experiences, he also became more accountable for the effects of his behavior on others and more willing to take initiative to maintain and repair his relationships.

Traditional gender socialization and institutional structures have made relationship maintenance a female responsibility. However, women's caring behaviors and focus on others tend not to be valued for the important relational functions they serve for families. Too often they are framed as personal pathology (i.e., codependent or enmeshed) rather than recognized as socially prescribed responsibilities or the result of holding lower societal power positions (Jack & Ali, 2010). Single mothers are often judged as inherently inadequate on their own, when their struggles are largely due to insufficient resources and lack of support from a nonresident father (see Anderson, Chapter 6, this volume).

Service providers are cautioned not to mirror societal expectations unreflexively, holding mothers to blame for the problems of their children or other family members (Walters, 1994). Given these societal expectations, women tend to feel responsible for the well-being of family members and the quality of relationships even though they may have limited power to shape their relationships or situations. This can be especially challenging for stepmothers, who suffer from negative stereotypes, while holding considerable responsibility for maintaining their families (Sweeney, 2010; see Pasley & Garneau, Chapter 7, this volume).

On the other hand, men's relational responsibility has historically been defined in terms of instrumental breadwinning and disciplinary functions, with few expectations to offer empathy or tend to the emotional needs of others (McGoldrick et al., 1989). Though most men desire to be relationally connected, adherence to male stereotypes of control and autonomy frequently limits their ability to do so. Lack of active efforts to maintain relational connection is a critical factor in male depression (Papp, 2003).

However, ideas that responsibility for relationships rests primarily on women are changing. As the roles of women and men in the larger society have become more equal, expectations for mutuality within marriage have increased (Coontz, 2005). Women today are less desperate to keep a relationship and more likely to be discontented and leave if their partners do not carry equal weight in sustaining the relationship. Though women's attitudes and behaviors are changing faster than men's, most young men also seek committed, lifelong relationships based on mutuality, respect, and shared responsibility (Gerson, 2010).

Interestingly, the young men and women in Gerson's (2010) study learned from observing their parents that achieving their connected, egalitarian ideal was not likely. However, they looked at the issue through gendered lenses, holding different "fallback positions" should their relationships fell short of expectations. Women concluded that they must not be dependent on men; that they need to be able to care for themselves and their children, and to not lose their personal identities. In contrast, most of the men expected to fall back on a neotraditional family model in which they would take backseats as caregivers in order to provide financially. Neither gender had confidence that men would be relationally responsible beyond breadwinning.

A study in California of 18- to 29-year-olds in the attraction phase of heterosexual relationships helps shed light on why many contemporary women and men have trouble realizing their egalitarian relationship ideals (Rusovick & Knudson-Martin, 2009). Most participants in the study used an image of peer relationships to explain their attraction to each other. But they also tended to accept sociocultural ideas that men and women innately communicate and behave differently. Though both women and men rejected images of male domination when describing their ideal relationships, few spoke about the more subtle, invisible aspects of gendered power or how these might limit relational reciprocity.

As a result, women still end up carrying the relational ball. As one exceptionally insightful man in the study explained, "It's pounded into your head, men and women are equal . . . unfortunately, I find that the more we get into our relationship, we're falling into a genderable [pattern]" (Rusovick & Knudson-Martin, 2009, p. 283). He ends up focusing less attention on her and she does most of the housework because he does not automatically do it.

Therapists can play an important role in helping parents socialize their children into greater gender flexibility, and women and men move toward shared relationship responsibility. What is needed is a relationship model that overcomes implicit gender expectations by explicitly placing equality at its core.

CONSTRUCTING EQUALITY

Contemporary discourse often uses the language of equality. Partners speak of "shared decisions," "give and take," or "being there for each other" (Knudson-Martin & Mahoney, 1998). But what these entail in daily life are seldom well developed (Coontz, 2005; Gerson, 2010). After looking at the many ways in which relationship equality has been defined in the literature, Anne Mahoney and I developed a model of equality based on four relationship dimensions: relative status, attention to the other, accommodation patterns, and well-being (Mahoney & Knudson-Martin, 2009b).

The model is useful in identifying and overcoming the gender and power issues in intimate relationships. It offers a framework for conversations about gender expectations, helps people to recognize ways in which their relationships might be out of balance, and forms a basis for developing new, more equal patterns. Since early gender socialization influences how women and men approach relationships, we also encourage parents to use this model to guide to what children and adolescents learn about themselves and relationships.

Relative Status

"Relative status" refers to who defines what is important; who has the right to have, express, and achieve goals, needs, and interests. It refers to whether both partners—and both sons and daughters—have the ability to use the relationship to support their interests. It has to do with the power of each to define relationship agendas. Traditional gender socialization encourages feelings of entitlement in men and an expectation that women will put family needs before their own. To the extent that boys and girls absorb this set of expectations, even if unconsciously, they set themselves to approach relationships from unequal positions (Silverstein et al., 2006). We explore relative status through questions such as the following:

- Whose interests shape what happens in the family?
- To what extent does each feel equally entitled to express and attain personal goals, needs, and wishes?
- How are low-status tasks like housework handled?
- Which adults listen to and validate the experiences of children?

Attention to Others

Part of the egalitarian model for relationships is an expectation that family members be emotionally present for and supportive of each other, that they be attuned to each other's needs and responsive to emotions and stresses. It is critical that these skills be valued in society and taught to both boys and girls. We explore attention to the other through questions such as the following:

- To what extent does each partner notice and attend to needs and emotions of their partner and other family members?
- Does attention go back and forth between adult partners? Does each give and receive?

- When attention is imbalanced, do partners express awareness of this and the need to rebalance?
- Are sons, as well as daughters, expected to tune into others, and are they validated for their efforts?

Accommodation Patterns

Accommodation to one another is a necessary part of family life. If influence in a relationship is equal, then accommodations tend to be reasonably balanced over time. When accommodations are not equal, the less powerful organize their lives more around the others. Accommodation by the lower-status person may feel natural or expected and may happen automatically. Parents need to raise their sons to learn that accommodation to others is valued, and to teach their daughters to expect reciprocity in relationships and to evaluate relational commitments accordingly. We explore accommodation through questions such as the following:

- Is one partner more likely to organize his or her daily activities around the other?
- Does accommodation often occur automatically, without anything being said?
- Do partners attempt to justify accommodations they make as being "natural" or the result of personality differences?
- Are sons, as well as daughters, expected to accommodate others, and are they validated for this behavior?

Well-Being

In equal relationships, burdens are shared and the well-being of each partner is supported equally, both in the short term and over the long haul. Even though equal well-being may not be possible all the time, both partners recognize a disparity when it occurs, acknowledge it, and work together to equalize it. Parenting goals are based on the expectations that both daughters and sons will integrate personal achievements in context of responsibility and commitment to the strength and stability of their relationships. We explore well-being through questions such as the following:

- Does one partner seem to be better off psychologically, emotionally, or physically than the other?
- Does one person's sense of competence, optimism, or well-being seem to come at the expense of the other?
- Does the relationship support the economic viability of each partner?
- Are daughters, as well as sons, encouraged to develop self-esteem for their strengths and accomplishments?
- Are sons, as well as daughters, encouraged to be aware of their feelings and to express their vulnerabilities and fears?

These relationship standards emphasize shared concern for mutual well-being and benefit in a relationship. Even though these aspects of equality may take on different meanings in various cultures and social contexts, we find that the idea of *mutually supportive relationships* is widely applicable and consistent with an almost universal norm of reciprocity. When we introduce these ideas in classroom, research and clinical settings, they stimulate exploration of equality in ways that transform gender away from rigid stereotypes to a more flexible range of options.

IMPLICATIONS

The importance of gender flexibility is a key research finding across studies. Families who move beyond the limits of traditional gender are more able to respond to contemporary life challenges (Gerson, 2010; Knudson-Martin & Mahoney, 2009). Children benefit developmentally when gender stereotypes are challenged and more possibilities are open to fit their needs and preferences (Eliot, 2009). Gender equality provides an important foundation for intimacy, relationship satisfaction, and family stability (Coontz, 2005; Jonathan & Knudson-Martin, 2012; Steil, 1997).

As illustrated in the examples at the beginning of the chapter, contemporary families are responding to multiple discourses on gender. Some promote gender equality; others reinforce destructive gender binaries. The processes through which some gender discourses are silenced and others are supported are thus inherently ethical concerns (Knudson-Martin & Huenergardt, 2010). Family members and the professionals who work with them are faced with an ongoing series of ethical choices regarding which sociocultural discourses they support and what other possibilities are or are not made visible.

In addition to the model of equality outlined earlier, the following suggestions can help identify the gender and power issues in family relationships and frame prevention and intervention issues:

1. *Value relational skills.* It is important to acknowledge and validate positive contributions to maintaining relationships. This is a societal issue, as well as a family matter. Relational skills are increasingly more important than muscle and dominance. Parents need to resist the "boys will be boys" mentality and help boys, as well as girls, learn to attune to others.

2. *Promote a wider range of gendered experience.* Move beyond binary thinking in families that fathers do this and mothers do that. Join with couples around their desires for egalitarian, mutually supportive relationships, and help parents support children in developing skills not automatically associated with their gender.

3. *Interrupt dominance patterns.* Allowing behaviors such as putting down girls and "feminine" boys sends an implicit message that male

dominance is an acceptable way to gain respect and privilege. Adult family members need to interrupt these "small" behaviors. Help single women and men recognize relationship patterns that lead to mutual well-being and interrupt the flow of power in adult relationships.

4. *Identify values that promote equality.* Do not assume that people from traditional cultures or religions have no interest in gender equality. Begin with the premise that people are likely to hold values such as mutual respect and a desire that family relationships support all members. Ask them about these cultural beliefs. Seek to understand their meaning in light of their religious faith and the history of the culture.

5. *Raise conversation about the social context.* Once societal influences are visible, families have more choice about how they want to respond. Conversation about what they learned about being male and female and how this affects their relationships is helpful. Ask how couples make decisions regarding roles and responsibilities; how they learned to attend to and accommodate; and what they learned about expressing their opinions, concerns, and wishes. Ask parents what they want to teach their sons and daughter about these issues.

6. *Help men attend.* Resist cultural messages that place relationship responsibility and vulnerability on women. Assume that men want to attend to their partners; that gender socialization and a male-dominant social structure get in the way. Encourage powerful male partners to initiate relational connection, and help fathers model this to their children.

7. *Support silenced voices.* Therapists should intentionally position themselves to enable marginalized voices in families to be heard. This includes looking for what female family members may hold back, accommodate to, or let go of in an attempt to maintain the family stability, as well as creating space for husbands and fathers to hear and be influenced by others.

8. *Help families develop their own model of equality.* Couples and families need to be able to identify what implementing gender equality would look like for them. Use their words. Walk through the details in their daily lives and future plans.

9. *Promote policies and practices that support gender equality.* Focusing on individual families misses the institutional nature of gender processes and gender inequality. Consider whether your practices engage both fathers and mothers, and whether diagnoses and assessment models value independence but pathologize focusing on others. Challenge workplace policies that constrain fathers from equal involvement in family life and those that frame work–family balance as women's issues.

10. *Be proactive.* Stereotypical gender norms and processes replicate themselves unless we consciously resist them. As family educators and practitioners, it is especially important to check our own values and assumptions

and to position ourselves, our work, and activism in ways that intentionally help to transform gender for the well-being of all family members.

REFERENCES

Almeida, R. V., Dolan-Del Vecchio, K., & Parker, L. (2008). *Transformative family therapy: Just families in a just society.* Boston: Pearson Education.

Amato, P. (2010). Research on divorce: Continuing trends and new developments. *Journal of Marriage and Family, 72,* 650–660.

Anderson, K. L. (2010). Conflict, power, and violence in families. *Journal of Marriage and Family, 72,* 726–742.

Bianchi, S. M., & Milkie, M. A. (2010). Work and family research in the first decade of the 21st century. *Journal of Marriage and Family, 72,* 705–725.

Brown, L. M., & Gilligan, C. (1992). *Meeting at the crossroads.* Cambridge, MA: Harvard University Press.

Carey, M., Walther, S., & Russell, S. (2009). The absent but implicit: A map to support therapeutic enquiry. *Family Process, 48,* 319–331.

Connolly, C. (2005). A qualitative exploration of resilience in long-term lesbian couples. *Family Journal, 13,* 266–280.

Coontz, S. (2005). *Marriage, a history: From obedience to intimacy or how love conquered marriage.* New York: Viking.

Cowdery, R. S., & Knudson-Martin, C. (2005). Motherhood: Tasks, relational connection, and gender equality. *Family Relations, 54,* 335–346.

Cowdery, R. S., Scarborough, N., Lewis, M. E., & Seshadri, G. (2009). Pulling together: How African American couples manage social inequalities. In C. Knudson-Martin & A. R. Mahoney (Eds.), *Couples, gender, and power: Creating change in intimate relationships* (pp. 215–233). New York: Springer.

Daneshpour, M. (2009). Steadying the tectonic plates: On being Muslim, feminist, academic, and family therapist. In S. A. Lloyd, A. L. Few, & K. R. Allen (Eds.), *Handbook of feminist family studies* (pp. 340–350). Los Angeles: Sage.

Dekel, R., Goldblatt, H., Keidar, M., Solomon, Z., & Polliack, M. (2005). Being wife of a veteran with posttraumatic stress disorder. *Family Relations, 54,* 24–36.

Eliot, L. (2009). *Pink brain, blue brain: How small differences grow into troublesome gaps.* New York: Houghton/Mifflin Harcourt.

Falicov, C. J. (1995). Training to think culturally: A multidimensional comparative framework. *Family Process, 34,* 373–388.

Ferree, M. M. (2010). Filling the glass: Gender perspectives on families. *Journal of Marriage and Family, 72,* 420–439.

Freedman, J., & Combs, G. (1996). *Narrative therapy: The social construction of preferred realities.* New York: Norton.

Gerson, K. (2010). *The unfinished revolution: How a new generation is reshaping family, work, and gender in America.* New York: Oxford University Press.

Goldner, V. (1989). Generation and gender: Normative and covert hierarchies. In M. McGoldrick, C. Anderson, & F. Walsh (Eds.), *Women in families: A framework for family therapy* (pp. 42–60). New York: Norton.

Goldner, V. (1994). Boys will be men: A response to Terry Real's paper. In K. Weingarten (Ed.), *Cultural resistance: Challenging beliefs about men, women, and therapy* (pp. 45–48). New York: Haworth.

Goodrich, T. J., (1991). Women, power, and family therapy: What's wrong with this picture? In T. J. Goodrich (Ed.), *Women and power: Perspectives for family therapy* (pp. 3–35). New York: Norton.

Gottman, J. M., Coan, J., Carrère, S., & Swanson, C. (1998). Predicting marital happiness and stability from newlywed interactions. *Journal of Marriage and the Family, 60*, 5–22.

Gray, J. (2004). *Men are from Mars, women are from Venus: The classic guide to understanding the opposite sex.* New York: Harper.

Greenberg, L. S., & Goldman, R. N. (2008). *Emotion-focused couples therapy: The dynamics of emotion, love, and power.* Washington DC: American Psychological Association.

Hare-Mustin, R. (1978). A feminist approach to family therapy, *Family Process, 17,* 181–194.

Hill, S. A. (2005). *Black intimacies: A gender perspective on families and relationships.* Walnut Creek, CA: AltaMira Press.

Hyde, J. S. (2005). The gender similarities hypothesis. *American Psychologist, 60,* 581–592.

Inclan, J. (2003). Class, culture, and gender in immigrant families. In L. Silverstein & T. Goodrich (Eds.), *Feminist family therapy: Empowerment in social context* (pp. 336–346). Washington, DC: American Psychological Association.

Jack, D. C., & Ali, A. (2010). Culture, self silencing, and depression: A contextual–relational perspective. In D. C. Jack & A. Ali (Eds.), *Silencing the self across cultures: Depression and gender* (pp. 3–18). New York: Oxford University Press.

Jonathan, N. (2009). Carrying equal weight: Relational responsibility and attunement among same-sex couples. In C. Knudson-Martin & A. R. Mahoney (Eds.), *Couples, gender, and power: Creating change in intimate relationships* (pp. 79–104). New York: Springer.

Jonathan, N., & Knudson-Martin, C. (2012). Building connection: Attunement and gender equality in heterosexual relationships. *Journal of Couple and Relationship Therapy.*

Kimmel, M. (2008). Guyland: *The perilous world where boys become men.* New York: Harper.

Kimmel, M. (2011). *The gendered society* (4th ed.). New York: Oxford University Press.

Knudson-Martin, C .(2003). Gender and biology: A recursive framework for clinical practice. *Journal of Feminist Family Therapy, 15*(2/3), 1–21.

Knudson-Martin, C. (2009a). Addressing gendered power: A guide for practice. In C. Knudson-Martin & A. R. Mahoney (Eds.). *Couples, gender, and power: Creating change in intimate relationships* (pp. 317–336). New York: Springer.

Knudson-Martin, C. (2009b). An unequal burden: Gendered power in diabetes care. In C. Knudson-Martin & A. R. Mahoney (Eds.), *Couples, gender, and power: Creating change in intimate relationships* (pp. 105–123). New York: Springer.

Knudson-Martin, C., & Huenergardt, D. (2010). A socio-emotional approach to couple therapy: Linking social context and couple interaction. *Family Process, 49,* 369–386.

Knudson-Martin, C., & Mahoney, A. R. (1998). Language and processes in the construction of equality in new marriages. *Family Relations, 47,* 81–91.

Knudson-Martin, C., & Mahoney, A. R. (2005). Moving beyond gender: Processes that create relationship equality. *Journal of Marital and Family Therapy, 31,* 235–246.

Knudson-Martin, C., & Mahoney, A. R. (Eds.). (2009). *Couples, gender, and power: Creating change in intimate relationships.* New York: Springer.

Laird, J. (1999). Culture and narrative as metaphors for clinical practice with families. In D. Demo, K. Allen, & M. Fine (Eds.), *Handbook of family diversity* (pp. 338–358). New York: Routledge.

Lev, A. I. (2010). How queer!—The development of gender identity and sexual orientation in LGBTQ-headed families. *Family Process, 49,* 268–290.

Maccoby, E. E., & Jacklin, C. N. (1974). *The psychology of sex differences.* Stanford, CA: Stanford University Press.

Maciel, J., van Putten, Z., & Knudson-Martin, C. (2009). Gendered power in cultural contexts: Part I. Immigrant couples. *Family Process, 48,* 9–23.

Mahoney, A. R., & Knudson-Martin, C. (2009a). The social context of gendered power. In C. Knudson-Martin & A. R. Mahoney (Eds.), *Couples, gender, and power: Creating change in intimate relationships* (pp. 17–29). New York: Springer.

Mahoney, A. R., & Knudson-Martin, C. (2009b). Gender equality in intimate relationships. In C. Knudson-Martin & A. R. Mahoney (Eds.), *Couples, gender, and power: Creating change in intimate relationships* (pp. 3–16). New York: Springer.

Marks, L. D., Hopkins, K., Chaney, C., Monroe, P., Nesteruk, O., & Sasser, D. D. (2008). "Together we are strong": A qualitative study of happy, enduring African American marriages. *Family Relations, 57,* 172–185.

Matta, D. S. (2009). Fathering: Disengaged or responsive? In C. Knudson-Martin & A. R. Mahoney (Eds.), *Couples, gender, and power: Creating change in intimate relationships* (pp. 149–170). New York: Springer.

McDowell, T. M., & Fang, S. S. (2007). Feminist-informed critical multiculturalism. *Journal of Family Issues, 28,* 549–566.

McGoldrick, M., Anderson, C., & Walsh, F. (Eds.). (1989). *Women in families: A framework for family therapy.* New York: Norton.

McGoldrick, M., & Hardy, K. V. (2008). Introduction: Revisioning family therapy from a multicultural perspective. In M. McGoldrick & K. V. Hardy (Eds.), *Revisioning family therapy: Race, culture, and gender in clinical practice* (2nd ed., pp. 3–24). New York: Guilford Press.

Moghadam, S., Knudson-Martin, C., & Mahoney, A. (2009). Gendered power in cultural contexts: Part III. Couple relationships in Iran. *Family Process, 48,* 41–54.

Papp, P. (2003). Gender, marriage, and depression. *Feminist family therapy: Empowerment in social context* (pp. 211–224). Washington, DC: American Psychological Association.

Pascoe, C. J. (2007). *Dude, you're a fag: Masculinity and sexuality in high school.* Berkeley: University of California Press.

Quek, K. M. (2009). We-consciousness: Creating equality in collectivist culture. In C. Knudson-Martin & A. R. Mahoney (Eds.), *Couples, gender, and power: Creating change in intimate relationships* (pp. 193–214). New York: Springer.

Quek, K., Knudson-Martin, C., Orpen, S., & Victor, J. (2011). Gender equality during the transition to parenthood: Longitudinal study of dual-career Singaporean couples. *Journal of Social and Personal Relationships*, 0265407510397989, first published on February 28, 2011 as doi: 10.1177/0265407510397989.

Rampage, C. (2003). Gendered constraints to intimacy in heterosexual couples. In L. Silverstein & T. J. Goodrich (Eds.), *Feminist family therapy: Empowerment in social context* (pp. 199–211). Washington, DC: American Psychological Association.

Risman, B. J., & Johnson-Summerford, D. (1998). Doing it fairly: Study of postgender marriages. *Journal of Marriage and Family, 60*, 23–40.

Rusovick, R., & Knudson-Martin, C. (2009). Gender discourse in relationship stories of young American couples. In C. Knudson-Martin & A. R. Mahoney (Eds.), *Couples, gender, and power: Creating change in intimate relationships* (pp. 275–294). New York: Springer.

Siegel, D., & Hartzell, M. (2003). *Parenting from the inside out: How a deeper self-understanding can help you raise children who thrive.* New York: Tarcher.

Siegel, D. J. (2007). *The mindful brain: Reflection and attunement in the cultivation of well-being.* New York: Norton.

Silverstein, L., & Goodrich, T. (Eds.). (2003). *Feminist family therapy: Empowerment in social context.* Washington, DC: American Psychological Association.

Silverstein, R., Bass, L. B., Tuttle, A., Knudson-Martin, C., & Huenergardt, D. (2006). What does it mean to be relational?: A framework for assessment and practice. *Family Process, 45*, 391–405.

Steil, J. (1997). *Marital equality: Its relationship to the well-being of husbands and wives.* Newbury Park, CA: Sage.

Stone, P. (2010). *Opting out: Why women really quit careers and head home.* Berkeley: University of California Press.

Sullivan, O. (2006). *Changing gender relations, changing families: Tracing the pace of change over time.* Lanham, MD: Rowman & Littlefield.

Sweeney, M. M. (2010). Remarriage and stepfamilies: Strategic sites for family scholarship in the 21st century. *Journal of Marriage and Family, 72*, 667–684.

Tichenor, V. J. (2005). *Earning more and getting less: Why successful wives can't buy equality.* New Brunswick, NJ: Rutgers University Press.

Umberson, D., Pudrovska, T., & Reczek, C. (2010). Parenthood, childlessness, and well-being: A life course perspective. *Journal of Marriage and Family, 72*, 612–629.

United Nations Division for the Advancement of Women, Department of Economic and Social Affairs. (2008, December). *The role of men and boys in achieving gender equality.* Retrieved May 15, 2011, from *www.un.org/womenwatch/daw/public/w2000andbeyond.html.*

Vachon, M., & Vachon, A. (2010). *Equally shared parenting: Rewriting the rules for a new generation of parents.* New York: Perigee.

Walsh, F. (1989). Reconsidering gender in the marital quid pro quo. In M. McGoldrick, C. Anderson, & F. Walsh (Eds.), *Women in families: A framework for family therapy* (pp. 267–285). New York: Norton.

Walsh, F., & Scheinkman, M. (1989). (Fe)male: The hidden gender dimension in models of family therapy. In M. McGoldrick, C. Anderson, & F. Walsh (Eds.), *Women in families: A framework for family therapy* (pp. 16–41). New York: Norton.

Walters, M. (1994). Service delivery systems and women: The construction of conflict.

In M. P. Mirkin (Ed.), *Women in context: Toward a feminist reconstruction of psychotherapy* (pp. 9–24). New York: Guilford Press.

Walters, M., Carter, B., Papp, P., & Silverstein, O. (1988). *The invisible web: Gender patterns in family relationships.* New York: Guilford Press.

Winslade, J. (2009). Tracing lines of flight: Implications of the work of Gilles Deleuze. *Family Process, 48,* 332–346.

Woods, S. J. (2010). Seeking safety with undesirable outcomes: Women's self-silencing in abusive intimate relationships and implications for health care. In D. C. Jack & A. Ali (Eds.), *Silencing the self across cultures: Depression and gender in the social world* (pp. 485–504). New York: Oxford University Press.

Zimmerman, T. S., Haddock, S. A., Ziemba, S., & Rust, A. (2001). Family organizational labor: Who is calling the plays. In T. S. Zimmerman (Ed.), *Balancing family and work: Special considerations in feminist therapy* (pp. 65–90). New York: Haworth.

CHAPTER 15

THE SPIRITUAL DIMENSION OF FAMILY LIFE

FROMA WALSH

S pirituality is a powerful dimension of human experience and family life. Spiritual beliefs and practices have anchored and nourished families over the millennia and across cultures. Today, the vast majority of families worldwide adopt some form of expression for their spiritual needs, both within and outside organized religion. This chapter addresses the role of spirituality in couple and family relationships, with attention to the growing diversity and complexity of spiritual beliefs and practices in society and within families. It examines the meaning and salience of spirituality in sociocultural context and its dynamic ebb and flow across the multigenerational family life cycle. Research and practice recommendations are offered to explore the spiritual dimension in couple and family relationships: to identify spiritual sources of distress and spiritual resources for coping, healing, and resilience, fitting families' values and preferences.

SPIRITUALITY: A DIMENSION OF HUMAN EXPERIENCE

To consider the role of spirituality in contemporary family life, it is important to clarify the concepts of *religion* and *spirituality* (Hill & Pargament, 2003). They are often blurred, mistakenly polarized, or conflated in research and public surveys.[1]

Religion can be defined as an organized, institutionalized faith system, with shared traditions, doctrine, practices, and a community of followers. Through sacred scriptures and teachings, religions provide standards and prescriptions for personal virtue, relational conduct, and family life. Congregational affiliation provides clergy guidance and a community of shared faith,

347

providing support in times of need. Rituals and ceremonies carry profound significance, connecting families with their larger community, its history, and its survival over adversity. Religious belief systems provide faith explanations of major events, personal experiences, and passage to an afterlife.

Spirituality, a broad overarching construct, refers to transcendent beliefs and practices lived out in daily life and relationships. Spirituality is "the heart and soul" of religion (Pargament, 2007) and can also be experienced outside religious structures through active investment in personal faith and in humanistic values by those who are not religious.

Spirituality can best be seen as a dimension of human experience. As such, it requires an expansion of systems theory, research, and practice to encompass biopsychosocial–spiritual influences and their interplay in personal and relational well-being and in suffering, healing, and resilience (Marks, 2005). Like culture or ethnicity, spirituality involves streams of experience that flow through all aspects of life, from multigenerational heritage to shared belief systems and their expression in ongoing transactions, spiritual practices, and responses to adversity. It ebbs and surges in significance over the life course. With neurobiological linkages, it involves the most profound and genuine connection within the self, thought of as one's inner spirit, center of being, or soul. It includes ethical values and a moral compass, expanding consciousness to responsibility for and beyond oneself, with awareness of our interdependency. Thus, spirituality transcends the self: It fosters a sense of meaning, wholeness, harmony, and connection with all others—from the most intimate bonds to extended kinship and community networks, and to a unity with all life, nature, and the universe. This perspective is at the core of spiritual belief systems of ancient indigenous peoples worldwide, as in Asian, African, Aboriginal, and Native American visions of the unity of all creation.

Spiritual nourishment can be found in varied ways, whether through religion or not. Many who are not affiliated with faith communities, and who may not consider themselves "religious," lead deeply spiritual lives. Personal faith may (or may not) involve a belief in a supreme being, a divine spirit within all living things, or a striving toward an ultimate human condition. Even among atheists and agnostics, most hold a transcendent set of values, such as secular humanism, that guides actions and relationships. Spiritual resources might include contemplative practices, such as prayer or meditation, and traditional healing rituals. Renewal and connection are found through nature and expression in the arts. Meaning and purpose are found in compassionate service to those in need and in social action to right injustice and to repair and improve conditions in our world. Spirituality is inherently relational and finds its most immediate expression in couple and family bonds.

Spiritual Diversity in a Changing Society

As families have become more diverse and complex over recent decades, so too have their approaches to their spiritual life. The patterns described here primarily reflect developments in the United States, yet similar changes are occurring in many societies. A broad multifaith and multidimensional perspective can have useful practice applications across cultures.

Religion has been central in family life throughout American history. In recent surveys, over 85% of all Americans report that religion is important in their lives; over half regard it as very important, and nearly one-third consider it the most important part of their lives (Gallup, Inc., 2008). By contrast, most northern Europeans and Australians are far more secular; among the British, only 17% take religion very seriously. Both the United States and Canada, which have been overwhelmingly Christian and Protestant until recent decades, are increasingly diverse in spiritual beliefs and practices.

The religious landscape in North America has been changing dramatically over recent decades, largely through immigration and the desire to seek varied spiritual pathways (Pew Forum on Religion and Public Life, 2008; 2009). Currently over 75% of Americans identify as Christian (Gallup, Inc., 2008). Denominational affiliations have been shifting from Roman Catholic (now 23%) and mainline Protestant (under 14%) to evangelical churches, many nondenominational (Lindner, 2008). Over 40% of Christians (3 in 10 Americans) now identify as evangelical, "born again," or fundamentalist, which are overlapping groups (Gallup, Inc., 2008; Greeley & Hout, 2006). Mormons (Church of Jesus Christ of Latter-Day Saints), nearing 2% of all adults, are the fastest growing religious group.

Non-Christians have steadily increased to over 15% of the population (Smith, 2002). Close to 2% identify as Jewish, yet vary widely from Orthodox, Conservative, and Reform branches to secular humanism and ethnic connection (Kadushin, Phillips, & Saxe, 2005). Buddhists, Muslims, and Hindus, approaching 1% each, are increasing. Others follow ancient traditions such as Native American, Sikh, Shinto, and Tao. Some are drawn to religions offering a universality of faiths, such as Unitarian/Universalist and Baha'i, which avows "many lamps; one light."

Formal denominational affiliation, congregational membership, and attendance at worship services have been declining (Lindner, 2008; Pew Forum, 2008). Currently, 62% of adults belong to a church or synagogue, yet only 38% attend services weekly (mostly older women); 27% seldom or never attend. Still, there are over 500,000 churches, temples, mosques, and other places of worship—from small storefronts to megachurches—drawing tens of thousands of congregants.

Common Religious Beliefs

The vast majority of Americans believe in God, a Higher Power, or a Universal spirit. Only 6% are atheists and 8% are agnostic, uncertain about the existence of God (Gallup, Inc., 2008). Conceptions of God vary widely, from a "force" that maintains a balance in nature to a personal God, who watches over and judges people, guiding them in making decisions. The closer believers feel to God, the better they feel about themselves and others. Most people say their religious beliefs help them to solve problems, to respect themselves and others, to help those in need, and keep them from doing things they know they should not do. Most believe in virtue and sin, to be rewarded or punished in an afterlife, according to varied conceptions of heaven and hell or reincarnation.

Most people's faith is stronger than their knowledge of their religion. Although over 90% of homes contain a Bible, 58% of Americans could not name five of the Ten Commandments; moreover, 10% thought Joan of Arc was Noah's wife. Nearly half of all teens thought Moses was one of the 12 Apostles (Prothero, 2007)!

Intertwining of Cultural and Spiritual Influences

Spiritual beliefs and practices are interwoven with sociocultural influences and vary greatly across and within ethnic groups. In the United States, African Americans are the most religious group, from personal faith to active congregational participation (Gallup & Lindsay, 2000). Some are involved in historically black churches that have been vital resources since the time of slavery. All look to their faith for strength in dealing with adversity (Boyd-Franklin & Lockwood, 2009; see Boyd-Franklin & Karger, Chapter 12, this volume).

Latino families, fervent in their prayer and congregational involvement, are increasingly reshaping the Catholic church and are turning to evangelical Christian churches, particularly Pentecostal and Charismatic spirit-filled movements, for more direct experience of God (Pew Hispanic Project, 2007). For the great majority of Latinos, God is an active force in everyday life. Many report experiences of direct revelations and divine healing and miracles; contact with deceased loved ones; and transpersonal encounters with angels, demons, and other spiritual visitations.

Immigrants from Latin America, Asia, and Africa often combine traditional spiritual beliefs and practices, such as *espiritismo*, with Christianity (Falicov, 2009). Most turn to the church for weddings, christenings, and funerals, yet may also maintain special relationships with spiritual guides or shamans and continue ancient practices and rituals. Many believe in an invisible world inhabited by good and evil spirits that influence human behavior: they can protect or harm, prevent or cause illness, and bring good luck or misfortune (Pew, 2009). Incense, candles, objects, herbal remedies, and powders with mystical properties are used to cure illness and ward off the "evil eye." Many believe that they can communicate directly with the spirits of ancestors who, if honored appropriately, will confer their blessings and protect them.

Eastern medicine and indigenous healing approaches are often turned to for physical and emotional distress alongside Western medicine and psychotherapy, but patients may not mention them if not asked. In therapy with refugee youth from Sudan, Kamya (2009) found that crucial in their trauma recovery and resilience were both their Christian faith in God and their prayers to ancestors and animist powers in nature and the spirit world (Mbiti, 1970). It is important for clinicians to respectfully explore these beliefs and practices. Too often, they have been neglected, depreciated, or pathologized in Western clinical settings.

Spiritual approaches in families also vary with generational cohorts, social class, education, and urban or rural setting. Religious, cultural, or racial discrimination in the larger society can lead family members to band together in solidarity, suppress identification, or marry out to assimilate. Families in impoverished communities find strength through their faith and congregational involvement to counter despair at blighted conditions and injustices. Aponte (2009) contends that those who have become *dispirited*, losing hope and faith in their chances for a better life, suffer at the core a wounding of the soul, with a pervasive sense of helplessness and rage. He urges therapists to attend to spiritual as well as practical needs to help marginalized youth and their families find meaning, purpose, and connection in their lives.

It is crucial to guard against stereotypes and not link religion and ethnicity reflexively. For instance, only one-third of Arab Americans are Muslim—most are Christian. Over half of American Muslims are not Arab; many are African American, and others have come from diverse ethnic groups around the world (Daneshpour, 1998). Most Muslim American immigrants are largely assimilated, moderate in their political views, and happy with their lives, yet they face strong discrimination (Pew Forum on Religion and Public Life, 2007).

In a predominantly Christian society with European origins, scholars and clinicians must be mindful not to superimpose that template of values on other belief systems and practices. It is crucial not to judge diverse faith orientations, particularly those of ancient and indigenous cultures, as inferior or primitive. Religious intolerance, persecution, and holy wars to convert or annihilate nonbelievers have had catastrophic consequences throughout human times (Marty, 2005). Early European American conquerors viewed Native tribes as savage heathens who practiced pagan witchcraft. In government and missionary programs, children were forcibly taken from their families to boarding schools to educate and acculturate them in Christianity and Western ways, stripping them of their cultural and spiritual heritage. A recent resurgence of Native American spirituality is reconnecting families and youth, especially those at high risk of substance abuse and suicide, with the spiritual roots of their ancestors (Bucko, 2007; Deloria, 1994).

Increasing Independence and Blending in Spiritual Life

In recent decades, as global crises, societal dislocations, and family structural transformations have rendered life less secure and more challenging, families are seeking greater coherence, meaning, and connectedness in their lives. Many turn to their cherished traditions, yet increasingly others forge new spiritual paths. As families' relationship patterns and trajectories over a lengthening life course become more varied and complex, so too are their approaches to religion and spirituality. In our rapidly changing society, religion is less often a given that people are born into and accept unquestioningly. Strikingly, 44% do not follow the religion of their upbringing in their families of origin (Lindner, 2008).

Recent surveys (e.g., Pew Forum on Religion and Public Life, 2008, 2009) reveal that people are increasingly independent in their spiritual lives, picking and choosing among aspects of their faith to fit their lives and relationships, a trend called "religion à la carte" by Canadian sociologist Bibby (2002). Many blend varied approaches, such as Eastern Buddhist and Hindu practices, with their Christian or Jewish faith. Others convert to other religions or nondenominational churches, searching new spiritual pathways. While 16% of adults are unaffiliated with any religion, most who are unaffiliated regard personal faith or a broader spirituality as important in their lives. Interfaith marriage and multifaith families are on the rise. Although survey data tend to be individually focused, these trends bring complexity to family dynamics. As individuals and couples attempt to shape their own meaningful spiritual paths, relational and intergenerational differences can fuel tensions, conflict, and estrangement (Walsh, 2010).

Public attitudes across social issues such as gay marriage, gay adoption and parenting, abortion, and euthanasia, have been moderating, with growing acceptance (Pew Forum, 2008). The most conservative on these issues tend to be evangelical Protestants, older adults, and those less educated. Yet we must be cautious not to assume that particular individuals or their loved ones adhere to doctrines of their religion. Those who have a friend or family member who is gay are twice as likely to be supportive of gay rights. On reproductive rights, across the ideological spectrum, two-thirds support finding common ground, for example, making abortion available but rare. Among Catholics, over 60% believe that those who have abortions can still be good Catholics. Over 75% of Catholics disagree with the Church refusal to sanction divorce and remarriage (Gallup & Lindsay, 2000). There is a growing gap between personal faith and adherence to institutionalized religious systems. Most people regard decisions such as birth control, abortion, divorce, and assisted-dying as a matter between them, their loved ones, and God. In summary, most Americans are highly independent in their spiritual lives (Pew Forum on Religion and Public Life, 2008). Still, such issues can cause contention in couple and family relationships.

SPIRITUAL BELIEFS AND PRACTICES IN FAMILY LIFE

Spirituality is deeply interwoven in most aspects of family life, yet research is only starting to clarify its influences. A growing body of research has been examining the influences of spiritual beliefs, practices, and congregational involvement on family functioning, parenting styles, family dynamics, and intergenerational bonds (e.g., Bailey, 2002; Dollahite & Marks, 2009; Lambert & Dollahite, 2006; Mahoney, 2005; Mahoney & Tarakeshwar, 2005; Marks, 2006; Snarey & Dollahite, 2001; Snider, Clements, & Vazsonyi, 2004; see Mahoney, 2010, for a critical review). Researchers who study highly religious families are examining the role of religion in couple conflict (Lambert & Dollahite, 2006; Marsh & Dallos, 2001) and parent–child interactions (Marks, 2004).

The preponderance of research has focused on couple relationships. Family research to date is limited: Studies tend to be cross-sectional, not permitting causal associations; to be conducted predominantly with highly religious, white Christian families; to be based on self-report of one family member; and to use only one or two items to measure religious variables (e.g., affiliation, attendance, self-rated importance, and Biblical conservatism; Mahoney, 2010). Overall, studies suggest positive benefits of religion in family functioning, child development, and the quality and stability of relationships. More in-depth research is needed to better illuminate the beliefs and practices that help or hinder family members and their relationships.

Public surveys find that those who regard religion as the most important influence in their lives and receive a great deal of comfort from their faith are far more likely to feel close to their families, to find their jobs fulfilling, and to be hopeful about the future (Gallup & Lindsay, 2000). Over 80% say that religion was important in their family of origin when they were growing up. Although many do not follow the faith of their upbringing, nearly 75% report that their current family relationships have been strengthened by religion in their home.

Shared Transcendent Values

Family process research has found that transcendent values foster healthy family functioning (Beavers & Hampson, 2003): A shared belief system that transcends the limits of family members' experience enables better acceptance of the inevitable risks and losses in living and loving fully. Members can view their particular life challenges, however painful and uncertain, from a larger perspective that makes some sense of events, fosters hope, and strengthens their bonds and common humanity with others.

Family values became a hotly debated issue in recent decades as religious conservatives contended that nontraditional family forms and gender roles would destroy the family and damage children. There is growing recognition that faith institutions need to adapt to the diversity of contemporary family life (Edgell, 2005). Holding a single, outdated family model as the "paragon of virtue" contributes spiritual distress to stigma already experienced by single parents, same-sex parents, and others. Abundant research finds that most children thrive when raised in a variety of kinship arrangements and by gay as well as straight parents (see Walsh, Chapter 1, and Part II chapters, this volume).

The vast majority of families raise their children with strong moral and spiritual values in stable, caring, and committed bonds. Most uphold traditional values of commitment, responsibility, and investment in raising healthy children. Morality in their family life involves the activity of informed conscience orienting relationships and judging right or wrong, based on principles of fairness, decency, generosity, and compassion (Anderson, 2009; Doherty, 2009). Most value a spiritual dimension in their lives that fosters personal and relational well-being, positive growth, and concern for others. Most are giving and forgiving in their personal relationships. Of note, survey respondents (Gallup & Lindsay, 2000) have ranked "family ties, loyalty, and traditions" as the main factors thought to strengthen the family; next were "moral and spiritual values," which far outranked "family counseling" and "parent training classes."

The Dynamic Nature of Spirituality Over the Family Life Cycle

Spirituality is at the heart of our earliest, longest-lasting, and most intimate bonds. It profoundly influences—and is affected by—both individual and family development through dynamic processes that ebb and flow, shifting in salience and meaning over the life course and across the generations (Worthington, 1989). From a systems perspective, there is a mutual influence between spirituality and the family over time: Meaningful spiritual beliefs and practices can strengthen family units, their members, and their bonds; in turn, their shared spiritual experiences strengthen members' faith. Likewise, harsh or oppressive spiritual convictions and practices can wound family members, their spirits, and their relationships; in turn, those who have been injured often turn away from their families and their faith.

A developmental systemic orientation is required to appreciate the dynamic nature of spirituality. This perspective attends to the intertwining of individual, couple, parent–child, and extended family influences over time. Family systems are meaning-making communities with directionality and a life of their own (Anderson, 2009). Rooted in cultural, spiritual, and multigenerational traditions, each family constructs its own spirituality, which is transmitted through ongoing transactions. From the miracle of birth to the mystery of death and afterlife, spiritual matters are at the heart of family relations. Spiritual considerations arise with each family life phase and with major transitions. Critical events may heighten their saliency or spark new directions.

Across diverse faiths, believers seek wisdom in making decisions about whom and when to marry, spousal roles, and childrearing (Onedera, 2008). In all religions, the family is central in sacred rites and those that mark the birth of a new member, entry into the adult community, marriage vows, and the death of a loved one. For instance, the practice of Judaism is centered on the family observance of rituals, from weekly Shabbat (Sabbath) to important holidays, such as Passover, in the Jewish calendar year, and rites of passage (e.g., bat/bar mitzvah) in the life cycle. Each ritual carries significant meaning, connecting family members with their larger community and with the history of the Jewish people and their covenant with God.

Couple Relationships

Marriage and commitment vows as life partners bring spiritual considerations to the fore. Conflict may arise over whether to have a religious ceremony. Even partners of the same faith may differ in how they were raised and in their expectations for the observance of doctrine, roles, and customs in their shared life. Families of origin may exert pressures for wedding plans and future family life in line with their own convictions. This can fuel intergenerational conflict and in-law triangles that reverberate over the years.

Marital and commitment vows are inherently spiritual, whether or not they conform to religious orthodoxy, incorporating core values of love, honor, mutual respect, loyalty, and trust. Many regard the formation and mainte-nance of a family as integral in their search for the sacred (Mahoney, 2010). Many same-sex couples report that their union has divine significance and meaning (Rostosky, Riggle, Brodnicki, & Olson, 2008), one reason for the importance of gaining marriage rights.

For older couples, spouses who are similar in religious affiliation, beliefs, and practices report greater personal well-being and relationship satisfaction, less conflict and abuse, and lower likelihood of divorce than those who differ (Myers, 2006). Relationships are enhanced when couples share meaningful spiritual practices and rituals (Fiese & Tomcho, 2001). Strong religious com-mitment can support fragile marital bonds through times of conflict (Lambert & Dollahite, 2006).

Interfaith Marriage. Traditionally prohibited by many religions, inter-faith marriage has become widespread. Currently, nearly 40% of Americans are married to someone outside their faith (Pew Forum on Religion and Public Life, 2008). Some may choose a spouse from a different religious background to differentiate from their family of origin. In some cases, this may express a rebellion or alienation from oppressive religious or parental upbringing. How-ever, most often this choice is a natural outgrowth of broader social contacts in our multicultural society. Acceptance has increased with the support of interfaith movements and the blurring of racial and ethnic barriers. However, family disapproval can have long-lasting reverberations in intergenerational relations.

When partners follow separate religions, strong faith differences can complicate ordinary couple relationship issues and create discord (Curtis & Ellison, 2002). Under stress, tolerance can erode, particularly if one religious approach is upheld as right, true, or morally superior. In raising children, some couples decide to choose one faith; others attempt to combine faith approaches; still others postpone decisions to let children choose their spiritual path as they develop. More complications arise when parents maintain different faith identities and practices, and are involved in separate faith communities. Differences that initially attracted partners or seemed unimportant can become contentious as decisions arise regarding significant rites, such as communion, baptism, or bar/bat mitzvah.

Divorce and Remarriage. Although religion can strengthen marital bonds, a sizable number of religiously affiliated people have been divorced, including more socially conservative Christians (Barna Group, 2008). Both divorce and remarriage can be fraught with religious complications. For Orthodox Jews, a divorced woman wishing to remarry must obtain a "get," or written permission, from her ex-spouse, although a man is not required to do so. The Catholic Church regards marriage as a sacrament that cannot be dissolved and only sanctions remarriage in cases of annulment. Catholics who leave their marriage often leave the church. Many who wish to remarry decide instead simply to cohabit with a new partner. Some petition the church for annulment when planning remarriage. Annulments are now commonly granted, even after a long marriage and over objections of a spouse and children, who may be deeply wounded that their prior family life and legitimacy are invalidated. It is crucial to explore such conflict-laden issues in practice.

With divorce in interfaith marriages, faith differences can become entangled with relational hurts, retaliation, and control issues (Walsh, 2010). While the custodial parent has the right to determine the continuing religious upbringing of children, this can become highly contentious, especially in joint custody situations. Furthermore, the nonresident parent usually has visitation on weekends, when most religious education and worship take place.

Parent–Child Relationships

From earliest childhood, convictional faith is shaped within caregiving relationships. With childrearing come parental decisions about spiritual upbringing. Over time, open discussions and further decision making are needed as children mature, as faith preferences change, or as spiritual questions arise. Sometimes children draw parents back to their religious roots. Grandparents may strongly voice their faith convictions for the spiritual development of their grandchildren. Those who previously accepted their child's nontraditional, interfaith, or same-sex commitment may shift to concern for their grandchildren. As one Christian grandmother expressed, "I thought I was OK with it all, but when I hold my grandbaby and see how precious and vulnerable she is, I worry that if something terrible happened to her, she wouldn't go to heaven."

Studies of highly religious families find a beneficial role of faith in parent–child interactions (Mahoney, 2010). Underscoring the importance of the "lived experience" of religion and spirituality, what matters most in childrearing is that parents practice what they preach (Marks, 2004). When parents are congruent in transmitting and following their spiritual values in parenting their children, and when they engage in meaningful spiritual practices together, children are more likely to internalize similar beliefs and practices, to find them to be a resource, and to feel more positive about their relationships. Children and adolescents most value spiritual practices that are shared and integrated into family life, as in family prayer, special rituals and holidays, community service, and family attendance at worship services (Bartkowski, Xu, & Levin, 2008). Youth across faiths and cultures express strong interest in discussing life's meaning and how to make moral decisions (Coles, 1997; Gallup & Lindsay, 2000), underscoring the importance of open communication and exploration of spiritual matters between parents and youth (Brelsford & Mahoney, 2008; Dollahite & Thatcher, 2008).

Limited research exists on the role of religion in vulnerable and distressed families. Studies of low-income and disproportionately single-parent minority families suggest that religion can facilitate positive parenting in stressful contexts (Mahoney, 2010). Greater religious involvement and personal salience of God or spirituality has been linked to more maternal satisfaction, efficacy, authoritativeness, and consistency, as well as less parental distress. Involvement in religious communities is a strong protective factor for at-risk adolescent single mothers and their children, with lower depression and child maltreatment, and with higher socioemotional adjustment and educational and job attainment (Carothers, Borkowski, Lefever, & Whitman, 2005). Data from the National Longitudinal Study of Adolescent Health (Pearce & Haynie, 2004) show that when mothers and their adolescent children both consider religion important and attend religious services together, the children are less often delinquent. Here, again, religion tends to be protective through shared beliefs and practices.

Family Relations in Adulthood and Later Life

Young adults—particularly college students—often distance themselves from their religious upbringing. Some simply drift away, while others more actively question their family's traditions. Many who are searching for greater meaning and commitment in their lives explore other spiritual pathways. Some who choose to convert or marry outside their faith may be seeking to differentiate from their family of origin or to distance from their ethnic or religious background. Parents may perceive such a choice as a rejection of themselves and all they value, which may not be the case. However, in some instances, such choices may express a rebellion against religious or parental authority that was experienced as harsh and oppressive. Such issues should be sensitively explored in clinical practice. Therapists can facilitate greater mutual understanding and acceptance of differences.

Middle to later life is a time of growing saliency of spirituality, as older adults and midlife family members increasingly face the illness and death of loved ones, and confront their own vulnerabilities and mortality. Whether or not they are religious, most grapple with questions about the meaning of life and reflect on their own personal and relational conduct and legacies (Walsh, 2011). In later life, there is a developmental striving toward *meaning*, connection, and continuity within older adults' multigenerational family system—those who came before and those who will come after them. Efforts to reconcile relational grievances (Fishbane, 2009) and gain a sense of *family integrity* (King & Wynne, 2004) generate a deep and abiding sense of peace and satisfaction with past, present, and future family relationships.

Facing Death and Loss

When families face end-of-life challenges, spiritual concerns can weigh heavily on life-and-death decisions (Walsh, 2009c). Now that medical advances and life support technology call into question just what is a "natural death," families face morally anguishing dilemmas and may grapple with religious prohibitions about hastening or assisting death. Those who believe in an afterlife may also be profoundly concerned about the fate of a loved one who has sinned or left the family's faith.

Coming to terms with death and loss involves multiple losses: the person; the spousal or family role; each unique relationship; and shattered hopes and dreams for the future (Walsh & McGoldrick, 2004). Death ends a life but not relationships, which are transformed from physical presence to ongoing spiritual connections, sustained through memory, dreams, rituals, conversations, stories, and legacies (Walsh, 2009c). Many believe that the spirits of ancestors may haunt or cause harm; however, if honored appropriately, they will confer their blessings and protection. How families handle loss can facilitate or hinder the adaptation of all members and their relationships. Spiritual beliefs, practices, and support of a faith community can facilitate coping, adaptation, and resilience (Greef & Joubert, 2007).

Continuity and Change

Across the family life cycle, spirituality in many families involves a lifelong, faithful adherence to a shared religious tradition. Yet, increasingly, spiritual expression assumes varied forms and substance as family members forge meaning and connection in life pursuits and significant relationships. Therefore, it is important to explore both continuities and changes over time, and help families respect differences and attempt to blend them.

Patriarchy and Changing Gender Role Relations

Patriarchy, an ancient and enduring cultural pattern embedded in most religious traditions, has been a dominant force in family life. At its worst, it has sanctioned—or it has been used to justify—the subjugation and abuse of women and harsh corporal punishment of children (Bottoms, Shaver,

Goodman, & Qin, 1995; Ellison & Anderson, 2001; Ellison & Broadshaw, 2009; Gunnoe, Hetherington, & Reiss, 2006; Murray-Swank, Mahoney, & Pargament, 2006). A legacy of the devaluation of females has been the abandonment, sexual trafficking, infanticide, and abortion of unwanted daughters in many parts of the world.

Within conservative religious groups, most women adhere to their deep faith convictions when they are treated with respect and valued for their centrality in family life as mothers, caregivers, and keepers of the hearth. However, when relationships are highly skewed in power, privilege, and control, men are more likely to act violently when conflict arises as women assert their needs or challenge authority (Kimball & Knudson-Martin, 2002). Some devout wives stay in abusive situations to adhere to religious precepts to keep their families intact. Increasingly, abuse of wives and children leads women to separate and divorce, which also alienate many from their religious roots. Many find new meaning and esteem through more progressive faith communities.

Over recent decades, traditional gender role relations and childrearing practices have been in transformation in couples and families worldwide (see Knudson-Martin, Chapter 14, this volume). Among Evangelical Christians, men tend to maintain patriarchal expectations for the husband/father to be the "spiritual head" of the family. Wilcox (2004) terms them "soft patriarchs": authoritative and strict, yet less authoritarian and more warm and expressive in interactions than past generations. Mainline Protestant men tend toward a more egalitarian position in marriage and in sharing household responsibilities (Anderson, 2009).

Sexual Orientation and Heterosexual Orthodoxy

The condemnation of homosexuality in religious doctrine has been a source of deep anguish for lesbian, gay, bisexual, and transgender (LGBT) persons. Some denominations have adopted a loving acceptance of gay persons as human beings created by God, yet abhor same-sex practices as unnatural and sinful, and oppose gay marriage and parenting. This dualistic position ("hate the sin, but love the sinner") perpetuates stigma and shame, producing a deep schism in an individual's gender identity and sexual orientation. Many have abandoned their childhood faith, feeling that to accept themselves, they must reject their religion. Increasingly, many religious clergy and congregations have been challenging institutional orthodoxy for the full acceptance of persons and relationships of diverse sexual orientation as human rights issues for equality and social justice. Yet LGBT persons may still confront heterosexist religiosity in their family or social networks and community. Family conflict and cutoff can be fueled by members' religious convictions or congregational stance.

The diversity among LGBT individuals, couples, and families requires an especially broad approach to spirituality. The challenges presented by religious dogma have not undermined the importance of spirituality for most (Tan, 2005). Some focus on their personal relationship with a God that loves them unconditionally (Lease & Shulman, 2003). Many seek out gay-inclusive faith communities, and focus on self-exploration and spiritual growth. Some turn to alternative approaches, such as earth-spirited faith (Smith & Horne, 2007) that emphasize personal versus institutional authority over spiritual matters.

SPIRITUAL RESOURCES IN FAMILY LIFE

Abundant research documents the powerful influence of spiritual beliefs and practices for well-being, recovery, and resilience (Koenig, 2005; Walsh, 2009b). Although affiliation and adherence to formal religion have been declining, what matters for most is a deep personal spirituality, guided by values that are lived out in daily lives and relationships (Wendel, 2003). Many, varied spiritual practices can enrich family relationships as they deepen the spiritual dimension of family life.

Contemplative Practices: Prayer, Meditation, and Shared Rituals

For most people, prayer originates in the family, is centered in the home, and grows in importance over the life course. Among Americans, 90% pray in some fashion at least weekly; three in four pray daily (Gallup, Inc., 2008). Prayer at bedtime and expressing gratitude before meals are common practices. Most people report that they pray whenever they feel the need. As one single parent said, "I talk to God to help my family get through hard times. We need that higher power to help us when we suffer illness or money problems or when my children get into trouble."

Families of all faiths value some form of prayer or meditation, which serves many functions. Almost all people pray for their family's health and happiness; very few pray for bad tidings for others. People commonly pray for strength, wisdom, or courage in facing life challenges. Many pray to seek forgiveness for sins, wrongdoing, or harm to others. Some request intercession or miracles in precarious situations, such as when a loved one's life is at risk. Others pray that God's will be done. Most who pray believe it makes them better persons. Nearly all report that their prayers have been heard and answered. Most say they received what they hoped for, as well as divine inspiration or a feeling of being led by God. Some (30%) have had long periods when they stopped praying, most because they got out of the habit. A few stopped because they had lost their faith, were angry with God or their church, or felt their prayers had not been answered (Gallup & Lindsay, 2000).

Contemplative practices generate feelings of tranquility, wholeness, hope, and peace. These may involve mindfulness practices, yoga, and other Eastern traditions; sacred or inspirational music or texts; chanting, reciting a rosary, use of prayer beads or a mantra; or rituals such as lighting candles or incense.

Catholics commonly offer prayers to patron Saints for guidance or intercession with God. Hindu meditation and offerings to various gods take place mostly in the home, before small statues and shrines. One of the five pillars of Islam is ritual prayer observance, five times daily. For Muslims, prayer expresses praise and gratitude for life itself and helps to keep life in perspective (Nasr, 2002). Many who are not religious value contemplative practices for physical, psychological, and spiritual well-being. Shared meditative experiences by couples and family members foster genuine and empathic relating, reduce defensive reactivity, and deepen bonds (Carson, Carson, Gil, & Baucom, 2004; Gale, 2009; Nhat Hahn, 2003).

Rituals and ceremonies connect individuals with their families and communities, as well as guiding them through life passage and times of adversity (Imber-Black, Roberts, & Whiting, 2003; see Imber-Black, Chapter 20, this volume). They facilitate unfamiliar transitions, script family actions, and comfort the dying and the bereaved. Rituals mark important events in family life and faith traditions. Couple relationships are enhanced by sharing meaningful spiritual rituals (Fiese & Tomcho, 2001). They also connect a particular joy or tragedy with all human experience, a birth or death with all others. In work with families, the observance, blending, and invention of meaningful rituals can be encouraged. This can be especially valuable for interfaith couples and multifaith families.

Involvement in Faith Communities

Congregations that flourish are vibrant communities of faith, offering a sense of belonging to a spiritual home and family (Kamya, 2009), as well as a wide range of programs to meet varied needs, through scripture reading groups, choir singing, potluck suppers, and community service. Many offer marriage and parenting skills workshops, youth mentoring, teen programs, job skills training, preventive health care, counseling, and meaningful involvement of seniors. Congregants in distress often turn to their clergy before mental health professionals. In religious study groups and support groups, as in other activities, members gain a sense of interdependence with others of shared values.

Communion with Nature

Many families, whether religious or not, find deep connection and nourishment through communion with nature—a walk at sunrise or the rhythm of waves on the shore; a camping trip; tending a garden or in a bond with a companion animal (Walsh, 2009a). Such immediate experiences take us into the moment and beyond ourselves, making us feel at one with other life and the universe. Many are drawn to visit places with high spiritual energy—sacred mountains, shrines, cathedrals, mosques, and temples; vistas of natural beauty and wonder. Living in harmony with nature and the environment is at the heart of the spirituality of indigenous communities.

Creative Arts Expression/Appreciation

Across cultures, people find inspiration in the creative arts, such as painting, poetry, and drama, that communicate our common humanity. Music in many forms can offer a powerful, transcendent experience. Native Americans say, "To watch us dance is to hear our hearts speak." African American gospel spirituals, blues, jazz, and soul music are creative expressions forged out of the cauldron of slavery, racism, and impoverished conditions, transcending those scarring experiences through the resilience of the human spirit.

Community Service/Social Activism

Engaging in community service or social activism can be a transformative expression of spirituality. Efforts to alleviate suffering and to mend the social fabric (e.g., Judaism's *tikkun olam*) are at the heart of all major faith traditions and humanistic movements (Perry & Rolland, 2009). When family members share in purposeful efforts, it strengthens their bonds as it deepens compassion and connection with others. A tragedy can spark new purpose. In one family, after the suicide of a beloved daughter who had suffered with bipolar disorder, the parents organized an annual community forum in her memory to advocate for mental health research, treatment, and prevention to benefit others. Therapists can listen for such inspiration: the urge to make a difference, to act so that something good might come out of a tragedy and in doing so further a family's own healing.

Intimate Bonds and Transcendent Connections

Intimate bonds with authentic communication are the most immediate and profound expressions of spirituality and offer pathways for spiritual and relational growth (Fishbane, 1998). We experience deep connections with "kindred spirits" and "soul mates." Caring bonds with partners, family members, and close friends can nourish spiritual well-being; in turn spirituality deepens and expands our connections with all others. It can be spiritually enriching to care for an infant or a frail elder, to befriend neighbors, or to offer kindness to strangers. Faith, intimacy, and resilience are interwoven: Love sustains lives, infuses them with meaning, and supports faith in overcoming adversity (Frankl, 1964/1984). Efforts to heal relational wounds and to seek or offer forgiveness are encouraged by all faith traditions (Fincham, Hall, & Beach, 2006; Hargrave, Froeschle, & Castillo, 2009; Legaree, Turner, & Lollis, 2007).

The transcendent connectedness of family and community is forged through shared values, commitment, and mutual support through adversity. In contrast to the highly individualized concept of human autonomy centered on the "self" in Western societies, most cultures and religions worldwide view the person as embedded within the family and larger community. Despite the diversity of perspectives, the broad aim of spirituality remains constant: to be open to the transcendent dimension of life and all relationships, both in ordinary, everyday activity and in the midst of adversity.

FROM MULTIFAITH DIVERSITY TO SPIRITUAL PLURALISM

The wide spectrum of faiths today attests to their strength and vitality. A broader spirituality is expected to continue in significance over the coming decades, shaped less by institutions and more by those who are seeking greater meaning and connection. In our rapidly changing world, religion is less often a given that people are born into and accept unquestioningly. Increasingly, individuals, couples, and families are forging their own spiritual paths, choosing among beliefs and practices to fit their life circumstances and relationships. This combining of varied elements has been likened to a platter of "religious linguini" (Deloria, 1994). Many are creating their own recipes for spiritual nourishment.

Our challenge is to move from a recognition of diversity to a spiritual pluralism (Eck, 2006). "Diversity" refers simply to many differences—splendid, colorful, perhaps threatening. "Spiritual pluralism" involves engagement and relationship with each other that creates a common society from multifaith diversity. Interfaith coalitions tackle shared concerns such as teen pregnancy, hunger, and homelessness, and galvanize support for disaster recovery and peace initiatives (see Harvard's Pluralism Project at *www.pluralism.org*).

With respect—more than the tolerance—of differences, pluralism requires understanding of both distinctiveness and commonalities. It involves broad inclusiveness of people of every faith, and of none, nurturing constructive dialogue, mutual understanding, and connectedness. Similarly, with growing spiritual diversity within families, members who follow different paths can strengthen bonds by engaging in dialogue, respect, and mutual understanding and coalescing around shared values and practices. With the increase of interfaith couples and multifaith families, this broad spiritual pluralism is all the more important (Walsh, 2010).

ADDRESSING THE SPIRITUAL DIMENSION IN CLINICAL PRACTICE

Spiritual beliefs and practices influence the ways that families deal with adversity, their experience of suffering, and the meaning of symptoms (Wright, 2009). They also influence how family members communicate about their problems; their explanatory assumptions and future expectations; their attitudes toward helpers—physicians, therapists, clergy, or faith healers; the treatments they seek; and their preferred pathways in recovery. To be most helpful to families, clinicians need to understand their suffering, and often its injustice or senselessness. Many therapists feel ill equipped in their training, constrained from broaching the subject with clients, and uncomfortable when it does arise. When clients sense that spirituality does not belong in the clinical context, they may censor themselves from bringing this aspect of their lives into the therapeutic conversation.

A collaborative, biopsychosocial–spiritual systems approach to practice is valuable in overcoming barriers to integrate spirituality in clinical practice, in particular:

1. *Forging linkages.* Viewing clinical and pastoral domains as complementary and important to bridge through mutual referral, consultation, and collaboration. It is also important for clinicians to become acquainted with local congregational resources and faith-based health care and human services that fit their clients' spiritual needs and preferences.

2. *Fostering collaboration and empowerment.* Inescapably, all therapeutic work involves the interaction of therapists' and clients' value systems. Therefore, clinicians need to deepen awareness of their own spiritual beliefs and biases, and be mindful not to impose them on vulnerable clients. Therapists best respect families by showing active interest in exploring and understanding *their* values, practices, and concerns, as with other sociocultural aspects of their lives. In working collaboratively, therapists reflect power back in ways that empower family members, strengthening family resilience (Walsh, 2006; see Walsh, Chapter 17, this volume).

In efforts to integrate the spiritual dimension of experience in clinical training and practice, the following guidelines are helpful:

- *Inquire respectfully about the meaning and importance of religious and/or spiritual beliefs and practices* in individual, couple, and family life and in relation to presenting problems and coping efforts.
  - Spiritual ecomaps, genograms, and other assessment tools can be helpful (Hodge, 2005; McGoldrick, Gerson, & Petry, 2008).
  - Convey a broad, multifaith perspective.
- *Explore spiritual sources of distress*, concerns that contribute to suffering or block personal and relational well-being:
  - Facilitate communication, understanding, and mutual respect around religious/spiritual conflicts in couples and families.
  - Facilitate compassion and possibilities for reconciliation and forgiveness in wounded relationships.

- *Identify spiritual resources* (current, past, or potential) that might contribute to healing and resilience. Encourage clients to draw on those—within or outside organized religion—that fit their values and preferences, including
  - Contemplative practices (prayer, meditation); rituals
  - Relationship with God or Higher Power
  - Involvement in faith community; pastoral guidance
  - Communion with nature
  - Expressive/creative arts
  - Service to others; social activism
  - Intimate bonds and connections.

With growing cultural and spiritual diversity among Americans, it is crucial not to make assumptions about personal beliefs and practices based on clients' religious identification or upbringing. It is important to explore the dynamic nature and significance of spirituality in their lives and relationships over time. If an upbringing has not been followed, how has that affected family relationships? If clients are not religious and do not think of themselves as "spiritual," how do they—or might they—find strength, meaning, connection, and nourishment in facing life challenges? What beliefs and practices could support their resilience, bolster their efforts, and strengthen their bonds? It is important to respect atheists' nonbelief in God or an afterlife, exploring their views of a meaningful life and fulfilling relationships (Smith-Stoner, 2007). Some who have not been religious find that a serious crisis becomes an epiphany, opening lives to a spiritual dimension previously untapped. It can crystallize important matters and spark a reappraisal and redirection of life priorities and pursuits, as well as greater investment in significant bonds.

Exploring Spiritual Sources of Distress

Many families who suffer emotional or relational problems are also in spiritual distress or unable to invest life with meaning, which can impede coping and mastery in the face of life challenges. In addressing spirituality in its clinical complexities, its potential for harm as well as healing should be considered (Elliott Griffith & Griffith, 2002).

Spiritual beliefs can become harmful, intentionally or not, if held too narrowly, rigidly, or punitively (Griffith, 2010). Overly harsh authoritarian parenting, summoning images of a wrathful, vengeful God, can alienate members from their family and faith. Injecting spiritual superiority into relational differences or triangling God into the middle of conflicts (i.e., supporting one side against the other) has a corrosive effect (Butler & Harper, 1994). An affair with a "soul mate" may be a devasating betrayal of one's spouse and children. A spiritual wound, as can occur with the relational trauma of sexual abuse, can block the ability to invest life with meaning or to trust others.

Religious ideations or experiences fostering guilt, shame, or worthlessness may contribute to addictions, destructive behavior, self-harm, or social isolation. Clinicians need to consider religious aspects of individual and family distress, such as concerns about sin, punishment, and afterlife.

Spiritual matters come to the fore with traumatic events, particularly with death and loss. Spiritual distress can spark relational conflict and complicate grief and adaptation for the family and all its members (Walsh, 2009c). The untimely death of an "innocent" child is often viewed as unjust and can affect the spiritual life of the bereaved. Religious condemnation of suicide compounds the anguish of families; final rites and cemetery burial may not be allowed. Such spiritual issues complicate an agonizing death and loss for the entire family and can spark intense conflict (Walsh & McGoldrick, 2004). Some draw closer to their faith, whereas others question or turn away from faith and family.

When patriarchal religious precepts are used to justify violence toward women and children, family therapists have an ethical responsibility to protect those in harms way and to address abusive behavior, whether rooted in family, ethnic, or religious beliefs and traditions. Therapists can engage in terms of transcendent values across faiths, which condemn violence and teach loving kindness, justice, and respect, honoring the dignity and worth of loved ones (Anderson, 2009). When the sexual orientation of a family member is a source of pain or cutoff in families that hold conservative religious views, therapists may be helpful in opening dialogue to facilitate understanding and loving acceptance. Unfounded fears of harm to children raised by gay parents can be allayed by information from research evidence of their well-being (see Walsh, Chapter 1, and Green, Chapter 8, this volume).

Many who seek help not only need to solve immediate problems but also yearn for greater meaning and purpose in life. Spiritual wellsprings can be tapped to offer a larger vision of humanity and meaningful connections that inspires their best potential. Clinicians can encourage clients to identify and draw on a wide range of potential spiritual resources that fit their values and preferences (Helmeke & Sori, 2006; Walsh, 2009d). As Pargament (2007) underscores, spiritual resources are not simply another problem-solving tool or set of therapeutic techniques. Instead, they are embedded in a larger worldview and facilitate the spiritual journey of an individual, couple, or family. They are resources for living and struggling with life's challenges and dilemmas. They can enable our clients to tap reservoirs of hope, meaning, and inspiration.

The growing diversity and complexity of contemporary families in their approach to religion and spirituality require a broadly inclusive, multifaith perspective in clinical practice. Despite differences of faith orientation, the overarching aim of spirituality is to be open to the transcendent dimension of life and all relationships, both in everyday practice and in adversity. With a spiritual pluralism and appreciative inquiry, therapists can respect the dignity, worth, and potential of all family members and support their spiritual journey in seeking greater meaning, connection, and fulfillment as they move forward in their lives.

NOTE

1. Pew and Gallup organizations conduct the most widely respected surveys on religion in the United States. Survey data offer valuable perspectives yet are often not directly comparable and variously report religious "identification," adherence," "affiliation," or "membership." Also, research that categorizes subjects by their stated religion does not capture intragroup variation, the lived experience of faith, or the dynamic and complex nature of spiritual life within and outside religion.

USEFUL WEBSITES

www.religions.pewforum.org—a major source of public survey data and links to news articles on wide range of topics concerning religion and spirituality.
www.pluralism.org/resources—Pluralism Project at Harvard; offers information on a wide spectrum of faith orientations, multifaith perspectives, and interfaith initiatives.
www.beliefnet.org—offers a wide variety of spiritual resources for the general public.

REFERENCES

Anderson, H. (2009). A spirituality for family living. In F. Walsh (Ed.), *Spiritual resources in family therapy* (2nd ed., pp. 194–211). New York: Guilford Press.
Aponte, H. (2009). The stresses of poverty and the comfort of spirituality. In F. Walsh (Ed.), *Spiritual resources in family therapy* (2nd ed., pp. 125–140). New York: Guilford Press.
Bailey, C. E. (2002). The effects of spiritual beliefs and practices on family functioning: A qualitative study. *Journal of Family Psychotherapy, 13*(1–2), 127–144.
Barna Group. (2008, March 31). New marriage and divorce statistics released. Retrieved December 20, 2010, from *www.barna.org/topics/faith-spirituality*.
Barnes, S., Brown, K. W., Krusemark, E., Campbell, W. K., & Rogge, R. D. (2007). The role of mindfulness in romantic relationship satisfaction and responses to relationship stress. *Journal of Marital and Family Therapy, 33*, 482–500.
Bartkowski, J. P., Xu, X. H., & Levin, M. L. (2008). Religion and child development: Evidence from the early childhood longitudinal study. *Social Science Research, 37*, 18–36.
Beavers, W. R., & Hampson, R. B. (2003). Measuring family competence: The Beavers Systems Model. In F. Walsh (Ed.), *Normal family processes* (3rd ed., pp. 549–580). New York: Guilford Press.
Bibby, R. W. (2002). *Restless Gods: The renaissance of religion in Canada*. Toronto: Stoddard.
Bottoms, B. L., Shaver, P. R., Goodman, G. S., & Qin, J. (1995). In the name of God: A profile of religion-related child abuse. *Journal of Social Issues, 51*, 85–111.

Boyd-Franklin, N., & Lockwood, T. W. (2009). Spirituality and religion: Implications for therapy with African American families. In F. Walsh (Ed.), *Spiritual resources in family therapy* (2nd ed., pp. 141–155). New York: Guilford Press.

Bucko, R. (2007). Native American families and religion. In D. S. Browning & D. A. Clairmont (Eds.), *American religions and the family* (pp. 70–86). New York: Columbia University Press.

Butler, M. H., & Harper, J. M. (1994). The divine triangle: God in the marital system of religious couples. *Family Process, 33,* 277–286.

Carothers, S. S., Borkowski, J. G., Lefever, J. B., & Whitman, T. L. (2005). Religiosity and the socio-emotional adjustment of adolescent mothers and their children. *Journal of Family Psychology, 19*(2), 263–275.

Carson, J. W., Carson, K. M., Gil, K. M., & Baucom, D. H. (2004). Mindfulness-based relationship enhancement. *Behavior Therapy, 35,* 471–494.

Coles, R. (1997). *The moral intelligence of children.* New York: Random House.

Curtis, K. T., & Ellison, C. G. (2002). Religious heterogamy and marital conflict: Findings from the national survey of families and households. *Journal of Family Issues, 23,* 551–576.

Daneshpour, M. (1998). Muslim families and family therapy. *Journal of Marital and Family Therapy, 24,* 355–368.

Deloria, V., Jr. (1994). *God is red: A native view of religion* (2nd ed.). Golden, CO: Fulcrum.

Doherty, W. J. (2009). Morality and spirituality in therapy. In F. Walsh (Ed.), *Spiritual resources in family therapy.* (2nd ed., pp. 215–228). New York: Guilford Press.

Dollahite, D. C., & Marks, L. D. (2009). A conceptual model of family and religious processes in a diverse, national sample of highly religious families. *Review of Religious Research, 51,* 373–391.

Dollahite, D. C., & Thatcher, J. Y. (2008). Talking about religion: How religious youth and parents discuss their faith. *Journal of Adolescent Research, 23,* 611–641.

Eck, D. (2006). *On common ground: World religions in America.* New York: Columbia University Press.

Edgell, P. (2005). *Religion and family in a changing society.* Princeton, NJ: Princeton University Press.

Elliott Griffith, M., & Griffith, J. (2002). Addresing spirituality in its clinical complexities: Its potential for healing, its potential for harm. *Journal of Family Psychotherapy, 13,* 167–194.

Ellison, C. G., & Anderson, K. L. (2001). Religious involvement and domestic violence among U.S. couples. *Journal for the Scientific Study of Religion, 40,* 269–286.

Ellison, C. G., & Broadshaw, M. (2009). Religious beliefs, sociopolitical ideology, and attitudes toward corporal punishment. *Journal of Family Issues, 20,* 87–113.

Falicov, C. J. (2009). Religion and spiritual traditions in immigrant families: Significance for Latino health and mental health. In F. Walsh (Ed.), *Spiritual resources in family therapy* (2nd ed., pp. 156–173). New York: Guilford Press.

Fiese, B. H., & Tomcho, T. J. (2001). Finding meaning in religious practices: The relation between holiday rituals and marital satisfaction. *Journal of Family Psychology, 15*(4), 597–609.

Fincham, F. D., Beach, S. R., Lambert, N. M., Stillman, T., & Braithwaite, S. (2008). Spiritual behaviors and relationship satisfaction: A critical analysis of the role of prayer. *Journal of Social and Clinical Psychology, 27,* 362–388.

Fincham, F. D., Hall, J., & Beach, S. (2006). Forgiveness in marriage: Current status and future directions. *Family Relations, 55*(4), 415–427.

Fishbane, M. (1998). I, thou, and we: A dialogical approach to couples therapy. *Journal of Marital and Family Therapy, 24,* 41–58.

Fishbane, M. (2009). Honor your father and your mother. In F. Walsh (Ed.), *Spiritual resources in family therapy* (2nd ed., pp. 174–193). New York: Guilford Press.

Frankl, V. (1984). *Man's search for meaning.* New York: Simon & Schuster. (Original work published 1946)

Gale, J. (2009). Meditation and relational connectedness: Practices for couples and families. In F. Walsh (Ed.), *Spiritual resources in family therapy* (2nd ed., pp. 247–266). New York: Guilford Press.

Gallup, G. H., Jr., & Lindsay, D. M. (2000). *Surveying the religious landscape: Trends in U.S. beliefs.* Harrisburg, PA: Morehouse.

Gallup, Inc. (2008). *Religion* (Survey data summaries). Retrieved March 14, 2008, from *www.gallup.com/poll/1690/religion.*

Greef, A. P., & Joubert, A. M. (2007). Spirituality and resilience in families in which a parent has died. *Psychological Reports, 100*(3), 897–900.

Greeley, A., & Hout, M. (2006). *The facts about conservative Christians.* Chicago: University of Chicago Press.

Griffith, J. L. (2010). *Religion that heals, religion that harms: A guide for clinical practice.* New York: Guilford Press.

Greef, A. P., & Joubert, A. M. (2007). Spirituality and resilience in families in which a parent has died. *Psychological Reports, 100*(3), 897–900.

Gunnoe, M. L., Hetherington, E. M., & Reiss, D. (2006). Differential impact of fathers' authoritarian parenting on early adolescent adjustment in conservative Protestant versus other families. *Journal of Family Psychology, 20,* 589–596.

Hargrave, T., Froeschle, J., & Castillo, Y. (2009). Forgiveness and spirituality: Elements of healing. In F. Walsh (Ed.), *Spiritual resources in family therapy* (2nd ed., pp. 301–322). New York: Guilford Press.

Helmeke, K., & Sori, K. (2006). *The therapist's notebook for integrating spirituality in counseling* (Vols. 1 & 2). New York: Haworth.

Hill, P. C., & Pargament, K. I. (2003). Advances in the conceptualization and measurement of religion and spirituality: Implications for physical and mental health research. *American Psychologist, 58,* 64–74.

Hodge, D. R. (2005). Spiritual assessment in marital and family therapy: A methodological framework for selecting from among six qualitative assessment tools. *Journal of Marital and Family Therapy, 31*(4), 341–356.

Imber-Black, E., Roberts, J., & Whiting, R. (Eds.). (2003). *Rituals in families and family therapy* (2nd ed.). New York: Norton.

Kadushin, C., Phillips, B. T., & Saxe, L. (2005). National Jewish Population Survey, 2000–2001: A guide for the perplexed. *Contemporary Jewry, 25,* 1–32.

Kamya, H. (2009). Healing from refugee trauma. In F. Walsh (Ed.), *Spiritual resources in family therapy* (2nd ed., pp. 286–300). New York: Guilford Press.

Kimball, L. S., & Knudson-Martin, C. (2002). A cultural trinity: Spirituality, religion, and gender in clinical practice. *Journal of Family Psychotherapy, 13*(1–2), 145–166.

King, D. A., & Wynne, L. C. (2004). The emergence of "family integrity" in later life. *Family Process, 43*(1), 7–21.

King, V. (2003). The influence of religion on fathers' relationships with their children. *Journal of Marriage and Family, 65*, 382–395.

Koenig, H. (2005). *Faith and mental health: Resources for healing.* Conshohacken, PA: Templeton Press.

Lambert, N., & Dollahite, D. (2006). How religiosity helps couples prevent, resolve, and overcome marital conflict. *Family Relations, 55*(4), 439–449.

Lease, S. H., & Shulman, J. L. (2003). A preliminary investigation of the role of religion for family members of lesbian, gay male, or bisexual individuals. *Counseling and Values, 47*, 195–209.

Legaree, T.-A., Turner, J., & Lollis, S. (2007). Forgiveness and therapy: A critical review of conceptualizations, practices, and values found in the literature. *Journal of Marital and Family Therapy, 33*, 192–213.

Lindner, E. W. (2008). *Yearbook of American and Canadian churches: 2008* (73rd ed.). New York: National Council of Churches in the USA.

Mahoney, A. (2005). Religion and conflict in marital and parent–child relationships. *Journal of Social Issues, 61*, 689–706.

Mahoney, A. (2010). Religion in the home 1999 to 2009: A relational spirituality perspective. *Journal of Marriage and Family, 68*, 292–304.

Mahoney, A., & Tarakeshwar, N. (2005). Religion's role in marriage and parenting in daily life and during family crises. In R. F. Paloutzian & C. L. Park (Eds.), *Handbook of the psychology of religion and spirituality* (pp. 177–198). San Francisco: Jossey-Bass.

Marks, L. (2004). Sacred practices in highly religious families: Christian, Jewish, Mormon, and Muslim perspectives. *Family Process, 43*(2), 217–231.

Marks, L. (2005). Religion and bio-psycho-social health: A review and conceptual model. *Journal of Religion and Health, 44*, 173–186.

Marks, L. (2006). Religion and family relational health: Overview and conceptual model. *Journal of Religion and Health, 45*(4) 603–618.

Marsh, R., & Dallos, R. (2001). Roman Catholic couples: Wrath and religion. *Family Process, 40*(3), 343–360.

Marty, M. E. (2005). *When faiths collide.* Malden, MA: Blackwell.

Mbiti, J. S. (1970). *African religions and philosophy.* Garden City, NY: Anchor.

McGoldrick, M., Gerson, R., & Petry, S. (2008). *Genograms: Assessment and intervention* (3rd ed.). New York: Norton.

Murray-Swank, A., Mahoney, A., & Pargament, K. I. (2006). Sanctification of parenting: Influences on corporal punishment and warmth by liberal and conservative Christian mothers. *International Journal of the Psychology of Religion, 16*, 271–287.

Myers, S. (2006). Religious homogamy and marital quality: Historical and generational patterns. *Journal of Marriage and Family, 68*(2), 292–304.

Nasr, S. H. (2002). *The heart of Islam: Enduring values for humanity.* New York: HarperCollins.

Nhat Hahn, T. (2003). *Creating true peace: Ending violence in yourself, your family, your community.* Berkeley, CA: Parallax Press.

Onedera, J. D. (Ed.). (2008). *The role of religion in marriage and family counseling.* New York: Routledge.

Pargament, K. I. (2007). *Spiritually integrated psychotherapy: Understanding and addressing the sacred.* New York: Guilford Press.

Pearce, L. D., & Haynie, D. L. (2004). Intergenerational religious dynamics and adolescent delinquency. *Social Forces, 82*(4), 1533–1572.

Perry, A. de V., & Rolland, J. S. (2009). Therapeutic benefits of a justice-seeking spirituality: Empowerment, healing, and hope. In F. Walsh (Ed.), *Spiritual resources in family therapy*. (2nd ed., pp. 379–396). New York: Guilford Press.

Pew Forum on Religion and Public Life. (2006, August 3). Public divided in social issues, but no "culture war." Retrieved May 7, 2007, from *religions.pewforum. org.*

Pew Forum on Religion and Public Life. (2007, May 22). *Muslim Americans: Middle class and mostly mainstream.* Retrieved March 14, 2008, from *religions.pewforum.org.*

Pew Forum on Religion and Public Life. (2008). U.S. Religious Landscape Survey. Retrieved January 24, 2010, from *religions.pewforum.org.*

Pew Forum on Religion and Public Life. (2009). *Many Americans mix multiple faiths: Eastern, new age beliefs widespread.* Retrieved January 24, 2010, from *religions.pewforum.org.*

Pew Hispanic Project. (2007, April). *Changing faiths: Latinos and the transformation of American religion.* Retrieved February 26, 2008, from *religions.pewforum.org.*

Prothero, S. (2007). *Religious literacy: What every American needs to know—and doesn't.* New York: HarperCollins.

Rostosky, S. S., Riggle, E. B., Brodnicki, C., & Olson, A. (2008). An exploration of lived religion in same-sex couples from Judeo-Christian traditions. *Family Process, 47,* 389–403.

Smith, T. (2002). Religious diversity in America: The emergence of Muslims, Buddhists, Hindus, and others. *Journal for the Scientific Study of Religion, 41,* 577–585.

Smith, B., & Horne, S. (2007). Gay, lesbian, bi-sexual, and transgendered (GLBT) experiences with earth-spirited faith. *Journal of Homosexuality, 52*(3/4), 235–249.

Smith-Stoner, M. (2007). End-of-life preferences for atheists. *Journal of Palliative Medicine, 10*(4), 923–928.

Snarey, J. R., & Dollahite, D. C. (2001). Varieties of religion–family linkages. *Journal of Family Psychology, 15*(4), 646–651.

Snider, J. B., Clements, A., & Vazsonyi, A. T. (2004). Late adolescent perceptions of parent religiosity and parenting processes. *Family Process, 43*(4), 489–502.

Tan, P. P. (2005). The importance of spirituality among gay and lesbian individuals. *Journal of Homosexuality, 49*(2), 135–144.

Walsh, F. (2006). *Strengthening family resilience* (2nd ed.). New York: Guilford Press.

Walsh, F. (2009a). Human–animal bonds I: The relational significance of companion animals. *Family Process, 48,* 462–480.

Walsh, F. (2009b). Integrating spirituality in family therapy. In F. Walsh (Ed.), *Spiritual resources in family therapy* (2nd ed., pp. 31–61). New York: Guilford Press.

Walsh, F. (2009c). Spiritual resources in family adaptation to death and loss. In F. Walsh (Ed.), *Spiritual resources in family therapy* (2nd ed., pp. 81–102). New York: Guilford Press.

Walsh, F. (Ed.). (2009d). *Spiritual resources in family therapy* (2nd ed.). New York: Guilford Press.

Walsh, F. (2010). Spiritual diversity: Multifaith perspectives in family therapy. *Family Process, 49*(3), 330–348.

Walsh, F. (2011). Families in later life: Challenges, opportunities, and resilience. In M. McGoldrick, B. Carter, & N. Garcia-Preto (Eds.), *The expanded family life cycle* (4th ed., pp. 261–277). Needham Heights, MA: Allyn & Bacon.

Walsh, F., & McGoldrick, M. (2004). *Living beyond loss: Death in the family* (2nd ed.). New York: Norton.

Wendel, R. (2003). Lived religion and family therapy: What does spirituality have to do with it? *Family Process, 42*(1), 165–179.

Wilcox, W. B. (2004). *Soft patriarchs, new men: How Christianity shapes fathers and husbands*. Chicago: University of Chicago Press.

Worthington, E. L., Jr. (1989). Religious faith across the lifespan: Implications for counseling and research. *Counseling Psychologist, 17,* 555–612.

Wright, L. (2009). Spirituality, suffering, and beliefs: The soul of healing with families. In F. Walsh (Ed.), *Spiritual resources in family therapy* (2nd ed., pp. 65–80). New York: Guilford Press.

PART IV

DEVELOPMENTAL PERSPECTIVES ON FAMILY FUNCTIONING

CHAPTER 16

THE FAMILY LIFE CYCLE

MONICA MCGOLDRICK
TAZUKO SHIBUSAWA

Until recently, therapists and researchers paid little attention to the family life cycle and its impact on human development (McGoldrick, Carter, & Garcia-Preto, 2011a). Most psychological theories have focused on the individual or, at most, on the nuclear family, ignoring the multigenerational context of family connections that pattern our lives over time. Yet a family life-cycle perspective is critical, because it enables clinicians to anticipate the future development of individuals and families, including risks, which in turn facilitates prevention. It is helpful to consider all clinical assessment within a life-cycle framework, which offers a flexible concept of predictable life stages and acknowledges the emotional tasks of individuals and family members, depending on their structure, time of life, and cultural and historical era. The old nuclear family model is insufficient because, as Dilworth-Anderson, Burton, and Johnson (1993) point out, "Important organizing, relational bonding of significant others, as well as socialization practices or socio-cultural premises are overlooked by researchers when the nuclear family structure is the unit of analysis" (p. 640).

Since the 1960s and 1970s, social norms that dictate life patterns and time tables for life transitions have continued to weaken, eroding the traditional model characterized by (1) the good provider role for men, (2) full-time homemaking on the part of women, and (3) universal marriage and childbearing (Kohli, 2007). The emergence of heterogeneous life patterns and the waning of conventional, standardized, and predictable life trajectories have been referred to as the "deinstitutionalization" of the life course (Wrosch & Freund, 2001). It is becoming increasingly difficult to define what family life-cycle patterns are "normal," adding stress for family members who have few models to to guide the passages they must negotiate. Furthermore, in our rapidly changing world, we need to recognize that life-cycle definitions and norms are relative, depending on the sociocultural context (McGoldrick et al., 2011a, 2011b; Falicov, 2011; Kliman & Madsen, 2011; Ashton, 2011; Hines, 2011; see McGoldrick & Ashton, Chapter 11, this volume). As the texture of life has become a more complicated fabric, research and therapeutic models must change to reflect this complexity, appreciating both the surrounding context as a shaping environment and the evolutionary factor of time on human development.

THE FAMILY AS A SYSTEM MOVING THROUGH TIME

Families comprise those who have a shared history and a shared future. They encompass the entire emotional system of at least three and frequently now four or even five generations, held together by blood, legal, and/or historical ties. Relationships with parents, siblings, and other family members go through transitions as they move along the life cycle. Boundaries shift, psychological distance among members changes, and roles within and between subsystems are constantly being redefined. It is extremely difficult, however, to think of the family as a whole because of the complexity involved. As a system moving through time, the family has basically different properties from all other systems. Families incorporate new members only by birth, adoption, commitment, or marriage, and members can leave only by death, if then. No other system is subject to these constraints. A business organization can fire members or, conversely, members can resign if the structure and values of the organization are not to their liking. In families, on the other hand, the pressures of membership with no exit available can, in the extreme, lead to psychosis. In nonfamily systems, the roles and functions of the system are carried out in a more or less stable way, by replacement of those who leave for any reason, and people move on into other organizations. Although families also have roles and functions, the main value in families is in the relationships, which are irreplaceable. If a parent leaves or dies, another person can be brought in to fill a parenting function, but this person can never replace the parent in his or her personal emotional aspects.

While people often act as though they can choose membership and responsibility in a family, there is little choice about whom we are related to in the complex web of family ties. Children, for example, have no choice about being born into a system, nor do parents have a choice, once children are born, adopted, or fostered, as to the existence of the responsibilities of parenthood, even if they neglect these responsibilities. Even for committed partners, the freedom to choose whomever one wishes is a recent option, and the decision to marry is probably much less freely made than people usually recognize at the time. While partners can choose not to continue a marriage relationship, if they have children they remain coparents and the former marriage continues to be acknowledged with the designation "ex-spouse." People cannot alter whom they are related to in the complex web of family ties over all the generations. Obviously family members frequently act as if this were not so—they cut each other off because of conflicts, or because they claim to have "nothing in common"—but when family members act as though family relationships are optional, they do so to the detriment of their own sense of identity and the richness of their emotional and social context.

Despite the current, dominant American pattern of nuclear families living on their own and often at great geographical distance from extended family members, they are still emotional subsystems, reacting to past, present, and anticipated future relationships within the larger, multigenerational family system. The many options and decisions to be made can be confusing: whether and whom to marry; where to live; how many children to have, if any; how to conduct relationships within the immediate and extended family; and how to allocate family tasks.

Cultural factors also play a major role in how families go through the life cycle. Not only do cultural groups vary greatly in their breakdown of family life-cycle stages and definitions of the tasks at each stage, but it is clear that even several generations after immigration the family life-cycle patterns of groups differ markedly (Falicov, 2011; McGoldrick, Giordano, & Garcia-Preto, 2005). The definition of "family" also differs according to cultures. For example, social support networks within the Black community serve as a vital buffer against a discriminating environment. Dilworth-Anderson et al. (1993) call for broadening ideas of what constitutes a family and its positive characteristics to allow for culturally relevant descriptions, explanations, and interpretations of the family.

Families' motion through the life cycle is profoundly influenced by the era in history at which they are living (Elder & Johnson, 2002). Family members' worldviews, including their attitudes toward life-cycle transitions, are influenced by the times in which they grow up. Those who lived through the Great Depression, those who experienced the black migration to the North in the 1940s, those in the "Baby Boomer" generation who came of age during the Vietnam War, and in Generation X who grew up in the 1970s and 1980s—all these cohorts have profoundly different orientations to the meaning of life, influenced by the eras through which they have lived.

We must also attend to the enormous anxiety generated by the chronic unremitting stresses of poverty and discrimination, especially as the economic and racial divide in our society widens. The traditional multigenerational extended family provided valuable mutual support and interconnectedness yet should not be romanticized, as it was supported by sexism, classism, racism, and heterosexism. In this traditional patriarchal family structure, respect for parents and obligations to care for elders were based on their control of the resources, reinforced by religious and secular sanctions against those who did not conform to the normative standards of the dominant group.

UNDERSTANDING THE LIFE CYCLE:
THE INDIVIDUAL, FAMILY, AND CULTURE

Families characteristically lack time perspective when they are having problems. They may be stuck in the past or magnify the present moment, overwhelmed and immobilized by their immediate feelings; or they become fixed on a moment in the future that they either long for or dread. They lose the awareness that life means continual motion from the past and into the future, with ongoing transformation of familial relationships. From a family life-cycle perspective, symptoms and dysfunction are examined within a systemic context and in relation to what the culture considers to be "normal" (i.e., expectable) functioning over time. From this perspective, therapeutic interventions aim at helping to reestablish the family's own developmental momentum, so that it can proceed forward to foster each member's development.

To understand how people evolve, we must examine their lives within the contexts of both the family and the larger culture, which change over time. Even within the diversity of family forms, there are some unifying principles we have used to define stages and tasks, such as the emotional disequilibrium generated by adding and losing family members during life's many transitions (Ahrons, 2011; McGoldrick et al., 2011a).

Each system (individual, family, and cultural) can be represented schematically (see Figure 16.1) along two time dimensions: One is historical (the vertical axis), and the other is developmental and unfolding (the horizontal axis). For the individual, the vertical axis includes the biological heritage and intricate programming of behaviors with one's temperament, possible congenital disabilities, and genetic makeup. The horizontal axis relates to the individual's emotional, cognitive, physical, and interpersonal development over the lifespan within a specific sociohistorical context. Over time, an individual's qualities can become either crystallized into rigid behaviors or elaborated into broader and more flexible repertoires. Certain individual stages may be more difficult to master, depending on one's genetic endowment and environmental influences (see Spotts, Chapter 22, this volume.).

At the family level the vertical axis includes the "family history," the patterns of relating and functioning that are transmitted down the generations, primarily through the mechanism of emotional triangling (Bowen, 1978). It includes all the family attitudes, taboos, expectations, labels, and loaded issues with which we grow up. These aspects of our lives are the hand we are dealt. What we do with them is the question. The horizontal flow at a family level describes the family as it moves through time, coping with the changes and transitions of the family's life cycle. This includes both the predictable developmental stresses and those unpredictable events, "the slings and arrows of outrageous fortune," that may disrupt the life-cycle process—untimely death, birth of a handicapped child, chronic illness, job loss, and so forth.

At a sociocultural level, the vertical axis includes cultural and societal history; stereotypes; patterns of power, privilege, and oppression; social

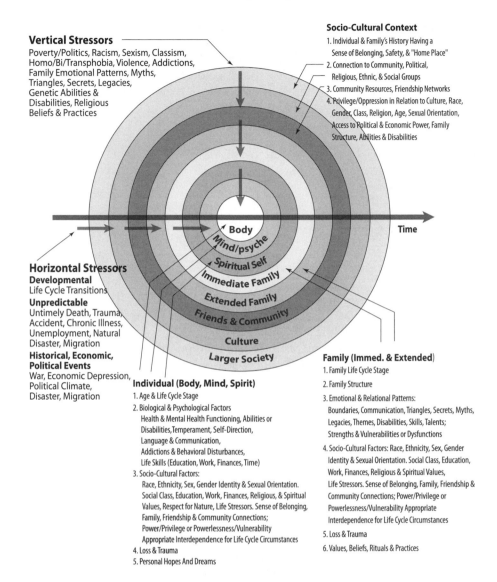

Socio-Cultural Context
1. Individual & Family's History Having a Sense of Belonging, Safety, & "Home Place"
2. Connection to Community, Political, Religious, Ethnic, & Social Groups
3. Community Resources, Friendship Networks
4. Privilege/Oppression in Relation to Culture, Race, Gender, Class, Religion, Age, Sexual Orientation, Access to Political & Economic Power, Family Structure, Abilities & Disabilities

Vertical Stressors
Poverty/Politics, Racism, Sexism, Classism, Homo/Bi/Transphobia, Violence, Addictions, Family Emotional Patterns, Myths, Triangles, Secrets, Legacies, Genetic Abilities & Disabilities, Religious Beliefs & Practices

Body
Mind/psyche
Spiritual Self
Immediate Family
Extended Family
Friends & Community
Culture
Larger Society

Time

Horizontal Stressors
Developmental
Life Cycle Transitions
Unpredictable
Untimely Death, Trauma, Accident, Chronic Illness, Unemployment, Natural Disaster, Migration
Historical, Economic, Political Events
War, Economic Depression, Political Climate, Disaster, Migration

Individual (Body, Mind, Spirit)
1. Age & Life Cycle Stage
2. Biological & Psychological Factors
   Health & Mental Health Functioning, Abilities or Disabilities, Temperament, Self-Direction, Language & Communication, Addictions & Behavioral Disturbances, Life Skills (Education, Work, Finances, Time)
3. Socio-Cultural Factors:
   Race, Ethnicity, Sex, Gender Identity & Sexual Orientation. Social Class, Education, Work, Finances, Religious, & Spiritual Values, Respect for Nature, Life Stressors. Sense of Belonging, Family, Friendship & Community Connections; Power/Privilege or Powerlessness/Vulnerability Appropriate Interdependence for Life Cycle Circumstances
4. Loss & Trauma
5. Personal Hopes And Dreams

Family (Immed. & Extended)
1. Family Life Cycle Stage
2. Family Structure
3. Emotional & Relational Patterns:
   Boundaries, Communication, Triangles, Secrets, Myths, Legacies, Themes, Disabilities, Skills, Talents; Strengths & Vulnerabilities or Dysfunctions
4. Socio-Cultural Factors: Race, Ethnicity, Sex, Gender Identity & Sexual Orientation. Social Class, Education, Work, Finances, Religious & Spiritual Values, Life Stressors. Sense of Belonging, Family, Friendship & Community Connections; Power/Privilege or Powerlessness/Vulnerability Appropriate Interdependence for Life Cycle Circumstances
5. Loss & Trauma
6. Values, Beliefs, Rituals & Practices

FIGURE 16.1. Multicontextual framework for assessing problems. From McGoldrick, Carter, and Garcia-Preto (2011a), *The Expanded Family Life Cycle: Individual, Family, and Social Perspectives, 4th Edition*, Copyright 2011. Printed and electronically reproduced by permission of Pearson Education, Inc., Upper Saddle River, New Jersey.

hierarchies; and beliefs that have been passed down through the generations. A group's history and, in particular, its legacy of trauma influences families and individuals as they go through life (e.g., the Holocaust for Jews and Germans; slavery for African Americans and colonizing, slave-owning groups; homophobic crimes for persons of diverse sexual orientation). The horizontal axis relates to community connections, current events, and social policies as they impact the family and the individual at a given time. It includes the consequences in people's present lives of the society's "inherited" (vertical) norms of racism, sexism, classism, and heterosexism, as well as ethnic and religious prejudices, as these are manifested in social, political, and economic structures that limit the options of some and support the power of others.

ANXIETY AND SYMPTOM DEVELOPMENT

Over time, stress is often greatest at transition points from one stage to another in developmental process as families rebalance, redefine, and realign their relationships. Hadley, Jacob, Milliones, Caplan, and Spitz (1974) found that symptom onset correlated significantly with the normal family developmental process of addition and loss of family members (e.g., birth, marriage, divorce, remarriage, death, launching). The clinical method of Murray Bowen (1978) tracks patterns through the family life cycle over several generations, focusing especially on nodel events and transition points to understand dysfunction at the present moment. Emotional issues and developmental tasks not resolved at appropriate stages will likely be carried along as hindrances in future transitions and relationships (McGoldrick et al., 2011a). Given enough stress on the horizontal, developmental axis (see Figure 16.1), any family can appear extremely dysfunctional. Even a small horizontal stress on a family whose vertical axis is full of intense stress will create great disruption in the system. The anxiety engendered where the vertical and horizontal axes converge, and the interaction of the various systems and how they work together to support or impede one another, are key determinants of how well the family will manage its transitions through life. It becomes imperative, therefore, to assess not only the dimensions of the current life-cycle stress but also their connections to family themes, and triangles coming down in the family over historical time. Although all normative change is to some degree stressful, when horizontal (developmental) stress intersects with vertical (transgenerational) stress, there tends to be a quantum leap in anxiety in the system. To give a global example, if one's parents were basically pleased to be parents and handled the job without too much anxiety, then the birth of the first child would produce just the normal stresses of a system expanding its boundaries. If, on the other hand, parenting were a loaded issue in the family of origin of one or both spouses, and has not been dealt with, the transition to parenthood might produce heightened anxiety for the couple. Even without any outstanding family-of-origin issues, the inclusion of a child could potentially tax a system if there is a mismatch between the temperaments of the child and the parents. Or if a child is conceived in a time of great economic or political upheaval that forces a family to migrate, leaving its roots and culture, then the child's birth might carry with it unresolved issues.

THE CHANGING STRUCTURE OF FAMILIES

The dramatic changes in families in the United States, described in Part I of this book, cannot be overestimated. Therapists must give up outdated norms and put a more positive conceptual frame around the broad spectrum and fluid life course of contemporary families. Transitional crises are common, and immediate distress does not result in permanent traumas for the vast majority of children and their families. We need to drop from our vocabulary pejorative phrases linked to the norms and prejudices of the past: children of divorce, out-of-wedlock child, fatherless home, working mother, and the like.

DEVELOPING A SELF IN CONTEXT

Gender, class, culture, race, sexual orientation, and spirituality structure our developing beliefs, values, relationships, and ways of expressing emotion. This context carries every child from birth and childhood through adulthood to death and defines his or her legacy for the next generation. Each generation or cohort is different, as cultures evolve through time, influenced by the social, economic, and political history of its era (Elder & Shanahan, 2006; Elder & Johnson, 2002; Gladwell, 2008). Healthy development requires establishing a solid sense of our cultural, spiritual, and psychological identity in the context of our connections to others. In many ways this involves the development of a sense of belonging, or "home," as we go through life. Developing an integrated sense of ourselves requires incorporating a sense of safety, belonging, and stability about who we are in relation to our closest family and social context.

THE NOTION OF "HOMEPLACE"

Researchers of African Americans and others who have been marginalized in our society have written often about a notion of "homeplace" and the need for belonging, for rootedness and connection to place and kin that is a crucible of affirmation for our sense of social and cultural identity (hooks, 1990). hooks describes homeplace as deriving from communal experiences anchored in a home, where "all that truly mattered in life took place, the warmth and comfort of shelter, the feeding of our bodies, the nurturing of our souls. There we learned dignity, integrity of being. . . . There we learned to have faith" (pp. 41–42). Linda Burton and her colleagues have urged us to take the concept of home into account in assessment and intervention (Burton, Winn, Stevenson, & Clark, 2004). Homeplace involves multilayered, nuanced individual and family processes anchored in a physical space that elicits feelings of empowerment, belonging, commitment, rootedness, ownership, safety, and renewal. This includes the ability to develop relationships that provide us with a solid sense of social and cultural identity. The notion of homeplace is relevant for people of all cultures throughout the life cycle. This is especially true for immigrant groups away from their homes, who form networks and communities that represent and celebrate their hometown rituals. Puerto Ricans on the mainland, for example, form social clubs with others from their hometowns on the island as a way to stay connected to their home. Homeplace also serves as the site of resistance against the oppressive forces of our society (Burton et al., 2004). Homeplace provides security and safety to develop self-esteem, political consciousness, and resilience in the face of societal invalidation, racism, and other barriers. Some may need adaptive strategies to find a place they can feel at home, because the very place that others rely on fundamentally may become a place of greatest danger, such as children whose families suffer from mental illness, violence, addictions, and other negative or disruptive forces.

We all need to experience a sense of belonging—to feel safe and secure— especially when living in a multicultural society where connecting with others who are different from us becomes particularly challenging. Indeed, the most challenging aspect of development involves our beliefs about, and interaction with, others who are different from ourselves: men and women; young and old; Black and white; wealthy and poor; heterosexual and gay. Our level of maturity on this crucial dimension of tolerance and openness to difference is strongly influenced by how our families of origin, communities, cultures of origin, and our society as a whole have dealt with difference—and how they are evolving into the future.

THE MYTHS OF AUTONOMY
AND SELF-DETERMINATION

Given the American focus on individualism and free enterprise, it is not surprising that autonomy and competitiveness have been considered desirable traits to instilled in child, leading to economic success in the marketplace. The people with the most privilege in our society—especially white men who have financial and social status—tend to be systematically kept unaware of their dependence on others (Coontz, 2005). In many hidden ways, society supports their so-called "autonomous" functioning. Those who are privileged develop connections amid a web of dissociations. Their privilege maintains their buffered position and allows them the illusion of complete self-determination. Those who are raised to deny their emotional interdependence face a terrible awakening during divorce, illness, job loss, or other adversities of life.

DEVELOPING A MATURE, INTERDEPENDENT SELF

We believe maturity depends on seeing past myths of autonomy and self-determination. It requires that we appreciate our basic interdependence with others and all of nature. Viewed from this perspective, in addition to self-direction, maturity involves skills such as the following:

1. The ability to connect and to feel safe in the context of the familiar *and* the unfamiliar or different.
2. The ability to read emotion in others, to practice self-control, to empathize, and to engage in caring for others and in being cared for by others.
3. The ability to accept one's self and simultaneously accepting differences in others, to maintain one's values and beliefs, and to relate generously to others, even if one is not receiving support for one's beliefs from them or from anyone else (defined by Murray Bowen as "differentiation").
4. The ability to consider other people and future generations when evaluating sociopolitical issues such as the environment and human rights.

We believe that children are best able to develop their full potential emotionally, intellectually, physically, and spiritually when they are exposed in positive ways to diversity and encouraged to embrace it. Children who are least restricted by rigid gender, cultural, or class role constraints have the greatest likelihood of developing an evolved sense of a connected self.

GENDERED DEVELOPMENT

Children's sense of security evolves through their connection and identification with those who care for them—mothers, fathers, siblings, nannies, grandparents, aunts, uncles, teachers, and all who participate in their caretaking. Twentieth-century formulations of child development ignored this rich context and offered a one-dimensional lens: through the mother–child relationship. In most cultures throughout history, mothers, with heavy work demands, have not been the sole, essential caretakers of their children. A narrow focus on mothers projects impossible expectations on them and ignores the richness of environments in which children grow up.

Most child development theories, even feminist theories (Chodorow, 1974; Gilligan, 1993), explained male development's focus on autonomy and independence as resulting from the child's (i.e., the son's) need to separate from his mother by rejecting feminine qualities. Like Maccoby (1999), Kimmel (2008), and many others (see Knudson-Martin, Chapter 14, this volume), we doubt that children's development of distinct styles of interacting has much to do with the fact that they are parented primarily by women. Parents, often outside of awareness, expect and reinforce different behaviors in their sons and daughters (Hastings, McShane, Parker, & Ladha, 2007). We need to help all children attain their full human potential and challenge the influences that limit it.

While separation and autonomy have been considered the primary values for male development, caring, ability to nurture others, interdependence, relationship, and attention to context have been viewed as the primary dimensions in female development (Gilligan, 1993). Values that were thought to be "feminine" were devalued by male theoreticians such as Erikson (1968, 1994), and Levinson (1978), while values associated with men were equated with adult maturity. Concern about relationships was seen as a weakness of women (and men) rather than a human strength. Valliant (2002), who studied the lives of male Harvard graduates across adulthood, concluded that relationships are the overriding key to men's positive development and life satisfaction. In fact, women have always defined themselves in the context of their changing relationships over the lifespan.

A life-cycle framework providing a perspective on self-in-relation offers a much more appropriate way to think of human development for both men and women (Jordan, 1997). Erikson's (1968, 1994) developmental model, based on observations of mid-20th-century middle-class men, ignored the evolution of our ability to communicate and to care for each other in times of need, just as other social animals do. It also neglected the interpersonal network of relationships in development and the reciprocity that is so powerful in "giving forward" in life. "Identity" was defined as having a sense of self *apart from* rather than *in relation to* one's family and said nothing about developing skill in relating to one's family or to others. In our view, all stages of the life cycle have both individual and interpersonal aspects. Our social brains enable us to coordinate our needs with those of people around us, fostering our flexibility (see Fishbane, Chapter 23, this volume). Taylor (2002) found that contrary to the "fight or flight" response to stress in studies of men, women's response is to "tend and befriend"—a more adaptive pattern for the future of our species.

NORMAL FAMILY PROCESSES IN CONTEXT

If the ideas of life-cycle norms are applied too rigidly, they lead to an anxiety that deviating from the norms is pathological. The opposite pitfall, overemphasizing the uniqueness of the "brave new world" faced by each new generation, can create a sense of historical discontinuity, devaluing the role of parenthood and the relationship between the generations. Our aim is to provide a view of the life cycle in terms of intergenerational connectedness in the family, for this is one of our greatest resources. This is not meant to oversimplify the complexity of life's transitions or to encourage stereotyping by promoting classifications of "normality" that constrict our view of human life but, rather, to expand clinicians' views of family problems and strengths.

In the following discussion, we present different stages of family life and what is required to accomplish the tasks at each stage. We remind readers that our schema is a mere approximation of complex processes, and not an affirmation of a "normal" model of fixed stages or ordered progression over the life course. For example, a child with severe developmental disabilities may not be able to launch in young adulthood, and parents do not transition out of their caregiving roles (see Rolland, Chapter 19, this volume). Families are often marginalized when they do not fit normative life-cycle expectations and need to take more initiative in managing their lives and charting their own life course to compensate for the lack of social structuring and support (Wrosch & Freund, 2001).

Generally speaking, major life-cycle transitions require a fundamental change in the system itself, rather than just incremental changes or rearrangements of the system, which go on continually throughout life. The central underlying processes to be negotiated are the expansion, contraction, and realignment of the relationship system to support the entry, exit, and development of family members in a functional way. We do not see individual or family stages as inherently age related (e.g., Levinson, 1978) or dependent on the structure of the traditional family (e.g., Duvall, 1977, and others). Nor do we view healthy maturation as requiring a single sequential pathway through marriage and childrearing. In contrast to the traditional view that not marrying is an "immature" choice, or that women who do not have children are unfulfilled, we hold a pluralistic view, recognizing many valid, healthy options and relationships over the life course.

BETWEEN FAMILIES: YOUNG ADULTHOOD

The primary tasks for young adults include coming to terms with their families of origin and entering the adult world of work and relationships. Families are powerful shapers of reality, influencing who, when, how, and whether young adults will marry and how they will carry out all succeeding stages of the family life cycle. But the economics of the 21st century are also powerful organizers of young adults' options. Adequate negotiation of this stage requires that the young adult separate from the family of origin, without cutting off or fleeing reactively to a substitute emotional refuge. This phase is a cornerstone. It is a time to formulate personal life goals and to become a "self" before joining with another to form a new family subsystem. The more adequately young adults can differentiate themselves from the emotional program of the family of origin at this phase, the fewer vertical stressors will follow them through their new family life cycle. This is the chance for them to sort out emotionally what they will take along from the family of origin, what they will leave behind, and what they will create for themselves.

Young adults may remain in an overly dependent position, unable to leave home, or they may rebel, breaking away in a pseudo-independent cutoff from their parents and families. Whereas for women the problems at this stage more often focus on short-circuiting their definition of themselves in favor of finding and accommodating to a mate, men more often have difficulty committing themselves in relationships, forming instead an incomplete identity focused around work. Only when the generations can shift their hierarchical relations and reconnect in a new way can the family move on developmentally. Among middle- and upper-middle-class families, an increasing challenge at this phase is the prolonged dependency that our technological society requires in order to prepare young adults for the work world, long after they would traditionally have been launched and married. Economic downturns can also prolong young adults' inability to achieve financial independence. This creates a difficult situation for both parents and children, who will have difficulty establishing appropriate boundaries, since it is almost impossible to be emotionally independent when one is still financially dependent as a student or unemployed.

Working with families at this phase of the life cycle is particularly rewarding because of the new options that arise when young adults are able to move toward new life patterns. Young men can be encouraged to develop themselves emotionally and expressively, exploring their connections with family and others. For men who have had few male role models or minimal relationship with their fathers, this is a time to reconnect. Because men's socialization so often does not facilitate their learning to achieve intimacy even in friendship, this period can also be a keystone to being proactive about the kind of friendships they want to nurture in life. It is important to help men make connections with other men in and outside their families, without having to forsake their mothers or devalue women. Interventions directed at helping young people reevaluate the gender roles of their parents and grandparents, so that they do not replicate previous relationships of inequality or dysfunction, may be especially valuable at this crucial formative phase. For both men and women, it is important to acknowledge all the unrecognized work by their mothers and grandmothers to raise their families and to keep a household going, in order to emphasize their courage, abilities, hard work, and strength as role models, since mothers are too often devalued and their contributions are typically hidden from history (herstory!). In general, both men and women can be helped to draw strength from each of their parents.

COUPLING: THE JOINING OF FAMILIES

Changing gender roles, frequent coupling of partners from widely different cultural backgrounds, increasing physical distance between family members, and emphasis on nuclear families place a much greater burden on couples to define their relationship for themselves than was true in traditional family structures (McGoldrick, 2011a). Although any two family systems always have different patterns and expectations, in our present culture, couples are less bound by family traditions and freer than ever before to develop intimate committed relationships, unlike those they experienced in their families of origin. Forming a couple tends to be misunderstood as a joining of two individuals. It really represents the changing of two entire systems, as well as an overlapping of systems to develop a third system. Women tend to turn back to their parents for more connection, whereas men may increase separation from their families of origin, seeing the couple relationship as a replacement of the family of origin. In fact, a daughter is also a daughter-in-law for the rest of her life, since she typically gains responsibility for the connectedness with and care of her husband's family as well.

Achieving a successful transition to couplehood may be an extraordinarily difficult proposition in our time, when we are in the midst of a transformation of male–female relationships in the direction of partnership educationally, occupationally, and in emotional connectedness. The transition to marriage is an important time for helping young couples look beyond the stereotypes that have been so problematic for family development (McGoldrick, 2011a). Yet although this transition is less marked than it used to be for many couples, who live together before (or instead of) marriage, many resist looking at the fallacies of their myths about marriage (Carter & Peters, 1997) until later, when predictable problems surface.

The failure to renegotiate family status with the family of origin may also lead to marital failure. Nevertheless, couples rarely present with extended family problems as the stated issue. Problems reflecting the inability to shift family status are usually indicated by defective boundaries around the new subsystem. In-laws may be too intrusive, and the new couple may be afraid to set limits, or the partners may have difficulty forming adequate connections with the extended systems, cutting themselves off in a tight twosome. At times the inability to formalize a marriage indicates that the partners are still too enmeshed in their own families to define a new system and accept the implications of this realignment. It is useful in such situations to help the system to move to a new definition of itself rather than to get lost in the details of incremental shifts over which the couple may be struggling (sex, money, time, etc.). Negotiating relationships with the family of origin can be extremely challenging for gay and lesbian couples whose families do not approve of their sexual orientation. Distancing from strongly disapproving parents does not necessarily result in negative consequences in couple relationships among gay men (LaSala, 2007; see Green, Chapter 8, this volume).

FAMILIES WITH YOUNG CHILDREN

With the transition to parenthood, the family becomes a threesome, which makes it a permanent system for the first time. If childless partners separate, they dissolve their family unit, but once they have children, they may end the couple bond but forever remain parents to their children, who also remain connected to both families of origin. Thus, symbolically, and in reality, this is a key transition in the family life cycle (see Cowan & Cowan, Chapter 18, this volume).

The shift to this stage of the family life cycle requires that adults now move up a generation and become caretakers to the younger generation. Typical problems that occur when parents cannot make this shift are struggles with each other about taking responsibility, or refusal or inability to behave as parents to their children. In some families, childhood symptoms may be more a function of the temperamental qualities and developmental needs of the child. Children who are temperamentally difficult create more discomfort for parents, making parenting more challenging, and decreasing couple and family functioning (see Spotts, Chapter 22, this volume).

For the modern two-paycheck family with small children, a central struggle during this stage of the life cycle is the handling of child care responsibilities and chores (see Fraenkel & Capstick, Chapter 4, this volume). The pressure of securing adequate child care, when affordable and satisfactory social provision is lacking, leads to several serious consequences: The woman may have to take two full-time jobs; the family may live in conflict and chaos; child care arrangements may be less than optimal; recreation and vacations may be sharply curtailed; or the mother may give up her job to stay home or work only part-time. The major research on the transition to parenthood indicates that it is accompanied by a general decrease in marital satisfaction, a reversion to more traditional sex roles even by dual-career couples, who previously had a more equitable relationship, and a lowering of self-esteem for women (Carter & Peters, 1997; Carter, McGoldrick, & Petkov, 2011). Even when fathers participate more actively in relating to children, mothers still tend to bear the major responsibility for meeting children's needs.

In many ways, the mid-20th-century normal family model not only encouraged but also required the overresponsibility of "homemaker" mothers for their children and the complementary underinvolvement of "breadwinning" fathers. Society, reinforced by psychoanalytic and developmental models, equated parenting with mothering in the earliest years of life, to the exclusion of other relationships or to later phases in the life cycle (McGoldrick, 2011). We urge a broader perspective on human development, viewing child development and this early stage in the richness of the network of multigenerational family relationships, and within social and cultural contexts. For a child's complete identity and development, a shift within society must be made to value, support, and reinforce the active inclusion of fathers and to appreciate the contributions of siblings, extended family members, and other caregivers as supportive resources, models and mentors (see Walsh, Chapter 17, this volume).

This is an important area for intervention with families at this life-cycle stage. Fathers who lack experience with small children need to learn these skills. Often this requires time alone with children to allow husbands to take primary responsibility and mothers to let go. Mothers may need assistance in allowing fathers to make mistakes. At this transition in the family's emerging development, many grandparents must shift to a back seat to allow their children to be the central parental authorities, while forming a new type of caring relationship with their grandchildren. At the same time, it is important to note that in low-income families, grandparents provide needed support for child care. There has also been an increase in kinship care households in which grandparents take on primary parenting roles, particularly when their adult children struggle with problems such as substance abuse, mental illness, and incarceration (see Engstrom, Chapter 9, this volume).

In working with families at this phase of life, it is important to explore boundaries and roles within the nuclear family and between the generations. How the system operates is an important variable in understanding family contribution and response to childhood problems. Careful history taking is imperative, examining both individual child development and family developmental history. Areas of assessment include problems around conception, pregnancy, and delivery; temperamental qualities of the infant; achievement of developmental milestones; and the onset and development of problems. One must carefully track the child's symptoms, inquiring about changes or stresses within the system that may relate to the problems; adjustment of all family members to the birth of the symptomatic child and to the evolution of symptoms; additional problems with other children; organization of the family; and the impact of family-of-origin issues—whom the child resembles, similar problems in the extended family, and how such problems have been dealt with by others.

Inquiry about household and job responsibilities, as well as the handling of finances and the specifics of childrearing and child care, can illuminate major stresses on the family and ineffective solutions. With attention to gendered role functioning, it is helpful to convey an awareness of responsibilities often taken for granted. We might ask whether both parents usually go to the children's school meetings, medical appointments, and sports events; how much time each parent spends alone with each child; and how money and domestic responsibilities are divided (see Knudson-Martin, Chapter 14, this volume).

FAMILIES WITH ADOLESCENTS

Adolescence marks a new era and definition of the children within the family, and of the parents' roles in relation to their children. Adolescents begin their transitions to adult roles and responsibilities, and parents must respond to their changing cognitive, emotional, physical, and social needs. While children become more autonomous and independent, close adolescent–parent relationships remain crucial to their emotional well-being. Parents need to establish qualitatively different boundaries than families with younger children, while maintaining trusting bonds and open communication so that their adolescents can turn to them for support and a sense of security. Adolescents who do not have close relationships with their parents are at greater risk for developing problems such as substance abuse and pregnancies (Liddle, Rowe, Diamond, Sessa, Schmidt, & Ettinger, 2000; Miller, 2002). Establishing strong yet permeable boundaries can be challenging, since parents can no longer maintain complete authority over adolescents. Adolescents can and do open the family to a whole array of new values as they bring friends and new ideals into the family arena. Families that become derailed at this stage may be rather closed to new values and threatened by them, and frequently are stuck on an earlier view of their children. New information and communication technology such as cell phones and social networking sites can have positive and negative effects for youth and their family relationships (Blinn-Pike, 2009). For example, cell phones can facilitate family contact and ease the process of teens' independence but also intensify parental monitoring and control (Lanigan, 2009).

Adolescence is also a period when gender roles become solidified. It is important not to reinforce this gender role stereotyping, but instead to encourage girls to develop their own opinions, values, aspirations, and interests, while discouraging them from developing competitive cliques that shun other girls. Likewise, boys need to be encouraged to communicate and express feelings, and discouraged from teasing and bullying other boys, or denigrating and disrespecting girls. Although conventional gender values are at an all-time high during adolescence, crucial life-shaping decisions are also made during this phase. Parents may not realize how much their teenagers need their help to learn about adult life, to discuss their concerns, and to help them make informed choices regarding education and relationships. Sexually transmitted diseases are rampant, and nearly 25% of teens report having had intercourse by 15 years of age (Klein & the Committee on Adolescence, 2005). Parents must teach responsible sexual attitudes and behavior to their sons, as well as their daughters.

During adolescence, daughters are particularly torn between pressures to conform to traditional societal roles as sex objects or family caretakers and striving for a life of their own. High rates of depression and suicide risk among Latino and Asian American female adolescents are attributed to these pressures (Yu & Vyas, 2009; Zayas, Lester, Cabassa, & Fortuna, 2005). Our society has also encouraged distancing between mothers and sons, with pernicious messages about the negative effects of mother–son bonding. Research indicates that rebellion against parents is only one way, and not the most common way, for adolescents to evolve an identity. Most teenagers of both sexes remain close to and admire their parents, and experience a minimum of conflict and rebellion. Fathers may need help to overcome inhibitions in relating emotionally to both sons and daughters.

Clinically, when working with adolescents and their families, it is important to ask about the roles each one is asked to play in the family. What are the chores and responsibilities of boys and of girls? Are sons encouraged to develop social skills, or are parents focused primarily on their achievement and sports performance? Are daughters encouraged to have high academic aspirations? Are both sexes given equal responsibility and encouragement in dealing with education, athletics, aspirations for the future, extended family relationships, buying gifts, and writing, calling, or caring for relatives?

Our society continues to give very different messages to our daughters than to our sons about their bodies, their minds, and their spirits, emphasizing for young women a highly sexualized physical attractiveness to men. Girls internalize messages from their environment that provide narrow views of female sexual attractiveness (American Psychological Association Task Force on the Sexualization of Girls, 2007). It is not surprising that girls have much higher rates of body dissatisfaction and eating disorders than adolescent males (Stice & Shaw, 2002). Boys still too often absorb the message that they have the right to treat girls as objects for their sexual pleasure and exploitation.

A common event in the parents' relationship at this phase is the "midlife crisis" of one or both spouses, with an exploration of personal, career, and marital satisfactions and dissatisfactions. This is especially important, because parents of adolescents tend to have the lowest marital satisfaction. An overfocus on parent–adolescent complaints in therapy may prevent the marital problems, an affair, or consideration of divorce from coming to the surface.

FAMILIES AT MIDLIFE:
LAUNCHING CHILDREN AND MOVING ON

This newest and longest phase in the family life cycle is in many ways the most problematic. In the past most families were occupied with raising their children for most of their active adult lives. Today, when young adults take longer to complete education, lead independent lives, and marry, most parents look forward to a longer postlaunching life expectancy. Parents must contract their household and reorient their attention and attachments. Some child-focused families seek to hold on to their children although, increasingly, they welcome the opportunity to explore new pursuits. The transition necessitates a restructuring of the marital relationship now that parenting responsibilities are no longer required.

The most significant aspect is that this phase is marked by the greatest number of exits and entries of family members. It begins with the launching of grown children and proceeds, for most, with the entry of their spouses and children. It is a time when grandparents often become ill and die. Parents must deal with the change in their own status as they make room for the next generation and prepare to move up to the position of grandparents. They must also forge a different type of relationship with their own parents, who may become dependent, giving them (particularly women) considerable caretaking responsibilities. For some families this stage is seen as a time of fruition and completion, and as a second opportunity to consolidate or expand by exploring new avenues and new roles. However, the current and forecasted economic climate may necessitate employment until a later age than anticipated and dash retirement dreams. In many families, the launching of young adults is impeded by financial constraints. When adult children cannot support themselves, or if they marry and then divorce, there is a kind of in-and-out process with their parents.

The emotional limitations of work and achievement lead more traditional, career-focused men to do important soul searching at this phase. They may regret the lack of intimacy in their marriages and turn to their children for closeness just as the children are moving away. Women today at midlife have been termed "the sandwich generation." Most are in the workforce, still attending to responsibilites for emerging young adults, as they take on primary caregiver roles for aging parents. Men who divorce at this phase tend to remarry rather quickly, usually to a younger woman. Some hope that starting over with a new family will give them a chance to "do it better." Women—who initiate most divorces at this phase—are less likely to remarry. In part this is because of the skew in availability of desirable partners, men's preference for younger partners, and women's reluctance to "settle," particularly for a traditional relationship that would involve extensive spousal caretaking.

Therapy at this phase is often aimed at helping family members redefine their lives and relationships, along with expanding and broadening their options, many of which may differ from those of the family in which they were raised—and from their own expectations. They need to envision new pathways for their lives that their parents possibly did not experience. There is also the difficult negotiation required when children return periodically to the nest, because of the complex and difficult economics of our times and society.

THE FAMILY IN LATER LIFE

Few of the visions of old age offered by our culture provide us with positive images for healthy later-life adjustment within a family or social context (Walsh, 2011). In contrast to traditional cultures, in which older adults are highly respected, they tend to be shunted aside and devalued in our youth-oriented modern society. Ageist stereotypes and pessimistic views of later-life decline and uncaring families prevail. In fact, most individuals between ages 65 and 80 are in good health and actively engaged in life pursuits. Only 4% of older adults live in institutions, typically with those over 85 requiring extensive care and lacking family resources. The vast majority of older adults maintain close connection with their family members and live within an hour of at least one child.

Among the tasks of families in later life are adjustments to retirement, which requires reorientation for retiring individuals and may strain the marital relationship, requiring renegotiation of household roles and postretirement plans. While the death of friends and relatives is a common distress at this phase, the loss of a spouse is the most difficult adjustment. Grandparenthood or other meaningful and generative involvements can, however, offer a new lease on life.

Declining health, financial insecurity, and dependence are common difficulties, particularly for older adult family members who value managing for themselves. With advanced age, chronic illness and disability pose significant family caregiving challenges, particularly with dementias, which affect nearly half of adults over 85. Especially anguishing for family members are the ambiguous losses with Alzheimer's disease, called "the long goodbye" (Boss, 2004). The inability to shift relational status can occur when older adults have difficulty accepting their lessening powers (e.g., refusing to give up driving when unsafe), or when they feel that the younger generation treats them disrespectfully or as incompetent. Even when older parents are quite frail, losing mental or physical capacities, this should not be seen as an intergenerational role reversal, nor should parents be labeled as "child-like." Parents always remain parents to their children in the generational hierarchy; they have many decades more life experience and can serve as models to the next generations for the phases of life ahead. Family members may need help in making appropriate shifts and to address discomfort or conflict concerning dependency and caregiving. The importance of dignity, respect, and meaningful involvement for older adults is paramount (Walsh, 2011).

Clinically, older family members rarely seek help for psychological problems, especially depression, and are more likely to consult physicians for somatic complaints. Often their adult children who seek help may not initially define their problem as relating to an older adult parent. Clinicians need to inquire about current extended family relationships and recent changes, such as concern about a parent who is no longer able to live independently, or who has parent's terminal illness. Such crises can also present opportunities for healing old relational wounds. Conjoint family life reviews can facilitate mutual understanding and update relationships frozen in the past, achieving a new level of "family integrity" (King & Wynne, 2004; Walsh, 2011).

DIVORCE, SINGLE PARENTING, AND REMARRIAGE

With the divorce rate at nearly 50%, and redivorce near 60%, divorce is a common interruption or dislocation of the traditional family life cycle, producing profound disequilibrium, with gains and losses in family membership.

There are crucial shifts in relationship status and important emotional tasks that must be dealt with by the members of divorcing families for healthy adaptation (see Greene et al., Chapter 5, this volume). As in other phases, emotional issues not resolved at this phase will be carried along as hindrances in future relationships.

Families in which divorce occurs must go through one or two additional phases of the family life cycle in moving forward developmentally. Many families go through the divorce phase and restabilize permanently as postdivorce families (Ahrons, 2011). Even more remarry and require negotiation of an additional phase of remarriage before long-term restabilization (see Pasley & Garneau, Chapter 7, this volume). Divorce and postdivorce family emotional process is a roller coaster with peaks of emotional tension at all transition points, including when the couple decide to separate; when the decision is announced to family and friends; when money, custody, and visitation arrangements are discussed; when separation takes place; when the actual divorce occurs; when separated spouses have contact to discuss money and their children; when each child graduates, marries, has children or becomes ill, and when either spouse has a new partner, marries, has other children, or dies. These emotional pressure peaks do not necessarily occur in the aforementioned order, and many of them take place repeatedly over the years. Adaptation requires mourning what is lost (including hopes and dreams) and dealing with hurt, anger, blame, guilt, shame, and loss in oneself, in the spouse, in the children, and in the extended family.

Clinical work aims to minimize the tremendous tendency toward cutoff of many relationships after a divorce. It is important to help divorcing spouses continue to relate as cooperative parents and permit maximum feasible contact among children, parents, and extended family. It usually takes a family several years and a great deal of effort after divorce to readjust to its altered structure, which may or may not include remarriage, since many families restabilize satisfactorily as single-parent households (see Anderson, Chapter 6, this volume). Families in which the issues of divorce are not adequately resolved can remain stuck emotionally for years, if not for generations. However, families who handle the challenges are not invariably damaged, as popular myths hold.

The family emotional process at the transition to remarriage consists of struggling with fears about investment in a new marriage and a new family; dealing with hostile or upset reactions of the children, the extended families, and the ex-spouse; struggling with the ambiguity of the new family structure, roles, and relationships; rearousal of intense parental guilt and concerns about the welfare of children; and rearousal of the old attachment to the ex-spouse (negative or positive). Triangles are common, such as when the new partners forge their bond by vilifying the ex-spouse, drawing the child into a loyalty conflict between parents, commonly expressed by acting out against the stepparent. It is important for therapists to realize that many of the problems are structural, not personal.

A FINAL CAVEAT

Most descriptions of the typical family life cycle, including our own, fail to convey the considerable effects of culture, ethnicity, race, religion, and sexual orientation on all aspects of how, when, and in what way a family experiences various phases and transitions. Although we may ignore these variables for theoretical clarity and focus on our commonalties, a clinician working with real families in the real world cannot afford to ignore them. The definition of "family" and the timing of life-cycle phases and the importance of transitions vary depending on a family's cultural background. It is extremely important for us as clinicians to help families develop rituals that correspond to their life choices and transitions, especially those that the culture has not validated (Imber Black, 2011; see Imber-Black, Chapter 20, this volume). The challenges of adaptation for multistressed low-income families in a stark political, social, and economic context have produced family life-cycle patterns that vary significantly from the middle-class paradigm that erroneously has been used to conceptualize their situation (Hines, 2011). Social class is another major definer of differences in life-cycle patterns (Kliman & Madsen, 2011), and the life cycles of gays and lesbians (Ashton, 2011), immigrants (Falicov, 2011), those who choose single parenting, and those who do not marry or have children (Berliner, Jacob, & Schwartzberg, 2011) offer significant variations on traditional definitions of the family life cycle that require us to expand our definitions of normality.

REFERENCES

Ahrons, C. R. (2011). Divorce: An unscheduled transition. In M. McGoldrick, B. Carter, & N. Garcia-Preto (Eds.), *The expanded family life cycle: Individual, family, and social perspectives* (4th ed., pp. 292–306). Boston: Pearson.

American Psychological Association Task Force on the Sexualization of Girls. (2007). *Report of the the Task Force on the Sexualization of Girls*. Washington, DC: American Psychological Association.

Ashton, D.. (2011). Lesbian, gay, bisexual and transgender individuals and the life cycle. In M. McGoldrick, B. Carter, & N. Garcia-Preto (Eds.), *The expanded family life cycle: Individual, family, and social perspectives* (4th ed., pp. 113–132). Boston: Pearson.

Berliner, K., Jacob, D., & Schwartzberg, N. (2011). The single adult and the family life cycle. In M. McGoldrick, B. Carter, & N. Garcia-Preto (Eds.), *The expanded family life cycle: Individual, family, and social perspectives* (4th ed., pp. 163–177). Boston: Pearson.

Blinn-Pike, L. (2009). Technology and the family: An overview from the 1980s to the present. *Marriage and Family Review, 45,* 567–575.

Boss, P. (2004). Ambiguous loss. In F. Walsh & M. McGoldrick (Eds.), *Living beyond loss: Death in the family* (2nd ed., pp. 237–246). New York: Norton.

Bowen, M. (1978). *Family therapy in clinical practice*. New York: Aronson.

Burton, L. M., Winn, D. M., Stevenson, H., & Clark, S. L. (2004). Working with African American clients: Considering the "homeplace" in marriage and family therapy practices. *Journal of Marital and Family Therapy, 30*(4), 397–410.

Carter, B., McGoldrick, M., & Petkov, B. (2011). Becoming parents: The family with young children. In M. McGoldrick, B. Carter, & N. Garcia-Preto (Eds.), *The expanded family life cycle: Individual, family, and social perspectives* (4th ed., pp. 211–231). Boston: Pearson.

Carter, B., & Peters, J. (1997). *Love, honor and negotiate: Building partnerships that last a lifetime.* New York: Pocket Books.

Chodorow, N. (1974). Family structure and feminine personality. In M. Z. Rosaldo & L. Lamphere (Eds.), *Woman, culture and society* (pp. 43–66). Stanford, CA: Stanford University Press.

Coontz, S. (2005). *Marriage: A history.* New York: Viking.

Dilworth-Anderson, P., Burton, L., & Johnson, L. B. (1993). Reframing theories for understanding race, ethnicity and families. In P. G. Boss, W. J. Doherty, R. LaRossa, W. R. Schumm, & S. K. Steinmetz (Eds.), *Sourcebook of family theories and methods: A contextual approach* (pp. 627–646). New York: Plenum.

Duvall, E. M. (1977). *Marriage and family development* (5th ed.). Philadelphia: Lippincott.

Elder, G. H., & Johnson, M. M. (2002). Perspectives on human development in context. In C. von Hofsten & L. Backman (Eds.), *Psychology at the turn of the millennium* (Vol 2, pp. 153–177). Florence, KY: Taylor & Frances/Routledge.

Elder, G. H., & Shanahan, M. J. (2006). The life course and human development. In R. M. Lerner & W. Damon (Eds.), *Handbook of child psychology* (Vol. 1, 6th ed., pp. 665–715). Hoboken, NJ: Wiley.

Erikson, E. (1968). *Identity: Youth and crisis.* New York: Norton.

Erikson, E. (1994). *Identity and the life cycle.* New York: Norton.

Falicov, C. (2011). Migration and the family life cycle. In M. McGoldrick, B. Carter, & N. Garcia-Preto (Eds.), *The expanded family life cycle: Individual, family, and social perspectives* (4th ed., pp. 336–347). Boston: Pearson.

Gilligan, C. (1993). *In a different voice.* Cambridge, MA: Harvard University Press.

Gladwell, M. (2008). *Outliers: The story of success.* Boston: Little, Brown.

Hadley, T., Jacob, T., Milliones, J., Caplan, J., & Spitz, D. (1974). The relationship between family developmental crises and the appearance of symptoms in a family member. *Family Process, 13,* 207–214.

Hastings, P. D., McShane, K. E., Parker, R., & Ladha, F. (2007). Ready to make nice: Parental socialization of young sons' and daughters' prosocial behaviors with peers. *Journal of Genetic Psychology, 168*(2), 177–299.

Hines, P. (2011). The family life cycle of African American families living in poverty. In M. McGoldrick, B. Carter, & N. Garcia-Preto (Eds.), *The expanded family life cycle: Individual, family, and social perspectives* (4th ed., pp. 89–100), Boston: Pearson.

hooks, b. (1990). *Yearning: Race, gender, and cultural politics.* Boston: South End Press.

Imber Black, E. (2011). Creating meaningful rituals for new life cycle transitions. In M. McGoldrick, B. Carter, & N. Garcia-Preto (Eds.), *The expanded family life cycle: Individual, family, and social perspectives* (4th ed., pp. 429–439). Boston: Pearson.

Jordan, J. V. (Ed.). (1997). *Women's growth in diversity: More writings from the Stone Center.* New York: Guilford Press.

Kimmel, M. S. (2008). *The gendered society* (3rd ed.). New York: Oxford University Press.

King, D. A., & Wynne, L. C. (2004). The emergence of "family integrity" in later life. *Family Process, 43*(1), 7–21.

Klein, J. D., & the Committee on Adolescence. (2005). Adolescent pregnancy: Current trends and issues. *Pediatrics, 116*(1), 281–286.

Kliman, J., & Madsen, W. (2011). Social class and the family life cycle. In M. McGoldrick, B. Carter, & N. Garcia-Preto (Eds.), *The expanded family life cycle: Individual, family, and social perspectives* (4th ed., pp. 75–88). Boston: Pearson.

Kohli, M. (2007). The institutionalization of the life course: Looking back to look ahead. *Research in Human Development, 4*(3–4), 253–271.

Lanigan, J. D. (2009). A sociotechnological model for family research and intervention: How information and communication technologies affect family life. *Marriage and Family Review, 45*, 587–609.

LaSala, M. C. (2007). Old maps, new territory: Family therapy theory and gay and lesbian couples. *Journal of GLBT Family Studies, 3*(1), 1–14.

Levinson, D. (1978). *The seasons of a man's life.* New York: Knopf.

Liddle, H., Rowe, C., Diamond, G. M., Sessa, F. M., Schmidt, S., & Ettinger, D. (2000). Toward a developmental family therapy: The clinical utility of research on adolescence. *Journal of Marital and Family Therapy, 26*(4), 485–500.

Maccoby, E. E. (1999). *The two sexes: Growing up apart: Coming together (the family and public policy).* Boston: Belknap Press.

McGoldrick, M. (2011a). Becoming a couple. In M. M. Goldrick, B. Carter, & N. Garcia-Preto (Eds.), *The expanded family life cycle: Individual family and social perspectives* (pp. 193–210). Boston: Pearson.

McGoldrick, M. (2011b). Women and the family life cycle. In M. McGoldrick, B. Carter, & N. Garcia-Preto (Eds.), *The expanded family life cycle: Individual, family, and social perspectives* (4th ed., pp. 42–58). Boston: Pearson.

McGoldrick, M., & Carter, B. (2011). Families transformed by the divorce cycle: Reconstituted, multi-nuclear, recoupled and remarried families. In M. McGoldrick, B. Carter, & N. Garcia-Preto (Eds.), *The expanded family life cycle: Individual, family, and social perspectives* (4th ed., pp. 317–331). Boston: Pearson.

McGoldrick, M., Carter, B., & Garcia-Preto, N. (Eds.). (2011a). *The expanded family life cycle: Individual, family, and social perspectives* (4th ed.). Boston: Pearson.

McGoldrick, M., Carter, B., & Garcia-Preto, N. (2011b). Overview: The life cycle in its changing context: Individual, family and social perspectives. In M. McGoldrick, B. Carter, & N. Garcia-Preto (Eds.), *The expanded family life cycle: Individual, family, and social perspectives* (4th ed., pp. 1–19). Boston: Pearson.

McGoldrick, M., Giordano, J., & Garcia-Preto, N. (Eds.). (2005). *Ethnicity and family therapy* (3rd ed.). New York: Guilford Press.

Miller, B. C. (2002). Family influences on adolescent sexual and contraceptive behavior. *Journal of Sex Research, 39*(1), 22–26.

Stice, E., & Shaw, H. E. (2002). Role of body dissatisfaction in the onset and maintenance of eating pathology: A synthesis of research findings. *Journal of Psychosomatic Research, 53*(5), 955–993.

Taylor, S. E. (2002). *The tending instinct*. New York: Holt.

Vaillant, G. (2002). *Aging well: Surprising guideposts to a happier life*. Boston: Little, Brown.

Walsh, F. (2011). Families in later life: Challenges, opportunities and resilience. In M. McGoldrick, B. Carter, & N. Garcia-Preto (Eds.), *The expanded family life cycle: Individual, family, and social perspectives* (4th ed., pp. 261–277). Boston: Pearson.

Wrosch, C., & Freund, A. M. (2001). Self-regulation of normative and non-normative developmental challenges. *Human Development, 44,* 264–283.

Yu, S. M., & Vyas, A. M. (2009). The health of children and adolescents. In C. Trin-Shevrin, N. S. Islam, & M. J. Rey (Eds.), *Asian American communities and health: Context, research, policy and action* (pp. 107–131). San Francisco: Jossey-Bass.

Zayas, L. H., Lester, R. J., Cabassa, L. J., & Fortuna, C. (2005). Why do so many Latina teens attempt suicide?: A conceptual model for research. *American Journal of Orthopsychiatry, 75*(2), 275–287.

CHAPTER 17

FAMILY RESILIENCE
Strengths Forged through Adversity

FROMA WALSH

C risis and challenge are inherent in the human condition. The concept of family resilience extends our understanding of family functioning to situations of adversity. *Family resilience* involves the potential for recovery, repair, and growth in families facing serious life challenges. Although some families are shattered by crisis events, disruptive transitions, or persistent hardship, what is remarkable is that many others emerge strengthened and more resourceful, able to love fully and raise their children well. This chapter presents an overview of a family resilience framework and outlines key processes, distilled from research on resilience and effective family functioning. Practice applications are briefly described to suggest the broad utility of this conceptual framework for intervention and prevention efforts to strengthen distressed and vulnerable families.

A SYSTEMIC VIEW OF RESILIENCE

Resilience—the ability to withstand and rebound from disruptive life challenges—has become an important concept in mental health theory, research, and practice over recent decades. It involves dynamic processes fostering positive adaptation within the context of significant adversity (Bonanno, 2004; Luthar, 2006; Masten, 2001). Beyond coping and adaptation, these strengths and resources enable recovery and positive growth.

The Interaction of Biopsychosocial Influences in Resilience

Most research to date has focused on individual resilience. Early studies found that the same adversity may result in different outcomes, which challenged the prevailing deterministic assumption that early traumatic experiences are inevitably damaging. Studies found, for instance, that most individuals who had experienced family abuse in childhood did not become abusive parents (Kaufman & Ziegler, 1987). As Rutter (1987) noted, no combination of risk factors, regardless of severity, gave rise to disorder in more than half the children exposed. Although many struggled in life, other individuals overcame similar, high-risk conditions and were able to lead loving and productive lives.

To account for these differences, early studies focused on intrapersonal traits for resilience, or hardiness, reflecting the dominant cultural ethos of the "rugged individual" (see Walsh, 1996). Initially, resilience was viewed as innate, as in the character armor of "the invulnerable child," who was impervious to stress, like a "steel doll" that would not break if mishandled (Anthony & Cohler, 1987). As studies were extended to a wide range of adverse conditions—impoverished circumstances, chronic illness, catastrophic life events, trauma, and loss—researchers recognized the interaction between nature and nurture in the emergence of resilience. It became clear that resilience involves the dynamic interplay of multiple risk and protective processes over time, with individual, interpersonal, socioeconomic, and cultural influences (e.g., Garmezy, 1991; Rutter, 1987). Psychobiological and genetic vulnerability or the negative impact of stressful life conditions could be counteracted by positive influences.

In a remarkable longitudinal study of resilience, Werner (Werner & Smith, 2001) followed the lives of nearly 700 multiethnic children of plantation workers living in poverty on the Hawaiian island of Kauai. One-third were classified "at risk" due to early life exposure to at least four additional risk factors, such as serious health problems and familial alcoholism, violence, divorce, or mental illness. By age 18, about two-thirds of the at-risk children had done as poorly as predicted, with early pregnancy, mental health problems, or trouble in school or with the law. However, one-third of those at high risk had developed into competent, caring, and confident young adults, with the capacity "to work well, play well, and love well," as rated on a variety of measures. In later follow-up studies through midlife, almost all were still living successful lives. Many had outperformed Kauai children from less harsh backgrounds; more were stably married and employed, and fewer suffered trauma effects of a hurricane that destroyed much of the island. Of note, several who had functioned poorly in adolescence turned their lives around in adulthood, most often crediting supportive relationships. These findings have important clinical implications, revealing that despite troubled childhood or teen years, there is potential to turn one's life around, developing resilience across adulthood.

Supportive Relationships Nurture Resilience

Notably, the positive influence of significant relationships stood out across many studies (Walsh, 1996). Individuals' resilience was nurtured in important bonds, particularly with role models and mentors, such as coaches and teachers, who were invested in their well-being, believed in their potential, supported their efforts, and encouraged them to make the most of their lives.

However, most early investigators studied individuals who thrived despite parental dysfunction and maltreatment, and held a narrow, pessimistic view of the family. The focus on parental deficits blinded many to potential family-wide resources, even when a parent's functioning was seriously impaired. Clinicians encouraged so-called "survivors" to cut off from their "dysfunctional families" and seek positive relationships elsewhere to counter the negative impact. Thus, families were seen to contribute to risk, but not to resilience.

A family systems orientation broadens attention to the entire relational network, identifying potential resources for resilience in the immediate and extended family. Positive contributions might be made by siblings, parents, and other caregivers; spouses or partners, grandparents and godparents, aunts and uncles; and other informal kin (Minuchin, Colapinto, & Minuchin, 2005; Ungar, 2004). Even in troubled families, islands of strength and resilience can be found.

THE CONCEPT OF FAMILY RESIILIENCE

Resilience in the Family as a Functional Unit

Beyond seeing individual family members as potential resources for individual resilience, the concept of family resilience focuses on risk and resilience in the family as a functional unit (Walsh, 1996, 2003, 2006). A basic premise in this systemic view is that serious crises and persistent adversity have an impact on the whole family, and in turn, key family processes mediate the adaptation of all members and their relationships. Major stressors or a pile-up of stresses can derail the functioning of a family system, with ripple effects for all members and their relationships. The family response is crucial: Key processes in resilience (described below) enable the family system to rally in troubled times to buffer stress, reduce the risk of dysfunction, and support optimal adaptation.

The concept of family resilience extends theory and research on family stress, coping, and adaptation (Hawley & DeHaan, 1996; Mackay, 2003; McCubbin & Patterson, 1983; Patterson, 2002; Simon, Murphy, & Smtih, 2005). It entails more than managing stressful conditions, shouldering a burden, or surviving an ordeal. It involves the potential for personal and relational transformation and growth that can be forged out of adversity. By tapping into key processes for resilience, families that are struggling can emerge stronger and more resourceful in meeting future challenges. Members may develop new insights and abilities. A crisis can be a wake-up call, heightening attention to important matters. It can become an opportunity for reappraisal of life priorities and pursuits, stimulating greater investment in meaningful relationships. Studies of strong families have found that when family members weathered a crisis together, their relationships were enriched and more loving than they otherwise might have been (Stinnett & DeFrain, 1985).

This family resilience perspective fundamentally alters the deficit-based lens from viewing struggling families as *damaged* and beyond repair to seeing them as *challenged* by life's adversities, with potential for fostering healing and growth in family members.

Ecological and Developmental Contexts of Family Resilience

A family resilience framework combines ecological and developmental perspectives to view family functioning in relation to its broader sociocultural context and evolution over the multigenerational life cycle.

Ecological Perspective

From a *biopsychosocial systems orientation*, risk and resilience are viewed in light of multiple, recursive influences. Human functioning and dysfunction are seen as resulting from an interaction of individual—and family—vulnerability or resilience in dealing with stressful life experiences and social contexts. Genetic and neurobiological predispositions (Feder, Nestler, & Charney, 2009) may be enhanced or countered by family processes and by sociocultural resources or disadvantages. Family distress may result from unsuccessful attempts to cope with an overwhelming crisis situation or a pile-up of stressors, such as traumatic loss in the family or the wider impact of a large-scale disaster (Walsh, 2007). The family, peer group, community resources, school or work settings, and other social systems can be seen as nested contexts for nurturing and reinforcing resilience.

The vital contribution of cultural and spiritual resources for resilience has been shown in many studies, especially for those facing discrimination and socioeconomic barriers, such as African Americans, Latinos, Native Americans, and Muslims (McCubbin & McCubbin, 2005; McCubbin, McCubbin, McCubbin, & Futrell, 1998; McCubbin, Thompson, Thompson, & Fromer, 1998; see Boyd-Franklin & Karger, Chapter 12; Falicov, Chapter 13; and Walsh, Chapter 15, this volume). Extensive research on resilience in Canadian Native populations (Kirmayer, Dandeneau, Marshall, Phillips, & Williamson, 2011) underscores the importance of a social–ecological systemic approach, incorporating indigenous cultural, historical, and spiritual values in mental health promotion, policy, and clinical practice. For instance, family and social transmission of stories and metaphors supports adaptation through relational, ecocentric, and cosmocentric concepts of self, personhood, and collective identity, and through agency in political activism, empowerment, and reconciliation. These sources of resilience, understood in dynamic terms, emerge from interactions between individuals and their families, their communities, and larger systems.

Falicov's (1995, 2007; see Chapter 13, this volume) multidimensional framework for considering cultural influences locates each family within a complex ecological niche, sharing borders and common ground with other families, as well as differing positions related to variables such as gender, economic status, life stage, and position vis-à-vis the dominant culture. Each family's experience will have common and unique features. A holistic assessment includes the varied contexts and aims to understand the constraints and possibilities in each family's position. A family resilience framework likewise seeks to identify common elements in an adverse situation and effective family responses, while also considering each family's unique perspectives, challenges, and resources.

Developmental Perspective

A developmental perspective is essential in understanding and fostering resilience. The impact of adversity varies over time and in relation to individual and family life-cycle passage.

Emerging Challenges and Responses over Time. Most major stressors are not simply a short-term single event, but rather a complex set of changing conditions with a past history and a future course (Rutter, 1987). Such is the experience of divorce, from an escalation of predivorce tensions to separation and reorganization of households and parent–child relationships. Most families undergo subsequent transitions, with relocation, remarriage, and stepfamily integration (see Greene, Anderson, Forgatch, DeGarmo, & Hetherington, Chapter 5; Pasley & Garneau, Chapter 7, this volume).

Given this complexity, no single coping response is invariably most successful; varied strategies may prove useful in meeting new challenges that emerge. In assessing the impact of stress events, it is crucial to explore how family members approached their situation: from proactive stance to immediate response and long-term strategies. Some approaches may be functional in the short term but rigidify and become dysfunctional over time or as conditions change. For instance, with a father's stroke, a family must mobilize resources and pull together to meet the crisis, but later they need to shift gears to adapt to chronic disability and attend to other members' needs (Walsh, 2011a; see Rolland, Chapter 19, this volume). Family resilience thus involves varied adaptational pathways extending over time, from a threatening event on the horizon through disruptive transitions, and subsequent shockwaves in the immediate aftermath and beyond.

Cumulative Stressors. Some families may do well with a short-term crisis but buckle under the cumulative strains of multiple, persistent challenges, such as chronic illness, conditions of poverty, or complex, ongoing trauma situations. A pile-up of internal and external stressors can overwhelm the family, heightening vulnerability and risk for subsequent problems (Patterson, 2002). Escalating conflict and the husband's heavy drinking brought one couple to therapy. It was essential to situate these problems in the context of the family's barrage of strains and losses over the past 2 years—including the husband's job loss and related loss of health benefits, and a stroke suffered by the maternal grandmother, who had been relied upon for help in raising their three children, one with developmental disabilities. The family was reeling from one crisis to the next, with pressures mounting and no respite. Therapy facilitated the couple's mutual support, role reorganization, and team efforts involving extended family members to master ongoing challenges.

Family Life-Cycle Perspective. Functioning and symptoms of distress are assessed in the context of the family system as it moves forward over the life course and across the generations (McGoldrick, Carter, & Garcia-Preto, 2011; see McGoldrick & Shibusawa, Chapter 16, this volume). A family resilience framework focuses on family adaptation around critical events, including complications with predictable, normative transitions, such as the birth of the first child (see Cowan & Cowan, Chapter 18, this volume), and unexpected disruptive events, such as divorce or the untimely death of a young parent (Gorell Barnes, 1999; Greeff & Human, 2004; Greeff & Van der Merwe, 2004; Walsh, 2009a). How a family prepares for an anticipated loss, buffers stress, manages disruption, effectively reorganizes, and reinvests in life pursuits will influence the immediate and long-term adaptation for all members and their relationships (Walsh & McGoldrick, 2004).

Distress is heightened when current stressors reactivate painful memories and emotions from past experiences, as in posttraumatic stress reactions. The convergence of developmental and multigenerational strains increases the risk for complications (McGoldrick et al., 2011). Family members may lose perspective, conflating immediate situations with past events, and become overwhelmed or cut off from painful feelings and connections. Experiences of past adversity, such as war-related and refugee trauma, influence future expectations: Catastrophic fears heighten risk of dysfunction, whereas stories of resilience can inspire positive adaptation (Hauser, 1999; Hernandez, 2002; Weingarten, 2004).

Advantages of a Family Resilience Framework

Assessment of family functioning is fraught with dilemmas. Clinicians and researchers bring their own assumptive maps into every family evaluation and intervention, embedded in cultural norms, professional orientations, and personal experience (see Walsh, Chapter 2, this volume). Moreover, with the social and economic transformations of recent decades and a growing multiplicity of family arrangements, no single model of family functioning is essential for children and families to thrive (see Walsh, Chapter 1, this volume).

Systems-oriented family process research over recent decades has provided some empirical grounding for assessment of effective couple and family functioning (see Lebow & Stroud, Chapter 21, this volume). However, family assessment typologies tend to be static and acontextual, offering a snapshot of interaction patterns but often not considering how they are related to a family's stressors, resources, and challenges over time and in the larger social environment. In clinical practice, families most often come in crisis periods, when distress and differences from norms are too readily assumed to be signs of family pathology.

A family resilience framework offers several advantages. First, by definition, it focuses on strengths forged under stress, in response to crisis, and under prolonged adversity. Second, it is assumed that no single model of healthy functioning fits all families or their situations. Functioning is assessed in context: relative to each family's values, structural and relational resources, and life challenges. Third, processes for optimal functioning and the well-being of members vary over time as challenges emerge and families evolve. Although most families might not measure up to ideal models, a family resilience perspective is grounded in a deep conviction in the potential of all families to gain resilience and positive growth out of adversity. Even those who have experienced severe trauma or very troubled relationships have the potential for healing and transformation across the life course and the generations (Tedeschi & Calhoun, 2004; Tedeschi & Kilmer, 2005).

KEY PROCESSES IN FAMILY RESILIENCE

The family resilience framework presented in Table 17.1 was developed as a conceptual map for practitioners to identify and target key family processes that can reduce stress and vulnerability in high-risk situations, foster healing and growth out of crisis, and empower families to surmount prolonged adversity. This framework is informed by over three decades of clinical and social science research seeking to understand crucial variables contributing to resilience and effective family functioning (Walsh, 2003, 2006). I have distilled and organized findings from the large research literature to identify key processes for resilience in three domains of family functioning: family belief systems, organizational patterns, and communication processes. These key processes are described briefly here (see Walsh [2006, 2007] for elaboration and application in clinical and community-based practice).

It is important to stress that this is not a typology of traits of a "resilient family." Rather these are *dynamic processes* involving strengths and resources that families can access and gain to increase family resilience. Practitioners can target key processes in intervention and prevention efforts. Various processes may be more relevant and useful in different situations of adversity, and family members may chart varying pathways in resilience depending on their values, resources, challenges, and aims.

TABLE 17.1. Key Processes in Family Resilience

Belief systems

1. Make Meaning of Adversity
   - Relational view of resilience
   - Normalize, contextualize distress
   - Sense of coherence: View crisis as meaningful, comprehensible, manageable challenge
   - Facilitative appraisal: Causal/explanatory attributions; future expectations

2. Positive Outlook
   - Hope, optimistic bias; confidence in overcoming odds
   - Courage/encouragement; affirm strengths; focus on potential
   - Active initiative and perseverance (can-do spirit)
   - Master the possible; accept what can't be changed; tolerate uncertainty

3. Transcendence and Spirituality
   - Larger values, purpose
   - Spirituality: Faith, contemplative practices, community; connection with nature
   - Inspiration: Envision possibilities; life dreams; creative expression; social action
   - Transformation: Learning, change, and growth from adversity

Organizational patterns

4. Flexibility
   - Open to change: Rebound, reorganize, adapt to new conditions
   - Stability to counter disruption: Continuity, dependability, predictability
   - Strong authoritative leadership: nurture, guide, protect
   - Varied family forms: Cooperative parenting/caregiving teams
   - Couple/coparent relationship: Mutual respect; equal partners

5. Connectedness
   - Mutual support, collaboration, and commitment
   - Respect individual needs, differences
   - Seek reconnection, repair cutoffs, grievances

6. Social and Economic Resources
   - Mobilize kin, social, and community networks; models and mentors
   - Build financial security; balance work/family strains
   - Larger systems: Institutional, structural supports

Communication/problem solving

7. Clear, Consistent Messages
   - Clarify ambiguous information; truth seeking

8. Open Emotional Expression
   - Share painful feelings; empathic response; tolerate differences
   - Pleasurable interactions, humor; respite

9. Collaborative Problem Solving
   - Creative brainstorming; resourcefulness
   - Share decision making; repair conflicts; negotiation; fairness
   - Focus on goals, take concrete steps: build on success; learn from failure
   - Proactive stance: Preparedness, planning, prevention

Family Belief Systems

Family belief systems powerfully influence how members view adversity, their suffering, and their options (Wright & Bell, 2009). Shared constructions of reality, influenced by multigenerational, cultural, and spiritual beliefs, emerge through family and social transactions. In turn, they organize family approaches to crisis situations and prolonged challenges, and they can be fundamentally altered by such experiences (Reiss, 1981). Adversity generates a crisis of meaning and potential disruption of integration. Family resilience is fostered by shared facilitative beliefs that increase effective functioning and options for problem solving, recovery, and growth. They help members make meaning of adverse situations; facilitate a hopeful, positive outlook; and offer transcendent or spiritual values and connections.

Making Meaning of Adversity

Well-functioning families approach a crisis or prolonged adversity as a *shared* challenge. In Gottman's research on couple relationships, successful couples approached problems as a team and partners emphasized the strength they drew from each other. They viewed hardships as trials to be overcome together and believed that their struggles made their relationship stronger; shared efforts and pride in prevailing brought them closer (see Driver, Tabares, & Gottman, Chapter 3, this volume). Professionals can foster this *relational view* of resilience.

By *normalizing* and *contextualizing* distress, family members can view their difficulties as understandable in light of their adverse situation. The tendency toward blame, shame, and pathologizing is reduced when problems are viewed as human dilemmas and complicated feelings are seen as common among those in similar predicaments—and in extreme or unjust situations, as normal responses to abnormal or inhumane conditions. Family resilience is also fostered by an evolutionary sense of time and becoming—a continual process of growth, challenge, and change over the life course and the generations (Beavers & Hampson, 2003). This family life-cycle perspective helps members see disruptive transitions as milestones or turning points in their life passage and links them with past and future generations.

In grappling with adversity, couples and families do best when helped to gain a shared *sense of coherence* (Antonovsky, 1993; Antonovsky & Sourani, 1988; Hansson & Cederblad, 2004) by recasting a crisis as a challenge that is comprehensible, manageable, and meaningful to tackle. It involves efforts to clarify the nature and source of problems and future expectations. Family members' subjective appraisal of their situation and their options influences their coping response and adaptation. They attempt to make sense of how things have happened through *causal or explanatory attributions*, and they look to their future with hopes and fears. Past negative experiences can load future expectations with catastrophic fears. To facilitate family members' reconstruction of meaning (Nadeau, 2001), practitioners can support their efforts to clarify understanding of their situation, to realistically appraise their challenges and options, and to plan active coping strategies.

Positive Outlook

Considerable research documents the strong neurophysiological effects of a positive outlook in coping with stress, recovering from crisis, and overcoming barriers to success. *Hope* is essential to the spirit: It fuels energy and efforts to rise above adversity. Hope is based on faith: No matter how bleak the present, a better future can be envisioned. In problem-saturated conditions, it is essential to rekindle hope from despair in order for family members to see possibilities, tap into potential resources, and strive to surmount obstacles. Hope for a better life for their children keeps many struggling parents from being defeated by their own life disappointments.

Epidemiologists have found that "positive illusions" sustain hope for those dealing with adversity, such as a life-threatening illness (Taylor, 1989). Unlike denial, there is awareness of a grim reality, such as a poor prognosis, and a choice to believe it is possible to overcome the odds against them. This positive stance supports efforts that can reduce risk and maximize the chances of success. Although studies have found that a positive outlook, in itself, does not necessarily lengthen life, it does enhance the quality of life and important relationships.

Well-functioning families tend to hold a more optimistic view toward life (Beavers & Hampson, 2003). Seligman's (1990) research on *learned optimism* has particular relevance for fostering resilience. His earlier studies on "learned helplessness" showed that with repeated experiences of futility and failure, individuals stop trying and become passive and pessimistic, generalizing the belief that bad things always happen to them, and that nothing they can do will matter. Seligman then demonstrated that optimism can be learned, and helplessness and pessimism unlearned, through experiences of successful mastery, building confidence that one's efforts can make a difference. He cautioned, however, that a positive mind-set is not sufficient for success if life conditions are relentlessly harsh, with few opportunities to rise above them. As Aponte (1994) stressed, many families who feel trapped in impoverished, blighted communities lose hope. This despair robs them of meaning, purpose, and a sense of future possibility. To be revitalized, a positive outlook must be reinforced by successful experiences and a nurturing social context.

The courage and determination shown by ordinary families in facing everyday hardships often go unnoticed. As a struggling single mother, working two jobs to support her children, avowed, "It's tough, but we all pitch in and we just don't give up." By *affirming family strengths and potential* in the midst of difficulties, clinicians can help multistressed families to counter a sense of helplessness, failure, and blame, while reinforcing pride, confidence, and a "can do" spirit. Offering *encouragement* bolsters courage to seize opportunities and persist in efforts. Interventions can help families *build confidence and new competencies* through experiences of successful mastery, learning that their efforts can make a difference. *Initiative and perseverance*—hallmarks of resilience—are fueled by this shared confidence through difficulties. One father, unemployed for over a year after his company downsized, reported, "We weren't sure how we would get through this, but we all pull together and keep believing we'll find a way." Families show confidence that they will do their best and support members' active participation in overcoming their challenges.

Mastering the art of the possible is a vital key to resilience (Higgins, 1994). For families, this involves taking stock of their situation—their challenges, resources, and aims—and then focusing energies on making the best of their options. This requires acceptance of that which is beyond their control and cannot be changed. Instead of being immobilized, or trapped in a powerless victim position, focus is directed toward ongoing and future possibilities. When events cannot be changed, they can be recast in a new light that fosters greater comprehension and healing. When future prospects are grim, such as a terminal illness, family members may not be able to control the outcome, but they can become meaningfully engaged, participate in caregiving, ease suffering, and make the most of their time together. Family members often report that by being more fully present with loved ones, this painful time became the most precious in their relationship (Walsh, 2006). In the aftermath of loss, survivors are helped to find ways to transform the living presence of a loved one into spiritual presence, through cherished memories, stories, and deeds that carry on the best aspects and aspirations of the deceased and their relationship.

Transcendence and Spirituality

Transcendent beliefs and practices provide meaning and purpose beyond a family's immediate plight. Most families seek strength, comfort, and guidance in troubled times through connections with their cultural and spiritual traditions, especially those facing barriers of poverty and discrimination (Walsh, 2009e; see Boyd-Franklin & Karger, Chapter 12; Falicov, Chapter 13; Walsh, Chapter 15, this volume). As a large body of research documents, spiritual resources, through deep faith, practices such as prayer and meditation, and congregational involvement, have all been found to be wellsprings for resilience (Walsh, 2009d). Rituals and ceremonies facilitate passage through significant transitions and linkage with a larger community and common heritage (see Imber-Black, Chapter 20, this volume). Many find spiritual nourishment outside formal religion, through secular humanism; deep connection with nature; creative expression in music and the arts; and social activism.

The paradox of resilience is that the worst of times can also bring out the best in the human spirit. A crisis can yield learning, transformation, and growth in unforeseen directions as documented in research on "posttraumatic growth" (Tedeschi & Calhoun, 2004; Tedeschi, Park, & Calhoun, 1996). It can awaken family members to the importance of loved ones or nudge them to heal old wounds and reorder priorities for more meaningful relationships and life pursuits. Many emerge from shattering crises with a heightened moral compass and sense of purpose in their lives, gaining compassion for the plight of others and sparking commitment to social, political, or environmental action. Professionals can support family efforts to envision a better future through their efforts and, where hopes and dreams have been shattered, to imagine new possibilities, seizing opportunities for invention, transformation, and positive growth.

Family Organizational Patterns

Contemporary families, with diverse structures and resources, must organize their households and relational networks in varied ways to meet life challenges. Resilience is strengthened by flexible structure, connectedness, and social and economic resources.

Adaptability: Flexibility and Stability

Flexibility, a core process in resilience, involves openness to adaptive change (Olson & Gorall, 2003). The ability to rebound is often thought of as "bouncing back," like a spring, to a preexisting shape or norm. However, after most serious crises and transitions, families cannot simply return to "normal" life as they knew it. A more apt metaphor might be "bouncing forward" (Walsh, 2002b): adapting to meet new challenges and constructing a "new normal." Families often need help in navigating uncharted terrain, recalibrating relationships, and reorganizing patterns of interaction to fit new conditions.

At the same time, families need to buffer and counterbalance disruptive changes to restore *stability*. Children and other vulnerable family members especially need assurance of *continuity, dependability*, and *predictability* through turmoil, and with separations and loss. Daily routines and meaningful rituals are important in such times, from regular bedtimes and shared mealtimes to regular events, such as Sunday brunch at Dad's house, and celebration of birthdays and milestones (see Imber-Black, Chapter 20, this volume).

Authoritative leadership, firm yet flexible, is generally most effective for family functioning and the well-being of children (Steinberg, Lamborn, Darling, Mounts, & Dornbush, 1994). Through stressful times, it is especially vital to provide *nurturance, protection*, and *guidance*. Strong parental leadership and dependability facilitate children's postdivorce adaptation as new single-parent household structures, visitation schedules, rules, and routines are set in place. Families with complex structures or dispersed living situations may need help in forging collaborative coparenting and caregiving teamwork across households or at a distance.

Connectedness

Connectedness is essential for relational resilience. A crisis or prolonged adversity can shatter family cohesion, leaving members unable to rely on each other. Resilience is strengthened by mutual support, collaboration, and commitment to weather troubled times together. As Gottman's research revealed, successful couples talk about their relationship in terms of mutual support and collaboration, regardless of their level of independence (see Driver et al., Chapter 3, this volume). At the same time, spouses and family members need to respect each other's individual differences, separateness, and boundaries. They may have varied reactions, coping styles, and time needed to process an adverse event, depending on variables such as the meaning and impact of the experience for each or the age of a child.

When family members are separated, for instance with foster care, parental absence, or communitywide disruption, it is important to sustain vital connections through photos, keepsakes, phone calls, and Internet contact. Adaptation and resilience of immigrant families are fostered by maintaining connection with kin and community, and with cultural and spiritual roots (Falicov, 2007; Chapter 13, this volume). In stepfamilies, parents can be encouraged to forge workable parenting coalitions within and across household boundaries and to knit together biological and steprelations, including extended families.

Intense pressures in troubled times can spark misunderstandings, conflicts, and cutoffs. Yet a crisis, such as a life-threatening situation, can also be seized as an opportunity for reconnection, reconciliation, and repair of wounded and estranged relationships. For instance, in later life, with the nearing of death and loss, aging parents and their adult children often develop new perspectives and impetus for resolving old grievances and achieving greater mutual understanding (Walsh, 2011a).

Social and Economic Resources

Kin and social networks, community groups, and faith congregations can be vital lifelines in times of trouble, offering practical and emotional support. The significance of role models and mentors for youth resilience is well documented. The importance of relational bonds for well-being and resilience, not only with loved ones and close friends but also with companion animals, is increasingly finding application in a wide range of programs for treatment and rehabilitation, and in care of older adults (Walsh, 2009b, 2009c).

The resilience and strengths of most families suffering economic hardship is remarkable (Orthner, Jones-Sanpei, & Williamson, 2004). However, financial security is vital for family well-being. Persistent unemployment or the loss of a breadwinner can be devastating. A serious or chronic illness can drain a family's economic resources. Serious financial strain is the most significant factor when children in single-parent families fare poorly (see Anderson, Chapter 6, this volume).

Most importantly, the concept of family resilience should not be misapplied to blame families that are unable to rise above harsh conditions by labeling them as not resilient. Just as individuals need supportive relationships for resilience, families need supportive institutional policies, structures, and programs in workplace, health care, and other larger systems. It is not enough to help vulnerable families "overcome the odds" against them; social policy must also "change the odds" to enable them to thrive (Seccombe, 2002).

Communication Processes

Communication processes facilitate resilience by bringing informational clarity to crisis situations, encouraging open emotional sharing, and fostering collaborative problem solving and preparedness. It must be kept in mind that cultural norms vary widely in sharing "bad news" and in emotional expression.

Clear Information

Clear and congruent messages facilitate effective family functioning (Epstein, Ryan, Bishop, Miller, & Keitner, 2003). In crisis and multistress conditions, communication easily breaks down. Ambiguity can block understanding, closeness, and mastery (Boss, 1999). Shared acknowledgment of the truth of a painful experience, such as relational abuse or torture, fosters healing, whereas denial, secrecy, and cover-up block authentic relating and can impede recovery (Walsh & McGoldrick, 2004). Well-intentioned families often avoid painful or threatening issues, wishing to protect each other from worry. They may say nothing about a precarious situation, such as a serious illness or a probability of divorce, until they are certain of the outcome. However, anxieties about the unspeakable can generate catastrophic fears and are often expressed in somatic or behavioral problems, especially in children. Parents or caregivers can help by keeping children and others informed as a situation develops and by openness to discussing questions or concerns. They may need guidance on age-appropriate ways to share information and can expect that, as children mature, they may revisit issues to gain greater comprehension or to bring up emerging concerns (Walsh, 2006).

In widespread disasters, ambiguous or mixed messages fuel anxiety and block understanding of what is happening, how it came about, and what can be expected. For instance, when the Louisiana Gulf oil spill occurred in 2010, multigenerational fishing families were devastated and left in limbo. Contradictory government and industry messages persisted over the following year about whether fish were safe to eat, and whether the fishing industry would survive or be destroyed for decades. When families can *clarify and share crucial information* about their situation and future expectations, it facilitates meaning making, informed decision making, and future planning.

Emotional Expression and Pleasurable Interactions

Open communication, supported by a climate of mutual trust, empathy, and tolerance for differences, enables family members to share a wide range of feelings that can be aroused by crisis events and chronic stress. Family members may be out of sync over time; one may continue to grieve a loss when others feel ready to move on. A parent or caregiver may suppress emotional reactions in order to keep functioning at work or for the family; children may stifle their own feelings and needs so as not to burden parents. For relational resilience, therapists can provide a safe haven for family members to share and process difficult feelings and facilitate empathic support. When emotions are intense, conflict can erupt and spiral out of control. Masculine stereotypes often constrain men from showing fear, vulnerability, or sadness, increasing risks of substance abuse, destructive behaviors, and relational conflict or estrangement. Combined individual and relational treatment approaches may be indicated.

Finding humor and laughter amid difficulties bolsters resilience (Wuerffel, DeFrain, & Stinnett, 1990). When family life is saturated with problems, suffering, or struggle, it is all the more crucial to create time and space for respite and to share pleasurable experiences for positive connection, fun, and joy to revitalize spirits and energies. It is especially important to celebrate birthdays and positive milestones, which often fall by the wayside under prolonged stressful conditions.

Collaborative Problem Solving and Preparedness

Creative brainstorming expands resourcefulness for surmounting adversity. Shared decision making and conflict management involve negotiation of differences with fairness and reciprocity over time. When overwhelmed by multistress conditions, it is important to set clear priorities and attainable goals, and to take concrete steps toward them. Practitioners can facilitate efforts to build on small successes and use failures as learning experiences.

A *proactive stance* is essential to meet future challenges. Struggling families need to shift from a crisis-reactive mode to prepare for anticipated challenges and avert crises. Encouraging members to consider a possible "Plan B" can enable them to rebound in the face of unforeseen challenges. When dreams have been shattered, families can be encouraged to survey the altered landscape and seek opportunities for meaningful growth in new directions.

Synergistic Influences of Key Processes in Resilience

These keys to resilience are mutually interactive and synergistic. For example, a relational view of resilience (belief system) supports—and is reinforced by—connectedness (organizational patterns) and collaborative problem solving (communication processes). A counterbalance of processes is also important, as when fluid shifts between stability and flexibility are required for both continuity and change.

Challenges for Research and Social Policy

Family research and social policy must be rebalanced from a focus on how families fail to how families, when challenged, can succeed if the field is to move beyond the rhetoric of promoting family strengths to support key processes in intervention and prevention efforts (Leadbeater, Dodgen, & Solarz, 2005). Mixed methods, combining quantitative and qualitative studies, are required to advance understanding of key variables in family resilience (Black & Lobo, 2008; Luthar & Brown, 2007).

The very flexibility of the construct of resilience complicates research efforts (Barton, 2005; Luthar, 2006). Unlike a static, singular family model or set of traits, resilience involves processes over time that may vary depending on adverse conditions and available resources. Different strengths might be called to the fore to deal with context-specific challenges, as with the death of a child or a parent's recurrent cancer, or the ongoing complex trauma of families in war zones or refugee camps. The family resilience framework presented here is being applied by researchers in many regions of the world (e.g., Yang & Choi, 2002), most often serving as a broad conceptual map for qualitative inquiry in interviews and questionnaires, each adapting particular questions and emphases to fit their research populations and the type of adversity under study. Continuing and future work is needed to clarify the most useful components of family functioning with varying adverse conditions and populations. A network of investigators and community mental health professionals interested in family resilience is currently being developed.

CLINICAL VALUE
OF A FAMILY RESILIENCE ORIENTATION

Over recent decades, the field of family therapy has refocused attention from family deficits to family strengths (see Walsh, Chapter 2, this volume). The therapeutic relationship has become more collaborative and empowering of client potential, with recognition that successful interventions depend more on mobilizing family resources than on therapist techniques. Assessment and intervention are redirected from how problems were caused to how they can be solved, identifying and amplifying existing and potential competencies.

This positive, future-oriented stance refocuses from how families have failed to how families can succeed.

A family resilience approach to practice draws on principles and techniques common among strengths-based models. It is distinct in attending more centrally to links between presenting symptoms and significant family stressors, and sociocultural and developmental contexts. It addresses symptoms of distress associated with highly stressful events and conditions, identifying and fortifying key processes for resilience (Walsh, 2003). This approach also gives greater attention to developmental processes over time, as families shift interactional patterns to meet emerging challenges and changing priorities. Principles guiding this approach are outlined in Table 17.2.

Resilience-Oriented Assessment

Families most often seek help in times of crisis or as chronic pressures mount, but they may not connect presenting problems with relevant stressors. A basic premise guiding this approach is that significant stresses reverberate throughout the family system and, in turn, key family processes mediate the adaptation of all members and their relationships.

In resilience oriented assessment, current distress is assessed in sociocultural and developmental contexts. A family system genogram and time line (McGoldrick, Gerson, & Petry, 2008) are valuable clinical and research tools to schematize relationship information, track system patterns, and guide

TABLE 17.2. Family Resilience: Principles for Clinical
and Community-Based Practice

- Relational view of human resilience (vs. "rugged individual")
  - o Family and social bonds; community, cultural, and spiritual resources
- Shift from deficit view of families
  - o Challenged by adversity; potential for repair and growth
- Grounded in developmental systemic theory
  - o Biopsychosocial–spiritual influences over life course, generations
- Crisis events, major stressors impact family system; family response influences
  - o Recovery of all members, relationships, and family unit
- Contextual view of crisis, distress, and adaptation
  - o Family, larger systems/institutional supports; sociocultural influences
  - o Temporal influences
    - Timing of symptoms vis-à-vis crisis/trauma events
    - Pile-up of stressors, disruptive transitions, persistent adversity
    - Varying adaptational challenges over time: immediate–long-term
    - Individual and family developmental phases, multigenerational patterns
- Varied pathways in resilience—No single model fits all families and situation
- Interventions have prevention value: In strengthening resilience, families become more resourceful; proactive in meeting future challenges

intervention planning. Because family structures and important bonds are so varied, it is important to map all significant relationships within and beyond the immediate household. This includes nonresidential parents, extended kin, and social networks. Many have knit together their own nurturing bonds for resilience with intimate partners and close friends whom they consider "family," such as the chosen families of many lesbian, gay, bisexual, and transgender persons (Oswald, 2002). Clincians attend to resources that have been lost and identify those torn by conflicts or estrangements that might be repaired.

Whereas clinical assessments tend to focus predominantly on problematic family patterns, a resilience-oriented approach prioritizes a search for positive influences—past, present, and potential. We ask about those members who might contribute strengths and resources in a team effort to overcome challenges. We identify potential role models and mentors in the kin network and are especially interested in hearing about resourceful ways family members have dealt with past adversity, such as stories about grandparents' "can-do spirit" through migration or economic hard times that might inspire efforts in mastering current challenges.

We explore how the timing of symptoms might be connected with highly stressful family transitions. Frequently, child symptoms coincide with anxiety-provoking transitions, such as parental separation with incarceration, transnational migration, or military service, which also involve family boundary shifts and role redefinition (MacDermid, 2010; MacDermid, Sampler, Schwartz, Nishida, & Nyarong, 2008).

Collaborative Intervention Process

In this practice approach, couples and family members work together, as a team, to find new possibilities in their problem-saturated situation and overcome impasses to change. The family resilience framework can serve as a valuable conceptual map to guide intervention and prevention efforts. In targeting and strengthening key processes as problems are addressed, risk and vulnerability are reduced. As families become more resourceful, they are better able to meet future challenges. Thus, building resilience is also a preventive measure.

Rather than rescuing so-called "survivors" from "dysfunctional families," this practice approach engages troubled families, with respect and compassion for their struggles; affirms their reparative potential; and seeks to bring out their best qualities. Family members are regarded as essential members of the healing team for recovery and resilience. Efforts aim both to reduce vulnerability and to enhance family functioning, with the potential to benefit all family members as they strengthen relational bonds and the family unit.

This collaborative approach readily engages "resistant" families, who are often reluctant to come for mental health services out of expectations (and prior experience) that they will be judged as disturbed or deficient and blamed for their problems. Instead, family members are viewed as intending

TABLE 17.3. Practice Guidelines to Strengthen Family Resilience

- Honor the dignity and worth of all family members.
- Convey conviction in their potential to overcome adversity through shared efforts.
- Use respectful language, framing to humanize and contextualize distress:
  o View as understandable, common in adverse situation (e.g., traumatic event—normal reactions to abnormal or extreme conditions).
  o Decrease shame, blame, stigma, pathologizing.
- Provide safe haven for sharing pain, concerns, challenges.
  o Show compassion for suffering and struggle.
  o Build communication, empathy, mutual support among members.
- Identify and affirm strengths, resources alongside vulnerabilities, limitations.
- Draw out and build potential for mastery, healing, and growth.
- Tap into kin, community, and spiritual resources—lifelines—to deal with challenges.
- View crisis as opportunity for learning, change, and growth.
- Shift focus from problems to possibilities.
  o Gain mastery, healing, and transformation out of adversity.
  o Reorient future hopes and dreams.
- Integrate adverse experience—including resilience—into individual and relational life passage.

to do their best for one another and struggling with an overwhelming set of challenges. Therapeutic efforts mobilize family and community resources, mastering challenges through collaborative efforts (see Table 17.3 for practice guidelines).

This approach is also valuable in therapeutic efforts toward the healing of relational wounds and reconciliation of estranged relationships (Walsh, 2006). A young adult might be helped to see an alcoholic, depressed parent in a new light by learning more about the trauma she experienced in her life, thereby gaining compassion for her struggles and appreciation of her courage, alongside her limitations. Without negating a client's own experience of neglect, one's view of a parent can be expanded and humanized. Not all individuals may be successful in overcoming life's adversities, but although they may have faltered, all are seen to have dignity and worth.

Broad Range of Practice Applications

A family resilience orientation can be applied usefully with a wide range of crisis situations, disruptive transitions, and multistress conditions in clinical and community services. A systemic assessment may be family-centered but include individual and/or group work with youth, single parents, or caregivers. Putting an ecological view into practice, interventions may involve coordination and collaboration with community agencies, religious communities, the workplace, schools, health care providers, and other larger systems.

Over the past 20 years, this family resilience orientation has guided the development of professional training, consultation, and services by the Chicago Center for Family Health (codirected by John Rolland and myself). Programs have been designed in partnership with community-based organizations to address a range of challenges (Rolland & Walsh, 2006; Walsh, 2002a, 2006, 2007, 2011b):

- Serious illness, disability challenges (e.g., "Resilient Partners" groups with multiple sclerosis; positive adaptation with diabetes; pediatric conditions)
- End-of-life challenges and complicated family bereavement
- Complex trauma, traumatic loss in war-torn regions and major disasters (Hurricane Katrina)
- Refugee trauma: multifamily groups (Bosnian and Kosovar)
- Divorce and stepfamily reorganization
- Family stresses with job loss and prolonged transition
- Family–school partnerships for success of at-risk youth
- Challenges for lesbian, gay, bisexual, and transgender persons, couples, families

Resilience-based family interventions can be adapted to a variety of formats, including family consultations or family counseling/therapy. Psychoeducational multifamily groups, workshops, and community forums offer social support and practical information, providing guidelines for crisis management, problem solving, and stress reduction as families navigate stressful periods and face future challenges. Family and community forums have been effective in widespread disaster situations (Landau & Saul, 2004; Walsh, 2007). Therapists or group facilitators may help families clarify specific stresses and develop effective coping strategies, and share pride and celebration in small successes. Brief, cost-effective psychoeducational "modules" timed for critical transitions or phases of a life challenge encourage families to digest manageable portions of a long-term recovery process. The following program descriptions are offered to illustrate this approach.

Facilitating Family Resilience with Job Loss and Prolonged Unemployment

One CCFH program was directed to the adaptation of displaced workers and their families when jobs were lost due to factory closings or company downsizing. Our faculty designed and implemented family resilience workshops and counseling services in partnership with a community-based agency specializing in job retraining and placement services. Job and income loss, as well as anxiety and uncertainty about prolonged unemployment and reemployment success, often fueled depression, substance abuse, and marital/family conflict. Cumulative stresses over many months, in turn, reduced the ability of spouses and family members to support worker efforts. In one case, when a large clothing manufacturing plant relocated, over 1,800 workers lost their jobs. Most were ethnic minority breadwinners for their families, many were single parents, and most had limited education and skills for employment in the changing job market.

Family resilience-oriented workshops addressed the personal and familial impact of losses and transitional stresses, attending to family strains, reorganizing role functions, and rallying family members to support the best efforts of the displaced worker. Group sessions focused on keys to resilience, such as identifying constraining beliefs (e.g., "No one will hire me, with all my deficiencies") to identify and affirm strengths, such as pride in doing a job well and personal qualities of dependability and loyalty in work and family life. For men whose sense of worth was diminished when losing the traditional male role as financial provider, it was important to broaden their contribution and value to their family. Fathers experienced new competencies and benefits through greater sharing of household and childrearing responsibilities and couple bonds were strengthened. Single parents, depressed and depleted, were encouraged to involve their children's aunts, uncles, and godparents, as well as grandparents, and to offer mutual services, such as exchanging childcare time, for respite from burdens. Members brainstormed ways to build in "family fun time" and to show daily appreciation of loved ones despite stresses. The family groups offered encouragement to take initiative and persevere in job search efforts, and celebrated small successes as they strengthened family bonds.

Fostering Family and Community Resilience in Response to Mass Trauma

The value of a community-based family resilience approach with refugees from war-torn regions was demonstrated in projects developed by the Chicago Center for Family Health in collaboration with the Center on Genocide, Psychiatry, and Witnessing at the University of Illinois (Walsh, 2006; Weine et al., 2005). In 1998–1999, multifamily groups were designed for Bosnian and Kosovar refugees who had suffered atrocities and traumatic loss of loved ones, homes, and communities in the Serbian "ethnic cleansing" campaign. Our family resilience approach was sought out because many refugees were suffering posttraumatic stress symptoms but would not use mental health services, feeling shamed and stigmatized by psychiatric diagnostic categories and the narrow focus on individual symptoms of disorder. This program, called CAFES for Bosnians and TAFES for Kosovars (Coffee/Tea And Family Education & Support), utilized a 9-week, multifamily group format. Families readily participated, because it tapped into the strong family-centered cultural values and was located in an accessible neighborhood storefront, where they felt comfortable. Offering a safe and compassionate setting to share stories of suffering and struggle, it also drew out and affirmed family strengths, such as their courage, endurance, and faith; strong kinship networks; deep concern for loved ones; and determination to rise above their tragedies to forge a new life. Paraprofessional facilitators from their community were trained to co-lead groups to foster collaboration and develop local resources. Families experienced this approach as respectful and empowering.

These projects led to the development of the Kosovar Family Professional Educational Collaborative (KFPEC) in Kosovo between local mental health professionals and an American team of family therapy consultants supported by the American Family Therapy Academy. The aim of this multiyear project was to enhance the capacities of mental health professionals and paraprofessionals to address the overwhelming service needs in their war-torn region by providing family-resilience-based services to foster recovery in the wake of widespread trauma and loss (Rolland & Weine, 2000). Recognizing that the psychosocial needs of refugees, other trauma survivors, and vulnerable persons in societies in transition far exceed the individual and psychopathological focus of conventional trauma mental health approaches, their approach built on family and cultural strengths. The consultants, sharing a broad multisystemic, resilience-oriented approach, encouraged Kosovar professionals to adapt the framework and develop their own practice methods to best fit local context and service needs.

The approach emphasized the importance of meeting with families to hear their stories, bearing witness to atrocities suffered, and eliciting each family's strengths and resources (Becker, Sargent, & Rolland, 2000). In one family, the mother had listened to the gunshots as her husband, two sons, and two grandsons were murdered in the yard of their farmhouse. She and her surviving family members talked with team members in their home about what has kept them strong:

The surviving son in the family responded, "We are all believers. One of the strengths in our family is from Allah . . . Having something to believe has helped very much."

INTERVIEWER: What do you do to keep faith strong?

SON: I see my mother as the 'spring of strength' . . . to see someone who has lost five family members—it gives us strength just to see her. We must think about the future and what we can accomplish. This is what keeps us strong. What will happen to him (pointing to his 5-year-old nephew) if I am not here? If he sees me strong, he will be strong. If I am weak, he will become weaker than me.

INTERVIEWER: What do you hope your nephew will learn about the family as he grows up?

SON: The moment when he will be independent and helping others and the family—for him, it will be like seeing his father and grandfather and uncles alive again. (p. 29)

In this family, the positive influence of belief systems was striking, in particular, the power of religious faith and the inspiration of strong models and mentors. In other families, team members noted that resilience was strengthened by their connectedness/cohesiveness and adaptive role flexibility:

> Everyone belongs to the family and to the family's homeland, alive or dead, here or abroad. Everyone matters and everyone is counted and counted upon When cooking or planting everyone moves together fluidly, in a complementary pattern, each person picking up what the previous person left off . . . A hidden treasure in the family is their adaptability to who fills in each of the absented roles. Although the grief about loss is immeasurable, their resilience [is] remarkable. (Becker et al., 2000, p. 29)

Family resilience-oriented intervention approaches are increasingly being developed for situations of mass trauma, war-related trauma, and natural disasters (Boss, 2006; Boss, Beaulieu, Wieling, Turner, & LaCruz, 2003; Boyd-Franklin, 2010; Cohen, Slonim, Finzi, & Leichtentritt, 2002; Girwitz, Forgatch, & Wieling, 2008; Hernandez, 2002; Knowles, Sasser, & Garrison, 2010; Landau, 2007; Landau & Saul, 2004; Rowe & Liddle, 2008; MacDermid, 2010; MacDermid et al., 2008; Walsh, 2007). In contrast to individual symptom-focused treatment programs, such multisystemic approaches build healing networks that facilitate individual, family, and community resilience. Programs create a safe haven for family and community members to support each other in sharing both deep pain and positive strivings. They help families and communities expand their vision of what is possible through collaboration, not only to survive trauma and loss, but also to regain their spirit to thrive.

Navigating New Challenges in a Changing World

A family resilience framework is especially timely in helping families with unprecedented challenges as the world around them changes at an accelerated pace (see Walsh, Chapter 1, this volume). Family cultures and structures are becoming increasingly diverse and fluid. Over an extended family life cycle, adults and their children are moving in and out of increasingly complex family configurations, with each transition posing new adaptational challenges. Amid social, economic, and political upheavals worldwide, families are dealing with many losses, disruptions, and uncertainties.

Yet, as Lifton (1993) contends, humans are surprisingly resilient. He compares our predicament and response to that of the Greek god Proteus: Just as he was able to change shape in response to crisis, we create new psychological, social, and family configurations, exploring new options and transforming our lives many times over the life course and the generations. Most families show remarkable resilience in creatively reweaving their family life. Yet stressful transitions and attempts to navigate uncharted territory can contribute to individual and relational distress. A resilience-oriented practice approach assesses individual, couple, and family distress in relation to this larger societal and global context. Families may need help to grieve their actual and symbolic losses as they "bounce forward" to adapt. Therapists can help families find coherence in the midst of complexity, and maintain continuities in the midst of upheaval as they journey into the future. Resilience does not mean bouncing back unscathed, but struggling well, effectively working through and learning from adversity, and integrating the experience into life's journey.

CONCLUSION

A family resilience orientation involves a crucial shift in emphasis from family deficits to family challenges, with conviction in the potential inherent in family systems for recovery and positive growth out of adversity. By targeting interventions to strengthen key processes for resilience, families become more resourceful in dealing with crises, navigating disruptive transitions, weathering persistent stresses, and meeting future challenges.

Although some families are more vulnerable or face more hardships than others, all are seen to have potential for gaining resilience in meeting their challenges, forging varied pathways. Beyond coping, adaptation, or competence in managing difficulties, resilience processes enable transformation and positive growth, which can emerge out of experiences of adversity. This research-informed conceptual framework can usefully be integrated with many strengths-based practice approaches and applied with a wide range of adverse conditions, with attunement to family and cultural diversity. Resilience-oriented services foster family empowerment as they bring forth shared hope, develop new and renewed competencies, and strengthen family bonds.

REFERENCES

Anthony, E. J., & Cohler, B. J. (Eds.). (1987). *The invulnerable child.* New York: Guilford Press.

Antonovsky, A. (1993). The structure and properties of the Sense of Coherence Scale. *Social Science and Medicine, 36*(6), 725–733.

Antonovsky, A., & Sourani, T. (1988). Family sense of coherence and family adaptation. *Journal of Marriage and Family, 50,* 79–92.

Aponte, H. (1994). *Bread and spirit: Therapy with the poor.* New York: Norton.

Barton, W.H. (2005). Methodological challenges in the study of resilience. In M. Ungar (Ed.), *Handbook for working with children and youth: Pathways to resilience across cultures and contexts* (pp. 135–147). Thousand Oaks, CA: Sage.

Beavers, W. R., & Hampson, R. B. (2003). Measuring family competence: The Beavers Systems Model. In F. Walsh (Ed.), *Normal family processes* (3rd ed., pp. 549–580). New York: Guilford Press.

Becker, C., Sargent, J., & Rolland, J. S. (2000). Kosovar Family Professional Education Collaborative. *AFTA Newsletter, 80,* 26–30.

Black, K., & Lobo, M. (2008). A conceptual review of family resilience factors. *Journal of Family Nursing, 14,* 33–55.

Bonanno, G. A. (2004). Loss, trauma, and human resilience: Have we underestimated the human capacity to thrive after extremely aversive events? *American Psychologist, 59,* 20–28.

Boss, P. (1999). *Ambiguous loss.* Cambridge, MA: Harvard University Press.

Boss, P. (2006). *Loss, trauma, and resilience: Therapeutic work with ambiguous loss.* New York: Norton.

Boss, P., Beaulieu, L., Weiling, E., & Turner, W. (2003). Healing loss, ambiguity, and trauma: A community-based intervention with families of union workers missing after the 9/11 attack in New York City. *Journal of Marital and Family Therapy, 29*(4), 455–467.

Boyd-Franklin, N. (2010). Families affected by Hurricane Katrina and other disasters: Learning from the experiences of African American survivors. In P. Dass-Brailsford (Ed.), *Crisis and disaster counseling: Learning from Hurricane Katrina and other disasters* (pp. 67–82). Thousand Oaks, CA: Sage.

Cohen, O., Slonim, I., Finzi, R., & Leichtentritt, R. (2002). Family resilience: Israeli mothers' perspectives. *American Journal of Family Therapy, 30,* 173–187.

Conger, R. D., & Conger, K. J. (2002). Resilience in Midwestern families: Selected findings from the first decade of a prospective, longitudinal study. *Journal of Marriage and Family, 64*(2), 361–373.

Epstein, N., Ryan, C., Bishop, D., Miller, I., & Keitner, G. (2003). The McMaster model: View of healthy family functioning. In F. Walsh (Ed.), *Normal family processes* (3rd ed., pp. 581–607). New York: Guilford Press.

Falicov, C. (1995). Training to think culturally: A multidimensional comparative framework. *Family Process, 34,* 373–388.

Falicov, C. J. (2007). Working with transnational immigrants: Expanding meanings of family, community and culture. *Family Process, 46,* 157–172.

Feder, A., Nestler, E. J., & Charney, D. S. (2009). Psychobiology and molecular genetics of resilience. *Nature, 10,* 1–12.

Garmezy, N. (1991). Resiliency and vulnerability to adverse developmental outcomes associated with poverty. *American Behavioral Scientist, 34,* 416–430.

Girwitz, A., Forgatch, M., & Wieling, E. (2008). Parenting practices as potential mechanisms for child adjustment following mass trauma. *Journal of Marital and Family Therapy, 34,* 177–192.

Gorell Barnes, G. (1999). Divorce transitions: Identifying risk and promoting resilience for children and their parental relationships. *Journal of Marital and Family Therapy, 25,* 425–441.

Greeff, A. P., & Human, B. (2004). Resilience in families in which a parent has died. *American Journal of Family Therapy, 32*(1), 27–42.

Greeff, A. P., & Van der Merwe, S. (2004). Variables associated with resilience in divorced families. *Social Indicators Research, 68*(1), 59–75.

Hansson, K., & Cederblad, M. (2004). Sense of coherence as a meta-theory for salutogenic family therapy. *Journal of Family Psychotherapy, 15,* 39–54.

Hauser, S. T. (1999). Understanding resilient outcomes: Adolescent lives across time and generations. *Journal of Research on Adolescence, 9*, 1–24.

Hawley, D. R., & DeHaan, L. (1996). Toward a definition of family resilience: Integrating lifespan and family perspectives. *Family Process, 35*, 283–298.

Hernandez, P. (2002). Resilience in families and communities: Latin American contributions from the psychology of liberation. *Journal of Counseling and Therapy for Couples and Families, 10*(3), 334–343.

Higgins, G. O. (1994). *Resilient adults: Overcoming a cruel past.* San Francisco: Jossey-Bass.

Kaufman, J., & Ziegler, E. (1987). Do abused children become abusive parents? *American Journal of Orthopsychiatry, 57*, 186–192.

Kirmayer, L.J., Dandeneau, S., Marshall, E., Phillips, M. K., & Williamson, K. J. (2011). Rethinking resilience from indigenous perspectives. *Canadian Journal of Psychiatry, 56*, 84–91.

Knowles, R., Sasser, D., & Garrison, M. E. B. (2010). Family resilience and resiliency following Hurricane Katrina. In R. Kilmer, V. Gil-Rivas, R. Tedeschi, & L. Calhoun (Eds.), *Helping families and communities recover from disaster* (pp. 97–115). Washington, DC: American Psychological Association Press.

Landau, J. (2007). Enhancing resilience: Families and communities as agents for change. *Family Process, 46*(3), 351–365.

Landau, J., & Saul, J. (2004). Facilitating family and community resilience in response to major disasters. In F. Walsh & M. McGoldrick (Eds.), *Living beyond loss: Death in the family* (2nd ed., pp. 285–309). New York: Norton.

Leadbeater, B., Dodgen, D., & Solarz, A. (2005). The resilience revolution: A paradigm shift for research and policy. In R. D. Peters, B. Leadbeater, & R. J. McMahon (Eds.), *Resilience in children, families, and communities: Linking context to practice and policy* (pp. 47–63). New York: Kluwer.

Lifton, R. J. (1993). *The Protean self: Human resilience in an age of fragmentation.* New York: Basic Books.

Luthar, S. (2006). Resilience in development: A synthesis of research across five decades. In D. Cicchetti & Cohen (Eds.). *Developmental psychopathology* (Vol. 3, 2nd ed., pp. 739–795). Hoboken, NJ: Wiley.

Luthar, S., & Brown, P. (2007). Maximizing resilience through diverse levels of inquiry: Prevailing paradigms, possibilities, and priorities for the future. *Development and Psychopathology, 19*, 931–955.

MacDermid, S. M. (2010). Family risk and resilience in the context of war and terrorism. *Journal of Marriage and Family, 72*, 537–556.

MacDermid, S. M., Sampler, R., Schwartz, R., Nishida, J., & Nyarong, D. (2008). *Understanding and promoting resilience in military families.* West Lafayette, IN: Military Family Research Institute at Purdue University.

Mackay, R. (2003). Family resilience and good child outcomes: An overview of the research literature. *Journal of New Zealand, 20*, 98–118.

Masten, A. (2001). Ordinary magic: Resilience processes in development. *American Psychologist, 56*(3), 227–238.

McCubbin, H., McCubbin, M., McCubbin, A., & Futrell, J. (Eds.). (1998). *Resiliency in African-American families.* Thousand Oaks, CA: Sage.

McCubbin, H., Thompson, E., Thompson, A., & Fromer, J. (Eds.). (1998). *Resiliency in Native American and immigrant families.* Thousand Oaks, CA: Sage.

McCubbin, H., & Patterson, J. M. (1983). The family stress process: The double ABCX model of adjustment and adaptation. *Marriage and Family Review, 6*(1–2), 7–37.

McCubbin, L. D., & McCubbin, H. I. (2005). Culture and ethnic identity in family resilience: Dynamic processes in trauma and transformation of indigenous people. In M. Ungar (Ed.), *Handbook for working with children and youth: Pathways to resilience across cultures and contexts* (pp. 27–44). Thousand Oaks, CA: Sage.

McGoldrick, M., Carter, B., & Garcia-Preto, N. (2011). *The expanded family life cycle: Individual, family, and social perspectives* (4th ed.). Boston: Pearson.

McGoldrick, M., Gerson, R., & Petry, S. (2008). *Genograms: Assessment and intervention* (3rd ed.) New York: Norton.

Minuchin, P., Colapinto, J., & Minuchin, S. (2005). *Working with families of the poor* (2nd ed.) New York: Guilford Press.

Nadeau, J. W. (2001). Family construction of meaning. In R. Neimeyer (Ed.), *Meaning reconstruction and the experience of loss* (pp. 95–111). Washington, DC: American Psychological Association.

Olson, D. H., & Gorall, D. (2003). Circumplex model of marital and family systems. In F. Walsh (Ed.), *Normal family processes* (3rd ed., pp. 514–544). New York: Guilford Press.

Orthner, D. K., Jones-Sanpei, H., & Williamson, S. (2004). The resilience and strengths of low-income families. *Family Relations, 53*, 159–167.

Oswald, R. F. (2002). Resilience within the family networks of lesbians and gay men: Intentionality and redefinition. *Journal of Marriage and Family, 64*(2), 374–383.

Patterson, J. (2002). Integrating family resilience and family stress theory. *Journal of Marriage and Family, 64*, 349–373.

Reiss, D. (1981). *The family's construction of reality.* Cambridge, MA: Harvard University Press.

Rolland, J. S. (1994). *Families, illness and disability: An integrative treatment model.* New York: Basic Books.

Rolland, J. S., & Walsh, F. (2006). Facilitating family resilience with childhood illness and disability [Special issue on the family]. *Pediatric Opinion, 18*, 1–11.

Rolland, J. S., & Weine, S. (2000). Kosovar Family Professional Educational Collaborative. *AFTA Newsletter, 79*, 34–35.

Rowe, C. L., & Liddle, H. A. (2008). When the levee breaks: Treating adolescents and families in the aftermath of Hurricane Katrina. *Journal of Marital and Family Therapy, 34*, 132–148.

Rutter, M. (1987). Psychosocial resilience and protective mechanisms. *American Journal of Orthopsychiatry, 57*, 316–331.

Seccombe, K. (2002). "Beating the odds" versus "changing the odds": Poverty, resilience, and family policy. *Journal of Marriage and Family, 64*(2), 384–394.

Seligman, M. E. P. (1990). *Learned optimism.* New York: Random House.

Simon, J., Murphy, J., & Smith, S. (2005). Understanding and fostering family resilience. *Family Journal, 13*, 427–436.

Steinberg, L., Lamborn, S. D., Darling, N., Mounts, N. S., & Dornbusch, S. M. (1994). Over-time changes in adjustment and competence among adolescents from authoritative, authoritarian, indulgent, and neglectful families. *Child Development, 65*, 754–770.

Stinnett, N., & DeFrain, J. (1985). *Secrets of strong families.* Boston: Little, Brown.

Taylor, S. (1989). *Positive illusions: Creative self-deception and the healthy mind.* New York: Basic Books.

Tedeschi, R. G., & Calhoun, L. G. (2004). Posttraumatic growth: Conceptual foundations and empirical evidence. *Psychological Inquiry, 15,* 1–18.

Tedeschi, R. G., & Kilmer, R. (2005). Assessing strengths, resilience, and growth to guide clinical interventions. *Professional Psychology: Research and Practice, 36*(3), 230–237.

Tedeschi, R. G., Park, L. C., & Calhoun, L. G. (1996). The Posttraumatic Growth Inventory: Measuring the positive legacy of trauma. *Journal of Traumatic Stress, 9,* 455–471.

Ungar, M. (2004). The importance of parents and other caregivers to the resilience of high-risk adolescents. *Family Process, 43*(1), 23–41.

Walsh, F. (1996). The concept of family resilience: Crisis and challenge. *Family Process, 35,* 261–281.

Walsh, F. (2002a). A family resilience framework: Innovative practice applications. *Family Relations, 51*(2), 130–137.

Walsh, F. (2002b). Bouncing forward: Resilience in the aftermath of September 11. *Family Process, 40*(1), 34–36.

Walsh, F. (2003). Family resilience: A framework for clinical practice. *Family Process, 42*(1), 1–18.

Walsh, F. (2006). *Strengthening family resilience* (2nd ed.). New York: Guilford Press.

Walsh, F. (2007). Traumatic loss and major disasters: Strengthening family and community resilience. *Family Process, 46*(2), 207–227.

Walsh, F. (2009a). Family transitions: Challenges and resilience. In M. Dulcan (Ed.), *Textbook of child and adolescent psychiatry* (pp. 675–686). Washington, DC: American Psychiatric Association Press.

Walsh, F. (2009b). Human–animal bonds I: The relational significance of companion animals [Special section]. *Family Process, 48*(4), 462–480.

Walsh, F. (2009c). Human–animal bonds II: The role of pets in family systems and family therapy. *Family Process, 48*(4), 481–499.

Walsh, F. (2009d). Integrating spirituality in family therapy: Wellsprings for health, healing, and resilience. In F. Walsh (Ed.), *Spiritual resources in family therapy* (2nd ed., pp. 31–61). New York: Guilford Press.

Walsh, F. (Ed.). (2009e). *Spiritual resources in family therapy* (2nd ed.). New York: Guilford Press.

Walsh, F. (2011a). Families in later life: Challenges, opportunities, and resilience. In M. McGoldrick, B. Carter, & N. Garcia-Preto (Eds.), *The expanded family life cycle* (4th ed., pp. 261–277). Boston: Allyn & Bacon.

Walsh, F. (2011b). Resilience in families with serious health challenges. In M. Kraft-Rosenberg & S.-R. Pehler (Eds.), *Encyclopedia of family health.* Thousand Oaks, CA: Sage.

Walsh, F., & McGoldrick, M. (Eds.). (2004). *Living beyond loss: Death in the family* (2nd ed.). New York: Norton.

Weine, S., Knafi, K., Feetham, S., Kulauzavic, Y., Klebec, A., Sclove, S., et al. (2005). A mixed methods study of refugee families engaging in multiple-family groups. *Family Relations, 54,* 558–568.

Weingarten, K. (2004). Witnessing the effects of political violence in families: Mechanisms of intergenerational transmission of trauma and clinical interventions. *Journal of Marital and Family Therapy, 30*(1), 45–59.

Werner, E. E., & Smith, R. S. (2001). *Journeys from childhood to midlife: Risk, resilience, and recovery.* Ithaca, NY: Cornell University Press.

Wright, L. M., & Bell, J. M. (2009). *Beliefs and illness: A model for healing.* Calgary: 4th Floor Press.

Wuerffel, J., DeFrain, J., & Stinnett, N. (1990). How strong families use humor. *Family Perspective, 24*, 129–142.

Yang, O.-K., & Choi, M.-M. (2001). Korean's Han and resilience: Application to mental health social work. *Mental Health and Social Work, 11*(6), 7–29.

CHAPTER 18

NORMATIVE FAMILY TRANSITIONS, COUPLE RELATIONSHIP QUALITY, AND HEALTHY CHILD DEVELOPMENT

PHILIP A. COWAN
CAROLYN PAPE COWAN

The transition to parenthood, especially when the child is a firstborn, represents one of the most profound joys and, at the same time, one of the most significant and stressful changes that is likely to occur in a lifetime. The disequilibration does not come simply from welcoming a new being into the family, one that comes without a user's manual, but rather from that fact that becoming a parent represents a major life transition, with both expected and unexpected changes for individuals and their relationships. Other major life transitions, such as beginning on a job or career track, have similar effects on individual family members and their relationships. In this chapter, we examine the concept of life transitions, offer a working model of how transitions affect *the family*, and show how interventions to alleviate the stresses of the transition can have a dual purpose. First, such interventions come at a time when family members are more likely to recognize the need for new coping strategies and are more open to accepting offers of help. Second, because transitions bring old and new family coping strategies into high relief, they provide an optimal context for researchers and scholars to expand our understanding of how family processes contribute to the healthy development of both adults and children. Our emphasis on "normative transitions"—those that are predictable and expectable for a substantial number of families—is not meant to imply that our interest is restricted to "normal" or nonclinical families.

We attempt to show that interventions to strengthen family relationships and enhance children's adaptation during life transitions can be helpful all along the spectrum, ranging from well-functioning to distressed families.

Most family theoretical models and intervention programs that have their eye on children's well-being emphasize the quality of parent–child relationships as the key to affecting child outcomes. While we, too, regard both mother–child and father–child relationships as centrally important in shaping children's development, we have come to focus on the relationship between the parents as a central risk or protective factor affecting how well the family copes with major life transitions. We include findings from three different intervention studies and cite several others in support of the claim that preventive interventions focused on the couple relationship early in the period of childrearing can be helpful. We conclude by discussing the implications of our formulation for designing *preventive, family-based* interventions, with the ultimate goal of enhancing the development of all family members in the early years of children's lives.

NORMATIVE FAMILY TRANSITIONS

The Definition of Major Life Transitions

Transition as Metaphor

The metaphor of "transition" as a voyage between stable states, originally used to describe the early years of development (Erikson, 1950; Freud, 1938; Piaget, 1968), included the notion that the passage from one shore to another *requires* a transitional period in which there is change, disequilibrium, and some psychological stress or confusion. A number of theorists then found the concept of transition useful to describe turning points in a life trajectory as a person takes on new life tasks (e.g., Neugarten, 1965; Vaillant & Koury, 1993). Unlike childhood transitions, those in adulthood, such as leaving school, entering the workforce, selecting a mate, or having a child, are expectable; they often involve some degree of choice and do not necessarily occur in sequence, especially given the departures from traditional family patterns over recent decades.

Studies tend to focus on either normative or non-normative transitions. Normative transitions are expectable and predictable based on biological, psychological, or social norms. Non-normative transitions are statistically less predictable and often unexpected, but this distinction is not always so clear in practice (e.g., is divorce normative or non-normative?). Moreover, what is normative in one subculture (e.g., adolescents becoming autonomous from parents) may not be normative in another. Here, we focus primarily on psychosocial transitions that are normative in contemporary American society and leave open the question of applicability of our conclusions for other cultures.

The Distinction between Change and Transition

Not all of the myriad changes made by individuals and families over a lifetime fit the definition of transition. We have proposed that major life transitions for individuals involve qualitative reorganizations of the self and the inner world, social roles, and close relationships (P. A. Cowan, 1991). For example, very different transitions, such as becoming an adolescent or growing old, involve shifts in the definition of who we are and will become. During transitions, roles change in different ways—by addition (e.g., becoming a parent), subtraction (e.g., becoming a widow), and revision (e.g., job reclassification). A shift in one's inner world and identity and a reorganization of major life roles are almost inevitably accompanied by disequilibrium in one's central relationships inside and outside the family. From a systemic view of individuals and their social environments, there are repercussions throughout the family system when an individual or a couple grapples with major life change (e.g., Walsh, 2006). For example, in our study of couples becoming parents (C. P. Cowan & Cowan, 2000), the addition of a new identity as parent and the reduction in identity as "partner" was paralleled by changes in the nature and quality of the division of family work for both spouses, and by shifts in the quality of their relationship as a couple.

Because transitions disrupt the status quo, the typical individual and family resistance to change may decline, and openness to trying new ways of coping may increase. Thus, life transitions signal opportune moments to consider preventive or therapeutic interventions that could be helpful in moving families closer to adaptive positions on their life trajectories (Falicov, 1988). As we show later, just as intervention studies provide potential benefits for family processes, they also allow researchers to test hypotheses about the impact of family processes on children's adaptation (P. A. Cowan & Cowan, 2001); that is, planned interventions (randomized clinical trial experiments) add weight to the natural experiments triggered by life transitions and help us understand some of the mechanisms that explain how family processes affect children's development.

A SYSTEMS MODEL OF FAMILY PROCESSES DURING MAJOR LIFE TRANSITIONS

In our first two longitudinal research and preventive intervention studies of couples making the transition to parenthood (C. P. Cowan & Cowan, 2000) and families with a first child making the transition to elementary school (P. A. Cowan, Cowan, Ablow, Johnson, & Measelle, 2005) we tested a six-domain model of family functioning. Based on a variety of descriptions of family systems (McGoldrick, Carter, & Garcia-Preto, 2011; Walsh, 2006), the model is consistent with other family researchers' attempts to show that understanding adaptation in one domain (e.g., the couple relationship or the child's development) requires an ecological (Bronfenbrenner, 1979) or contextual analysis of multiple aspects of family life (e.g., Belsky, 1984; Heinicke, 2002).

The six interacting domains of family life in our model are (1) the well-being or distress of individual family members; (2) the quality of relationship between parents and *their* parents; (3) the quality of relationships between each parent and child(ren); (4) the quality of relationships between siblings; (5) the balance of life stress and social supports available to the family; and the central focus in our own studies, (6) the quality of relationship *between* the parents.

Figure 18.1 presents a schematic representation of the connections among five of the six family domains. We have omitted sibling relationships because of our initial focus on the first child, but we do not mean to discount the important influence of sibling relationships in children's development (e.g., Dunn & Plomin, 1990). The model represented in Figure 18.1 contains central features of family systems approaches to analyses of development and psychopathology (Wagner & Reiss, 1995). The structure or organization of family relationships affects the quality of the relationship between any two family members, and vice versa. The double-headed arrows signify that causality is circular rather than linear; parents affect children, and children affect parents;

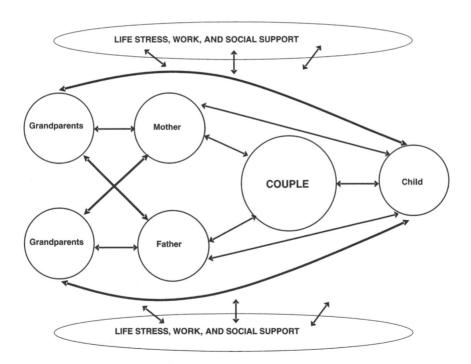

FIGURE 18.1. Domains of family life associated with children's development.

marital relationships affect parenting, and parenting affects marital relationships; grandparents from both sides of the family affect parents and children, and vice versa. Like cybernetic systems, family systems are self-regulating in that a perturbation of the system sets forces in motion that attempt to reach a new, more adaptive equilibrium.

One important feature of the systemic model is that family relationships have both direct and indirect effects. A cold, unforgiving relationship between grandparent and parent can affect the grandchild directly in terms of what the child observes, and indirectly in its impact on the parents as individuals and as a couple, and on the way they treat the child. We use this model to look at two major family transitions to show how variation in multiple domains contributes to our understanding of the dynamic connections among marital adaptation, parent–child relationship quality, and children's development.

NORMAL FAMILY PROCESSES
IN COUPLES BECOMING PARENTS

Over 40 years ago, sociologist LeMasters (1957) made the startling claim that having a first child produced a moderate or severe crisis in the marriages of 83% of the couples he interviewed, a view that generated wide controversy at the time. Here, we provide a selective update of this claim, largely supporting the LeMasters statement, with more detail. Most studies have focused on heterosexual couples having babies, but more recent studies bring attention to processes in same-sex couple relationships (see Goldberg & Perry-Jenkins, 2007, and Green, Chapter 8, this volume). We expect that future research will find that similar relational processes operate in major transitions in gay and lesbian couples, with added complexities of adoption or surrogacy, gender role socialization, legal obstacles, and social prejudice.

What Happens to Men, Women, and Marriage around the Birth of a First Child?

Shifts in the Sense of Self

Using a model of development derived from Erikson (1980), many writers have suggested that the disequilibrium involved in the transition to parenthood can precipitate an intrapsychic crisis leading to adaptation or dysfunction. Most assertions about the impact of having a child *on the parent*— positive or negative—come from therapy case studies and remain untested in systematic research. On the positive side, becoming a parent can lead to an increased sense of maturity, and a more differentiated and integrated approach to life, with more perspective on the connections between oneself and the world, increased vitality and commitment, and a greater ability to control one's impulses in the service of caring for others (P. A. Cowan, 1988). Despite extensive writing about the reawakening inner conflicts (Anthony & Benedek, 1970), the only well-established finding about negative effects of the transition on individual adaptation is an increased risk of clinical depression in postpartum women—approximately 10% of women in one study (Campbell, Cohn, Flanagan, & Popper, 1992). Two more recent studies find an increase in depressive symptoms from pregnancy into the first year of parenthood for both partners (Pancer, Pratt, Hunsberger, & Gallant, 2000; Paulson, Sharnail, & Bazemore, 2010).

Clearly, for many new parents this transition represents a marked restructuring of the self and a shifting sense of well-being. Nevertheless, an emphasis on change obscures the fact that people are likely to be consistent over time; expectant parents with low self-esteem before the birth were most likely to have low self-esteem as new parents at 6- and 18-months postpartum, and those whose relationships were highly satisfying were likely to be so after having a first baby (C. P. Cowan et al., 1985).

Shifts in Relationships with Families of Origin

Bringing a first child into the family requires a shift in family roles and relationships across the generations (see McGoldrick & Shibusawa, Chapter 16, this volume). As the baby's due date approaches, and especially after the birth, there tends to be more contact between the new parents and their families of origin (C. P. Cowan & Cowan, 2000). The increased calls and visits are not always positive, especially if the relationships were strained or ambivalent before the pregnancy was announced (Hansen & Jacob, 1992). We found several common sources of stress between the generations in the early postpartum period, especially for couples who lived far from their families of origin. Many new parents in our study were troubled by questions of how and when to arrange visits, how to respond to grandparents' criticism—direct or implied—about their handling of the baby, and whether or when new mothers should return to work. Some new parents expected that relationships between the generations would improve when they had a child. Although in a few cases the hoped-for improvement did occur (e.g., one new father reestablished contact with his parents after not talking to them for 10 years), relationships on the whole continued pretty much as they had before the babies were born. While there are notable shifts in the intensity of connection, the positive or negative valence of the relationship tends to remain unchanged.

Shifts in Relation to the Child

While forming a new family unit by adding a child to the couple system leads to a structural change in the family (from dyad to triad), it also adds new roles (mother, father) and new relationships (parent–child, grandparent–grandchild) to the system, some of which take some adjustment for all parties. The quality of the relationships with the baby may be affected by not only the parents' reaction but also the child's biological and psychological characteristics (see Spotts, Chapter 22, this volume). An infant's easy or difficult temperament makes a difference to parents' equilibrium and is related, in turn, to both individual and marital adaptation in the early postpartum months (Klinnert, Gavin, Wamboldt, & Mrazek, 1992).

Changes in Stress and Social Support

In our study of primarily middle-class couples from several ethnic backgrounds, men and women described no significant increase in overall stressful life events *outside* the nuclear family between pregnancy and 6- and 18-months postpartum (C. P. Cowan & Cowan, 2000). Other researchers (Levy-Shiff, Dimitrovsky, Shulman, & Har-Even, 1998) found an increase in parents' stress from pregnancy to 1-month postpartum, a decline in stress by 6-months postpartum, followed by another decline at 12 months.

One central issue for couples to resolve is their level of involvement in work outside the home during their child's first months of life. Most husbands described their work involvement as stemming directly from their desire to be good providers, but wives often viewed husbands' work as an avoidance of involvement in the family. In the context of contemporary U.S. culture, where working outside the home is now normative for mothers of young children, mothers who went back to work during the first 18-months postpartum (about 50%) reported feeling torn by wanting to care for their infants and toddlers, while mothers who stayed home by choice felt conflicting desires to care for their children, to ease the family's new financial burdens, and to pursue their careers (Hochschild & Machung, 1990; see Fraenkel & Capstick, Chapter 4, this volume).

Changes in the Couple

We asked each participant in our study to fill out a questionnaire we called "The Pie" (C. P. Cowan et al., 1985), by indicating on a blank circle how large each aspect of self feels (not how much time it takes). The increased psychological space allocated to men's and women's identity as new parents seemed to come at the expense of the aspect of the self they labeled "partner" or "lover." In our study, data from questionnaires were buttressed by interviews in which a recurrent theme was parents' reports of placing their couple relationship on the back burner while they coped with the realities and ambiguities of life with a newborn whose requests for nurturance required extensive decoding, and whose sleep and waking patterns were often unpredictable. Parental fatigue and anxiety, the need to juggle family and work life, and simply the presence of a new resident in the household clearly reduced the time, opportunity, and actual experience of marital intimacy.

A number of investigators have found that role arrangements that constitute a couple's division of family labor become more traditional when partners
become parents. Despite a growing *ideology* of egalitarianism in marriage
over the past 40 years, men still tend to do less family work after the birth
of a baby than they did before, and fewer of the daily tasks of caring for the
children than they predicted they would (see Fraenkel & Capstick, Chapter 4,
and Knudson-Martin, Chapter 14, this volume). This shift in roles appears to
spill over into communication between husbands and wives as marital conflict
increases and the "Who does what?" of daily life becomes the number one
issue of conflict between them (C. P. Cowan & Cowan, 2000).

Not surprisingly, then, for the average couple making the transition to
first-time parenthood, marital satisfaction declines from pregnancy into the
early childrearing years—for women, in the first year of parenthood, and for
men in the second. Let us be clear: New parents' satisfaction with marriage
does not plummet from the heights of happiness to the depths of despair.
The average decline is quite modest but very consistent across many studies. It is also important to note that marital satisfaction rises for 18–30% of
couples after having a baby, which is a significant proportion (C. P. Cowan &
Cowan, 1995). Nevertheless, with the exception of three studies that report
no significant change, results of more than 50 longitudinal studies conducted
between the late 1970s and the turn of the 21st century in different regions
of the United States (Gotttman, 1994; Shapiro, Gottman, & Carrère, 2000;
Twenge, Campbell, & Foster, 2003), Israel (Levy-Shiff et al., 1998), England
(Parr, 1997), and Germany (Gloger-Tippelt & Huerkamp, 1998) reveal that
a substantial majority of couples show significant declines in marital satisfaction after having a first baby.

Most transition to parenthood studies, including our own, find that
the best predictor of marital quality after having a baby is the quality of the
couple's relationship before the baby arrived (C. P. Cowan & Cowan, 1995).
Babies do not bring couples previously experiencing high unresolved conflict
closer, nor do they drive apart couples whose relationships were highly satisfying and compatible. This point deserves more attention in discussions of the
transition to parenthood. A central feature of life transitions is that even in a
context of small but important before-and-after changes, the central core of
individual and relationship functioning remains in place. Moreover, substantial predictability of pre- to postbirth characteristics means that it is possible
to identify families and children at risk for relationship difficulties before the
child's birth. This increases the possibility of providing targeted interventions
to help parents make the transition more successfully and to facilitate the
healthy development of their children in the long term.

One prebirth risk factor for marital decline emerged clearly in our study.
The ways couples collaborated on the planning of the pregnancy was predictive of what happened to their relationship after having a baby. When we
asked in partners' sixth or seventh month of pregnancy how they came to be

having a baby at this time, we found that approximately 50% of the couples deliberately planned the timing of their first pregnancy, and 20% accepted the news of a pregnancy as "fate." Most did reasonably well in terms of their satisfaction as couples in the first 3 years of parenthood. Another 20% of the couples, who described moderate ambivalence about the prospect of becoming parents, showed a sharp decline in marital satisfaction in the early years of parenthood. Another 10% of the couples, when interviewed in their third trimester of pregnancy, were divided, with one partner wanting a child and the other not feeling ready. Out of those nine couples, two, in which the man wanted the baby and the woman was the reluctant partner, reported high marital conflict 3 years later. In all seven couples in which the woman wanted the baby but the man did not feel ready to become a father, the partners had divorced by the time their child entered kindergarten. Data from other studies (e.g., Cox, Paley, Payne, & Burchinal, 1999) support the conclusion that disagreement about whether or when to have a child signals risk for the parents' couple relationship during the early childrearing years.

An important marker of marital adaptation is the tendency for marriages to remain intact or dissolve. Our own data correspond with national surveys, which suggest that about 20% of all divorces occur within 5 years after the birth of a first child (Bumpass & Rindfuss, 1979). *This means that almost half of all couples with children who divorce will have done so before their first child enters kindergarten.* Before rushing to conclude that the strains inherent in the transition to parenthood are responsible for early marital dissolution, the statistics on marital stability–divorce reveal that couples without children tend to divorce at an even higher rate than those in early parenthood, with the rates evening up only during the second decade of marriage. In our sample that included some couples who had not yet decided whether to have a baby, compared with the 20% divorce rate in new parents, 50% of those who did not have a baby were separated or divorced 5 years after the study began. This suggests that despite increased marital stresses that accompany the transition to parenthood, the presence of a child appears to help keep couples together in the early family-making years.

Two methodological points about research on the transition to parenthood are worth noting. First, studies rarely include a comparison group of couples that have not had a baby, to control for the possibility that marital decline is attributable to the erosion of intimacy over time. Our own results (C. P. Cowan et al., 1985) and those of Shapiro et al. (2000) reveal that, compared with childless couples, new parents showed a sharper drop in marital satisfaction over the 2-year period surrounding the transition to parenthood. Second, relatively little is known about this transition in samples defined as being at high risk by virtue of youth, low income, and single parenthood (C. P. Cowan & Cowan, 1995). Studies have been conducted with high-risk mothers—many one-time cross-sectional studies (Brooks-Gunn & Chase-Lansdale, 1995), several with longitudinal designs (Olds et al., 1998)—but all began after childbirth, and none compared new mothers with childless women in the same general life circumstances. Therefore, we have almost no information on how much of the stress attributed to low-income single motherhood may reflect the normative challenges involved in making the transition to parenthood, and how much additional stress can be explained by economic and social conditions associated with poverty (see Anderson, Chapter 6, this volume). Furthermore, it is important to investigate what happens to not only the mothers themselves as they become parents but also their intimate relationships. Studies have ignored the fact that a majority of contemporary single mothers giving birth are in romantic relationships with the child's father, making it possible to study the impact of the transition on the couple in most "single parent" families (McLanahan, Garfinkel, Reichman, Teitler, Carlson, & Audigier, 2003).

In summary, although new studies are needed, especially of families not in the middle class, we can conclude from many studies that becoming a parent is a major life transition, with significant changes in men's and women's self-views, roles, and relationships. Despite the pleasures associated with this transition, research provides consistent support for the hypothesis that it is normal for normative family transitions to create changes in new parents' relationships, especially in their relationship as a couple, in the direction of increasing conflict, dissatisfaction, and disappointment.

Couples Group Interventions for Partners Becoming Parents

The Becoming a Family Project, begun in 1979, was a preventive intervention in the form of couples groups for first-time parents (C. P. Cowan & Cowan, 2000). At the time of its inception we did not have all of the data that now strongly support the need to help couples through this normative transition. Couples were recruited for a study of what happens during this important life transition; they were randomly invited to participate in a couples group or a no-treatment control condition. Because they did not know about the intervention when they entered the study, they were not couples seeking help with problems. The couples groups, led by trained mental health professionals, were 2 hours long and met weekly for 24 weeks. Group discussions, which were partially structured and partially open-ended, covered salient topics in each of the family domains in Figure 18.1 (e.g., feelings about themselves as individuals, issues with parents and in-laws, developmentally appropriate discipline of children, stress at work, conflict between the parents, and strengths and successes in each of these aspects of family life). Because we were interested in what was working for families during this life transition, the leaders encouraged the parents' exploration of their successes and difficulties.

Although some couples offered advice, and leaders sometimes made suggestions about handling a marital or parenting issue, the groups were not didactic sessions in which specific skills were taught to parents. The intent was to provide a safe, containing environment in which men and women could (1) listen to their partners and others facing similar problems and dilemmas at the same stage of family life, (2) discuss differences or impasses under the guidance of mental health professionals who would help them express ideas and feelings but prevent high levels of conflict from escalating in ways that erode marital relationships over time, and (3) find examples of successful coping with the challenges of life as parents and partners. Couples in both treatment and control conditions were assessed in midpregnancy, and again at 6, 18, 36, and 60 months postpartum (during the transition to kindergarten). The most salient outcome was that, consistent with the nonintervention literature, couples randomly assigned to the control condition declined in marital satisfaction over the first 5 years of parenthood, whereas couples participating in the groups from late-pregnancy through the early months of parenthood maintained their marital satisfaction over the next 5 years (Schulz, Cowan, & Cowan, 2006).

A few recent studies of middle-class couples with follow-ups from 1–2 years postpartum show similar positive effects on marital satisfaction (Feinberg, Kan, & Goslin, 2009; Gottman, Gottman, & Shapiro, 2009; Halford, Petch, & Creedy, 2010). Finally, preliminary results from a large national study of unmarried couples—Building Strong Families (Wood, McConnell, Quinn, Clarkwest, & Hsueh, 2010)—indicate that only one of eight sites that specifically focused on couples having children produced significant positive results. We have, then, clear indications that, for middle-class families, becoming a parent is a normative transition that brings some associated risks for the couple, and that group interventions attended by both partners may provide a buffer that reduces risks for the participants and prevents or reduces the expectable slide in couple relationship quality. We need much more information about who benefits most from these interventions and whether they are equally effective for low-income families.

FAMILY FACTORS IN CHILDREN'S TRANSITION TO SCHOOL

In the years that follow couples' transition to parenthood, individuals and families may undergo a number of transitions—having a second child, moving, changing jobs, starting their children in day care, separation or divorce, and so on. Even so, in Western cultures, the next *universal* normative transition after the birth of a first child occurs when the child begins formal education. We focus here on children's transition to elementary school, and on family processes that facilitate or impede children's development and adaptation. We rely centrally on our own work (P. A. Cowan, Cowan, Ablow, et al., 2005), because very few studies have followed families longitudinally from the preschool through the early school period, with systematic observation-based information about family processes before and after children make the transition to formal schooling.

On the first day of elementary school, it is clear that the children's sense of self, roles, and relationships are changing. They are entering a new institution with new rules and demands. Even those with extensive preschool experience are required to take the role of student in a larger social environment with few close friends and adults who know and understand them. In the Schoolchildren and Their Families study, we had ample opportunity to hear about parents' (1) preoccupation with the choice of schools, (2) disagreements about who would obtain school information and what decisions they need to make, (3) worries about whether the child would "get along" with peers and teachers, (4) reawakened emotional issues about ways their own parents had or had not helped them, and (5) questions about whether the child's entrance to school provides some opportunity, especially for women, to consider new work arrangements. This was also a period in which two-thirds of the families had already had a second child, and several were about to have a third. Siblings, too, felt the pressure of the family focus on the oldest child as he or she would be going off to "the big school." In short, parents talked about concerns in each of the domains of family life represented in our six-domain model.

Study Design

The Schoolchildren and their Families Project drew on a population quite similar to that of our earlier study of couples in transition to parenthood. More than 200 couples with children in preschools and day care centers in 28 cities and towns in the San Francisco Bay area initially filled out a questionnaire and agreed to be interviewed. They were randomly invited to participate in one of three conditions: (1) a 16-session couples group meeting weekly, led by male–female teams of trained mental health professionals who emphasized marital issues during the open-ended part of each meeting, when couples brought their own issues; (2) a 16-week couples group in which the leaders emphasized parent–child issues when couples discussed their own issues; or (3) a chance to consult our clinically trained staff once each year over the next 3 years. The third condition constituted our "low dose" control sample. In the longitudinal study, 100 couples agreed to take part—about half in one of the two variations of the couples groups. We describe the groups briefly below (see P. A. Cowan, Cowan, & Heming, 2005).

As in our earlier study, about 16% of this sample of parents were members of ethnic minorities (Hispanic, African American, Asian American), and 84% were European American. When their first child was 4 years old, the parents were in their mid-to-late 30s, most with fairly comfortable incomes, although 22% of the families were below the median income for dual-earner families. These were "nonclinical" families in the sense that couples responded to a request for participants in a study of family factors in children's adaptation to school. Only after they had filled out an initial questionnaire were they randomly offered a couple group or the consultation condition.

Family Processes Predicting Children's Adaptation to School

Because we were interested in the outcomes of the couple groups for children, we focused on three indices of the child's adaptation to school: (1) academic achievement, as measured by achievement tests; (2) externalizing (aggressive and hyperactive) behavior problems; and (3) internalizing (depressed and shy/withdrawn) behavior problems, as measured by a checklist filled out by teachers on every child in their class, including the study child. We looked at several aspects of family life as risk or protective factors that have been associated with these outcomes for children. We first observed parent–child interaction in our project playroom in order to assess authoritative parenting style—a combination of warmth, responsiveness, and age-appropriate structure and limit setting (Baumrind, 1980). Variations in mothers' and fathers' parenting style during the preschool period accounted for about 15% of the variance in children's adaptation to kindergarten and first grade.

We assessed the quality of the parents' marital relationship using each parent's self-report, observations of the parents in two 10-minute problem-solving discussions, and coparenting as parents interacted with each other when both were working and playing with the child in our playroom. To add the child's perspective, we used the Berkeley Puppet Interview (Ablow & Measelle, 1993) to ask the children whether their parents fought a lot, and whether they felt their parents' fights were about them. Adding information about the quality of marital interaction as perceived by observers and by the children before they entered kindergarten allowed us to account for *another* 10–15% of the variance in the children's later school adaptation (Ablow, 2005; P. A. Cowan, Bradburn, & Cowan, 2005). When parents were described by project staff as being high in displeasure, coldness, anger, disagreement, and competition with each other, and when their children described their parents as fighting a lot, the children tended to score especially high in externalizing aggressive behavior in kindergarten and first grade, higher in internalizing behavior, and somewhat lower in academic achievement as assessed by their teachers than children of parents with lower scores on negative interaction and fighting as a couple.

Yet another family context was provided by the parents' experiences in their families of origin, measured by systematically coding parents' memories of their early relationships with their parents on the Adult Attachment Interview (George, Kaplan, & Main, 1985). With this information, we could predict an *additional* 15% of the variance in the children's academic achievement and externalizing or internalizing behaviors in kindergarten and first grade (P. A. Cowan, Bradburn, & Cowan, 2005).

Finally, we included information from two additional domains of family life: Parents' symptoms on the Brief Symptom Inventory (Derogatis & Melisaratos, 1983) contributed especially to predictions of their children's internalizing–depression, whereas parents' perceptions of stressors in their life outside the family added a small but significant amount of predictive power to links between preschool family functioning and children's adaptation to the first 2 years of school (P. A. Cowan & Cowan, 2005; Schulz, 2005).

When we combined information about how parents and children are faring as individuals and the quality of their relationships in the preschool period, we could explain from 32 to 65% of the variance in the children's academic competence and quality of relationships with peers and teachers in the first 2 years of school, depending on the specific outcome and when it was measured. Again, we saw that despite changes associated with transitions, there is a strong degree of consistency in level of adaptation from before to after transitions occur. This means that it is possible to identify individuals and families at risk for difficulties in the early elementary school years based on what we know about them before the child enters kindergarten. This kind of consistency is evident in both cross-sectional and longitudinal studies of children at other ages (Cummings, DeArth-Pendley, Du Rocher Schudlich, & Smith, 2001; Hetherington, 1999; Parke & Buriel, 1998). The findings suggest that without intervention, children and families entering transitions at a disadvantage are likely to continue on that trajectory over the next few years.

A Couples Group Intervention to Facilitate Children's Adaptation to School

In a randomized clinical trial design, we assigned couples to a group intervention very similar in approach to the Becoming a Family intervention described earlier, or to a low-dose consultation (P. A. Cowan, Cowan, & Heming, 2005). The major difference was random assignment to two variations of a couples group, one set of groups that focused more in the unstructured part of each evening on couple relationships and another that focused more on parent–child relationships. For example, leaders might ask how a disagreement about the child's evasion of limits was affecting the partners' relationship as a couple, or about how each parent was dealing with discipline, and work on those issues. Whether the focus was on the couple or the parent–child relationship, the leaders tried to draw out what worked well for one couple, and to see whether any adaptations of that strategy could be useful for other couples in the group. The comparison of the couples versus parenting emphasis of the group was initially designed to explore whether a direct focus on parenting was necessary to influence children's development, or whether improvement in the relationship between the parents would spill over in positive ways to affect parent–child relationships and, ultimately, the children's adaptation to school.

When couples from the ongoing groups were compared with those in the consultation control group, we found significant positive effects of the two kinds of ongoing group interventions. Parents in the marital-focus groups were observed to fight less in front of their children in the year after the groups ended. Parents in the parenting-focused groups were observed to be warmer and more structuring (i.e., more authoritative) with their children. Children whose parents had been in either kind of couples group were at an advantage in kindergarten and first grade compared to children in the control group: According to teachers, who were not aware of which students were in the study, the children of parents who participated in the 16-week groups had higher academic achievement, less aggression, and fewer symptoms of depression.

Although early systemic models assumed that changes in any domain of family life affect every other domain (the double-headed arrows in Figure 18.1), not all members of a system have equal influence on other individuals, relationships, and the system as a whole, and changes in some aspects of a relationship may be more influential than others (McGoldrick, Anderson, & Walsh, 1989). In our intervention study, when the men and women in the groups that emphasized parenting improved in their parenting skills, their marital interaction did not change systematically. By contrast, when couples in the groups that emphasized couple relationship issues reduced their conflict in front of the children, their parenting effectiveness improved too. New data (Cowan, Cowan, & Barry, 2011) show that the effects of the couples group interventions conducted during the preschool period extended for 10 years. Couples who participated in both kinds of groups during the kindergarten transition, especially the couples-focused groups, were more satisfied with their marriages as their children entered high school, and their children were described by their high school teachers as significantly less hyperactive and less aggressive than children in the control group families. Thus, beyond the information that marital and parent–child relationship quality are correlated, intervention designs can tell us something about how family systems operate. *In two-parent families, the "engine" of parent–child relationships appears to be fueled by the quality of the relationship between the parents.* We know that this is also true for divorcing families (see Greene et al., Chapter 5, this volume). Future research could well examine whether this marital-to-parenting influence holds at different stages of the family life cycle, for different normative and non-normative transitions.

APPLICATIONS OF THIS APPROACH TO LOW-INCOME FAMILIES

Participants in the two intervention studies we have described, and those in many other studies of couples-focused intervention (Blanchard, Hawkins, Baldwin, & Fawcett, 2009) were primarily middle-class in income and education. In 2004, the California Office of Child Abuse Prevention invited us to create an intervention program that would enhance and maintain low-income fathers' positive involvement in the daily lives of their young children (Cowan, Cowan, Pruett, Pruett, & Wong, 2009). Prevailing ideas about involving fathers, especially low-income fathers, center around the notion of creating groups of fathers with male group leaders, so men can support each other and encourage more active, positive involvement in family life. We started with another approach. Based on the fact that the quality of a father's relationship with the mother of the child is the best predictor of father involvement (Carlson & McLanahan, 2006; Cummings, Goeke-Morey, & Raymond, 2004), we decided to compare the traditional fathers group approach to work with fathers and the mothers of their children in couples groups, led by male–female coleader teams, as we had in our earlier intervention studies. Each of these couples was raising a child together; a majority was married, some were living together, and a few of the fathers were not living in the home.

The Supporting Father Involvement (SFI) project was housed in local family resource centers (FRCs) in five California counties, four rural and one urban. Parents who expressed interest in the program were invited to take part in one of the following on a random basis: (1) a group for fathers that met for 16 weeks (32 hours); (2) a group for couples that met for 16 weeks (32 hours); or (3) a one-time informational meeting (3 hours)—the low-dose control group. All three variations of the SFI program were delivered by clinically trained male–female pairs of group leaders. All families were also offered the support of a case manager/family worker to help with referrals to other services as needed during their time in the project. When we discovered at later follow-ups that the families who attended the one-time informational meeting were not doing as well as families who took part in the ongoing groups for fathers or couples, we stopped offering the informational meetings.

The curriculum for both fathers and couples groups was identical, with the content, structure, and format adapted from our earlier intervention studies. A major assumption of the program is that if we can (1) reduce parents' distress and foster their satisfaction and well-being individually, as a couple, and as coparents; (2) encourage satisfying relationships with their children, each other, and other family members; and (3) help them use support more effectively when they feel stress in their lives, their family relationships will be healthier and their distress levels lower, which should lessen the risk of abusive and neglectful behavior.

A majority of the first 279 families in the SFI study were Mexican American; most of the remaining families were European American. The second set of 270 families included a majority of Mexican American families, some European American families, and 40 African American families. Their children ranged in age from 0 to 7 years, with the typical age of the youngest child being 2½ years. Two-thirds of the families were at the lower end of the income scale. *None of these families was involved with the child welfare system when they entered the study.*

The study results from the first 279 families (Cowan et al., 2009) show that fathers or mothers who participated in the *informational meeting* did not show any positive changes over 18 months; they showed some negative changes over time and described their children as increasing in aggression, hyperactivity, depression, and social isolation. By contrast, participants in *fathers or couples groups* benefited from significant positive advantages over

18 months. The fathers were more involved in hands-on child care than before, and the children showed no change in problematic behaviors over 18 months. Participants in the *couples groups* showed even more positive changes over 18 months. Their stress as parents decreased significantly, and unlike couples in many other studies whose satisfaction declined over time, these couples maintained their satisfaction with their couple relationship. Parents reported these gains regardless of their ethnic group, income, or marital status (married or cohabiting). In this study, then, the couples group intervention was more effective than the fathers group in stimulating father involvement *and* improving family relationships. Here we have another example of the power of couples-focused interventions to affect families during the early years of childrearing.

As yet unpublished results with a new set of 270 families in groups for fathers and couples reveal positive results equal to or better than those just described. Furthermore, the ongoing group interventions produced positive effects on couple relationship quality, fathers' involvement, and children's behavior in the African American sample, as it had in the earlier Mexican American and European American samples. *The positive effects were strongest in families with nonresident fathers.* This is noteworthy because the literature suggests that interventions for families with nonresident fathers have not been successful in increasing father involvement.

Systematic evaluations of couples-focused interventions have only recently included low-income families. There are two ongoing, very large, federally funded studies of couple group interventions offering "marriage education" for low-income unmarried couples (Building Strong Families; Wood, McConnell, Moore, Clarkwest, & Hsueh, 2010) and low-income married couples (Supporting Healthy Marriage; Knox & Fein, 2009), but so far neither has released results examining effects on the children. When the studies are completed, we will have a much better idea of the general applicability of interventions designed to improve couple relationships and their potential effects on children. Until then, based on our own results, we remain cautiously optimistic about the possibility that working with both more and less economically advantaged couples during the transition to parenthood and the early childrearing years can have benefits for the family relationship system in ways that enhance children's well-being.

IMPLICATIONS FOR THEORY AND PRACTICE

What Do the Findings Tell Us about Normal Family Processes? What Do We Still Need to Know?

The Major Messages

One of the central messages in recent family studies of major life transitions is virtually identical to core tenets endorsed by family systems clinicians for the past five decades. Various domains of family life are interconnected; to explain adaptation or dysfunction in children, we need information beyond parenting quality about relationships between the parents and across the generations. Another major message is certainly consistent with the views of family clinicians. Transitions are useful times to study families, especially because they signal opportunities for preventive interventions to strengthen normal family processes in ways that facilitate adults' and children's development. A third message links the first two. While many different kinds of interventions may be helpful to parents of young children during major life transitions, targeting the relationship between the parents may be an important place to start. The coparenting relationship may be thought of as a thermostat that regulates perturbations in the system to amplify or reduce their effects. It may be wise to frame the intervention as one designed to foster the children's development and well-being to avoid initial resistance to focusing directly on the couple, until trust has been established with the leaders and other group members.

The Normality of Nonclinical Families

We return to the issue of "normal" families that Walsh raises in each edition of *Normal Family Processes*. At this point in the history of family theory and research, it is not surprising to find that early family life is normally stressful—and for some, debilitating. In our study examining the transition to school in a "low-risk" sample, 20–30% of the parents scored above the clinical cutoff on a standard measure of depression, and 30% showed low levels of marital satisfaction. Furthermore, by the time they had completed kindergarten, 10% of their children had entered the mental health system with problems that required assessment or treatment.

Our research findings have led to concerns that the difficulties encountered by ordinary couples with young children are getting lost in the attention paid to "families at risk"—those with the least financial, social, and psychological resources. Although too many normal, relatively advantaged families are showing strains similar to those already in the mental health system, it is clear that resources are not being made available to them, because they are assumed to be "doing fine."

Speculative Extension of This Analysis to Other Normative and Non-Normative Transitions

Because family studies rarely provide prospective information with systematic assessments of family relationships at different points in time, we do not really know what happens to the whole family system when mothers return to work after their children are in school, when children become teenagers or leave home, or when parents retire. And because prospective studies are even more difficult to conduct when the focus is on non-normative transitions (job loss, onset of physical or mental illness in a family member, death of a parent or child), there is even less solid evidence of how self, roles, and relationships change over time. One exception is exemplary research program by Hetherington (1999) that has enriched our understanding of the myriad changes and influences in adaptation to divorce over time (see Greene et al., Chapter 5, this volume).

Still, the model of family transitions we have presented could serve as a checklist for researchers and clinicians. For example, if we are concerned about the potential impact on a child of a mother's descent into depression, we need to look beyond her self-image and parenting style to examine changes in the relationships with her partner, her parents and extended family members, and other sources of stress and support outside the family. Similarly, studies of the impact of job loss must focus on not only the individual out of work but also the reverberations for the worker's spouse and children, and their relationships. Transitions differ depending on how the subsystems are affected, and on the family system's adaptive response to challenges. Findings from both research and clinical investigations using a systemic framework might have a better chance of identifying specific aspects of the family to target for preventive interventions if the hoped-for outcome is the prevention of children's distress or the enhancement of child and family adaptation.

Thinking about Family-Based Preventive Interventions

The links between the quality of key family relationships and children's academic, social, and emotional development, along with the intervention results, suggest that therapeutic interventions can be targeted to reduce risk and promote resilience in order to reduce the probability of dysfunction and increase the probability that transitions will stimulate positive developmental change for all family members. It would be advantageous to make these interventions available to all who undergo stressful life transitions. Unfortunately, the time is not ideal for government support of large-scale intervention programs. The findings of almost every investigator mentioned in this chapter make clear that we know how to identify individuals and families who are most likely to be in difficulty after a major life transition. Despite the fact that transitions trigger shifts in views of one's sense of self, family, roles, and close relationships, we know that without intervention, individuals, couples, and families tend to stay in the same relative position on measures of adaptation after a transition that they held before the transition began. For those at the well-functioning end of the continuum, this is reassuring news. For families at the low end of the adaptation continuum, there is cause for concern.

Of course, the rule of consistency is far from absolute. Some individuals and families that were not faring well at one time do manage to improve the quality of their relationships or their mental health over time (Block & Haan, 1971; P. A. Cowan, Cowan, Ablow, et al., 2005). Both for theory development and intervention planning, we need more research to discover which processes naturally buffer children from the negative effects of troubling family transactions (e.g., marital conflict, authoritarian parenting), and which processes increase children's vulnerability to distress, even when risks seem relatively low.

We are not arguing that all families need help with all family transitions. We are suggesting that if we want to optimize families' ability to provide the kinds of environments and processes that foster children's well-being and development, then preventive and therapeutic interventions focused on couples and offered during normative and non-normative transitions can help us seize the opportunity when new challenges and confusion can be expected to strain family relationships and threaten family equilibrium. If these interventions help parents make positive shifts in their relationships with their children *and* their partners, it seems clear that their children will reap the benefits academically, socially, and emotionally.

REFERENCES

Ablow, J. (2005). When parents conflict or disengage: Understanding links between marital distress and children's adaptation to school. In P. A. Cowan, C. P. Cowan, J. Ablow, V. K. Johnson, & J. Measelle (Eds.), *The family context of parenting in children's adaptation to elementary school* (pp. 189–208). Mahwah, NJ: Erlbaum.

Ablow, J., & Measelle, J. (1993). *The Berkeley Puppet Interview: Administration and scoring system manuals.* Unpublished manuscript, University of California, Berkeley.

Anthony, E. J., & Benedek, T. (1970). *Parenthood: Its psychology and psychopathology.* Boston: Little, Brown.

Baumrind, D. (1980). New directions in socialization research. *American Psychologist, 35*(7), 639–652.

Belsky, J. (1984). The determinants of parenting: A process model. *Child Development, 55*(1), 83–96.

Blanchard, V. L., Hawkins, A. J., Baldwin, S. A., & Fawcett, E. B. (2009). Investigating the effects of marriage and relationship education on couples' communication skills: A meta-analytic study. *Journal of Family Psychology, 23*(2), 203–214.

Block, J., & Haan, N. (1971). *Lives through time.* Berkeley, CA: Bancroft Books.

Bronfenbrenner, U. (1979). *The ecology of human development: Experiments by nature and design.* Cambridge, MA: Harvard University Press.

Brooks-Gunn, J., & Chase-Lansdale, P. L. (1995). Adolescent parenthood. In M. H. Bornstein (Ed.), *Handbook of parenting: Vol. 3. Status and social conditions of parenting* (pp. 113–149). Hillsdale, NJ: Erlbaum.

Bumpass, L., & Rindfuss, R. R. (1979). Children's experience of marital disruption. *American Journal of Sociology, 85,* 49–65.

Campbell, S. B., Cohn, J. F., Flanagan, C., & Popper, S. (1992). Course and correlates of postpartum depression during the transition to parenthood. *Development and Psychopathology, 4*(1), 29–47.

Caplan, G. (1964). *Principles of preventive psychiatry.* New York: Basic Books.

Carlson, M., & McLanahan, S. (2006). Strengthening unmarried families: Could enhancing couple relationships also improve parenting? *Social Service Review, 80,* 297–321.

Cowan, C. P., & Cowan, P. A. (1995). Interventions to ease the transition to parent-hood: Why they are needed and what they can do. *Family Relations: Journal of Applied Family and Child Studies, 44*(4), 412–423.

Cowan, C. P., & Cowan, P. A. (2000). *When partners become parents: The big life change for couples.* Mahwah, NJ: Erlbaum.

Cowan, C. P. Cowan, P. A., & Heming, G. (2005). Two variations of a preventive intervention for couples: Effects on parents and children during the transition to elementary school. In P. A. Cowan, C. P. Cowan, J. Ablow, V. K. Johnson, & J. Measelle (Eds.), *The family context of parenting in children's adaptation to elementary school* (pp. 277–312). Mahwah, NJ: Erlbaum.

Cowan, P. A. (1988). Becoming a father: A time of change, an opportunity for devel-opment. In P. Bronstein & C. P. Cowan (Eds.), *Fatherhood today: Men's chang-ing role in the family* (pp. 13–35). New York: Wiley.

Cowan, P. A. (1991). Individual and family life transitions: A proposal for a new definition. In P. A. Cowan & E. M. Hetherington (Eds.), *Family transitions* (pp. 3–30). Hillsdale, NJ: Erlbaum.

Cowan, P. A., Bradburn, I. S., & Cowan, C. P. (2005). Parents' working model of attachment: The intergenerational context of problem behavior in kindergarten. In P. A. Cowan, C. P. Cowan, J. Ablow, V. K. Johnson, & J. Measelle (Eds.), *The family context of parenting in children's adaptation to elementary school.* Mahwah, NJ: Erlbaum.

Cowan, P. A., & Cowan, C. P. (2001). What an intervention reveals about how par-ents affect their children's academic achievement and behavior problems. In M. Bristol-Power (Ed.), *Parenting and the child's world: Influences on intellectual, academic, and social–emotional development.* Mahwah, NJ: Erlbaum.

Cowan, P. A., & Cowan, C. P. (2005). "Mega-models" of parenting in context. In P. A. Cowan, C. P. Cowan, J. Aglow, V. K. Johnson, & J. Measles (Eds.), *The fam-ily context of parenting in children's adaptation to elementary school* (pp. 315–333). Mahwah, NJ: Erlbaum.

Cowan, P. A., Cowan, C. P., Ablow, J., Johnson, V., & Measelle, J. (Eds.). (2005). *The family context of parenting in children's adaptation to school.* Mahwah, NJ: Erlbaum.

Cowan, P. A., Cowan, C. P., & Barry, J. (2011). Couples' groups for parents of pre-schoolers: Ten-year outcomes of a randomized trial. *Journal of Family Psychol-ogy, 25*(2).

Cowan, P. A., Cowan, C. P., Pruett, M. K., Pruett, K. , & Wong, J. (2009). Promot-ing fathers' engagement with children: Preventive interventions for low-income families. *Journal of Marriage and the Family, 71*(3), 663–679.

Cowan, P. A., & Heming, G. (2005). Change, stability, and predictability in family members during children's transition to school. In P. A. Cowan, C. E. Cowan, J. Ablow, V. K. Johnson, & J. Measelle (Eds.), *The family context of parenting in children's adaptation to elementary school.* Mahwah, NJ: Erlbaum.

Cox, M. J., Paley, B., Payne, C. C., & Burchinal, M. (1999). The transition to parent-hood: Marital conflict and withdrawal and parent–infant interactions. In M. J. Cox & J. Brooks-Gunn (Eds.), *Conflict and cohesion in families: Causes and consequences* (pp. 87–104). Mahwah, NJ: Erlbaum.

Cummings, E. M., DeArth-Pendley, G., Du Rocher Schudlich, T., & Smith, D. A. (2001). Parental depression and family functioning: Toward a process-oriented model of children's adjustment. In S. R. H. Beach (Ed.), *Marital and family processes in depression: A scientific foundation for clinical practice* (pp. 89–110). Washington, DC: American Psychological Association.

Cummings, E. M., Goeke-Morey, C., & Raymond, J. (2004). Fathers in family context: Effects of marital quality and marital conflict. In M. E. Lamb (Ed.), *The role of the father in child development* (4th ed., pp. 196–221). Hoboken, NJ: Wiley.

Derogatis, L. R., & Melisaratos, N. (1983). The Brief Symptom Inventory: An introductory report. *Psychological Medicine, 13*(3), 595–605.

Dunn, J., & Plomin, R. (1990). *Separate lives: Why siblings are so different.* New York: Basic Books.

Erikson, E. H. (1950). *Childhood and society.* New York: Norton.

Erikson, E. H. (1980). *Identity and the life cycle.* New York: Norton.

Falicov, C. J. (Ed.). (1988). *Family transitions: Continuity and change over the life cycle.* New York: Guilford Press.

Feinberg, M. E., Kan, M. L., & Goslin, M. C. (2009). Enhancing coparenting, parenting, and child self-regulation: Effects of family foundations 1 year after birth. *Prevention Science, 10*(3), 276–285.

Freud, S. (1938). *The basic writings of Sigmund Freud* (A. A. Brill, Trans.). New York: Modern Library.

Gloger-Tippelt, G. S., & Huerkamp, M. (1998). Relationship change at the transition to parenthood and security of infant–mother attachment. *International Journal of Behavioral Development, 22*(3), 633–655.

Goldberg, A. E., & Perry-Jenkins, M. (2007). The division of labor and perceptions of parental roles: Lesbian couples across the transition to parenthood. *Journal of Social and Personal Relationships, 24*(2), 297–318.

George, C., Kaplan, N., & Main, M. (1985). *The Adult Attachment Interview.* Unpublished manuscript, University of California, Berkeley.

Gottman, J. M. (1994). *What predicts divorce?: The relationship between marital processes and marital outcomes.* Hillsdale, NJ: Erlbaum.

Gottman, J., Gottman, J., & Shapiro, A. (2009). A new couples approach to interventions for the transition to parenthood. In M. S. Schulz, M. K. Pruett, P. K. Kerig, & R. D. Parke (Eds.), *Strengthening couple relationships for optimal child development: Lessons from research and intervention* (pp. 165–179). Washington, DC: American Psychological Association.

Halford, W. K., Petch, J., & Creedy, D. K. (2010). Promoting a positive transition to parenthood: A randomized clinical trial of couple relationship education. *Prevention Science, 11*(1), 89–100.

Hansen, L. B., & Jacob, E. (1992). Intergenerational support during the transition to parenthood: Issues for new parents and grandparents. *Families in Society, 73*(8), 471–479.

Heinicke, C. M. (2002). The transition to parenting. In M. H. Bornstein (Ed.), *Handbook of parenting: Vol. 3. Being and becoming a parent* (2nd ed., pp. 363–388). Mahwah, NJ: Erlbaum.

Hetherington, E. M. (1999). *Coping with divorce, single parenting, and remarriage: A risk and resiliency perspective.* Mahwah, NJ: Erlbaum.

Hochschild, A. R., & Machung, A. (1990). *The second shift.* New York: Avon Books.

Klinnert, M. D., Gavin, L. A., Wamboldt, F. S., & Mrazek, D. A. (1992). Marriages with children at medical risk: The transition to parenthood. *Journal of the American Academy of Child and Adolescent Psychiatry, 31*(2), 334–342.

Knox, V., & Fein, D. (2009). Designing a marriage education demonstration and evaluation for low-income married couples. In H. E. Peters & C. M. Kamp Dush (Eds.), *Marriage and family: Complexities and perspectives*. New York: Columbia University Press.

LeMasters, E. E. (1957). Parenthood as crisis. *Marriage and Family Living, 19,* 352–355.

Levy-Shiff, R., Dimitrovsky, L., Shulman, S., & Har-Even, D. (1998). Cognitive appraisals, coping strategies, and support resources as correlates of parenting and infant development. *Developmental Psychology, 34*(6), 1417–1427.

McGoldrick, M., Carter, B., & Garcia-Preto, N. (Eds.). (2011). *The expanded family life cycle: Individual, family, and social perspectives* (4th ed.). Boston: Pearson.

McLanahan, S., Garfinkel, I., Reichman, N., Teitler, J., Carlson, M., & Audigier, C. N. (2003). *The fragile families and well-being study: Baseline national report.* Princeton, NJ: Center for Research on Child Well-Being.

Neugarten, B. L. (1965). Personality and patterns of aging. *Anthropology and Medicine, 13*(4), 249–256.

Olds, D., Henderson, C. R., Jr., Cole, R., Eckenrode, J., Kitzman, H., Luckey, D., et al. (1998). Long-term effects of nurse home visitation on children's criminal and antisocial behavior: 15-year follow-up of a randomized controlled trial. *Journal of the American Medical Association, 280*(14), 1238–1244.

Pancer, S. M., Pratt, M., Hunsberger, B., & Gallant, M. (2000). Thinking ahead: Complexity of expectations and the transition to parenthood. *Journal of Personality, 68*(2), 253–280.

Parke, R. D., & Buriel, R. (1998). Socialization in the family: Ethnic and ecological perspectives. In N. Eisenberg (Ed.), *Social, emotional, and personality development* (5th ed., Vol. 3, pp. 463–552). New York: Wiley.

Parr, M. (1997). Adjustment to family life. In C. Henderson (Ed.), *Essential midwifery* (pp. 131–140). London: Times/Mirror.

Paulson, J. F., Sharnail, D., & Bazemore, M. (2010). Prenatal and postpartum depression in fathers and its association with maternal depression. *Journal of the American Medical Association, 303*(19), 1961–1969.

Piaget, J. (1968). *Six psychological studies* (A. Tenzer, Trans.). New York: Random House.

Schulz, M. (2005). Parents' work experiences and children's adjustment to kindergarten. In P. A. Cowan, C. P. Cowan, J. Ablow, V. K. Johnson, & J. Measelle (Eds.), *The family context of parenting in children's adaptation to elementary school* (pp. 237–253). Mahwah, NJ: Erlbaum.

Schulz, M. S., Cowan, C. P., & Cowan, P. A. (2006). Promoting Healthy Beginnings: A randomized controlled trial of a preventive intervention to preserve marital quality during the transition to parenthood. *Journal of Consulting and Clinical Psychology, 74*(1), 20–31.

Shapiro, A. F., Gottman, J. M., & Carrère, S. (2000). The baby and the marriage: Identifying factors that buffer against decline in marital satisfaction after the first baby arrives. *Journal of Family Psychology, 14*(1), 59–70.

Twenge, J. M., Campbell, W. K., & Foster, C. A. (2003). Parenthood and marital satisfaction: A meta-analytic review. *Journal of Marriage and Family, 65*(3), 574–583.

Vaillant, G. E., & Koury, S. H. (1993). Late midlife development. In G. H. Pollock & S. I. Greenspan (Eds.), *The course of life: Vol. 6. Late adulthood* (pp. 1–22). Madison, CT: International Universities Press.

Wagner, B. M., & Reiss, D. (1995). Family systems and developmental psychopathology: Courtship, marriage, or divorce? In D. Cicchetti & D. J. Cohen (Eds.), *Developmental psychopathology* (Vol. 1, pp. 696–730). New York: Wiley.

Walsh, F. (2006). *Strengthening family resilience* (2nd ed.). New York: Guilford Press.

Wood, R. G., McConnell, S., Quinn, M., Clarkwest, A., & Hsueh, J. (2010). *Strengthening unmarried parents' relationships: The early impacts of building strong families*. Washington DC: Mathematic Policy Research, Inc.

CHAPTER 19

MASTERING FAMILY CHALLENGES IN SERIOUS ILLNESS AND DISABILITY

JOHN S. ROLLAND

A NORMATIVE SYSTEMIC HEALTH PARADIGM

Illness, disability, and death are universal experiences in families. The real question is not "if" we will face these issues, but when in our lives, under what kinds of conditions, how serious they will be, and for how long. With major advances in medical technology, people with formerly fatal conditions are living much longer. Cancer, heart disease, diabetes, and now AIDS are just a few examples. Many children with chronic conditions that were previously fatal or necessitated institutional life are now reaching adulthood, and, with the help of new policies, they are assimilating into mainstream adult life. This means that ever-growing numbers of families are living with chronic disorders over an increasingly long time span and often coping with multiple conditions simultaneously.

The extension of later life has heightened the strain on sons and daughters who must contend with divided loyalties and a complex juggling act between caregiving for aging parents and grandparents, childrearing, and providing financially for the family. They must achieve these ends in a society in which over 50 million were uninsured in 2010 (with projections by the Congressional Budget Office that 23 million will remain uninsured after implementation of current health care reform legislation), and 62% of bankruptcies currently are linked to illness and medical bills (Himmelstein Thorne, Warren, & Woolhandler, 2009). Families are geographically dispersed, most have woefully inadequate coverage for long-term care, and health care disparities continue to increase for minority and lower socioeconomic status populations (U.S. Bureau of the Census, 2009).

Given these changes, how can we best describe the normative challenges of serious illness and optimal family coping and adaptation? We are advancing past stereotypical definitions of "the family" and the view of normal family life as "problem-free" to recognize that all families are challenged by adversity. In the same way, when serious illness strikes, we need to move beyond an outdated, rigid, and often romanticized version of coping.

This chapter provides a normative, preventive model for psychoeducation, assessment, and intervention with families facing chronic and life-threatening conditions (Rolland, 1984, 1987, 1990, 1994a, 1998, 2002). This model offers a systemic view of healthy family adaptation to serious illness as a developmental process over time in relation to the complexities and diversity of contemporary family life, modern medicine, and flawed models of health care delivery and access to care. Before I describe the model, some basic constructs are useful.

First, we need to broaden the unit of care from the medical model's narrow focus on the ill individual to the family or caregiving system (McDaniel, Hepworth, & Doherty, 2012). Systemically, an effective biopsychosocial model needs to encompass all persons involved in the family unit and caregiving, which in turn can influence the course of an illness and the well-being of the affected person. By using a broad definition of "family" as the caregiving system, we can describe a model of successful coping and adaptation based on family system strengths.

Second, we need to describe the complex mutual interactions among the illness, ill family member, and family system within a normative framework. There is a vast literature describing the impact of chronic disorders on individuals and families. However, the impact of individual and family processes on disease has historically been defined in terms of psychosomatic processes and almost invariably in pathological terms. The definition of a condition as "psychosomatic" is a shame-laden label associated with pejorative cultural meanings that imply family dysfunction and negative influences that exacerbate symptoms and suffering.

The framework presented here describes psychosomatic processes in more holistic, interactive, and normative terms. All illnesses can be viewed as having a psychosomatic interplay in which the relative influence of biological and psychosocial factors varies over a range of disorders and illness phases. In a psychosomatic interplay, psychosocial factors, not just biomedical interventions, can be important influences in well-being and disease course. With this approach, professionals can undercut pathologizing family and cultural beliefs, and help families approach a psychosomatic interaction as an opportunity to make a positive difference. This increases their sense of control and overall quality of life.

Family research in the area of chronic illness, like studies of the individual, has tended to emphasize pathological family dynamics associated with poor disease course or treatment compliance (Campbell, 2003; Martire, Lustig,

Schulz, Miller, & Helgeson, 2004; Weihs, Fisher, & Baird, 2001). This focus on illness-based family systems and so-called "psychosomatic" families has narrowed attention to one end of a continuum of family functioning and does not clarify what constitutes healthy family coping and adaptation to illness. At the other end of the continuum, especially in the popular literature, there has been a focus on the exceptional patient (Siegel & Sander, 2009). Numerous personal accounts highlight the "superstar" patient or family. Although these provide a refreshing relief from descriptions of pathological patients and families, they often err toward superhuman, epic descriptions that leave the average family without a reference point. The average family is vulnerable to double jeopardy. Its members can feel deficient either by noting any similarities with severely dysfunctional families or by not measuring up to the exceptional one. This leaves families with a view of healthy adaptation that is rarely achieved and perpetuates self-judgments of deficient performance, infused with blame, shame, and guilt. The inspirations of the exceptional and the warning signs of dysfunction need to be grounded by descriptions of typical experiences. More recently investigators have shifted attention toward the influences of social support and a range of family processes that enhance coping and adaptation. A growing literature is examining the positive impact of individual and family functioning on health/well-being and, in the context of illness, the quality of life for all family members, as well as disease course and outcome (Carr & Springer, 2010; D'Onofrio & Lahey, 2010; Weihs et al., 2001).

Finally, outdated, rigid, gender-based models of the normal family invariably define a narrow range of roles and strategies for coping with illness and disability. Traditional models of patient and caregiver roles can shackle families—especially the designated female caregiver—in the face of the protracted strains of illness and threatened loss. A broad multigenerational and multicultural conception of the family that evolves over the life cycle (McGoldrick, Carter, & Garcia-Preto, 2011) is essential to constructing a normative model.

The family-centered model described in this chapter views a broad range of family forms and processes as normative and uses as its central reference point the idea of goodness of fit between the psychosocial demands of the illness in relation to family challenges and resources over time. For example, high versus low family cohesion is not viewed as inherently healthy or unhealthy. Rather, the organizing principle becomes relative: What degree of family cohesion will work optimally with this illness now, and how might that change in future phases of the condition?

A basic task for families is to create a meaning for the illness situation that preserves their sense of competency and mastery. At the extremes, competing ideologies can leave families with a choice between a biological explanation or one of personal responsibility (bad things happen to bad people). Families desperately need reassurance that they are handling the illness normally (bad things do happen to good people). Without a psychosocial map, many families, particularly those with untimely disorders, find themselves in unfamiliar territory and without guides. This highlights the need for a preventive, psychoeducational approach that helps families anticipate normative illness-related developmental challenges over time in a fashion that maximizes a sense of control and mastery.

To create a normative context for their illness experience, families need the following foundation. First, they need a psychosocial understanding of the condition in systems terms. This means learning the expected pattern of practical and affective demands of a disorder over the course of the condition. This includes a time frame for disease-related developmental tasks associated with different phases of an unfolding disorder. Second, families need to understand themselves as systemic functional units. Third, they need an appreciation of individual and family life-cycle patterns and transitions to facilitate their incorporation of changing developmental priorities for the family unit and individual members in relation to evolving challenges of a chronic disorder. Finally, families need to understand the cultural, ethnic, spiritual, and gender-based beliefs that guide the type of caregiving system they construct. This includes guiding principles that delineate roles, rules of communication, definitions of success or mastery, and fit with beliefs of the health care providers. Family understanding in these areas facilitates a more holistic integration of the disorder and the family as a functional family–health/illness system evolving over time.

FAMILY SYSTEMS HEALTH MODEL

A normative, preventive model has been developed for psychoeducation, assessment, and intervention with families facing chronic and life-threatening disorders (Rolland 1984, 1987a, 1987b, 1990, 1994a, 1998). This model is based on the concept of a systemic interaction between an illness and family that evolves over time. The goodness of "fit" between the psychosocial demands of the disorder and the family style of functioning and resources is a prime determinant of successful versus dysfunctional coping and adaptation. The model distinguishes three dimensions: (1) psychosocial "types" of disorders, (2) major phases in their evolution, and (3) key family system variables (Figure 19.1). A scheme of the systemic interaction between illness and family might look like the diagram in Figure 19.2. Family variables given particular emphasis include (1) the family and individual life cycles, particularly in relation to the time phases of a disorder; (2) multigenerational legacies related to illness and loss; and (3) belief systems.

Psychosocial Types of Illness

The standard disease classification used in medical settings is based on purely biological criteria that are clustered in ways to establish a medical diagnosis

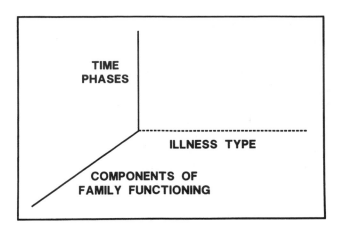

FIGURE 19.1. Three-dimensional model representing the relationship between illness type, time phases, and family functioning. From Rolland (1987a). Reprinted by permission.

and treatment plan, rather than on psychosocial demands placed on patients and their families. I have proposed a different classification scheme that provides a better link between the biological and psychosocial worlds, and thereby clarifies the relationship between chronic illness and the family (Rolland, 1984, 1994a). The goal of this typology is to define meaningful and useful categories with similar psychosocial demands for a wide array of chronic illnesses affecting individuals across the lifespan.

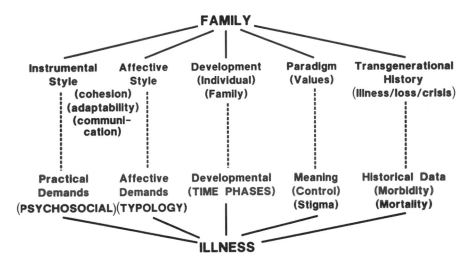

FIGURE 19.2. Interface of chronic illness and the family. From Rolland (1987b). Reprinted by permission.

Onset

Illnesses can be divided into those that have either an acute onset, such as strokes, or gradual onset, such as Alzheimer's disease. For acute-onset illnesses, affective and practical changes are compressed into a short time, requiring more rapid family mobilization of crisis management skills. Families able to tolerate highly charged emotional situations, exchange roles flexibly, problem-solve efficiently, and utilize outside resources will have an advantage in managing acute-onset conditions. Clinicians can facilitate this process.

Course

The course of chronic diseases can take three general forms: progressive, constant, or relapsing/episodic. Varying levels of uncertainty overlay these forms. With a *progressive* disease such as Alzheimer's disease, the family is often faced with a perpetually symptomatic family member whose disability worsens in a stepwise or gradual way. The family must live with the prospect of continual role change and adaptation to continued losses as the disease progresses. Increasing strain on family caregiving is caused by exhaustion, with few periods of relief from demands of the illness, and with more caregiving tasks over time. Diabetes is an example of a progressive disease with a much longer and unpredictable course.

With a *constant* course illness, the occurrence of an initial event, such as a one-time heart attack or spinal cord injury, is followed by a stable biological course. Typically, after an initial period of recovery, the illness is characterized by some clear-cut deficit or limitation. The family is faced with a semipermanent change that is stable and predictable over a considerable time span. The potential for family exhaustion exists without the strain of new role demands over time.

Relapsing- or *episodic-*course illnesses, such as disk problems and asthma, are distinguished by the alternation of stable low-symptom periods with periods of flare-up or exacerbation. Families are strained by both the frequency of transition between crisis and noncrisis, and the ongoing uncertainty of *when* a recurrence will occur. This requires family flexibility to alternate between two forms of family organization. The wide psychological discrepancy between low-symptom versus flare-up periods is a particularly taxing feature unique to relapsing diseases.

Outcome

The extent to which a chronic illness leads to death or shortens one's life expectancy has profound psychosocial impact. The most crucial factor is the *initial expectation* of whether a disease is likely to cause death. On one end of the continuum are illnesses that do not typically affect the lifespan, such as disk disease or arthritis. At the other extreme are clearly progressive and fatal illnesses, such as metastatic cancer. An intermediate, more unpredictable category includes both illnesses that shorten the lifespan, such as heart disease, and those with the possibility of sudden death, such as hemophilia. A major difference between these kinds of outcome is the degree to which the family experiences anticipatory loss and its pervasive effects on family life (Rolland, 1990).

Incapacitation

Disease and disability can involve impairment of cognition (e.g., Alzheimer's disease), sensation (e.g., blindness), movement (e.g., stroke with paralysis), stamina (e.g., heart disease), disfigurement (e.g., mastectomy), and conditions associated with social stigma (e.g., AIDS) (Olkin, 1999). The extent, kind, and timing of disability imply sharp differences in the degree of family stress. For instance, the combined cognitive and motor deficits often caused by a stroke necessitate greater family role reallocation than that for a spinal cord injury in which cognitive abilities are unaffected. For some illnesses, such as stroke, disability is often worst at the beginning. For progressive diseases, such as Alzheimer's disease, disability looms as an increasing problem in later phases of the illness, allowing a family more time to prepare for anticipated changes and an opportunity for the ill member to participate in disease-related family planning while still cognitively able (Boss, 1999).

By combining the kinds of onset, course, outcome, and incapacitation into a grid format, we generate a typology that clusters illnesses according to similarities and differences in patterns that pose differing psychosocial demands (Table 19.1).

The *predictability* of an illness, and the degree of uncertainty about the specific way or rate at which it unfolds, overlays all other variables. For illnesses with highly unpredictable courses, such as multiple sclerosis, family coping and adaptation, especially future planning, are hindered by anticipatory anxiety and ambiguity about what family members will actually encounter. Families able to put long-term uncertainty into perspective are best prepared to avoid the risks of exhaustion and dysfunction.

Time Phases of Illness

Too often, discussions of "coping with cancer," "managing disability," or "dealing with life-threatening illness" approach illness as a static state and fail to appreciate the evolution of illness processes over time. The concept of *time phases* provides a way for clinicians and families to think longitudinally and to understand chronic illness as an ongoing process with normative landmarks, transitions, and changing demands. Each phase of an illness poses its own psychosocial challenges and developmental tasks that may require significantly different strengths, attitudes, or changes for family adaptation. Core psychosocial themes in the natural history of chronic disease can be described as three major phases: crisis, chronic, and terminal (Figure 19.3).

TABLE 19.1. Categorization of Chronic Disorders by Psychosocial Type

	Incapacitating		Nonincapacitating	
	Acute	Gradual	Acute	Gradual
FATAL				
Progressive		Lung cancer CNS metastases Bone marrow failure Amyotrophic lateral sclerosis	Pancreatic cancer Metastatic cancer (e.g., breast, lung, liver)	
SHORTENED LIFE SPAN / POSSIBLY FATAL				
Progressive		Parkinson's disease Emphysema Alzheimer's disease Multi-infarct dementia AIDS Multiple sclerosis (late) Chronic alcoholism Huntington's disease Scleroderma		Type 1 diabetes[a] Malignant hypertension Insulin-dependent Type 2 diabetes
Relapsing	Angina	Early multiple sclerosis Episodic alcoholism	Sickle cell disease[a] Hemophilia[a]	Systemic lupus erythematosus[a]
Constant	Stroke Moderate/severe myocardial infarction	PKU and other inborn errors of metabolism	Mild myocardial infarction Cardiac arrhythmia	Hemodialysis-treated renal failure Hodgkin's disease

(cont.)

TABLE 19.1. (cont.)

	Incapacitating		Nonincapacitating	
	Acute	Gradual	Acute	Gradual
NONFATAL Progressive		Rheumatoid arthritis Osteoarthritis		Non-insulin-dependent type 2 diabetes
Relapsing	Lumbosacral disk disease		Kidney stones Gout Migraine Seasonal allergy Asthma Epilepsy	Peptic ulcer Ulcerative colitis Chronic bronchitis Other inflammatory bowel diseases Psoriasis
Constant	Congenital malformations Spinal cord injury Acute blindness Acute deafness Survived severe trauma and burns Posthypoxic syndrome	Nonprogressive mental retardation Cerebral palsy	Benign arrhythmia Congenital heart disease (mild)	Malabsorption syndromes (controlled) Hyper/hypothyroidism Pernicious anemia Controlled hypertension Controlled glaucoma

Note. Adapted from Rolland (1984). Copyright 1984 by the American Psychological Association. Adapted by permission.

[a]Early.

460

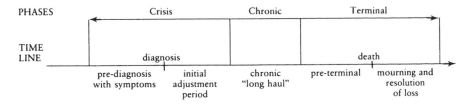

FIGURE 19.3. Timeline and phases of illness. From Rolland (1984). Copyright 1984 by the American Psychological Association. Reprinted by permission.

The *crisis* phase includes any symptomatic period before diagnosis and the initial readjustment period after a diagnosis and initial treatment planning. This phase holds a number of key tasks for the ill member and family. Moos (1984) describes certain universal, practical, illness-related tasks that include (1) learning to cope with any symptoms or disability; (2) adapting to health care settings and any treatment procedures; and (3) establishing and maintaining workable relationships with the health care team. Also, there are crucial tasks of a more general, existential nature. Families optimize well-being when they can (1) create a meaning for the illness that maximizes a sense of mastery and competency; (2) grieve for the loss of normal "life" before illness; (3) gradually accept the illness as long term, while maintaining a sense of continuity between their past and future; (4) pull together to cope with the immediate crisis; and (5) in the face of uncertainty, develop flexibility toward future goals.

During this initial crisis period, health professionals have enormous influence over a family's sense of competence and strategies to accomplish these developmental challenges. Initial meetings and advice given at the time of diagnosis can be thought of as a "framing event." Because family members are so vulnerable at this point, clinicians need to be extremely sensitive in their interactions with them and aware of messages conveyed by their behavior. Who is included or excluded (e.g., the patient) from a discussion can be interpreted by the family as a message of how they should plan their communication for the duration of the illness. For instance, if a clinician meets with family members separately from the patient to give them information about the illness diagnosis and prognosis, they may assume that they are being instructed implicitly to exclude the patient from any discussion of the illness. Meeting only with a spouse or primary caregiver may fuel anxiety about whether and how to share information with children or other members. Clinicians also need to be careful not to undercut a family's attempt to sustain a sense of competence by implicitly blaming the patient or the family for an illness (e.g., delay in seeking an appointment, negligence by parents, poor health habits) or by distancing themselves from the family.

The *chronic* phase, whether long or short, is the time span after the initial diagnosis/readjustment. This era can be marked by constancy, recurrence (e.g., heart attack), progression, or episodic flare-ups. It has been referred to as "the long haul," or "the day-to-day living with chronic illness" phase. Often the patient and family have come to grips psychologically and organization-ally with long-term changes and have devised an ongoing coping strategy. The ability to maintain the semblance of a normal life with a chronic illness and heightened uncertainty is a key family task in this phase. If the illness is fatal, this is a time of "living in limbo." For certain highly debilitating but not clearly fatal illnesses, such as a massive stroke or dementia, the family can feel saddled with an exhausting problem "without end." Paradoxically, a family may feel its hope to resume a so-called "normal" life can only be realized after the death of its ill member. The maintenance of maximum autonomy for all family members in the face of protracted adversity helps offset these trapped, helpless feelings. Clinicians can help families develop new priorities and see opportunities for relationship growth within a "new normal."

For long-term disorders, customary patterns of intimacy for couples become skewed by discrepancies between the ill member and the well spouse/caregiver (Rolland, 1994b). As one young husband lamented about his wife's cancer, "It was hard enough 2 years ago to absorb that, even if Ann was cured, her radiation treatment would make pregnancy impossible. Now, I find it unbearable that her continued slow, losing battle with cancer makes it impossible to go for our dreams like other couples our age." Normative ambivalence and escape fantasies often remain underground and can contribute to survivor guilt. Psychoeducational family interventions that normalize such emotions related to threatened loss can help prevent destructive cycles of blame, shame, and guilt.

In the *terminal* phase of an illness, the inevitability of death becomes apparent and dominates family life. Now the family must cope with issues of separation, death, mourning, and resumption of family life beyond the loss (Walsh & McGoldrick, 2004). Family members adapt best to this phase when able to shift their view of mastery from controlling the illness to a successful process of "letting go." Optimal coping involves emotional openness, as well as dealing with the myriad practical tasks at hand. This includes seeing this phase as an opportunity to share precious time together, to acknowledge the impending loss, to deal with unfinished business, to say good-byes, and to begin the process of family reorganization. If they have not been determined beforehand, the patient and key family members need to decide about things such as a living will; the extent of medical heroics desired; preferences about dying at home, in the hospital, or at a hospice; and wishes about a funeral or memorial service and burial or cremation.

Critical *transition periods* link the three time phases. Transitions in the illness course are times when families reevaluate the appropriateness of their previous life structure in the face of new illness-related developmen-tal demands. Helping families resolve unfinished business from the previous phase can facilitate movement through the transitions. Families can become permanently frozen in an adaptive structure that has outlived its utility (Penn, 1983). For example, the usefulness of pulling together in the crisis phase can become maladaptive and stifling for all family members through the chronic phase.

The interaction of the time phases and illness typology provides a framework for a normative psychosocial developmental model for chronic disease that resembles models for human development. The time phases (crisis, chronic, and terminal) can be considered broad developmental periods in the unfolding of chronic disease. Each period has certain basic tasks, independent of the type of illness. Each "type" of illness has specific supplementary tasks.

The New Genetics and an Extended Illness Timeline

With the mapping of the human genome, burgeoning scientific knowledge is rapidly increasing our understanding of the mechanisms, treatment, and prevention of disease. New genetic technologies enable physicians to test for increased risk of developing a serious and life-threatening illness before it actually occurs. This means that individuals and families now can be living with illness risk information long before they or loved ones have developed symptoms of those illnesses (Miller, McDaniel, Rolland, & Feetham, 2006). This significantly increases the amount of time and energy that families spend considering an illness, and lengthens the illness time line to include nonsymptomatic phases (Rolland & Williams, 2005). The nonsymptomatic phases include awareness, pretesting, testing/posttesting, and long-term adaptation. These phases are distinguished by questions of uncertainty. Fundamental issues include the potential amount of genetic knowledge medically available, decisions about how much of that information various family members choose to access, and living with the psychosocial impact of those choices.

For some, the nonsymptomatic crisis phase begins when predictive testing becomes available, continuing through the decision to pursue testing and initial posttesting adaptation. For others, this phase begins as individuals reach significant developmental milestones and begin to consider testing. Sometimes, plans to have children raise fears of passing on a mutation and spark an interest in testing. Some women decide to be tested for hereditary breast and ovarian cancer genes when they reach an age that coincides with the age when another blood relative—a mother, aunt, or older sister—was diagnosed. During the posttesting phases, families need to accept the permanence of the genetic information and develop meanings that preserve their sense of competency in the face of future uncertainty or loss (Rolland, 2006a; Werner-Lin, 2008).

The involvement of the health care system is very different with predictive testing than with a diagnosed illness. Despite the potentially enormous psychosocial impact of positive testing results, families usually have limited contact with health professionals after initial testing. This highlights the need for ongoing, family-centered, collaborative approaches to prevent isolation, anxiety, and depression.

We can orient families to the value of prevention-oriented consultations at key future life-cycle transitions, when the experience of genetic risk will likely be heightened. Concerns about loss may surface that family members either postponed or thought were "worked through." It is vital to prepare family members that their concerns about genetic risk and decisions about whether to pursue genetic testing will be more activated with upcoming transitions, such as launching young adults, marriage or partner commitments, or starting a family. Also, such feelings can be reactivated by critical events, such as genetic testing of another family member, diagnosis of a serious illness in immediate or extended families or friends, or death of a loved one. Clinicians can help family members decide when further family discussion would be helpful, who would be appropriate to include, and how to discuss genetic risk with children or adolescents.

Genomics, distinguished from traditional genetics, goes beyond the study of single genes to the function and interaction of all genes in the human genome, including their interactions with environmental factors. Most illnesses are thought to be affected by multiple genes and environmental factors that include life experience, social context, and interpersonal relationships. Thus, as most families learn more about their own genetic risks, members need not adopt a fatalistic, deterministic mind-set. Rather, family members will have varying degrees of control to influence the onset, course, and severity of disease expression. Recent research suggests family interaction can be an important protective factor counterbalancing genetic risk related to mental health conditions (Reiss, Neierhiser, Hetherington, & Plomin, 2000; Tienari et al., 2004; see Spotts, Chapter 22, this volume). This kind of complex interaction may operate in common physical disorders as well.

As the new genetics unfolds, families and clinicians are facing unprecedented and complex clinical and ethical challenges (Miller et al., 2006). Families will increasingly be able to choose genetically informed knowledge of their future health risks or fate. Some key research questions include the following: Which individuals and families will benefit by genetic risk screening and knowledge of their health risks or fate? How can we best help family members reach decisions about whether to pursue predictive testing? Who are the relevant family members to include in these decisions? Spouses or partners? Extended family? Our societal fixation on "the perfect healthy body" could meld seamlessly with technology and eugenics, forcing families living with disability, illness, or genetic risk to hide their suffering further, in order to demonstrate the value of their lives and avoid increased stigmatization (Rolland, 1997; 1999).

Clinical Utility of Framework

This model provides a framework for clinical practice by facilitating an understanding of chronic illness and disability in psychosocial terms. Attention to features of onset, course, outcome, and incapacitation provides markers that focus clinical assessment and intervention with a family. For instance, acute-onset illnesses demand high levels of adaptability, problem solving, role reallocation, and balanced cohesion. In such circumstances, helping families to maximize flexibility enables them to adapt more successfully.

An illness time line delineates psychosocial developmental phases of an illness, with each phase having its own salient developmental challenges. In particular, mastering initial crisis phase-related tasks provides a foundation for successful adaptation over the long haul. Attention to time allows the clinician to assess family strengths and vulnerabilities in relation to present and future phases of the illness.

The model clarifies treatment planning. Goal setting is guided by awareness of the aspects of family functioning most relevant to the particular type or phase of an illness. Sharing this information with the family and deciding on specific goals offer a better sense of control and realistic hope. This process empowers families in their journey of living with a chronic disorder. Also, it educates family members about warning signs that alert them to seek help at appropriate times for brief, goal-oriented treatment. The framework is useful for timing family psychosocial checkups to coincide with key transition points in the illness.

Preventively oriented multifamily psychoeducational or support groups and workshops for patients and their families (Gonzalez & Steinglass, 2002; Steinglass, 1998) provide cost-effective preventive services that decrease family isolation, increase networking, and can identify high-risk families. Multifamily groups can be designed to deal with different types of conditions (e.g., progressive, life-threatening, relapsing). Brief psychoeducational "modules," timed for critical phases of particular "types" of diseases, enable families to digest manageable portions of a long-term coping process. In time-limited (e.g., four sessions) or one-day formats, couples and families can increase coping skills and discuss common disease-related relationship challenges with others in similar situations. For instance, through the Chicago Center for Family Health, we have developed programs in partnership with local medical centers to help families dealing with diabetes and cystic fibrosis and, in collaboration with the MS Society, the Resilient Partners Program, for couples living with multiple sclerosis.

FAMILY ASSESSMENT

As chronic conditions become incorporated into the family system and all its processes, family coping is influenced by illness-oriented family processes that concern the dimension of time and belief systems.

Multigenerational Legacies of Illness, Loss, and Crisis

A family's current behavior, and therefore its response to illness, cannot be adequately comprehended apart from its history (Bowen, 1993; Byng-Hall, 1995; McGoldrick et al., 2011; Walsh & McGoldrick, 2004). Clinicians can use historical questioning and construct a genogram and time line (McGoldrick, Gerson, & Petry, 2008) to track key events and transitions to gain an understanding of a family's organizational shifts and coping strategies as a system in response to past stressors and, more specifically, to past illnesses. Such inquiry helps explain and predict the family's current style of coping, adaptation, and meaning making. A multigenerational assessment helps to clarify areas of strength and vulnerability. It also identifies high-risk families, burdened by past unresolved issues and dysfunctional patterns, that cannot absorb the challenges presented by a serious condition.

A chronic illness-oriented genogram focuses on how a family organized itself as an evolving system specifically around previous illnesses and unexpected crises. A central goal is to bring to light areas of consensus and "learned differences" (Penn, 1983) that are sources of cohesion, resilience, and potential conflict. Patterns of coping, replications, shifts in relationships (i.e., alliances, triangles, cutoff), and sense of competence are noted. These patterns are transmitted across generations as family pride, myths, taboos, catastrophic expectations, and belief systems. Also, it is useful to inquire about other forms of loss (e.g., divorce, migration), crisis (e.g., job loss, traumatic event), and protracted adversity (e.g., poverty, racism, war, political oppression). These experiences can provide transferable sources of resilience and effective coping skills in the face of a serious health problem (Walsh, 2006). Clinicians need to ask specifically about positive family-of-origin experiences with illness and loss that can serve as models to adapt to the current situation.

Illness Type and Time Phase Issues

Whereas a family may have certain standard ways of coping with any illness, there may be critical differences in its style and success in adaptation to different "types" of diseases. It is important to track prior family illnesses for areas of perceived competence, failure, or inexperience. Inquiry about different illness types may reveal, for instance, that a family dealt successfully with non-life-threatening illnesses but reeled under the weight of metastatic cancer. Such families might be well equipped to deal with less severe conditions but be particularly vulnerable if another life-threatening illness were to occur.

Tracking a family's coping capabilities in the crisis, chronic, and terminal phases of previous chronic illnesses highlights legacies of strength as well as complication in adaptation related to different points in the illness course. One man who grew up with a partially disabled father with heart disease witnessed his parents' successful renegotiation of traditional gender-defined roles when his mother went to work, while his father assumed household responsibilities. This man, now with heart disease himself, has a positive legacy about gender roles from his family of origin that facilitated a flexible response to his own illness. Another family with a member with chronic kidney failure functioned very well in handling the practicalities of home dialysis. However, in the terminal phase, their limitations with emotional expression left a legacy of unresolved grief. Tracking prior illness experiences in terms of time phases helps clinicians see both the strengths and vulnerabilities in a family, which counteracts the assignment of dysfunctional labels that emphasize the difficult periods.

Couples' hidden strengths, not just unresolved issues, can remain dormant and suddenly reemerge when triggered by a chronic illness. For any significant illness in either adult partner's family of origin, a clinician should try to get a picture of how those families organized to handle the range of disease-related affective and practical tasks. What role did each play in handling these tasks, and did they emerge with a strong sense of competence or failure? Such information can help to anticipate areas of conflict, consensus, and similar patterns of adaptation.

Although many families have healthy multigenerational family patterns of adaptation, any family may falter in the face of multiple disease and other major stressors that impact in a relatively short time. With progressive, disabling diseases or the concurrence of illnesses in several family members, a pragmatic approach that focuses on expanded or creative use of supports and resources outside the family is most productive.

Interweaving of Illness, Individual, and Family Development

A developmental lens provides a powerful way to construct a normative framework for serious illness. To place the unfolding of chronic disease into a developmental context, it is vital to understand the intertwining of three evolutionary threads: illness, individual, and family development.

Concepts of human and family development have evolved from models that centered on a basic, somewhat invariant sequence and unfolding of phases to ones that are more varied, fluid, and multidimensional, consistent with contemporary individual and family life course trajectories. Serious health conditions are one example of major, often unexpected, life challenges that can significantly alter the sequence and character of a family and its members' life course. For purposes of this discussion, *life structure*, a useful central concept for both family and individual development, refers to core elements (e.g., work, childrearing, caregiving) of an individual's or family's life at any phase of the life cycle. Individual and family development have in common the notion of phases (each with its own developmental priorities) and are marked by the alternation of life structure-building/maintaining (stable) and -changing (transitional) phases (Levinson, 1986). The primary goal of a building/maintaining phase is to form a life structure and enrich life within it based on the key choices an individual–family made during the preceding transition. Transition phases are somewhat more fluid, because previous individual, family, and illness life structures are reappraised in the face of new developmental challenges that may involve major changes rather than minor alterations (see Cowan & Cowan, Chapter 18, this volume).

At a macro level, the family life cycle can be viewed as oscillating between phases in which family developmental tasks require intense bonding or relatively higher cohesion, as in early childrearing, and phases such as families with adolescents, in which the external family boundary is loosened, with increasing personal identity and autonomy (Combrinck-Graham, 1985). Ethnic and racial differences influence the specific cultural expression of these phases.

These unifying concepts provide a foundation for understanding the experience of chronic disorders. The life cycle contains alternating transition and life structure-building/maintaining phases. And particular phases can be characterized as requiring relatively greater or lesser degrees of family cohesion. Illness, individual, and family development each pose priorities and challenges that move through phases of being more or less in sync with each other.

Generally, serious disorders exert an inward cohesive pull on the family system. Analogous to the addition of a new family member, illness onset sets in motion an inside-the-family focused process of socialization to illness. Symptoms, loss of function, the demands of shifting or acquiring new illness-related roles, and the fears of further disability and/or death, all push a family to focus inward.

The need for family cohesion varies enormously with different illness types and phases. The tendency for a disease to pull a family inward increases with the level of disability or risk of progression and death. Progressive diseases over time inherently require greater cohesion than constant course illnesses. The ongoing addition of new demands with illness progression keeps a family's energy focused inward, often impeding the development of other members. After an initial period of adaptation, a constant course disease (without severe disability) permits a family to get back on track developmentally. Relapsing illnesses alternate between periods of drawing a family inward and times of release from immediate demands of disease. But the on-call nature of many such illnesses keeps part of the family focus inward despite asymptomatic periods, hindering the natural flow between phases of development.

Diagnosis of a serious illness can precipitate a family transition in which one of the family's main tasks is to accommodate the anticipation of further loss and possibly untimely death. If illness onset coincides with launching or postlaunching phases in family development, it can derail a family's natural momentum. For an affected young adult, it may require a heightened dependency and return to the family of origin for disease-related caregiving. The autonomy and individuation of parents and child can be jeopardized. Separate interests and priorities may be relinquished or put on hold. Family processes, as well as disease severity, influence whether the family's reversion to a childrearing-like structure is a temporary detour or a long-term reversal.

When disease onset coincides with a phase in family development requiring higher cohesion (e.g., early childrearing), it can prolong this period. At worst, the family can become enmeshed and developmentally stuck. Alternatively, with chronic disorders, there is a risk of the label *enmeshment* when the normative lengthening of developmental phases for child and family is disregarded. Often, families coping with a chronically ill child are tentative about giving the child more autonomy, not because of inherent family dysfunction, but because of anticipation of further loss, coupled with a lack of preventive psychoeducation from professionals.

With major health conditions, previous norms concerning family organization may need greater flexibility. Enmeshment with blurred generational boundaries is overdiagnosed as family dysfunction. Yet the very real demands on older children and adolescents to assume more adult functions, in the interest of family well-being, need to be distinguished from rigid pathological descriptions of "parentified" children. For instance, when a parent develops a serious disorder during a childrearing phase of development, a family's ability to stay on course is most severely taxed. The impact is twofold: A new family burden is added, with some loss of parental functioning. To meet simultaneous childrearing and caregiving needs, an older child or grandparent may need to assume parental responsibilities. These forms of family adaptation are appropriate if structural realignments are flexible, shared, and sensitive to competing age-related developmental needs. Strong extended kin networks facilitate family adaptation.

When illness onset coincides with a transition in the individual or family life cycle, issues related to existing and anticipated loss tend to be magnified. Transition periods are often characterized by upheaval, rethinking of prior commitments, and openness to change. Such times often hold a greater risk for the illness to become either embedded or ignored in planning for the next life phase. During a transition period, the process of thinking through future commitments can bring to the forefront family norms regarding loyalty through sacrifice and caregiving. The following example highlights this point.

In one Latino family, the father, a factory worker and primary financial provider, had a mild heart attack. He also suffered from emphysema. At first his impairment was mild and stabilized, allowing him to continue his work. The family, including the oldest son, age 15, seemed relatively unaffected. Two years later, the father experienced a second, more life-threatening heart attack and became totally disabled. His son, now 17, had dreams of going away to college. The specter of financial hardship and the perceived need for a "man in the family" created a serious dilemma for the son and the family. Moreover, the parents had worked hard to move out of the housing projects and to ensure that their children could get a good education for a better future. There was a clash among simultaneous transition periods: (1) the illness transition to a more incapacitating progressive course; (2) the son's individual transition to early adulthood with individuation, leaving home, and educational pursuits; and (3) the family developmental transition in the family life cycle, with dreams for the future. It also illustrates the significance of the type of illness: One that was less incapacitating and life-threatening might have interfered less with individual and family developmental priorities.

It is essential to situate these developmental issues in the context of cultural values, socioeconomic considerations, availability of family or community resources, and access to health care. In many cultures, as in this Latino family, a strong emphasis on loyalty to family needs would normatively take priority over individual goals, especially with a major illness or disability. Also, a lack of community and health care resources can severely constrain family adaptation options.

Illness onset that coincides with a life structure-building/maintaining developmental phase presents a different challenge. These phases are characterized by living out choices made during the preceding transition. Relative to transition phases, family members try to protect their own and the family unit's current life structure. Milder conditions may require some revision but not a radical restructuring. A severe condition (e.g., traumatic brain injury) can force families into a more complete transition at a time when individual–family inertia is to preserve the momentum of a stable phase. To navigate this kind of crisis successfully, family adaptability often requires the ability to transform the entire life structure to a prolonged transitional state.

Systemically, at the time of diagnosis, it is important to know the life-cycle phases of the family and each member, not just the ill one. Chronic disease in one family member can profoundly affect developmental goals of another member. For instance, an infant disability can be a serious roadblock to parents' preconceived ideas about competent childrearing, or a life-threatening illness in a young, married adult can interfere with the well spouse's readiness to become a parent. Also, family members frequently adapt in varied ways. Each member's ability to adapt, and the rate at which he or she does so, is related to his or her own developmental phase and role in the family. When family members are in tune with each other's developmental processes, while promoting flexibility and alternative means to satisfy developmental needs, successful long-term adaptation is maximized.

The timing of chronic illness in the life cycle can be normative (e.g., expectable in relation to chronological and social time) or non-normative (e.g., "off-time"). Chronic illness is considered a normally anticipated challenge in later adulthood, whereas its occurrence earlier is "out of phase" and developmentally more disruptive (Neugarten, 1976). For instance, chronic diseases that occur in the childrearing phase can be more challenging because of their potential impact on family childrearing responsibilities. The actual impact depends on the "type" of illness and preillness family roles. Families with flexible gender-influenced rules about financial provision and childrearing tend to adjust better.

The concept of "out of phase" illnesses can be refined to highlight patterns of strain over time. Because diseases have an inward pull on most families, they can be more disruptive to families in a launching children phase of development. If the particular illness is progressive, relapsing, increasingly incapacitating, and/or life-threatening, then the unfolding phases of the disease will be punctuated by numerous transitions. Under these conditions, a family will need to alter its life structure more frequently to accommodate shifting and increasing demands of the disease. This level of demand and uncertainty keeps the illness in the forefront of a family's consciousness, constantly impinging on its attempts to get back "in phase" developmentally.

Finally, the transition from the crisis to the chronic phase is the key juncture at which the intensity of the family's socialization to living with chronic disease is lessened. In this sense, it offers a window of opportunity for the family to reestablish or sometimes chart a "new normal" developmental course.

An overarching goal is to deal with the developmental demands of the illness without family members sacrificing their own or the family's development as a system over time. It is important to determine whose life plans have been or might be cancelled, postponed, or altered, and when plans put on hold and future developmental issues will be addressed. In this way, clinicians can anticipate developmental nodal points related to "autonomy within" versus "subjugation to" the condition. Family members can be helped to strike a healthier balance, with life plans that resolve feelings of guilt, overresponsibility, and hopelessness, and find family and external resources to enhance freedom both to pursue personal goals and to provide needed care for the ill member.

HEALTH/ILLNESS BELIEF SYSTEM

When illness strikes, a primary developmental challenge for a family is to create a meaning for the illness experience that promotes a sense of mastery and competency. Because serious illness is often experienced as a betrayal of our fundamental trust in our bodies and belief in our invulnerability (Kleinman, 1988), creating an empowering narrative can be a formidable task. Family health beliefs help us grapple with the existential dilemmas of our fear of death, our tendency to want to sustain our denial of death, and our attempts to reassert control when suffering and loss occur. They serve as a cognitive and interpersonal road map guiding decisions and action; they provide a way to approach new and ambiguous situations for coherence in family life, facilitating continuity of past, present, and future (Antonovsky & Sourani, 1988; Reiss, 1981). Our appreciative inquiry to understand family beliefs is perhaps the most powerful foundation stone of collaboration between families and health professionals (Wright & Bell, 2009).

In the initial crisis phase, it is valuable for clinicians to inquire about key beliefs that shape the family's illness narrative and coping strategies. This includes tracking beliefs about (1) normality; (2) mind–body relationship, control, and mastery; (3) meanings attached by a family, ethnic group, religion, or the wider culture to symptoms (e.g., chronic pain; Griffith & Griffith, 1994), types of illnesses (e.g., life-threatening), or specific diseases (e.g., HIV/AIDS); (4) assumptions about what caused an illness and what will influence its course and outcome; (5) multigenerational factors that have shaped a family's health beliefs; and (6) anticipated nodal points in illness, individual, and family development when health beliefs will likely be strained or need to shift. Clinicians should also assess the fit of health beliefs among family members, as well as between the family and health care system, and the wider culture.

Beliefs about Normality

Family beliefs about what is normal or abnormal, and the importance members place on conformity and excellence in relation to the average family, have far-reaching implications for adaptation to chronic disorders. When family values allow having a "problem" without self-denigration, it enables members to seek outside help yet maintain a positive identity. When families define help seeking as weak and shameful it undercuts this kind of resilience. Essentially, with chronic disorders in which problems are to be expected, and the use of professionals and outside resources is necessary, a belief that pathologizes this normative process adds insult to injury.

Two useful questions elicit these beliefs: "How do you think other *average* families would deal with a similar situation to yours?" and "How would families *ideally* cope with your situation?" Families with strong beliefs in high achievement and perfectionism are prone to apply standards that are impossible to achieve in a situation of illness. Particularly with untimely conditions that occur early in the life cycle, there are additional pressures to keep up with socially expectable developmental milestones of age peers. The fact that life goals may take longer or need revision requires a flexible belief about what is normal and healthy. To sustain hope, particularly with long-term adversity, effectively, families need to embrace a flexible definition of normality.

The Family's Sense of Mastery in Facing Illness

It is vital to determine how a family defines *mastery* or *control* in general, and in situations of illness. Mastery is similar to the concept of *health locus of control* (Lefcourt, 1982), which can be defined as the belief about influence over the course/outcome of an illness. It is useful to distinguish whether a family's beliefs are based on the premise of internal control, external control by chance, or external control by powerful others.

An internal locus-of-control orientation means that individuals or families believe they can affect the outcome of a situation. Such families believe they are directly responsible for their health and have the power to recover from illness (Wallston, 2004). An external orientation entails a belief that outcomes are not contingent on the individual's or the family's behavior. Families that view illness in terms of chance believe that when illness occurs, it is a matter of luck, and that fate determines recovery. Those who see health control as being in the hands of powerful others view health professionals, God, or sometimes "powerful" family members as exerting control over their bodies and the illness course.

A family may adhere to a different belief about control when dealing with biological as distinct from typical, day-to-day issues. Therefore, it is important to inquire about a family's (1) core values, (2) beliefs about control of serious illness, and (3) the specific disease. For instance, regardless of the actual severity or prognosis in a particular case, cancer may be equated with "death" or "no control" because of medical statistics, cultural myth, or prior family history. Alternatively, families may have enabling stories about a relative or friend, who, in spite of cancer and a shortened lifespan, lived a "full" life centered on effectively prioritizing the quality of relationships and goals. Clinicians can highlight these positive narratives as a means to help families counteract cultural beliefs that focus exclusively on control of biology as defining success.

A family's beliefs about mastery strongly affect its relationship to an illness and to the health care system. Beliefs about control can affect treatment adherence and a family's preferences about participation in the ill member's treatment and healing process. When families view disease course/outcome as a matter of chance, they tend to establish marginal relationships with health professionals and may not adhere to treatment recommendations, largely because their belief system minimizes the importance of their own or the professional's impact on a disease process. Also, poor minority families too often receive inadequate care or lack access, leading to a fatalistic attitude and lack of engagement with health care providers, who may not be trusted to help. Because any therapeutic relationship depends on a shared belief system about what is therapeutic, a workable accommodation among the patient, family, and health care team in terms of these fundamental beliefs is essential. Families that feel misunderstood by health care professionals are often reacting to a lack of engagement at this basic value level.

The goodness of fit in family beliefs about mastery can vary depending on the illness phase. For some disorders, the crisis phase involves protracted care outside the family's direct control. This may be stressful for a family that prefers to tackle its own problems without outside control and "interference." The patient's return home may increase the workload but allow members to reassert more fully their competence and leadership. In contrast, a family guided more by a preference for external control by experts can expect greater difficulty when their family member returns home. Recognition of such normative differences in belief about control can guide an effective psychosocial treatment plan tailored to each family's needs and affirming rather than disrespecting core values.

In the terminal phase, a family may feel least in control of the biological course of disease and the decision making with regard to the overall care of the dying member. Families with a strong belief about being involved in a member's health care may need to assert themselves more vigorously with health providers. Effective decision making about the extent of heroic medical efforts requires a family–provider relationship that respects the family's basic beliefs (Lynn, Schuster, Wilkinson, & Simon, 2007).

Clinicians must be cautious about judging the relative usefulness of minimization versus direct confrontation with and acceptance of painful realities. Often both are needed. The healthy use of minimization or selective focus on the positive and timely uses of humor should be distinguished from the concept of denial, regarded as pathological (Walsh, 2006). As distinct from denial, Taylor's research underscores that with "positive illusions," information about a stressful situation, such as major illness, has been understood and its implications incorporated (Taylor, Kemeny, Reed, Bowers, & Gruenwald, 2000). The skilled clinician can support both the usefulness of hope and the need for treatment to control the illness or a new complication. Families can be helped to confront denial and illness severity when there is hope that preventive action or medical treatment can affect the outcome, or when an illness is entering a terminal phase. Yet to cope with an arduous, uncertain course, families often simultaneously need to acknowledge the condition and to minimize treatment risks or the likelihood of a poor outcome.

Family Beliefs about the Cause of an Illness

When a significant health problem arises, many wonder, "Why me (or us)?" and "Why now?" (Roesch & Weiner, 2001). We attempt to construct an explanation or story that helps us organize our experience. With the limits of current medical knowledge, tremendous uncertainties persist about the relative importance of myriad factors, leaving individuals and families to make idiosyncratic attributions about what caused an illness. A family's causal beliefs need to be assessed separately from its beliefs about what can influence the outcome. It is important to ask each family member for his or her explanation. Responses generally reflect a combination of medical information and family mythology. Beliefs about cause might include punishment for prior misdeeds (e.g., an affair), blame of a particular family member ("Your drinking made me sick!"), a sense of injustice ("Why am I being punished? I have been a good person"), genetics (e.g., cancer runs on one side of the family), negligence of the patient (e.g., careless driving) or of parents (e.g., sudden infant death syndrome), religious beliefs (punishment for sin), or simply bad luck.

Optimal family narratives respect the limits of scientific knowledge, affirm basic competency, and promote the flexible use of multiple biological, psychosocial, and spiritual healing approaches. In contrast, causal attributions that invoke blame, shame, or guilt are particularly important to uncover, as they can derail family coping and adaptation. With a life-threatening illness, a blamed family member may be held accountable if the patient dies. A mother who is blamed by her husband for their son's leukemia may be less able to stop a low-probability experimental treatment for their dying child. A husband who believes his drinking caused his wife's coronary and subsequent death may increase self-destructive drinking in his profound guilt.

Belief System Adaptability

Because illnesses vary enormously in their responsiveness to psychosocial factors, *both families and providers* need to distinguish between beliefs about their overall participation in a long-term disease process, beliefs about their ability to control the biological progression of an illness, and flexibility in applying these beliefs. Families' experience of competence or mastery depends on their grasp of these distinctions. Optimal family and provider narratives respect the limits of scientific knowledge, affirm basic competency, and promote the flexible use of multiple biological and psychosocial healing strategies.

A family's belief in its participation in the total illness process can be thought of as independent of whether a disease is stable, improving, or in a terminal phase. Sometimes, mastery and the attempt to control biological process coincide, such as when a family tailors its behavior to help maintain the health of a member with cancer in remission. This might include changes in family roles, communication, diet, exercise, and balance between work and recreation. Optimally, when an ill family member loses remission, and the family enters the terminal phase of the illness, participation as an expression of mastery is transformed to a successful process of letting go that eases suffering and allows palliative care to be provided. Families can play an important role in easing suffering by both providing comfort through pleasurable visits and outings, and openness to healing and repairing old grievances and relationship wounds.

Families with flexible belief systems are more likely to experience death with a sense of equanimity rather than profound failure. The death of a patient whose long, debilitating illness has heavily burdened others can bring relief, as well as sadness, to family members. Relief over death, even when it ends patient suffering, and family caregiving and financial burdens, can trigger massive guilt reactions that may be expressed through symptoms such as depression and family conflict. Clinicians need to help family members accept mixed feelings they may have about the death being natural, as well as often an end to the suffering of a loved one.

Thus, flexibility both within the family and the health care team is a key variable in optimal family functioning. Rather than linking mastery in a rigid way with biological outcome (survival or recovery) as the sole determinant of success, families can define control in a more "holistic" sense, with involvement and participation in the overall process as the main criteria defining success. This is analogous to the distinction between curing "the disease" and "healing the system." Psychosocial–spiritual healing may influence the course and outcome, but a positive disease outcome is not necessary for a family to feel successful. This flexible view of mastery permits the quality of relations within the family, or between the family and health care professional, to become more central to criteria of success. The health care provider's competence becomes valued from both a technical and caregiving perspective not solely linked to the biological course.

Ethnic, Spiritual, and Cultural Beliefs

Ethnic, racial, and spiritual beliefs and dominant cultural norms can strongly influence family values concerning health and illness (McGoldrick, Giordano, & Garcia-Preto, 2005; Rolland, 2006b; Walsh, 2009). Significant ethnic differences regarding health beliefs often emerge at the time of a major health crisis. Although American families are a continuum that frequently represents a blend of different ethnic, racial, and spiritual beliefs, health professionals need to be mindful of the diversity of belief systems of various subpopulations in their community, particularly as these are expressed in different behavioral patterns. Cultural norms vary in areas such as the definition of the appropriate "sick role" for the patient; the kind and degree of open communication about the disease; who should be included in the illness caregiving system (e.g., extended family, friends, professionals); who is the primary caretaker (most often wife/mother/daughter/daughter-in-law); and the kind of rituals viewed as normative at different illness phases (e.g., hospital bedside vigils, healing, and funeral rituals). This is especially true for racial minority groups (e.g., African American, Asian, Hispanic) that experience discrimination or marginalization from the prevailing European American culture. Illness provides an opportunity to encourage role flexibility and shift from defining one female member as the caregiver to a collaborative caregiving team that includes male and female siblings/adult children.

Clinicians need to be mindful of these cultural differences in themselves, the patient, and the family to forge a workable alliance that can endure a long-term illness (Seaburn, Gunn, Mauksch, Gawinski, & Lorenz, 1996). Effective collaboration occurs when professionals explore and understand families' cultural and spiritual beliefs about illness and healing. Disregarding these issues can lead families to wall themselves off from health care providers and available community resources—a major source of adherence issues and treatment failure. Sometimes professionals may need the flexibility to suspend their need to be "in charge," especially in relation to family/cultural beliefs that proscribe certain standard forms of medical care (e.g., blood products for Jehovah's Witness). This requires an acceptance that patients, not physicians, retain final responsibility for decisions about their bodies.

Fit among Clinicians, Health Systems, and Families

It is a common, but unfortunate, error to regard "the family" as a monolithic unit that feels, thinks, believes, and behaves as an undifferentiated whole.

Clinicians should inquire both about the level of agreement and tolerance for differences among family members' beliefs, and between the family and the health care system.

Family beliefs that balance the need for consensus with diversity and innovation are optimal and maximize permissible options. If consensus is the rule, then individual differentiation implies disloyalty and deviance. If the guiding principle is "We can hold different viewpoints," then diversity is allowed. This is adaptive, because it facilitates bringing to the family novel and creative forms of problem solving that may be needed in a situation of protracted adversity, such as serious illness. Families also need open communication and effective conflict resolution when members differ on major health care/treatment decisions.

The same questions concerning beliefs asked of families are relevant to the health care team:

1. What are health professionals' attitudes about their own and the family's ability to influence the course/outcome of the disease?
2. How do they see the balance between their own and the family's participation in the treatment process?
3. If basic differences in beliefs about control exist, how can these differences be bridged?

Because of the tendency of most health facilities to disempower individuals and thereby foster dependence or alienation, utmost sensitivity to family values is needed to forge a therapeutic alliance. Many breakdowns in relationships between "noncompliant" or marginal patients and their providers can be traced to natural disagreements at this basic level that were not addressed.

Normative differences among family members' health beliefs may emerge into destructive conflicts during a health crisis, as in the following case:

> When Stavros, a first-generation Greek American, became ill with heart disease, his mother kept a 24-hour bedside vigil in his hospital room, so she could tend to her son at any hour. His wife Dana, from a Scandinavian family, greatly resented the "intrusive behavior" of her mother-in-law, who in turn criticized Dana's emotional "coldness" and relative lack of concern. Stavros felt caught between his warring mother and wife, and complained of increased symptoms.

In such situations, clinicians need to sort out normative cultural differences from pathological enmeshment. In this case, all concerned behaved according to their own cultural norms. In Greek culture, it is normal to maintain close ties to one's family of origin after marriage and expected that a mother would tend to her son in a health crisis. A son would be disloyal not to allow his mother that role. This sharply differs from the wife's northern European traditions. Each side pathologized the other, creating a conflictual triangle, with the patient caught in the middle. In such situations, the clinician who affirms multicultural differences promotes a transformation of process from blaming or demonizing to accommodating varied cultures respectfully.

It is common for differences in beliefs or attitude to erupt at any major life-cycle or illness transition. For instance, in situations of severe disability or terminal illness, one member may want the patient to return home, whereas another may prefer long-term hospitalization or transfer to an extended care facility. Because the primary caregiver role is typically assigned to the wife/ mother, she is apt to bear most burdens in this regard. Anticipating the collision of gender-based beliefs about caregiving with the potential overwhelming demands of home-based care for a dying family member can help families flexibly modify their rules and avert the risk of family caretaker overload, resentment, and deteriorating family relationships.

The murky boundary between the chronic and the terminal phase highlights the potential for professionals' beliefs to collide with those of family members. Physicians can feel bound to a technological imperative that requires them to exhaust all possibilities at their disposal, regardless of the odds of success. Family members may not know how to interpret continued lifesaving efforts, and may assume real hope where virtually none exists. Health care providers and institutions can collude in a pervasive societal tendency to deny death as a natural process truly beyond technological control (Becker, 1973). Endless treatment can represent medical team members' inability to separate a general value placed on controlling diseases from their beliefs about participation (separate from cure) in a patient's total care, which includes biopsychosocial–spiritual well-being.

CONCLUSIONS

Facing the risks and burdens of a serious illness, the "healthiest" families are able to harness that experience to improve the quality of life. Families can achieve a healthy balance between accepting limits and promoting autonomy and connectedness. For illnesses with long-range risks, including genomic disorders, families can maintain mastery in the face of uncertainty by enhancing the following capacities: acknowledge the possibility of loss; sustain hope of medical advances; and build flexibility into family life-cycle planning that conserves and adjusts major goals, and helps circumvent the forces of uncertainty. The systemic model described here, which integrates the psychosocial demands of disorders over time with individual and family development and belief systems, provides a foundation for such a normative perspective.

A serious illness or brush with death provides an opportunity to confront catastrophic fears about loss. This can lead family members to develop a better appreciation and perspective on life that results in clearer priorities and closer relationships (Walsh, 2006). Seizing opportunities can replace procrastination for the "right moment" or passive waiting for the dreaded moment. Serious illness, by emphasizing life's fragility and preciousness, provides families with an opportunity to heal unresolved issues and develop more immediate, caring relationships. For illnesses in a more advanced stage, clinicians should help families emphasize quality of life by defining goals that are attainable more immediately and that enrich their everyday lives.

Imber-Black, Roberts, and Whiting (2003) have underscored the importance of rituals for many families dealing with chronic and life-threatening disorders and loss (see Imber-Black, Chapter 20, this volume). Heightened uncertainty and loss increase awareness that each family gathering may be the last together. Clinicians can help families dealing with serious illness by promoting the timely creation and use of rituals of celebration, transition, and inclusion. A family reunion can invigorate members and serve to coalesce healing energies to support the ill member and key caregivers. With a serious illness, holidays and family traditions offer an opportunity to affirm, strengthen, and repair all family relationships.

Finally, clinicians need to consider their own experiences and feelings about illness and loss (McDaniel, Hepworth, & Doherty, 1997). Awareness and ease with our own multigenerational and family history with illness and loss, our health beliefs, and our current life-cycle passage will enhance our ability to work effectively with families facing serious illness.

REFERENCES

Antonovsky, A., & Sourani, T. (1988). Family sense of coherence and family adaptation. *Journal of Marriage and Family, 50,* 79–92.

Becker, E. (1973). *The denial of death.* New York: Free Press.

Boss, P. (1999). *Ambiguous loss: Learning to live with unresolved grief.* Cambridge, MA: Harvard University Press.

Bowen, M. (1993). *Family therapy in clinical practice.* New York: Aronson.

Byng-Hall, J. (1995). *Rewriting family scripts.* New York: Guilford Press.

Campbell, T. (2003). The effectiveness of family interventions for physical disorders. *Journal of Marital and Family Therapy, 29*(2), 263–281.

Carr, D., & Springer, K. W. (2010). Advances in families and health research in the 21st century. *Journal of Marriage and Family, 72*(3), 743–761.

Combrinck-Graham, L. (1985). A developmental model for family systems. *Family Process, 24*(2), 139–150.

D'Onofrio, B. M., & Lahey, B. B. (2010). Biopsychosocial influences on the family: A decade review. *Journal of Marriage and Family, 72*(3), 762–782.

Gonzales, S., & Steinglass, P. (2002). Application of multifamily discussion groups in chronic medical disorders. In W. R. McFarlane (Ed.), *Multifamily groups in the treatment of severe psychiatric disorders* (pp. 315–340). New York: Guilford Press.

Griffith, J., & Griffith, M. (1994). *The body speaks.* New York: Basic Books.

Himmelstein, D., Thorne, D., Warren, E., & Woolhandler, S. (2009). Medical bankruptcy in the United States, 2007: Results of a national study. *The American Journal of Medicine, 122,* 741–746.

Imber-Black, E., Roberts, J., & Whiting, R. (Eds.). (2003). *Rituals in families and family therapy* (2nd ed.). New York: Norton.

Kleinman, A. M. (1988). *The illness narratives: Suffering, healing and the human condition.* New York: Basic Books.

Lefcourt, H. M. (1982). *Locus of control* (2nd ed.). Hillsdale, NJ: Erlbaum.

Levinson, D. J. (1986). A conception of adult development. *American Psychologist, 41,* 3–13.

Lynn, J., Schuster, L. L., Wilkinson, A., & Simon, L. N. (2007). *Improving care for the end of life: A sourcebook for health care managers and clinicians* (2nd ed.). New York: Oxford University Press.

Martire, L., Lustig, A., Schulz, R., Miller, G., & Helgeson, V. (2004). Is it beneficial to involve a family member?: A meta-analysis of psychosocial interventions in chronic illness. *Health Psychology, 23,* 599–611.

McDaniel, S., Hepworth, J., & Doherty, W. (Eds.). (1997). *The shared experience of illness: Stories of patients, families, and their therapists.* New York: Basic Books.

McDaniel, S. H., Hepworth, J., & Doherty, W. J. (2012). *Medical family therapy* (2nd ed.). New York: Basic Books.

McGoldrick, M., Carter, E., & Garcia-Preto, N. (Eds.). (2011). *The expanded family life cycle: Individual, family, and social perspectives* (4th ed.). Boston: Allyn & Bacon.

McGoldrick, M., Gerson, R., & Petry, S. (2008). *Genograms in family assessment* (3rd ed.). New York: Norton.

McGoldrick, M., Giordano, J., & Garcia-Preto, N. (Eds.). (2005). *Ethnicity and family therapy* (3rd ed.). New York: Guilford Press.

Miller, S., McDaniel, S., Rolland, J., & Feetham, S. (Eds.). (2006). *Individuals, families, and the new genetics.* New York: Norton.

Moos, R. H. (Ed.). (1984). *Coping with physical illness: Vol. 2. New perspectives.* New York: Plenum.

Neugarten, B. (1976). Adaptation and the life cycle. *Counseling Psychologist, 6*(l), 16–20.

Olkin, R. (1999). *What psychotherapists should know about disability.* New York: Guilford Press.

Penn, P. (1983). Coalitions and binding interactions in families with chronic illness. *Family Systems Medicine, 1*(2), 16–25.

Reiss, D. (1981). *The family's construction of reality.* Cambridge, MA: Harvard University Press.

Reiss, D., Neierhiser, J., Hetherington, M., & Plomin, R. (2000). *The relationship code: Deciphering genetic and social influence on adolescent development.* Cambridge, MA: Harvard University Press.

Roesch, S., & Weiner, B. (2001). A meta-analytic review of coping with illness: Do causal attributions matter? *Journal of Psychosomatic Research, 50*(4), 205–219.

Rolland, J. S. (1984). Toward a psychosocial typology of chronic and life-threatening illness. *Family Systems Medicine, 2*(3), 245–263.

Rolland, J. S. (1987a). Chronic illness and the life cycle: A conceptual framework. *Family Process, 26*(2), 203–221.

Rolland, J. S. (1987b). Family illness paradigms: Evolution and significance. *Family Systems Medicine, 5*(4), 467–486.

Rolland, J. S. (1990). Anticipatory loss: A family systems developmental framework. *Family Process, 29*(3), 229–244.

Rolland, J. S. (1994a). *Families, illness, and disability: An integrative treatment model.* New York: Basic Books.

Rolland, J. S. (1994b). In sickness and in health: The impact of illness on couples' relationships. *Journal of Marital and Family Therapy, 20*(4), 327–349.

Rolland, J. S. (1997). The meaning of disability and suffering: Socio-political and ethical concerns. *Family Process, 36*(4), 437–440.

Rolland, J. S. (1998). Families and collaboration: Evolution over time. *Families, Systems and Health, 16*(1), 7–25.

Rolland, J. S. (1999). Families and genetic fate: A millennial challenge. *Families, Systems, and Health, 16*(1), 123–133.

Rolland, J. S. (2002). Managing chronic illness. In M. Mengel, W. Holleman, & S. Fields (Eds.), *Fundamentals of clinical practice: A textbook on the patient, doctor and society* (2nd ed., pp. 233–268). New York: Plenum.

Rolland, J. S. (2006a). Living with anticipatory loss in the new era of genetics: A life cycle perspective. In S. Miller, S. McDaniels, J. Rolland, & S. Feetham (Eds.), *Individuals, families, and the new era of genetics: Biopsychosocial perspectives* (pp 139–172). New York: Norton.

Rolland, J. S. (2006b). Genetics, family systems, and multicultural influences. *Families, Systems and Health, 24*(4), 425–442.

Rolland, J. S., & Williams, J. K. (2005). Toward a biopsychosocial model for 21st century genetics. *Family Process, 44*(1), 3–24.

Seaburn, D., Gunn, W., Mauksch, L., Gawinski, A., & Lorenz, A. (Eds.). (1996). *Models of collaboration: A guide for mental health professionals working with physicians and health care providers.* New York: Basic Books.

Siegel, B., & Sander, J. (2009). *Faith, hope, and healing: Lessons learned from people living with cancer.* Hoboken, NJ: Wiley.

Steinglass, P. (1998). Multiple family discussion groups for patients with chronic medical illness. *Families, Systems and Health, 16*(1–2), 55–71.

Taylor, S., Kemeny, M., Reed, G., Bowers, J., & Gruenwald, T. (2000). Psychological resources, positive illusions, and health. *American Psychologist, 55*(1), 99–109.

Tienari, P., Wynne, L. C., Sorri, A., Lahti, I., Laksy, K., Moring, J., et al. (2004). Genotype–environment interaction in schizophrenia-spectrum disorder: Long-term follow-up study of Finnish adoptees. *British Journal of Psychiatry, 184*(3), 216–222.

U.S. Bureau of the Census. (2009). *Statistical abstract of the United States.* Washington, DC: U.S. Government Printing Office.

Wallston, K. A. (2004). Control and health. In N. Anderson (Ed.), *Encyclopedia of health and behavior* (Vol. 1, pp. 217–220). Thousand Oaks, CA: Sage.

Walsh, F. (2006). *Strengthening family resilience* (2nd ed.). New York: Guilford Press.

Walsh, F. (Ed.). (2009). *Spiritual resources in family therapy* (2nd ed.). New York: Guilford Press.

Walsh, F., & McGoldrick, M. (Eds.). (2004). *Living beyond loss: Death in the family* (2nd ed.). New York: Norton.

Weihs, K. Fisher, L., & Baird, M. (2001). *Families, health, and behavior* (Commissioned Report: Institute of Medicine, National Academy of Sciences). Washington, DC: National Academy Press.

Werner-Lin, A. (2008). Beating the biological clock: The compressed family life cycle of young women with BRCA gene alterations. *Social Work in Health Care, 47*(4), 416–437.

Wright, L. M., & Bell, J. M. (2009). *Beliefs and illness: A model for healing.* Calgary: 4th Floor Press.

CHAPTER 20

THE VALUE OF RITUALS IN FAMILY LIFE

EVAN IMBER-BLACK

The familiar and the mysterious, the dimly lit past and the unknown future, our despair and our celebration—all may be held and expressed through ritual. As with no other aspect of family, community, and cultural life, rituals braid continuity and change, at once anchoring us in where we may come from, while simultaneously enabling transformation of self, relationships, and community. Living in our fast-forward 21st century, our rituals allow us to make and mark transitions from the small rituals of everyday life to the profound rituals of birth and death. The marvelous elasticity of rituals, the capacity of rituals to change and adapt to changing life circumstances, places them at the core of our lives and our relationships.

In this chapter I provide a ritual framework for family and community life, highlighting concepts with illustrations from both clinical and nonclinical situations involving common dilemmas and challenges.

LOCATING RITUALS

Rituals are omnipresent. They occur in the daily lives of families, including rituals of parting in the morning, reentering the home at the end of a school or work day, meals, and bedtime. Rituals distinguish annual intrafamily events, such as birthdays, anniversaries, family reunions and vacations. They celebrate the seasons, and secular and religious holidays. Rituals make and mark life-cycle transitions, including birth, adolescence, committed adult relationships, and death. And in our changing world, never before seen rituals paradoxically provide guidance as families make their way with new birth technologies, bicultural marriage, migration and reunion, or terror attacks (Imber-Black, 2011).

RITUAL PURPOSES: HOW RITUALS WORK IN FAMILIES

We have learned in working with families over three decades that it is useful to illuminate five purposes of rituals (Imber-Black & Roberts, 1993; Imber-Black, Roberts, & Whiting, 2003):

1. Relating—shaping, expressing, maintaining, and altering relationships
2. Changing—making and marking transitions
3. Healing—recovering from relationship loss, trauma, or betrayal
4. Believing—voicing beliefs and making meaning
5. Celebrating—affirming deep joy and honoring life with festivity

Rituals in family systems may include an entire intergenerational network, such as a family reunion; involve just the immediate household, such as a weekly Sunday dinner; focus on a subsystem, such as a father's bedtime ritual with his 6-year-old daughter, or a couple's anniversary; or highlight an individual's milestone within a family and a community, such as a high school graduation. All such rituals may embody one purpose, but more often any given ritual expresses several purposes.

Relating

Rituals, by virtue of who initiates and plans, and who attends, immediately begin to inform a family about their relationships. Closeness and distance, involvement and disengagement may be seen through the lens of a ritual. Something as seemingly simple as an adolescent who cannot make the regular family dinner hour because of sports or a job signals change in the parent–child relationship. A grown sibling, who refuses to attend a niece's wedding, announces a relationship cutoff without words. Relationship change may be stated silently by virtue of where a ritual occurs. For instance, following the death of a parent who always hosted holidays, a sibling may proclaim, "Thanksgiving will be at my house." The lack of conversation and negotiation may then be experienced as a shift in decision-making power among all of the siblings.

Rituals do not just shape and express relationships. They can also be vehicles to alter relationships with deliberation. In a recently remarried family, a carefully constructed weekly dinner can ease the transition of the new stepparent and stepchildren (Whiteside, 2003). A sacrosanct time for Sunday brunch can build a necessary boundary around a far too busy dual-career couple. A grown child's announcement that he will spend Thanksgiving with his father and stepmother for the first time since becoming an adult signals a difficult but necessary shift in his relationship with his mother.

When people express painful memories of rituals from their families of origin, it is usually the troubled relationships within these rituals that they are recalling. And when people reflect on beautiful memories of childhood rituals, they are most often calling forth generative relationships. Storytelling in therapy can lead to transforming past painful rituals in the present.

A New Bedtime Ritual

When Elana and Bill came to family therapy, one of their many struggles involved how to get their 8-year-old son Billie to go to bed. Every night, Billie resisted, cried, and refused to go to bed until finally falling in a heap at 11:00 P.M. In the middle of the night, he would frequently crawl in to his parents' bed. A year of individual child therapy focusing on dimensions such as fears and nightmares yielded no change. By the time Elana and Bill came to family therapy, they were fighting nightly over how best to get their son to sleep. Elana wanted to read quietly to Billie and soothe him; Bill insisted this was "babying" and that Billie needed to "toughen up." A session was devoted to the question, "What was your bedtime ritual like when you were Billie's age?"

"What bedtime ritual?" Bill exploded. Bill grew up with his divorced and very unhappy father. His mother left the family when Bill was 5, and he never saw her again. "If I disobeyed my father the way Billie disobeys us, I was beaten, plain and simple. Why can't Billie just grow up?" It became clear that bedtime was an especially terrible time in Bill's young life, as his father had usually been quite drunk by that time every night.

Elana listened with tears in her eyes. She knew some of her husband's story, but the abuse he suffered at the hands of his own father was seldom discussed. She and Bill were both proud that he had not physically abused their son, but "words can sometimes be destructive, too," Elana said sadly. Her own bedtime ritual memories were very different, and would prove to be a resource.

"I grew up with my grandmother in the Dominican Republic. My mother also left, but my grandmother was so loving to me. Every night she held me in her lap and told me stories. She could not read, so she made up the most wonderful, magical tales. I actually remember some of them. I would love to tell these to Billie. I think you could make up great stories for him, too, Bill. They would be different—hero stories from your work." Bill was a firefighter who had saved lives.

Bill remarked that he had never heard the story of Elana's bedtime ritual. He was clearly touched by the image of a caring grandmother spinning yarns for her little granddaughter. The therapist suggested that they alternate evenings telling stories to Billie, and that they frame this with him as a new way to close the day.

They returned to family therapy the following week and reported that Billie had gone to bed calmly and by 9:00 P.M. each night. Elana said, "Billie told us he was happy we had stopped fighting, and that we tell better stories than his teacher!"

This work, anchored in a ritual framework, focused on the relating purpose of rituals. The absent bedtime ritual for Bill, coupled with the fear engendered by his own father's abuse and the delight of Elana's memory of her grandmother's arms and words in a bedtime ritual that made her feel safe and loved, combined to open a door to a new ritual in the present. This new ritual held the beginnings of fresh relationship opportunities among the three of them.

Changing

Rituals make and mark transitions, including simple daily transitions—from home to school or work and back again, dinner, and bedtime; annual transitions—birthdays, anniversaries, and holidays; and life-cycle transitions—birth, adolescence, commitment to another in an adult relationship, retirement and aging, illness and death. When such transitions occur, rituals enable us to make the transition, providing not only guidance from the past, familiarity, and repetition but also sufficient space for the novelty and imagination of the never before seen or done. Rituals also mark the transition—parting in the morning with a hug or a repeating phrase, sharing an evening meal to shift from work to home, a special cake to signify a birthday, a wedding ceremony to announce a committed relationship. With such transitions, and the rituals accompanying them, come change in self, relationships, family, and community. The ritual both announces the change and creates the transformation.

Change can often provoke anxiety regarding the unknown. Rituals can make change manageable through familiar enactment. For instance, the ritual of *Quinceanera*, marking the shift from childhood to young womanhood for a Latina girl, makes what could be an otherwise fearful change knowable and predictable. Here it is important to note that change is occurring for not only the girl but also her parents, the wider extended family, and their community (Alvarez, 2007).

An Elementary School Graduation: Making and Marking Change

One family developed a ritual as part of their twin children's graduation from elementary school. Most of their friends were receiving expensive tech toys or fancy cell phones as graduation gifts from their parents. Instead, in this family, the parents began a new ritual to mark the change from childhood to adolescence. The parents took them to the local bank and opened an account in each child's name. Money for the accounts would come from holiday and birthday gifts from parents and other relatives. The children were told that every 6 months they could make new decisions about the funds in the account, with the rule that one-third must be saved, one-third could be spent on items they wanted, and one-third would go to a charity of their choice. In one permission-giving stroke, the parents were able to offer their children a shift to adolescence and a glimpse of young adulthood, while foreshadowing and later experiencing their own changed roles as parents.

Healing

Rituals accompany us when we need to heal. Whether from a death, a divorce, or a relationship betrayal, rituals have the capacity to facilitate healing. Every culture and religion has rituals to initiate healing after a death. Many have annual rituals to remember a loved one and further the healing process. Such annual healing rituals confirm that recovering from loss is not a quick fix but an ongoing process of integration and transformation. Wide and deep community losses such as those the attacks of September 11, 2001, are commemorated with annual healing rituals (Imber-Black, 2003).

No life is lived without loss. Healing rituals simultaneously mark the death, honor a person's life, allow for the expression of grief, and begin to point the way to continuity for the living. Often such rituals involve rich storytelling, together with comforting those who are bereaved.

In contemporary Western cultures, death often occurs in a hospital or institutional setting, severing the connection of death to the ongoing cycle of life. Rituals to enable healing are urgently needed, but often missing in our speeded up society. When healing rituals are absent, family relationship may cease to unfold in the present. A family may become stuck in repetitive interactions. Silence replaces necessary storytelling. In family therapy, a family may be helped to create a new healing ritual.

Melting Frozen Grief

When Carol, 36, came to family therapy with her son Kevin, 8, and her daughter Elisa, 10, the family appeared frozen. Carol's husband Ben had died unexpectedly and mysteriously 4 years earlier, when he was 40. There were no family conversations about the father, his life, or his death. When the therapist asked about him, everyone began to sob as if the death had happened yesterday, but no one could speak about him or tell stories of his life and relationships.

The therapist invited the family to bring photographs that included the father to the next session. In this meeting, the children laughed as they remembered fun times and vacations with Dad. As they told these stories, however, their mother grew more sullen and silent. What was going on?

In a session alone with the mother, the therapist discovered several disturbing secrets. The father had been an alcoholic who viciously beat the mother, followed by apologies and vows never to hurt her again. He died following a fall while drunk. The children did not know this information, or so Carol thought. In the next family meeting, Elisa spoke movingly of witnessing her father beat her mother, of getting in between to make him stop, of toys he would bring them and promises he would make after such terrible episodes.

The children had not been allowed to go to their father's funeral, because Carol thought she could shield them from sadness. His ashes were hidden in a closet at home, a metaphor for his life and death. Slowly, the therapy became a place to tell stories to hold and express the complexities. Ben had been a wonderful and loving husband and father until he lost his job and began to drink. The children heard their mother's sadness and bewilderment for the first time. The true story of Ben's death emerged. With the help of the therapist, the family began to fashion a healing ritual that involved scattering some of Ben's ashes in the ocean, as he loved boating, and putting the remainder in the ground in their yard, where they planted a tree to symbolize a new beginning. This healing ritual necessarily followed time in therapy devoted to developing a complex view of the father and husband.

Believing

All rituals express beliefs. Whether in words or actions, the sheer act of participating in a given ritual is a commentary on our beliefs. Often the beliefs are obvious, such as when a family goes to church every Sunday. But sometimes the expression of beliefs and values in a ritual is more nuanced.

In two different families, an adolescent declares that she has become a vegetarian. In the first family, the parents react with anger and refuse to adapt the family dinner to meet their daughter's request. Every night there is an argument as she refuses to eat the meat served, and she often storms away from the table. Without direct words, the parents are telling their daughter, "In this family, we believe we must all think and act the same." In the second family, the parents accept their daughter's request. Some in the family continue to eat meat, while the teenager is allowed to prepare a vegetarian meal as long as she joins the family for dinner. Occasionally, the whole family eats a vegetarian meal. Here the parents are telling their daughter, "In our family, it is OK to be different. Being together has a higher value than what each of us prefers to eat."

Rituals that remain alive and meaningful for us are those that continue to express our deeply held beliefs. When a ritual feels routine or devoid of meaning, it likely has ceased to carry authentic beliefs. The marvelous ability of rituals to change and grow with changing circumstances, while still anchoring us to where we come from, to our shared history, allows us to express new beliefs through our rituals.

Negotiating Beliefs through Rituals

Newly developed rituals can allow the negotiation of differing beliefs. In couple therapy, a couple arguing over seemingly intractable differences may be asked to design and implement a conversation ritual. Anna and Barbara came to therapy, unable to stop arguing over Anna's wish to adopt a child and Barbara's refusal. Their polarization prevented each from hearing anything her partner was saying. In order to reduce their opposition which was now contaminating the best parts of their relationship, the therapist suggested a "two-part conversation" ritual. The partners were asked to find a place in their apartment that each liked, to meet there, and bring one another a cup of each one's differing favorite tea. During the first conversation, each was to speak about all of the good reasons to adopt a child. During the second conversation, held 2 days later, each was to express all of the good reasons to remain child-free. The therapist asked the women to end each conversation with an expression of appreciation for the other.

When Anna and Barbara returned the following week, they appeared calm and connected to one another. They reported that these two conversations allowed an experience they had not had before in their relationship over this issue—the experience of really listening to one another and the sense of being truly heard. As is so often true when couples polarize about an issue, neither partner had dared to voice doubts in their ferociously staked-out position. During this ritual, each could give expression to the previously unspoken. While Anna had heard over and over about Barbara's aunt, who had adopted a child who turned on the family, this time she also heard Barbara speak about a wonderful and successful adoption by an old friend. And Barbara heard Anna express concerns about her career, and how it might be affected by childrearing. "We saw each other and heard each other as full people and not as the stereotypes we had become," Anna remarked. "We've realized that what we need right now is to have more of these sorts of talks with each other," said Barbara, "and then we can decide what to do." The women went on to say that they had ended the first conversation with a hug of appreciation, and the second, with a hug and an exchange of a yellow rose, the flower they carried at their commitment ceremony.

Celebrating

Rituals marking individual and relationship transformation—weddings, births, graduations, funerals, rituals for holidays, and those distinguishing the passage of time, such as birthdays and anniversaries—all involve celebrating. The celebration theme of rituals announces who we are and who we may become, and connects us with what has come before us and with our larger community. All cultures have rituals of celebration.

The elasticity of rituals means that some rituals may simultaneously hold celebration and further healing of a loss. Annual memorial rituals often entail the honoring of a life in a complex context of sadness and joy. Annual holiday gatherings often contain moments to remember those who have died.

In contemporary Western society, many of our rituals are freighted with unrealizable expectations for celebration. Following a holiday such as Christmas, many express some version of "I thought it would be better, more fun, happier." This may be an important signal to begin to talk over what we really want in a given ritual.

Some families abandon celebration rituals following a terrible loss or because of differing beliefs that feel too difficult to negotiate. In one family, following an adolescent's suicide, the father declared that there would be no more celebrations of holidays. Holidays came and went with no celebration, no special meals, and no discussion of their terrible loss. This went on for 4 years, until the mother decided to organize Christmas once more. She put up a tree, brought out her son's favorite ornaments, and edited a video of his life. At first the father was furious. He tried to walk out of the room when his wife turned on the video, but she implored him to stay. He sobbed through most of it. At the end, he got up and hugged his wife, and asked if they could please have Christmas dinner.

Bicultural and interfaith couples face particular dilemmas regarding celebration rituals. Expectations of each partner's family of origin over the "right" way to celebrate, struggles over preferred foods, the meanings of gifts, and questions about how to maintain and honor connections to each other's heritage all can contribute to a sense that celebrating is "just too much trouble." It helps when couples talk over these dilemmas before making a commitment, but most do not. Only later, when arguments ensue or when children arrive, do many couples begin to engage the differences. Unlike previous generations, when it was expected that one partner would convert (Walsh, 2010) and adopt all of the rituals of his or her mate, couples today find ways to incorporate the differences that enable each partner to maintain his or her beliefs and rituals, while also creating new, meaningful rituals. In one Jewish–Christian intermarriage, the couple, like many, celebrated Hanukah and Christmas, with each taking the lead for his or her particular holiday. Just before New Year's Day they marked a new and idiosyncratic holiday they called "Celebrating Our Differences Day," enabling each to reexamine what he or she believed and valued, communicate this to their children, and mark the day with newly invented festivities and never tried before recipes.

Weaving Multiple Ritual Purposes

Most rituals fulfill more than one of the purposes described earlier. A celebration ritual surely involves relating and believing. When a ritual for celebration intentionally includes a moment to remember departed family members, healing is enhanced. A healing ritual, such as the New Orleans memorial event marking the anniversary of Hurricane Katrina, simultaneously defines a community, reminds people of all that was lost, and celebrates the spirit of renewal and resilience with jazz and dancing in the streets. A religious holiday whose primary purpose may be to express beliefs holds elements of celebration and relationship.

Cal and Jimmy Make a Ritual

Cal, age 54, and his son Jimmy, age 27, came to family therapy to work on their chronically unhappy and conflicted relationship. They had lived together as a duo ever since Jimmy's mother abandoned them when he was 7. Currently

Cal manages a fast-food restaurant. Jimmy is unemployed. The family is Irish American. While Cal comes from a large family, the family members are scattered all over the country and see little of each other. Cal and Jimmy argue daily. These conflicts occur when Cal returns home from a 12-hour shift, following a 90-minute commute. "I enter the apartment and the first thing I see is that Jimmy has done nothing all day—no housework, no laundry, no dinner prepared for us," Cal complained. "He never even says 'hello' to me—just criticism from the moment he walks in," Jimmy retorted. "Even if he doesn't say anything, I watch his face and I know he's angry." Cal agreed that the first thing on his tired mind was all that Jimmy had not done that day.

Clearly, this unhappy father and son had many problems to tackle. Jimmy, a bright and talented young man, had dropped out of college, and Cal spent each evening drinking beer. They had no friendships. Money was tight. Their one point of connection was their dog Ella. Despite Jimmy's inability to function during the day, he always walked Ella. He groomed her and made sure she was fed. At night, after arguing with Jimmy and before drinking, Cal walked Ella. With the television as their backdrop, the two men and Ella sat together in the living room.

The two men had created an unhappy reentry ritual. Their main point of daily contact was the argument that ended in separation. Each ate alone in stony silence, then Cal left to walk Ella.

Many families today have entirely abandoned reentry rituals: A husband goes to his computer, a wife is ordering in dinner, children are playing video games, and no one reconnects. Busy dual-earner families or single-parent households are scrambling just to keep up with children's after school activities and growing piles of homework. Often, a fight replaces a satisfying and brief ritual. Since most people do not fight with strangers, daily conflict becomes a way to say, "we are family."

In therapy, Cal and Jimmy agreed to try a new reentry ritual. They both loved their dog Ella, and knew that their arguing upset her; she would stand between them and bark and growl (see Walsh, 2009, on the role of animals in relational dynamics and therapy). After a conversation in therapy about the importance of reentry rituals to set a tone for the evening, Jimmy suggested that, when Cal returned, before a moment of argument could ensue, they go out together with Ella for a half-hour walk. Their focus would be Ella and not what Jimmy had or had not done that day. Cal joked, "Can I still yell at him when we get back?"

In fact, once they implemented this reentry ritual, the yelling stopped. Jimmy surprised his father by starting to do the necessary chores. The therapy could turn to the far more profound matters of the core sadness in the two men, Jimmy's future, Cal's drinking and exhaustion, and their need for outside friendships.

This simple reentry ritual braided several purposes—opening the relationship of father and son, beginning to heal chronic daily conflict, and marking the transition at the end of the day in a new way.

SHAPING RITUALS

Rituals differ from mere routines in our life. They carry meaning and express values. They may be handed down intergenerationally, created to meet a new circumstance, or utilize the past in a never before seen way (Fiese, 2006). While rituals differ from family to family, community to community, and culture to culture, they contain some common elements:

1. Symbols
2. Symbolic actions
3. Special time
4. Special space
5. Structured parts
6. Open parts

Symbols

The symbols in rituals give voice to meanings without words. Many varied meanings may be contained in a single symbol. For Cal and Jim, Ella symbolized love, warmth, caring, and connection in a household otherwise fraught with conflict and unhappiness. The symbols in our rituals may hold diverse meanings for different family members. A symbol may express and hold the contradictions in a ritual. When Carol and her children put some of Ben's ashes out to sea, burying the rest and planting a tree, Carol remarked, "I could finally let go of all that I hated in him and embrace all that I loved."

Symbols may carry meanings from childhood, implying an entire ritual—a special birthday cake, pumpkins, *matzoh*. Food served during rituals often symbolizes relationships and evokes memories. Jewish women in a concentration camp during World War II drew strength from writing down and sharing memories of favorite recipes from their former family lives—a powerful contradiction in the midst of starvation (de Silva, 2006).

Newly joined couples often need help to incorporate differing symbols in their new ritual life together. If he brings his beloved grandmother's china, a pattern his new wife hates, they need to have a conversation about how to honor what the china symbolizes for him and how to incorporate this in some of the rituals they create. When Andy and Rich began to live together, Andy was appalled by the angel Rich insisted must go at the top of their Christmas tree. Neither man was religious. The angel just made no sense to Andy until Rich explained that it belonged to his deceased mother. "For my mom it was a Christian symbol. For me, it is a symbol of my mom and all of the joyful Christmases I had with her," Rich said.

While many of our symbols have broadly agreed upon meanings—a Christmas tree, a turkey for Thanksgiving, an Easter egg, a national flag—these same symbols often have special meanings in a given family. The Thanksgiving turkey might elicit a humorous reminiscence: "Remember the year when

Dad was slicing the turkey and it slipped off the platter and landed in Mom's lap?" Just seeing the turkey brings peals of warm laughter to this family long after Dad and Mom had died. For one family, displaying the national flag may express their pride and pain in the recent loss of their loved one in military combat. For another family, it might express their underlying patriotism in opposing a war.

Most families develop unique symbols for their rituals—newly designed wedding rings for a reconciled couple, a special scrapbook to hold an unfolding family history, Shabbat candlesticks that a grandmother brought from Europe after the Holocaust, or a platter that comes out just once a year to mark Greek Easter. Children may contribute to a family's treasure trove of symbols with drawings and computerized certificates, as in one family in which the grown children presented their parents with a framed diploma for "graduating from parenthood" as a jocular way to tell them that the time for advice giving had stopped. The symbols in a family's rituals may be passed from one generation to the next, or they may be newly created to mark a special transition. When Bob stopped smoking after years of failed attempts, his children created a ritual of celebration to mark his 1-year anniversary, burned all of his smoking paraphernalia, and put it in a special box decorated with pictures of healthy men.

A critical aspect of symbols is their capacity to hold and express multiple meanings. A key dimension of family and community relationship well-being includes the ability to accept differences among members, to be simultaneously separate and connected. The symbols in our rituals are one vehicle for such synchrony.

Symbolic Actions

Rituals contain "symbolic actions"—the behaviors in a ritual that are capable of holding and expressing multiple meanings. When we sit in the same seats for a nightly supper with family, exchange wedding rings, walk across a stage for graduation, raise a bride up on a chair, hunt for Easter eggs, or open gifts, we are engaging in symbolic actions. Spoken words, written letters, seating arrangements, music, dance, creating art, processions—all these and more are symbolic actions in rituals. When Cal and Jimmy go for their nightly walk with Ella, they take the same path. Over time they added a component for each to find something new to point out to the other on their stroll. "I think the new discovery, which started as a game, became a way for us to tell each other that our relationship was new and growing," Jimmy remarked.

Symbolic action involves doing, not simply saying. When a child graduates high school, she dons a cap and gown, participates in a procession, collects her diploma, moves her tassel from one side of the mortar board to the other, and together with her class throws her cap in the air at the end. Think how empty it would be, in contrast, if we simply said, "You've graduated."

The symbolic actions in our rituals may be small ways to part in the morning, such as when my husband says to me, "Walk Good," a repeated phrase in our 30 years together that holds both humor and a benediction. Or they may be large markers for gender patterns, such as when men and women are separated in a ritual. In a wedding scene in *Fiddler on the Roof*, a man breaks centuries of tradition when he changes the symbolic action of segregated dancing and insists on dancing with his wife.

Like symbols, symbolic actions in a ritual provide depth and express multiple meanings and values. As such, there must be room in our rituals for adding, deleting, and changing the symbolic actions in order to express relationship growth.

Special Time

Rituals take place in special time. Whether the ritual is a daily, 30-second reconnection at the end of a busy day, a weekly special dinner, a birthday or anniversary, a secular or religious holiday, or a life-cycle ritual, *when* a ritual occurs helps us to know we are demarcating between special time and regular time.

When families have no time set aside for any daily rituals, they often experience a sense of chaos in their lives, because there are no markers to help shift from home to work or school, to reenter at the end of a day, to share a meal or close the day.

Couples who lose track of important annual rituals in one another's lives, such as birthdays or anniversaries, often speak of a sense of emptiness, disappointment, and disconnection.

The special time dimension in our rituals provides us with an anchor, reminding us where we have been. Simultaneously, it gives us a compass, pointing the way to where we are going.

In religions, the times for particular life-cycle rituals are often prescribed. In Christianity, a baby is baptized in infancy. Mormons, in particular, wait until a child is 8 days old. Greek Orthodox babies are baptized and later take part in a special ceremony when they are 5, using candles saved from the original baptism. Observant Jewish families circumcise their sons 8 days after birth. Orthodox Jews mark the passage from babyhood to toddlerhood for boys with a special haircut at age 3 (Cohen, 1991). Similarly, rituals to mark a death involve culturally and religiously prescribed times, such as Nine Nights in many Caribbean cultures or Shiva in Judaism.

The special time dimension in rituals includes a time for preparation, a time for the ritual per se, and a time after the ritual to incorporate changes and return to regular life (Van Gennep, 1960). The time leading up to a ritual may involve making arrangements, choosing clothing and food, and passing on new knowledge. The ritual itself is a special time to experience new roles and relationships, such as the shift to adult religious responsibilities conferred in a Bar Mitzvah, or the change from two single people to a committed couple created in a wedding. Here it is important to note that changes are happening for not only those who are most central, such as the newlywed couple, but also the people in an entire network of relationships, with new connections as in-laws and friends. A ritual to welcome a new baby, whether secular or religious, also marks a shift in generations, and with a first child, the profound move to parenthood and grandparenthood. The time following a ritual event consolidates the changes. Following a life-cycle ritual, such consolidation may take place over several months as family and community members experience themselves in new roles and relationships.

Special Space

Rituals occur in special space. This location may be secular, spiritual, or religious space—a living room, a kitchen, a child's bedroom, a backyard, a river bank, a cemetery or the Selma to Montgomery Bridge, the Vietnam Memorial Wall, Ground Zero, or a synagogue, mosque, temple or church. When we enter the space of a ritual, we sense the demarcation from ordinary life.

While religious rituals often prescribe the special space, most rituals center on the family, and many are conducted in the home, giving families the capacity to choose a meaningful space. For Jews, the dining room is especially important for Shabbat dinners. Hindu or Buddhist families choose a space for a small shrine for prayers and dedication to ancestors. Special space becomes one of the inventive elements in meaningful rituals. In her qualitative research on Bar Mitzvah, Davis (2003) describes a divorced family intent on making sure that their son would celebrate his Bar Mitzvah wrapped in love and loyalty from both sides of his family. After much relational work to assuage bitterness, they carefully chose a hotel for guests with a large hospitality suite for a Friday night dinner, a Sunday brunch, and an informal gathering that would bring all of their son's relatives together to celebrate him and their ability to make genuine room for everyone.

Special space can be a planned part of a ritual, or it may simply rise up in spontaneous and unspoken agreement. Following the September 11, 2001, attacks in New York City, the streets of Manhattan were suddenly papered with photographs of the missing. Citizens who had not lost a person stood in silence or wrote messages of love and support. For a short period of time, the city became special space (Imber-Black, 2003; Sella, 2001). Over time, the area at "Ground Zero" became widely considered as a sacred space and hallowed ground containing the remains of so many who perished.

Where a ritual occurs can become a fraught issue for families, particularly when the space must shift due to illness or death. Many annual rituals, such as Passover or Christmas, occur in the special space of the home of the older generation. When the ritual maker, often a grandmother, becomes ill or dies, a period of confusion regarding the space of a ritual often takes place.

In many families, there is no open conversation of this crucial developmental shift. One sibling may simply claim the ritual, while others respond with silent resentment or vote with their feet and refuse to come. Sometimes, decades of beautiful tradition can be lost. Encouraging open discussion of where the special space will now be is critical.

Changing Special Time and Special Space in a New Anniversary

Following a 6-month couple therapy focused on healing years of painful interaction and a period of separation, Shafali and Bill decided to reconcile. "We need a new anniversary," Bill proclaimed. "The first wedding didn't work," Shafali said, reflecting on the bitter disputes of their parents over this young, mixed-religion couple. The planning for their original wedding had been filled with parental arguments over where the wedding would take place, because Bill came from a Catholic family and Shafali's family was Hindu. In the end, Bill's parents prevailed because they had money and were paying for the wedding. "Bill and I are not particularly religious," Shafali said, "but my parents felt erased." Both confirmed that their anniversary every year brought back sad memories.

Since Bill and Shafari had been wed in the winter, they selected a date in April for their new anniversary, citing spring as a time of new beginnings. "I want our celebration to be outdoors at the Botanical Garden," Bill stated. "This space symbolizes our values."

Structured Parts and Open Parts

Rituals hold our history. They connect us to where we come from and provide us with a sense of continuity and constancy. The repetition in our rituals, through familiar symbols and symbolic actions, and agreed-upon special time and special space provide a touchstone. Links to previous generations, critical historical events in a culture, and expressions of long-held values all reside in the repeated parts of rituals. Comfort in what is already known marks the structured parts of rituals.

However, if rituals only contain structured, familiar, and repeated parts, with no room for newness or novelty, they can become rigid, boring, and obsolete. No longer able to express the present and an imagined future, the ritual grows steadily obligatory. In order for rituals to stay alive and to enable the transformations required by both expected life-cycle changes and unexpected events, they must contain room for open parts, for difference and surprise.

The open parts in rituals both mirror and facilitate change. These may be massive alterations, such as those brought to Catholic rituals by Vatican II, or they may be the local changes, such as when a newly divorced mother sits in the father's chair at the head of the dinner table, announcing without words that the shape of the household and the structure of the family unit has changed.

CONCLUSIONS

While rituals can sometimes feel magical, they are not, in fact, magic. They are a knowable, accessible, and changeable resource in our lives. Helping families to consider their rituals carefully, to question whether their rituals are working well for them, and to help them create newly needed rituals and redesign existing rituals that are rich with meaning offers new opportunities for families in their communities and in therapy.

Rituals express and enable relationships, transitions, healing, beliefs, and celebration. To do so with authenticity they must simultaneously hold continuity and change, connecting us with the past and leading us to an as yet unknown future.

REFERENCES

Alvarez, J. (2007). *Once upon a Quiñceanera: Coming of age in the USA.* New York: Viking Press.

Cohen, D. (1991). *The circle of life: Rituals from the human family album.* San Francisco: HarperCollins.

Davis, J. (2003). Mazel tov: The bar mitzvah as a multigenerational ritual of change and continuity. In E. Imber-Black, J. Roberts, & R. Whiting (Eds.), *Rituals in families and family therapy* (rev. ed., pp. 182–216). New York: Norton.

de Silva, C. (2006). *In memory's kitchen: A legacy from the women of Terezin.* Lanham, MD: Rowman & Littlefield.

Fiese, B. (2006). *Family routines and rituals.* New Haven, CT: Yale University Press.

Imber-Black, E. (2003). September 11th: Rituals of healing and transformation. In E. Imber-Black, J. Roberts, & R. Whiting (Eds.), *Rituals in families and family therapy* (rev. ed., pp.333–344). New York: Norton.

Imber-Black, E. (2011). Creating meaningful rituals for new life cycle transitions. In M. McGoldrick, B. Carter, & N. Garcia-Preto (Eds.), *The expanded family life cycle* (4th ed., pp. 429–439). Boston: Pearson.

Imber-Black, E., & Roberts, J. (1993). *Rituals for our times: Celebrating, healing and changing our lives and our relationships.* New York: HarperCollins.

Imber-Black, E., Roberts, J., & Whiting, R. (Eds.). (2003). *Rituals in families and family therapy* (rev. ed.). New York: Norton.

Sella, M. (2001, October 7). Missing: How a grief ritual is born. *The New York Times Magazine,* pp. 48–51.

Van Gennep, A. (1960). *The rites of passage.* Chicago: University of Chicago Press.

Walsh, F. (2009). Human–animal bonds: II. The role of pets in family systems and family therapy. *Family Process, 48,* 481–499.

Walsh, F. (2010). Spiritual diversity: Multifaith perspectives in family therapy. *Family Process, 49,* 330–348.

Whiteside, M. (2003). Creation of family identity through ritual performances in early remarriage. In E. Imber-Black, J. Roberts, & R. Whiting (Eds.), *Rituals in families and family therapy* (rev. ed., pp. 300–332). New York: Norton.

PART V

ADVANCING FAMILY SYSTEMS RESEARCH AND PRACTICE

CHAPTER 21

ASSESSMENT OF EFFECTIVE COUPLE AND FAMILY FUNCTIONING

Prevailing Models and Instruments

JAY LEBOW
CATHERINE B. STROUD

We live in a world in which research on mental health primarily focuses on individuals rather than families and on pathology rather than health. With the dominance of the medical model in the funding of large-scale research, evidence-based models of normal family functioning are dwarfed by innumerable models and measures of individual depression and other disorders in DSM-IV-TR. In this chapter, we assume a much different lens from that focused on individual pathology and look at the state of the art in empirical assessment of family functioning. Each of these efforts creates a model of the dimensions crucial to family functioning and a set of scales or subscales to assess these dimensions. There have been many laudable efforts, though only a few have gained widespread usage. In this chapter, we provide a review of measures of family and couple functioning, and discuss the strengths and limitations of the models.

Before launching our consideration of models and measures, it is essential to consider the multiple meanings of "normality" in the context of empirical research (see Walsh, Chapter 2, this volume). Through one lens, "normal" is operationalized as being within some range of the center of the distribution (e.g., one or two standard deviations from the mean). Most of the models and measures below are based in this methodology. Yet, for example, with a near 50% divorce rate, it would be an error to view successful marriage as merely approximating the mean of the marital distribution. Through another lens, what is "normal" is operationalized by some other standard, such a being free of symptoms or major difficulties. Yet, from this vantage point, normality would only apply to problem-free families, leaving us with that well-known cartoon of the empty auditorium at the convention of so-called "normal families." A third perspective on normality has compared families to a single ideal model with socially desirable characteristics. From all these reference points, one is left with the vital question of how to determine the context for family assessment: Are we comparing a family to families worldwide, in our society, or in a specific subculture or social class? What is "normal" may be quite different in these different contexts. And in contemporary societies, the diversity and complexity of family structures and life challenges render any single model of family normality to be of questionable relevance.

MEASURES OF FAMILY FUNCTIONING

In this section, we present the most frequently used measures of whole family functioning that (1) demonstrate acceptable reliability and validity (for reviews, see also Alderfer et al., 2008; Carlson, 2003; Kaufman, Tarnowski, Simonian, & Graves, 1991; Novack & Gage, 1995), and (2) have been employed most in empirical studies, including studies of family therapy outcomes (see also Sanderson et al., 2009, for a review).

Measurement of family functioning involves several distinct decisions. There is the question of what aspects of family life are viewed as worthy of evaluation. Numerous family variables have been posited as crucial to family functioning in family theories and have emerged as significant in family research (e.g., adaptability, cohesion, conflict, monitoring, and expressiveness). Because family models begin with different views of what is essential to evaluate, measures not only overlap but also tend often to have very different foci. This complexity is also reflected in understanding the importance of perspective. Family members each have a perspective on life in their family. These *insider perspectives* often differ from one another. Others, who may be individuals involved with the family (e.g., teachers, therapists, or neighbors) or trained to rate families, have *outsider perspectives*. Insiders and outsiders both have value in understanding family processes. Their perspectives are expected to differ and do so when such comparisons are made. For a complete picture, both insider and outsider measures are needed.

In the early days of the family therapy movement and family science, there was little in the way of reliable and valid instruments to study families. The building of a true family science depended on the creation of such instruments. Without such measures to assess families, the characteristics of families were often largely in the eye of the beholder. Sometimes this resulted in keen insights and at other times, in faulty hypotheses. Thus, for example, families in which one member has schizophrenia were thought to engage in "double-bind" communication, a concept that never could be reliably or validly operationalized, and was discredited. To create a family science, reliable and valid measures had to be created and tested that assess complex concepts.

Constructing such instruments has been an enormous endeavor; the work of several of the best social scientists over a lifetime.

Family system measures build on family system models, operationalizing systems concepts into forms in which aspects of families can be systemically evaluated. The best family system measures are multidimensional, capturing the complexity of family interaction processes, which are inherently multidimensional. Although there remain studies that examine the relationship of a single aspect of family life, such as warmth to some other individual or family variables, the complexity of family life necessitates complex measures.

Scales may offer *insider perspectives* in self-reports by family members (often the family score is a sum or average of individual ratings) or *outsider perspective* in ratings by observers of family interaction (e.g., clinician or investigator). Ratings from either perspective can be molecular, such as counts of individual behaviors, or more subjective molar ratings of an aspect of family interaction, such as warmth or humor.

There also has been a range of ways to gather data that allow the rating of families on the measures, and the use of such data as independent or dependent measures in research. Sometimes family members simply rate their own behaviors or each other's behaviors over a specified period of time. Other times, families are observed for short periods, live or on tape, and their behaviors are rated by others. Still other times, structured tasks are created in which family members participate to provide a sample of behavior that can be rated and compared to other families more systematically.

Hovering always are the questions of generalizability: How well do the dimensions and measures apply to families beyond those around whom the model was developed and the scale validated? This is a crucial question given the wide range of family forms; varied family resources and challenges; ethnic, racial, gender, and socioeconomic differences; and larger cultural contexts. Ideally, from a research standpoint, measures and models would be applicable across cultures and families, yet many years of research have suggested that variables may differ in meaning and salience, and that the factor structures of instruments and cutoffs for normality often vary across cultures. Thus, research instruments always need to be considered in the context of the culture in which they are utilized, and in the best idealized (and, we have to add, most expensive) version of this work tested and normed in the context of specific cultures.

Family systems measures are perhaps the richest and most treacherous of instruments, because they seek to capture the essence of important yet difficult to operationalize concepts. These measures also present complexity in their analysis. What are we to do, for example, when father and mother and child (or two siblings) differ radically in their reports of family cohesion, or when all agree, yet outside observer ratings on scales assessing behavior in a standard task look quite different than those of family members? Thankfully, evaluation of such measures has led to complex statistical techniques for their evaluation that account for such factors as the expected covariation of multiple reports on the same family. Yet the complexity of these measures and multiple reporters also has benefits that outweigh the inherent difficulties involved. After examining a family through such a systemic lens, we hope that it becomes more difficult to accept the findings of a study in which a single family member reports on one aspect of family life, as this process raises questions about what others in the family may report, and what other unmeasured variables may impact, and even explain, the results.

Ultimately, we must be realistic about what family measures can tell us. No one family study or set of measures can examine all aspects of family life or all perspectives. Family science progresses incrementally through the use of these measures to study families, with each measure and study providing valuable information that can be incorporated into a scientific understanding of families. Each measure offers something toward a full "picture of the elephant" as long as we know there are other pictures and perspectives that have relevance. It is the nature of this science, and the clinical practice in which it is rooted, that many of these endeavors focus on specific aspects of family life. The key is to keep a systemic perspective in viewing what is in focus; all of the variables studied are operating in the real world and part of the human condition.

FAMILY SYSTEM MODELS
WITH MULTIMETHOD MEASURES

The Circumplex Measures

The circumplex model of marital and family systems (Olson & Gorall, 2003) and associated assessment instruments conceptualize and measure couple and family functioning along three dimensions: cohesion, flexibility, and communication.

"Cohesion," defined as the emotional bonding or connectedness among couple and family members, focuses on how systems balance separateness and togetherness. Specific variables include closeness, boundaries, coalitions, shared time, space, friends, decision making, interests, and recreation. Five levels of cohesion range from disconnected/disengaged to overly connected/enmeshed extremes. More balanced couple and family systems (three moderate levels of connectedness and separation) tend to be more functional. The second dimension, "flexibility," reflects the quality and expression of leadership and organization, role relationship, and relationship rules and negotiations. This dimension focuses on how well systems balance stability with change, for family integration and adaptability. Extremes (inflexible/rigid or chaotic) tend to be problematic over an extended period of time, whereas midrange ("balanced") scores (moderate in flexibility and structure) tend to be more functional. The third dimension, "communication," viewed as a facilitating dimension, comprises positive skills that enable families to alter their levels of cohesion and flexibility to meet developmental and situational demands (see

Olson, 2011). Positive skills include listening, speaking, self-disclosure, clarity, tracking, and respect/regard.

Based on this model, families can be plotted on a Couple and Family Map that describes 25 relationship types. Discussion can relate patterns to past and future multigenerational family issues. These types and levels are seen as dynamic, with families able to shift to become more functional and satisfying. Across the family life cycle, functional shifts are needed, for instance, from the early childrearing to the adolescent phase, or with a family crisis or a member's illness (see also Rolland, Chapter 19, this volume).

A number of assessment instruments based on the Circumplex Model have been developed over the past two decades. Initially standardized with white, middle-class, two-parent families with adolescents, the scales have increasingly been used in research and counseling with diverse samples of couples and families in terms of ethnicity/race, family structure, sexual orientation, and social class. Five scales can be found in the Family Inventories Package (FIP) (Olson, Gorall, & Tiesel, 2006; *www.facesiv.com/studies/ fip.html*), including the most recent version of the Family Adaptability and Cohesion Evaluation Scales (FACES-IV) and its companion scales, the Family Communication Scale (FCS) and the Family Satisfaction Scale (FSS). The FACES-IV is a 42-item self-report measure, with subscales to assesses the full range of the cohesion and flexibility dimensions. Initial investigations with the FACES-IV suggest very good reliability and validity. The FCS and FSS are both 10-item self-report measures that assess communication and satisfaction with the current family system; the Family Strengths Scale (Olson, Larsen, & McCubbin, 1989) taps family characteristics and dynamics that promote resilience and effective managing of family problems. Finally, the Family Stress Scale (adapted from the Coping and Stress Profile; Olson, 1997) measures the current level of stress experienced in the family. More than 250 studies, most of which used the FACES-IV self-report scale to compare clinical families with various emotional symptoms and problems to nonclinical families, have supported the central hypothesis of the Circumplex model: Balanced couples and families function more adequately than couples and families at extremes on adaptability and cohesion; highly rated communication is associated with better individual and family functioning (Olson & Gorall, 2003).

The Circumplex Clinical Rating Scale (CRS), an observational assessment tool, was designed for therapists or researchers to rate couples and families based on clinical interviews or observation of their interaction, with specific clinical indicators on the three dimensions of the model. Nearly a dozen studies using the CRS have also supported the central tenet that balanced families function more adequately than unbalanced families.

The Circumplex Measures have been widely used in research and clinical settings for both assessment and treatment planning. FACES has been employed in randomized clinical trials of family therapy. For example, in a systematic comparison of multisystemic therapy (MST) versus treatment as usual for juvenile sex offenders, the FACES-II was completed by each family member to measure perceptions of family relations, and results suggested that MST was more effective in increasing cohesion and adaptability than treatment as usual (Borduin, Schaeffer, & Heiblum, 2009). Among outcome variables in couple and family therapy intervention research, FACES is third in frequency of use for whole family measures (Sanderson et al., 2009).

The McMaster Measures

The McMaster Model of Family Functioning, developed by Epstein, Baldwin, and Bishop (1983), is based in a systems approach and focuses on the family's ability to accomplish Basic Tasks (instrumental issues, such as shelter), Developmental Tasks (e.g., changes over time), and Hazardous Tasks (e.g., handling crises). Six core dimensions are postulated to have the most impact on negotiating tasks effectively. The first, *problem solving*, reflects a family's ability to resolve instrumental and affective problems efficiently and easily to maintain effective family functioning. The second, *communication*, refers to a family's pattern of verbal exchanges, with direct and clear communication in both instrumental and affective areas reflecting effective functioning. The third, *role functioning*, reflects patterns of behavior by family members in ability to fulfill family functions such as provision of resources, nurturance, and support. Role allocation and role accountability are seen as crucial aspects of effective family functioning, without overburdening family members and with clear accountability. The fourth, *affective responsiveness* reflects a family's range of emotional responses to one another, with the quality and degree appropriate to stimuli seen as optimal. The fifth, *affective involvement*, refers to the degree to which a family shows interest in and values individual family members, ranging from a lack of interest to extreme involvement. Empathetic involvement, or interest and involvement for the sake of the other family members, is conceptualized as most effective. Finally, *behavior control*, reflects the standards and rules set by the family, ranging from rigid behavior control to chaotic behavior control. Flexible behavior control, with reasonable and flexible standards depending on the context, is seen as most effective (see Epstein, Ryan, Bishop, Miller, & Keitner, 2003).

The McMaster model has led to the development of three assessment instruments, including the Family Assessment Device (FAD; Epstein et al., 1983), the McMaster Structured Interview of Family Functioning (McSIFF), and the McMaster Clinical Rating Scales (MCRS; Epstein, Baldwin, & Bishop, 1982; Miller et al., 1994).

The FAD is a 60-item self-report instrument designed to measure family functioning. It yields a score for each of six core dimensions and one score for general functioning, with scores ranging from healthy to unhealthy on a 4-point scale. The FAD has demonstrated good reliability and validity, but there remains considerable debate about its factor structure, as many of the items load significantly on other subscales, which they were not designed to tap (see Aarons, McDonald, Connelly, & Newton, 2007, for a review).

Although the FAD has been used extensively internationally, some research has raised concerns about its use cross-culturally, as its reliability and validity may be lower with international samples (Shek, 2002) and with nonwhite families in the United States (e.g., Hispanic families; Aarons et al., 2007). The FAD has been used in research studies of family therapy, including randomized clinical trials. For instance, Kolko and colleagues used the FAD in a randomized controlled trial of treatment of adolescent depression, demonstrating that systemic-brief family therapy influenced family conflict and parent–child relationship problems more than cognitive-behavioral therapy (Kolko, Brent, Baugher, Bridge, & Birmaher, 2000). According to a recent review of outcome variables in couple and family therapy treatment research, the FAD is the most widely used measure of whole family functioning in couple and family therapy treatment research (Sanderson et al., 2009) .

The McSIFF, a 2-hour structured interview of all family members, assesses the six dimensions of the McMaster Model, as well as general functioning. The MCRS, an assessment tool completed by the interviewer, is used to quantify the information obtained in the interview (from observation of the family members during the interview and information yielded from the questions), scoring seven subscales (the six dimensions and general functioning) on 7-point Likert scales.

A large body of research supports the construct validity of the McMaster Model and measures. Of relevance here is the considerable research documenting its ability to capture normal family functioning (see Epstein et al., 2003). For instance, using the Behavior Control and Communication scale to tap family functioning in a nonclinical sample ("normal"), Maziade, Bernier, Thivierge, and Côté (1987) showed that what the scale defined as a normal level of functioning matched the functioning of most nonclinical families in the sample. The measures have also produced interesting findings relevant to their correlation with individual psychopathology. For example, the General Functioning scale of the FAD was the best predictor of a psychiatric diagnosis in a child in a sample of 1869 families in the Ontario Child Health Study (Byles, Byrne, Boyle, & Offord, 1988).

The Mealtime Interaction Coding System (MICS; Dickstein, Hayden, Schiller, Seifer, & San Antonio, 1994) is an additional observational assessment tool based upon a slightly modified version of the McMaster Model, by other researchers (see also Alderfer et al., 2007, for review). The MICS was developed to assess family interaction at mealtime in a naturalistic setting. Families are videotaped in their homes (without the presence of an experimenter), and adapted versions of the MCRS scales are used to code the interactions.

The Beavers Systems Measures

The Beavers Systems Model (Beavers & Hampson, 2003) describes current family functioning along two dimensions: (1) *Family competence* describes family organization and management (continuum from severely dysfunctional to optimal); and (2) *family style* describes the orientation of the family on a continuum from extremes of either "centripetal" (mostly seeking satisfaction within the family) or "centrifugal" (mostly seeking satisfaction outside the family), through midrange, average families to optimally functioning families at the high end. Highly functioning families tend to balance needs for connection and separateness; two-parent families demonstrate more egalitarian power, competent leadership, and skilled negotiation, taking children's needs into account. Extremely centripetal families mistrust the outside world; they tend to deny negative and hostile emotions by emphasizing positive feelings for unity; children are slower to individuate and have more internalizing problems (Beavers & Hampson, 2003). Extremely centrifugal families are uncomfortable with affection, and negative or angry feelings prevail; children often run away or are expelled and show more externalizing symptoms (Beavers & Hampson, 2003). Family functioning is characterized by plotting families according to their ratings on these two dimensions, with family competence on the horizontal axis and family style on the vertical axis.

The Beavers Systems Model has yielded three instruments (Beavers & Hampson, 2003). Two of the instruments, comprising the Beavers Interactional Scales (BIS; Beavers & Hampson, 2003), are observational clinical rating scales completed by observers of the families' interactions. One instrument, the Beavers Interactional Competence Scale (BICS) uses 10-point scales to rate how well families organize and manage themselves. It includes the following subscales: Structure, Family Mythology, Goal-Directed Negotiation, Autonomy, Family Affect, and Global Health and Pathology. The second, the Beavers Interactional Style Scale (BISS), uses 5-point scales to assess Meeting Dependency Needs, Managing Conflict, Use of Space, Appearance to Outsiders, Professed Closeness, Managing Assertion, Expression of Feelings, and Global Style. The BIS scales have demonstrated good reliability and validity (Beavers & Hampson, 2003).

The third instrument, the Beavers Self-Report Family Inventory (SFI), a 36-item, Likert-style self-report measure, taps individual family members' perceptions of Health/Competence, Conflict, Cohesion, Leadership and Emotional Expressiveness. All of the subscales, except the Leadership subscale, yield adequate psychometric properties (though reported in non-peer-reviewed formats; see also Alderfer et al., 2007).

Together the three instruments of the Beavers Systems Models assess levels of families' health/dysfunction. The combination of observational and self-report methods facilitates a comparison of insider and outsider perspectives. The measures have both clinical and empirical applications, and some measures have been used in randomized clinical trials of family therapy. For example, the Global Health and Pathology scale of the BICS was employed to measure changes in family functioning in a randomized controlled trial of multidimensional family therapy (MDFT) for adolescent drug use. Observers rated videotaped interactions of families on three standardized family interaction tasks using the BICS scale. Although the results indicated significant improvements in symptoms and drug use in all three interventions studied, in addition, families who received MDFT became more functional over the course of treatment, and gains were sustained during follow-ups. Thus, the results supported the notion that MDFT facilitates adaptive family functioning, thereby reducing family processes that likely contribute to adolescent drug use (e.g., Liddle et al., 2001).

SELF-REPORT MEASURES

Family Assessment Measure

The Family Assessment Measure (FAM-III; Skinner, Steinhauer, & Sitarenios, 2000) is a self-report measure designed to assess the seven constructs of the Process Model of Family Functioning: Task Accomplishment, Role Performance, Communication, Affective Expression, Involvement, Control, and Values and Norms. The Process Model proposes that understanding the interrelations of these seven dimensions at multiple levels of analysis is imperative to understanding family functioning. Thus, the FAM provides scores of family strengths and weaknesses from three different perspectives, including the family as a system (50-item General Scale), various dyadic relationships (42-item Dyadic Scale) and individual family members (42-item Self-Rating Scale). Each scale contains the same subscales (one for each of the seven constructs), allowing for the comparison of family functioning at multiple levels of the family system. Alternatively, combining the three scales provides clinicians and researchers with a richer and more detailed understanding of the family than that achieved by assessing only one level of analysis. The General Scale also includes Social Desirability and Defensiveness subscales. The FAM can be interpreted either objectively (using standardized scores in comparison to a nonclinical population as a percentile) or subjectively to formulate hypotheses regarding family functioning for clinical purposes. The FAM has demonstrated very good reliability and validity (see Skinner et al., 2000). It has also established utility as an assessment tool in clinical and research settings, and as a measure of therapy process and outcome, ranking fourth in use among whole family measures employed in couple and family therapy outcome studies (Sanderson et al., 2009). For use in clinical settings, norming data are available for numerous clinical groups and special circumstances, from families of children suffering with cystic fibrosis to families with anxiety disorders among family members, to families with adopted children. This permits the comparison of family functioning with norms tailored to the specific circumstances of the family. Illustrating the varied and specific populations in which the FAM has been used to measure family functioning, the impact of acquired brain injury on family functioning was assessed using the FAM. Patients with an acquired brain injury and their family members completed the FAM. Interestingly, family members, but not the patients themselves, described their family functioning in the distressed range on all scales compared to population norms. This highlights the impact of acquired brain injury on the family system and the importance of including families in intervention efforts (Gan & Schuller, 2002).

Family Environment Scale

The Family Environment Scale (FES), which originated from social systems ecological theory to assess the unique environment of the family, is a self-report measure developed through observations and interviews with white, middle-class families (Moos & Moos, 1994). The developers proposed that three primary areas and underlying specific dimensions differentiate among families: (1) Interpersonal Relationships (e.g., degree of cohesion) reflects family members' subjective perceptions of the stable patterns of interaction among family members and includes three subscales, Cohesion, Conflict, and Expressiveness; (2) Personal Growth (e.g., degree of achievement or moral–religious emphasis) reflects the degree to which families promote members' personal growth and is tapped by five subscales: Independence, Achievement Orientation, Intellectual–Cultural Orientation, Active–Recreational Orientation, and Moral–Religious Emphasis; (3) Family Structure reflects the degree of emphasis on systems maintenance and is assessed by the Organization and Control subscales. These three dimensions are assessed by 90 true–false questions completed by each available family member. The FES has been widely used in empirical studies that include with clinical populations such as families with individuals abusing alcohol (e.g., Sanford, Bingham, & Zucker, 1999) and those with unipolar depression (e.g., Billings, Cronkite, & Moos, 1983). The FES, because of its easily administered and scored questionnaire format, has been the most widely utilized research measure of family functioning, used in over 500 studies (Plake & Impara, 2001). Furthermore, among outcome variables in couple and family therapy, it is second in use (Sanderson et al., 2009). However, there has been serious concern about the adequacy of its reliability, with scales demonstrating only poor to good internal consistencies, and its factor structure (e.g., Sanford et al., 1999). True–false questionnaire items also force responses that are more nuanced on scaled measures. Question construction has also been criticized for prompting socially desirable responses and reflects norms of mid-20th-century society and family models. Therefore, its validity and relevance for contemporary families are problematic.

Family Relations Scale

The Family Relations Scale (Tolan, Gorman-Smith, Huesmann, & Zelli, 1997) was developed in the context of examining risk and reliance in inner-city families, specifically in relation to buffering risks for delinquent and antisocial behavior. First, although extensive empirical research and theory suggest that family processes are relevant to risk for antisocial and other disorders in youth, few risk models incorporate family functioning constructs. Second, many existing measures of family functioning are limited by poor psychometric properties, and others fail to test and develop measures using diverse samples. Thus, Tolan and colleagues reviewed empirical, theoretical, and clinical literature to identify family processes relevant to risk for the development of child antisocial behavior, depression, and psychopathology. Based on the review, two major constructs were seen as influencing risk: (1) behavioral routines (family relations that imply rules about behavior) and (2) family beliefs (values shared by the family and the meanings attached to family processes). To this end, the authors developed the Family Relations Scale by pooling items from existing self-report family measures to tap relevant family processes (Tolan et al., 1997). The 92-item scale combines the report of at least two family members (e.g., a child and his or her primary caregiver), and assesses family beliefs and daily family interactions, tapping six dimensions/Family Beliefs, Emotional Cohesion, Shared Deviant Beliefs, Support, Organization, and Communication—that load on three higher order factors (Cohesion, Beliefs, and Structure). The scale's reliability, factor structure, and predictive validity have been demonstrated in several samples of urban racially and ethnically diverse families (e.g., Henry, Tolan, & Gorman-Smith, 2001), and research using the Family Relations Scale has greatly contributed to our understanding of families living in poor urban neighborhoods.

For example, Gorman-Smith, Tolan, Henry, and Florsheim (2000) examined patterns of family functioning and adolescent outcomes in economically disadvantaged inner-city African American and Mexican American male adolescents and their families. Of note, their longitudinal investigation demonstrated that when socioeconomic status was controlled, the associations between patterns of family functioning and youth outcomes over time were similar regardless of race or ethnicity. Furthermore, youth from the families that functioned best exhibited significantly better outcomes regardless of race or ethnicity, suggesting that within poor, urban social communities positive family functioning buffers the impact of stressors specifically associated with this environmental context, contributing to resilience in youth in high-risk social environments (Gorman-Smith et al., 2000). Research using the Family Relations Scale is relevant to both intervention and prevention efforts.

CLINICAL RATING SCALES

A number of scales primarily designed for clinical research have assessed family functioning associated with presenting problems in individuals or relationships. These measures, developed from efforts to attend to the family systems of those with individual or relationship difficulties, also offer scales that assess functioning, and may suggest positive directions for symptom reduction and more functional and satisfying relationships.

Systematic Therapy Inventory of Change

The Systematic Therapy Inventory of Change (STIC) measurement system (Pinsof et al., 2009) was developed to measure change in couple, family, and individual therapy from a multisystemic and multidimensional perspective, and to be used in the context of assessing progress on a session-by-session basis over the course of treatment. This measurement system was constructed in the context of client-focused progress research, the study of how people change in psychotherapy. The measurement system comprises four components: (1) the STIC INITIAL (completed prior to the first session); (2) the INTERSESSION STIC (completed at each subsequent session); (3) three scales included at the end of the INTERSESSION STIC for assessing and tracking the Integrative Psychotherapy Alliance (Pinsof, Zinbarg, & Knobloch-Fedders, 2008); and (4) a software package and website that provide electronic INITIAL and INTERSESSION STIC data for therapists and researchers.

The INITIAL STIC includes five subscales. The first, Individual Problems and Strengths, taps individual adult and adolescent functioning. The second, Family of Origin, assesses adults' recollections of their family of origin growing up. The third, Relationship with Partner, measures clients' relationships with their spouse or partner in a committed relationship. The fourth, Family/Household, taps adults' and adolescents' current experiences with their families. Finally, Child Problems and Strengths, is a scale completed by parents regarding their child's or children's functioning in several domains. The Family of Origin and Family/Household scales tap similar constructs. Subscales within these measures include Positivity, Family Pride, Decision Making, Negativity, Boundary Clarity, Misunderstood, and Feeling.

The subscales of the INITIAL STIC were empirically derived and although current empirical data are limited, most have demonstrated strong construct validity and adequate-to-good reliabilities in diverse samples (see Pinsof et al., 2009, 2010). The INTERSESSION STIC, a brief version of the INITIAL STIC, is completed at each session to track individual and relational change over the course of therapy. The INITIAL STIC accurately differentiates between treatment-seeking (clinical) and non-treatment-seeking ("normal") samples, has been used in diverse populations, and has empirically derived norms that allow clinicians and researchers to evaluate statistically and clinically significant change. The STIC has been normed on a national, stratified random sample of Americans.

INTERVIEW MEASURES

The Global Assessment of Relational Functioning Scale (GARF; American Psychiatric Association, 1994) was developed as a measure of relational health and functioning, placed on the Axis IV of the *Diagnostic and Statistical Manual of Mental Disorders* (DSM-IV), the Global Assessment of Functioning

Scale. It is a simple rating scale on which any relational unit (i.e., couple, family, or other grouping) can be rated by clinicians for its functionality on a 100-point scale. The goal is to assign a single number that describes the quality of functioning of a relationship system. The model suggests that family functioning can be conceived of simply as linear and assigned a value. The GARF taps Problem Solving, Organization, and Emotional Climate. There is little empirical work investigating the psychometric properties of the GARF, but some evidence supports its validity (e.g., Stein, Hilsenroth, Pinsker-Aspen, & Primavera, 2009), suggesting it may be useful for relational diagnosis and treatment planning.

OBSERVATIONAL MEASURES

Structural Family Systems Ratings (SFSR)

The Structural Family Systems Ratings (SFSR; Szapocznik, Hervis, Rio, & Mitrani, 1991) measure was developed to assess structural family change as part of a psychotherapy research program for brief strategic family therapy (BSFT), which targets Hispanic youth with behavior problems and their families. The SFSR defines family structure in terms of six interrelated dimensions, including structure, flexibility, resonance, developmental stage, identified patienthood, and conflict resolution. The SFSR measure is derived from observing families completing three tasks (e.g., planning a menu) based on the Wiltwyck Family Tasks (Minuchin, Rosman, & Baker, 1978), which are videotaped and rated by independent observers on six subscales (the six dimensions listed earlier) using 5-point Likert scales. The SFSR has demonstrated good reliability and validity with urban Hispanic families (Szapocznik et al., 1991), and frequently has been used in empirical studies examining the efficacy of BSFT (Szapocznik & Prado, 2007). For example, in one investigation, BSFT demonstrated significantly greater pre- to postintervention improvement in observed–rated family functioning, measured by the SFSR, and adolescent- and parent-reported family functioning, measured with the FES, compared to adolescent group counseling in a study of Hispanic adolescents with problem behaviors and their families (Santisteban et al., 2003). Using the SFSR along with other measures of family functioning has allowed investigators to show that BFST is not only effective in reducing targeted symptoms but also positively affects family functioning.

Family Process Code

The Family Process Code (FPC; Dishion, Gardner, Patterson, Reid, & Thibodeaux, 1983) is a real-time microcoding system of family interactions empirically developed over the past 40 years through ongoing research at the Oregon Social Learning Center (*www.oslc.org*). The original coding system was followed by the Interaction Coding System (ICS) and the Multidimensional

Observations of Social Adjustment in Children (MOSAIC) code. The FPC comprises three dimensions: (1) Activity: the general setting in which the participant is observed (six categories: Work, Play, Read, Eat, Attend and Unspecified); (2) Content: describes behaviors as they change through time (25 content codes), which are defined as positive, negative, or neutral and divided into verbal, vocal, nonverbal, physical, and compliance behaviors; and (3) Valence: emotional tone of the content behaviors (six ratings: Exuberant, Positive, Neutral, Negative, Unrestrained Negative, and Sad Affect). Each recorded content behavior is qualified by both setting and valence.

Observations are made in families' homes, and all family members are present during the interactions. The observation includes a series of segments, and coding is completed by using toggle switches on a keyboard. Each coded segment is recorded in five parts: the initiator of the behavior, the activity code, the content code, the valence, and the recipient of the behavior. The system allows the observer to record the sequence of all behaviors and their duration. The coding manual includes a detailed description of all codes with examples (Dishion, Gardner, Patterson, Reid, & Thibodeaux, 1983).

The FPC and its earlier versions have been used extensively in empirical research. Studies using these family interaction coding systems have been extremely influential in understanding the role of family interactions in the areas of adolescent delinquency and aggression, as well as in describing normal developmental patterns of family interaction. This is highlighted by recent work examining changes over time in the structure of family interactions during early adolescence in a five-wave longitudinal study of boys from childhood until age 18 and their parents. At each time point, boys and their parents were videotaped in problem-solving interactions, which were coded using the FPC, and state space grids were created at each wave to capture the trajectory of real-time behavior. As predicted, results indicated that the structure of family interactions was characterized by more variability during the period of early adolescence, extending previous research that has documented changes in content and frequency of behaviors during this period (Granic, Hollenstein, Dishion, & Patterson, 2003).

Iowa Family Interaction Rating Scales

The Iowa Family Interaction Rating Scales (IFIRS; Melby et al., 1998) is a macro-level observational coding system that draws upon social interactional, behavioral, and social contextual theories, was developed for use in research settings. The IFIRS was designed to assess the behavior and emotions of individuals, exchanges between family members, and characteristics of the overall family process across diverse age and relationship types. The IFIRS score behavioral processes in a number of different types of interaction tasks, including parent–child discussion tasks, family problem-solving tasks, couple problem-solving tasks, sibling interaction tasks, and marital and couple interaction tasks. The latest edition of the IFIRS (fifth edition) also includes activity-based tasks (parent–child teaching task and a cleanup task), designed to code the interactions of parents and young children. Typically the interactions are videotaped in the families' homes and the tasks selected depend on the nature of the research project and participants. There are 60 rating scales, most of which are 9-point Likert scales, on four different measurement levels (individual, dyadic interaction, dyadic relationship, and group interaction). Thirty-five scales are included in the General Interaction Rating Scales, which rates behavioral interactions at all four measurement levels noted earlier. The two specialty scales (Parenting and Problem Solving) measure interactions in specific types of tasks. The number and type of scales employed depend on the type of interaction task being scored. In general, the psychometric properties of the IFIRS have been strong (Melby & Conger, 2001).

The IFIRS is widely used in research. For instance, in a prospective longitudinal study, observer ratings using the IFIRS predicted divorce over and above self- and partner-reports, suggesting that observer ratings captured important aspects of family functioning not elucidated in family member's self-reports (Matthews, Wickrama, & Conger, 1996). The IFIRS has also been used in a number of different research studies, including as an outcome measure in intervention studies (Spoth, Redmond, Haggerty, & Ward, 1995). It has also been used extensively to predict adolescent adjustment and symptoms. For example, observer ratings that tapped warmth, hostility, and discipline predicted adjustment problems of 10th graders, even after researchers controlled for seventh graders' depressive symptoms and delinquent behavior (Ge, Best, Conger, & Simons, 1996). Although originally developed with a sample of white families, the IFIRS has subsequently been studied with diverse populations, including African American and Native American families (Melby & Conger, 2001).

Coparenting and Family Rating System

The Coparenting and Family Rating System (CFRS; (McHale, Kuersten-Hogan, & Lauretti, 2001) was designed to examine everyday coparenting interactions among families from the community samples in which at least two adults are regularly involved with the children. The CFRS was developed using both family systems theory and research. Play interactions involving at least two adults and one child are videotaped, and trained coders make five global ratings using 5-point Likert scales. The global rating scales include Cooperation, Coparental Competition, Verbal Sparring (conflict), Coparental Warmth, and Adult versus Child Centeredness (reflecting who drives the family interaction). In addition to the global scales, there are two "constructed ratings," generated from coding the parent–child interactions at the dyadic level. First, five parenting variables are coded to capture Positive Parenting: warmth, investment, sensitivity and timing of interventions, provision of structure, and (low) negativity. Discrepancy scores (Parenting Discrepancies) on these variables capture differences in positive parenting in the interaction.

The second constructed rating is Family Warmth, combining the Positive Parenting warmth code for each parent with the Coparental Warmth Global Rating code.

The CFRS has demonstrated adequate reliability and validity, but more work is needed to examine whether it is valid cross-culturally (McHale, Kuersten-Hogan, & Lauretti, 2001). The CFRS has been employed in several empirical studies of families with young children, demonstrating cross-sectional and longitudinal associations with marital distress and varied measures of child outcomes (e.g., McHale et al., 2001). For example, McHale (1995) employed the CFRS to rate marital and triadic interactions of couples with infants. Interestingly, the links between the observed marital behavior and coparenting behavior varied according to the gender of the infant; that is, maritally distressed parents of boys tended to exhibit hostile–competitive coparenting behavior in the triad, whereas maritally distressed parents of girls tended to exhibit discrepant levels of parenting involvement. Thus, use of the CFRS has contributed to our understanding of the role of coparenting in the family system.

MODELS AND MEASURES OF COUPLE FUNCTIONING

In this review, we emphasize measures of whole family functioning rather than include a comprehensive review of measures of couple functioning. Numerous reviews of this literature exist (e.g., Snyder, Heyman, & Haynes, 2005). In this section we describe two of the most widely used self-report measures in research and clinical practice.

Dyadic Adjustment Scale

The Dyadic Adjustment Scale (DAS; Spanier, 1976) is the most widely used self-report measure of dyadic functioning. Based on the premise that dyadic adjustment is an ever-changing process of movement along a continuum, it can be evaluated at any point in time along a dimension from well adjusted to maladjusted (Spanier, 1976). The DAS is a 32-item self-report inventory designed to measure the levels of satisfaction in couple relationships. The items load on four factors: (1) Dyadic Consensus (extent to which the couple agrees or disagrees on several issues); (2) Dyadic Cohesion (frequency of positive interactions); (3) Dyadic Satisfaction (perceived stability and conflict management); and (4) Affectional Expression (degree of agreement on the ways affection is expressed). In addition, there are a number of shorter forms of the DAS, including a 14-item version (Busby, Crane, Larson, & Christensen, 1995).

The DAS has exhibited strong psychometric properties. Indeed, a recent meta-analysis of 91 studies employing the DAS, which included 25,000 participants, showcased the exceptional reliability of the DAS (Graham, Liu, & Jeziorski, 2006). The DAS has been used extensively in basic applied research and in outcome studies of couple therapy, including randomized clinical trials. In their review of outcome measures of couple and family therapy, Sanderson and colleagues (2009) found that the DAS had the highest frequency of use of all outcome measures. For example, the DAS was used as a crucial outcome measure in a 5-year longitudinal study examining traditional versus integrative behavioral couple therapy in chronically and seriously distressed couples (Christensen, Atkins, Baucom, & Yi, 2010).

Marital Satisfaction Inventory—Revised

The Marital Satisfaction Inventory—Revised (MSI-R; Snyder & Aikman, 1999) was designed to measure the nature and intensity of relationship distress in several distinct areas of interaction deemed to be crucial for successful marriage. The MSI-R is a multidimensional measure that includes 150 true–false questions. Ten subscales assess specific areas of relationships, one global satisfaction scale, and two validity scales. The 10 subscales include Affective Communication, Problem-Solving Communication, Aggression, Time Together, Disagreement about Finances, Sexual Dissatisfaction, Role Orientation, Family History of Distress, Dissatisfaction with Children, and Conflict over Childrearing.

In over 25 years of research, the MSI-R shows good internal consistency, test–retest reliability, and discriminant validity (Snyder & Aikman, 1999). The MSI-R has been translated into numerous languages and has exhibited the ability to capture functioning in couples with diverse ethnic backgrounds, and in cohabitating same-sex and heterosexual couples (Means-Christensen, Snyder, & Negy, 2003; Snyder et al., 2004). The MSI-R has been utilized frequently as an outcome measure of couple and family interventions (see Sanderson et al., 2009) and in basic research. Notably, recent research using the MSI-R examined the nature of marital satisfaction and discord in a nationally representative sample of 1,020 clinical and community couples (Whisman, Beach, & Snyder, 2008). Results indicated that marital discord is "taxonic"; that is, discordant couples differ qualitatively, not just quantitatively, from nondiscordant couples. In this work, Whisman and colleagues developed clinical cutoffs that accurately discriminated between clinical and community couples and corresponded with therapists' ratings of relationship discord. This research supports the notion that the use of categorical and continuous measurement of marital discord may provide the most comprehensive assessment of this construct.

Prepare/Enrich

Olson and Gorall (2003) have also developed PREPARE/ENRICH Couple Inventories to assess strengths and growth in 20 content areas found to be critical to healthy or problematic functioning in couple relationships (PREPARE–Cohabiting Couple, PREPARE–Marriage with Children, ENRICH for married couples, and MATE for couples over age 50). In predictive validity, PREPARE for premarital couples has been found to predict with 80–85% accuracy in 3-year longitudinal studies couple satisfaction and which couples will divorce. ENRICH has discriminated happy, nonclinical couples from clinical couples with 90% accuracy. These scales have been widely used in premarital and marital counseling programs nationally and internationally, and with diverse couples. Feedback from the inventory computer scores and report, along with a workbook for couples, *Building a Strong Relationship*, are integrated into couple discussion, counseling, and experiential exercises.

QUALITATIVE METHODS

Although most measures of family functioning are quantitative, recent work has begun to create scientifically grounded qualitative methods that add to our base of knowledge. Quantitative and qualitative measures each have distinct strengths and contribute different information. We offer two examples of such merging qualitative scales.

Family Narrative Consortium Coding System

The Family Narrative Consortium Coding System (Fiese, Sameroff, Grotevant, Dikstein, & Fravel, 2001)is a multidimensional system rooted in narrative psychology. It is designed to capture family members' narratives in order to understand family functioning and processes. The coding system contains three dimensions, conceptualized to be the central components of family narratives. First, Narrative Coherence refers to the ability of individuals' to construct and organize a story. It includes four scales: Internal Consistency, Organization, Flexibility, and Congruence of Affect and Content. Second, Narrative Interaction reflects how well couples work together to construct the narrative. The Narrative Interaction component is only used to code joint interviews, and it contains four scales. Two scales are scored for the couple as a unit: Couple Narrative Style (style and character of the narrative produced by the couple) and Coordination (how well the partners work together to produce shared solutions and perceptions). Confirmation/Disconfirmation, scored separately for each partner, reflects the degree of confirmation or disconfirmation of partners' ideas. Third, Relationship Beliefs taps the ways families' construction of the social world is conveyed in the narrative content and interview. This dimension contains two scales, Relationship Expectations and Interviewer Intimacy. The former is scored separately for each partner and reflects whether partners' view their current families and their families of origin as manageable, reliable, and safe. The latter taps the degree of openness and willingness of individuals to share material with the interviewer. Family narratives can be collected using a variety of methods, such as interviews and story-stem procedures (Fiese &

Spagnola, 2005). The coding system is used to code interviews in a multistep process using both audio- or video recordings and transcripts. Emerging work suggests that the family narrative coding system is reliable and valid, and the system is currently being employed in a number of empirical studies (see Fiese, Winter, Anbar, Howell, & Poltrock, 2008).

Interpretive Phenomenological Analysis

Interpretive phenomenological analysis (IPA; Smith & Osborn, 2003; Smith, Flowers, & Larkin, 2009) is a qualitative approach that aims to understand how participants' make sense of events and experiences in their lives, while also acknowledging the role of the researcher in interpreting participants' subjective experiences. The IPA researcher obtains a small, homogeneous sample through purposive rather than random sampling in order to find a defined group in which the research question will be significant. Typically, participants are interviewed with semistructured interviews, although IPA has also been employed to analyze data obtained in structured interviews, personal accounts, and diaries. Using the interview transcripts, a detailed, systematic case-by-case analysis of each transcript is conducted in order to identify themes. Subsequently, connections are made across transcripts to obtain superordinate themes for the group of participants. The superordinate themes are described in narrative form using quotes from participants' transcripts, and these results are followed by a discussion section linking the themes to the literature. IPA has been used extensively in the health psychology literature. In this context, it has produced a number of interesting findings relevant to understanding how families cope with illness.

OTHER RECENT DEVELOPMENTS

With increasing sophistication of video technology and computerized data analysis, observational methods are better able to capture complex family processes. For instance, the UCLA Center on the Everyday Lives of Families (CELF) has conducted in-home observational studies of daily interaction in dual-earner middle-class families (with varied ethnic/racial backgrounds and sexual orientation) (e.g., Campos, Graesch, Repetti, Bradbury, & Ochs, 2009). Their naturalistic studies have also incorporated daily diary and physiological measures to offer new insights into families' everyday stress response and coping processes (Repetti, Wang, & Saxbe, 2009). In Switzerland, Fivaz-Depeursinge and Favez (2006) have demonstrated fascinating triadic interaction patterns involving infants with both parents. In Italy, Fruggeri and colleagues are analyzing verbal and nonverbal patterns of microtransitions in normal family life (Molinari, Everri, & Fruggeri, 2010). Such examples suggest the growing potential of observational studies.

DISCUSSION

As we noted in our introduction, although the evidence-based identification and assessment of the crucial dimensions of family functioning have lagged well behind such efforts focused on individuals, there is no shortage of models and methods. This is a rich and creative body of work, deriving notions of the crucial dimensions of family life, then building methods to assess those dimensions. All show some ability to distinguish functional and dysfunctional family processes, yet most studies have focused on two-parent, middle-class families with adolescents. More attention is needed to varied family forms, such as single-parent households; varied developmental phases and stressful life challenges, such as coping with chronic illness or disability; and contextual influences, such as migration or prolonged unemployment, socioeconomic status, and community resources; and larger system supports, such as health care and child care, for families to thrive.

Many elements of family life, such as a fair and consistent family structure and adequate communication, frequently appear across the models. Such research can usefully inform family intervention and community prevention approaches. For instance, Walsh's (2003) family resilience framework, synthesizing common elements found across studies of effective family functioning and resilience, identifies key processes that practitioners can facilitate to strengthen families dealing with adversity (see Walsh, Chapter 17, this volume).

Yet some variables are idiosyncratic to certain models (see Bray, 2004). Some models are simple, focusing on two or three variables, while others are multidimensional in understanding the difference between families being functional or dysfunctional. Some measures are constructed as curvilinear (moderate levels are functional, and extremes are dysfunctional); others are linear, with extreme scores distinguishing lowest–highest functioning. In addition, different theoretical traditions have fed into various models, with, for instance, systems theory and social exchange theory leading to somewhat different emphases in the models. No doubt there is enormous complexity and richness in family interaction, presenting a challenge to modeling and measuring development, as well as research examining the family context.

Method variance is also important to consider. Family members phenomenologically have a sense of their own being and what matters to them. Every member has a subjective experience and a narrative about how well family life works and why it does or does not work. Instruments that structure responses onto delimited spaces necessarily prioritize those dimensions. Though still seen through the eyes of the family member, they may seem more or less relevant to their situation. Measures that rate family behavior in the context of standardized tasks or in the natural family environment add yet a different perspective, one that is often more objective about the behavior but also somewhat removed from the underlying shared belief systems. This body of work clearly requires multiple perspectives from family members and from observers to obtain multiple pictures of family life, and a recognition that assessment at a certain moment is a snapshot. The currents of family interaction ebb and flow over time, with changes in family composition and emerging life demands that can best be understand with a developmental perspective and with longitudinal study.

Additionally, there is the thorny issue of how well an overall rating of family functioning on a dimension can capture the processes occurring within the family. Family systems comprise subsystems that may vary considerably in the degree or salience of key family variables and in alliances or coalitions in particular relationships. For example, although we can speak of a family with a high level of cohesion, family dynamics enter in, so there may be high cohesion among three members—parents and one child—and little cohesion with another child who has distanced from the family. They may be close to extended family members on the mother's side but distant from those on the father's side. With divorce and remarriage, there even are questions about how the family unit is defined and measured. Clearly, interactional patterns are more complex and require more assessment across households than is found in assessment of intact first families, and cannot simply be combined together. When a divorced father of adolescents remarries and has another child, the family processes are more complex, involving two developmental phases and step- and half-sibling relations. Despite great advances in statistical methods that can help with such dilemmas, the complexity of contemporary family relationships is an ever-present challenge in such work.

In order for a scale to be valid across a wide range of families regardless of ethnicity, class, and sexual orientation (among others), the measure needs to be developed, tested and normed using individuals from underrepresented segments of the population. Without this process, the ability of measures to tap family processes and functioning across varied individuals and families is questionable (see Tolan et al., 1997). There has been some progress in this domain, with some groups developing, testing, and standardizing measures in diverse samples. The Family Relations Scale (Tolan, Gorman-Smith, Huesmann, & Zelli, 1997) and the SFSR (Szapocznik et al., 1991) are exemplify this progress. Nonetheless, many have called into question the ability of current family assessment models and measures to describe accurately and capture family functioning in diverse populations (e.g., Aarons et al., 2007). For example, Green and colleagues have questioned the applicability of Olson's concept of too much cohesion as dysfunctional when high connectedness and caregiving are typical (normative) and functional in crisis situations, in many ethnic/cultural groups, and in lesbian couples with satisfying relationships (Green, Harris, Forte, & Robinson, 1991; Green & Werner, 1996). Similarly, Chao (1994) has identified aspects of structuring in parenting that have much different meanings in some Asian traditions. Clearly, the ability to capture family functioning in families of varied compositions (e.g., single-parent families, unmarried couples, same-sex couples and families), ethnic and racial backgrounds, levels of socioeconomic status, and levels of functioning is crucial as we continue to advance our understanding of families.

Perhaps because of these complexities, measures of whole family functioning are infrequently used in empirical studies of family therapy. For instance, Sanderson and colleagues (2009) provided a comprehensive review of outcome variables in couple and family therapy intervention research. Of 480 different outcome measures employed in 274 different studies, no measure of whole family functioning was used more than 10 times. The FAD was most often utilized; followed by the FES, FACES, and the FAM. Nonetheless, as advocated by Sanderson and colleagues, it is imperative to develop a core battery of measures. The use of family functioning measures in intervention research can demonstrate the influence of family therapy on individual symptoms, but more importantly, how effective family processes can reduce risk and promote greater well-being in intervention and prevention programs.

In applied work with families, these measures and models remain underutilized. Family-oriented clinicians infrequently use standardized assessment measures (e.g., Snyder et al., 2005), despite many advantages (e.g., see Bray, 2004). Although the various models and measures differ in their scales and emphasis, a few constructs, such as family cohesion, adaptability, communication, affection, and effectiveness, converge as important across these many models and measures; indicating their transcendent importance. In the clinical setting, the utilization of measures to tap these dimensions, and changes occurring along them, have great potential value. Only a few treatment models, such as the McMaster Model, have built such forms of assessment into their methods. Yet, broadly, measures such as those reviewed here have great utility for helping us understand and work with disturbed or vulnerable families. As a practical consideration, it seems clear that the many competing models and measures have made it difficult for one or two standard measures to emerge, which in turn constrains wider adoption. So, too, does the length of many of these measures, which may cause some to be reluctant to complete instruments, and the complexity involved in ratings made by nonfamily members.

It should be noted that the development of family assessment measures over the last two decades has occurred primarily in the mental health and social science research environment in the United States. Funding for the time-consuming and expensive research processes has largely come from government agencies focused predominantly on the study of dysfunction, such as the National Institute of Mental Health. As a result, many measures have been steered toward family dysfunction in both content and descriptive language (e.g., problematic relational patterns). While this has also contributed to the development of measures to study a continuum of functioning, we want to underscore Walsh's call (Chapter 2, this volume) for research funding to focus on not only how families fail but, more importantly, also how they can succeed.

In summary, the evidence-based assessment of families and associated models of normal family functioning has created a base of many state-of-the-art methods and models. This set of efforts reveals highly salient, yet complex, areas of family life. However, existing methods are also subject to influence from the dimensions selected, as well as questions of validity and generalizability owing to the complexity of constructs and broad diversity of contemporary families. None can be expected to convey the entirety of a vision of what constitutes health in family life. Yet together they have much to say about what works in families, and each alone can help to grasp what is going on in key dimensions of family life. The field has moved from the search for one overarching, simple model or "the normal family" to describe the rich texture of normal family processes, and to appreciate what the multiple viewpoints and methods can contribute to our understanding. Much work remains in continuing to develop measures that are valid and meaningful for the diversity of families, and to expand their application in varying contexts of research and practice.

REFERENCES

Aarons, G., McDonald, E., Connelly, C., & Newton, R. (2007). Assessment of family functioning in Caucasian and Hispanic Americans: Reliability, validity, and factor structure of the Family Assessment Device. *Family Process, 46*(4), 557–569.

Alderfer, M., Fiese, B., Gold, J., Cutuli, J., Holmbeck, G., Goldbeck, L., et al. (2008). Evidence-based assessment in pediatric psychology: Family measures. *Journal of Pediatric Psychology, 33*(9), 1046–1061.

American Psychiatric Association. (1994). *Diagnostic and statistical manual of mental disorders* (4th ed.). Washington, DC: Author.

Beavers, R. W., & Hampson, R. B. (2003). Measuring family competence: The Beavers Systems Model. In F. Walsh (Ed.), *Normal family processes: Growing diversity and complexity* (3rd ed., pp. 549–580). New York: Guilford Press.

Billings, A., Cronkite, R., & Moos, R. (1983). Social–environmental factors in unipolar depression: Comparisons of depressed patients and nondepressed controls. *Journal of Abnormal Psychology, 92*(2), 119–133.

Borduin, C., Schaeffer, C., & Heiblum, N. (2009). A randomized clinical trial of multisystemic therapy with juvenile sexual offenders: Effects on Youth Social Ecology and Criminal Activity. *Journal of Consulting and Clinical Psychology, 77*(1), 26–37.

Bray, J. (2004). Models and issues in couple and family assessment. In L. Sperry (Ed.), *Assessment of couples and families: Contemporary and cutting-edge strategies* (pp. 13–29). New York: Brunner/Routledge.

Busby, D., Crane, D., Larson, J., & Christensen, C. (1995). A revision of the Dyadic Adjustment Scale for use with distressed and nondistressed couples: Construct hierarchy and multidimensional scales. *Journal of Marital and Family Therapy, 21*(3), 289–308.

Byles, J., Byrne, C., Boyle, M., & Offord, D. (1988). Ontario Child Health Study:

Reliability and validity of the General Functioning subscale of the McMaster Family Assessment Device. *Family Process, 27*(1), 97–104.

Campos, B., Graesch, A. P., Repetti, R., Bradbury, T., & Ochs, E. (2009). Opportunity for interaction?: A naturalistic observation study of dual-earner families after work and school. *Journal of Family Psychology, 23*(6), 798–807.

Carlson, C. (2003). Assessing the family context. In C. R. Reynolds & R. W. Kamphaus (Eds.), *Handbook of psychological and educational assessment of children: Personality, behavior, and context* (2nd ed., pp. 473–492). New York: Guilford Press.

Chao, R. (1994). Beyond parental control and authoritarian parenting style: Understanding Chinese parenting through the cultural notion of training. *Child Development, 65*(4), 1111–1119.

Christensen, A., Atkins, D., Baucom, B., & Yi, J. (2010). Marital status and satisfaction five years following a randomized clinical trial comparing traditional versus integrative behavioral couple therapy. *Journal of Consulting and Clinical Psychology, 78*(2), 225–235.

Dickstein, S., Hayden, L. C., Schiller, M., Seifer, R., & San Antonio, W. (1994). *Providence Family Study Mealtime Family Interaction Coding System: Adapted from the McMaster Clinical Rating Scale.* East Providence, RI: E. P. Bradley Hospital.

Dishion, T. J., Gardner, K., Patterson, G. R., Reid, J. B., & Thibodeaux, S. (1983). *The Family Process Code: A multidimensional system for observing family interaction* [Unpublished technical report]. (Available at Oregon Social Learning Center, 207 E. Fifth Ave., Suite 202, Eugene, OR 97401)

Epstein, N., Ryan, C., Bishop, D., Miller, I., & Keitner, G. (2003). The McMaster Model: A view of healthy family functioning. In F. Walsh (Ed.), *Normal family processes: Growing diversity and complexity* (3rd ed., pp. 581–607). New York: Guilford Press.

Epstein, N. B., Baldwin, L. M., & Bishop, D. S. (1982). *The McMaster Clinical Rating Scale (MCRS).* Providence, RI: Brown University Family Research Program.

Epstein, N. B., Baldwin, L. M., & Bishop, D. S. (1983). The McMaster Family Assessment Device. *Journal of Marital and Family Therapy, 9,* 171–180.

Fiese, B. H., Sameroff, A. J., Grotevant, H. D., Wamboldt, H. D., Dikstein, S., Fravel, D. L. (2001). Observing families through the stories they tell: A multidimensional approach. In P. K. L. Keirg (Ed.), *Family observational coding systems: Resources for systematic research* (pp. 259–271). Mahwah, NJ: Erlbaum.

Fiese, B. H., & Spagnola, M. (2005). Narratives in and about families: A critical look at definitions, methods, and application to family psychology. *Journal of Family Psychology, 19,* 51–61.

Fiese, B. H., Winter, M. A., Anbar, R. D., Howell, K. J., & Poltrock, S. (2008). Family climate of routine asthma care: Associating perceived burden and mother–child interaction patterns. *Family Process, 47,* 63–79.

Fivaz-Depeursinge, E., & Favez, N. (2006). Exploring triangulation in infancy: Two contrasted cases. *Family Process, 45,* 3–18.

Gan, C., & Schuller, R. (2002). Family system outcome following acquired brain injury: Clinical and research perspectives. *Brain Injury, 16*(4), 311–322.

Ge, X., Best, K., Conger, R., & Simons, R. (1996). Parenting behaviors and the occurrence and co-occurrence of adolescent depressive symptoms and conduct problems. *Developmental Psychology, 32*(4), 717–731.

Gorman-Smith, D., Tolan, P., Henry, D., & Florsheim, P. (2000). Patterns of family functioning and adolescent outcomes among urban African American and Mexican American families. *Journal of Family Psychology, 14*(3), 436–457.

Granic, I., Hollenstein, T., Dishion, T., & Patterson, G. (2003). Longitudinal analysis of flexibility and reorganization in early adolescence: A dynamic systems study of family interactions. *Developmental Psychology, 39*(3), 606–617.

Graham, J., Liu, Y., & Jeziorski, J. (2006). The Dyadic Adjustment Scale: A reliability generalization meta-analysis. *Journal of Marriage and Family, 68*(3), 701–717.

Green, R., Harris, R., Forte, J., & Robinson, M. (1991). Evaluating FACES-III and the circumplex model: 2,440 families. *Family Process, 30*(1), 55–73.

Green, R.-J., & Werner, P. D. (1996). Intrusiveness and closeness–caregiving: Rethinking the concept of family "enmeshment." *Family Process, 35,* 115–136.

Henry, D., Tolan, P., & Gorman-Smith, D. (2001). Longitudinal family and peer group effects on violence and nonviolent delinquency. *Journal of Clinical Child Psychology, 30*(2), 172–186.

Kaufman, K., Tarnowski, K., Simonian, S., & Graves, K. (1991). Assessing the readability of family assessment self-report measures. *Psychological Assessment: A Journal of Consulting and Clinical Psychology, 3*(4), 697–700.

Kissane, D., McKenzie, M., Bloch, S., Moskowitz, C., McKenzie, D., & O'Neill, I. (2006). Family focused grief therapy: A randomized, controlled trial in palliative care and bereavement. *American Journal of Psychiatry, 163*(7), 1208–1218.

Kolko, D., Brent, D., Baugher, M., Bridge, J., & Birmaher, B. (2000). Cognitive and family therapies for adolescent depression: Treatment specificity, mediation, and moderation. *Journal of Consulting and Clinical Psychology, 68*(4), 603–614.

Liddle, H., Dakof, G., Parker, K., Diamond, G., Barrett, K., & Tejeda, M. (2001). Multidimensional family therapy for adolescent drug abuse: Results of a randomized clinical trial. *American Journal of Drug and Alcohol Abuse, 27*(4), 651–688.

Matthews, L., Wickrama, K., & Conger, R. (1996). Predicting marital instability from spouse and observer reports of marital interaction. *Journal of Marriage and Family, 58*(3), 641–655.

Maziade, M., Bernier, H., Thivierge, Y., & Côté, R. (1987). The relationship between family functioning and demographic characteristics in an epidemiological study. *Canadian Journal of Psychiatry, 142,* 943–946.

Maziade, M., Côté, R., Boutin, P., & Bernier, H. (1987). Temperament and intellectual development: A longitudinal study from infancy to four years. *The American Journal of Psychiatry, 144*(2), 144–150.

McHale, J. (1995). Coparenting and triadic interactions during infancy: The roles of marital distress and child gender. *Developmental Psychology, 31*(6), 985–996.

McHale, J., Kuersten-Hogan, R., Lauretti, A., & Rasmussen, J. (2000). Parental reports of coparenting and observed coparenting behavior during the toddler period. *Journal of Family Psychology, 14*(2), 220–236.

Means-Christensen, A., Snyder, D., & Negy, C. (2003). Assessing nontraditional couples: Validity of the Marital Satisfaction Inventory—Revised with gay, lesbian, and cohabiting heterosexual couples. *Journal of Marital and Family Therapy, 29*(1), 69–83.

Melby, J. N., & Conger, R. D. (2001). The Iowa Family Interaction Rating Scales: Instrument summary. In P. Kerig & K. M. Lindahl (Eds.), *Family Observational*

Coding Systems: Resources for systemic research (pp. 33–58). Mahwah, NJ: Erlbaum.

Melby, J. N., Conger, R. D., Book, R., Rueter, M., Lucy, L., Repinski, D., et al. (1998). *The Iowa Family Interaction Rating scales* (5th ed.). Unpublished manuscript, Institute for Social and Behavioral Research, Iowa State University, Ames.

Miklowitz, D., Axelson, D., George, E., Taylor, D., Schneck, C., Sullivan, A., et al. (2009). Expressed emotion moderates the effects of family-focused treatment for bipolar adolescents. *Journal of the American Academy of Child and Adolescent Psychiatry, 48*(6), 643–651.

Miller, I. W., Kabacoff, R. I., Epstein, N. B., Bishop, D. S., Keitner, G. I., Baldwin, L. M., et al. (1994). The development of a clinical rating scale for the McMaster Model of Family Functioning. *Family Process, 33,* 53–69.

Minuchin, S., Rosman, B. L., & Baker, L. (1978). *Psychosomatic families: Anorexia nervosa in context.* Cambridge, MA: Harvard University Press.

Molinari, L., Everri, M., & Fruggeri, L. (2010). Family microtransitions: Observing the process of change in families with adolescents children. *Family Process, 49*(2), 236–251.

Moos, R., & Moos, B. (1994). *Family Environment Scale manual* (3rd ed.). Palo Alto, CA: Consulting Psychologists Press.

Novack, T., & Gage, R. (1995). Assessment of family functioning and social support. In L. A. Cushman & M. J. Scherer (Eds.), *Psychological assessment in medical rehabilitation* (pp. 275–297). Washington, DC: American Psychological Association.

Olson, D. H. (1997). Family stress and coping: A multi-system perspective. In S. Dreman (Ed.), *The family on the threshold of the 21st century* (pp. 258–282). Mahwah, NJ: Erlbaum.

Olson, D. H. (2011). FACES IV and the circumplex model: Validation study. *Journal of Marital and Family Therapy, 37,* 64–80.

Olson, D. H., & Gorall, D. M. (2003). Circumplex model of marital and family systems. In F. Walsh (Ed.), *Normal family processes: Growing diversity and complexity* (3rd ed., pp. 514–548). New York: Guilford Press.

Olson, D. H., Gorall, D. M., & Tiesel, J. W. (2006). *FACES IV package.* Minneapolis, MN: Life Innovations.

Olson, D. H., Larsen, A., & McCubbin, H. I. (1989). Family strengths. In D. H. Olson, H. I. McCubbin, H. Barnes, A. Larsen, M. Muxen, & M. Wilson (Eds.), *Family inventories* (pp. 21–42). St. Paul: Family Social Science, University of Minnesota.

Pinsof, W. M., Zinbarg, R.E., Durbin, C. E., Latta, T., Knobloch-Fedders, L. M., Lebow, J., et al. (2010). *Confirming and norming the factor structure of the STIC INITIAL: Enhancing multi-systemic progress research in family, couple and individual therapies.* Unpublished manuscript. Family Institute at Northwestern University, Evanston, IL.

Pinsof, W., Zinbarg, R., & Knobloch-Fedders, L. (2008). Factorial and construct validity of the Revised Short Form Integrative Psychotherapy Alliance Scales for family, couple, and individual therapy. *Family Process, 47*(3), 281–301.

Pinsof, W., Zinbarg, R., Lebow, J., Knobloch-Fedders, L., Durbin, E., Chambers, A., et al. (2009). Laying the foundation for progress research in family, couple, and individual therapy: The development and psychometric features of the initial Systemic Therapy Inventory of Change. *Psychotherapy Research, 19*(2), 143–156.

Plake, B. S., & Impara, J. C. (Eds.). (2001). *The fourteenth mental measurements yearbook*. Lincoln, NE: Buros Institute of Mental Measurements.

Repetti, R., Wang, S., & Saxbe, D. (2009). Bringing it all back home. How outside stressors shape families' everyday lives. *Current Psychological Directions in Science, 18*, 106–111.

Sanderson, J., Kosutic, I., Garcia, M., Melendez, T., Donoghue, J., Perumbilly, S., et al. (2009). The measurement of outcome variables in couple and family therapy research. *American Journal of Family Therapy, 37*(3), 239–257.

Sanford, K., Bingham, C., & Zucker, R. (1999). Validity issues with the Family Environment Scale: Psychometric resolution and research application with alcoholic families. *Psychological Assessment, 11*(3), 315–325.

Santisteban, D., Perez-Vidal, A., Coatsworth, J., Kurtines, W., Schwartz, S., LaPerriere, A., et al. (2003). Efficacy of brief strategic family therapy in modifying hispanic adolescent behavior problems and substance use. *Journal of Family Psychology, 17*(1), 121–133.

Shek, D. (2002). Assessment of family functioning in Chinese adolescents: The Chinese version of the Family Assessment Device. *Research on Social Work Practice, 12*(4), 502–524.

Skinner, H., Steinhauer, P., & Sitarenios, G. (2000). Family Assessment Measure (FAM) and Process Model of Family Functioning. *Journal of Family Therapy, 22*(2), 190–210.

Smith, J. A., Flowers, P., & Larkin, M. (2009). *Interpretative phenomnological analysis: Theory, method, and research*. London: Sage.

Smith, J. A., & Osborn, M. (2003). Interpretative phenomnological analysis. In J. A. Smith (Ed.), *Qualitative psychology: A practical guide to methods* (pp. 53–80). London: Sage.

Snyder, D., Cepeda-Benito, A., Abbott, B., Gleaves, D., Negy, C., Hahlweg, K., et al. (2004). Cross-cultural applications of the Marital Satisfaction Inventory—Revised. In M. E. Maruish (Ed.), *The use of psychological testing for treatment planning and outcomes assessment: Volume 3: Instruments for adults* (3rd ed., pp. 603–623). Mahwah, NJ: Erlbaum.

Snyder, D., Heyman, R., & Haynes, S. (2005). Evidence-based approaches to assessing couple distress. *Psychological Assessment, 17*(3), 288–307.

Snyder, D. K., & Aikman, G. G. (1999). The Marital Satisfaction Inventory—Revised. In M. E. Maruish (Ed.), *The use of psychological testing for treatment planning and outcome assessment* (2nd ed., pp. 1173–1210). Mahwah, NJ: Erlbaum.

Spanier, G. (1976). Measuring dyadic adjustment: New scales for assessing the quality of marriage and similar dyads. *Journal of Marriage and Family, 38*(1), 15–28.

Spoth, R., Redmond, C., Haggerty, K., & Ward, T. (1995). A controlled parenting skills outcome study examining individual difference and attendance effects. *Journal of Marriage and Family, 57*(2), 449–464.

Stein, M., Hilsenroth, M., Pinsker-Aspen, J., & Primavera, L. (2009). Validity of DSM-IV Axis V Global Assessment of Relational Functioning Scale: A multimethod assessment. *Journal of Nervous and Mental Disease, 197*(1), 50–55.

Szapocznik, J., Hervis, O., Rio, A., & Mitrani, V. (1991). Assessing change in family functioning as a result of treatment: The Structural Family Systems Rating scale (SFSR). *Journal of Marital and Family Therapy, 17*(3), 295–310.

Szapocznik, J., & Prado, G. (2007). Negative effects on family functioning from psychosocial treatments: A recommendation for expanded safety monitoring. *Journal of Family Psychology, 21*(3), 468–478.

Tolan, P., Gorman-Smith, D., Huesmann, L., & Zelli, A. (1997). Assessment of family relationship characteristics: A measure to explain risk for antisocial behavior and depression among urban youth. *Psychological Assessment, 9*(3), 212–223.

Walsh, F. (2003). Changing families in a changing world: Reconstructing family normality. In F. Walsh (Ed.), *Normal family processes: Growing diversity and complexity* (3rd ed., pp. 3–26). New York: Guilford Press.

Walsh, F. (2003). *Normal family processes: Growing diversity and complexity* (3rd ed.). New York: Guilford Press.

Whisman, M., Beach, S., & Snyder, D. (2008). Is marital discord taxonic and can taxonic status be assessed reliably?: Results from a national, representative sample of married couples. *Journal of Consulting and Clinical Psychology, 76*(5), 745–755.

CHAPTER 22

UNRAVELING THE COMPLEXITY OF GENE–ENVIRONMENT INTERPLAY AND FAMILY PROCESSES

ERICA L. SPOTTS

F indings from the past two decades of quantitative genetic research suggest that genes and environment frequently operate on individual behaviors and family relationships in an interactive and nonlinear fashion. More recently, epigenetic and gene expression studies are revealing that genes and their expression can be influenced by nongenetic factors, both negative and positive, including key relationships and life experiences. The field has made significant strides in the effort to begin to peel apart the layers of this human behavioral complexity.

The discovery that genetic factors account for a significant portion of variation in virtually every human behavior was an essential first step in addressing the broad issue of behavioral complexity. Twin, family, and adoption studies have confirmed moderate to substantial genetic influence on widely varying conditions such as schizophrenia, neurotic disorders, and autism (see review by McGuffin, Owen, O'Donovan, Thapar, & Gottesman, 1994), as well as social responsibility (Neiderhiser, Reiss, & Hetherington, 1996), cognition (Plomin & DeFries, 1999), and optimism (Plomin et al., 1992).

Likewise, the discovery of genetic contributions to family *relationships*, such as parenting (Deater-Deckard, 2000; Elkins, McGue, & Iacono, 1997) and sibling relationships (Rende, Slomkowski, Stocker, Fulker, & Plomin, 1992), advanced our understanding of the complicated interplay between genes and family environment. Such findings confirm, again, the complexity of human behavior, namely, that most behaviors occur within the context of reciprocal, long-term relationships, which are themselves a representation of a very intricate pattern of interactions between people, formed over time.

So, when a mother treats her adolescent harshly, and that adolescent displays unruly behavior, we have learned that this association may reflect more than the psychological impact of the mother and the child on one another. Numerous alternatives now exist to account for such an association: Perhaps the adolescent's genetic propensity toward externalizing behavior plays a large role in evoking maternal negativity; perhaps these genetic tendencies toward impulsive behavior are ones the child shares with one or both biological parents, a phenomenon called *passive gene–environment (GE) correlation*. Alternatively, perhaps the heritable traits that impact the parent–child relationship most are those of the child, a phenomenon called *evocative/active GE correlation*.

Although the concept of GE correlation is not new (Bussell & Reiss, 1993), most genetically informed studies of parenting have been unable to isolate whether or not the GE correlation is evocative or passive. Consequently, we have been unsure about whose genes are really more important to the relationships of interest. In other words, are children's behaviors associated with those of their biological parents because of their 50% genetic similarity to one another? Or because the children's own, heritable traits *shape* their parents' behaviors toward them? The answer to this question has implications for many disciplines, in both basic science and clinical practice, since it speaks to the issue of the mechanisms underlying major family subsystems. If heritable behaviors of the child evoke parental negativity, then clinical efforts might be directed toward intervening more at the parent level. There is accumulating evidence that favorable environmental conditions can dramatically alter or eliminate the impact of the same genetic factors that can cause psychopathology in unfavorable environments. In this sense, findings of genetic influence on family subsystems in no way suggest a hopeless scenario for families in distress. Nor does knowledge of genetic influence on behaviors imply that the home, or one's rearing environment, is not important. As we shall see, both shared and nonshared family environments play important and distinct roles in human development.

The ability to distinguish between types of GE correlation in parent–child relationships is just one example of how the field of quantitative genetics has made significant gains in clarifying the mechanisms underlying genetic and environmental influences on family relationships. Other equally important examples include identification of GE interactions, isolation of specific sources of sibling-specific environmental variation in behavior, and a focus on the potential for shared environment to moderate these sibling-specific associations. The purpose of this chapter is to provide an overview of some of the conceptual and methodological advances that have occurred within the field over the past decade. Information relevant to the study of family systems and processes is covered, with a particular focus on the following areas: (1) sensitivity of the family environment to variation in genotype (GE correlation), (2) sensitivity of genotype to the environment (GE interaction), (3) sibling-specific (or nonshared) environments, and (4) the role of environmental factors shared by family members in shaping family relationships. Prior to discussion of recent findings, a brief definition and description of each conceptual area is provided.

INTRODUCTION TO
FOUR KEY QUANTITATIVE GENETIC CONCEPTS

Gene–Environment Correlation

GE correlation refers broadly to the estimated association between a person's environment (and the people in it) and that person's genetically influenced behaviors, and may be partitioned into three types (Scarr & McCartney, 1983). Briefly, *passive GE correlation* refers to a correlation between a measure of the environment (e.g., parenting) and a genotype (e.g., that of a child), which is due to the 50% genetic-relatedness of the two. For example, a father may pass on to his child those genes that contribute to his own depression. A passive GE correlation could explain genetic influences on parent–child negativity in this example, because the depression genes shared by the father and the child also contribute to making the relationship strained and negative in tone. The two alternative types of GE correlation, *evocative* and *active*, represent the possibility that children's genetically influenced characteristics play an important role in shaping the environments. *Evocative GE correlation* refers to the reaction of others (who need not be genetically related) to someone based on some genetically influenced trait of that person. For example, a husband may be overly critical toward a wife who is genetically predisposed to being gloomy and depressed. Or an adoptive mother may respond negatively to the difficult temperament of a newly adopted child. *Active GE correlation* refers to an individual's seeking out a particular environment based upon a genetically influenced characteristic. For example, Manke, McGuire, Reiss, Hetherington, and Plomin (1995) found that there are strong genetic influences on the quality of an adolescent's peer group, suggesting that heritable factors shape the choice of peer groups.

A number of quantitative genetic studies have examined GE correlation directly. Such studies rely mainly on information regarding the characteristics of children adopted away at birth, their adoptive parents, and at least one biological parent. These adoption designs are ideal tools for assessing evocative GE correlation, because information on the psychiatric, biological, and criminal histories of the biological parent serves as a proxy for the adopted child's genetic characteristics. Because adoptive parents share none of their segregating genes (genes that cause human variation) with their adopted child, adoptive parents represent an environment entirely separate from the adopted child's genes. Finding an association between the heritable behaviors of an adopted child (e.g., the psychiatric or criminal characteristics of the biological parent) and the parenting of that child by his or her adoptive parents, then, suggests the presence of an evocative GE correlation.

Gene × Environment Interaction

G × E interaction occurs when the environment has an impact on the degree to which genetic influences are expressed. For example, one study of G × E interaction in the development of antisocial behavior found that adolescent adoptees at genetic risk for becoming antisocial (indicated by the presence of an impulsive disorder in at least one birth parent) were much more likely to do so when placed into adoptive homes in which the environment was characterized by adverse factors, including a depressed adoptive mother or marital discord between the adoptive parents (Cadoret, Cain, & Crowe, 1983). Such a finding suggests that the compounded effect of genes and environment may outweigh the single, main effect of each, at least for certain behaviors.

Nonshared Environment

The term *nonshared environment* refers to those nongenetic factors that make family members different from each other. Siblings from the same household are frequently just as *different* from one another, due to environmental factors, as they are *similar* to one another for genetic reasons, with both sources of influence accounting for approximately half of the variation in a variety of human behaviors (see review by Plomin, Chipuer, & Neiderhiser, 1994). This is one of the most remarkable and robust findings to come out of genetic explorations of the family environment.

Nonshared environmental influences may include different peer groups or friendships, different parenting, different experiences of trauma, different work environments, and different romantic partners or spouses. The difficulty has been in finding evidence of the substantial and systematic impact of any of these variables on sibling differences. Understanding the nonshared environment remains a topic of considerable interest in the field of quantitative genetic research because it has been shown to be important to a wide array of behaviors across the entire lifespan, yet its *systematic* causes remain elusive (Turkheimer & Waldron, 2000). In a subsequent section on nonshared environment, recent efforts to identify sources of nonshared environmental influence on behaviors, including some preliminary analyses of nonshared associations using an adult-based twin study, are examined. Then new advances in genetic technology that can also advance understanding of the family environment are discussed.

Shared Family Environment

Historically, the field of quantitative genetics did not consider the general family environment a very important determinant of variations in children's outcomes (Bussell & Reiss, 1993). That conclusion was based on the quantitative genetic finding that when young siblings are similar with respect to constructs such as IQ (Scarr & Weinberg, 1983) and personality (Loehlin, Willerman, &

Horn, 1987), it is usually for *genetic* reasons, and not because of shared influences within their environment, such as common parenting, common friends, or family socioeconomic scale level. For many phenotypes (i.e., observable characteristics of individuals resulting from genetic plus environmental factors), shared environmental influences do account for less variation in behavior than nonshared ones.

However, a recent meta-analysis of genetic and environmental contributions to child and adolescent psychopathology may have the field rethinking that stance on the shared environment (Burt, 2009). Findings from this study strongly suggest that shared environmental factors contribute 10–30% of the variance of many common forms of child and adolescent psychopathology (with the exception of attention-deficit/hyperactivity disorder). These potentially fundamental contributions to the risk of a broad range of psychopathology warrant further examination, so that specific risk factors can be identified, such as parental divorce and aspects of the parent–child relationship.

CONCEPTUAL AND METHODOLOGICAL ADVANCES

Gene–Environment Correlation

Evidence for the association between one's genotype and characteristics of his or her social environment has been accumulating over many years (Deater-Deckard, 2000; Ge et al., 1996; O'Connor, Deater-Deckard, Fulker, Rutter, & Plomin, 1998; van Os, Park, & Jones, 2001). Although such studies have been relatively rare, they are relevant to research concerned with family process because most theories linking child adjustment to family environment, including parenting behaviors, have presumed that these associations were caused by environmental mechanisms, due, primarily, to their reliance on data collection designs lacking information on genetic influences. Most often, any observed correlations between the two have been interpreted as evidence of socialization. What we know now from twin studies suggests that the influence of children's genetic factors on their own behavior is roughly equal to the influence of their family environment. More importantly, these same genetic factors have been shown to correlate with behaviors exhibited by family members toward the child, which may indicate the role of children's heritable characteristics in shaping their own family environment.

For example, a cross-sectional examination of adopted adolescents and their families found that the association between parenting and negative adolescent outcome could be explained by evocative GE correlation (Ge et al., 1996). Study results indicate that the same genes that contribute to antisocial behavior in adolescents also seem to evoke specific parenting practices in their adoptive parents. In other words, it was the children's genes that accounted for the association between parenting and child outcome. Another adoption study confirmed the presence of a GE correlation mechanism for the same parent–child relationship construct, employing a longitudinal design (O'Connor et al., 1998). Investigators found that 7- to 12-year-olds who were at genetic risk for becoming antisocial, assessed by measuring antisocial behavior in their biological parents, were more likely to evoke negative parenting from their adoptive parents than were those adopted children not at genetic risk. Such a finding confirms that we can predict problematic relationships between adopted children and their adoptive parents from knowledge of psychopathology in their birth parents. Interestingly, the same study found that a range of the adopted children's *internalizing* behaviors, although significantly heritable and associated with parenting, did *not* account for negative parenting patterns of their adoptive parents. In most instances, the more salient heritable characteristics of children, such as externalizing or aggression, are most likely to evoke reaction from parents (although an exception is discussed below).

The GE correlation mechanism observed in those two studies (Ge et al., 1996; O'Connor et al., 1998) is thought to account for at least some of the genetic influence often observed on certain measures traditionally considered to be environmental. The process is likely reciprocal and cumulative, such that externalizing behavior is only intensified by the negative parenting it evokes, causing a further increase in parental negativity, and so on. A more recent publication made this parent–child reciprocity, or mutuality, the explicit focus of genetic analysis (Deater-Deckard & O'Connor, 2000). This study was also noteworthy in finding GE correlation between *positive* child and parent behaviors. Three aspects of mother–child dyadic mutuality, including cooperation, emotional reciprocity, and responsiveness, were assessed in two separate, genetically informed samples of young children. Results of genetic analyses of these relationship constructs showed both substantial genetic and nonshared environmental influences on all three aspects of mother–child mutuality. In other words, within each family, the two siblings' relationships with their mothers were both similar to and different from (i.e., relationship-specific) one another. When they were similar, it was due to the impact of some aspect of the children's genetically influenced behavior on the mother's parenting, and not to the children's similar rearing experiences, or shared environment. This inference was based on the finding that siblings who were most genetically similar to one another (e.g., identical twins) had more similar relationships with their mothers than did siblings who were less genetically similar (e.g., fraternal twins). These results suggest the potential for evocative GE correlation mechanisms to play a role in the interactions between children as young as 3 years old and their parents.

Such findings are consistent with earlier work that confirms children and adolescents are not merely passive recipients of parenting efforts, but instead often actively elicit and affect parents' behaviors through the children's own heritable traits (Lytton, 1980; Scarr & McCartney, 1983). But what about the potential for GE correlation to occur within other family relationships? Such instances have implications for the workings of normal family processes to the extent that they impact the various subsystems that characterize families. Although research examining GE correlation within family subsystems has been concerned primarily with parent–child associations, there have been reports of GE correlation among other family subsystems, including sibling (Plomin, Reiss, Hetherington, & Howe, 1994; Stocker & Dunn, 1994) and marital (Block, Block, & Gjerde, 1986) relationships. However, such publications have focused on circumstances surrounding the *child* for whom genetic and environmental data have been collected. Findings from an adult-based twin study provides one example of ongoing efforts to identify and describe GE correlation patterns in *adult* family subsystems.

The Twin and Offspring Study in Sweden (TOSS), a study of adult twins and their spouses, examined the role of twin women's heritable characteristics on their own reports as well as their spouses' reports of marital quality (Spotts et al., 2004). There was a strong phenotypic correlation between spouses' reports of their overall marital satisfaction. Interestingly, both wife *and* husband reports show moderate genetic influence on their reports of a satisfying marriage. Genetic influences on the husband's perceptions indicate the influence of the *wife's* genetic characteristics because there is no genetic information on the husband's genetic characteristics in this study. Therefore, genetic characteristics of the wife not only influence her perceptions of the marriage but are also reflected in her husband's reports of marital satisfaction. While it is possible that this association merely reflects assortative mating (i.e., the wife has sought out a husband compatible with her heritable characteristics), it is more likely that the husband is *responding* to some heritable trait of the wife, and that this response leads him to feel a certain way about the marriage. Further study of the mechanisms underlying both the husband's and wife's perceptions of the marital subsystem will shed light on this important distinction.

Since publication of the third edition of this volume, great methodological strides have been made in understanding GE correlation. Not only have researchers intuited ways to extract information about the nature of GE correlation (Neiderhiser et al., 2004), but they have also developed new methods capitalizing on two different types of existing family designs.

First, the children of twins design capitalizes on the fact that children of monozygotic (MZ) twins are more similar to each other than the children of dizygotic (DZ) twins, and that the children of MZ twins are as genetically similar to their own mother as they are to their aunt (i.e., the mother's twin sister). This method has been used to tease apart pathways through which parental factors (e.g., divorce, age at first sex, maternal smoking, and perinatal effects) influence child outcomes. For example, a study by D'Onofrio and colleagues (2007) examined the mechanism underlying the association between parental divorce and child psychopathology. In controlling for genetic and environmental factors that might account for these associations, they found different mechanisms for child substance use and internalizing disorders. Results were consistent with causal pathways linking divorce with substance abuse. However, results were consistent with a shared genetic liability between the parents and offspring accounting for the increased risk for internalizing problems following parental divorce. Another study (Narusyte, Andershed, Niederhiser, & Lichtenstein, 2007) examined the robust association between conflictual parent–child relationships and adolescent aggression, supporting the hypothesis that genetically influenced aggression in the adolescent evokes criticism from the parents. This is in contrast to an alternative hypothesis suggesting that parental criticism and adolescent aggressions are influenced by the same genes shared by parents and offspring.

Second, adoption designs have been revisited. The Early Growth and Development Study is innovative in that it measures families longitudinally from the infant age of 3 months, collects extensive observational and self-report data, collects data on birth mothers and fathers, and has gone to great lengths to be as representative as possible in the sample size (361 linked triads) and the extent of its measurement (very young children, birth and adoptive families, birth fathers). Through the use of this natural design, this study has begun to tease apart the effects of genes, environment, and how genes and environments interact and correlate. For example, this study revealed some very complicated pathways related to the development of externalizing behavior, whereby maternal structured guidance interacted with child's temperament and genetic risk in varying ways (Leve et al., 2009). The results from these studies, along with the growing body of work using the same methods, highlight the importance of taking both genetic and environmental factors into account to understand fully the dynamic pathways involved in family relationships.

Gene × Environment Interaction

In animal studies, researchers can cross-foster offspring (i.e., remove offspring from biological parents to be raised by surrogates). In fact, some of the most useful information we have obtained concerning the potential relevance of the early rearing environment to gene expression has come from rearing experiments using nonhuman primates (Suomi, 2000). Most Old World monkeys (e.g., rhesus) and chimps share approximately 90–95 and 99%, respectively, of their genes with human beings, with many conserved regions of the genome across species. This means that while the analogue is not perfect, animal models of biological/gene–behavioral links constitute an indispensable part of human studies.

Take, for example, the problem of childhood aggression which is frequently the focus of family therapy intervention. A series of animal studies shows biological evidence of strong associations between the serotonergic functioning and highly aggressive behavior of a group of preadolescent rhesus monkeys (Champoux, Higley, & Suomi, 1997; Mehlman, Higley, Faucher, Lily, Tau, Vickers, et al., 1994). The studies found that low levels of a particular serotonin metabolite (5-HIAA) in the cerebrospinal fluid (CSF) of these monkeys are highly predictive of certain patterns of extremely aggressive and often deadly behaviors. Furthermore, it appears that individual differences in rhesus monkey levels of 5-HIAA are genetically influenced (Higley, Thompson, Champoux, Goldman, Hasert, Kraemer, et al., 1993). These findings are particularly interesting in light of other work suggesting that an identical biological mechanism may account for acts of aggression in human children and adults.

Even more provocative are findings from a prospective study with rhesus monkeys demonstrating a moderating effect of early rearing environment on this well-documented association between genetic propensity toward low CSF 5-HIAA levels and aggressive behaviors (Bennett et al., 1998). Whether or not monkeys develop a relationship *with their mother* is a critical factor in determining the expression of their genetic risk toward aggression. For instance, the study found an association between a polymorphism and negative behavioral outcomes for the monkeys. Specifically, having a short version of a transporter gene implicated in serotonergic activity was associated with depressed serotonergic functioning and increased alcohol consumption for those monkeys reared by their peers. Notably, being raised by one's mother seemed to serve as a buffer to these negative effects of the same short version of the gene, reducing the risk for excessive alcohol consumption and high social dominance.

Although animal experiments are certainly better suited to assess specific GE interactions, numerous studies have demonstrated the usefulness of human adoption designs for uncovering GE interactions among humans, focusing on psychiatric illnesses ranging from depression and alcoholism (Cadoret, 1995; Cadoret et al., 1996) to schizophrenia (Tienari et al., 1994; Tsuang, Stone, & Faraone, 2001) and antisocial personality disorder (Bohman, 1996). The basic premise of most of these studies is that children adopted at a young age into a new environment, or home, come with genetic characteristics that can be indexed by the psychiatric status of their biological parent. If the environment is capable of constraining or modifying their genetic tendencies, then developmental trajectories of individuals with the same genetic propensities (e.g., toward antisocial behavior) should *differ* as a function of whether they are placed into a supportive or a disruptive adoptive home.

Notably, Bohman (1996) found that male children with a genetic propensity toward criminality (as indexed by criminal behavior of a biological parent) who experienced unstable preadoptive (e.g., multiple temporary placements) or adverse adoptive conditions (e.g., low socioeconomic status) evidenced much higher rates of petty criminality than did those children with the same genetic risk placed into stable adoptive conditions. Similarly, symptoms of schizophrenia appear among children at genetic risk for the disease who are raised in a home with a parent with schizophrenia (Kinney et al., 1997), and full-blown schizophrenia is present among those adopted into homes with multiple problems (Tienari et al., 1994). Remarkably, there is an absence of these symptoms among adoptees who have a genetic liability toward schizophrenia but were adopted into well-adjusted families.

As Suomi has stated in reference to his primate work: "It is hard to imagine that the situation would be any less complex for humans" (2000, p. 253).

While this area of human research is still developing, observations thus far make at least one point very clear: Having a genetic propensity toward a particular behavior—good or bad—is not a recipe for expression of that behavior. If genetics has taught us anything, it is that genetic endowment does not determine outcome. Knowledge of an individual's genotype, combined with early intervention at the level of the family environment, may well prove to be the critical combination for preventing serious psychopathology.

The Search for Nonshared Environmental Associations

The topic of nonshared environmental variation in behavior has been of primary interest to quantitative geneticists for some time, prompted by the fact that across a very wide range of individual characteristics and behaviors, children raised in the same home are more often different from one another than they are similar (Reiss et al., 1994). Most importantly, these behavioral differences are the product of some aspect of the children's environment and not differences in their genes. Just as genetic influences on behaviors are inferred from comparisons of different sibling types, so can nonshared environmental outcomes be detected through similar comparisons. For example, identical twins are 100% genetically identical, which means that when identical twins exhibit different behaviors, these differences cannot be due to genetic differences and must be the result of differential effects of factors within the twins' respective environments.

Prior to a review of some of the more recent efforts to identify nonshared environmental associations, a brief discussion of an important distinction is necessary. While it is clear that nonshared environmental differences are substantial for most behaviors, until recently, the *sources* of these differences have remained anonymous; that is, quantitative genetic analyses of individual behaviors at one time point can only tell us that siblings are different because of factors in their environments. An example using the MZ twin methodology (cited earlier) clarifies this point. If the adjustment behavior of interest is depression and there are substantial differences in levels of depression within MZ twin pairs, then a nonshared environmental influence on depression is indicated. To understand what factors are causing or contributing to within-family behavioral differences, a growing number of studies have examined nonshared environmental associations between proposed environmental factors (e.g., peer relations) and adjustment (e.g., depression; see review in Turkheimer & Waldron, 2000). The following section provides a brief overview of major findings from our project.

The Nonshared Environment in Adolescent Development (NEAD) project (Reiss et al., 1994; Reiss, Neiderhiser, Hetherington, & Plomin, 2000) was undertaken to clarify environmental sources of sibling differences. Despite the presence of nonshared environmental influence on both adolescent adjustment and parenting at specific time points (influences on sibling relationships were due almost entirely to shared environment), there was virtually no systematic impact of differential parenting practices on sibling differences in adjustment across the interval of early to late adolescence. This conclusion was based on (among results of other, more complex analyses) the observation that MZ twin differences in adolescent adjustment were not substantially associated with differences in the way their parents treated them. It had been expected that the factors contributing to differential parenting would also contribute to, or at least correlate with, factors influencing differential sibling adjustment. Findings from the NEAD project suggested otherwise: Differential sibling adjustment in adolescence is apparently the result of factors in the environment other than differential parenting. For example, quantitative genetic studies have turned their focus toward the impact of extrafamilial influences, such as peers (Iervolino et al., 2002; Manke et al., 1995).

The MZ twin difference method is ideal in its relative simplicity and its stringency. Yet very few quantitative genetic analyses have employed MZ differences. Of those that have, the reported associations have almost exclusively relied on self-reports of both the environment, which are often retrospective, and current psychological adjustment. While this does not diminish the importance of their findings, exclusive reliance on correlations between two measures reported by the same informant is more likely to represent rater bias than more objective, across-reporter correlations.

However, one MZ difference analysis of nonshared environmental influences on the socioemotional development of preschool children provides evidence for at least moderate and, in some cases, substantial nonshared environmental family associations using parent, interviewer, and observer ratings (Deater-Deckard et al., 2001). In this study, across-rater MZ difference correlations between interviewer reports of parental harshness and parent reports of the children's problem behaviors, emotionality, and prosocial behavior were significant (.36, .38, and −.27, respectively). Cross-rater MZ difference correlations were also significant for a number of associations between parental positivity/negativity and several measures of child outcome. These findings offer evidence that the differential parental treatment of very young siblings living in the same family matters—and it matters *apart from any genetic traits of the child*. For example, when a parent is harsh toward one child and less harsh to the other, the child receiving the harsh discipline is more likely to have behavior problems, be more emotionally labile, and be less prosocial than the sibling.

Of course, one alternative explanation (not directly testable with cross-sectional data) is that differences in the children's behaviors elicit differences in the parents, or that the relationship is reciprocal. As an interesting and related aside, preliminary analysis of parent–child data from the TOSS sample (described earlier) shows several substantial cross-rater MZ difference correlations between the differential parenting patterns of adult twin women and characteristics of their adolescent children. Although directionality cannot be confirmed in this cross-sectional sample either, such findings in an *adult-based* sample imply that differences in the children are contributing to nonshared environmental influences in parenting behaviors of the mothers, because the mothers' genes and environment are the focus of assessment.

Regardless of the direction of effect, the associations reported by Deater-Deckard and colleagues (2001) are remarkable for at least two reasons. First, nonshared environmental differences for at least certain traits have been shown to increase over time—and to be less easily detected in early childhood, when parents are more likely to treat their children similarly (McCartney, Harris, & Bernieri, 1990; Scarr & Weinberg, 1983). Finding associations between differential parenting (a family environment variable) and childhood behaviors with a sample of 3½-year-old children is notable and has implications for clinical intervention efforts, discussed later in this chapter. Second, the fact that these associations exist across three different raters lends validity to the associations: They cannot be attributed entirely to the bias of a single reporter. Third, unlike univariate analyses of nonshared environment, analyses of multivariable associations minimize the amount of measurement error in the estimate of nonshared environment.

Since the publication of the third edition of this volume, work has been done on the genetic and environmental influences on marital quality. Univariate analyses have shown that marital quality is heritable, but the largest portion of the variance is accounted for by nonshared environmental influences (Spotts et al., 2004). These findings held for men and women, and for Swedish and American samples (Spotts, Prescott, & Kendler, 2006). Work on a longitudinal American sample found that over three time points, nonshared environmental influences on marital quality were largely stable (Spotts, unpublished data, 2007). The likely source of these stable nonshared environmental influences is, of course, the spouse. These results are notable in that this is one of the first, if not the only, finding of stable, nonshared environmental influences.

Aside from this example, there is a general inability to isolate *systematic* sources of nonshared environmental influences on behavior, which are so prevalent. In other words, when single studies have succeeded in specifying sources of sibling differences, there has been a general failure to replicate these findings across samples. A recent meta-analysis of the effect produced by specific sources of nonshared environment on behavior found the average effect size of studies using genetically informed designs to be roughly 2% (Turkheimer & Waldron, 2000). Revelations of this kind have stirred discussion about the definition of nonshared environment itself (Maccoby, 2000; Rowe, Woulbroun, & Gulley, 1994), and some researchers have begun to examine directly the issue of *how* nonshared environment may operate by examining the interplay between shared and nonshared environmental events (Jenkins, Rasbash, & O'Connor, 2001; McHale & Pawletko, 1992; Turkheimer, Haley, Waldron, D'Onofrio, & Gottesman, 2003). At the crux of the issue for those who question the traditional approach to searching for nonshared environmental influence on behavior is the issue of whether attention should be focused only on environmental events, factors, or people unique to each sibling—or whether environmental factors (e.g., family socioeconomic status) that are *shared* among siblings might also impact the extent of differences between them. This leads us to our discussion of a reconceptualization of shared environment.

Shared Environment: Revisited

Despite failure among quantitative genetic studies to replicate most nonshared environmental associations, there has certainly been success in replicating a separate but related phenomenon: the relative lack of importance of shared environmental influences on a broad range of outcomes. Shared environmental influences are indicated by findings of sibling similarity in behavior across all sibling types, regardless of the siblings' genetic similarity. For example, if adopted-together siblings, who share 0% of their segregating genes, are very similar in behavior, then this indicates that factors in the siblings' common environment are making them similar. For example, one might expect that marital discord would have a relatively similar impact on children living in the same household. If this were the case, we would expect an association between marital distress in the home and the extent to which *multiple* siblings within the same family are well adjusted. In the case of a shared environmental effect, we would not expect marital satisfaction to have a differential impact on within-family sibling adjustment. As it happens, the importance of factors we might assume to be experienced as shared by immediate family members— parental socioeconomic status, parental education, marital discord, and family size—does not appear to have the shared effect on family members we would predict (Plomin & Bergeman, 1991), in that they do not cause family members to be similar to one another in their behaviors. But might they cause at least some family members to be *different* from each another?

Several sets of analyses from separate laboratories suggest that this seeming contradiction is not only a possibility but also an often untested (and thus undetected) reality. The National Longitudinal Survey of Children and Youth (NLSCY) is a design that includes some 3,860 families from various Canadian provinces, each family with two to four children, ages 4–11 years. An investigation of the role of child- and family-level effects on differential parenting patterns within this sample showed that differential parenting (the prototypical nonshared environmental variable) was itself a function of, or moderated by, shared environmental factors (Jenkins et al., 2001). Notably, the study found that *differential parental positivity* (e.g., more praise directed) toward one child than the other) was *more frequent* in homes characterized by low socioeconomic status, high marital dissatisfaction, and larger family size. In addition, the study found differential parental negativity to be highest among single-parent families and families in which marital dissatisfaction was great.

The National Perinatal Collaborative Study also examined the effects of socioeconomic status (a shared environmental factor) on genetic and environmental variation in child IQ (Turkheimer et al., 2003). The study showed that in families with low socioeconomic status, the amount of variation in child IQ due to nonshared environment was large. In other words, siblings in families with low socioeconomic status were more likely to *differ* in their IQ levels than were siblings from high socioeconomic status households. Among families in which financial stress was absent (i.e., high socioeconomic status), sibling IQ differences caused by the environment seemed to dissipate. Findings such as these suggest that there may be a false dichotomy in conclusions about the relative influence of shared and nonshared environment on behavior. Just as most behaviors are influenced by both genes and environment, so it may prove to be the case that many of our behaviors are influenced by both shared and nonshared environmental factors.

One final example of this concept is an analysis of peers as nonshared environmental influences on child and adolescent behaviors (Rowe et al., 1994). It is generally assumed that siblings within the same family associate with *different* peers. However, data from the Arizona Sibling Study, a survey of siblings ranging from 10 to 16 years in age, showed that the siblings' frequency of contact with friends classified as "mutual" to both siblings within a pair was actually quite high (47.4% of brother pairs, 34.5% of sister pairs, and 24.8% of mixed-gender sibling pairs) It was suggested that variables such as the amount of time spent with mutual friends, or the number of mutual friends, should be assessed as potential *moderators* of nonshared associations between peer networks and adolescent adjustment. In other words, the impact of a mutual friend on a sibling's adjustment may depend on the amount of time the friend and the sibling spend together. Thus, it may be the intricacies of an experience, and the nature of the relationship under study, that matter—and not simply whether the experience is shared or nonshared within a sibling pair.

Beyond Heritability

In recent years, technology has forged ahead, allowing researchers to examine the family at ever more fine-grained levels of analysis. Advances are allowing us to get a taste of how the social environment affects biology and "gets under the skin" through genomewide scans and the assessment of epigenetics and gene expression. This section briefly focuses on human and nonhuman research that has moved beyond studies of anonymous genetic influences to understand more finely defined areas of the genome and how they relate to human social behavior. An advantage to animal studies is that researchers can randomly vary rearing conditions and other social contexts in ways that they cannot in humans. Additionally, the biological pathways through which genes exert their effects can be experimentally assessed via paradigms such as knockout genes, cross-fostering, and so forth. These studies of specific genes, epigenetic marks, and differences in gene expression may serve as the bridge between human and nonhuman research. In this section are several examples of cross talk between human and nonhuman research that is furthering our understanding of human social behavior by exploiting analogues across species.

The natural progression from basic heritability by environment studies mentioned earlier is to use measurement of specific genes, and work has begun on associating candidate genes with aspects of the family environment, as well as examining candidate gene × environment associations. This area has exploded since Caspi and Moffitt's (e.g., Caspi, Sugden, Moffitt, Taylor, Craig, Harrington, et al., 2003) observational studies. Although their work has received criticism (Risch et al., 2009), experimental work from the neuroscience and neurogenetic fields supports their findings. There is a great appeal for social scientists to search for gene × environment interactions because it better explains how the social environment and biology can both have an effect on behavior. Such findings also suit the needs of prevention and intervention science by suggesting targets for intervention. Given that humans have evolved as a social species, it makes sense that genes would be responsive to varying social environments.

Candidate genes have also been directly associated with familial behaviors. Since there are many regions of the genome conserved across, across species, work with specific genes can help bridge human and nonhuman work. An example comes from our growing understanding of vasopressin, a peptide involved in the neural processing of social information. The work of Young and others on voles has shown that vasopressin receptor genes play a large role in the regulation of social behavior in these animals (see Donaldson & Young, 2008, for a review). Specifically, vasopressin facilitates social contact, partner preferences, parental behaviors, and variation in sexual and social fidelity in voles (e.g., Ophir, Wolff, & Phelps, 2008). There is not a direct genetic homolog in humans, but three repetitive sequences in the AVPR1A region are polymorphic. Previous work suggested associations between AVPR1A polymorphisms and social phenomena such as autism (Kim et al., 2002), age at first sexual intercourse (Pritchard, MacKinnon, Jorm, & Easteal 2007), and altruism (Knafo et al., 2007). This work sparked interest in finding out whether or not AVPR1A is associated with relationship quality and pair-bonding in human males in the TOSS sample. Findings indicated pair-bonding for men, but not women, was significantly associated with the RS3 alleles of the vasopressin receptor gene. Additionally, pair-bonding varied by what allele the men were carrying, with lower bonding if men carried the 334 allele. This allele had a dose-dependent effect depending on how many copies the man was carrying. Men carrying the 334 allele were more likely than carriers of other alleles to have experienced a marital crisis or threat of divorce in the past year and to be in a cohabiting relationship without being married. There was also a dyadic effect, in that the wives of male carriers of the 334 allele were less satisfied in their marriages than wives of noncarriers. While hardly conclusive, this study sets the stage for future work examining the effects of specific genes on social behavior, and suggests biological pathways that influence human interpersonal interactions.

Epigenetic work has also bridged the gap between human and nonhuman research. A large body of work on rats has indicated that epigenetic regulation is a likely mechanism through which the effects of caregiving behaviors are transmitted to offspring and through which they have long-lasting effects. This work, reviewed extensively elsewhere (e.g., Champagne, 2011), is reviewed briefly here. Variation in rodent nurturing behaviors, such as licking and grooming of offspring, leads to variation in neural pathways in the offspring brains. Cross-fostering studies have shown that the quality of care received in infancy predicts offspring behaviors and can be passed along through several generations. This apparent inheritance has been shown to occur via epigenetic pathways. While the brain is most sensitive to these social stimuli during infancy, social enrichment or isolation in the juvenile stage also impacts subsequent maternal care. What is particularly fascinating is that researchers have intervened postinfancy to reverse successfully the epigenetic effects created by earlier parenting. Because the effects found in this line of research are neural, and because epigenetic marks seem to be tissue specific, it is difficult to translate this research to humans. As a proxy, Szyf and his colleagues (McGowan, Sasaki, Huang, Unterberger, Suderman, Ernst, et al., 2008) looked at methylation in the brains of suicide and nonsuicide deaths in individuals with early maltreatment. They found that the suicide victims were more highly methylated in the hippocampus than in the cerebellum. This is significant because the hippocampus is the center of stress hormone regulation, whereas the cerebellum directs motor control. The researchers then compared abused and nonabused suicide victims with nonabused sudden death victims (McGowan et al., 2009). The abused suicide victims had substantially different methylation patterns than the other two groups. While this research certainly is not conclusive, it is highly suggestive that early life events have the potential to influence later outcomes via epigenetic pathways.

Looking at gene expression is another way to examine how social factors influence and shape biological mechanisms. Suomi, who is beginning to augment his work on GE interactions in primates (described earlier) with gene expression work, is finding differential expression for peer-reared versus other-reared infants. In the human arena, a recent example can be found in some exploratory work on gene expression in individuals with high versus low social isolation (Cole et al., 2007). Findings suggest differing patterns of up-regulation and down-regulation by level of isolation. Genes that were identified as being differentially expressed were ones that made biological sense; for example, those involved in the immune system. This work used a very small sample, so replication is essential. However, this looks to be a promising beginning to understanding further the biological effects of social environments.

Genomewide studies of social behaviors will open up new possibilities for integration of biology and social science. For example, the population-based Health and Retirement Study is in the process of completing a genomewide scan of 20,000 subjects; more studies are likely to follow. Through the creation of resources like this one, more researchers will have access to data that permit testing of a broad range of theories of behavioral and social science, and arrive at new leads for biological underpinnings of social behavior.

CONCLUSIONS

Over the past decade, great advances in genetics and genetic technologies have moved our understanding of health and behavior forward. These advances have increased the number of tools available to social researchers for better understanding the interplay between the social and the biological. One of the most important uses of this wealth of genetic options is to better understand the environment by controlling for genetic factors. That said, many unanswered questions remain, requiring further attention.

I have discussed examples of recent advances in our understanding of four quantitative genetic concepts that are highly relevant to understanding how families function. I have described two mechanisms that may account for a major part of the interaction between genetic and social processes, both between and within parent–child and couple subsystems. I have also focused on *specific* environmental mechanisms that most likely act as supplements to, or in conjunction with, GE correlation and interactions. To account for these related but distinct mechanisms in terms of a comprehensive developmental theory of family process, much more longitudinal research is needed to confirm the sequence and timing of genetic and environmental interplay among family members.

However, findings from both studies of GE correlation and interaction in parent–child relationships, and studies of specific environmental influence lend support to a nonadditive, reciprocal theory of family adjustment, in contrast to a one-way, additive model of influence. Findings from the few longitudinal studies to date suggest the potential for a "family relations–effects" model (Reiss et al., 2000), by which a genetically influenced child behavior sparks a reaction (either negative or positive) from a parent. The parental response in turn serves to reinforce the initial child behavior, and so on. According to this model, a family subsystem (e.g., parent–child) is capable of *mediating* the often observed genetic influence on adolescent adjustment behaviors. Research showing the ability of 3-year-olds to evoke positive responses within a mother–child interaction, in addition to evidence for strong genetic influence on temperament in infancy, suggests the basis for such a developmental trajectory.

If these early, heritable behaviors do indeed turn out to be genetic precursors to subsequent adjustment of the child, then what needs be demonstrated is the mediating role of parenting. Longitudinal analyses from the NEAD project (described earlier) provide some indirect support for this part of the family relations equation. It is interesting to speculate about what may be occurring when those who are genetically predisposed to antisocial behavior do not do as poorly as expected. Whatever the mechanism, the implications for early intervention are clear: The parental response to the child in early adolescence appears to have the effect of *protecting* the child from a pathway to full-blown antisocial characteristics.

While the family relations–effects model accommodates behavioral genetic evidence of child genetic effects on family environment, the model must also account for the large body of psychosocial evidence that family influence on child and adolescent adjustment is substantial. While the longitudinal NEAD findings give us some clues about the *order* of GE interplay, analyses of GE interaction and specific shared and nonshared environmental influences on behaviors are critical for isolating the effects of environment on family processes. Recall the MZ difference analysis that suggested a strong impact of differential parenting on childhood adjustment, *independent* of child genetic effects (Deater-Deckard et al., 2001). It is noteworthy that some of the same differential parent–child relationships were also observed in a separate MZ difference study of parenting and adolescent adjustment (Pike, Reiss, Hetherington, & Plomin, 1996). Results such as these, along with findings from studies showing that family environment may actually *moderate* both genetic propensities and nonshared environment, are evidence that family environment does matter. On a related note, part of the influence that parents have on their children may well be grounded in heritable behaviors of the *parents* (Neiderhiser et al., 2004), which may or may not be shared with a given child because parents and children share only 50% of their genes. Parent-based genetic designs, in which the parents are the twins or siblings of interest, are needed to reveal the extent of such influence. Work that has incorporated epigenetic and gene expression methods also support the importance of the social environment, but in a slightly different way. These studies remind us that the social environment is the context in which genes are expressed and may thereby have a substantial impact on individual outcomes.

We are just beginning to understand the complexities of GE operations within the family. As the enigma surrounding the issue of nonshared environment illustrates well, the challenge in linking specific influences to family process constructs has been to do so *consistently* across samples. Longitudinal work on marital quality has show that this is not impossible. Undoubtedly, there is so much about human nature that escapes even our most sophisticated methodology: The distinction between actual behaviors and people's subjective perceptions of behavior patterns testifies to this challenge, complicating the search to explain what is predictable about human behavior.

This being said, three goals of human developmental psychology are the description, explanation, and optimization of behavior (Baltes, Reese, & Lipsitt, 1980). Part of meeting these goals necessarily entails a thorough assessment of factors that shape development over the entire lifespan. For example, behavioral genetic evidence to date suggests entirely different mechanisms underlying the link between *children's* own adjustment patterns and behaviors of their parents toward them, and that between *parents'* relationships with their spouses and their children. In the former, genetic factors emanating from the child appear to be important. In the latter, those factors in the environment that make siblings different from one another (perhaps the children and spouses themselves) are most important in determining the quality of adult marriages and parent–child relationships (Spotts et al., 2004).

So far, study of nonshared environmental associations within the family (with the exception of work from the TOSS project) has been limited almost exclusively to analyses of children and adolescents. As noted earlier, it has been observed that nonshared environmental influences on at least certain characteristics increase with age (McCartney et al., 1990). This makes intuitive sense because siblings often go their separate ways after they leave home. Once this happens, a whole host of new people and experiences in the siblings' respective environments may influence their behaviors. It seems a viable possibility that primary sources of nonshared environmental influence on behavior are to be found in adulthood. Analyses from the TOSS project indicate that the majority of the covariation in reports of marital satisfaction by middle-age adult women and their husbands is due to some aspect of the nonshared environment of the twin women (Spotts et al., 2004) and that this nonshared environmental influence is stable over time (Spotts, unpublished data, 2007).

Finally, our success in quantifying the relative impact of GE factors (and their mutual interplay) on human behavior has profound implications for therapeutic intervention. For example, the goal of many types of therapy is often to produce changes in individuals' social environments. These therapies may be all the more effective when based on the knowledge that it is possible to alter the mechanisms of genetic expression for a particular trait. Such knowledge may enable clinicians to target an intervention toward eliminating the *evocative* effects of extreme problem behaviors in young children, which are a function of the heritability of these behaviors. Many scholars are thinking about the best ways to use genetically informative studies to inform intervention efforts and are laying out steps to guide this process (Leve, Harold, Ge, Neiderhiser, & Patter, 2010). In fact, some research has examined whether behavioral interventions might ameliorate the risk for risky behavior incurred by *5-HTTLPR*, a serotonin transporter gene. As noted, researchers found that participation in the Strong American Families Program, a long-standing prevention program for at-risk African Americans, reduced the rate of risky behaviors in genetically at-risk youth (Brody, Beach, Philibert, Chen, & Murry, 2009). Awareness of the different genetic mechanisms underlying both individual traits and relationships will also help to inform clinicians about why certain forms of intervention are effective in treating some problems but not others. The task before us is to begin to expand our search for the genetic and environmental factors underlying individual behaviors to include the interactive GE bridges between various subsystems of the family.

In order to further our understanding of family and social relationships, and the role that genetics and other biological processes play in these relationships, we need to foster integrative research combining all relevant domains.

Science is currently moving at such a rapid pace that we cannot expect scientists to be fully versed in both the biological and the behavioral sciences. Just as we encourage good communication in families, we need to encourage and develop a common language that will facilitate communication across various areas of science in order to make this possible.

REFERENCES

Baltes, P. B., Reese, H. W., & Lipsitt, L. P. (1980). Life-span developmental psychology. *Annual Review of Psychology, 31*, 65–110.

Bennett, A. J., Lesch, K. P., Heils, A., Long, J., Lorenz, J., Shoaf, S. E., et al. (1998). Serotonin transporter gene variation, strain, and early rearing environment affect CSF 5-HIAA concentrations in rhesus monkeys (*Macaca mulatta*). *American Journal of Primatology, 45*, 168–169.

Block, J. H., Block, J., & Gjerde, P. F. (1986). The personality of children prior to divorce: A prospective study. *Child Development, 57*, 827–840.

Bohman, M. (1996). Predispositions to criminality: Swedish adoption studies in retrospect. In G. R. Bock & J. A. Goode (Eds.), *Genetics of criminal and antisocial behavior: Ciba Foundation Symposium 194* (pp. 99–114). Chichester, UK: Wiley.

Braungart, J. M., Plomin, R., DeFries, J. C., & Fulker, D. W. (1992). Genetic influence on tester-rated infant temperament as assessed by Bayley's Infant Behavior Record: Nonadoptive and adoptive siblings and twins. *Developmental Psychology, 28*(1), 40–47.

Brody, G. H., Beach, S. R., Philibert, R. A., Chen, Y. F., & Murry, V. M. (2009). Prevention effects moderate the association of 5-HTTLPR and youth risk behavior initiation: Gene x environment hypotheses tested via a randomized prevention design. *Child Development, 80*(3), 645–661.

Burt, S. A. (2009). Rethinking environmental contributions to child and adolescent psychopathology: A meta-analysis of shared environmental influences. *Psychological Bulletin, 135*, 608–637.

Bussell, D. A., & Reiss, D. (1993). Genetic influences on family process: The emergence of a new framework for family research. In F. Walsh (Ed.), *Normal family processes* (2nd ed., pp. 161–181). New York: Guilford Press.

Cadoret, R. J. (1995). Familial transmission of psychiatric disorders associated with alcoholism. In H. Begleiter (Ed.), *Alcohol and alcoholism* (pp. 70–81). New York: Oxford University Press.

Cadoret, R. J., Cain, C. A., & Crowe, R. R. (1983). Evidence for gene–environment interaction in the development of adolescent antisocial behavior. *Behavior Genetics, 13*(3), 301–310.

Cadoret, R. J., Winokur, G., Langbehn, D., Troughton, E., Yates, W. R., & Stewart, M. A. (1996). Depression spectrum disease: I. The role of gene–environment interaction. *American Journal of Psychiatry, 153*(7), 892–899.

Caspi, A., Sugden, K., Moffitt, T. E., Taylor, A., Craig, I. W., Harrington, H., et al. (2003). Influence of life stress on depression: Moderation by a polymorphism in the 5-HTT gene. *Science, 301*, 386–389.

Champagne, F. A. (2011). *Nurturing nature: Social experiences and the brain.* Topical briefing #33 for the British Society for Neuroendocrinology. Available at *www. neuroendo.org.uk/content/view/100/11/*.

Champoux, M., Higley, J. D., & Suomi, S. J. (1997). Behavioral and physiological characteristics of Indian and Chinese–Indian hybrid rhesus macaque infants. *Developmental Psychobiology, 31*, 49–63.

Cole, S. W., Hawkley, L. C., Arevale, J. M., Sung, C. Y., Rose, R. M., & Cacioppo, J. T. (2007). Social regulation of gene expression in human leukocytes. *Genome Biology, 8*, 1–13.

Deater-Deckard, K. (2000). Parenting and child behavioral adjustment in early childhood: A quantitative genetic approach to studying family processes. *Child Development, 71*(2), 468–484.

Deater-Deckard, K., & O'Connor, T. G. (2000). Parent–child mutuality in early childhood: Two behavioral genetic studies. *Developmental Psychology, 36*(5), 561–570.

Deater-Deckard, K., Pike, A., Petrill, S. A., Cutting, A. L., Hughes, C., & O'Connor, T. G. (2001). Nonshared environmental processes in socio-emotional development: An observational study of identical twin differences in the preschool period. *Developmental Science, 4*(2), F1–F6.

Donaldson, Z. R., & Young, L. J. (2008). Oxytocin, vasopressin, and the neurogenetics of sociality. *Science, 322*, 900.

D'Onofrio, B. M., Turkheimer, E., Emery, R. E., Maes, H. H., Silberg, J., & Eaves, L. J. (2007). A children of twins study of parental divorce and offspring psychopathology. *Journal of Child Psychology and Psychiatry, 48*(7), 667–675.

Elkins, I. J., McGue, M., & Iacono, W. G. (1997). Genetic and environmental influences on parent–son relationships: Evidence for increasing genetic influence during adolescence. *Developmental Psychology, 33*(2), 351–363.

Ge, X., Conger, R. D., Cadoret, R. J., Neiderhiser, J. M., Yates, W., Troughton, E., et al. (1996). The developmental interface between nature and nurture: A mutual influence model of child antisocial behavior and parent behaviors. *Developmental Psychology, 32*(4), 574–589.

Higley, J. D., Thompson, W. T., Champoux, M., Goldman, D., Hasert, M. F., Kraemer, G. W., et al. (1993). Paternal and maternal genetic and environmental contributions to CSF monoamine metabolites in rhesus monkeys (*Macaca mulatta*). *Archives of General Psychiatry, 50*, 615–623.

Iervolino, A. C., Pike, A., Manke, B., Reiss, D., Hetherington, E. M., & Plomin, R. (2002). Genetic and environmental influences in adolescent peer socialization: Evidence from two genetically sensitive designs. *Child Development, 73*, 162–174.

Jenkins, J. M., Rasbash, J., & O'Connor, T. (2001, April). *Understanding the sources of differential parenting: The role of child and family level effects.* Paper presented at the biennial meeting of the Society for Research in Child Development, Minneapolis, MN.

Kim, S.-J., Young, L. J., Gonen, D., Veenstra-VanderWeele, J., Courchesne, R., Courchesne, E., et al. (2002). Transmission disequilibrium testing of arginine vasopressin receptor 1A (AVPR1A) polymorphisms in autism. *Molecular Psychiatry, 7*, 503–507.

Kinney, D. K., Holzman, P. S., Jacobsen, B., Jansson, L., Faber, B., Hildebrand, W., et al. (1997). Thought disorder in schizophrenic and control adopters and their relatives. *Archives of General Psychiatry, 54*, 475–479.

Knafo, A., Israel, S., Darvasi, A., Bachner-Melman, R., Uzefovsky, F, Cohen, L., et al. (2008). Individual differences in allocation of funds in the dictator game associated with length of the arginine vasopressin 1a receptor (AVPR1a) RS3 promotor-region and correlation between RS3 length and hippocampal mRNA. *Genes, Brains, and Behavior, 7*(3), 66–75.

Leve, L. D., Harold, G. T., Ge, X., Neiderhiser, J. M., & Patterson, G. (2010). Refining intervention targets in family-based research: Lessons from quantitative behavioral genetics. *Perspectives on Psychological Science, 5*, 516–526.

Leve, L. D., Harold, G. T., Ge, X., Neiderhiser, J. M., Shaw, D., Scaramella, L. V., et al. (2009). Structured parenting of toddlers at high versus low genetic risk: Two pathways to child problems. *Journal of the American Academy of Child and Adolescent Psychiatry, 48*, 1102–1109.

Loehlin, J. C., Willerman, L., & Horn, J. M. (1987). Personality resemblance in adoptive families: A 10-year follow-up. *Journal of Personality and Social Psychology, 53*, 961–969.

Lytton, H. (1980). *Parent–child interaction: The socialization process observed in twin and single families.* New York: Plenum.

Maccoby, E. E. (2000). Parenting and its effects on children: On reading and misreading behavior genetics. *Annual Review of Psychology, 51*, 1–27.

Manke, B., McGuire, S., Reiss, D., Hetherington, E. M., & Plomin, R. (1995). Genetic contributions to adolescents' extrafamilial social interactions: Teachers, best friends, and peers. *Social Development, 4*, 238–256.

McCartney, K., Harris, M. J., & Bernieri, F. (1990). Growing up and growing apart: A developmental meta-analysis of twin studies. *Psychological Bulletin, 107*(2), 226–237.

McGowan, P. O., Sasaki, A., D'Alessio, A. C., Dymov, S., Labonte, B., Szyf, M., et al. (2009). Epigenetic regulation of the glucocorticoid receptor in human brain associates with childhood abuse. *Nature Neuroscience, 12*, 342–348.

McGowan, P. O., Sasaki, A., Huang, T. C. T., Unterberger, A., Suderman, M., Ernst, C., et al. (2008). Promoter-wide hypermethylation of the ribosomal RNA gene promoter in the suicide brain. *PLoS ONE, 3*(5), e2085.

McGuffin, P., Owen, M. J., O'Donovan, M. C., Thapar, A., & Gottesman, I. I. (1994). *Seminars in psychiatric genetics.* London: Gaskell Press.

McHale, S., & Pawletko, T. M. (1992). Differential treatment of siblings in two family contexts. *Child Development, 63*(1), 68–81.

Mehlman, P. T., Higley, J. D., Faucher, I., Lily, A. A., Tai. D. M., Vickers, J., et al. (1994). Low CSF 5-HIAA concentrations and severe aggression and impaired impulse control in nonhuman primates. *American Journal of Psychiatry, 151*, 1485–1491.

Narusyte, J., Andershed, A.-K., Neiderhiser, J. M., & Lichtenstein, P. (2007). Aggression as a mediator of genetic contributions to the association between negative parent–child relationships and adolescent antisocial behavior. *European Journal of Child and Adolescent Psychiatry, 16*, 128–137.

Neiderhiser, J., Reiss, D., & Hetherington, E. M. (1996). Genetically informed designs for distinguishing developmental pathways during adolescence: Responsible and antisocial behavior. *Development and Psychopathology, 8*, 779–791.

Neiderhiser, J. M., Reiss, D., Pedersen, N., Cederblad, M., Hansson, K., Lichtenstein, P., et al. (2004). Genetic and environmental influences on mothering of adolescents: A comparison of two samples. *Developmental Psychology, 40*(3), 335–351.

O'Connor, T. G., Deater-Deckard, K., Fulker, D., Rutter, M., & Plomin, R. (1998). Genotype–environment correlations in late childhood and early adolescence: Antisocial behavioral problems and coercive parenting. *Developmental Psychology, 34*(5), 970–981.

Ophir, A. G., Wolff, J. O., & Phelps, S. M. (2008). Variation in neural V1aR predicts sexual fidelity and space use among male prairie voles in semi-natural settings. *Proceedings of the National Academy of Sciences, 105*(4), 1249–1254.

Pike A., Reiss, D., Hetherington, E. M., & Plomin, R. (1996). Using MZ differences in the search for nonshared environmental effects. *Journal of Child Psychology and Psychiatry, 37*(6), 695–704.

Plomin, R., & Bergeman, C. S. (1991). The nature of nurture: Genetic influence on "environmental" measures. *Behavioral and Brain Sciences, 14*(3), 373–427.

Plomin, R., Chipuer, H. M., & Neiderhiser, J. M. (1994). Behavioral genetic evidence for the importance of nonshared environment. In E. M. Hetherington, D. Reiss, & R. Plomin, (Eds.), *Separate social worlds of siblings: The impact of non-shared environment on development* (pp. 1–31). Hillsdale, NJ: Erlbaum.

Plomin, R., & DeFries, J. C. (1999). The genetics of cognitive abilities and disabilities. In S. J. Ceci & W. M. Williams (Eds.), *The nature–nurture debate: The essential readings* (pp. 177–195). Malden, MA: Blackwell.

Plomin, R., Reiss, D., Hetherington, E. M., & Howe, G. W. (1994). Nature and nurture: Genetic contributions to measures of the family environment. *Developmental Psychology, 30*(1), 32–43.

Plomin, R., Scheier, M. F., Bergeman, C. S., Pedersen, N. L., Nessleroade, J. R., & McClearn, G. E. (1992). Optimism, pessimism and mental health: A twin/adoption analysis. *Personality and Individual Differences, 13*(8), 921–930.

Pritchard, Z. M., MacKinnon, A. J., Jorm, A. F., & Easteal, S. (2007). AVPR1A and OXTR polymorphisms are associated with sexual and reproductive behavioral phenotypes in humans. *Human Mutation Mutation in Brief, 28*(11), 1150.

Reiss, D., Neiderhiser, J. M., Hetherington, E. M., & Plomin, R. (2000). *The relationship code: Deciphering genetic and social influences on adolescent development.* Cambridge, MA: Harvard University Press.

Reiss, D., Plomin, R., Hetherington, E. M., Howe, G. W., Rovine, M., Tryon, A., et al. (1994). The separate worlds of teenage siblings: An introduction to the study of the nonshared environment and adolescent development. In E. M. Hetherington, D. Reiss, & R. Plomin (Eds.), *Separate social worlds of siblings: The impact of nonshared environment on development* (pp. 63–109). Hillsdale, NJ: Erlbaum.

Rende, R. D., Slomkowski, C. L., Stocker, C., Fulker, D. W., & Plomin, R. (1992). Genetic and environmental influences on maternal and sibling interaction in middle childhood: A sibling adoption study. *Developmental Psychology, 28*, 484–490.

Risch, N., Herrel, R., Lehner, T., Liang, Y.-K., Eaves, L., Hoh, J., et al. (2009). Interaction between the serotonin transporter gene (5-HTTLPR), stressful life events, and risk of depression: A meta-analysis. *Journal of the American Medical Association, 301*(23), 2462–2471.

Rowe, D. C., Woulbroun, J., & Gulley, B. L. (1994). Peers and friends as nonshared environmental influences. In E. M. Hetherington, D. Reiss, & R. Plomin (Eds.),

Separate social worlds of siblings: The impact of nonshared environment on development (pp. 159–173). Hillsdale, NJ: Erlbaum.

Scarr, S., & McCartney, K. (1983). How people make their own environments: A theory of genotype–environment effects. *Child Development, 54,* 424–435.

Scarr, S., & Weinberg, R. A. (1983). The Minnesota Adoption Studies: Genetic differences and malleability. *Child Development, 54,* 260–267.

Spotts, E. L., Neiderhiser, J. M., Towers, H., Hansson, K., Lichtenstein, P., Cederblad, M., et al. (2004). Genetic and environmental influences on marital relationships. *Journal of Family Psychology, 18*(1), 107–119.

Spotts, E. L., Prescott, C. A., Kendler, K. S. (2006). Examining the origins of gender differences in marital quality: A behavior genetic analysis. *Journal of Family Psychology, 20*(4), 605–613.

Stocker, C., & Dunn, J. (1994). Sibling relationships in childhood and adolescence. In J. C. DeFries, R. Plomin, & D. W. Fulker (Eds.), *Nature and nurture during middle childhood* (pp. 214–232). Oxford, UK: Blackwell.

Suomi, S. (2000). A biobehavioral perspective on developmental psychopathology: Excessive aggression and serotonergic dysfunction in monkeys. In A. J. Sameroff, M. Lewis, & S. M. Miller (Eds.), *Handbook of developmental psychopathology* (2nd ed., pp. 237–256). New York: Kluwer Academic/Plenum.

Tienari, P., Wynne, L. C., Moring, J., Lahti, I., Naarala, M., Sorri, A., et al. (1994). The Finnish adoptive family study of schizophrenia: Implications for family research. *British Journal of Psychiatry, 23*(Suppl. 164), 20–26.

Tsuang, M. T., Stone, W. S., & Faraone, S. V. (2001). Genes, environment and schizophrenia. *British Journal of Psychiatry, 178*(Suppl. 40), S18–S24.

Turkheimer, E., Haley, A., Waldron, M., D'Onofrio, B., & Gottesman, I. I. (2003). Socioeconomic status modifies heritability of IQ in young children. *Psychological Science, 14*(6), 623–628.

Turkheimer, E., & Waldron, M. (2000). Nonshared environment: A theoretical, methodological, and quantitative review. *Psychological Bulletin, 126*(1), 78–108.

van Os, J., Park, S. B. G., & Jones, P. B. (2001). Neuroticism, life events and mental health: Evidence for person–environment correlation. *British Journal of Psychiatry, 178*(Suppl. 40), S72–S77.

CHAPTER 23

NEUROBIOLOGY AND FAMILY PROCESSES

MONA DEKOVEN FISHBANE

The multisystemic discourse of family systems theory is enhanced by recent research in neurobiology and relationships. Current studies in neuroscience address the mutually recursive flow among body, brain, relationships, and context. The science is constantly evolving; the neurobiological data presented here are sure to evolve as well, and are presented as current knowledge. This chapter focuses on the interaction between neurobiology and relationships in families throughout the life cycle.

In the past decade, the field of neuroscience has been transformed through new technologies that allow scientists to observe the brain in action. In addition to the older methods of brain research—animal studies, evaluation of human functioning in the presence of brain damage or disease, and electroencephalographic (EEG) studies—newer scanning techniques such as functional magnetic resonance imaging (fMRI) have allowed unparalleled access to the human brain. The fMRI measures blood flow to the brain; as an area of the brain becomes active, it requires oxygen, which is reflected in blood flow. Thus, as a person lies in a scanner, and is shown a picture of a loved one, a terrifying scene, or an angry encounter, the fMRI identifies what parts of the brain are active. And what the scanner reveals about the human brain is remarkable.

THE SOCIAL BRAIN

Our understanding of the human brain in context has been enriched by both neuroscientists and key synthesizers of neurobiology research as it applies to human development, relationships, and therapy (e.g., Cozolino, 2006, 2008;

Damasio, 1994; Doidge, 2007; LeDoux, 1996; Schore, 2003; Siegel, 2010a, 2010b). This body of work points to our deeply social nature: Our brains are wired through connection with others, and we are wired for connection (Fishbane, 2007). Terms such as "interpersonal neurobiology" (Siegel, 2010b) and "social neuroscience" (Cacioppo & Berntson, 2004) capture the fundamental interconnectedness of human neurobiological processes. Likewise, neuroscience highlights the importance of emotion in our functioning; "affective neuroscience" (Panksepp, 1998) studies emotions as evolutionary processes for survival.

From the viewpoint of interpersonal neurobiology, the narrative of the rugged individualist, fostered by the dominant U.S. culture and by older theories of development and therapeutic approaches, misses the mark. Research indicates that from birth to death we need others for our well-being; interdependence is central to human functioning. Neuroscientists have found that social rejection triggers physical pain centers in the brain (Eisenberger & Lieberman, 2004). Indeed, "[social] exclusion could be a death sentence" to our ancestors (Goleman, 2006, p. 113), since we evolved as a social species. Humans are wired to read others' intentions and motivations beneath awareness. Much of this communication is nonverbal, mostly through reading others' faces and eyes in particular (Baron-Cohen, 2004). The pain of others is felt in the pain centers of one's own brain (Decety & Jackson, 2004). This deep interconnectedness contributes to health—in positive and negative ways. Positive relationships and social support correlate with physical and emotional health; unhappy or toxic relationships negatively affect health (Kiecolt-Glaser & Newton, 2001; Kim, Sherman, & Taylor, 2008). Loneliness is associated with lower immune function and with illness (Cacioppo & Patrick, 2008). The attachment literature interfaces with neuroscience research in emphasizing the importance of safe, attuned, well-attached relationships at all stages of family life.

Neuroscientists have found that nature and nurture are inextricably intertwined. Erik Kandel (2006) won the Nobel Prize for his discovery that learning changes the brain. Many studies have explored how the brain is changed through learning and experience throughout life. This change occurs at both the level of connections between neurons (brain cells), and at the genetic level: Experience influences the expression of genes, a process called epigenetics (see Spotts, Chapter 22, this volume). Early experience is particularly crucial to the baby's growing brain, as it is being wired through interactions with caregivers. The impact on the brain of interconnection with others continues at all ages.

BRAIN: THE BASICS

Humans have approximately 100 billion neurons; each connects to up to 10,000 other neurons at synapses, the space between neurons. There are trillions of synaptic connections in the human brain, making it the most complex entity in the known universe. Neurons are fundamentally social; they survive by connecting with other neurons to form networks. The neurons that do not connect die, through a normal process called apoptosis. Babies are born with many more neurons than they will need; it is the creation of networks and the pruning of disconnected neurons that shape brains and determine function.

Through evolution, the newer, uniquely human brain was built upon older, more primitive forms. The "triune brain" (MacLean, 1990) is composed of brain stem (reptilian brain), limbic system (mammalian brain), and neocortex (human brain). Because we carry our evolutionary history in our heads, our animal self is part of the human experience. Humans are not purely rational creatures; lower brain processes are very active, especially in emotional experience. We share 98% of our DNA with chimpanzees. The 2% difference is mostly in the prefrontal cortex (PFC), which Daniel Siegel (2010a) has called the "cortex humanitas." The brain stem, limbic system, and cortex are intertwined with multiple connections and feedback loops between brain areas. Most human activities—emotion, behavior, thought—do not activate just one brain area, but rather are reflected in circuits of interconnected activity.

One of the key circuits underlying emotional and relational functioning is that of the limbic system–PFC. The limbic system, or emotional brain, has at its core the amygdala, which sets off the fight-or-flight response if it senses threat. The amygdala is constantly scanning for danger. If it gets a whiff of threat, it sets in motion a full-body readiness to flee or to fight, activating the sympathetic nervous system and the HPA (hypothalamic–pituitary–adrenal) axis, which produces cortisol, a chemical in the stress response. When the amygdala is in fight-or-flight mode, it often overwhelms the PFC, which becomes quiet. The amygdala is much faster at processing information (at times erroneously) than the PFC. In a position of high emotional threat, the amygdala "highjacks the brain" (Goleman, 1995). While this system is highly efficient for sudden, life-threatening situations, it can cause crises in couple and family interaction as one person experiences the other as critical or abandoning and goes into full battle mode. The amygdala does not distinguish between threat in the jungle and threat to our well-being or self-esteem in our current relationships. Danger is danger.

One of the reasons the amygdala can so easily overwhelm the PFC is that there are more fibers running from amygdala up to PFC than there are from PFC to amygdala (LeDoux, 1996). Thus, it can be hard to rein in the threat response and respond reasonably. To complicate matters further, it has been proposed that the vagus nerve, which runs between the viscera (heart and intestines) and brain stem in both directions, participates in responding to threat or safety. According to the Polyvagal Theory (Porges, 2007), when safety is assessed, the "smart vagus," the more recently evolved part of the vagal system, signals the body and facial muscles to relax and engage with others. If danger is sensed, the amygdala fight-or-flight response is initiated through the sympathetic nervous system. If the danger is perceived to be life threatening, with no possibility of escape or defeating the enemy, the more primitive vagus nerve takes over, activating the "freeze" response, including fainting and dissociation.

While these processes run on automatic pilot, and mostly beneath awareness, humans do have access to higher brain processing; we have a PFC that comes online and interfaces with our limbic system, calming the amygdala and gaining perspective. The PFC can inhibit amygdala reactivity and bring thoughtfulness, self-regulation, response flexibility, and compassion to shape responses. The more these prefrontal capabilities are cultivated, the more fibers grow from PFC to amygdala. Then, in a potential moment of escalation or reactivity, one can more quickly calm down and gain perspective. But even the most evolved individuals will have irrational moments, amygdala takeovers. Part of the reason for this is that the amygdala holds emotional memories; when a current situation feels threatening, memories of an older, painful experience can become activated. This process has survival value; but it can stress couple and family relationships.

Humans have two brain hemispheres. As currently understood, the left specializes in logic, language, linear thinking, and details. The right specializes in emotions, nuance, and gestalt perception. The right hemisphere is online and functioning at birth; the left develops in the first years of life. The right hemisphere is responsible for much of our automatic and conscious self-regulation, modulation of emotion, and knowledge of how our body feels. The "interpreter" part of our brain (Roser & Gazzaniga, 2004) is a left prefrontal function, narrating and justifying our experience, including our emotional reactions. The corpus callosum connects the two hemispheres and allows for the creation of coherent narratives of life experiences. Integration is key in this and other areas of brain life.

EMOTIONS AND EMPATHY

Neurobiologists have identified the centrality of emotion as well as cognition in human experience; it has been suggested that a counterbalance to Descartes' famous dictum, "I think therefore I am" would be "I feel therefore I am" (Cacioppo & Patrick, 2008). Emotions are body states; feelings occur when these body cues are read and named (Damasio, 1994). The brain is embodied, with a bidirectional flow of input and influence. The vagus nerve carries information from heart and intestines to brain, giving literal meaning to "gut feelings" and "a broken heart." The insula specializes in interoception, reading one's inner body states, and in perceiving pain in self and other. Many important brain processes are subcortical, automatic, and beneath awareness; they involve the limbic system and brain stem, in interface with body processes. The PFC catches up in recognizing and naming these physical sensations as feelings. Some individuals are unable to name their emotions, to read their body cues. This alexithymia can severely impair interpersonal functioning and personal well-being.

To experience emotions fully and safely, humans need the empathy of others. Indeed, emotions are not just interior, individualized states; they are communications with others. Through fine-tuned facial muscles that communicate feeling and intention, and through neurons that specialize in reading the faces and emotions of others, intertwined attunement between self and other is central to emotional life. Parental attunement is particularly crucial to the baby's brain development. Infants come hardwired for empathy; babies cry when another baby is crying in the nursery. Even some primates demonstrate rudimentary empathy (de Waal, 2009). Empathy is considered a necessary ingredient in human well-being throughout life.

The neurobiology of empathy includes several components (Decety & Jackson, 2004). The first is resonance, an automatic process in which one feels what the other feels. Some neuroscientists emphasize the role of "mirror neurons," special neurons that read the actions and intentions of others by creating the same experience in one's own brain–body. First discovered in monkeys, the human mirror neuron system has been mapped by scientists in recent years (Iacoboni, 2008). Other scholars point to different mechanisms of resonance, in which the somatosensory cortex or the insula is activated when one experiences pain or disgust, for example, and when one sees another exhibiting pain or disgust. With this resonance, we feel what the other feels "from the inside out" (Siegel & Hartzell, 2003). We read others—and are affected by them—beneath awareness. This can be salutary, as we share the emotions of others, and can support and help them with empathy. But this "emotional contagion" (Hatfield, Cacioppo, & Rapson, 1993) can be problematic; when family members become reactive with each other, they may be picking up and reacting to each other's emotions before they are aware of what is happening. In a circular process, or vicious cycle, each reaction can intensify the reactions of others, escalating the level of distress for all. Conversely, attuned and positive responses can calm emotions, facilitating a virtuous cycle.

The second component of empathy, cognitive empathy, entails consciously putting oneself in the other's shoes. This prefrontal capacity brings thoughtfulness to the subcortical process of resonance. Individuals differ with regard to their "empathic accuracy" (Ickes, Gesn, & Graham, 2000). Third, empathy requires identification with the other, while maintaining a boundary between self and other. When seeing another in pain, pain centers in one's own brain light up; yet the overlap is not complete. Parts of the brain that are active when one experiences pain do not become activated when watching another in pain (Decety & Jackson, 2004). The brain is wired to know the difference between self and other. This crucial differentiation of self from other—otherwise known as healthy boundaries—allows for empathic connection with another without losing one's self in the process. Finally, empathy requires that one not become overwhelmed with the other's pain. The ability to self-regulate in the face of another's distress is crucial in the empathic process.

A key neurochemical in empathy is oxytocin. Both a hormone and a neurotransmitter, oxytocin is released with orgasm, childbirth, nursing, massage, touch, and empathy. Oxytocin is associated with trust and generosity in laboratory experiments, and it reduces cortisol, the stress hormone. Oxytocin, the "cuddle chemical" (Taylor, 2002), helps modulate attachment. Women have more oxytocin receptors than men; in males, vasopressin, a related hormone, is more plentiful. Oxytocin and vasopressin have been studied in prairie voles, monogamous rodents that live in the Midwest (Carter, 2003). These neurochemicals are key to male–female pair-bonding and monogamy; when oxytocin and vasopressin receptors are blocked, pair-bonding yields to promiscuity. Oxytocin prompts female voles to seek out other females when stressed, while vasopressin prompts males to engage in mate guarding and territory protection.

Oxytocin has also been associated with the "tend and befriend" response (Taylor, 2002). Taylor's data suggest that the fight-or-flight response has been overemphasized in the human response to threat. The amygdala does indeed set off a survival-based sympathetic nervous system response when danger is detected. Taylor proposes that the tend-and-befriend response, or "care and connection system," is equally important in the face of danger. Just as female voles turn to each other and protect their young when faced with threat, female humans often do the same. Research on the interplay between this system and the fight-or-flight system in humans is ongoing. The dynamics of care (identified by neuroscientist Jaak Panksepp [1998] as one of the seven basic emotional operating systems in the brain) are central to family relationships. This "protective urge" is an important factor in intimate relationships (Fishbane, 1998, 2005). Looking for "resources of trustworthiness" (Boszormenyi-Nagy & Ulrich, 1981) in families nurtures this care-and-connection system. This system needs to be studied more fully in both neuroscience and family theory.

STRESS AND TRAUMA

When danger is severe or chronic, care is lacking or inconsistent, or attunement and attachment are distorted or unavailable, the stress response can become overactive. Humans evolved to deal with acute, short-term stress. The sympathetic nervous system and cortisol signal the body to route its resources to the threat at hand. As Sapolsky (2004) wryly notes, on the savannah, a zebra either escapes or becomes another animal's lunch. The stress is intense and short term. We humans, however, often live in conditions of chronic stress. And long-term stress can impair the immune system. It can also impair memory, since cells in the hippocampus (mediator of explicit or conscious memory) are highly affected by cortisol. If the stress is long-lasting and severe enough, cells in the hippocampus die, leading to hippocampal shrinkage and impairment of memory and cognitive function.

Trauma—especially interpersonal trauma—is the most toxic form of stress for humans. Severe abuse and neglect affect the young child's developing brain and can cause long-term cognitive and memory impairment, as well as problems in self-regulation and social relating (Perry, 2001, 2002). Traumatic memories are often held in the brain in the implicit memory system. This system, online at birth, holds memories without conscious awareness. It is only with the development of the hippocampus, around age 2, that the explicit or conscious memory system develops. Implicit memories—for nontraumatic as well as traumatic events—are processed in the right hemisphere and can affect one in the present even if the event is not consciously remembered.

Stress and trauma often arise from the larger context in which the family is embedded. Poverty, war, living in violent neighborhoods, or experiencing discrimination can negatively affect even well-attached parents and children. While research on the impact of poverty on the developing human brain is new, data point to the negative impact of poverty-related stress for child development (Hackman & Farah, 2009).

HABITS AND CHANGE: NEUROPLASTICITY AND HUMAN ADAPTATION

Humans are creatures of habit. The human brain, an "anticipation machine" (Siegel, 2010a), is an organ structured for habit. Habits reflect circuits of interconnected neurons firing over and over again. This process is captured in Hebb's theorem: "Neurons that fire together wire together" (Siegel, 1999). The more a neuronal network fires, the more likely the whole network will fire when one of the neurons fires in the future. This process underlies habits, behaviors, thoughts, and feelings. The more we do, think, or feel something, the more likely we will do so in the future. In that sense, we are what we do, as the brain changes and rewires to reflect our repetitive behaviors. Indeed, habits are hard to change for this very reason.

Humans are also creatures of change and adaptation. The brain mechanism for change is neuroplasticity, the ability of neurons to create new synaptic connections with other neurons. In addition, through neurogenesis, new neurons are created from stem cell neurons. The old assumption was that neural growth and change were only possible in youth, that the adult brain was unchangeable. However, it is now well established that adults are capable of both neuroplasticity and neurogenesis throughout the life course. For adult neuroplasticity to flourish, we need to be open to new experience, learn new things, pay attention, and exercise both physically and mentally (as children do naturally). Being stuck in our (neural) ruts, living with "hardening of the categories" (Cozolino, 2008), and being physically inactive will not facilitate neuroplastic change as we age.

Neuroplasticity is the basis for resilience in human functioning, for change in therapy, and for transformation in couple and family relationships. For new habits to take hold and override old habits, "massed practice" (Doidge, 2007) is necessary, as new neuronal networks are activated over and over again to become the new default position. Neuroplasticity and brain development, especially in the prefrontal cortex, continue throughout life—if we nurture them and are open to new possibilities.

CULTURE AND THE BRAIN

Current thinking in cultural neuroscience emphasizes the mutually reciprocal influences between the biological and the sociocultural, between brain and culture (Zhou & Cacioppo, 2010). Indeed, "human brains are biologically prepared to acquire culture" (Ames & Fiske, 2010, p. 72), and are shaped by culture. From perception to neurobiological correlates of the self-concept, culture affects brain processes (Ames & Fiske, 2010). Research comparing Eastern (Asian) and Western (European and American) subjects finds that while Western perception favors figure over ground, Eastern perception emphasizes context and a holistic view. Self-concept, as revealed in both psychological studies and fMRI scans, focuses on the independent self-versus-other view in Western subjects, and on the interdependent, self-and-other view among Asian subjects (Zhu, Zhang, Fan, & Han, 2007). Similarly, definitions of self and of family include a wide network of others, kin and nonkin, in African American culture, captured in the African saying, "We are, therefore I am" (Hines & Boyd-Franklin, 2005, p. 88).

The "contact zone" (Wexler, 2006) between cultures and races has been studied in recent years. Empathy, as measured by fMRI, was found to be higher in subjects observing faces of their own in-group undergoing pain than faces of other races (Xu, Zuo, Wang, & Han, 2009). Culturally learned racial prejudice is evidenced in amygdala activation; the greater the implicit prejudice, the greater the amygdala activity (Phelps et al., 2000). However, conscious social goals can ameliorate these amygdala activations (Wheeler & Fiske, 2005).The interplay between automatic and controlled cognitive processes of perceiving others (including racial prejudice) is a current topic in neuroscience.

Immigration from one culture to another can pose neurobiological challenges, as the environment in which one's brain was shaped is left behind (Wexler, 2006): "Culture shock is brain shock" (Doidge, 2007, p. 299). Immigrants often create mini-versions of their home country in the new land, " 'as if' environments" that "help transform the receiving culture into more familiar places" (Falicov, 2003, p. 293). Recent conceptualization of immigration identifies creative and ongoing adaptations that integrate the two cultures; in an age of easy communication, the Internet, and transportation, "transnationals" maintain relations that transcend geographic borders, creating "flexible bicultural identities" (Falicov, 2008). The ongoing process of "selective adaptation" to the new culture (Garcia-Preto, 2008) continues to reshape the brain as immigrants find creative ways to "construct the bridges they need for this journey between cultures" (Garcia-Preto, 2008, p. 273).

Even within the same culture, evolving social practices and technology such as the Internet affect the plastic brain. The Internet and its distractions are reshaping the ways we think, leading to greater distractibility and multitasking, and less access to "deep reading" and sustained attention (Carr, 2010). The easy accessibility of Internet pornography is affecting couples' relationships. Individuals who become addicted to porn are rewiring their own brains, and are often unable to relate sexually to their real-life partners (Doidge, 2007). The far-reaching impacts of technology on the brain and on culture are yet to be determined. The Internet, social networks, smartphones, and constant (non-face-to-face) connection that constitute our new context will surely reshape our brains that evolved to navigate face-to-face communication.

NEUROBIOLOGY AND PARENT–CHILD INTERACTIONS

The child's brain is shaped by early family experience: "Parents are the active sculptors of their children's growing brains" (Siegel & Hartzell, 2003, p. 34). In infancy, most of this occurs through right-brain to right-brain interaction (Schore, 2003). The infant's right brain is functioning at birth; this hemisphere processes nonverbal cues and emotions, and is prepared for the "protoconversations" (Trevarthen, 1995), the lilting prosody of give-and-take between parents and baby in early preverbal life. Infants are not blank slates; they are born with specific genetic potential, temperament, and limitations. Much of a child's genetic potential is then shaped by experience as nature meets nurture. The newborn is immature neurobiologically and requires intensive adult care. Fortunately, infants come ready to connect, endowed with reflexes that allow parents, grandparents, and other caregiving adults to fall in love with the baby. The earliest infant smile is a reflex; the social smile develops later. But the smile reflex makes the caregiver feel loved by the baby, bringing the adult into the loving loop that is so necessary for the infant's survival (Tronick, 2007). Through this "lyrical duet" (Cozolino, 2006) of sound, touch, and eye contact, endogenous opioids are released in the child's brain (Schore, 2003) as the bonds of attachment are formed and oxytocin is released in both child and adult.

Matching states, or "contingent communication" (Siegel & Hartzell, 2003), is central to this lyrical duet, as parent and infant coregulate each other. In a series of studies, Tronick (2007) examined this coregulation and found that parents and infants are in a constant process of responding to each other nonverbally, each one's behavior evoking the other's. While well-attached pairs enjoy the attunement and attachment of their bond, research has found these parent–baby pairs to be mismatched or out of sync 70% of the time (Tronick, 2007). What matters is what comes after the mismatch: the repair. Well-attached babies and parents repair their break, their out-of-sync moment, and come back together into sync. Child development researchers have suggested that these breaks in attunement allow the child to develop a sense of confidence and mastery in interpersonal repair, a capacity that is vital for healthy adult functioning. Most studies of attachment in early childhood focus on dyadic relationships (especially between mother and baby). However, recent systemic research points to the baby's competence in handling triadic interactions, navigating differences in contingent communication between two parents (Fivaz-Depeursinge & Favez, 2006).

Babies are born with the necessary equipment for attachment, and are active participants in the dance of attachment with parents. Newborns can differentiate mother from father from stranger within days of birth. The baby relies on parents or other adult caregivers for affect regulation. As the adult responds and soothes the infant's distress—a process of dyadic regulation— the baby's brain is developing structures that ultimately allow that child to learn self-regulation, an internalization of the parent's soothing. While these right-brain processes of attunement, attachment, and emotion regulation are developing, as the child grows, the PFC, left hemisphere, and hippocampus develop as well, making possible the acquisition of language and development of explicit memory in the first and second years of life.

The baby's brain is in a constant state of attention and curiosity; all is new to the infant. The nucleus basalis in the brain, necessary for paying attention, is in the "on" position in infants, releasing acetylcholine, which promotes learning (Doidge, 2007). The infant is born with many more neurons than exist in the adult brain. Through early experience, some of these neurons form networks with other neurons; the neurons that do not connect die off through a process called pruning or apoptosis (programmed cell death). Thus, the baby's brain comes ready to engage and be shaped by experience, most especially by the family. Early life experience matters; attuned caregiving matters.

Throughout the child's life, attunement and attachment with parents and other family members are vital for development of brain and self. Connections are not perfect and constant, however, even in the best of circumstances. As with babies, there will be many moments of mismatch between the parents' and the child's needs and states. Indeed, the oscillation between connection– disconnection–reconnection is part of the flow of any intimate relationship. The key is *repair* throughout childhood. Even in healthy relationships, parents may become reactive with their child in the face of current stress overload or as old implicit memories from their childhood—held in the amygdala— are triggered while they struggle in the current moment. A dispute between parents can spill over, or be deflected, into upset with a child. Parents can be reduced to the level of a screaming toddler while reexperiencing a sense of helplessness and rage felt as a young child or in other situations beyond their control. In trying to repair these moments with their child, parents should wait until their own reactivity has calmed; trying to hold a repair conversation while still emotionally flooded is likely to fail (Siegel & Hartzell, 2003). The activated amygdala does not easily share airspace with a reasonable PFC, and the fight can quickly reignite if parents have not had time to regroup and regain some calm. Later, after the storm, reflective conversation is called for as parents and child revisit their reactivity and repair the connection.

THE ADOLESCENT BRAIN:
CHALLENGES FOR FAMILY LIFE

From a neurobiological perspective, adolescence is a second period of exuberant brain growth and transformation. There is a disparity between early changes brought on by puberty that heighten emotional arousal and intensity, and later adolescent brain development that allows for greater self-regulation and control. With puberty, emotional intensity and reactivity increase, along with sexual urges and romantic interest. Risk taking, sensation seeking, and sensitivity to peer influence rise dramatically as well (Dahl, 2004). In later adolescence, changes in the PFC allow for greater emotion regulation and executive functioning. Synaptic pruning and myelination (the development of a fatty sheath around the axon of the neuron, which provides speed and efficiency in the transmission from one neuron to the next) within the PFC continue from adolescence through the mid-20s. So the young adolescent is subject to massive doses of hormones, intense affect, and heightened responsiveness to social pressure, while prefrontal processes of "regulatory competence" (Steinberg, 2005), planning, and impulse control are slower to develop. The adolescent brain is at particular risk for substance abuse, because of both its fluid nature during this second pruning and rewiring process, and the social pressures on youths to engage in risky behavior. Sexual urgency may trump common sense or caution, as the PFC has difficulty catching up to the exuberance of the emotional brain, sexual urges, and peer pressure.

The desire for independence often outruns the adolescent's capacity to self-regulate, think carefully, plan, and use good judgment (all prefrontal functions). Parents at times need to lend their PFC to their adolescents, helping them make better choices. This is easier said than done with an adolescent who wants nothing more than freedom and autonomy. Cross-culturally, adolescents do best in close, nonconflictual families with authoritative (firm, warm) parenting that nurtures both their autonomy and connection (Garcia-Preto, 2011; Steinberg, 2001). Adolescents use this "social scaffolding" (Dahl, 2004), involvement and monitoring by parents and other adults, while they learn the necessary skills of emotion regulation and self-control. Such monitoring of adolescents by responsible adults in the community is especially important, for example, for African American youth in high-crime neighborhoods (APA Task Force, 2008).

While current research departs from the "storm-and-stress" model of normal adolescence, this period in the family life cycle can be stressful, especially for parents dealing with their critical or oppositional adolescents (Steinberg, 2001). Relationship plasticity, made possible by neuroplasticity and flexibility in response to changing circumstances, is key for adolescent and parents as they evolve and develop a more mature and complex connection. It is precisely this evolving connection with parents—along with greater autonomy—that characterizes healthy adolescence, not a radical separation from parents. Likewise, the adolescent is not becoming "independent" in the sense of a solo actor; rather, the teenager's need for connection is largely transferred to the peer group. The social brain does not stop needing others in adolescence. While the change processes at this time of life can be daunting for the whole family, understanding the normal developmental trajectory of the adolescent—and of the teenage brain—can give perspective and potentially some wisdom during this challenging time.

ADULTHOOD: NEUROBIOLOGICAL MATURITY AND FLEXIBILITY

The PFC continues to evolve throughout the lifespan. These changes allow for growing maturity with age. With myelination of the PFC, greater thoughtfulness, judgment, and response flexibility are possible, and it appears that myelination, along with neuroplasticity, continues into adulthood (Siegel, 2010b). In the normal maturing brain the PFC develops greater control over the reactive amygdala; with intentional practice, this influence can increase. Since experience changes the brain by creating new neuronal connections, practices that activate the PFC can build new pathways to the amygdala, thus increasing emotion regulation. Mindfulness meditation in particular has been found to impact emotion and well-being positively, facilitating compassion, positive mood, and immune functioning (Davidson et al., 2003).

Self-regulation and self-soothing (achieved through processes of dyadic regulation with parents and in transactions with others in childhood and adolescence) are important aspects of adult emotional competence. While the PFC does exert an inhibitory role on the amygdala, this is not a suppression of emotion. Rather, it is a collaborative working with and soothing of emotion that constitute neurobiological maturity. Identifying or naming an emotion, reading body cues, and labeling the feeling give one the ability to shape it—we "name it to tame it" (Siegel, 2010a). Naming the emotions activates the PFC. This self-regulation has been called "parenting yourself from the inside out" (Siegel & Hartzell, 2003). Siegel (2007) has noted that intrapersonal attunement, reading one's own emotions and sensations, uses the same resonance circuitry as interpersonal empathy. The skills of empathy for self and other are central to emotional and social intelligence in adulthood.

Neurobiological maturity dovetails with the family systems concept of differentiation (Bowen, 1978). Differentiation requires self-regulation, so one can engage with others in a nonreactive, thoughtful, compassionate manner without losing oneself, responding with heart and mind in a calm way (McGoldrick & Carter, 2001). Differentiation involves integration of PFC and limbic system, thought and feeling, left and right hemispheres, mind and body, self and others. Differentiation is an ongoing developmental process, not a state achieved at one time. Changing circumstances in the family, new perspectives, and ongoing prefrontal development all provide challenges and opportunities for further growth. Flexibility, aided by neuroplasticity, allows for adaptation to new challenges in the family system and in one's own life course. Siegel (2010b) offers the image of navigating the "river of integration," without landing on either the bank of rigidity or the bank of chaos. Research on family functioning emphasizes the importance of flexibility in couple and family well-being and resilience (Walsh, 2003).

Flexibility in current relationships can be undermined when one becomes reactive in an interpersonal encounter as old, implicit memories in the amygdala are activated. The past can haunt an individual (and relationships) in the present. Working through unfinished business with one's family of origin can liberate a person from the grip of these old patterns of reactivity. As myelination of the PFC continues through the mid-20s and beyond, life experience combined with brain maturity allows an adult child to view parents with a more sympathetic and curious perspective. "Waking from the spell of childhood" (Fishbane, 2005, p. 550) enables one to see parents as real people with their own strengths and limitations. Holding "interactional awareness" (Byng-Hall, 2008) of parents' experience and feelings as well as one's own, facilitates this shift. Using this perspective to invite parents to a "loving update" of relationships (Fishbane, 2005) can be empowering and transformative for both generations.

In this process, outdated, constraining narratives give way to new narratives of resilience and possibility. From a neurobiological perspective, a transformative narrative integrates thoughts and feelings. Indeed, attachment research has found that having a coherent narrative about one's childhood, incorporating the positives and the negatives, integrating both thought and feeling, is predictive of having children with a secure attachment (Siegel, 2010b). Even when adults have had difficult, painful childhoods, if they have wrestled with past issues and come to a more integrative, differentiated intergenerational perspective, they can parent well and create a secure bond with children.

INTIMATE COUPLE BONDS

Our need for connection with others is intensely expressed in adult love relationships. Neurobiology sheds light on many of the dynamics of adult love. According to Fisher (2004), love relationships entail three separate stages, each fueled by different brain chemicals, and each serving a different evolutionary purpose. Lust is fueled by testosterone in both men and women. Romantic love, which focuses on a specific person with great intensity, is associated with dopamine and norepinephrine. And long-term couple attachment is fueled by oxytocin and vasopressin. As Fisher points out, sometimes these systems work against each other; for example, attachment neuromodulators may dampen lust at times. Fisher, studying madly-in-love people in the fMRI machine as they looked at a picture of their beloved, found that the brain circuits for this state are the same as the addictive cocaine state: Love is a drug high. Studying the recently jilted, she found that their brains fire like those in withdrawal from drugs. She points out that this romantic drug high can only last so long in the brain; at some point (around 18 months or so into the relationship) it yields to a saner, more realistic approach to the partner. For many people, however, the loss of the romantic high is interpreted to mean that one is with the wrong partner, and that it is time to move on. The assumption that one "falls in love" or "falls out of love" is a remarkably passive description, in which the lover has no power or responsibility. Understanding the brain processes of romantic love can facilitate a more mature and proactive way of loving. Nurturing passion in long-term relationships can be challenging, but is important. Touch, massage, and sex all release oxytocin, the neurochemical that both facilitates attachment and reduces cortisol, the stress hormone.

The power of intimate relationships to heal or to harm is enormous. The strain of unhappy love relationships is associated with morbidity and mortality (Robles & Kiecolt-Glaser, 2003; Slatcher, 2010). Happy couples come to look like each other over the years, as their facial muscles are co-sculpted through ongoing synchrony with each other. The happier the relationship, the more the partners resemble each other (Iacoboni, 2008). Holding a loving partner's hand lessens the experience of physical pain (Coan, Schaefer, & Davidson, 2006). Unhappy relationships, by contrast, can be deleterious to health, as can loneliness (Kiecolt-Glaser & Newton, 2001; Cacioppo & Patrick, 2008). Unhappy couples tend to dysregulate each other, setting each other off in a "limbic tango" (Goleman, 1995). As each feels vulnerable, automatic survival strategies are triggered (Scheinkman & Fishbane, 2004), fueled by the amygdala's fight-or-flight reaction.

Adult love entails an oscillation between connection–disconnection–reconnection. Like well-attached parent–infant bonds, secure adult partner attachments include many moments of out-of-sync experiences; what is key in both cases is repair. Happy couples have conflict, but they repair well and often (Gottman & Gottman, 2008; see Driver, Tabares, Shapiro, & Gottman, Chapter 3, this volume). When reactive, with amygdala activation, partners are unable to repair successfully. Using a time-out to calm down is essential before beginning the repair process. Flooding, or DPA (diffuse physiological arousal; heart rate over 100 beats per minute) interferes with the ability to think clearly and solve problems (Gottman & Gottman, 2008).

The power of repair is crucial to successful relationships. Relational wounds (Johnson, Makinen, & Milliken, 2001), when not addressed by the couple, tend to fester and get retriggered over and over as the amygdala associates a current slight to an older, unprocessed wound in the relationship. The normative need to be understood by one's partner fuels repeated attempts to get through to the partner about one's pain. These attempts may misfire as the wounded partner speaks in an angry, accusatory tone, leading to a defensive response in the other. Learning to speak without attacking and to hear without becoming defensive are key processes for successful relationships.

Empathy is key to repair. "Feeling felt" (Siegel & Hartzell, 2003) allows one to relax, to be held by the partner emotionally, and to let down one's neurobiological guard. One mechanism for feeling felt is eye contact, which activates the medial prefrontal and orbitofrontal cortex, among other areas

(Senju & Johnson, 2008). Early in a relationship, as partners are falling in love, each looks in the lover's eyes and sees the self reflected back in a loving, affirming gaze. The mutual empathy of partners can soothe distress, an interpersonal process of coregulation. While self-regulation and differentiation are crucial in relational functioning, soothing each other is a powerful source of well-being in happy couples (Greenberg & Goldman, 2008). The balance between coregulation and self-regulation is part of the dynamic of a healthy relationship.

AGING BRAINS, AGING FAMILIES

Given that families change with the evolving developmental needs of their members, it is good news that neuroplasticity can continue throughout the life course. Even as young adults are navigating their new lives with changing brains, their parents, in middle age and beyond, need to adjust their expectations and behaviors accordingly. It can be difficult for parents of young adults to learn that their children no longer welcome advice or guidance unless requested. Young adults want to be accepted by parents and are sensitive to perceived criticism. Yet they often need emotional and financial support, and may even need to return home to live with parents in harsh economic times. At this phase of family life, parents often find that they have little leverage over their adult children and need to mind their boundaries and their manners—a delicate balancing act. Navigating relationships with adult children, sons- or daughters-in-law, and grandchildren can be daunting for parents who have been responsible for guiding their children's entire development and ensuring their well-being.

The aging brain is more resilient and capable of change than previously thought. While there is cognitive and memory loss with age, the resilient mature brain compensates—for example, using both hemispheres for a task in which younger brains use one hemisphere. These adaptations in the aging brain can foster greater integration and wisdom (Cozolino, 2008). Older adults tend to approach problems in a more positive, integrative, and thoughtful manner, achieving greater perspective (Cacioppo & Patrick, 2008; Mather & Carstensen, 2005). Emotion regulation and social processing—tasks involving the middle PFC—often improve with age. "The taming of the amygdala may be one of the primary gifts of aging and an important component of becoming a wise elder" (Cozolino, 2008, p. 154). Thoughtfulness about the meaning of one's life and efforts to achieve "family integrity" (King & Wynne, 2004) in intergenerational relationships are key processes in successful aging. This focus on integration and meaning reflects the capacities of the mature brain and can enhance well-being in the whole family.

Resilience, wisdom, and neuroplasticity in the aging brain are not guaranteed, however. Luck plays a role, as do genes and life circumstances; disease or injury can limit neural capacity with aging. And lifestyle habits matter:

Regular exercise, nutrition, and healthy habits in middle age can affect later brain plasticity (Ratey, 2008; Strauch, 2010). Mental exercise and exposure to new challenges also promote neuroplasticity, as does paying attention. Whereas paying attention, modulated by the nucleus basalis, is the baby's natural state, for the older adult, attention needs to be more intentional. Recall that the human brain is an anticipation machine, always predicting what will happen based upon past experience; there is a pull for relying on old habits in the adult brain as it ages. For the aging brain to keep growing and adapting, it needs stimulation—cognitive, social, and emotional. Attention, curiosity and a readiness for surprise prime the aging brain for adaptability and change. Focus, new learning, and practice affect neuroplasticity: "Use it or lose it" characterizes adult brain function. How we live affects our brain, which in turn affects our life choices. Keeping vital, alert, socially connected, and active, both cognitively and physically, enables neuroplasticity to flourish into old age.

For all the positive news of brain potential, there are undeniable losses associated with aging. Memory and cognitive loss, even in the absence of dementia, can have painful impacts on functioning and self-esteem. And dementia rates rise with age. Loss of a spouse can be a traumatic blow that affects the survivor's health and longevity, and is a neurobiological challenge as well, as the intimate environment to which the brain has adapted is lost (Wexler, 2006). The loneliness of old age as partners, friends, and relatives die can leave the older adult without the social supports so necessary for healthy functioning. Losses due to illness can be debilitating for the whole family. When an older adult is ill or experiences dementia, the primary caregiver in the family, often a spouse or an adult daughter, can experience massive stress that negatively affects the caregiver's immune system (Kiecolt-Glaser, Dura, Speicher, Trask, & Glaser, 1991). Yet old age and the challenges of caregiving offer opportunities for care and repair in the multigenerational family system (Walsh, 2011). Utilizing the care-and-connection system (Taylor, 2002) can enhance the well-being of elders and their adult children,

IMPLICATIONS FOR CLINICAL WORK

Clients come to therapy to change, yet they may be ambivalent about change. Neuroscience sheds light on this dynamic. Some difficulties with change stem from neural wiring and the tenacity of habits. Understanding how habits or behavioral ruts reflect—and reinforce—neural ruts enables therapists and clients to have more compassion for the challenges of change. In other language, clients' survival strategies, which have helped them navigate the world in the past, may be interfering with current relationships (Scheinkman & Fishbane, 2004); but survival strategies are protective and deeply wired. Helping clients build on their own strengths and addressing change in a collaborative manner allows them to balance the stability of their familiar modes of coping with the flexibility of new adaptations. Offering "neuroeducation" (Fishbane, 2008) about the challenges of change and neuroplasticity in the adult brain can be empowering. Maintaining new habits can be difficult, as old habits tend to reappear in times of stress. Therapists can normalize this and suggest that overlearning and "massed practice" (Doidge, 2007) are often necessary for new behaviors to become wired as the "new normal" in relationships. Thus, neuroeducation can be used both to normalize setbacks and to offer hope and a blueprint for change.

Emotional reactivity and power struggles can pose dilemmas in couple and family therapy. Mutual escalation and blame often ignite quickly as family members become dysregulated and resort to attacking or stonewalling behavior. Partners in unhappy relationships may turn away from or against each other rather than turning toward each other (Gottman & Driver, 2005; see Driver et al., Chapter 3, this volume). This dynamic has neurobiological underpinnings. According to the Polyvagal Theory (Porges, 2007), we automatically assess for safety or danger with others. A sense of safety prompts social engagement (turning toward); threat prompts turning against or turning away—fight or flight. The freeze response may be activated in situations of extreme threat or trauma. It can be empowering to help clients identify the neurobiological underpinnings of their reactive moments, to give them a "peek inside" their own brains.

If couples or family members are caught up in a recursive pattern of criticism–defense, with each becoming dysregulated, the therapist can help them calm down, become more thoughtful about their own reactivity and mutual escalation, and learn how to self-regulate when upset. Techniques such as focused breathing, mindfulness meditation, naming one's feeling with compassion, or holding a hand on one's heart can soothe the agitated amygdala and bring the PFC back online. Imagery work, such as picturing one's own PFC soothing one's rowdy amygdala, promotes resilience in the face of interpersonal upset (Fishbane, 2007). These techniques help family members become more relationally competent and empowered, and less prone to power struggles with each other (Fishbane, 2010, 2011).

For clients who become agitated and hyperaroused, or for those who shut down and go to hypoarousal, expanding the "window of tolerance" for affect (Fosha, 2000; Siegel, 2010b) is important. Learning to read and label one's own emotions is key; the PFC–limbic system circuit is activated in this process. Likewise, learning to speak one's needs respectfully in a relationship is important. Therapists can encourage clients to "make a relational claim" (Fishbane, 2001), in which they speak their needs while holding the needs of their partner and of the relationship at the same time. These skills involve integration of PFC and limbic system, mind and body, left and right hemispheres, and self and other. Siegel (2010b) considers these levels of integration key to mental health.

Helping family members listen to each other with empathy can be transformative in mind and body, since empathy releases oxytocin, which reduces cortisol, the stress hormone. The therapist can frame empathy as a skill that can be learned. Indeed, empathic accuracy has been shown to increase with motivation (Ickes et al., 2000). Clients who find empathy difficult can develop this skill by learning to pay attention to their body cues, through guided body visualizations and body scans (Kabat-Zinn, 1990; Siegel, 2010b), and by explicit empathy-building exercises such as the speaker–listener technique. Family members can also be encouraged to offer each other gentle hugs and other forms of safe touch, which release oxytocin and lower the stress hormone cortisol. Facilitating the care-and-connection system in the family offers an antidote to cultural messages of competition and individualism that contribute to reactivity and polarization in relationships.

Neuroscience points to our fundamentally social nature. Helping couples and families to utilize the social contexts in which they are embedded and to seek out additional social resources is key in therapy. The impact of poverty, marginalization, racism, isolation, or violence can be devastating. The therapist must use a wide lens to understand clients-in-context. Social support is vital to mental and physical health; however, forms of social support may differ culturally (Kim et al., 2008). Therapists must be attuned to clients' cultural traditions, beliefs, and expectations in order to facilitate new adaptations while building on resources and strengths within the family and larger community.

Therapy often challenges clients' familiar modes of operating, beliefs, and survival strategies. Deep internal or relational change—the work of therapy—can feel at times like venturing into foreign territory. Learning new skills, shifting perspectives, and changing constraining practices can feel disorienting. The therapist's respect, acceptance, and empathy ground this process of transformation. For clients to work toward rewiring their brains, habits, and relationships, they need to feel safe. It is imperative for the therapist to create a shame-free, blame-free zone in the therapeutic setting (Fishbane, 2010), so clients can risk the journey of change. When working with couples or families, extending "multilateral partiality" (Boszormenyi-Nagy & Spark, 1973), concern and care, to all of the individuals involved promotes safety and facilitates change. To do therapy with the brain in mind, to participate in neurobiological change, the therapist joins clients in the limbic zone, bringing prefrontal thoughtfulness to the process of personal, relational, and contextual transformation.

REFERENCES

Ames, D. L., & Fiske, S. T. (2010). Cultural neuroscience. *Asian Journal of Social Psychology, 13*, 72–82.

APA Task Force on Resilience and Strength in Black Children and Adolescents. (2008). *Resilience in African-American children and adolescents: A vision for optimal development*. Washington, DC: American Psychological Association.

Baron-Cohen, S. (2004). *The essential difference: Male and female brains and the truth about autism.* New York: Basic Books.

Boszormenyi-Nagy, I., & Spark, G. M. (1973). *Invisible loyalties: Reciprocity in intergenerational family therapy.* New York: Harper & Row.

Boszormenyi-Nagy, I., & Ulrich, D. (1981). Contextual family therapy. In A. S. Gurman & D. P. Kniskern (Eds.), *Handbook of family therapy* (pp. 159–186). New York: Brunner/Mazel.

Bowen, M. (1978). *Family therapy in clinical practice.* New York: Aronson.

Byng-Hall, J. (2008). The crucial roles of attachment in family therapy. *Journal of Family Therapy, 30,* 129–146.

Cacioppo, J. T., & Berntson, G. G. (Eds.). (2004). *Essays in social neuroscience.* Cambridge, MA: MIT Press.

Cacioppo, J. T., & Patrick, W. (2008). *Loneliness: Human nature and the need for social connection.* New York: Norton.

Carr, N. (2010). *The shallows: What the Internet is doing to our brains.* New York: Norton.

Carter, C. S. (2003). Development and consequences of oxytocin. *Physiology and Behavior, 79,* 383–397.

Coan, J. A., Schaefer, H. S., & Davidson, R. J. (2006). Lending a hand: Social regulation of the neural response to threat. *Psychological Science, 17,* 1032–1039.

Cozolino, L. (2006). *The neuroscience of human relationships: Attachment and the developing social brain.* New York: Norton.

Cozolino, L. (2008). *The healthy aging brain: Sustaining attachment, attaining wisdom.* New York: Norton.

Dahl, R. E. (2004). Adolescent brain development: A period of vulnerabilities and opportunities. *Annals of the New York Academy of Sciences, 1021,* 1–22.

Damasio, A. (1994). *Descartes' error: Emotion, reason, and the human brain.* New York: Penguin.

Davidson, R. J., Kabat-Zinn, J., Schumacher, J., Rosenkranz, M., Muller, D., Santorelli, S. F., et al. (2003). Alterations in brain and immune function produced by mindfulness meditation. *Psychosomatic Medicine, 65,* 564–570.

Decety, J., & Jackson, P. L. (2004). The functional architecture of human empathy. *Behavioral and Cognitive Neuroscience Reviews, 3,* 71–100.

de Waal, F. (2009). *The age of empathy: Nature's lessons for a kinder society.* New York: Harmony.

Doidge, N. (2007). *The brain that changes itself.* New York: Penguin.

Eisenberger, N. I., & Lieberman, M. D. (2004). Why rejection hurts: A common neural alarm system for physical and social pain. *Trends in Cognitive Neurosciences, 8,* 294–299.

Falicov, C. J. (2003). Immigrant family processes. In F. Walsh (Ed.), *Normal family processes* (3rd ed., pp. 280–300). New York: Guilford Press.

Falicov, C. J. (2008). Transnational journeys. In M. McGoldrick & K. V. Hardy (Eds.), *Re-visioning family therapy: Race, culture, and gender in clinical practice* (2nd ed., pp. 25–38). New York: Guilford Press.

Fishbane, M. D. (1998). I, Thou, and We: A dialogical approach to couples therapy. *Journal of Marital and Family Therapy, 24,* 41–58.

Fishbane, M. D. (2001). Relational narratives of the self. *Family Process, 40,* 273–291.

Fishbane, M. D. (2005). Differentiation and dialogue in intergenerational relationships. In J. Lebow (Ed.), *Handbook of clinical family therapy* (pp. 543–568). Hoboken, NJ: Wiley.

Fishbane, M. D. (2007). Wired to connect: Neuroscience, relationships, and therapy. *Family Process, 46*, 395–412.

Fishbane, M. D. (2008). "News from neuroscience": Applications to couple therapy. In M. E. Edwards (Ed.), *Neuroscience and family therapy: Integrations and applications* (pp. 20–28). Washington, DC: American Family Therapy Academy Monograph Series.

Fishbane, M. D. (2010). Relational empowerment in couple therapy: An integrative approach. In A. S. Gurman (Ed.), *Clinical casebook of couple therapy* (pp. 208–231). New York: Guilford Press.

Fishbane, M. D. (2011). Facilitating relational empowerment in couple therapy. *Family Process, 50*, 337–352.

Fisher, H. (2004). *Why we love: The nature and chemistry of romantic love.* New York: Little, Brown.

Fivaz-Depeursinge, E., & Favez, N. (2006). Exploring triangulation in infancy: Two contrasted cases. *Family Process, 45*, 3–18.

Fosha, D. (2000). *The transformng power of affect: A model for accelerated change.* New York: Basic Books.

Garcia-Preto, N. (2008). Latinas in the United States: Bridging two worlds. In M. McGoldrick & K. V. Hardy (Eds.), *Re-visioning family therapy: Race, culture, and gender in clinical practice* (2nd ed., pp. 261–274). New York: Guilford Press.

Garcia-Preto, N. (2011). Transformation of the family system during adolescence. In M. McGoldrick, B. Carter, & N. Garcia-Preto (Eds.), *The expanded family life cycle: Individual, family, and social perspectives* (4th ed., pp. 232–246). Boston: Pearson.

Goleman, D. (1995). *Emotional intelligence.* New York: Bantam.

Goleman, D. (2006). *Social intelligence: The new science of human relationships.* New York: Bantam.

Gottman, J. M., & Driver, J. L. (2005). Dysfunctional marital conflict and everyday marital interaction. *Journal of Divorce and Remarriage, 43*, 63–77.

Gottman, J. M., & Gottman, J. S. (2008). Gottman method couple therapy. In A. S. Gurman (Ed.), *Clinical handbook of couple therapy* (4th ed., pp. 138–164). New York: Guilford Press.

Greenberg, L. S., & Goldman, R. N. (2008). *Emotion-focused couples therapy: The dynamics of emotion, love, and power.* Washington, DC: American Psychological Association.

Hackman, D. A., & Farah, M. J. (2009). Socioeconomic status and the developing brain. *Trends in Cognitive Sciences, 13*, 65–73.

Hatfield, E., Cacioppo, J. T., & Rapson, R. L. (1993). Emotional contagion. *Currrent Directions in Psychological Science, 2*, 96–99.

Hines, P., & Boyd-Franklin, N. (2005). African American families. In M. McGoldrick, J. Giordano, & N. Garcia-Preto (Eds.), *Ethnicity and family therapy* (3rd ed., pp. 87–100). New York: Guilford Press.

Iacoboni, M. (2008). *Mirroring people: The science of empathy and how we connect with others.* New York: Farrar, Straus & Giroux.

Ickes, W., Gesn, P. R., & Graham, T. (2000). Gender differences in empathic accuracy: Differential ability or differential motivation? *Personal Relationships, 7,* 95–109.

Johnson, S. M., Makinen, J. A., & Millikin, J. W. (2001). Attachment injuries in couple relationships: A new perspective on impasses in couples therapy. *Journal of Marital and Family Therapy, 27,* 145–155.

Jordan, J. V., Kaplan, A. G., Miller, J. B., Stiver, I. P., & Surrey, J. L. (1991). *Women's growth in connection: Writings from the Stone Center.* New York: Guilford Press.

Kabat-Zinn, J. (1990). *Full catastrophe living: Using the wisdom of your body and mind to face stress, pain, and illness.* New York: Delta.

Kandel, E. (2006). *In search of memory: The emergence of a new science of mind.* New York: Norton.

Kiecolt-Glaser, J. K., Dura, J. R., Speicher, C. E., Trask, O. J., & Glaser, R. (1991). Spousal caregivers of dementia victims: Longitudinal changes in immunity and health. *Psychosomatic Medicine, 53,* 345–362.

Kiecolt-Glaser, J. K., & Newton, T. L. (2001). Marriage and health: His and hers. *Psychological Bulletin, 127,* 472–503.

Kim, H. S., Sherman, D. K., & Taylor, S. E. (2008). Culture and social support. *American Psychologist, 63,* 518–526.

King, D. A., & Wynne, L. C. (2004). The emergence of "family integrity" in later life. *Family Process, 43,* 7–21.

LeDoux, J. (1996). *The emotional brain: The mysterious underpinnings of emotional life.* New York: Simon & Schuster.

MacLean, P. D. (1990). *The triune brain in evolution.* New York: Plenum.

Mather, M., & Carstensen, L. L. (2005). Aging and motivated cognition: The positivity effect in attention and memory. *Trends in Cognitive Sciences, 9,* 496–502.

McGoldrick, M., & Carter, B. (2001). Advances in coaching: Family therapy with one person. *Journal of Marital and Family Therapy, 27,* 281–300.

Panksepp, J. (1998). *Affective neuroscience: The foundations of human and animal emotions.* New York: Oxford University Press.

Perry, B. D. (2001). The neurodevelopmental impact of violence in childhood. In D. Schetky & E. P. Benedek (Eds.), *Textbook of child and adolescent forensic psychiatry* (pp. 221–238). Washington, DC: American Psychiatric Press.

Perry, B. D. (2002). Childhood experience and the expression of genetic potential: What childhood neglect tells us about nature and nurture. *Brain and Mind, 3,* 79–100.

Phelps, E. A., O'Connor, K. J., Cunningham, W. A., Funayama, E. S., Gatenby, J. C., Gore, J. C., et al. (2000). Performance on indirect measures of race evaluation predicts amygdala activation. *Journal of Cognitive Neuroscience, 12,* 729–738.

Porges, S. (2007). The polyvagal perspective. *Biological Psychology, 74,* 116–143.

Ratey, J. J. (2008). *Spark: The revolutionary new science of exercise and the brain.* New York: Little, Brown.

Robles, T. F., & Kiecolt-Glaser, J. K. (2003). The physiology of marriage: Pathways to health. *Physiology and Behavior, 79,* 409–416.

Roser, M. & Gazzaniga, M. S. (2004). Automatic brains—interpretive minds. *Current Directions in Psychological Science, 13,* 56–59.

Sapolsky, R. M. (2004). *Why zebras don't get ulcers* (3rd ed.). New York: Holt.

Scheinkman, M., & Fishbane, M. D. (2004). The vulnerability cycle: Working with impasses in couple therapy. *Family Process, 43,* 279–299.

Schore, A. (2003). *Affect regulation and the repair of the self.* New York: Norton.

Senju, A., & Johnson, M. H. (2008). The eye contact effect: Mechanisms and development. *Trends in Cognitive Sciences, 13,* 127–134.

Siegel, D. J. (1999). *The developing mind: How relationships and the brain interact to shape who we are.* New York: Guilford Press.

Siegel, D. J. (2007). *The mindful brain: Reflection and attunement in the cultivation of well-being.* New York: Norton.

Siegel, D. J. (2010a). *Mindsight: The new science of personal transformation.* New York: Bantam/Random House.

Siegel, D. J. (2010b). *The mindful therapist.* New York: Norton.

Siegel, D. J., & Hartzell, M. (2003). *Parenting from the inside out.* New York: Penguin.

Slatcher, R. B. (2010). Marital functioning and physical health: Implications for social and personality psychology. *Social and Personality Psychology Compass, 3,* 1–15.

Steinberg, L. (2001). We know some things: Parent–adolescent relationships in retrospect and prospect. *Journal of Research on Adolescents, 11,* 1–19.

Steinberg, L. (2005). Cognitive and affective development in adolescence. *Trends in Cognitive Sciences, 9,* 699–674.

Strauch, B. (2010). *The secret life of the grown-up brain.* New York: Viking.

Taylor, S. E. (2002). *The tending instinct: Women, men, and the biology of our relationships.* New York: Holt.

Trevarthen, C. (1995). The child's need to learn a culture. *Children and Society, 9,* 5–19.

Tronick, E. (2007). *The neurobehavioral and social-emotional development of infants and children.* New York: Norton.

Walsh, F. (2003). Family resilience: A framework for clinical practice. *Family Process, 42,* 1–18.

Walsh, F. (2011). Families in later life. In M. McGoldrick, B. Carter, & N. Garcia-Preto (Eds.), *The expanded family life cycle: Individual, family, and social perspectives* (4th ed.). Boston: Pearson.

Wexler, B. E. (2006). *Brain and culture.* Cambridge, MA: MIT Press.

Wheeler, M. E., & Fiske, S. T. (2005). Controlling racial prejudice: Social-cognitive goals affect amygdala and stereotype activation. *Psychological Science, 16,* 56–63.

Xu, X., Zuo, X., Wang, X., & Han, S. (2009). Do you feel my pain?: Racial group membership modulates empathic neural responses. *Journal of Neuroscience, 29,* 8525–8529.

Zhou, H., & Cacioppo, J. (2010). Culture and the brain: Opportunities and obstacles. *Asian Journal of Social Psychology, 13,* 59–71.

Zhu, Y., Zhang, L., Fan, J., & Han, S. (2007). Neural basis of cultural influence on self-representation. *NeuroImage, 34,* 1310–1316.

INDEX

f indicates a figure; t indicates a table; n indicates a note.